The
SCRIBNER
HANDBOOK
for Writers

Fourth Edition

Robert DiYanni
New York University

Pat C. Hoy II
New York University

PEARSON
Longman

New York   San Francisco   Boston
London   Toronto   Sydney   Tokyo   Singapore   Madrid
Mexico City   Munich   Paris   Cape Town   Hong Kong   Montreal

Senior Vice President and Publisher: Joe Opiela
Development Manager: Janet Lanphier
Development Editor: Adam Beroud
Executive Marketing Manager: Ann Stypuloski
Senior Supplements Editor: Donna Campion
Production Manager: Charles Annis
Project Coordination, Text Design, and Electronic Page Makeup: Pre-Press Company, Inc.
Cover Designer/Manager: Nancy Danahy
Cover Image: ©PhotoDisc/Getty Images
Manufacturing Buyer: Lucy Hebard
Printer and Binder: Quebecor World Taunton
Cover Printer: Coral Graphic Services

For permission to use copyrighted material, grateful acknowledgment is made to the copy-right holders on pp. 827–828, which are hereby made part of this copyright page.

Library of Congress Cataloging-in-Publication Data
DiYanni, Robert, Robert.
  The Scribner handbook for writers / Robert DiYanni, Pat C. Hoy II--4th ed.
    p. cm.
  Includes bibliographical references and index.
  ISBN 0-321-16389-3
    1. English language--Rhetoric--Handbooks, manuals, etc. 2. English
language--Grammar--Handbooks, manuals, etc. 3. Report writing--Hanbooks, manuals,
etc. I. Hoy, Pat C. II Title.

PE1408.D59 2003
808'.042--dc21   2003051425

Copyright © 2004 by Pearson Education, Inc.

Please visit our Web site at http://www.ablongman.com

ISBN 0-321-16389-3

4 5 6 7 8 9 10—QWT—06 05

Contents

PART **4**   **Clear and Effective Sentences**

Instructor Preface

This is a handbook for writers. It begins by discussing what writing is and how to do it well. It goes on to offer suggestions for writing essays, papers, and reports in different disciplines and for taking essay exams. It shows how an understanding of words and sentences, paragraphs and punctuation, grammar and usage helps writers with the work of writing.

We wrote *The Scribner Handbook for Writers* because we wished to create a college handbook that would be useful not only as a reference guide to grammar and language, but also as a guide to writing. We wanted to provide an accurate and comprehensive demonstration of how writers actually write. The discussions of writing we found in other handbooks seemed to oversimplify the often messy and complex process of writing. Instead of the realities of writing—and its intimate connections with reading and thinking—we found formulas and procedures that described a finished product rather than a method for showing students how to become involved successfully in the intricate and exciting process of writing college essays.

We wrote this book also because we wanted a college handbook to include discussion of the kind of reading and thinking required of students in college. We believe that reading and writing are mutually supportive and that they should be taught together. We also believe that there can be no real writing and no inferential, interpretive reading without creative and logical thinking. And so we have striven to connect reading with writing and writing with thinking. As a result, this *Handbook* is also about making connections.

The Scribner Handbook for Writers, thus, is both a complete handbook of English grammar, style, punctuation, and usage and a thorough guide to writing. Between the covers of the handbook, students will find what they need to use language accurately and effectively. And they will find guidance in using the latest technology and Internet resources to research and write effectively.

A handbook that shows how writers write

Writing Essays and Paragraphs

The first three chapters of *The Scribner Handbook* discuss the connections between writing and reading. In these chapters, students will find practical suggestions for doing the work of college writing *and* reading. Chapters 4–8 describe the writing process. Chapter 4 begins the process by detailing four techniques for developing ideas. Chapter 5 addresses paragraph development, a skill we believe to be essential to successful academic writing. This chapter explains how to write unified and coherent paragraphs, how to organize paragraphs, and how to develop ideas within and across paragraphs. It also describes how paragraphs function at the beginning, middle, and end of essays. Chapters 6–8 provide start-to-finish instruction on how to write three different types of essays: exploratory, argumentative, and literary. These chapters include exemplary student writing that demonstrates how writers discover and develop their ideas. The three chapters provide context-based models of how to write essays, following student writers as they move from preliminary thinking to finished products.

Taken together, the first eight chapters, on the reading/writing connection and on the paragraph and the essay, offer clear, thorough, and honest descriptions of the techniques students may use to write essays that fulfill their own interests *and* their academic requirements.

Reading: Process and Practice

We have devoted two chapters to reading because we believe that reading and writing are indissolubly interconnected and because we know that students need practice and guidance in how to get more out of what they read. Chapter 2, on critical reading, leads students to formulate a written interpretation of a text. Discussion of the experience of reading illustrates how to question a text, engage it on the writer's terms, and consider a writer's ideas and evidence in light of a reader's knowledge, experience, and values. The chapter demonstrates the recursiveness of reading while simultaneously introducing concepts of critical and creative thinking. It also invites students to participate actively in making meaning from the different kinds of texts they read. The principles delineated in this chapter are intimately connected with those explained in all of our writing chapters and are additionally reinforced in our chapters on research writing and on writing in the disciplines. Chapter 3, "Reading (and Writing about) Visual Texts" (new to this edition) offers advice on how to interpret and critically respond to images, be they the everyday advertisements encountered in print and electronic media or works of art such as paintings and photographs.

The Importance of Thinking

We have integrated thinking into many sections of *The Scribner Handbook for Writers*. In the chapters on writing, for example, readers encounter repeated instances of student and professional writing where ideas are foregrounded and evaluated. The essay writing chapters show how students can construct essays that develop ideas in exploratory, argumentative, and literary modes. Several chapters focus on how thinking and reading inform writing, including Chapter 4, "Developing Ideas," Chapter 5, "Fundamentals of Paragraphs Development," and Chapter 40, "Writing the Research Essay." These chapters give students advice on enriching the ideas of their essays and developing and supporting the ideas with precision and care.

Grammar

Grammar is presented not as an isolated system, but as a living element of language intimately bound up with speaking, thinking, and writing. The focus remains on using grammatical structures and elements in writing. Examples of this practical focus include the numerous Usage Notes and Writing Hints students will find throughout the grammar section. Usage Notes guide students through some of the trickier aspects of applied grammar, emphasizing situations in which common problems occur. Writing Hints provide guidance in how to use different grammatical principles in academic writing. Along with an emphasis on using grammar in writing, students will encounter throughout these chapters a supportive, encouraging tone. They are shown how to use grammar to increase their repertoire of sentence forms, types, and patterns. They are also shown how to write grammatically rather than being presented with numerous examples of failings that need correction.

Coverage of grammar in *The Scribner Handbook for Writers* is extensive. The grammar chapters are arranged for maximum ease of use as a reference guide. Those who need work on grammatical structures or elements will find abundant examples and numerous exercise items that range not only across the academic disciplines but also across topics representing experiences from everyday life. The exercises and examples throughout these chapters balance the familiar and the new, the academic and the everyday, references to majority culture with various minority multicultural perspectives.

English as a Second Language

Chapter 15, "Grammar for ESL Writers," emphasizes the grammatical structures that many speakers and writers of English as a Second Language find troublesome. Carefully chosen examples offer students advice on usage coupled with clear explanations of basic grammatical concepts. Exercises provide numerous opportunities for students to practice using the various grammatical structures.

Style: Playing with Words and Sentences

The Scribner Handbook for Writers deals extensively with style, a critical aspect of writing for college students but one often neglected or given only cursory treatment. Two examples of our special treatment of style include the extensive coverage of diction and the display of sentence structures in our chapter on parallelism. Our chapters on words offer detailed examples of how words are used in various social contexts, how they carry not only lexical and social intonations but also regional information and figurative implications. We also address language bias, devoting attention to avoiding gender and race bias in language, but considering as well how to avoid other forms of biased language such as that directed against age, region, religion, sexual orientation, and physical characteristics.

Since understanding the connotation of words is crucial for students who are learning how to be more perceptive readers, more able writers, and better critical thinkers, we have created exercises that invite students to think about language, to analyze it, and to stretch their imaginations in a series of playful but instructive examples. We consistently connect our discussion of connotation (and the other aspects of diction) with reading, writing, and thinking.

One of the more unusual things we do in teaching sentence style is to set off parallel sentence elements in stacks or layers to provide a visual illustration of sentence organization. Our goal throughout the chapters on language and style is to help students express themselves with accuracy and grace.

Research

The six research chapters illustrate the complexity of the writing processes outlined in earlier chapters (especially Chapters 1–8) and they reinforce in cogent ways the important concepts developed in our reading chapters (Chapters 2 and 3). The first of the research chapters (Chapter 39) lays out the fundamentals of directed research. Primary emphasis is on showing students how to become efficient and effective researchers in the library and in the field. Chapter 40 shows students how to make use of that research—how to restrict a topic, read and evaluate sources, take notes, develop a reasonable thesis, consider audience and organization, draft an essay, incorporate evidence, and prepare a final manuscript. We have included a separate chapter on plagiarism because of the continued growth of this problem in academic writing and persistent student confusion about its precise nature. Chapter 41 (new to this edition) explains both intentional and accidental plagiarism and informs students how to avoid this academic crime by correctly documenting all of their sources. Chapter 42 explains how to use the Internet for research, especially for deepening and extending research and for using it in conjunction with print sources. To make these chapters more illustrative of the recursive processes of researching and writing, we show students how first-year student Ericka Kostka used library and Internet resources to become knowledgeable enough to write a research essay, and how she developed that essay.

In Chapter 43 students find the help they need to document their research essays and papers, whether they use MLA, APA, CMS, or CSE format. Our coverage of these documentation styles is complete and up-to-date, offering thorough coverage of MLA and APA and numerous examples of documenting in the sciences and documenting electronic sources. In Chapter 44 students can see how to document both MLA and APA essays. Ericka Kostka's complete essay appears in MLA form along with extensive annotations that highlight principles of research and writing from earlier chapters. Excerpts from Rosette Schleifer's essay illustrate the basic format for APA papers and reveals the nature and scope of her research.

Teaching and reference features to aid understanding

Examples of Student Writing

The Scribner Handbook for Writers contains more extensive and more instructive student writing than any handbook or writing guide currently available. Complete student essays and lengthy excerpts from many others appear in the essay chapters (6–8) and the final research chapter (44). In all, eight complete pieces of student writing, some of them fairly extensive, are complemented by numerous shorter examples of student writing ranging from a sentence or two to several paragraphs. These student examples provide a demonstration of how writers write. In showing the decision-making and revising processes in action, these writers help students understand the complex process of writing and its close connections to reading and thinking.

In addition, this *Handbook* offers many excellent examples by reputable writers, ranging from sample sentences to complete brief essays. These models throughout the text reinforce key principles in the chapters on reading, writing, and thinking in the opening parts of the *Handbook*.

Engaging Exercises, Individual and Collaborative

Exercises in *The Scribner Handbook for Writers* are numerous and various. Students will find exercises ranging from readily accessible practice materials to intellectually provocative and challenging writing assignments that call for creative and critical thinking and that encourage students to stretch their imaginations. Many exercises can be performed individually while others invite collaboration. Teachers who use collaborative teaching strategies will find ample opportunity to encourage students to work together on exercises and assignments throughout the *Handbook*. In all collaborative exercises, student writers are encouraged to seek feedback from their classmates, to share ideas, to open themselves to other points of view—all with an eye to returning to their individual writing tasks with additional ideas for revision.

Artwork in Color as Cues to Thinking and Writing

Students will find that color reproductions of a painting by van Gogh and black-and-white photographs by Richard Avedon, Tina Barnes, and New York University student Anna Norris are included as part of the pedagogy in our chapters on reading visual texts and developing ideas. The inclusion of Richard Avedon's photo, for example, serves as a stimulus for a lesson in questioning one's way to an idea. The pedagogy that accompanies the artwork shows students how to use guiding questions to discover an idea.

Vincent van Gogh's *The Starry Night* is discussed in Chapter 3, "Reading (and Writing about) Visual Texts." Students are led into the painting through a series of carefully sequenced exercises that invite their personal responses, their observations and inferences, and their evaluation of the interpretive ideas of others. As with the photographs, van Gogh's painting is included to stimulate thinking. The works of art serve as evidence for ideas that student writers develop in response to looking at artwork, learning about it, and thinking about what they see and learn in the context of their own lives.

The reproductions are an integral part of the pedagogy of Chapters 3 and 4. Working through this pedagogy reminds students that learning to make observations from evidence is central to interpretation, and that moving from observations to connections and inferences can lead to viable and defensible interpretations. We have found that students write well about visual images when they are encouraged to look carefully at details, describe accurately what they see, and reflect thoughtfully on their observations. Students also seem to enjoy writing and thinking about paintings and photographs.

Charts and Lists for Ready Reference

More than one hundred charts and lists are included in *The Scribner Handbook for Writers*. These compact reference aids—displayed in accessible categories on the back endpaper—provide handy summaries of key points for students to study and review as they learn and write. Some of the charts function as overviews, some as summaries, some as aids to memory. All offer a succinct visual counterpart to the discussions they abstract and condense. Overall, these strategically placed charts are designed to make concepts and information optimally accessible to students.

Changes in this edition

Throughout this new edition of *The Scribner Handbook for Writers*, we have maintained the features that distinguished the previous editions. We have added elements that will aid teachers in helping students become better writers, readers, and thinkers in a range of academic contexts.

In this fourth edition, we have created three new chapters. Chapter 3, "Reading (and Writing about) Visual Texts," explains how to interpret and critically respond to images. Chapter 41, "Avoiding Plagiarism," shows students how to avoid plagiarism in their writing. Chapter 48, "Writing and Making Oral Presentations," offers students simple guidelines for public speaking.

We have also added new material to other chapters. Chapter 7, "The Argumentative (Persuasive) Essay" now devotes considerable attention to the logic of reasonable arguments, detailed treatment that includes a discussion of logical fallacies. This chapter now provides two model essays, a shorter argument in the vein of the editorial and a longer, critical argument supported by written sources. Chapter 8, "The Literary (Analytical) Essay," synthesizes material from the third edition's chapters on the analytical essay and on writing about literature and adds new material about interpreting and responding to poetry.

Part Eight, "Research," has been updated to accommodate the latest developments in researching with electronic information databases and CD-ROM technology. Student research essays contain examples of documenting Internet sources. Chapter 43, "Documenting Sources," explains how to document the newest additions to Internet and electronic media sources.

While we have added much to the fourth edition, anyone comparing its table of contents with that of the previous edition will see that there are five fewer chapters in the new edition. This change reflects the synthesis of certain chapters, streamlining of the contents, and tightening of the writing. Our aim was both to update *The Scribner* and to distill it down to its essentials, making it a more practical and accessible resource for users.

Acknowledgments

From beginning to end, writing *The Scribner Handbook for Writers* has been a collaborative effort. We acknowledge here the help we have given one another in writing this book. We wish to thank our collaborators around the country who evaluated our initial plans and drafts, offering sound advice.

We thank these reviewers for their constructive comments on various parts of the manuscript: Virginia Johnson Anderson, Towson State University; Deborah C. Andrews, University of Delaware; Tamara Andrews, Iowa State University; Linda Anstendig, Pace University; David Bartholomae, University of Pittsburgh; Patsy Callaghan, Central Washington University; Cherie Castillo, University of Wisconsin–Fox Valley; John Chaffee, LaGuardia Community College; Carolyn Channell, Southern Methodist University; Dr. Mary Jane Clerkin, Berkeley College; Joseph J. Comprone, Arizona State University West; Thomas A. Copeland, Youngstown State University; Lauren Coulter, University of Tennessee; Bobby Cummings, Central Washington University; Carol David, Iowa State University; Mark DeFoe, West Virginia Wesleyan College; R. Scott Evans, University of the Pacific; James Farrelly, University of Dayton; Michael C. Flanigan, University of Oklahoma; Mark Gallaher, Freelance Ink Chrysanthy; M. Grieco, Seton Hall University; Dr. Elizabeth Howells, Armstrong Atlantic State University; Christine Hult, Utah State University; Douglas Hunt, University of Missouri, Columbia; William B. Lalicker, Murray State University; Mark Lester, Eastern Washington University; Miriam P. Moore, University of South Carolina; Mary Morse, Rider University; Roxanne Munch, Joliet Junior College; William Peirce, Prince Georges Community College; Nancy Porter, West Virginia Wesleyan College; Annette T. Rottenberg, University of Massachusetts, Amherst (Emerita); Alice M. Roy, California State University, Los Angeles; Jean Sorensen, Grayson County College; Barbara Stout, Montgomery College; John W. Taylor, South Dakota State University; William Vaughn, Central Missouri State University; Richard Veit, University of North Carolina, Wilmington; and Linda Woodson, The University of Texas at San Antonio.

Thanks also to many instructors who responded to surveys that were helpful to our design of this book: Libby Bay, Rockland Community College, SUNY; Kathleen Beauchene, Community College of Rhode Island; Peter G. Beidler, Lehigh University; Pam Besser, Jefferson Community College, Louisville; Wendy Bishop, Florida State University; Lynn Z. Bloom, University of Connecticut; John Boe, University of California, Davis; Alice Glarden Brand, SUNY Brockport; Alice Brekke, California State University, Long Beach; Stuart C. Brown, New Mexico State University; Thomas A. Brunell, Rutgers University, Newark, Dolores M. Burton, Boston University; Lee C. Carter, Wake Forest University; Donald A. Daiker, Miami University; John A. R. Dick, University of Texas, El Paso; Mimi Still Dixon, Wittenberg University; Jane Dugan, Cleveland State University; Penelope Dugan, Richard Stockton College of New Jersey; Lisa Ede, Oregon State University; Theresa Enos, University of Arizona; Christine Farris, Indiana University; Gary

Fincke, Susquehanna University; John Fugate, J. Sargeant Reynolds Community College; Susan Galloway, St. Mary's University; Michelle Gibson, Ohio University; Muriel Harris, Purdue University; Andrea W. Herrmann, University of Arkansas, Little Rock; Rosalie Hewitt, Northern Illinois University; Elizabeth Hodges, Virginia Commonwealth University; Francis A. Hubbard, Marquette University; Sally L. Joyce, Keene State College; Joyce Kinkead, Utah State University; Mary Levitt, North Adams State College; Marty Lewis, University of Texas, Brownsville; Tom MacLennan, University of North Carolina at Wilmington; Lynne C. McCauley, Western Michigan University; Susan H. McLeod, Washington State University; Nikki Lee Manos, Marymount College, Tarrytown; T. A. Marshall II, Robert Morris College; Janet Marting, University of Akron; Emily P. Miller, Virginia Military Institute; Kevin Morris, Greenville Technical College; Robert M. Otten, Indiana University, Kokomo; Susan Palo, University of California, Davis; Deepika Petraglia-Bahri, Bowling Green State University; John Woodrow Presley, University of Michigan, Dearborn; Jeanie Page Randall, Austin Peay State University, Clarksville; Ruth Ray, Wayne State University; Marjorie Roemer, Rhode Island College; Duane H. Roen, Arizona State University; William J. Schang, Ripon College; Charles I. Schuster, University of Wisconsin, Milwaukee; Nancy S. Shapiro, University of Maryland, College Park; Phillip Sipiora, University of South Florida; John W. Taylor, South Dakota State University; and Irene Ward, Kansas State University.

A number of colleagues deserve special thanks for their contributions, including: Linda Anstendig, Pace University; Chris Baker, Armstrong State College; Anne Bliss, University of Colorado, Boulder; Cherie Castillo, University of Wisconsin–Fox Valley; Cherie Clark, Miami Dade Community College; Boyd Creasman, West Virginia Wesleyan College; Michael Day, Northern Illinois University; Charles E. DeBose, California State University, Hayward; Ray Dumont, University of Massachusetts, Amherst; Maurice Duperre, Midlands Technical College; Jack Ferstel, University of Southwestern Louisiana; Jill Goodman Gould, Santa Clara University; Carol Jamison, Armstrong Atlantic State University; Nancy Krimmel, Midlands Technical College; Lee Anne Mauno, Indiana University; Susan Moore, Scottsdale Community College; Viki Pettijohn, Southwest Oklahoma State University; Linda Quillian, Benedict College; and Carol Schiess, Boise State University. Thanks to Alleen Pace Nilsen of Arizona State University, who reviewed the three sections on biased language in Chapter 26, making extensive suggestions and contributing generously to our work there. Thanks also to Margaret Bonner, who developed a rich chapter on English as a Second Language (Chapter 15) and to Rick Branscomb of Salem State College for his useful Chapter 42, "Using the Internet for Research." And thanks as well to those who helped us develop and update our research documentation chapter, especially Joseph Law of Texas Christian University.

Special gratitude must also be expressed to two other professional colleagues: Bill Lalicker of Murray State University and Robert Funk of Eastern Illinois University. Professor Lalicker has been with us on this project from the beginning, when we presented our initial ideas for the book. He has reviewed each of our drafts, offering consistently wise counsel, which we have incorporated gratefully in our revisions. Professor Funk gave us the benefit of his extensive knowledge of grammar by scrupulously reviewing our grammar chapters revising them to clarify explanations, add and replace exercises, and provide sound ways to illustrate grammatical and stylistic distinctions. We thank Bill Lalicker and Robert Funk for their help.

At Longman we have had the good fortune to work with Joseph Opiela. We also benefited from the perceptive assistance of development editor Adam Beroud; from Charles Annis, our production manager; from Ann Stypuloski, our marketing manager; and from Doug Day, field marketing specialist in English.

Finally, we owe a profound debt of gratitude to our wives, Mary Hammond DiYanni and Ann Burns Hoy for their loving support and their steadfastness during these years of labor. Thanks also to our children, Karen and Michael DiYanni, and Patrick and Tim Hoy, whose contributions appear in countless, anonymous ways in these pages.

ROBERT DIYANNI
PAT C. HOY II

Student Preface

How to Use this Book:
A Guide to Special Features

Quick access features for reference

The Scribner Handbook for Writers is a reference work to consult about matters of grammar, punctuation, mechanics, and style as well as a guidebook for your writing processes. This section shows you the features that will help you locate the information you need to use this *Handbook*.

Use these information locators.

- Front endpapers: The compact contents chart provides an overview of the section and page numbers of key topics you will need.
- Main contents: A detailed listing of sections and pages for all topics.
- Revision symbols—-back endpaper: This chart guides you to the revision symbols likely to be used by instructors or peers annotating your paper. The symbols are cross-referenced to appropriate *Handbook* sections, where you will see the symbols also used at the head of each page.
- A list of useful checklists, charts, and boxes—back endpaper: This listing is a convenient tool for locating the special boxed panels of checklists and guidelines for every stage of writing and revision.

Look for these features on each page:

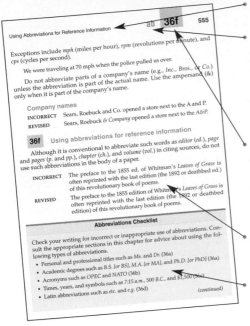

The *Header* briefly describes chapter and section topics.

The *Tab* identifies the section number for every topic. A symbol by the tab shows the revision symbol likely to be used by instructors or peers annotating your paper. These symbols are also listed on the back endpaper.

The *Chapter Number* and *Section Letter* for each heading are included in the tab. These are the section number references to follow when you look for cross-references throughout the *Handbook*.

Revision Examples identify common writing problems and suggest revision solutions.

Explanations describe how or why writing guidelines operate. **Bold type** identifies key terms. *Cross-references* provide section numbers that index related topics.

Handy boxes quickly sum up the writing steps and guidelines that you need

Users of *The Scribner Handbook for Writers* have taken advantage of the abundant box panels throughout the book. These distinctive panels do more than overview the high spots in grammar and writing—they sum up and provide step-by-step checklists to help walk you through the writing and revision processes that are most important. Especially in working with writing processes, you can start with the box summaries listed in the back endpapers, and then look at the text and student sample papers for a full understanding of how a writing process works. Take a look at the following examples, and then follow how these processes are explained in Chapters 2 and 40.

your notes for your own ideas about the evidence. Let your ideas guide you. Be especially careful to separate your own thoughts from those of your sources. Doing so will also help ensure that you do not plagiarize. The tips in the accompanying chart will keep you on track as you incorporate evidence into your essay.

Guidelines for Incorporating Evidence

- Clearly introduce and conclude each summary, paraphrase, or quotation in such a way that readers know where it begins and ends.
- Ensure that the incorporated material blends smoothly into your sentences and paragraphs (see 40i-1). Avoid shifts in verb tense or awkward phrasing that would contrast sharply with the incorporated evidence, making your sentences difficult to read and understand.
- Provide a parenthetical citation within the essay to document the source of your evidence and avoid plagiarism. That in-text citation will correspond to the source list at the end of the essay (see Chapter 13).
- Explain the incorporated evidence so that readers can understand how the evidence relates to a paragraph's main idea and, when appropriate, to your thesis (see 40i-2).

Here are some guidelines for using supporting evidence in your paper.

1 Integrating source material

When you put information from your notes int[o]
duce that material by identifying the author or tit[le]
also identify the author's special credentials if you a[re]
authority to help you establish your claim.

At the end of each summary, paraphrase, or q[uotation]
about the source in parentheses. Parenthetical info[rmation]
the author's last name (unless you have already ci[ted]
graph) and relevant page numbers. The title (or a [para-]
graph) also appear as a part of the parenthetical citatio[n]
by that author appears in your list of sources, or [the]
author. This parenthetical information signals fo[r]
incorporated material. (See Chapter 43 for mor[e]
ing references.)

---

3 Using a double-column notebook

To create a **double-column notebook**, simply divide your page in half. One half is for summarizing and interpreting what you read. Use this side of the page to record as accurately as you can your understanding of what the text says. Use the other side to respond to what you have read, to think about its implications, and to relate it to other things you have read or otherwise experienced.

The advantage of a double-column notebook is that it encourages you to be an active reader, to think about what you read and to make connections

Highlights of the Double-Column Notebook

SUMMARY	COMMENTS
Summarize the text.	Respond to your summary.
Interpret the author's ideas.	Reflect on the author's ideas.
Explain the ideas succinctly.	Consider whether you agree or disagree—and why.
Identify important details.	Raise questions about the details you have observed.
Relate the details to the central idea.	Relate the text and the writer's main idea to other things you have read and to your own experience.

Here's an example of a box on critical reading.

Computer Tip

Using Separate Windows for Writing

You can work on more than one document at a time by using separate windows for each document. You can view documents simultaneously as you can switch between them. You may wish, for example, to add material from one document into another, perhaps material from an earlier draft into a later one, or perhaps notes from a brainstorming document into a draft, which elaborates those notes. You can also view the documents at the same time by selecting the VIEW or WINDOW feature of your word processing program.

Ways to get ideas and develop them into a solid essay

Users of *The Scribner Handbook for Writers* have a unique advantage in looking for reliable methods of developing writing ideas and applying them to successful writing assignments. This *Handbook* shows you how to select and apply any of four methods for developing ideas (Chapter 4); how to use reading skills to find ideas from evidence (Chapter 2); how to work with your ideas to form a thesis with sound support, and how to develop your ideas into essay projects of exploration, argumentation, or literature (Chapters 6, 7, and 8). Here's an overview of four ways to develop ideas:

1. *Inferring ideas by creative and logical thinking and questioning of evidence.* Section 4a shows you how to look for key features and significant patterns within the evidence, to seek underlying relationships that weren't at first obvious but that can be used to build inferences and ideas for your paper, and to decide how you feel about the evidence before you.

2. *Letting your ideas evolve through stages of writing and revising.* Section 4b shows how you can work from sketchy freewriting or brainstorming exercises to find a usable starting point for your essay. This discussion also helps you test your intentions and the implications of your draft from new angles by redrafting, questioning, and connecting to alternate possibilities until you have a developed essay. Excerpts from a student essay and from a paragraph by E. B. White show you how this revising can be done.

3. *Looking for creative connections and relationships in your material to find ideas.* Section 4c shows how questioning and writing about evidence can lead to a connection-making process. This process will help you respond to one idea (an assignment or a provocative statement) in relation to another statement, image, text, or experience that has moved you. As you put together the ideas you discover when making these connections, you can form a significant essay that says something important to you.

4. *Discovering writing ideas from looking at controversies that interest you.* Section 4d shows you how to work with evidence about conflicting points of view. This section covers ways to line up opposing viewpoints and look for questions, weaknesses, and connections among parts of the controversy until you have formed what can become a reasonable conclusion of your own. This section also shows how to use your conclusion as a basis or thesis for your own essay.

Ways to form ideas into essay assignments you will meet in your courses

The Scribner Handbook for Writers shows you how to work within the forms your writing is likely to take for most of the assignments you encounter in college. The *Handbook* also shows how an essay evolves in stages rather than by any simple application of a formula. Whether your writing ideas evolve from personal experience, from a close reading of a text, or from observing and studying a set of objects, college essays that develop these ideas are likely to become one of these three types of essays:

Exploratory Essay (Chapter 6). An exploratory essay strives to share with readers the writer's process of inquiring into an interesting but often hard-to-define idea. When you write an exploratory essay, you develop an idea, often from experience that has become familiar in your or another person's life and you shape this experience into a coherent form that allows you to use stories as evidence.

Argumentative Essay (Chapter 7). Developing an argument in an essay involves a relatively formal process of discovering a claim that can be developed and supported with careful reasoning and sound evidence. This process requires careful consideration of counterarguments and competing viewpoints.

Literary Essay (Chapter 8). The main goal of literary essays is to share with readers an interpretation of a "text"—a set of written, experienced, or observed events—that is complex and in need of explanation.

Full-length student samples show you realistic ways to develop essays

A distinctive feature of *The Scribner Handbook for Writers* is its exceptionally generous sampling of real student research papers and essays that have been developed using the methods described in the *Handbook*. You can learn how real writers build assignments by analyzing how the sample essays are constructed and by reading the *Handbook*'s generous commentary about these essays. In research as well as essay writing, the *Handbook* offers a step-by-step demonstration of how revision and the process of rethinking ideas affects writing.

One research paper using the MLA documentation style.

- Ericka Kostka develops evidence from written and electronic sources to write about the controversy over retaining gray wolves in Yellowstone National Park, and keeping them on the endangered species list.

One primary-source student paper on a literary topic.

- Ruth Chung writes on Virginia Woolf's "Old Mrs. Grey."

One research paper using the APA documentation style.

- Rosette Schleifer does a research piece on intimate relationships.

Four student essays show you how to write exploratory, argumentative, and literary essays. Each of the complete essays is shown in various stages of revision. Many examples of student writing illustrate the effective use of visual sources (reproduced in the *Handbook*).

An argumentative essay by Matthew Weishar highlights an effective revision process.

Applied grammar demonstrations show you how the rules work in real writing situations

The Scribner Handbook for Writers helps you look beyond the grammar rules to see why conventions of usage and grammar work to your advantage as you craft sentences that say what you mean.

- Grammar and Writing sections explain why the rules work to your advantage.

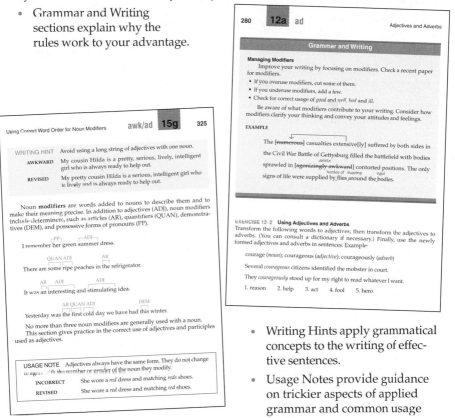

280   **12a**   ad   Adjectives and Adverbs

Grammar and Writing

Managing Modifiers

Improve your writing by focusing on modifiers. Check a recent paper for modifiers.

- If you overuse modifiers, cut some of them.
- If you underuse modifiers, add a few.
- Check for correct usage of *good* and *well, bad* and *ill.*

Be aware of what modifiers contribute to your writing. Consider how modifiers clarify your thinking and convey your attitudes and feelings.

EXAMPLE

The [~~numerous~~] casualties extensive[ly] suffered by both sides in the Civil War Battle of Gettysburg filled the battlefield with bodies sprawled in [~~agonizingly awkward~~] *delete* contorted positions. The only signs of life were supplied by *hordes of buzzing rigid* flies around the bodies.

EXERCISE 12-2   Using Adjectives and Adverbs

Transform the following words to adjectives; then transform the adjectives to adverbs. (You can consult a dictionary if necessary.) Finally, use the newly formed adjectives and adverbs in sentences. Example:

courage (*noun*); courageous (*adjective*); courageously (*adverb*)

Several *courageous* citizens identified the mobster in court.

They *courageously* stood up for my right to read whatever I want.

1. reason   2. help   3. act   4. fool   5. hero

Using Correct Word Order for Noun Modifiers   awk/ad **15g**   325

WRITING HINT   Avoid using a long string of adjectives with one noun.

AWKWARD   My cousin Hilda is a pretty, serious, lively, intelligent girl who is always ready to help out.

REVISED   My pretty cousin Hilda is a serious, intelligent girl who is lively and is always ready to help out.

Noun **modifiers** are words added to nouns to describe them and to make their meaning precise. In addition to adjectives (ADJ), noun modifiers include determiners, such as articles (AR), quantifiers (QUAN), demonstratives (DEM), and possessive forms of pronouns (PP).

 ┌─PP─┐ ┌─ADJ─┐
I remember her green summer dress.

 ┌QUAN ADJ┐   ┌AR┐
There are some ripe peaches in the refrigerator.

 ┌AR┐ ┌ADJ┐   ┌ADJ┐
It was an interesting and stimulating idea.

 ┌AR QUAN ADJ┐   ┌DEM┐
Yesterday was the first cold day we have had this winter.

No more than three noun modifiers are generally used with a noun. This section gives practice in the correct use of adjectives and participles used as adjectives.

USAGE NOTE   Adjectives always have the same form. They do not change to agree with the number or gender of the noun they modify.

INCORRECT   She wore a *red* dress and matching *reds* shoes.

REVISED   She wore a *red* dress and matching *red* shoes.

- Writing Hints apply grammatical concepts to the writing of effective sentences.

- Usage Notes provide guidance on trickier aspects of applied grammar and common usage problems.

References and tools for computer-based writing and research

648   **42b**   accessing   Using the Internet for Research

Computer Tip

Using the Internet to Find a Topic
You can pursue a topic that interests you by using a search engine such as Excite or InfoSeek, which has subject areas or categories arranged hierarchically. First, find categories that seem relevant to your area of interest or your topic. Within a broad area such as *politics*, for example, you might find the topic *government*, and within that area, *elections*. As you follow the subject tree into more specific topics, jot down other related topics that might be either interesting to you or relevant to your assignment.

Kostka decided to pursue the topic "Endangered Species," with 75 sites listed, and while a click to that page did not reveal a separate category for wolves, she found several sites with further links on endangered species, and three sites with relevant government documents.

When Kostka went through a similar range of hierarchical topics on the HotBot search engine, she found a useful topic, "Environmental Monitoring," where she was able to receive a number of "Site Recommendations" that would provide detailed information about this subject. With such sequences of subject searching, Kostka was able to move quickly from general to more restricted and specific topics.

http://www.lib.berkeley.edu/ TeachingLib/Guides/ Internet/FindInfo.html
Offers valuable guidance on searching the Internet.

Another useful resource for pursuing subjects and subtopics is the *Library of Congress Subject Headings* (LCSH) reference, a three-volume book that lists all of the subject headings used to classify library books (see 39e-1-2 on library catalogs and key word searches). Using the key terms from this listing, Kostka was able to pursue some relevant subject topics by means of a key word search.

2   Key word searches

After you have selected key words that are closely related to your chosen area of research, you are ready for additional searching on the Web. Enter

* Computer Tips provide practical advice for word processing, writing, and researching.
* Weblinks provide citations for more than one hundred World Wide Web sites, which offer guidance on every aspect of the writing process.

Narrowing and Refining Your Search   accessing   **42b**   647

WebCrawler
http://webcrawler.com/info.wbcrwl   Fast and complete search engine. Includes newsgroups and e-mail. *Subject area, key word, and Boolean searching.*

Yahoo!
http://www.yahoo.com   Includes news, e-mail, and chat rooms. *Subject area and key word searching. No Boolean searching.*

42b   Narrowing and refining your search

Because there is so much information on the Web, you will almost certainly need to limit your searches so that you are only identifying information that is directly related to your research area. There are three primary ways to facilitate and narrow your searches: subject area, key word, and Boolean searches.

1   Subject area searches

You can look for Web sites according to subject areas in many of the search engines (see the listing above), pursuing subjects arranged in a hierarchy that allows you to narrow your search by topic and subtopic. Because each search engine develops its own list of topical sites based on editorial judgment and experience, search engines can vary widely in both the number and quality of sites offered for selection by subject area. One of the most comprehensive subject listings for Web sites is offered by Yahoo! However, Google, HotBot, InfoSeek, and Lycos have extensive lists as well.

When Ericka Kostka needed some information about the gray wolf reintroduction program in Yellowstone, she looked at the Yahoo! site which contained broad subject areas, such as "Arts & Humanities," "Business & Money," "Health," "Reference," and "Science"—the last of which offered a subtopic of "Animals." Clicking on this subtopic allowed her to find and click again on a subtopic of "Wildlife," a page with 413 topics and special descriptive site listings, many with links to other wildlife sites. On this page

* *Searching for fresh research material on the Internet.* Chapter 42 describes reliable guidelines, step-by-step processes, and applied examples of Internet research procedures. Section 42b shows you how using search engines can be a productive way to find information for your paper. This section also explains how to consider the tradeoffs of time and effort needed for Internet research by critically evaluating the flood of sources available on the Internet.

References and tools for document design

Chapter 46, "Writing and Designing for the World Wide Web," explains how to compose a Web page.

Other handy computer-oriented references features:

Chapter 45, "The Visual Design of Documents," illustrates how to use space and graphic elements to communicate more effectively in

- Reports
- Proposals

Chapter 47, "Business Writing," includes:

- Formatting résumés
- Writing e-mail correspondence
- Preparing scannable and Web-based résumés

Other extras give you help where you need it

The Scribner Handbook for Writers helps you solve writing problems beyond the basics of developing and revising an essay. Here are some key areas where you can find helpful guidelines and examples:

- *Models and guidelines for the writing you'll use in the workplace.* Chapter 47 highlights résumés, job application correspondence, and business letters and memos.

- *Finding help with the English language for international students, regional speakers, or writers seeking to avoid biased language.* Chapter 15 gives a complete reference for international students needing a refresher on troublesome features of the English language. Chapter 26 provides helpful guidelines for regional and dialect speakers in making decisions about forms of English to use in writing and also addresses issues of biased language.

- *Getting extra help with grammar and usage trouble spots. The Scribner Handbook for Writers* provides extensive exercises, many of them fascinating thinking and writing activities, as well as supplements in key areas of grammar and usage.

PART 1

THE WRITING, READING, THINKING CONNECTION

 # Writing – A Way of Expressing Ideas

1a Becoming a writer

Becoming a good writer depends on your becoming a good reader and thinker. Writing, reading, and thinking are so closely related that it is difficult to imagine one without the others. Knowledge provides the basis for your writing—knowledge that you gain from thinking or reflecting about what you read, experience, and observe.

Discovering ideas can be exciting. Studying and writing, you find that you know enough about a subject to make judgments and draw conclusions. You discover possibilities that no one else has imagined quite the way you have. With something to write about, you begin to understand that you are not a recorder, transcribing what others have said. Rather, you are a *thinker*— a writer with ideas of your own to express. You have the power to cause others to sit up and take notice. You know something, and you know how to say it.

As a writer, you often want to move as quickly as possible from coherent sentences to good paragraphs and then on to full-length pieces of writing such as interesting essays or reports. But you can gain a great deal by moving gradually and deliberately instead of leaping ahead too fast. Reviewing the fundamentals can help you write better. Another look at the basics about sentences can reveal not only how to write different kinds of sentences but also how to vary sentences to interest your readers and to help you develop ideas. Reconsidering the fundamentals of paragraph writing can show you how paragraphs, like good essays, vary according to purpose and rely on different kinds of evidence depending on the nature of your idea.

Reviewing these fundamentals, you can become aware of just how exciting words and syntax (the arrangement of words into sentences) can be. Consider these two sentences:

> The woman walked down the trail.

> The frail woman walked with a slight limp as she made her way down the narrow, winding trail, looking, as she went along, for the thief who had assailed her when first she turned round the bend, the thief who had been dogging her for nearly a mile as she made her way home, deep in the woods, way out beyond help and the telephone and the police.

Each of these sentences has its own special qualities. Neither is preferable. The simplicity and directness of the first, complemented by the surprising revelations of the second, suggest possibilities available to you as a writer. The first sentence conveys information. The second also conveys information but suggests as well an idea—the idea that movement deeper into the woods is movement toward isolation and danger. The writer does not declare that idea straight out but implies it in the details of the sentence. Like a good story, the second sentence draws you into it, inviting you to decipher its meaning. The sentence conveys more than the writer states.

When you write, you have options, endless possibilities for helping your readers understand what you have to tell them. Learning about the options and variations by writing and practicing, you will begin to discover how satisfying it is to find an idea and express it so that others know just what you know. Therein lie the writer's most gratifying rewards.

1b   An overview of the writing process

The **writing process** often begins with a fleeting hunch about something you want to write about and ends with a completed essay. Writing that essay depends very much on your ability to think, read, and take notes, but it also depends on your capacity to complete a series of related tasks: accumulating evidence, formulating ideas, considering audience and purpose, preparing, organizing, drafting, revising, editing, and proofreading. We will look closely at these tasks in this chapter.

Computer Tip

Getting Online Help

Throughout this book you will find numerous references to Web sites that offer online writing help. These online writing labs, or OWLs, provide assistance on every aspect of writing, including finding a topic, refining a thesis, developing paragraphs, drafting essays, revising, editing, proofreading, and more. One of the most popular is the OWL at Purdue University: http://owl.english.purdue.edu

---

But to suggest that the writing process is linear—that you go through these tasks step by step, the same way every time—would be to deny its most important characteristic: flexibility. You may discover differences in the process almost every time you write an essay.

Writing an essay can be, and most often is, a messy business. Thinking and reading and drafting and rethinking and revising and rereading go on and on as you write. The process moves back and forth; it is recursive. It usually involves some false starts as well as botched endings, jumbled middles, and muddled ideas. Do not be dismayed by the complications. You will get better and more efficient as you learn to be more comfortable with the writing process and its interesting complications. All writers face them, no matter what their level of experience. In Chapter 4, you can watch E. B. White, a professional essayist, struggling to develop an idea in a single paragraph about the first moon walk. But you can tell that the struggle is accompanied by the pleasure of getting the words right, finally.

http://www.writing.
colostate.edu/references/
Provides an introduction to
the writing process with an
emphasis on developing ideas.

1c   Accumulating evidence and formulating ideas

To become a good writer, you need the two kinds of knowledge you have just read about—knowledge about how to write and knowledge of a subject. You will accumulate knowledge about how to write as you study writing and as you write. You can acquire knowledge about a given subject much more deliberately, by way of experience, of course, but also through concentrated study. Let us consider briefly the subject *civil disobedience*—disobeying seemingly unjust laws through passive resistance—and how you might begin to acquire knowledge and evidence about it to gain insight that will lead to ideas.

Reading about civil disobedience, you discover that people often have to make complex choices in the face of the law. As you read and think about civil disobedience and then start to write about it, you discover how disobedience can be civilized and nonviolent, how it can affect lives, and how it can lead to violence, just as it can lead to changes in laws that a community considers unjust.

Studying such a controversial issue, you begin to realize that you have something to say about it that no one else has imagined quite the way you have. Your acquired knowledge provides the foundation for your ideas and eventually becomes the **evidence** you use in your essays.

Ideas and evidence have a symbiotic relationship; they feed off each other. Stephen Jay Gould, an evolutionary biologist, makes some interesting observations about his own science that should help you understand more clearly the relationship between evidence and ideas:

> Well, evolution *is* a theory. It is also a fact. And facts and theories are different things, not rungs in a hierarchy of increasing certainty. Facts are the world's data. Theories are structures of ideas that explain and interpret facts. Facts do not go away when scientists debate rival theories to explain them. Einstein's theory of gravitation replaced Newton's, but apples did not suspend themselves in mid-air pending the outcome. . . . In science, "fact" can only mean "confirmed to such a degree that it would be perverse to withhold provisional assent."
>
> —Stephen Jay Gould, "Evolution as Fact and Theory"

An **idea** accounts for evidence, provides a theory about it. An idea is your sense of what the evidence means, your explanation or interpretation of the facts. Your essay will be shaped and controlled by a leading idea (often called a **thesis**).

Think again about the topic *civil disobedience.* It is not a new concept. The United States was founded on disobedience, not all of it civil. Looking back at U.S. history, you can find numerous examples of important changes brought about by disobedience and revolution. But the term acquired new meaning during the civil rights demonstrations in the late 1950s and early 1960s in the United States when African Americans began to speak out against racial injustice. If, as a writer, you choose to look into the matter of civil disobedience, you might focus on what has already happened, or you might focus on what is going on in the United States today. Wherever you look, you will find **controversy**—disagreement about past events or about future courses of action. When you find such controversy, you are probably on the scent of an idea.

http://www.powa.org/
whtfrms.htm
Helps with deciding what
to write about, with finding
a viable topic.

The evidence you assemble about civil disobedience leads to questions: Under what conditions is it permissible to break the law? What is justifiable violence? How should oppressed citizens respond to unjust laws? At first, such questions lead to a search for more evidence, but then those questions lead to answers, to your interpretation of what the evidence means. That interpretation is your idea, something you reason or intuit from the evidence.

As a writer, your dual tasks are to create a good idea from the available evidence and to find an interesting way to express that idea, often in an essay. You can never be sure about that available evidence—where it will come from, what you will think about it once you find it, how you will use it in your essay. At the outset, you cannot predict where your search for evidence will take you. Every time you begin the process of writing an essay, you are on the trail of discovery, on the scent of something new, something you can discover and express in words.

An **essay** is your attempt to express an idea through writing so that readers can understand and accept what you have discovered. As you have just seen, the knowledge you acquire through study becomes the evidence you need in your essay to illustrate and develop your leading idea.

When you begin to decide how best to explain your idea and your reasons for believing it, you will have to select evidence from all that acquired knowledge. You have to consider what you know, think about your purpose, and think about what your readers need to know so that you can choose only the specific evidence that will help you present your idea. You will also have to organize your presentation into the form of an essay.

1d Assessing audience and purpose

1 How audience influences writing

Your readers, those people you are trying to reach with your writing, constitute your **audience**. The relationship between your audience's needs—based on its knowledge and level of expertise—and your own selection and presentation of evidence is important. Much of what you say and how you say it depends on whether your audience is a group of experts or a more general audience consisting of diverse people interested in your topic.

Even the way you organize your writing and the amount of detail you include (the terms you define, the amount of context you provide, the level of your explanations) depend in part on what your audience needs to know. If you are writing about civil disobedience for a group of historians, you can assume that because they are experts they know the meaning of civil disobedience and know its history. At the outset of your essay, you would need to remind them only of key points important to the development of your idea. But if you are writing about the same subject for a general audience with little expert knowledge (e.g., your English class), you may have to prepare your audience by filling in important background information and defining basic terms. You have to establish context so they can understand your idea.

As a writer, you must always consider what your audience needs to know to understand your essay. It pays to think often of that audience. Think about what assumptions you share with your readers and what you might disagree about. Use the Audience Checklist on p. 9 to help you think about your audience and make decisions on how best to communicate with that audience.

2 How to assess audience feedback

Often in a college course your instructor will be your primary audience, providing written feedback and guidance as you develop your papers. Your instructor may also designate classmates as your audience and at the same time ask them to be your collaborators. They will provide feedback during the time that you are drafting and revising. You will not have to imagine their response as you often do with other audiences. They will tell you how well they understand what you have written.

Your instructor and your classmates serve as important reminders that you rarely write just for yourself. Unless you are writing a personal journal, you are writing to reveal your thoughts to someone else, so you always have to put yourself to the test of your readers' understanding. To put yourself in your readers' place takes practice and skill at separating yourself from what you have written. But it is not only a matter of learning to stand apart from your drafts and see them objectively; it is also a matter of learning to spot gaps even as you write. Develop the good habit of pausing occasionally as you write to ask yourself whether you think your audience will be able to understand your point.

3   How to influence an audience—Purpose and tone

You write for any number of reasons or **purposes**—to provide information; to persuade others to accept your point of view; to explain an event that you witnessed, a poem that you read, or a movie that you saw; to entertain—but beneath all of these reasons for writing is the desire to be understood. You also often write to get a response.

You may simply want your readers to know something—to respond by understanding—but you may also want to stir them to action. Whatever your purpose, you are not likely to accomplish it without carefully considering your own relationship to your audience. When you write, you not only provide evidence and explanation so that your audience can follow along and understand what you have to say; you also provide a crucial sense of your own attitude to that audience through the **tone** of your writing. Tone conveys your attitude toward your subject and your sense of how best to approach your audience according to your purpose. Tone, therefore, includes strategy. Let us consider a few of your options by examining four professional writers at work. All of these writers are targeting a general audience.

In the following example, the writer's tone is conversational, light, and humorous. The writer's purpose is to interest his readers in a subject of great interest to him—his own writing.

Occasionally I write familiar essays. When I send them to editors, I usually explain that I am trying to write my way to a new car, adding that I have done well recently and have earned the front half of a station wagon, the automatic transmission, power brakes, and a luggage rack.

> Of course, that's not true. My essays will never earn me a new car. Besides I am happy with my 1973 Pontiac.
>
> —Samuel Pickering, "Being Familiar"

The tone of the following example is biting, witty, and angry, and the author's purpose is to evoke awareness. Carter is having a bit of fun about women's makeup, but anger lurks behind her playfulness, anger intended to evoke awareness and perhaps to change habits. Hers is a serious cultural argument.

> White-based lipsticks, colourless glosses, or no lipstick at all, were used in the 1960s. Now the mouth is back as a bloody gash, a visible wound. This mouth bleeds over everything, cups, ice-cream, table napkins, towels. Mary Quant has a shade called (of course) "Bloody Mary," to ram the point home. We will leave our bloody spoor behind us, to show we have been there.
>
> —Angela Carter, "A Wound in the Face"

In the passage that follows, the author uses a clear, unemotional tone. She also uses images to lull her readers into awareness and understanding about the relationship between the stark beauty of winter and winter's effect on the mind. The transparent, unemotional flatness here leads her audience to accept a revelation at the end of the paragraph.

> Winter is smooth-skulled, and all our skids on black ice are cerebral. When we begin to feel cabin-feverish, the brain pistons thump against bone and mind interrupts—literally invading itself—unable to get fresh air. With the songbirds gone only scavengers are left: magpies, crows, eagles. As they pick on road-killed deer we humans are apt to practice the small cruelties on each other.
>
> —Gretel Ehrlich, "The Smooth Skull of Winter"

Finally, the tone of the following passage is technical and academic but inviting. The author seeks to interest a general audience in a technical experiment, but without becoming so technical and formal that he turns away all but the experts. Heinrich tries to figure out how he will gather experimental data that will in turn allow him to explain how the sphinx moth regulates its body temperature during flight.

My problem was now specific: Is heat loss regulated by way of the circulatory system? I couldn't stay away from the lab for more than a few hours at a time. Once I went to camp out for a weekend in the Sierras, but my mind was in the lab and I didn't see the birds or flowers. My measurements of heat production (oxygen consumption rate) and thoracic temperature showed that the moths thermoregulated by as much as tripling their rate of heat loss during flight at high air temperatures. But how could you measure heat loss facilitated by blood flow in a flying moth? Sphinx moths are extremely fast. You can't trail them in flight with instruments attached. I decided to mimic the overheating that normally occurs in flight and to control it myself.

—Bernd Heinrich, "The Thesis Hunt"

The four preceding passages give you a glimpse of how you can vary tone to suit your purpose. Academic writing often has a formal and technical tone, and it should always be reasonable and objective, serious and thoughtful. It should also avoid contractions such as *they're, we'll,* and *you're,* and casual expressions such as "I'd thought long and hard about Sylvia Plath's

---

Audience Checklist

- Who are my readers? Are they experts or are they generalists?
- What reasonable assumptions can I make about what my audience knows? Do I need to provide detailed background information? Can I assume that my audience will understand the technical terms and language?
- What sort of audience response do I hope for?
- If my audience's response is hostile, what can I say to make my readers more receptive? What concessions can I make to them without compromising my own position? If my audience is friendly, how can I keep their interest?
- What can I discover by looking at my writing objectively—that is, by reading my writing as if I am a member of the audience? What evidence or explanations have I left out?
- What tone would be most appropriate and produce the desired effect with this audience?

images." Write instead, "Sylvia Plath expresses her sense of despair in a number of images that form a pattern within her poem," and then go on to discuss each of those images and explain the pattern in clear, direct analytical language.

Despite its formality, academic writing can, at appropriate times, accommodate humor, personal experience, and even satire. But it is not ordinarily as conversational or personal as Samuel Pickering's is in the preceding passage from "Being Familiar." Your tone will depend on your subject, but it will depend as well on your purpose and your sense of what your audience will be most receptive to. No formula specifies what tone to use for what effect. You will learn what is appropriate by experimenting, by practicing, and by studying how other writers use tone effectively.

1e   Preparing to write

Most of the evidence for your essays will come from actual experience and from reading, so it is useful to keep journals. It will also help to know other preparatory strategies.

1   Keeping a reading journal

Try to become an active reader who not only questions and thinks about what you read but also keeps ongoing records of those questions and reflections. Such written records may turn out to be your best source of ideas. Because remembering and reflecting can add to and enhance your preparation for writing, read with pen in hand. Keep track of your mind's play by noting what interests you and by jotting down your thoughts in a **reading journal** as you read.

The format for your reading journals can vary. If you are reading a book or copies of articles that you own, you can record your observations directly on the printed pages—highlighting or underlining what seems important, writing down questions that occur to you as you read, making note of connections you see within the piece you are reading and of connections with other books or articles you have read or with observations from your field research. The book or article itself becomes a journal that you can go back to, studying both it and your reflections all in one place.

At times you will need more space than the printed page provides. In that case, you can keep a journal in a separate notebook, on a pad of paper,

Computer Tip

Using Your Computer to Brainstorm

You can brainstorm to find ideas by creating a document expressly for that purpose and saving it, updating it as you think of new ideas. First, type what you know about your topic, using listing, freewriting, and other quick-writing techniques. Then, jot down questions you have that you need to investigate. Save the document for review and revising later, as a prompt to further thinking.

or in your computer. This type of journal would consist of your **freewriting**. This is writing in which you let your mind play more expansively over what you have read, recording your thoughts in whatever way they occur. Or you can keep a double-column notebook in which you can align your reflections with your summary of the text you are reading. Simply divide your notebook pages so that in one column you summarize what you have read and in the facing column you reflect on what you have summarized.

Reviewing your journals should help you get your bearings, suggesting the importance of what you have read and of your reflections about that reading. That record helps prepare you for writing, reminding you of how you made sense of what you read, of your questions, of tentative connections you made, of controversies that seemed intriguing, of other books you have read that seem to relate to the assigned or chosen reading. Most important, however, is that your reading journals help you discover your own ideas.

2 Keeping a personal journal

You will not, of course, depend solely on evidence that you have gleaned from reading. Sometimes, when writing essays, you will make use of your own experiences, such as in an exploratory essay. Those experiences will actually constitute much of the evidence from which you develop ideas.

Keep a record of interesting experiences in a **personal journal**. You should be especially mindful of moments that stop you in your tracks and make you take notice—a little walled-in enclosure with a tiny headstone just off the side of a quiet country road; the shimmering effect of the breeze on the

Computer Tip

Using a Computer Notepad

You can use your computer to "take notes" while you are reading online and to "make notes" when you write with a computer. If you have access to separate windows, you can read a text in one window and write notes about it in another—or write your essay or paper in one window and jot additional notes and thoughts in a second window. When writing on a single screen, you can jot questions and thoughts as you write. But surround them with *** or ### to distinguish them from your actual essay. Later, when you revise, you can develop them and incorporate them into your writing, or you can delete them.

leaves of the birch trees outside your window; a scene you saw on television or at the movies; music you heard on the radio or at a concert. Think of yourself as a writer trying to remember the essence of what you have seen. You are less interested in creating a detailed report of what happened than in conveying what the event meant to you. You want to account for why it struck you so powerfully.

As you make notes about those events, remember to describe how you felt about them and what you thought about those feelings. Later, when you sit down to write, these memories may come back to mind when you least expect them, and if they do, you will be able to turn to your journal for details. As your mind plays over the moment and as you consider your recorded evidence, you may begin to connect those recorded events with books you have read, with other experiences, with movies or songs or visual images. Connecting those pieces of evidence can create the trace of an idea.

3   Using other preparatory strategies

Besides journal writing, a number of other important strategies can help you prepare to write and can lead you to develop ideas. The accompanying list identifies those strategies and refers you to the sections of the *Handbook* that discuss and illustrate them.

Preparatory Strategies that Will Lead You to Ideas

- Outlining and mapping (see 1f)
- Questioning (see 2b-1, 4a, and 8a-3)
- Writing to discover ideas (see 4b)
- Developing ideas by making connections (see 4c)
- Using controversy to find ideas (see 4d)
- Listing details and observations (see 8a-2)

EXERCISE 1–1   **Recording Your Ideas**

1. Create a reading journal. Select a textbook from your syllabus and read a portion of it. Then make a list of two or three major ideas you found in the book. Reflect on those ideas, writing down what you think about them. Finally, see if those ideas lead you to an idea of your own or to questions that you would like answered.

2. Create a personal journal. Make observations about interesting details for about a week. Remember also to keep track of how those observations affected you.

3. After you have kept your personal journal for several days, look back through it for connections between two events that you recorded, events that might not on the surface seem related. If you see such connections, add notes to your journal about them. Look back to your reading journal as well. Make notes about the connections you see between what you have been reading and what you have been observing. Let your imagination have free rein; let your mind play over this recorded evidence. Begin to write, preparing two typed pages in which you try to reveal your discoveries to a general audience.

1f   Organizing

After you have become knowledgeable about an assigned subject or one you have selected on your own, and after you have begun to develop an idea about your evidence (gathered from reading, field research, your own experiences and observations, and so forth), you will have to figure out how to convey that idea to your readers. To do this, you will have to answer two interesting questions:

1. How do I decide what evidence to select from all of the evidence I have accumulated?
2. In what order do I present the evidence to my readers?

The answers to these questions are quite simple: You select the evidence that will, in your mind, help your audience see what it is that you want to convey. You then present that evidence—along with your explanation of it—in a way that you think will make it easy for your audience to follow.

How then should you go about organizing your evidence and your essay? Each essay you write will have a basic, three-part organizational structure—a beginning, a middle, and an ending—that will give shape to your

http://www.powa.org/orgnfrms.htm
Explains a variety of organizational strategies for essays.

essay and help readers understand your idea. Each part of the essay serves a particular function:

The *beginning* introduces your leading idea.

The *middle* presents evidence and develops the idea.

The *ending* offers a closing perspective on the idea and reminds readers of your main supporting points.

The beginning and the ending lead readers into and out of the essay. They are relatively short and easy to organize. The middle can be more difficult because you have to deal with those vexing questions about selecting and presenting evidence.

Organizing an essay has to do with how you finally decide to present your idea. Will you provide historical background information—a context for understanding—just after your introduction, or will you spread the information throughout your essay? Will you present your best evidence first, or should you save it for last? Do you need to define an important term such as *civil disobedience* early in your essay, or will your audience already know a great deal about it? These kinds of practical, organizational decisions will depend on the kind of essay you decide to write, on the essay's purpose, and on your imagined or targeted or assigned audience—what the members of that audience already know about your subject, whether they are likely to be hostile or friendly to your idea, and whether you will try to get them involved in an inquiry about that idea or whether you want to do everything in your power to convince them of the truth of what you have discovered.

A number of organizational methods can help you present ideas and organize evidence within paragraphs of an essay. These methods include organizing from general to specific or from specific to general, climactic order, time order, and spatial order. Two of these methods—climactic order and time order—also have broad application to the organization of entire essays. They help you decide in what order to present your supporting ideas.

When you use **climactic order**, you present your least important idea first and move toward your most important, most convincing idea. Or, you present simpler ideas first and move toward more complex ones. The overall effect of using climactic order is to build your essay toward an emphatic climax. Climactic order is especially effective for analytical and argumentative essays. When you use **time order**, you present your ideas in accordance with a time sequence, narrating how the ideas themselves developed or accounting for the actual order in which events occurred. Organizing the presentation of your ideas will ultimately depend on your subject, your evidence, your essay's purpose, and your sense of how your audience will respond.

1 Outlining

There are two main types of outlines—informal and formal. An informal outline is a sketch consisting of a few key terms or phrases listed in an order that will guide you as you write or as you think about what you have written. This type of outline does not follow the conventions of a formal outline. (See 1f-2 for examples of two types of informal outlines.)

Outlines can also be detailed and formal, written out in complete sentences (a *sentence outline*) or with words and phrases (a *topic outline*) and organized into units that show the structure of every section of the essay. A **formal outline** reveals the logical relationships among the various sections of the essay; those relationships are only suggested by an informal outline.

The following example of a conventional formal outline shows how to organize major and subordinate headings. As you can see, major headings are designated by roman numerals, while subordinate headings are signaled by indented capital letters, arabic numbers, or lowercase letters. The headings indicate the level of importance of your ideas and evidence and their relationship with each other. Note that outline headings should always contain at least two parts (e.g., if you have an *A* heading you should also have a *B* heading).

FORMAL OUTLINE FORMAT

Leading idea

I. First major idea
   A. First supporting idea
      1. First illustration or explanation (your supporting evidence)
      2. Second illustration or explanation
   B. Second supporting idea
      1. First illustration or explanation
      2. Second illustration or explanation
      3. Third illustration or explanation
II. Second major idea
   A. First supporting idea
      1. First illustration or explanation
      2. Second illustration or explanation
         a. First additional illustration or explanation
         b. Second additional illustration or explanation
   B. Second supporting idea

As the formal outline shows, a well-developed essay often has a hierarchy of ideas—a leading idea that you are presenting and developing, along with a number of supporting ideas that contribute to your readers' understanding of the leading idea. Each subordinate idea must be illustrated or explained by evidence that clarifies it. The relationship of each supporting idea to the leading idea must also be clear if your essay is to be persuasive and coherent.

2   Mapping

Some writers like to use an outline to begin thinking and getting organized, but others prefer to use a different method—a diagram that results from keeping up with the mind as it plays over a given subject. **Mapping** can lead to sketchy, informal outlines, to drafting, and then, perhaps, to a more formal outline that will accompany the final essay submitted to the instructor. (Instructors often require that a formal outline accompany a research essay.)

You begin mapping by choosing a piece of evidence—a quotation, a discovery from an experiment, a recollected experience, a cliché—and writing it in the center of a blank piece of paper. Then you begin to think about it, keeping track, mapping the mind's play as

in the accompanying example. The sample *mind map* traces how one student, Robin Dumas, was motivated to write an essay about skiing. By mapping her thoughts about a cliché—"Nothing lasts forever"—she came up with a subject and a question she wanted to answer. She went directly from her mind map to an informal outline because she got an idea about teaching intermediate skiers how to ski moguls—the small mounds that form on a ski slope and present a challenge to skiers. Robin saw right away how to organize her thoughts, but

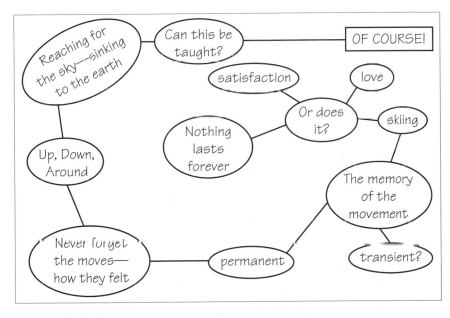

Example of a Mind Map

she could just as well have started another mind map, beginning with the words *Of course,* placing that new starting point in the center of the map and venturing out to other discoveries about skiing as her mind played over her experiences. What you do and how you get organized depend on what works best for you.

Writers who prefer to begin with a mind map often say they find a linear outline too structured and confining. They want to explore their imagination and express their findings in a diagram. But an outline is not necessarily confining; it can be quite flexible. An outline, like a mind map, can help you get organized and discover ideas. In fact, mind maps and outlines are useful, complementary techniques.

Robin went from mapping to this informal outline:

> Purpose: To convince the intermediate skier that mogul skiing is within reach
> Moguls
> Turning and sliding
> Riding the troughs
> Rhythm

After mapping and outlining, Robin wrote a preliminary draft and then reconstructed what she had written (to think about it) by outlining again. She recorded her concerns within the outline so she could consider them with her instructor when they met to discuss her draft.

> Beginning:　Introduce readers to the subject of mogul skiing and the essay's purpose--to convince the intermediate skier that mogul skiing is within reach. Define moguls.
> Middle:　Approaching the mogul--like stopping.
> Initiating the turn, reaching for the sky--nothing new for an intermediate.
> Compressing, sinking down to earth--a brief rest on the way up again.
> Repeating the process--up, down, around.
> Getting the rhythm--speed in the troughs.
> Concerns:　Should I use sketches within my essay? Do I need photographs to illustrate each phase of the turning? How technical should the terms be? Do I need to get into the physics of it all?

Ending: Pull the essay together, emphasizing the ease of the transition from intermediate to expert. Point out the joys of skiing rather than the sore back and wobbly legs that follow. Reveal what it's like to sit in the lodge at the end of the day talking about skiing the bumps.

As you can see from Robin's more detailed informal outline, she has a good idea of how she intends to develop her essay. She will use this outline like a road map, aware that she will also navigate side roads and alternate routes to reach the final destination—a well-developed essay. She does not want to exclude alternate routes altogether, but, like all of us, she does want to be able to begin her essay with a clear sense of direction, reserving the right to change her course if necessary. Good writers know that changes in direction can lead to new insights and greater clarity.

EXERCISE 1–2   **Mapping and Drafting**

1. Select a cliché (*You can't teach an old dog new tricks; No pain, no gain; What can't be cured must be endured*) that you have been carrying around in your memory. Write it in the center of a blank piece of paper and circle it. Let your mind play over the cliché. Devise a mind map, keeping track of where your mind takes you, jotting down the thoughts and memories you associate with the cliché. Model your efforts on the mapping diagram in 1f.

2. Look at the evidence you recorded about your cliché on the mind map— your thoughts and associated memories—and see if you can form an idea, something new and fresh to say, about that old cliché (see 1c on evidence and ideas).

3. Write a draft paragraph about your idea.

1g   Drafting and revising

Writers almost never get the words right the first time. They are always drafting and revising. **Drafting** involves successive attempts to say what you mean and to say it clearly. **Revising** involves going over what you have written, rethinking it with an eye to whether your audience can understand you. Drafting and revising also lead to ideas.

When you set out to write the draft of an essay, you are not trying to produce letter-perfect writing. It is to be expected that your punctuation and grammar might not be perfect and that your spelling may not always be correct. You will get a chance to fine-tune those details later in the writing process. You can make notations to correct any errors as you are revising. But deal with them when you edit and proofread your work, not when you draft. When drafting, you want to write your way to a clear expression of your idea. This process takes time and, often, successive efforts. Trying to make everything perfect from the beginning will almost surely divert you from your larger purpose: developing your idea so that your readers can understand it.

http://wp.rutgers.edu/
courses/301/tutorama/
revision_strategies.html
Provides strategies and
tips for revision.

Your first draft—your first effort to create the essay—is always an exploration, so you should expect to get off track. Your mind does not like to be controlled. Turn it loose with a pen in your hand or a keyboard at your fingertips, and you can expect it to take detours away from the main idea. Let that happen. Let your mind have free rein as you write the initial draft.

Set your first draft aside for a few hours and return to it later to revise it. Come back and ask probing questions: Does this draft make sense? Have I stayed on track? Was that diversion really illogical, or is there something in that wayward paragraph I need to think more about? As you read your draft, you will undoubtedly find problems: fuzzy sentences, a need for an illustration to help clarify a point, an important paragraph that needs to be moved, a connection that needs more explanation. You can also try reading your essay

Computer Tip

Writing without Seeing

As a kind of game you can play to see what you write without keeping track of it as you go, turn off your computer screen and write "in the dark." One reason for doing this is to free yourself from worrying about making corrections. Another is to help you write freely without worrying about transitions and logical connections from sentence to sentence and paragraph to paragraph. Such freedom allows you to shift direction and let your thinking direct your writing.

Drafting and Revising Guidelines

- Read your first draft carefully, looking for signs of a good idea.
- Determine whether you can see a clear relationship between each paragraph and the idea you are trying to develop in your essay. Are those relationships logical?
- Pause over sentences that are not clear. Then revise for clarity.
- Consider key words in your draft. Check the dictionary for the meanings of words and then revise if necessary.
- Begin another draft, taking your direction from the idea you discovered in the first draft. Think more about your audience now. Explain and develop your idea for that audience.
- Pause occasionally to let your mind make connections with new evidence that occurs to you. Write about those connections.
- Question your evidence. Consider what it might mean to someone whose ideas may differ from yours.
- Put the draft aside for a few hours or, if you can, for a few days. Get some distance from your writing, and then reread what you have written. Think about the relationship between your evidence and your idea. Clarify wherever you can.
- If you have work groups in class, ask the group to read your draft and identify its strengths and weaknesses. If you do not have a work group, ask a classmate to read the draft.
- Write other drafts if you still need to clarify your thinking.

aloud; often you will become aware of errors that you could not spot reading silently. A sentence that is hard to read aloud usually needs revising.

If you give your draft to a fellow student or collaborator to read, or talk about it with your instructor, you are likely to get additional insight about what you have done and what needs to be revised. Out of these helpful readings, you get direction for revising your draft and creating another one.

Revising leads to new writing and often results in reorganizing, more reading, gap filling—new drafts. As you draft and revise, you want to improve what you have already written. When you discover a gap in your explanation, you sometimes must do additional reading, which in turn leads

---

Computer Tip

Manipulating Text for Easier Revising

You can change the way your text is formatted to help you revise. Adjust the spacing of the text to spread it out more on the page, and increase the font size for easier viewing. If you arrange to have one paragraph per page, it will encourage you to add more details, more examples, more evidence to support each paragraph. You might wish to print out a copy in one or more of these altered modes and then insert ideas for revision in the extra space available on each page.

---

to further reflection and additional changes. As you fill the gaps and make your presentation clearer, you can begin to pay attention to the way you use words, to the structure of your sentences, to the way in which your sentences flow from one to the other, and to the transitions between paragraphs.

http://owl.english.purdue.edu/handouts/general/gl_proof.html
Discusses revision priorities, from large-scale through small-scale aspects of revising.

How, then, you ask, does a writer know when to stop drafting and revising? There is no conclusive answer, but when you can say "yes" to the following questions, you have likely reached your final draft.

1. Can my readers follow my train of thought?
2. Have I made my points clearly and convincingly?
3. Have I included sufficient evidence to illustrate what I mean and to convince my readers?
4. Am I satisfied with what I have written?

Remember to refer to the Drafting and Revising Guidelines (p. 21) at this stage in the writing process.

1h Collaborating

During the processes of drafting and revising, you can benefit from the help of your instructor and your classmates—in the form of **collaboration**.

Your instructor can assist you as you draft and revise, responding occasionally to your drafts and helping you answer tough questions and make important decisions. Your instructor may also ask you to do collaborative writing in a work group in class so that you and your classmates can help each other become better writers. You might work in a small group within the class at times specified by your instructor, or on a one-to-one basis outside of class, reading and responding to each other's writing. Nothing can spur you on like a friendly but critical collaborator who is willing to give you an honest reaction to your writing. That collaborator can save you the misery of self-doubt by pointing out strengths in what you have done. That person can also help you identify troubling gaps in your writing and offer constructive suggestions for improvement. Most writers thrive on collaborative feedback.

http://ec.hku.hk/
writing_turbocharger/
collaborating/
Explains how to exchange drafts and do peer editing with a computer.

Writing is a lonely act only up to a certain point. Few good writers stay isolated from readers during the entire process. Collaboration can bring you out of hiding and remind you that you are writing for an audience, that there is someone outside your head who wants to understand what is going on inside.

The Guidelines for Collaboration on page 24 will help you provide feedback about written texts. (Also see 1d-2 on audience feedback.)

Computer Tip

Sharing Drafts Online

All writers need feedback, and the best time to get that feedback is just after or shortly after you have completed a draft. You can ask friends or colleagues at your school or at other schools to read your work and give you feedback simply by sending them an e-mail with a file attachment that they can download. You can also send your draft as a paste-up into an e-mail message. This use of the computer can speed up the entire drafting, feedback, and revising process.

Guidelines for Collaboration

- Work in a small group of two to five students so that everyone has a chance to be heard. Your task is to provide feedback to the other writers—a genuine response to what you have read. That feedback can be about ideas, about the cited evidence, or about the overall effectiveness of the student's text.

- Write the word *nice* in the margin or insert a check mark (√) to identify the most satisfying parts of the essay: a fine sentence, a telling detail, a good paragraph, an arresting line of dialogue, a sentence or two that give you a clear sense of the essay's meaning.

- In the margin of the paper, write the word *gap* where you believe you need more information. If you are confused at some point, write a brief marginal note explaining what troubles you.

- Write specific questions in the margin as you read: *What do you mean? Please explain. What does this passage or this paragraph have to do with your leading idea?*

- Always write a note to the student (at the bottom of the page or on the reverse side) saying what you think the essay is about. Try to restate the essay's idea in your own words, whether that idea is expressed explicitly or implicitly.

- Offer constructive comments about how you think the essay could be revised. Refer back to the gaps or your marginal questions.

- Remember that as a collaborator, you are serving as both audience and editor—offering advice and feedback about your reaction to the essay. Be friendly and evenhanded, but talk back, giving your writer a chance to hear an audience response.

1i   **Editing and proofreading**

Once you have a typed final draft, you should edit and proofread it to identify and correct errors that might distract your readers. Surface errors in your writing are quite different from the problems you address while drafting and revising your essay. These sur-

http://www.ualr.edu/~owl/
tipsforproofreading.htm
Provides a list of useful
suggestions for effective
proofreading.

Editing Guidelines

- Check your grammar (Chapters 9–21).
- Check your sentences (Chapters 22–25).
  - —Do you avoid sentence errors such as fragments (Chapter 16) and misplaced and dangling modifiers (Chapter 18)?
  - —Are your sentences parallel (Chapter 23), varied (Chapter 24), and concise (Chapter 25)?
- Check the appropriateness of the words you use (Chapter 26).
  - —Do you avoid biased language (Chapter 26)?
  - —Are all words spelled correctly (Chapter 27)?
- Check your use of punctuation marks (Chapters 28–33).
- Check your use of capitalization, italics, abbreviations, numbers, and hyphens (Chapters 34–38).

How to Proofread

- Carefully read the final draft, line by line.
- Use a ruler to help you stay focused on individual sentences and words rather than on your idea and how it is expressed.
- Try reading backward to stay focused on the details.
- Check the final draft against the edited draft, sentence by sentence.
- Read the final draft aloud to hear and detect any remaining errors.

Look for omitted words or letters, misspellings, punctuation errors, illegible type, and anything that does not look neat. Retype or reprint the essay if you find too many errors.

---

face errors have to do with grammar, spelling, usage, punctuation, mechanics, and format rather than with the more conceptual revision of your idea. During **editing** you read specifically to identify and correct surface errors; in **proofreading** you ensure that you have corrected those errors and that your

Computer Tip

Avoiding Widows and Orphans

When you print out text, be careful to avoid leaving either a widow—one short line alone at the top of a page or column—or an orphan—a single word alone on a line at the end of a paragraph. Why? Because widows and orphans make for an unattractive appearance. Your word processor very likely includes an option to correct for widows and orphans. If it doesn't, you should revise your text to avoid them.

final draft is in near-perfect shape. The guidelines on page 25 will help you with these tasks.

If you use a computer when you are writing your paper, edit first on the computer screen using the computer's special features, such as the spell checker. Then check the printed copy of your paper for errors. You can often spot mistakes in the printed copy that you did not notice on the computer screen.

EXERCISE 1–3   Revising and Collaborating

1. After setting it aside for a few hours or a day, look at your paragraph from Exercise 1–2. Reread it, and think about what you could change to make it easier for someone else to understand your idea. Make those revisions.

2. Write a letter or e-mail to a friend explaining your idea. In the letter, try to interest your friend in the idea. Finally, ask for feedback: What do you like about the idea? Is it confusing? Did I convince you about my idea?

2 *Critical Reading*

The reading you do in college most often is critical reading; it requires careful analysis and thoughtful response. More specifically, **critical reading** involves reacting to what you read, analyzing it, interpreting it, and evaluating its ideas and assessing its values. The word *critical* in this approach to reading does not mean "being critical of" in the familiar sense of disapproval. Critical reading is more encompassing than this, involving a wider range of possible judgments and a deeper sense of understanding. This chapter provides an approach to reading that incorporates the major aspects of critical reading that are outlined in the chart below.

Critical Reading: An Overview

- Adjusting to different kinds of reading material (2a)
- Writing while reading to record your reactions and reflections (2b)
- Analyzing the texts you read—observing details and connecting them (2c)
- Interpreting texts by making inferences and drawing conclusions (2d)
- Evaluating texts by judging their quality and considering their ideas and values (2e)

2a   Adjusting to different kinds of texts

Reading a written text critically requires knowing what kind of work you are reading. Your expectations and response derive from the nature of the text you are reading and your purpose in reading it. Different kinds of texts require different ways of reading. You may skim a magazine article to pick up essential information. You may read a popular novel swiftly to discover what happens. You read your textbooks more slowly, taking time to absorb information, understand concepts, and consider questions. You read a newspaper editorial or an article in a serious journal carefully to analyze its argument and evaluate the evidence used to support it.

In the same way that we analyze a written text we can analyze the constructed "text" of an object, an action, a work of art, or a historical event. Thus a **text** can be something made or socially constructed, something that happens, as well as something written. Texts include works of art such as paintings, drawings, sculptures, and architectural monuments. They also include historical events, such as the Vietnam War. And they include other kinds of actions and events such as sports contests, beauty pageants, social celebrations (such as wedding ceremonies and receptions), and public cere-monies (such as presidential inaugurations).

You take a different approach to reading stories and poems than to read-ing informative essays and popular and scientific articles in periodicals. Fic-tion and expository prose make their points in different ways. Whereas expository writing presents ideas directly, fiction does so indirectly. In expos-itory prose, the writer's ideas are usually stated and described explicitly. But in fiction you must often infer a writer's implied idea or interpret the mean-ing of a story or novel.

2b Writing from reading

You can expect much of your college reading to lead to writing assign-ments such as essays, research papers, and reports. To develop those assign-ments, it helps to write both while and after you read. React to what you read by making marginal notes or annotations (only if you own the text, of course). Afterward, do some reflective writing, such as freewriting. Either keep a double-column notebook or a reading journal, or write a summary. The kind of writing you do will be determined by your purpose. But what-ever your purpose, you can begin responding to what you read by using the following writing techniques.

1   Reacting to a text with annotations

Annotations are brief notes you write about a text while reading it. You can underline and circle words and phrases that strike you as important. You can highlight passages. You can make marginal comments that reflect your attitude toward the text. Your annotations might also include arrows that identify related points, question marks that indicate your confusion, and exclamation marks to express your surprise. Annotations can be single words or brief phrases; they can be statements, exclamations, or questions. Depending on how extensively you annotate a text, your annotations may form a secondary text that reminds you of the text you are reading. Annota-tions used this way serve as an abbreviated outline of what the text says and what you think about it.

As you read the following passage, notice the various types of annota-tions and add some of your own.

To be called beautiful is thought to name something   1
essential to women's character and concerns. (In contrast
to men—whose essence is to be strong, or effective, or
competent.) It does not take someone in the throes of
advanced feminist awareness to perceive that the way
women are taught to be involved with beauty encourages
narcissism, reinforces dependence and immaturity. Everybody (women and men) knows that. For it is "everybody,"
a whole society, that has identified being feminine with
caring about how one *looks*. (In contrast to being masculine—which is identified with caring about what one *is* and
does and only secondarily, if at all, about how one looks.)
. . .

It is not, of course, the desire to be beautiful that is   2
wrong but the obligation to be—or to try. What is accepted by most women as a flattering idealization of
their sex is a way of making women feel inferior to what
they actually are—or normally grow to be. For the ideal
of beauty is administered as a form of self-oppression.
Women are taught to see their bodies in *parts*, and to evaluate each part separately. Breasts, feet, hips, waistline, neck,
eyes, nose, complexion, hair, and so on—each in turn is
submitted to an anxious, fretful, often despairing scrutiny.
Even if some pass muster, some will always be found
wanting. . . .

In men, good looks is a whole, something taken in at a   3
glance. It does not need to be confirmed by giving measurements of different regions of the body; nobody encourages a
man to dissect his appearance, feature by feature. As for
perfection, that is considered trivial—almost unmanly.

—Susan Sontag, "A Woman's Beauty: Put-Down or Power Source?"

The types of annotations used most often include the following:

1. Restating the language of the text
2. Asking questions about the text
3. Challenging the text's ideas or details
4. Comparing and contrasting the text with other things

2   Reflecting on a text in freewriting

Your initial impressions of a text, which you can record with annotations, will often lead you to further thoughts about it. You can develop these thoughts with **freewriting**. Like annotating, freewriting is an invention technique that serves as a source of ideas for writing. In freewriting, you record your ideas, reactions, or feelings about a text without arranging them in any special order. You simply write down what you think about the passage, without worrying about spelling or grammar. The point is to get your ideas down on paper and not to censor or judge them prematurely. Freewriting, in fact, offers you a way to pursue an idea, to develop your thinking to see where it may lead.

Both annotation and freewriting precede the more intricate and deliberative work of analysis, interpretation, and evaluation (see 2c–e). Annotation and freewriting also provide a convenient way to prepare for writing essays, papers, and reports. These two informal techniques work well together; the brief, quickly noted reactions of annotation complement the more leisurely paced reflections of freewriting.

Here is an example of one reader's freewriting about the preceding annotated passage by Susan Sontag. Notice how the writer uses the freewriting exercise to reflect on and ask questions about the passage.

Example of Freewriting

Interesting questions. Women do seem to think more about their looks than men do. But since it's men women wish to please by looking good, men may be responsible (some? much?) for women's obsession with appearance. How far have women bought into the beauty myth? How far are they responsible for obsessing about beauty? How about money and profit? And at whose expense?

Why don't men <u>need</u> to be beautiful? To please parents--employers? To attract a mate? To be considered "normal"? Sontag says that beauty is irrelevant to men-- men judged by different measures--strength, effectiveness, competence. She doesn't mention power, money, status. She leaves things out--intelligence and moral qualities, kindness, decency, generosity. How important are these?

Distinction between <u>desiring</u> to be beautiful (perhaps to be desired or admired) and <u>needing</u> to be. There's nothing wrong with women wanting to be attractive, to look their best. The problem occurs when desire becomes <u>obligation</u>, wasting women's talents, minimizes them, keeps them subservient.

Parts and whole--are women concerned with <u>parts</u> of their bodies--certain parts? Their overall appearance? Their sense of self? Silicone breast implants? Cosmetic surgery generally? (But: men have nose jobs, facelifts, even pectoral implants.) Men are concerned with <u>some</u> parts of their bodies more than others.

What about the words used to describe good-looking women--or good-looking men? A "beautiful" woman but a "handsome" man. A "foxy" lady, a "gorgeous" woman (guy?), an "attractive" girl, a ??? And what of men? "Handsome" does most of the work. So too does "good-looking." Though we also have "pretty boy" and "hunk"--derogatory? Hmm. Statuesque? Powerfully built? A real he-man?

EXERCISE 2–1   Annotating and Freewriting

Annotate one of the following passages. Then develop your initial thoughts about the passage by freewriting.

1. Americans are at last realizing that the acquisition of goods is not the whole of life. Consumption, on one level, is turning insipid, especially as the quality of the artifacts themselves seems to be deteriorating. On another level, consumption is turning sour. There is a growing guilt about the masses of discarded junk—rusting automobiles and refrigerators and washing machines and dehumidifiers—that it is uneconomical to recycle. Indestructible plastic hasn't even the grace to undergo chemical change. America, the world's biggest consumer, is the world's biggest polluter. Awareness of this is a kind of redemptive grace, but it doesn't appreciably lead to repentance and a revolution in consumer habits.

   —Anthony Burgess, "Is America Falling Apart?"

2. I am a cripple. I choose this word to name me. I choose from among several possibilities, the most common of which are "handicapped" and "disabled." I made the choice a number of years ago, without thinking, unaware of my motives for doing so. Even now, I'm not sure what those motives are, but I recognize that they are complex and not entirely flattering. People—crippled or not—wince at the word "cripple," as they do not at "handicapped" or "disabled." Perhaps I want them to wince.

   —Nancy Mairs, "On Being a Cripple"

3   Using a double-column notebook

To create a **double-column notebook**, simply divide your page in half. One half is for summarizing and interpreting what you read. Use this side of the page to record as accurately as you can your understanding of what the text says. Use the other side to respond to what you have read, to think about its implications, and to relate it to other things you have read or otherwise experienced.

The advantage of a double-column notebook is that it encourages you to be an active reader, to think about what you read and to make connections

Highlights of the Double-Column Notebook

SUMMARY	COMMENTS
Summarize the text.	Respond to your summary.
Interpret the author's ideas.	Reflect on the author's ideas.
Explain the ideas succinctly.	Consider whether you agree or disagree—and why.
Identify important details.	Raise questions about the details you have observed.
Relate the details to the central idea.	Relate the text and the writer's main idea to other things you have read and to your own experience.

Computer Tip

Using Separate Windows for Writing

You can work on more than one document at a time by using separate windows for each document. You can view documents simultaneously, or you can switch between them. You may wish, for example, to add material from one document into another, perhaps material from an earlier draft into a later one, or perhaps notes from a brainstorming document into a draft, which elaborates those notes. You can also view the documents at the same time by selecting the VIEW or WINDOW feature of your word processing program.

with your reading and experience rather than to consider a text in isolation. You can use the double-column notebook to think further about your earlier reactions, which you may have recorded in annotations or freewriting, and to sustain a conversation with the writer and with yourself. The chart on the opposite page outlines how to use a double-column notebook.

Here is an example of the double-column notebook. Notice how one side of the two-column notebook summarizes and interprets Sontag's idea and how the other side raises questions, offers judgments, and makes connections.

SUMMARY	*COMMENTS*
Sontag argues that beauty is an essential attribute of women but that it is an incidental attribute of men.	Does she mean that people always consider beauty in looking at women? What replaces beauty in looking at men—their height? Strength? Power?
Sontag suggests that women's concern for beauty makes them narcissistic—preoccupied with themselves and fascinated with their looks.	Is this necessarily the case? Can't a woman be beautiful—or not—and know it, but not be preoccupied with beauty?
Sontag emphasizes the way women's concern for beauty makes them appear immature and dependent.	Dependency on other people's views of them. Immaturity because beauty is superficial.
Society—men and women—hold women to a high standard of beauty—focus first on how women look.	Men are to "blame" for expecting women to be as beautiful as they can be. Women are complicit in going along, and thus are also to "blame"?
Women are viewed by their parts—figure, face, eyes, legs, breasts, lips, etc. Men are viewed as a whole. Women have great legs, hair, breasts, complexion etc. Men aren't dissected this way.	A man's parts are "private"—not viewed and commented on. Other things matter more for men—money and status and power.

Sample Double-Column Notebook

EXERCISE 2–2   Beginning a Double-Column Notebook

Create your own double-column notebook by following Highlights of the Double-Column Notebook. You may use a passage from a reading required for one of your courses or choose a reading selection from this book. Then consider how your double-column notebook entries might prepare you to write an essay or report.

4 Writing a summary

A **summary** is a compressed version of a text in which you explain the author's meaning in your own words. You summarize a text when you need to give your readers the gist of what it says. A summary should present the author's text accurately and represent his or her views fairly. Although there is no rule for how long or short a summary should be, a summary of a text is always shorter than the text itself. Your goal in summarizing a text is to render a writer's ideas accurately and fairly.

A **paraphrase,** which is similar to a summary, tends to be nearly as long as the text paraphrased. When you paraphrase a poem, for example, you explain its meaning in your own words, line by line or stanza by stanza. Unlike a summary, a paraphrase follows the order of ideas, images, and details in the original text.

Writing a summary requires essentially two kinds of skills: identifying the idea of the text you are summarizing and recognizing the evidence that supports that idea. One strategy for writing a summary is to find the key points that support the main idea. You can do this by looking for clusters of sentences or groups of paragraphs that convey the writer's meaning. Because paragraphs work together, you cannot simply summarize each paragraph independently. You may need to summarize a cluster of paragraphs to convey the idea of a text effectively.

The accompanying chart explains what you need to do.

How to Write a Summary

1. Read the text carefully, looking for the main idea and important supporting points.
2. Write a sentence that identifies the writer's main idea.
3. Write a few sentences that explain the key supporting points from different paragraphs or paragraph clusters.
4. Write a draft of your summary by putting together the sentences you wrote for steps 1–3, in the order you wrote them.
5. Revise your summary by adding transitional words and phrases to link your sentences. Add introductory and concluding sentences as necessary.

Here is an example of the process at work on the passage about women's beauty by Susan Sontag (see 2b-1).

General idea of passage: Women are seen as superficial and trivial, concerned with surface beauty rather than with deeper qualities of character. Women are viewed as beautiful objects, valued for how they look rather than for who and what they are.

Key supporting points:

- Women's preoccupation with their beauty is a sign of their self-absorption and inconsequentiality.
- Women's concern for beauty is a form of enslavement that results from their need to always care about their appearance, all the while being objectified as mere body parts.
- Men are less concerned about their appearance, especially with trying to perfect their outward look.

To create a smooth summary from these sentences, it is necessary to add introductory and concluding sentences. Transitional wording is also needed. Basically, however, you can follow the order devised for the passage as reflected in the sentences for the main idea and key supporting points.

Here is a revised version that avoids direct quotation from the original text. Also avoided are opinions or judgmental words and phrases. Notice, too, how the writer and text are identified in the opening sentence.

Revised Summary

In her essay "A Woman's Beauty: Put-Down or Power Source?" Susan Sontag explains how women's need to appear beautiful trivializes them, making them concerned with superficial appearances and identifying them as creatures preoccupied with how they look rather than who and what they really are. Sontag suggests that women's preoccupation with physical beauty is a sign of their self-absorption and lack of power. Through being taught to see themselves as mere body parts, women become both objectified and ridden with anxiety that their parts may not measure up. Unlike women, men are viewed for their good looks overall rather than for the beauty of their particular parts. Also unlike women, men are perceived as more serious, more sure of themselves, and more powerful than the women who anxiously labor to be beautiful to please them.

A final note: When you are working with readings for a research essay or project, you have a choice of summarizing, paraphrasing, and quoting the text. For advice about deciding when to summarize, paraphrase, or quote, see 41d.

EXERCISE 2–3   **Writing a Summary**
Write a summary of a passage of your choice.

2c   Analyzing what you read

When you **analyze** a text, you isolate and look closely at its parts (the beginning, middle, and ending of an essay or article, for example, or the sequence of events in a story). You focus on one element at a time, observing its details. Then you look for connections and relationships among those details. Your goal in analyzing a text is to understand it, to see how its parts fit together to make sense as a whole.

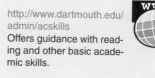

http://www.dartmouth.edu/admin/acskills
Offers guidance with reading and other basic academic skills.

Your analysis of a text can only be as good as the evidence that supports it. And that evidence begins with what you notice or observe in the text. It is crucial, then, to learn to look carefully, to notice details, and to make accurate observations about the texts you read.

1   Observing details

The kinds of observations you make about a text will depend on the kind of text you are reading. If you are reading a scientific report, you will observe its argument and the evidence that supports it. If you are reading a psychological abstract, you will attend to the purpose and limits of the study as well as to the kind of field research it may involve. In reading literary works you will consider such elements as diction and imagery (especially for poetry), character and conflict (especially for fiction and drama), and style and structure.

Here are some observations you might make about the Sontag piece.

- Sontag focuses throughout on surface beauty—on appearance.
- She distinguishes between beauty in women and men.

- She sees women's obsession with beauty as dangerous.
- She describes men as strong and competent.
- She italicizes certain words.
- She places some sentences in parentheses.
- She puts certain words in quotation marks.
- She punctuates heavily with dashes.

2   Connecting the details

It is not enough, however, simply to observe details about a text. You must also connect them with one another. To make a connection is to see one thing in relation to another. You may notice that some details reinforce others, or that the writer repeats certain words. Perhaps the writer sets up a contrast (as Sontag contrasts women's and men's attitudes toward beauty).

While you are noticing aspects of a text, you can also begin making connections among its details. Your goal is to see how the connected details help you make sense of the text as a whole. Making observations about a text and establishing connections among them form the basis of analysis. From that basis you begin to consider the significance of what you observe and proceed to develop an interpretation.

EXERCISE 2–4   **Making Observations and Connections**

Read the passage by Susan Sontag and make at least two new observations about it. Relate these observations to one another or to any you made earlier. As you begin to group your observations, identify the connections that emerge.

 2d   Formulating an interpretation

An **interpretation** is a tentative or provisional conclusion about a text based on your analysis of it (your observations and connections). To arrive at an interpretation, you need to make inferences based on your observations. An **inference** is a statement you make based on what you have observed. You infer a writer's idea or point of view, for instance, from the examples and evidence he or she provides. Inferences drive the interpretative process. They push you beyond making observations toward explaining them and the text.

1   Making inferences

You make inferences in everyday life all the time, and there is nothing mysterious about the process of making them. If you see someone at 8 A.M. with a large ring of keys opening a classroom door in a university building, you may infer that he or she is a member of the school staff whose job it is to unlock classroom doors. You may, of course, be right or wrong about your inference, but you will have made a reasonable inference nonetheless.

The same is true when you make inferences about a text. Your inferences are a way of understanding the text by "reading between the lines," by discovering what is implied rather than explicitly stated.

The freewriting about the Sontag passage contains examples of inferences. Here are a few additional inferences a reader could draw from the Sontag passage.

- Sontag thinks the double standard by which women are judged for their beauty and men by other qualities is wrong (paragraph 1).

- She implies that few women can meet the high standards for beauty that society imposes (paragraph 2).

- She seems to approve of the way masculine beauty is considered as a sum of each feature of a man's appearance and implies that this would be better for women as well (paragraph 3).

Sontag does not say any of these things explicitly, but readers might infer them. Remember that an inference can be right or wrong, and thus different readers might debate the reliability of these or other inferences. The important thing is not to be afraid to make an inference because you think a particular inference might be challenged or questioned. Critical reading involves thinking. Thinking involves making inferences. Making inferences and thinking about what you read help you arrive at an interpretation of a text.

2   Arriving at an interpretation

The step from drawing inferences to arriving at an interpretation is small. An interpretation is a way of explaining the meaning of a text; it represents your way of understanding the text expressed as an idea.

Your goal in interpreting any text is to understand it so that you can explain its meaning accurately. Informative texts, such as newspaper reports about current events or textbook material about scientific processes, require factual understanding and accuracy. Literary texts demand accurate observations and defensible inferences. Persuasive interpretations are characterized by these qualities.

When you arrive at an interpretation, look back at the text's details to reconsider your initial **observations** as well as to review the **connections** you established to see if they still make sense. Consider whether your **inferences** are defensible—that is, whether you can offer support on their behalf. Look also to see if additional details can support your inferences, or whether you wish to make different inferences that may lead to another interpretation.

Steps to Interpretation

- Make observations about the details of a text (2c-1).
- Relate your observations, looking for connections (2c-2).
- Develop inferences based on the related observations (2d-1).
- Arrive at an interpretation based on your inferences (2d-2).

2e   Evaluating a text

In reading to interpret, you give the author a chance to make a point or to develop an idea without judging the merit of that point or the value of that idea. You thus recognize the writer's meaning as paramount and your primary aim to understand what the writer says. In reading to **evaluate**, however, you want to both understand and assess the writer's idea. If you find yourself disagreeing with the writer's idea, you may refuse to accept other dimensions of the text, including the values it reflects.

Evaluating a text involves making judgments about it. You consider its effectiveness, and you assess the cultural values it embodies. When you evaluate a text, then, you make two kinds of judgments: one about quality, the other about values.

Your evaluation of a text grows out of your interpretation of it. To make fair and reasoned judgments about a text, you first need to be clear about what it says. You can evaluate the quality of a text only after you understand its meaning. And you can evaluate the cultural values of a text only after you understand the cultural values it embodies or promotes.

Evaluating a text requires more than interpreting it reasonably. You also need to be alert to your own personal and cultural values. This is so in part because evaluation is affected by your likes and dislikes, by what attracts you or repels you, as well as by your knowledge of what the text reveals. Your evaluation of a text may also be entangled with your feelings about its subject.

Consider the following brief passage by Ernest Hemingway, a vignette based on a war experience.

> While the bombardment was knocking the trench to pieces at Fossalta, he lay very flat and sweated and prayed oh jesus christ get me out of here. Dear jesus please get me out. Christ please please please christ. If you'll only keep me from getting killed I'll do anything you say. I believe in you and I'll tell every one in the world that you are the only one that matters. Please please dear jesus. The shelling moved further up the line. We went to work on the trench and in the morning the sun came up and the day was hot and muggy, and cheerful and quiet. The next night back at Mestre he did not tell the girl he went upstairs with at the Villa Rossa about Jesus. And he never told anybody.
>
> —Ernest Hemingway, *In Our Time*

In the process of interpreting this passage, consider your personal response to the events it describes. If you are repelled by the soldier's behavior, ask yourself why. Is it because he acts cowardly? Is it because he prays out of desperation? Is it because once out of danger he forgets his promise, or because he visits a prostitute? Perhaps you are not bothered by his behavior or by his language. Do not be surprised if your reaction to this text differs from the reactions of others—in fact, be prepared for it. Every reader has a unique perspective on what a text reveals and a unique set of personal values to bring to Hemingway's text.

Here is one reader's evaluation of the Hemingway passage. The evaluation includes judgments about both its effectiveness and the cultural and moral values the text suggests.

Evaluation

In his brief vignette from In Our Time, Ernest Hemingway describes some realities of war. The young soldier in the trenches is terrified of the artillery shells exploding near the trench, where he lies praying to God for deliverance. Instead of behaving heroically or courageously, the young soldier bargains desperately with God. His behavior is far from the ideal not only in the way he prays, but also in the way he breaks his promise. He is neither courageous nor honest. And his visit to a prostitute degrades the ideal of love as his earlier behavior degraded the ideals of war and faith.

The image of war Hemingway describes in the vignette is brutally realistic. He avoids glorifying war or idealizing the soldier's behavior. And yet even though some may find the soldier's behavior repugnant, Hemingway does not explicitly condemn that behavior. In fact, it might be argued that he helps readers understand the young soldier's predicament. His visit to the prostitute, given the circumstances, is convincing. The passage brings readers into the soldier's mind so they can understand how he feels. In its refusal to idealize war, it convinces us of its truth.

Evaluating this vignette or any text is not easy. Readers will disagree about both the cultural values this passage displays and how well the writer has described the soldier's predicament. Readers also will disagree in their judgments of the soldier, some finding his behavior inexcusable and morally reprehensible, others finding it neither extraordinary nor troubling—given the situation. Making your own judgments about the text is what is important. Equally important, however, is to make those judgments responsibly, by grounding your evaluation in a thoughtful consideration of meaning.

Guidelines for Evaluation

- Consider your initial reaction to the text and why you react as you do.
- Interpret the text, using the Steps to Interpretation on page 39.
- Decide whether you agree with what the text argues or illustrates.
- Identify and respond to the cultural values the text presents.
- Decide whether the text relates an idea or an experience effectively.

EXERCISE 2–5 Evaluating a Text

Write one paragraph identifying the cultural values in the Sontag passage. Write another paragraph in which you evaluate the strengths and successes of either text.

Guidelines for Critical Reading

- Read actively, annotating the text.
- Read attentively, focusing on each paragraph or section.
- Reflect on the text and question it.
- Interpret the text by observing and connecting details, drawing inferences, and formulating a conclusion.
- Evaluate the text, considering its effectiveness, its persuasiveness, and its cultural values.

EXERCISE 2–6   **Reading Evaluatively**

Read the following passages carefully. Then write a couple of paragraphs in which you evaluate what the two writers are saying.

1. I have always disliked being a man. The whole idea of manhood in America is pitiful, in my opinion. . . . Even the expression "Be a man!" strikes me as insulting and abusive. It means: Be stupid, be unfeeling, obedient, soldierly, and stop thinking. Man means "manly"—how can one think about men without considering the terrible ambition of manliness? And yet it is part of every man's life. It is a hideous and crippling lie; it not only insists on difference and connives at superiority, it is also by its very nature destructive— emotionally damaging and socially harmful.

   —Paul Theroux, "Being a Man"

2. I am demanding something of you that takes more courage than entering a battle: not to enter the battle. I am asking you to say *no* to the values that have defined manhood through the ages—prowess, competition, victory— and to grow into a manhood that has not existed before. If you do, some men and women will ridicule and even despise you. They may call you spineless, possibly even (harshest of curses) womanish. But your life depends on it. My life depends on it.

   —Nancy Mairs, "A Letter to Matthew"

3   *Reading (and Writing about) Visual Texts*

Reading and interpreting visual texts is similar in many ways to reading and interpreting written texts. You make observations and connections; you draw inferences and formulate an interpretive conclusion for visual images—photographs, paintings, Web pages, advertisements—just as you do for written texts. In fact, some visual texts, advertisements, and Web pages, for example, often include both visual and verbal elements.

The proposed advertisement on page 44, for example, includes both written and visual elements that only convey their full meaning when read together as a whole. The first thing one notices in this ad is the skeleton in the center of the picture. The picture's setting is a desert, clearly a dangerous place if we are to believe what we see. Indeed, images of bleached bones lying under the hot sun are so common as to be cliché. What makes this particular image unique is the cell phone clutched in the skeleton's bony hand. Presumably, one can call for help with a cell phone, but not in this case. Why?

The ad's written message answers this question. In addressing the reader directly, the headline clarifies the picture's meaning: "Can't find a signal?" That poor soul lying there isn't just anybody: it's you, the reader, a figurative dead person in a figurative desert. If only you could have found that signal, you could have made the call that would have made the difference. As the ad's clincher implies, the fault isn't your own, it's your current cell phone company. "Come in from out of the desert." Clearly, the ad suggests you can find a signal and avoid a terrible fate, but only by using Conover Communications.

The next advertisement is a Web page for Verizon Wireless, the wireless telecommunications company. Notice how the visual image and the words work together to convey a single impression. The words emphasize the ways customers can gain access to help. The picture similarly emphasizes service—with a smile.

Can't find a signal?

Come in from out of the desert.
CONOVER COMMUNICATIONS

EXERCISE 3–1 **Comparing Web Pages**

Write two paragraphs comparing the Web page for Verizon on page 45 with the Sprint Web page on page 46. Be sure to comment on the pictures and the words for each. Explain the main idea of each Web page, and explain which company's Web page you find more enticing, and why.

3a Responding to a Painting

The techniques you have been using to analyze ads and Web pages in this chapter and those you used to analyze verbal texts in Chapter 2 can be applied now to a painting by the nineteenth century painter Vincent van Gogh, whose *The Starry Night* is one of the best known of all modern paintings. Van Gogh painted *The Starry Night* in 1889 in St. Remy, located in southern France. After spending a few minutes looking carefully at Van Gogh's painting on page 47, use the following questions to formulate a response to

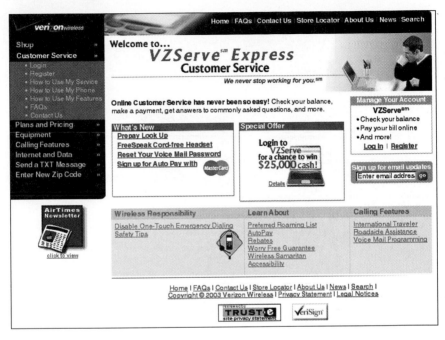

© 2003 Verizon Wireless. Used with permission.

Van Gogh's art. Use one or more of the techniques discussed in Chapter 2—annotating, freewriting, and the double-column notebook—to record your response. The questions in the following exercise can help you get started.

EXERCISE 3–2   Responding to *The Starry Night*

1. What is your first reaction to van Gogh's painting? Why?

2. What strikes you most about *The Starry Night*?

3. What is your overall impression of the painting? How can you characterize its mood?

4. Do you like van Gogh's choice of colors? Their intensity? Why or why not?

◆ *Sprint.* One Sprint. Many Solutions.™   Sprint.com | Personal | Business | About Sprint

Contact Us

How can we help you? Can't find what you are looking for or want to send us a question?

Select one of the categories below to talk to us by phone, email, or at one of our many Sprint Stores.

Personal / Residential Accounts

> PCS Service

Find Sprint Store locations, answers to frequently asked questions, and contact information.

> Long Distance Service

For help with moving, dialing long distance or international numbers, understanding your long distance bill, and contacting a Sprint representative.

Business Accounts

> PCS Service

Locate contact information, answers to frequently asked questions, and find Sprint Store locations.

> Long Distance and Data

Want more information about Sprint national business products and services? Contact a qualified sales representative with your questions.

FEEDBACK

5. How do you respond to the painting's swirling cyclical lines? To the thick brushstrokes?

6. Would you prefer a painting of the night sky that more closely resembled a photograph? Why or why not?

3b   Writing to interpret a visual work

When you write to interpret a work of art, or a visual image, you must go beyond first impressions. It is not enough simply to state your opinion of the work or to express your feelings about it. Nor is it enough to offer an

Gogh, Vincent van (1853–1890). *The Starry Night*. 1889. Oil on canvas, 29x36x¼. Acquired through the Lillie P. Bliss Bequest. The Museum of Modern Art, New York.

interpretation without providing evidence in its support. You need to explain why readers or viewers should understand the work as you do. Your evidence derives from your analysis or close scrutiny of the work's elements.

To arrive at an interpretation you must also come up with an *idea* about the work. That idea will be based on connections you discover among your observations about the work's details and inferences you draw from those observations.

When you interpret, you ask what a work *means*, not how you feel about it. Interpretation aims at understanding, at intellectually comprehending a work rather than simply reacting to it. To arrive at an interpretation, you will need to move beyond your personal reaction to a broader understanding of the work's significance. One way to do this is to relate the work you are interpreting to other works by the same artist, to similar works by different artists, and to your own knowledge—what you know about the subject being analyzed. Another approach is to do some research.

A condensed version of the interpretive process follows. Here you will see how these steps can be applied in an interpretation of Vincent van Gogh's painting *The Starry Night.*

Steps in Interpreting Works of Art

1. Make observations about the work's details (3b-1 and 2c-1).
2. Establish connections among your observations (3b-2 and 2c-2).
3. Develop inferences based on those connections (3b-3 and 2d-1).
4. Formulate an interpretation based on your inferences (3b-4 and 2d-2).
5. Relate the work (and your interpretation of it) to other works (2b)

---

1   Observing

To begin understanding a work, you must *observe* its details closely. In looking at a painting or photograph, you observe the shape, size, and color of its figures. You notice their relative positions in the foreground or background. You pay attention to shape, line, and color (and in a painting such as van Gogh's *The Starry Night,* to brushstroke as well). You look, in short, at the elements or characteristic features of works of literature and art.

In viewing Vincent van Gogh's painting *The Starry Night,* for example, you will likely notice the intensity of its colors. You might notice as well the thickness of its brushstrokes. And you might also observe the way van Gogh surrounds each star with a circular burst of light, the cypress trees in the left foreground, and the whitish disc of the sun. You are likely to notice many other details as well. To interpret *The Starry Night,* however, you will also need to establish connections and discover patterns among your many observations.

2 Connecting

Once you observe the details and other aspects of a work, whether a painting or a work of art or literature, you should look for *connections* among your observations. Try to relate the things you see to one another as you look for both similarities and differences. Making connections is essential to analysis and interpretation: it helps you begin thinking about works of literature and art. Without connections you have only a series of fragmented observations.

In the van Gogh painting, for example, you might notice how the dark and quiet village in the bottom quarter of the painting contrasts with the bright sky. You might relate the shape of the cypress trees to that of the stars since both convey an intense image of burning. You might notice that the village's scale is small compared with the sky and stars. And you might begin to reflect on the significance of such connections, asking yourself why the artist depicted these things as he did.

3 Inferring

By considering the significance of a work's related details, you will be leaping to the third interpretive stage—*inference*. There is no way around drawing inferences when you interpret a work. If you do not draw inferences, you may wind up saying "I have no idea what this artist is doing." And while particular works may stump you, you need to move beyond making observations and connections to thinking about their significance.

In the van Gogh painting, for instance, you might notice how much of the painting is occupied by moon, stars, and sky and how little space is accorded the village. On the basis of that contrast in scale you might wonder whether van Gogh's painting describes the overwhelming power of nature, its potential to wreak destruction on helpless human inhabitants. In connecting van Gogh's portrayal of the stars, moon, and sun with his depiction of the cypress as a flame shooting into the sky, you might see the painting as an image of an imminent conflagration. But you might see it in other ways as well.

EXERCISE 3–3 **Analyzing and Interpreting** *The Starry Night*

Answer the following questions about van Gogh's *Starry Night*. Try to use the questions in conjunction with your own observations about the painting and the connections you make among those observations.

1. Since van Gogh does not depict the night sky realistically, what feeling or attitudes might he be expressing with his bright colors, thick brushstrokes, and swirling forms?

2. What can you infer from the painting about the artist's state of mind?

3. How might someone from a culture in which stars are seen as sacred symbols, perhaps even as supernatural beings, interpret van Gogh's work?

4. How might knowledge about van Gogh's life and work aid you in understanding what he is portraying in *The Starry Night?* What kinds of information might be helpful in interpreting his painting?

4 Interpreting

Once you make observations, establish connections among those observations, and start to draw inferences, you are ready to formulate an interpretation of the work. Your interpretation should convey your understanding of the work. The evidence that supports your interpretation should come from the work's details, whether you are interpreting van Gogh's painting or another work of art or literature. Your interpretation may also be informed by what you have learned from consulting secondary sources.

Following is a short sample interpretation of *The Starry Night*. It is based on an analysis of the work's elements along with information and ideas gleaned from reading about van Gogh's life and work. Notice how the interpretation is organized. The authors begin by describing what they see. They then build on those observations to arrive at an interpretation, which they place in the final sentence of their paragraph for emphasis.

The artist is looking down on a village from an imaginary viewpoint. It [the painting] is framed by his newly discovered motifs: at left a cypress towers skywards, at right a group of olive trees clusters into a cloud, and against the horizon run the undulating waves of the Alpilles [a mountain range]. Van Gogh's treatment of his motifs prompts associations with fire, mist and the sea; and the elemental power of the natural scene combines with the intangible cosmic drama of the stars. . . . The church spire seems to be stretching up into the elements, at once an antenna and a lightning conductor, like some kind of provincial Eiffel Tower. . . . van Gogh's mountains and trees (particularly the cypresses) seemed to crackle with an electric charge. Confident that he had grasped their natural appearance, van Gogh set out to remake their image in the service of the symbolic. Together with the firmament, these landscape features are singing the praises of Creation in this painting.

—Ingo F. Walther and Rainer Metzger, *Van Gogh: The Complete Paintings II*

Although the authors did research to arrive at their interpretation of *The Starry Night,* you do not necessarily need to know a great deal about the artist's life, about his other paintings, or about how his work relates to that of other artists. Such additional knowledge, however, can give you a different understanding of a work.

Here, for example, is some additional information about the painting, taken from one of van Gogh's letters.

To look at the stars always makes me dream as simply as I dream over the black dots of a map representing towns and villages. Why, I ask myself, should the shining dots of the sky not be as accessible as the black dots on the map of France? . . .

I go out at night to paint the stars . . . I have a terrible lucidity at moments when nature is so beautiful; I am not conscious of myself any more, and the pictures come to me as in a dream . . .

That does not keep me from having a terrible need of—shall I say the word—religion. Then I go out at night to paint the stars.

—*The Complete Letters of Vincent van Gogh*

Sources such as van Gogh's letters and Walther and Metzger's comments can help you better understand van Gogh's work. They may lead you to see *The Starry Night* (or another work) in a way you might not have arrived at by simply viewing the painting. Consider, too, how the following interpretations that have been made of van Gogh's painting influence your own interpretation of *The Starry Night.*

1. The painting is a realistic account of the position of the stars in June 1889 in St. Rémy, France (where van Gogh painted this nocturnal scene).

2. The painting expresses van Gogh's personal agony and suffering during an especially trying time of his life.

3. The painting is an attempt to express a state of shock, to convey the inner turmoil of the artist's mind and spirit.

4. The painting portrays the power and grandeur of nature, conveying simultaneously a sense of its beauty and its terror.

5. The painting expresses van Gogh's sense of apocalypse, of the biblical end, and the imminent destruction of the world.

To arrive at your own understanding of the painting, you could consider these interpretations along with your own observations. You could also go to the library to read more of van Gogh's letters as well as books about his life and art.

EXERCISE 3–4   Interpreting *The Starry Night*
Use your own observations along with the information and interpretive leads presented to develop a 500–750-word interpretation of van Gogh's *Starry Night.* Use the artist's own remarks if you wish, or do additional research.

EXERCISE 3–5   Writing an Interpretation of a Visual Work
Look carefully at a work of fine art—a painting, sculpture, or work of architecture. Using the four stages of interpretation discussed earlier, develop an interpretation of the work. Document any secondary sources you use, following the guidelines in Chapter 43.

Genre, medium, form

In writing about a visual work (as in writing about a verbal text) you need to determine just what kind of work you are looking at—its genre. Genre refers to the type or category of a work. A painting, for example, might belong to the genre of landscape, still life, or portrait, and so on. Leonardo da Vinci's famous *Mona Lisa* combines elements of portrait and landscape. Van Gogh's *The Starry Night* is a portrayal of nature, though it includes human elements as well. In any work that combines elements of different genres, you should consider the relationship between them, as you did in your analysis of van Gogh's painting. The following questions provide some suggestions for what to focus on when looking at paintings.

1 Painting (Portraits)

- How much of the figure(s) is portrayed?
- What do the figure's clothing and accessories reveal?
- What do the figure's expression and posture convey? In portraits of two or more figures, how do the figures interact, and what is the significance of that interaction (or lack of interaction)?
- To what extent is the figure individualized?
- To what extent is the figure symbolic or representative of some political or social ideal?

2 Paintings (Landscapes)

- What does the landscape suggest about the natural world?
- What relationship is shown between human figures and nature?
- To what extent can the landscape be considered symbolic?

3 Photographs

We are so familiar with photographs that we may not look carefully at them or ever really consider them to be works of art. In fact, most photographs we look at are typical snapshots taken without much preparation and without artistic intent. But photographs taken with intent and thoughtful planning are worth a closer look. Consider the photograph on the following page, by Tina Barney, which presents a picture of a family. Notice how each family member is isolated in his or her own space, and how each is occupied with his or her own thoughts and actions.

A photograph from the most casual snapshot to the most artistically arranged picture is always a selection of the details desired by the photographer from the multitude of details available. It is important also to recognize that photographers alter their photographs by cropping them. In this and

other ways photographers control and shape the images they provide, just as painters do.

In addition to the questions provided for looking at paintings, here are some others to guide your viewing of photographs.

- What is the subject of the photograph?
- What details are visible? What details are emphasized? How?
- What kind of lighting does the photograph exhibit?
- What is conveyed through the photo's color or lack of color?
- What is the relationship of the figures depicted?
- Who took the photograph and for what purpose?
- What is its title, and who provided it when?
- What is the overall impression conveyed by the photograph?

EXERCISE 3–6   Writing about a Visual Text

Select a visual text—a photograph, advertisement, or Web page with a visual image, or a reproduction of a painting. Use the techniques of observing, connecting, inferring, and concluding along with the questions provided for paintings and photographs to analyze the visual text. Then write a few paragraphs in which you offer your interpretation of it.

PART 2

THE PARAGRAPH
AND THE ESSAY

4 *Developing Ideas*

Developing ideas is an eternally interesting process. Ideas are never fixed; they have about them a certain elasticity. They can be stretched, modified, made more interesting. They are, as one student told us, "always capable of further analysis." Ideas come from a variety of sources: your reading, your consideration of a painting or a photograph, your own lived experiences. They take shape as your mind plays over such sources and begins to make sense of them.

This chapter presents four techniques that can help you formulate and develop ideas as you think about your evidence and begin your essays: questioning, writing, connecting, and considering controversies. These four techniques should help you as you move *from* sources *to* ideas *to* essays. The techniques are highly effective when you use them concurrently, letting them guide your mind's play toward ideas. We begin with questioning, but we could just as easily begin with one of the other techniques. They are related, and, in practice, you are likely to use the techniques simultaneously. We separate them now so that you can more clearly understand them.

4a Questioning evidence to find an idea

Questioning follows from a natural human curiosity about what something means. Much questioning can take place in your mind as you mull over the evidence you have collected, but writing about the evidence even before you have developed your idea often leads to more questions and helps you clarify what the evidence means. As you write, your mind surprises you; it reaches back into memory or leaps from one piece of evidence to another, making connections, helping you discover meaning.

1 Inferring—A logical process

Ideas evolve in your mind as you consider the evidence, but the acts of the mind that lead you from evidence to ideas are not part of a magical process. Although no formula ensures insight every time you examine a body of evidence, you can learn the logical process that leads from evidence to idea.

Consider this example: an elderly couple lives in the house across the street from you. For a week you notice that newspapers are accumulating in their yard. By the end of the week the grass needs mowing, and you know from past experience that the Spencers always keep their yard in perfect order. After noticing these changes, your curiosity is aroused, and you begin to pay attention to other signs around the house and to question their meaning. You wonder why the shades remain at the same position day after day and why the lights go out each night at the same time in all of the rooms except one. The Spencers do not come out for their usual walks in the late afternoon, and you do not see them in the reading room at the local library on Saturday morning. You wonder why. As you watch their house for other signs, you begin to make inferences about what might have happened to the Spencers. Those signs constitute your evidence, and you decide to try to figure out what it means.

Try always to formulate the simplest explanation that will account for the evidence. Here are four possibilities:

1. The Spencers have changed their habits.
2. The Spencers have gone away on vacation.
3. The Spencers are sick.
4. The Spencers have died.

These inferences are not forced by the evidence; they are not *necessarily* true. Put another way, the evidence itself does not spell out the answer; *you have to develop the theory or the idea that will account for the evidence.* As you gather more evidence—in this case, as you continue to observe what is going on around the Spencers' house—one of your ideas might become more plausible than another. You might, for example, read in the local newspaper that the Spencers won a trip to Asia. That piece of information would seem to confirm your second inference. But given what you know without that information, any one of your theories seems plausible, and without more evidence you have to consider which idea seems most convincing based on the available evidence. To reach a higher degree of certainty about your idea, you would have to gather more evidence.

The evidence you consider as a writer will often be less conclusive than that given here about the Spencers. Nevertheless, you attempt to develop an idea that accounts for the evidence you are examining. Rarely does an idea acquire the certainty of a fact.

Consider again civil disobedience (the topic we first looked at in 1c). If you read Thoreau's "Civil Disobedience," you may come away thinking that civil disobedience is not only a positive moral action but also a civic duty. If you then consider historical and contemporary events, such as the American Revolution and the more recent women's movement, you might reasonably conclude that civil disobedience leads to beneficial results. But if you look further, you can discover that civil disobedience does not always produce results pleasing to everyone. Demonstrators for and against abortion commit acts of civil disobedience, so whichever side you take, you see the other side as guilty of unjustifiable civil disobedience. In short, evidence gathered as a basis of writing is likely to be not only less conclusive than the details about the Spencers, but also fiercely contradictory. Considering and reconciling the evidence is part of the challenge and excitement of writing.

Preliminary Questions to Ask Yourself about Evidence

1. What do I first notice about the evidence? What is most obvious?
2. How do I feel about what I am seeing or reading?
3. Are any patterns obvious in the evidence?
4. When I look again, do I realize some deeper meaning that was not so obvious on first consideration? What can I logically infer about the evidence?

2 Questioning a photograph—A student example

To illustrate how curiosity might lead you to interesting questions that can, in turn, guide you to ideas, let us consider a photograph that seems to offer, at first glance, little more than an arresting image of a young man in motion. His name is Killer Joe Piro; the photograph is by the well-known photographer Richard Avedon.

Instead of turning directly to the image itself, let Kristina Wilson's re-creation of her first encounter with Joe Piro help you conjure up his image in your own imagination. When Wilson saw Avedon's photograph of Piro at the Whitney Museum in New York City, she had been dragged there on a Sunday morning by her father. Wilson would eventually study at New York University's Tisch School of the Arts, but that morning she had gone to the Whitney unwillingly. Piro grabbed her attention:

We inched our way through the huge gray steel doors and eventually found our way into the exhibit itself. I walked through the entrance with my head down and my eyes averted, ironically making a show of my apathy. When something finally provoked me to look up--an elbow in my side, a person in front of me, what it was, I'm not quite sure--I came face to face with an image that has rarely left me since that morning.

A huge enlargement of Avedon's portrait of the dancer Killer Joe Piro confronted me, stared at me, commanded me to really <u>see</u> for once in my life. He threw his head back and his entire face rushed upward. His hair became a solid black mass with edges of velvet grain, and a cowlick of dagger-sharp spikes pointed downward from the left side of his head. A bit of his bangs fell forward onto his face, melding and becoming one with the shadows between the bridge of his nose and his left eye. Black eyes raced upward as well, reflections of light in the pupils carving burning paths in front of him like dividing lines on a highway. He seemed to have four eyes, six, and at the same time, none at all. Joe's nose, along with his forehead, cheeks and chin, were white hot, scorched into pure whiteness by intense light, and came together to make a negative-space cross. . . . His teeth were playing the same game as his eyes--multiplying and dividing until they became one and a thousand at the same time. Those white forms reached upwards and downwards like stalactites and stalagmites in the dank cave of Killer's mouth, interspersed with a few needle-thin light smears. His dynamic head rested upon a seemingly stable half circle of complete darkness, surrounded by a hint of white collar that disappeared into the stark white background and the deep black of Killer's sweater. An ascot ran down an inch or so from his chin, taking on the look of wood grain as it was smeared, as if by the hand of some small child, down into the darkness and off the print.

Never before had I been so enraptured by a single image, but Killer Joe sucked me in--into the massive fine grain that made up his blurring face, into his upward motion, and into photography.

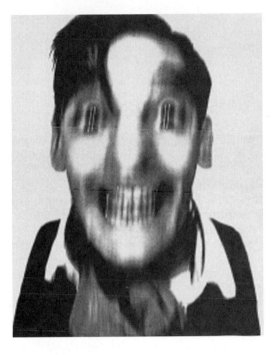

Photograph by Richard Avedon
Killer Joe Piro, dancer
New York City January 3, 1962
© 1962 Richard Avedon

I stood in front of him for a long time, trying to unlock his secrets--how was he moving? How had he been captured? How could *I* do work like this? I finally moved on to view the rest of the exhibit, which astounded me as well, but I kept finding myself in front of Joe again, as I do now.

3   Questioning to address the writing requirement

Kristina Wilson had been asked in a second-semester freshman writing class to select an image (a photograph, a painting, or a sculpture) and bring it to class, described in her own words so that others could see it as she saw it. The exercise was a preliminary step that would lead to an essay about the relationship between an artist and her or his work. To write the essay, Wilson would need an *idea;* to find an idea, she would need *evidence* to consider.

The re-created image—the word-picture brought by the student to class—was to be the first piece of evidence that students would investigate. Their task was to look at this initial piece of evidence—the image itself—to question it, and to look again to see what else it might reveal. That questioning should lead eventually to an idea.

Wilson's response—Questioning to find an idea

As you can see, Wilson's vivid description of the photograph ends with a series of interesting questions. Even as she describes her encounter with the photograph, she is already seeing Piro's image as a source of inspiration for her own work as a photographer. She sees motion and light.

In subsequent writing as she questions the photograph and tries to keep her mind on the essay requirement—the one that asks her to try to account for Avedon's relationship to the photograph—Wilson worries first about whether she has, in the two years since she first saw the photograph, "seen too much of Killer Joe, if I've exhausted a seemingly inexhaustible resource." She has a T-shirt with Joe on it and a book about Avedon's photography by Jane Livingston. Killer Joe has "popped up" in her papers and conversations and her thoughts often. She worries about whether there is anything fresh to see. She questions whether too much knowledge gets in the way of seeing.

Looking at the photograph, she also begins to question whether her own work is being "polluted" by the opinions of others. That question leads to another, one more directly related to her essay assignment. Here is Wilson's account:

> In investigating the pollution that has occurred in my work, and in my view of Killer Joe, I begin to wonder if Avedon perhaps has the same problem. I would imagine that he does, and in much more profusion than I--after all, hundreds of critiques have been written about his work, and I have been privy to only a few. Avedon's portraits have been said to be about "being caught out of character, about the matter of transforming personality and disguising motive" (Livingston 11)--a theory we can certainly find support for in his blurred, dynamic portrait of Killer Joe. Joe is most definitely being caught at something here--his entire body in motion and his eyes glaring maniacally at us.

Taking her cue from a 1995 PBS documentary that she had seen about Avedon's life, Wilson questions whether his photographs are not in some way self-portraits, whether all photographs are self-portraits, no matter what the subject. From the documentary, she recalls Avedon's struggle with "his strong Jewish roots coupled with his lack of native culture or religion and his sense of being the 'loneliest person on earth.'" She concludes tentatively: "So perhaps there is a piece of the photographer in his portrait of Killer Joe—the fleeting moment, the slight look of desperation in Joe's eyes, but I wonder—now that this fact has been revealed to him, how it is that he can continue to photograph so remarkably? How does he, how can *I*, get around knowing too much?"

Looking for a leading question or idea

That last question is the one that intrigues Wilson, and it is the one she tries to answer in her essay. Can photographers not be overwhelmed by too much self-knowledge and too much technical knowledge when they go out into the world to take their photographs? She concludes that they can get around knowing too much, that there is a way:

> Over time, old visions and theories will be worn down and pushed away by the gentle running of new ones over the old, like stones in a meandering stream. Eventually a small, polished smooth piece of <u>something</u> will remain, ready to be pulled out of one small branch of the massive, intricate system of waterways that are our minds.

Let's highlight the process that Wilson used and then infer additional guidelines for questioning evidence.

- Recall that Wilson began with evidence that she was genuinely interested in. Even though she had looked at that photograph of Piro many times, she chose to look at it again, to see if there was something there she had not seen before.

- She was also looking at the photograph in connection with the requirements of her writing course; that course gave her a line of inquiry, a question to begin with. As she looked and wrote about her questions, she asked more questions.

- She found two other sources of evidence: Jane Livingston's book about Avedon and the PBS documentary. Those sources came into play as she continued to question the photograph.

- Finally, the questioning led to an idea that she eventually developed in her essay, using as evidence the photograph as well as information from the Livingston book, the documentary, and several other essays that she read in the course.

Developing Questions from Evidence

1. Begin with evidence that interests you.
2. Study it. Look at it again and again to try to understand what it means. Use the guidelines about evidence on p. 59.
3. Think about the evidence and the assignment together. What questions do they suggest?
4. As you begin to ask questions, try to answer them in terms of what you already know. Write out these tentative answers. Then question your answers.
5. As you formulate answers, consider other related information that you remember or that comes from assigned readings in your course.
6. Look for the question that most intrigues you. Work with it; write about it. The answer to that question could turn out to be the idea you develop in your essay.

EXERCISE 4–1   Questioning an Image
Select one of the paintings or photographs in this book, other than the one of Killer Joe Piro. Using the guidelines above, question the image. Answer your own questions by writing about them. Keep a list of new questions that follow from your questions and your writing about them. Which question would you most want to keep investigating? What would you hope to learn from that investigation?

EXERCISE 4–2   Reconsidering *Killer Joe Piro*
Having read Kristina Wilson's description of Avedon's photograph of Killer Joe, what can you see in the photograph that Kristina Wilson did not mention? What does the image remind you of? What questions does it raise for you? Try to answer the most interesting of those questions by writing about it. Keep track of new questions and connections that come to you as you write.

EXERCISE 4–3   Questioning Advertising
1. Select from a magazine any advertisement for a beauty product. Question that advertisement using the guidelines above. Look especially for the way the written part of the advertisement fits in with the images it presents. Then consider how questioning led you to discover the advertisement's underlying assumptions about beauty. Discuss your responses to the photograph with others in the class. How do those responses help you *see* more?

2. Look at several other advertisements for beauty products. Question them and try to find an idea about them that you would like to investigate and develop in an essay.

4b   Writing about evidence to find an idea— Drafting and revising

E. B. White, essayist, storyteller, and grammarian, once said, "I always write a thing first and think about it afterward, which is not a bad procedure, because the easiest way to have consequential thoughts is to start putting them down." White seems to have followed his own sound advice in **drafting** several versions of one paragraph (attempting in writing to catch hold of an idea and to express that idea clearly). If you look carefully at his various drafts, you will see how, even in the construction of a single paragraph, White wrote and rewrote to clarify his thinking. (See 1g for a general discussion of drafting and revising.)

Watching White work his way through three drafts of a paragraph about the first moon walk, you will see that even professional writers do not get their ideas formulated on the first try. **Revising**—rewriting, redrafting, rethinking—is the watchword. White revises within a given draft to clarify a tentative idea that he is trying to express, and then he does more extensive revision from draft to draft as he becomes more certain about what he wants to say. Always, it seems, his desire to clarify and present an idea guides such revision.

Looking on the following pages at these drafts (three of the six drafts he wrote), you will see that White does not simply edit his work to correct errors or to make minor word changes within his sentences. Rather, he *explores* as he writes, trying to figure out exactly what that space walk he saw on television meant to him and what he wanted his audience to understand about what he saw.

White's drafts change considerably, and they suggest how you might also draft and revise. The guidelines on p. 66, Writing to Discover and Clarify an Idea, give you a sense of what good writers do when they write to clarify an interesting idea.

1   White's first draft—Finding an idea

White began with what he saw on television one night in 1969, when Neil Armstrong and Buzz Aldrin stepped out of a lunar module onto the surface of the moon. That televised event constituted White's evidence.

Writing to Discover and Clarify an Idea

1. Look carefully at the evidence, then begin writing about whatever notion strikes you as interesting.

2. At the outset, open your mind to intrusions—to new notions that want to be let into what you are writing.

3. Stop. Consider what you have written. See what your writing has revealed to you about the evidence.

4. Write another draft, beginning this time with your revelations about the evidence. See if you can clarify them by writing about them.

5. Make connections. If the revelation reminds you of other things you know or have read, write down those connections. See what they reveal to you.

6. Question your draft as if you are a member of your audience. Ask yourself questions about the relationship between the evolving idea and the evidence.

   • Is that relationship clear to an audience that has to read about it without the benefit of all that I know?
   • Are my intentions clear?
   • Are there deeper implications in the evidence than I have expressed, other aspects of the idea that need to be clarified?
   • What else might I learn about my idea if I examine my own draft according to Preliminary Questions to Ask Yourself about Evidence (p. 59)?

Watching the astronauts, White was struck with a notion about the American flag that they planted on the moon. Thinking and writing about that notion, he clarified it and eventually turned it into a clear idea about universality and conquest. It took several drafts to get the words right.

Let us consider three of the six drafts of "Moon Landing" that White wrote. Look first at his initial draft (pp. 67–68). Although this first draft is rough, it lets you see how White got his initial thoughts down on paper and then modified them.

What can you learn about your own drafts from reading and thinking about White's? In his first draft, you can glimpse how a writer takes up one notion and then moves to another and then another, all in the space of one paragraph. White's first draft is his initial attempt to say something about the evidence.

[handwritten top:] ...tionauts would never have reached their goal. But they sent along something that might better have been left behind —

white

comment

Planning a trip to the moon, ~~isxxxxxxxiaiiyxxx~~

~~differ~~   differs in no ~~esstial~~ essential respect from planning a trip
along,
to the beach. You have to decide what to take ^ what to leave

behind.   Should the thermos jug go?   The child's rubber horse?
The dill pickles?
~~These are sometimes~~ fateful decisions ~~,~~ on which the success or
failure
outing
~~inxhappixness~~ of the whole ~~expedition~~ turns.   Something goes

along that spoils everything because it is always in the way.

Something gets left behind that spoils everything because it is
for   ~~were saddled with the~~
desperately needed ~~for comfort or~~ ^ safety.   The men who had to
send
decide what to ~~take~~ along ^ to the moon must have pondered long and
Should the vacuum cleaner go? The peanut butter?   *really*
hard, drawn up many a list.   ~~We're not sure~~ they planned well,
when they included the
~~forxviiuyxxiextsdxxsvbakexxxxng~~ the little telescoped flagpole and
artificially stiffened
the ~~stiffnxxdx~~ American flag, ~~artifimxxixxxtiffxxxd~~ so that it
would fly to the breeze that didn't blow.
flew to the breeze that didn't blow.   The Stars and Stripes on

the moon undoubtedly gave untold satisfaction to millions of
But   *d*
~~When~~ As we watched the Stars and Stripes planted on the surface of

the moon, we experienced the same sensations of pride ~~and~~ that

must have filled the hearts of millions of Americans.   But it

the emotion soon turned to *stone in our stomach*
Here   a   *to be something vast, and unparalleled in all history.*
~~This was our~~ great chance, and we muffed it.   The ~~meen~~ men who
were
stepped out onto the surface of the moon are in a class by
to sum up by the   *of men and women everywhere*
themselves---pioneers of what is universal.   They saw the
dark sky
~~earth~~ whole---just as it is, a round ball in a   But they *filled*
instruction and
~~colored~~ the moon red, white, and blue ~~0---good colors all---but~~
the sun that is out of the realm of nationality by its very position.
~~out of place in that setting.~~   The moon still ~~influences~~ the
still
tides, and the tides lap on every shore, right around the globe.

still holds the key to madness

Kiss in every land

The moon stil belongs to lovers, and lovers are everywhere--not

just in America. What a pity we couldn't have planted some
                precisely   this unique, this incredible
emblem that ~~exactly~~ expressed the occasion, even if it were

nothing more than a white banner, with the legend: ~~XXXXXXXXXXXX~~-y."

"At last!"   *that simply said I*

handkerchief, symbol of the common std
which, like the moon, belongs of all
marking

White's First Draft

At first, he emphasizes that the astronauts must have made fairly elaborate preparations for taking a little American flag to the moon. He devotes
nearly two-thirds of his paragraph to developing a picnic analogy. But then
he becomes *critical* about the planting of the flag and, when he does so, when
he makes that *judgment* about the flag, he is on the scent of an idea.

White thinks the planners and the astronauts "muffed it" when they
planted the flag. Instead of being nationalistic, the astronauts should have
done something with more universal appeal, something that would have
been a more fitting tribute to all people. Having written his way to that idea,
White begins to think about what the moon actually stands for, and his mind

seems to reach out for a symbol as universal as the moon, "even if it [that symbol] were nothing more than a white banner."

The most striking feature of White's first draft is the way his mind moves from *picnic analogy* to *judgment* to *symbol*. One notion leads him to another, as he follows his own leads. But we can learn even more from his draft. White's corrections (both typed and handwritten) suggest that even as he wrote the draft, he moved away from his work to read it and think about it. On occasion, he realized that he needed to clarify what he had written, and he made those corrections you see—as he went along.

White was not content to let sentences stand as they were even though he was only drafting and laying out his idea. It was as if fixing a sentence allowed him to clarify his thinking and go forward. There is no better example of that kind of thoughtful revision than in the handwritten correction of the last sentence in this first draft. White makes the "white banner" more specific, more concrete; it becomes a "handkerchief, symbol of the common cold which, like the moon, belongs to all mankind." That correction puts White on the track for a subsequent revision.

2 White's revised draft—Changing tone

Read White's revised draft on page 71. As you can see, the controlling idea about universality is again at the heart of White's paragraph, but he gets to that idea much sooner in the revised version and is much less harsh in his criticism of the flag planting. Nothing like "we muffed it" appears in his revision. White softens his tone—his expressed attitude about the event—even though he remains critical of the flag.

A lesson about audience is embedded in White's change in tone. He is trying to reach a general audience, so he does not want to alienate his readers by criticizing too harshly that amazing accomplishment he witnessed on television. If his audience is proud of the accomplishment and White belittles it, he might turn readers away.

The following two versions of the same sentence reflect White's change in tone as he shifts from his harsh judgment to the idea about universality so closely related to that judgment.

FIRST DRAFT

The men who stepped out onto the surface of the moon were in a class by themselves—pioneers of what is universal, of men and women everywhere. They saw the earth whole—just as it is, a round ball in a dark sky.

REVISED DRAFT

Yet the two men who stepped out on the surface of the moon were in a class by themselves and should have been equipped accordingly: they were of the new breed of men, those who had seen the earth whole.

Locate this sentence within White's revised draft, and try to figure out why the beginning word *Yet* is so important. How does it help change the tone of the entire paragraph? Think too about why White decides to call the astronauts a "new breed of men." Were they actually a new breed, or is this White's way of making readers think in a new way? Consider why the writer might have decided that the astronauts had "seen the earth whole" instead of as a "round ball in a dark sky."

White's subtle revisions of details are suggestive. He *speaks* to you indirectly through detail. White asks you to think and imagine as you confront his work.

White not only suggests something important about universality through these revised subtleties; he also makes other striking changes in the revised draft. In his last sentence, for example, the new phrase "Iwo Jima scene" clarifies his thinking about nationalism.

FIRST DRAFT

What a pity we couldn't have planted some emblem that precisely expressed this unique, this incredible occasion, even if it were nothing more than a white handkerchief, symbol of the common cold which, like the moon, belongs to all mankind, that simply said: "At last!"

REVISED DRAFT

What a pity we couldn't have forsworn our little Iwo Jima scene and planted instead a banner acceptable to all—a simple white handkerchief, perhaps, symbol of the common cold, which, like the moon, affects us all!

When White recalls Iwo Jima—a scene near the end of World War II when American soldiers raised the U.S. flag to signal victory and conquest (captured permanently in the Iwo Jima memorial sculpture at Arlington National Cemetery)—he has in mind nationalism, a symbolic, victorious act characteristic of postwar America. By changing "planted some emblem" to the more specific "Iwo Jima scene," White clarifies his judgment against the nationalistic act of flag planting and leans in the direction of a simpler, less-charged universal symbol—a white handkerchief—that does not make

white

comment

Planning a trip to the moon differs in no essential respect from planning a trip to the beach. You have to decide what to take along, what to leave behind. Should the thermos jug go? The child's rubber horse? The dill pickles? These are sometimes fateful decisions on which the success or failure of the whole outing turns. Something goes along that spoils everything because it is always in the way; something gets left behind that is desperately needed for comfort or for safety. The men who drew up the moon list for the astronauts planned long and hard and well. (Should the vacuum cleaner go, to suck up moondust?) Among the *inevitable* items they sent along, of course, was the little jointed flagpole and the flag that could be stiffened to the breeze that did not blow. (It is traditional among explorers to plant the flag.) Yet the two men who stepped out on the surface of the moon were in a class by themselves and should have been equipped accordingly: they were of the new breed of men, those who had seen the earth whole. When, following instructions, they colored the moon red, white, and blue, they were fumbling with the past---or so it seemed to us, who watched, trembling with awe and admiration and pride. This moon plant was the last *chapter* scene in the long book of nationalism, one that could well have been omitted. The moon still holds the key to madness, which is universal, still controls the tides that lap on shores everywhere, still guards lovers that kiss in every land under no banner but the sky. What a pity we couldn't have forsworn our little Iwo Jima scene and planted instead a banner acceptable to all---a simple white handkerchief, perhaps, symbol of the common cold, which, like the moon, affects us all.

White's Revised Draft

the astronauts look like American conquerors on the moon. Consider too how the words *pity* and *forsworn* convey White's judgment in the revised sentence.

White's revisions in this paragraph—his earlier emphasis on the idea about universality, his change of tone, the subtle alterations in detail, the addition of a new example—suggest the possibilities open to you as you revise your own work. Revision is never simply changing a word or a sentence here and there. It involves rethinking and reconstructing—*changing for the sake of clarifying and strengthening your presentation of the idea.*

3   White's final draft—Refining the idea

Scott Elledge, White's biographer, tells us that after White sent that revised version of the paragraph to *The New Yorker* (where the complete essay was published in 1969), he had a change of mind and composed three other drafts. White eventually phoned the final draft to his editor after he had telegraphed this message: "My comment [by which he means the 'revised draft' you just considered] is no good as is. I have written a shorter one on the same theme but different in tone."

In White's final draft, you can see how he went even further to soften his tone and turn the moon walk into a festive occasion, marred only by the flag planting. Instead of blaming the astronauts, however, White shifts the blame for that nationalistic act to the planners. The astronauts were just doing what someone else told them to do. Now White tells us that the astronauts were "universal men, not national men" and that they "should have been equipped accordingly."

But perhaps the most significant lesson you can learn from White's final revision is about letting go of evidence that in the beginning of your exploration seemed so important but in the end has no place in the piece. The picnic analogy does not appear in White's final draft. At the outset, it led him to his idea, but as he began to emphasize that idea, the picnic analogy became less and less important. We know that it is in the background even in this final draft—in the lighthearted spirit of the paragraph—but packing and planning are much less important in the final draft. Festive sharing of a great moment occupies White's mind. He wants to make that moon walk a moment for everyone in the world.

White demonstrates in these three drafts how much freedom you have to revise as you write. His drafts show you as well *how to explore to find an*

white

comment

       The moon, it turns out, is a great place for
men. One-sixth gravity must be a lot of fun, and when Armstrong and Aldrin went into their bouncy little dance, like
two happy children, it was a moment not only of triumph but of
gaeity. The moon, on the other hand, is a poor place for flags.
Ours looked stiff and awkward, trying to float on the breeze
that does not blow. (There must be a lesson here somewhere.)
It is traditional, of course, for explorers to plant the flag,
but it struck us, as we watched with awe and admiration and
pride, that our two fellows were universal men, not national
men, and should have been equipped accordingly. Like every
great river and every great sea, the moon belongs to none and
belongs to all. It still holds the key to madness, still controls the tides that lap on shores everywhere, still guards the
lovers that kiss in every land under no banner but the sky.
What a pity that in our moment of triumph we did not forswear
the familiar Iwo Jima scene and plant instead a device acceptable
to all: a limp white handkerchief, perhaps, symbol of the
common cold, which, like the moon, affects us all, unites us
all.

White's Final Draft

idea and how to be responsible to both your idea and your audience. The changes
that he makes do not come automatically to any writer. They evolve as you
write and think about your idea. White's work reminds you that you have to
stay with the task, sometimes through several drafts, to get the words—and
the idea—right.

EXERCISE 4–4 **Thinking about Drafting and Revising**

1. Read back through each of White's three drafts and identify other revisions that seem significant to you. How exactly do these revisions help you understand White's idea? In two typed pages, describe the inferences you made about the writing process from studying White's revisions.

2. Consider the final draft of White's paragraph in terms of today's audience. Would his message about universality be undermined by his language? Does the term "universal men" contradict White's idea about universality? Did women have a place in all that moon planning and exploration? Revise White's final draft to eliminate the sexist language (see 26k).

EXERCISE 4–5 **Drafting and Revising a Paragraph**

1. Select an event that stirs your imagination—something you saw on television, or read in the newspaper, or remember—and write a paragraph about it. Begin by writing freely about the event, letting your writing lead you to an idea. Then follow the guidelines in 4b (and White's example), and draft and revise until you have a paragraph that you want to present to your class about that idea.

2. Have your in-class work group or another classmate comment on your idea, questioning it as a way of helping you clarify it.

4c   Connecting—Another way to an idea

You have examined two techniques that lead writers to interesting ideas. That examination showed you how to begin thinking about evidence—how you can look at something and begin to let your mind play over that material in search of an idea. Curiosity leads you to question the evidence, and questioning leads to the kind of writing that helps clarify ideas. Those two techniques—questioning and writing—can also lead you to make **connections,** to think about one thing in relation to another. Noticing relationships, you begin to notice ideas.

As a general rule, you can better understand one thing by relating it to another. Noticing connections, you begin comparing and contrasting, accounting for likenesses and differences. Even when connecting similar subjects—the playing style of the Boston Celtics and the New York Knicks, the paintings of Picasso and Van Gogh, the corporate environment at Ford and General Motors—you begin to distinguish one from the other. In the process, you not only understand each of those subjects better but also begin to see that the comparison can lead you to ideas. By comparing and contrasting seemingly unrelated subjects, you may find even more interesting ideas.

1   Scientific research—Discoveries through connecting

Consider the unlikely connection between dolphins and chimpanzees that led to important scientific research. In "The Social Lives of Dolphins," William Booth, a science writer, relates a story about a place in western Australia where "wild bottlenosed dolphins swim into knee-deep water and allow tourists to stroke their flanks and feed them frozen fish." This site on the shores of Sharks Bay is now being compared to the Gombe Stream Reserve in Africa, where Jane Goodall studied chimpanzees. Researchers from the Gombe site were drawn to Sharks Bay because they were interested in comparing "the social lives of these two big-brained mammals."

The research into social communities began when two graduate students observed that dolphins at Sharks Bay showed evidence of "begging behavior similar to that exhibited by wild chimpanzees." Their comparison attracted the interest of other scientists and led to extensive research on the social lives of dolphins and chimpanzees. Here is a glimpse of some of their many findings about the way these mammals form communities.

Within the community, dolphins have a tendency to associate with members of the same sex and age, except in the case of females and young calves. Mothers and offspring form some of the tightest bonds in the community, remaining together until the calf is weaned between the ages of three and four years.

Indeed, like chimpanzees, sons and daughters may often closely associate with their mothers years after weaning. Wells [researching as far away as Florida] reports that he has watched older offspring return to their mother's side for the birth of a sibling. "They seem to want to check out the new arrival," says Wells.

Female dolphins with calves are extremely cooperative. The mothers will often form "playpens" around youngsters and allow them to interact within the protective enclave. Episodes of "baby-sitting" are also common, where one female will watch another's calf while the mother is occupied elsewhere.

—William Booth, "The Social Lives of Dolphins"

Once you have read a few of these observations, you begin to make your own connections and ask your own questions. If chimpanzees exhibit social behavior similar to that exhibited by dolphins, what do these patterns of behavior tell you in general about big-brained mammals? Is their gender-related behavior learned or inherited? What might this information tell us about humans? These kinds of questions lead to further research and eventually to ideas. (See 4d for more on looking at controversies to find ideas.)

The simple connection made by the graduate students opened up a whole new world of research. You can see from that experience what you, too, might do. But you do not have to be off at a remote research site to reap the benefits of such connections. You need only be alert to your mind's work. When you think of a connection or a comparison, pursue it.

2   Academic exploration—A student connecting and searching

Let us turn now to the kind of connecting that can serve you in your courses, the kind of connecting that can lead you to a good idea of your own. Begin by thinking about what your mind can do for you if you allow it to move (sometimes leap) toward whatever connections it wants to make. Your precise understanding of what your mind has done will come after the fact, after you have written your thoughts down and turned back to see what your writing reveals to you. Joan Didion, a novelist and essayist, says, "I write entirely to find out what I'm thinking." Respecting that exploratory notion of Didion's, consider what can happen when you write with no other purpose at the outset than letting your mind make connections.

The writing assignment

We will consider work done by Anna Norris during a freshman writing class as a way of seeing how a process of connecting can lead to ideas. In her writing class, Norris was asked first to think and read about three abstract concepts—truth, representation, and value—and then to interpret what those concepts might mean to her in concrete terms, as a student or as a citizen living in the world.

In one of her other courses, Norris was studying photography, so she chose to think of those three abstract concepts as they might relate to her own photographs or to photography in general. Eventually she would need to find an idea related to those concepts so that she could write an essay for the writing course, but at the outset her primary business was connecting.

Photograph by Anna Norris.
Whispering Wall, Soho 1996.
Collection of Anna Norris.

Norris's response—Reading, writing, connecting

As Norris began to think about the kind of representing that photographers do in their photographs—the way they represent themselves and the way they represent the world—she was able to call on reading that she was doing in her photography course and on her own experience. When she came to her writing instructor for an early conference, he suggested that she take preliminary notes about the connections that occurred to her as she thought and read about truth, representation, and value, and that she could take full advantage of the work and the reading she was doing in her other course. He encouraged her *to give free rein to her thoughts but to try to keep up with them,* making a list of ideas and reading notes as she worked. Here is an excerpt from Norris's list of notes based on her own photos, those of others, song lyrics, and her reading:

- Photography is a means to play and explore representation. It is done for the love of the medium itself—of fascination with pictures. From the beginning, love and fascination. My imagination, as in my photo of hands. The images [of hands] are fabricated, wispy, fanciful. [See Norris's photograph of hands within the photograph *Whispering Wall, Soho 1996* on the previous page.]

- The photograph's truth is made up of nothing that has its representation in the surface of the image; any search for the truth behind the image would result in a synopsis of the method I used to arrive at these pretty fabrications.

- What's the use of pictures to anyone who didn't make them?

- Coffee table images. Stock photos. In their case, they gain meaning with context. As everything does, I would think. The story: the Polaroid show where my images were shown; images seem meaningless beyond the activity that went into them. Significance through context.

- "Meaning is discovered in what connects, and cannot exist with development." "When we find a photograph meaningful, we are lending it a past and a future" (quotes from book by Berger 89).

- "Photographs do not translate from appearances. They quote from them" (quote from Berger 96).

- "I have a photograph—preserve your memories, they're all that's left you"—Simon and Garfunkel, *Bookend's Theme.*

- The muse of photography is memory—depend on and equally oppose the passing of time—stimulate and are stimulated by the interconnectedness of events (Berger 280).

- Don't look at this [photo of hands] with admiration, and then search for meaning! It is a trick of light, and the result of a playful period of time spent in the creation of this fabrication of mine. Watch what happens when the same sort of image, created in the same spirit, occupies a different space within a different context:

  POLAROID SHOW: assigned meaning, assigned worth

  OUTSIDE GALLERY: a place marker for the conflict with the city

- Collected and seen by a few people, the image's worth then is as an icon for something that happened to it. I can speak this way about [the photographs of hands] because they are my own photos, and though I can't really know their effect, I know the story and reasons for their conceptions.

This was not Norris's complete list, but it shows how her mind moved *from* general thoughts about photography *to* the quotations from *Another Way of Seeing* (John Berger's book) *to* Simon and Garfunkel *to* her own photographs and her thoughts about them. Obviously journal notes based on hearing Garfunkel and reading Berger influenced her thinking. (See reading journal, in 1e-1.) Probably journal notes on two or three other photographers and critics who appear in subsequent notes were important. (See 1e-2 on personal journals.)

Norris's idea—Connecting and more writing

It is productive for writers to read back through their notes, paying particular attention to key themes and ideas. In this example, notice the way Norris switches to her own photographs in the last section, beginning with "Don't look at this [picture] with admiration, and then search for meaning!" By that time in her thinking and writing, she had discovered an idea; it had evolved through the listing and the connecting and the writing. Some writers might accomplish these connections through mapping, listing, or outlining (see 1f).

Here in the beginning section of an essay she wrote later, "Photographic Assertions," you can see where the list and the idea led her. If you refer to the composite photograph of the hands that is included within *Whispering Wall, Soho 1996* (p. 77), you will see that this photograph of the hands is the image Norris refers to in the following passage:

> Do not look at this image with admiration for some dreamed-up intrinsic value! It is a trick of light. Don't look at it with admiration for its aesthetics, and then search for meaning. Any search for the meaning of the image, as it stands here, would result in a synopsis of the method I used to arrive at this pretty fabrication. An explanation of the mechanics would not bring anyone closer to an understanding of the image's effects, or its worth to anyone else. This image, alone within the frame of a page, asserts very little.
>
> The image exists as a medium; meaning will come from other sources. As John Berger explains, meaning lies in the connections that we make between an object or event or set of data, and its place within the set of information that we base our thoughts and judgments on, not in those things themselves, as isolated objects (89). Under this framework, it seems as if the photographer's role is

inconsequential; why bother making an image at all, if perhaps a random object found in nature could spark just as valid a response at the viewer's whim? But the photographer's influence does not end with this isolated image, stranded, at the mercy of a viewer's set of individualized inferences and colorations; she still has the authority to change her image by placing it in a context. She then changes the image from a rectangle of light-sensitive materials, so contained in itself as to be bordering on solipsistic self-referentiality, into a powerful communicative medium.

If you look again at the *Whispering Wall* photograph, you can see the hands photo in a new context—the context of a city wall that gave it still another meaning. Norris's purpose in looking at her photos is to reveal her leading idea: *Seeing a photograph is complicated business. Isolated and alone a photograph may seem to represent one thing, but in a gallery show or in the context of a city, it may seem to represent another. Context changes meaning.*

In this next section of her essay, you can see Norris beginning to develop her idea:

With the understanding, then, that pretty pictures are worthless for their own sake, watch what happens when the same sort of image, created in the same spirit, occupies a different space within a different context. I make a Polaroid photograph of a delicate, wispy hand appearing twice on the pure black background as it moves across the frame. For a few months its only activity was in being taped to my wall as decoration, speaking nothing and asserting no new viewpoint. Then I made it a frame, as a way to make it seem more formal and serious and less like the playful experiment that it began as, and I entered it in a group show for exhibition in SoHo. The theme was "Instant Visions: Polaroid Photographs by and about Women in New York."

Now, without any change to the image itself, it becomes a representation of what it is to be a woman in New York. One might read the image as speaking of meditative, fanciful, ephemeral night-dreams that occupy a woman's mind as she escapes from daily drudgery. Perhaps it is the promise of learning to fly, before she realizes that she is still anchored by a body and its needs and her responsibilities. I could speculate to no end because within this established context, the image guides viewers to their own conclusions. Within this context the image held significance for someone; it sold within the first half-hour of the exhibition.

Connecting and writing led Norris to her idea about context and meaning. You can do what Norris did; the process is neither intimidating nor complicated. Yet there are no hard-and-fast rules to make that kind of connecting take place, just as there is no established, foolproof process that could lead Anna Norris from her general comments about photography to the written texts and then to her idea. But there are some general principles embedded in her work that can help you make connections and discover ideas.

The accompanying Guidelines for Making Connections will help you. They encapsulate what Norris did. Follow one guideline at a time, giving yourself the opportunity to complete one before going on.

Guidelines for Making Connections

1. Begin always with an aspect of your chosen or assigned topic that interests you most. Select this aspect after you have thought about the topic and have perhaps done some reading about it.

2. List your thoughts, allowing your mind free rein as you make your list. As connections occur, jot them down. Connections can be to related thoughts, to course readings, to other kinds of texts—photographs, movies, poems.

3. Question your preliminary list. See if reading through that list all at once might generate new insights, new connections.

4. Give yourself space to write notes in the margins beside the list—add thoughts, other connections, questions.

5. Look over the list and the notes to see what you have discovered. Does that discovery stand up to the *test of a good idea:* When you state the idea outright, might it cause others to want to know more?

EXERCISE 4–6   Formulating Ideas

What other ideas do you see emerging from Norris's list (p. 78)? If you work within a discussion group in class, write down your ideas and compare them with ideas recorded by other members of your group. Try to reach some consensus about an idea related to context and meaning. If you are working alone, see if you can capture an idea of your own about context and meaning, in two or three sentences.

EXERCISE 4–7   Making Connections

1. Turn to Norris's photograph, *Whispering Wall, Soho 1996* (p. 77). The photograph is a picture of what she considered her "gallery," a wall in Soho where artists put pictures; she put hers there and left them for people to take or do

with what they wanted. Consider the broader social context for "Whispering Wall" as Norris describes it: "During the time that I was operating my 'gallery,' a conflict came into play between the street artists and the New York City government, wherein the city repeatedly and illegally arrested artists for selling their works on the sidewalk." Make as many connections as you can between what Norris has told you and what you can see in the picture. Give your imagination free rein. Make a list of the connections. See if you can discover an idea of your own as you make connections and write about them.

2. Now look again at the photograph. This time, look with critic Joel Eisenger's remark in mind: "Captions change, the context of display changes, the times change. In the end, photographs have no fixed meaning; they float free of any anchor in discourse, offering endless possibilities for speculation." To what extent do you agree or disagree with Eisenger? Formulate a one-paragraph answer in light of Norris's story about the hands photo (described in 4c-2), Eisenger's remark, and your own experience with the way objects either change meaning in different contexts or stay relatively the same over time. Try to work both Norris and Eisenger into your paragraph.

EXERCISE 4–8   Comparing as a Way of Connecting
Consider two fields of study that interest you. Start by writing an impersonal and objective paragraph comparing and contrasting the two fields. Then prepare two or three other paragraphs about the fields, making these more subjective and personal. Recall how you first became interested in each of the fields. Next, consider the impersonal comparison in terms of the more personal exploration. What are the relative merits of each? Finally, let one of those personal accounts, the one you like best, lead you to other connections and ideas. Do not restrict the play of your mind in this final phase of the exercise. Let your mind take its own direction.

4d   Looking at controversies to find ideas

The writing examples presented thus far suggest not only how questioning, writing, and connecting can help you find an interesting idea but also how close at hand such ideas can be. You need not go far to find evidence based on your own experiences and observations, and it can lead you to an idea worth writing about.

Of course, as a student you will have to find other types of evidence. You saw an example of the kind of evidence that comes from research when you considered the connections between dolphins and chimpanzees made earlier in this chapter. Evidence from research may come from the field (as with the dolphins and chimpanzees), or it may be found in the library.

1 Finding a thesis within controversies

Typically, when doing assigned research, you will be asked to develop a leading idea in the form of a **thesis**—a point of view about your subject. That thesis, like a good idea, is nothing more than your conclusion about what the evidence means. One effective way to discover your own point of view is to consider what others have written about your subject. In the sources you consult, look always for differing points of view because they usually signal a topic worthy of your consideration; they point to the heart of controversy.

For every controversial issue, you are sure to find special-interest groups that insist on your seeing the issue the way they see it. You have to sort out the issues and try to resolve the controversy.

Because neither you nor anyone else can be expected to have the range of experience each special-interest group represents, you have to supplement your own limited experience with research. You have to broaden your understanding of the issues, turning to other **sources** for help: books and articles; published interviews and personal interviews (i.e., those you conduct with experts and others affected by the issue or problem you are investigating); newspapers; government studies; documentaries; pamphlets; and any other source that might give you a clearer understanding of the controversy.

A thorough consideration of the appropriate and available sources should help you decide what you think about the controversy. Your reasonable conclusion will become the thesis for your essay.

Considering the gray wolf controversy

Let us see how a consideration of conflicting points of view can help you develop an idea. When Ericka Kostka, a student, began her research, she was concerned about the disappearance of the gray wolf from the United States. She decided to limit her inquiry to Yellowstone National Park, even though the wolf problem exists elsewhere.

Kostka's research pinpointed several special-interest groups, chiefly environmentalists, who wanted to restore the wolf population, and stockgrowers, who feared the wolves would endanger their stock. As she uncovered the competing points of view, she had to weigh one against the other. To do so, she had to locate as best she could a reliable account of each group's vested interest. No single source provided a solution. Kostka had to search through written accounts for answers. That search gave purpose to her research, focused her effort, and led to an idea about the gray wolf.

2 Arriving at a thesis

Behind Kostka's search for a clear resolution of the wolf controversy was a guiding question that focused her research: To what extent does it seem reasonable, given the conflicting interests, to make an effort to try to maintain the restored wolf population in Yellowstone? As Kostka gathered evidence and considered the conflicting points of view, that question kept her on track. It could not be answered with a simple "yes" or "no"; it required her to think about *reasonableness* as she developed her thesis.

To reach a conclusion, Kostka had to consider those opposing points of view. She had to learn enough about each special-interest group to know how to formulate her thesis—the idea that would give purpose and unity to her essay. Here is her thesis.

> Given that the evidence strongly indicates that wolf populations are important to the predator-prey balance of nature [in Yellowstone] and that the details of repopulation can be viable for both the gray wolf and its opponents, I believe that we should reverse the one-sided concessions that we reforced upon a now-endangered population by supporting the program to restore wolves in the park and by keeping their endangered classification until the population is fully restored.

Kostka did not bring the thesis to the assignment. Rather, it evolved through learning and writing, as she considered conflicting points of view, wrote about them, questioned them, and, finally, reached her own conclusion.

In Chapter 40, you can see in detail how Kostka questioned those points of view, resolved the controversy, and wrote a research essay to present and defend her thesis. Her complete essay appears in 44a.

3 Using your own investigations to resolve controversies

Kostka's methods can also serve you well when you do directed research to develop a thesis for your own essays. This recursive process, which takes you from library sources to drafting and back to the sources, moves back and forth until you can formulate a thesis that you feel confident defending. The accompanying checklist, Considering Controversies to Find Ideas, will guide you. (See also Chapter 7 on argumentative essays and Chapter 40 on the research essay.)

Considering Controversies to Find Ideas

1. Select a controversy that interests you.

2. Go to the library. Locate sources for conflicting points of view. (See Chapter 39 on researching.) Outline each special-interest group's concerns.

3. Question sources. Look for weaknesses and connections in the various arguments.

4. Begin to formulate what you think is a reasonable conclusion about the controversy. Write down your thesis and your reasons for believing it. List questions that still need to be answered.

5. Broaden your reading to help answer remaining questions and test your conclusion, making sure that you have not overlooked important evidence.

6. Modify your conclusion in light of the evidence and formulate your thesis—the clear-headed statement that you will set down and defend in an essay.

EXERCISE 4–9   Locating and Investigating a Controversy

1. Read the local or state newspaper for three or four days looking for a story about a controversial topic that is important enough to require coverage for more than one day. Read the coverage carefully, looking for signs of special-interest groups. List the groups and their opinions. Which group do you side with? Why?

2. Investigate one of the groups that you did not side with—by reading other newspapers, by interviewing people involved in the controversy, by discussing the subject with others in your writing class. Try to be open minded about that other group's point of view, but question their ideas, looking for their value as well as their weakness. Write a paragraph about the other group's special interest. Question what you have said about the group's point of view. Does this preliminary research change your mind about the controversy? Explain.

5 *Fundamentals of Paragraph Development*

In effective paragraphs, unity and coherence go hand in hand with a tight organization and the development of an idea. Everything in a paragraph helps achieve those four requirements of effective paragraphing: the flow of the sentences; their variety; the paragraph's evidence, including details, examples, and images; and the way in which evidence and explanation are arranged and presented.

5a Creating unified and coherent paragraphs

A **unified paragraph** develops a single idea. A **coherent paragraph** is one in which all of the parts—sentences, evidence, thinking, explanations— come together in a near-perfect fit to express that idea. To write unified and coherent paragraphs you need to stay focused and make all parts of the paragraph stick together.

Following is a unified and coherent paragraph taken from a speech given before the United Nations by Václav Havel, president of the Czech Republic. As you read the paragraph, notice how Havel carries forward the idea expressed in the first sentence, how each sentence builds on the one before it, and how the sentences clarify and amplify the meaning of that first sentence.

Without a global revolution in the sphere of human consciousness, nothing will change for the better in the sphere of our being as humans, and the catastrophe toward which this world is headed—be it ecological, social, demographic or a general breakdown of civilization—will be unavoidable. If we are no longer threatened by world war or by the danger that the absurd mountains of accumulated nuclear weapons might blow up the world, this does not mean that we have definitely won. We are still incapable of understanding that the only genuine backbone of all our actions, if they are to be moral, is responsibility. Responsibility to something higher than my family, my country, my company, my success—responsibility to the order of being where all our actions are indelibly recorded and where and only where they will be properly judged.

—Václav Havel, "Global Responsibility"

Although the first sentence contains the germ of Havel's idea, his meaning is not altogether clear until you reach the end of the paragraph, where you learn what he means by a "revolution in the sphere of human consciousness." There, at the end of the paragraph, he calls for a higher sense of responsibility among nations as he brings the ideas of revolution and responsibility together. Each sentence in the paragraph enlarges our sense of Havel's idea.

http://www.uottawa.ca/ academic/arts/writcent/ hypergrammar/paragrph.html Explains clearly and accessibly how to write and revise paragraphs.

When the parts of a paragraph do not fit together, the paragraph seems out of kilter, confusing. The defect usually results when a writer fails to stay focused or fails to clarify the relationships among the sentences in the paragraph. Consider this paragraph from an editorial that argues against limiting terms for members of Congress.

As a college student in a constant struggle to balance coursework, extracurricular activities, and sleep, I often find it difficult to keep up with a constantly fluctuating world. However, there has always been something that never seems to change, American politics. It still seems to be as ineffective as ever. The stagnation on Capitol Hill has led to a situation where most of the exigencies of this country are not being met. It has turned into a bureaucratic black hole where everything is proposed but nothing is done. Most people suffer from intense feelings of anger and frustration when it comes to the government. It is easy to understand and sympathize with these people, many of whom have decided to wage a war on Congress. Recently, however, it seems as though the people's anger has been misdirected. It seems as though many have been swept up in the entire anti-incumbent fever.

—Anshul Patel, student (draft paragraph)

In the first two sentences, Patel seems to be trying to relate a personal experience to a problem he senses in politics, but he neither makes that relationship clear nor establishes its importance. He is not focused; he does not lead his readers to the paragraph's main point about anti-incumbent fever. Now consider what happens when he focuses his argument.

As a result of the November 3rd election, at least 110 new faces will join the 103rd Congress. According to the *Congressional Quarterly,* this turnover, affecting nearly a quarter of the House, is the largest since 1948. The turnover was largely due to the anti-incumbency fever that swept the nation earlier this year. The stagnation on Capitol Hill had disillusioned most people in the electorate. Their anger was further fueled by revelations that hundreds of members of Congress had routinely overdrawn their House Bank accounts without penalty. The checking scandal and others like it seemed to symbolize just how out of touch senators and representatives were. All of this disenchantment lit a fire under the movement for term limits. The movement culminated on November 3rd when voters passed term limitation bills in fourteen states. However, it seems as though most people were so frustrated with Congress that they jumped onto the term-limitation bandwagon unaware of all its implications. Their anger was misdirected by term limiters who took full advantage of America's disgust with its government. It is imperative that we realize that term limitations will only worsen the situation on Capitol Hill.

—Anshul's revised paragraph

This focused paragraph is also unified; every sentence leads to the next, carrying the reader forward to Patel's main idea—in this case, expressed in the last sentence of the paragraph (reread Václav Havel's paragraph, where the main idea appears in the first sentence). The sentence containing a paragraph's main idea is referred to as a **topic sentence.** Topic sentences provide focus and clarify meaning; they contain the essence of each paragraph. These sentences can also point beyond the paragraph to the essay itself. Patel's main idea will be developed and defended in the middle paragraphs of his essay.

5b   Achieving paragraph unity

You can achieve paragraph unity by staying focused on the main idea expressed in your topic sentence and by clearly explaining the relationship between your evidence and the idea you are developing.

1 Staying focused on the idea

One of the surest ways to keep your paragraphs unified is to stay focused on your main idea so that everything you put in the paragraph contributes to your readers' understanding of that idea.

Here is a paragraph that seems unsure of its controlling idea. Readers, therefore, have to guess about the paragraph's meaning, choosing between at least two possible ideas. About halfway through this draft paragraph, the writer seems to change her focus, moving from one idea to another. See if you can detect the shift.

> On the left side of the room, facing in from the doorway, is my boudoir. There is a bed and a vanity in the corner. It's kind of fun; I can play the leading lady who gives her long golden tresses one hundred strokes before retiring for the night. Only I don't have long hair. And it's not blonde. Besides, the mirror is all but obscured by photos, postcards, and other miscellany. There's my family, my best buddies, and the men in my life: Dizzy, Charlie Parker, and the Count.
>
> —Cindy Fujita, student (draft paragraph)

Cindy Fujita begins the paragraph on an interesting note, calling her bedroom a "boudoir"—a woman's bedroom or private sitting room. This first part of the paragraph suggests that the bedroom is a place for acting out fantasies. But about halfway through the paragraph—starting with "Only"—Fujita veers from fantasy into reality. She confesses that she does not have long blonde hair and that the mirror, the photos, and the postcards get in the way of the fantasy. So at the end of the paragraph, readers are confused about what Fujita thinks about her bedroom. Is the bedroom a place of fantasy or a place that brings Fujita to her senses?

To answer that question, you would have to read Fujita's full essay, where she writes about the importance of fantasy; that is her essay's main idea. Thus, her paragraph should stay focused on fantasy.

> On the left side of the room, facing in from the doorway, is my boudoir, nothing so private as to be shocking, but special, very special, nevertheless. There is a bed and a vanity in the corner. It's kind of fun. I can play the leading lady who gives her long tresses one hundred strokes before retiring for the night, and when I look in my mirror it doesn't faze

me that I see short, black hair. All around my face in the mirror, I see my friends, their faces, and their messages sent me from around the world. There's my family, my best buddies, and the men in my life: Dizzy, Charlie Parker, and the Count. As I sit and stroke my hair, I hear them playing for me, hear the sax and the piano and know that in this lair, I am the leading lady, waiting for them . . . or they are waiting for me to join them—out through the back door, only steps away from that other world.

—Fujita's revised paragraph

Unifying the draft paragraph required little more than a clear sense of what the evidence in the "boudoir" was supposed to suggest. Fujita had to decide whether the mirror was a help or a hindrance, whether the pictures and postcards distracted her from her fantasy or enhanced it.

As a writer, you can make your selection of detail—your evidence—say what you want it to say. The choice is yours. But a paragraph must be unified, the relationship between evidence and idea clear. Also, the complete essay must be unified.

Rules of Thumb for Writing Unified Paragraphs

- Be sure your paragraphs focus on one idea and state that idea in a topic sentence (5b-1).

- Place your topic sentence effectively within your paragraph. Let the purpose of your paragraph and the nature of your evidence guide you (5b-2).

- Let your paragraph's evidence—the selected details, the examples—illustrate or clarify the idea expressed in your topic sentence (5b-3).

- Make sure you explain the relationship between your evidence and your idea so that it is clear to readers (5b-3).

- Think about unity among paragraphs when writing essays. Be sure your paragraphs are related, that they fit together and clarify your essay's idea.

EXERCISE 5–1   **Writing Paragraphs**

1. Select a space that intrigues you—a room, a spot outdoors, a state of mind—and write a paragraph about it. When you begin writing, do not worry about an idea; try only to convey through selected details what the space is like.

Then look at what you have written and decide what you want your readers to know about that space. Revise your paragraph so that it conveys your idea about the space. Bring both versions of your paragraph to class for consideration by your work group or by another reader.

2. Read both versions of your paragraph to the work group or aloud to yourself, and explain the differences between the two versions. Explain why you made the changes you did.

3. Exchange revised paragraphs with a classmate. Read one another's paragraphs and comment in writing about whether the evidence (the selected details) is explained sufficiently to allow you to understand the idea.

2 Placing the topic sentence

The topic sentence, which states the paragraph's main idea, can be placed anywhere in the paragraph, depending on how you want to lead your readers to understand your main idea. Consider the following options for placing the topic sentence.

Topic sentence at the beginning of a paragraph

If you place your topic sentence at the beginning of a paragraph, as Václav Havel did (5a), your readers will know immediately what your paragraph will be about. They will then be able to see how each subsequent sentence contributes to the development of your main idea.

This placement will serve you well when you are writing argumentative essays (see Chapter 7) or responding to essay examination questions (see Chapter 49). In those cases, you are defending your position on a given subject; it is helpful if your readers can see prominently at the outset what your idea is.

Topic sentence at the end of a paragraph

Placing the topic sentence at the end of a paragraph, as Anshul Patel did (5a), lets you lead your readers through your evidence and your reasoning to your conclusion. You will hold that clarifying topic sentence until the end to leave readers with a clear and emphatic reminder of your main idea.

This placement is effective when you use stories as evidence and want to lead readers through a fairly complex inquiry, as you would in an exploratory (narrative) essay (see Chapter 6). In this type of essay, you want to maintain some suspense about your idea. When you clarify meaning at the end of the paragraph, you leave readers with a clear sense of what the stories mean to you and what they have to do with your idea.

In the following paragraph, the main idea (a judgment about the Sioux Indians) does not become clear until the last sentence of the paragraph.

> In 1890, the year of the final defeat of the Sioux at Wounded Knee, the Ghost Dance was sweeping the plains. Begun by a few leaders, especially the Paiute seer Wovoka, the Ghost Dance promised its practitioners among the warriors that the buffalo would return and the white man would be defeated. Ghost Dancers believed that their ceremonial dancing and the shirts they wore would make them proof against the white man's bullets. Among the Sioux warriors at Wounded Knee, the willing suspension of disbelief was complete. It made the warriors reckless and abandoned, throwing normal caution and survival strategy to the wind.
>
> —Diana Hume George, "Wounded Chevy at Wounded Knee"

Everything in this paragraph contributes to our understanding of that last sentence. That topic sentence calls attention to the unity of the paragraph because it lets us see how every other sentence in the paragraph contributes to its meaning.

A final note: topic sentences that appear at the end of an essay's beginning paragraph often become the essay's thesis—the main idea that gets developed in much greater detail in the middle of the essay.

Topic sentence in the middle of the paragraph

Occasionally, you will need to prepare your readers with some background information before they can understand your topic sentence, and then you will want to offer further evidence and explanation before you bring the paragraph to a close.

Here is an example of an effective paragraph on the legacy of a mother's hard work. The topic sentence falls near the middle of the paragraph.

> But she did not raise me to respect her way of offering love and to believe that hard work is often the irreducible factor for survival, not something to avoid. Her woman's work produced a reliable home base where I could pursue the privileges of books and music. Her woman's work invented the potential for a completely different kind of work for

us, the next generation of Black women: huge, rewarding hard work demanded by the huge, new ambitions that her perfect confidence in us engendered.

—June Jordan, "In Our Hands"

Implied topic sentence

A paragraph's main idea need not be stated explicitly; it can be implied. Paragraphs with implied topic sentences ask more of readers because the details of the paragraph only suggest the main idea. The reader must infer that idea from the details.

The following paragraph with an implied topic sentence is easier to understand if you have some knowledge of the rest of the essay. But if you pay attention to the details, you can infer a great deal from them. The paragraph recounts the writer's experience and reflections as she paddled around a lake observing the change of season from summer to fall. See if you can infer the paragraph's main idea.

As I drift aimlessly, ducks move out from the reeds, all mallards. Adaptable, omnivorous, and hardy, they nest here every year on the two tiny islands in the lake. After communal courtship and mating, the extra male ducks are chased away, but this year one stayed behind. Perhaps he fathered a clutch on the sly or was too young to know where else to go. When the ducklings hatched and began swimming, he often tagged along, keeping them loosely together until the official father sent him away. Then he'd swim the whole circumference of the lake alone, too bewildered and dignified to show defeat.

—Gretel Ehrlich, "This Autumn Morning"

It may help you to know the main idea of Ehrlich's essay, stated in an earlier paragraph: "To long for love, to have experienced passion's deep pleasure, even once, is to understand the mercilessness of having a human body whose memory rides desire's back unanchored from season to season." With that sentence in mind, you can see more easily how Ehrlich sees her own plight in the duck's as the season turns from the dryness of summer to the fullness and fecundity of autumn. Ehrlich, too, finds herself alone, longing and bewildered but too "dignified to show defeat."

3   Explaining the idea

As you have just seen, developing paragraphs around a single idea, often expressed in a topic sentence that you can present in a variety of ways, helps you achieve paragraph unity. However, you need to be sure that you do not rely solely on your topic sentence to carry the weight of your idea. Always offer sufficient explanation throughout a paragraph to make your idea clear to your readers. And be sure that the sentences in your paragraph include evidence—examples and details—that is clearly related to your idea. (See 1c on evidence and ideas.) Always explain your main idea so that readers will know what you want them to know.

5c   Achieving paragraph coherence

So far, we have concentrated on paragraph unity. But unity alone does not make a good paragraph. The key to focusing and explaining your idea is a coherent presentation. Let us now consider five ways to fit the various parts of a paragraph together to express your idea coherently.

Ways to Achieve Paragraph Coherence

- Use pronouns to replace nouns (5c-1).
- Repeat and develop key terms (5c-2).
- Link sentences with transitional words (5c-3).
- Create visual clarity (5c-4).
- Use parallel structures (5c-5).

As you think about the guidelines and begin to understand what each one means, keep in mind that they represent techniques experienced writers eventually use almost unconsciously. Be aware of these techniques; try them as you write. In the long run, you will find yourself using them automatically.

1   Using pronouns

Let us begin with a paragraph that has unity of idea but lacks coherence. Something in this paragraph makes it difficult to read. The sentences, even though related to one another, stand apart. There is no easy movement from one sentence to another. See if you can detect the cause of the problem as you read out loud Patrick Cleburn's paragraph from an essay entitled "Leadership."

> During the attack, Lieutenant Sothoron did something very important. Lieutenant Sothoron gave the saving performance. Although Sothoron had been schooled in leadership and knew about the skills of soldiering, what Sothoron did that night was like drama. It was more like drama than leadership. Sothoron became someone else. Sothoron wore the mask of the warrior. That night in Vietnam, Lieutenant Sothoron played out his appointed part. Other soldiers participated in the fight, but Sothoron was responsible for what happened. He inspired them.
>
> —Patrick Cleburn, student (draft paragraph)

The main idea in Cleburn's paragraph is clear: Lieutenant Sothoron gave an unusual performance in combat, and his performance inspired other soldiers. Everything fits together; everything contributes to the unified expression of the idea. But the halting, choppy rhythm of the paragraph makes it difficult for the reader to grasp that idea.

One way to create smoother transitions from sentence to sentence is to substitute a pronoun for a noun. (See Chapter 11 for more on pronouns.) In Cleburn's paragraph, for example, try substituting the pronoun *he* for either *Sothoron* or *Lieutenant Sothoron*. The pronoun should serve as a linking device, pulling the sentences together and making the paragraph easier to read and understand. Make sure the reader can always identify the person for whom the pronoun stands (its antecedent).

Notice the way the pronouns—italicized in Cleburn's revised paragraph—improve the rhythm and link the sentences, making the paragraph more coherent.

> During the attack, Lieutenant Sothoron did something very important. *He* gave the saving performance. Although Sothoron had been schooled in leadership and knew about the skills of soldiering, what *he* did that night was like drama. It was more like drama than leadership. Sothoron became someone else. *He* wore the mask of the warrior. That night in Vietnam, *he* played out his appointed part. Other soldiers participated in the fight, but Sothoron was responsible for what happened. *His* performance inspired them.
>
> —Cleburn's revised paragraph

EXERCISE 5–2 Using Pronouns

1. Try other pronoun substitutions in Patrick Cleburn's revised paragraph. Can you substitute *he* for *Sothoron* in other places without creating confusion?

2. Write a paragraph about one of your heroes or heroines. Try to convey to your readers the one thing that you think is most important about that person. After you complete your draft, revise to make the paragraph more coherent, paying particular attention to the way you use pronouns.

2   Repeating key terms

Repeating important terms can positively affect paragraph coherence. In the revised paragraph about Lieutenant Sothoron, you can see that the terms *leadership* and *drama* are very important to the paragraph's idea. The term *leadership* appears twice to remind readers of the importance of that concept. These two terms appeared in the first version of the paragraph, too, but the unnecessary repetition of the name *Sothoron* so dominated the paragraph that the other words were somewhat obscured, and coherence was destroyed.

In the revised version of Cleburn's paragraph, you can see more easily how the key terms *leadership* and *drama* contribute to the paragraph's main idea. As you reread the paragraph, notice how Patrick develops the notions of leadership and drama by introducing other related words, such as *soldiering, mask, warrior,* and *performance,* to help you understand his idea. You need not simply repeat a single term to reap the benefits of repetition—including related words can also clarify meaning and give the paragraph a forward momentum while drawing the parts into a coherent whole.

As a general rule, repeat words sparingly. Use repetition to develop your idea and to keep readers' attention on the paragraph's evolving meaning. Avoid excessive repetition; it can obscure your idea and create paragraphs that are difficult to read.

EXERCISE 5–3 Repeating and Developing Key Terms

1. Select one of the following words and write for ten minutes about that word: *woman, man, paragraph, heroism, leadership.* Do not feel obligated to define the word as the dictionary would; rather, use the word in a sentence and keep writing, trying to illustrate what the word means to you.

2. Look over what you wrote in the preceding exercise and identify what seem to be key terms in the passage. Pick out an idea that you see embedded in

the passage, and think about the relationship between the key terms and the idea. Write a paragraph repeating the key terms to help you develop your idea.

3 Linking sentences with transitional expressions

Often, you can create coherence within a paragraph by linking closely related sentences with **transitional expressions.** Such linking often tightens paragraphs and clarifies meaning. Transitional words such as *although, therefore, thus, but,* and *yet* indicate the relationships among sentences and among the ideas in sentences; they refer to surrounding sentences, pulling the paragraph together. (See 24b-1 for more on transitions.) The chart on p. 98 provides a select list of commonly used transitional words and expressions.

As a writer, you cannot simply turn to a list of transitional expressions, select two or three of them, and insert them in paragraphs to create coherence. Rather, you must use transitions to convey a relationship that already exists among ideas. Transitions, by themselves, cannot create such relationships.

Consider the following paragraph about the differences between masculine and feminine discourse. In it, David Reich links sentences by using transitional words, but you can also see that those words signify the relationship among ideas about the two types of discourse. Those transitional words (shown in italics) and the movement of his thinking pull Reich's paragraph together and make it more coherent.

Another thing that makes masculine discourse unimportant in a literary way, *besides* the fact that it is so marginal, is that it is, according to Joyce Carol Oates, "a story without words." Boxing, *for example,* allows for the "public embrace of two men who otherwise, in public or in private, could never approach each other with such passion." *But* however communicative the embrace, the language of masculinity is emphatically a physical language and not a language of words, *so that* masculinity, for the most part, is not a literary idea in the same way that femininity is. Civilized conversation, *though,* tends more toward words and ideas—the province of femininity rather than masculinity. *Because* feminine discourse has something to say about words and ideas, *whereas* masculine discourse has very little to say, women are bound by expectations and subtexts that they themselves didn't create, *while* men are more free to

Transitional Words and Expressions

To Suggest Continuity and Sequence
again, also, and then, besides, finally, furthermore, in the first place, moreover, next

To Illustrate with Examples
after all, for example, for instance, specifically, such as, that is, the following example

To Suggest Comparison
also, in the same way, likewise, once more, similarly

To Indicate Contrast
although, but, despite, even though, for all that, in spite of, instead, nevertheless, notwithstanding, on the contrary, on the other hand, yet

To Show a Result
as a result, because, consequently, hence, so, then, therefore, thus, to this end

To Signal Time
after a few days, after a while, afterward, at that time, before, earlier, immediately, in the meantime, in the past, lately, later, now, presently, shortly, simultaneously, since, when

To Indicate Place
above, below, beyond, closer to, elsewhere, nearby, opposite, out there, there, to the left, to the north, to the right, under

To Offer Concessions
although, but I admit, granted, it may seem that, let me concede that, of course

To Clarify and Conclude with Emphasis
as we have seen, finally, in any event, in conclusion, in other words, in summary, let me reiterate, notwithstanding, on the whole, therefore, thus, to put it differently, to sum up

approach civilization from a "neutral" perspective, to live first of all as human beings and only secondarily as manly men.

—David Reich, student

Consider how difficult it would be to follow Reich's paragraph without the transitional words. Reread the paragraph and skip over the transitional words and consider the difference. Without them, the sentences bear no clear relationship to one another; as a result, the paragraph is incoherent. It makes little sense and does not clearly reflect Reich's judgments about masculine and feminine discourse.

EXERCISE 5–4   Writing and Revising Using Transitional Words
Respond to David Reich's paragraph in one of your own, developing the idea about either masculine or feminine discourse. Include both your ideas and Reich's in your paragraph. Revise for more coherence, using transitional words to link your thoughts.

4   Including visual details

Often, when you are trying to make your reader understand an idea in a paragraph, it helps to provide visual details or images. Joseph Conrad, the novelist, said he only wanted to make his readers *see*. Psychologists tell us that images elicit ideas. Because visual details can clarify meaning, they can also pull ideas in a paragraph together and make it more coherent.

In the following paragraph, novelist Toni Morrison relies on visual details to get at an elusive concept; she tries to make you, the reader, see what she means by "flooding."

You know, they straightened out the Mississippi River in places, to make room for houses and livable acreage. Occasionally the river floods these places. "Floods" is a word they use, but in fact it is not flooding; it is remembering. Remembering where it used to be. All water has a perfect memory and is forever trying to get back to where it was. Writers are like that: remembering where we were, what valley we ran through, what the banks were like, the light that was there and the route back to our original place. It is emotional memory—what the nerves and the skin remember as well as how it appeared. And a rush of imagination is our "flooding."

—Toni Morrison, "The Site of Memory"

Morrison uses the image of flooding both literally and imaginatively to help readers visualize and understand the idea that writers are always trying to get back to some original place and to remember and render it. The visual detail of the flood not only clarifies the idea; it also makes the paragraph coherent because it draws together the ideas of remembering, flooding, and imagining in a way that shows you their close relationship.

EXERCISE 5–5   **Writing with Images**
Think of something you care a great deal about but that is hard to get across to someone else—a mathematical concept, a scientific principle, a notion about love, the texture of someone's hair, a political principle—and write a paragraph about it, using one or two images or visual details to help you clarify what you think.

5   Using parallelism

Repeating parallel structures is yet another way to make your paragraphs coherent. **Parallelism** results when you repeat a grammatical form. You can use parallel structures within your paragraphs to call attention to an important aspect of your idea and to create a pleasing, emphatic rhythm that underscores your idea and carries your reader forward.

Consider the italicized parallel phrases in the following paragraph. As you read the paragraph, listen to the words to hear how rhythm develops through repetition and how that rhythm moves through the paragraph and helps you stay focused on the accumulating meaning. Sound and sense combine to create coherence.

Animals give us their constant, unjaded faces and we burden them with our bodies and civilized ordeals. We're both humbled by and imperious with them. We're comrades who save each other's lives. *The horse we pulled* from a boghole this morning bucked someone off later in the day; one stock dog refuses to work sheep, while another brings back a calf we had overlooked while trailing cattle to another pasture; *the heifer we doctored* for pneumonia backed up to a wash and dropped her newborn calf over the edge; *the horse that brings us home safely* in the dark kicks us the next day. On and on it goes.

—Gretel Ehrlich, "Friends, Foes, and Working Animals"

Note the way Ehrlich identifies a "job" of each of the working farm animals, and how each of the working animals makes more work for the humans. The humans have to pull the horse out of a boghole, but later in the day, the horse bucks off the human. That pattern of work begetting work repeats itself throughout the paragraph and suggests some tension within the "odd partnership" between humans and animals that Ehrlich is writing about. The parallel structures in the paragraph contribute to our understanding of its meaning and help pull the parts of the paragraph together coherently. (See also Chapter 23 on parallelism.)

EXERCISE 5–6   Working with Parallel Structures

1. Underline the parallel structures in the following paragraph. Then write a paragraph of your own explaining how those parallel structures contribute to coherence and meaning.

   Women of Color in America have grown up within a symphony of anger, at being silenced, at being unchosen, at knowing that when we survive, it is in spite of a world that takes for granted our lack of humanness, and which hates our very existence outside of its service. And I say symphony rather than cacophony because we have had to learn to orchestrate those furies so that they do not tear us apart. We have had to learn to move through them and use them for strength and force and insight within our daily lives. Those of us who did not learn this difficult lesson did not survive. And part of my anger is always libation for my fallen sisters.
   —Audre Lorde, "The Uses of Anger"

2. Start drafting a paragraph in which you try to achieve coherence by repeating a grammatical structure at least three times. Begin without a particular plan in mind. Through writing, discover a word, phrase, or clause worth repeating. Then write a coherent paragraph that uses your discovery.

5d   Organizing paragraphs

Paragraphs must be organized so that readers can follow the development of your idea and can understand the relationship between your evidence and the idea. Logically organized paragraphs are coherent paragraphs. A disorganized paragraph is difficult for your readers to comprehend. Always remember that your aim is to make it easy for your reader to follow your thinking.

The five organizational patterns identified in the accompanying chart represent logical and familiar ways to order paragraphs. Whether you have thought much about them or not, they have probably been serving you well for a long time. Think about them now as organizational options available to you.

In all likelihood, you will not sit down and decide that a paragraph needs a general-to-specific order or a climactic one. Instead, you will probably decide subconsciously how to organize paragraphs as you are writing or after you have done some drafting. Once you write your initial draft paragraph, always stop and think about how you have organized it. And then when you revise, use the organizational pattern that seems most appropriate for your purpose. Let your purpose and an organizational pattern shape your revision.

> **www**
> http://webserver.maclab.comp.uvic.ca/writersguide/Pages/paragraphsTOC.html
> Provides advice on how to develop and organize paragraphs.

Five Ways to Organize Paragraphs

1. From general to specific (5d-1)
2. From specific to general (5d-2)
3. Climactic order (5d-3)
4. Time order (5d-4)
5. Spatial order (5d-5)

1 From general to specific

Paragraphs using the **general-to-specific order** move from a general statement of a problem to a very specific solution, or they move from a general claim about a fairly broad subject to a more specific claim about it. Here is an example of the latter.

> What we casually call "English," less and less defers to England and its "gentlemen." "English" is no longer a specific matter of geography or an element of class privilege; more than thirty-three countries use this tool as a means of "intranational communication." Countries as disparate as Zimbabwe and Malaysia, or Israel and Uganda, use it as their

non-native currency of convenience. Obviously, this tool, this "English," cannot function inside thirty-three discrete societies on the basis of rules and values absolutely determined somewhere else, in a thirty-fourth other country, for example.

—June Jordan, "Nobody Means More to Me than You
and the Future Life of Willie Jordan"

This paragraph begins with the general claim that the English language cannot be too narrowly associated with England and class privileges. The paragraph ends with a very specific claim that adhering to such a restricted view of English would make the language unfit for use in all those other countries Jordan alludes to.

2 From specific to general

Paragraphs that use the **specific-to-general order** move from some specific detail (or group of details) to a general conclusion. Here is such a paragraph from an essay by Loren Eiseley, an anthropologist.

I have seen a tree root burst a rock face on a mountain or slowly wrench aside the gateway of a forgotten city. This is a very cunning feat, which men take too readily for granted. Life, unlike the inanimate, will take the long way round to circumvent barrenness. A kind of desperate will resides even in a root. It will perform the evasive tactics of an army, slowly inching its way through crevices and hoarding energy until someday it swells and a living tree upheaves the heaviest mausoleum. This covert struggle is part of the lifelong battle waged against the Second Law of Thermodynamics, the heat death that has been frequently assumed to rule the universe. At the hands of man that hoarded energy takes strange forms, both in the methods of its accumulation and in the diverse ways of its expenditure.

—Loren Eiseley, "The Last Neanderthal"

Eiseley begins this paragraph with a specific detail about a tree root bursting a rock face. But what really interests him is the force of life that expresses itself in that bursting. From his initial observation, he begins to generalize, explaining as he goes along how that hoarded energy manifests itself and what happens to that energy in human hands.

EXERCISE 5–7 **Organizing Your Own Paragraphs**
Try to develop two different paragraphs about the same topic—sewing, running, fighting, creating, or eating, for example. Use the general-to-specific pattern in one paragraph and the specific-to-general pattern in the other. Does one pattern seem more appropriate than the other for organizing your particular idea? Explain your answer.

3 Climactic order

It often makes good sense to present a paragraph in **climactic order,** moving from the least important information to the most important, leaving the most telling bit of knowledge for the end. Here is an example.

> So it was that I stood above the mat and heard myself sigh and then felt myself let go, dropping through the quiet air, crutches slipping off to the sides. What I didn't feel this time was the threat of my body slipping into emptiness, so mummified by the terror before it that the touch of air preempted even death. I dropped. I did not crash. I dropped. I did not collapse. I dropped. I did not plummet. I felt myself enveloped by a curiously gentle moment in my life. In that sliver of time before I hit the mat, I was kissed by space.
>
> —Leonard Kriegel, "Falling into Life"

Climactic ordering is particularly useful within a single paragraph when your idea is too complex to present all at once. In that case, you need to introduce an aspect of that idea and then develop it as you go along, saving your most important point until the very end of the paragraph.

What is true for paragraphs is true for entire essays. An effective argumentative essay will almost always present the least important evidence first and the most important last, becoming more convincing and emphatic as it moves along (see 7d).

EXERCISE 5–8 **Writing Toward a Climax**
1. Reread Kriegel's paragraph carefully and then answer these questions.
   a. What is the effect of the last sentence on the sentences that come before it?
   b. How does the last sentence change your sense of their meaning? Explain your answer.

c. Consider what the paragraph might be like if it began this way: "The first time I fell after I contracted polio, it felt as though I had been kissed by space." Which version seems more effective to you? Explain your answer.

2. This paragraph is from Kriegel's essay (it follows the paragraph from 5d-3). Read this paragraph and answer the questions that follow it.

> My body absorbed the slight shock and I rolled onto my back, braced legs swinging like unguided missiles into the free air, crutches dropping away to the sides. Even as I fell through the air, I could sense the shame and fear drain from my soul, and I knew that my sense of my own cowardice would soon follow. In falling, I had given myself a new start, a new life.
>
> —Leonard Kriegel, "Falling into Life"

To what extent is this paragraph organized like Kriegel's earlier paragraph? Do the paragraphs themselves follow a climactic order? Explain your answer.

3. Write a paragraph that is organized climactically. Use one of the topics identified in Exercise 5–7 or another of your own choosing.

4 Time order

The passage of time provides a context for understanding. You no doubt use it to explain how an event happened. Time, or chronology, helps us order events. Using **time order** to organize your paragraphs also makes it easier for readers to follow along with your thinking. You lead your readers through time to your idea.

Consider the following paragraph, in which the references to time are underlined.

> I have lived this way since I abandoned the city. Before that, I began my day by bending to the mail slot of the front door of Fig Tree House and picking up the *Guardian* and the *Times* of London, and before that by stepping onto the fragrant front porch of our house on Upperline Street in New Orleans and picking up the *Times-Picayune*. I had trained all my life to be a city person, learning tennis manners and cocktail English. When I reached New Orleans, I assumed, as the people of that city do, that I would never move again. I became as mellow as an Orleanian, and was happy. Then I fled. There was an interlude in London, but even then

I was in the act of flight. I landed in the Ozarks, in my native state. A rocky hillside farm became my home.

—Roy Reed, "Abandoning the City"

The chronological sequencing provides order in Reed's paragraph and helps you sense the significance of the idea that Reed associates with time passing—the idea that after all this time and traveling, after spending years training himself to be a city person, he had to return to the farm to find home.

You, too, can use chronology to orient your readers and help them understand your idea. Time may have something to do with your idea, as it does for Reed, or it may simply be an ordering device for your paragraph.

EXERCISE 5–9   Using Time Order
Write a paragraph explaining how you completed a challenging task such as conducting a chemistry experiment, preparing a meal, or programming a VCR. Revise your paragraph to organize it chronologically.

5   Spatial order

Often you want your readers to survey a place so that they can actually see what you want them to see. You may want them to see the space from a distance, from close up, or from top to bottom so that they can understand what happened there. Or you may want to "put them into" a space so they can know what it felt like to be there. Such arrangements use **spatial order,** and they go hand in hand with descriptive paragraphs—those that appeal to the senses and evoke sight, touch, taste, or smell to create ambience, or those that try to describe a place exactly as it is without emotional overtones. Vivid or exacting descriptions of a space orient readers and help you clarify your idea about that place or what happened there. (See also 5e-9 on description.)

Notice how description and spatial ordering work together in this paragraph to give you a sense of what is happening in the room.

One of the women from the cluster has walked away. Moving along the side of the studio, she maneuvers to avoid the clutter of easels and stacks of paintings. She pauses near the platform at the front of the studio. Meanwhile, among the others the discussions have ended and have been replaced by the gathering of pencils, charcoal, and paper. At the platform, the woman has begun to transform herself. As the clothes fall away from her body and she stretches out upon the platform, she becomes a model. The others become artists, intently observing. I become tense.

—Senta Wong, student

EXERCISE 5–10   Bringing Order and Idea Together

1. Reread Senta Wong's paragraph. How do her selection of detail and her description of the room make the revelation in the last sentence effective? Explain your answer. Then change the time order of the paragraph by moving the last sentence to the beginning of the paragraph. How does that change your response to the paragraph? Explain your answer.

2. Re-create in words a space or place where something unusual happened to you. Orient your readers by using spatial order, but also try to convey through your description and selection of details the effect of that experience.

5e   Developing ideas within paragraphs

In addition to the methods you have considered for achieving paragraph unity and coherence and for organizing paragraphs, other traditional and familiar techniques are available for developing ideas within paragraphs. Without a well-developed idea in which the relationship between the idea and the evidence is clearly explained, paragraphs run the risk of being dull and ineffective; they do little more than relay information. Fully developed ideas not only make paragraphs more interesting, but also bind the parts of a paragraph together. (See 5b-3.)

Computer Tip

Paragraphing with the TAB Key
Be sure to use the TAB key when you indent for paragraphs in your writing. Tapping the space bar key five times can create spacing problems when you print your work, or when you send it to others for conversion and downloading. The TAB key is quick and easy—a single stroke—and it is consistent in the space it provides throughout, regardless of typesize, typeface, typestyle, and other formatting settings.

Rarely do you use just one developmental technique within a paragraph. As you will see, a paragraph can combine several techniques or can depend more on one technique than another. The important thing to remember is that you have options, and that as you learn the techniques and practice using them, they will, over time, become second nature. You will be able to use them without thinking about them just as you write various kinds of sentences without announcing to yourself beforehand that you will create a simple sentence, a compound one, or even a compound-complex one. The accompanying chart lists ten ways you can develop ideas within your paragraphs.

Techniques for Developing Ideas within Paragraphs

- Enumeration (5e-1)
- Illustration by example (5e-2)
- Definition (5e-3)
- Cause-and-effect analysis (5e-4)
- Process analysis (5e-5)

- Comparison and contrast (5e-6)
- Classification (5e-7)
- Division and analysis (5e-8)
- Description (5e-9)
- Analogy (5e-9)

---

1   Enumeration

A basic method for developing paragraphs involves listing or enumerating a series of points. But when you develop paragraphs using enumeration, take care not simply to list your points without explaining or connecting them.

In the following paragraph, the British philosopher Bertrand Russell accounts for why he sought love.

> I have sought love, first, because it brings ecstasy—ecstasy so great that I would often have sacrificed all the rest of life for a few hours of this joy. I have sought it, next, because it relieves loneliness—that terrible loneliness in which one shivering consciousness looks over the rim of the world into the cold unfathomable lifeless abyss. I have sought it, finally, because in the union of love I have seen, in a mystic miniature, the prefiguring vision of the heaven that saints and poets have imagined. This is what I sought, and though it might seem too good for human life, this is what—at last—I have found.

—Bertrand Russell, "What I Have Lived For"

Notice that Russell explains each reason as he gives it, avoiding the pitfall of merely listing for the sake of providing a list. His list develops and explains his ideas about the nature and rewards of love.

EXERCISE 5–11　**Writing a Paragraph by Enumerating**
Write a paragraph in which you list your reasons for something you believe, you think, or you are planning to do. Be sure to explain your list and the relationship among the elements of the list as you develop an idea.

2　Illustration by example

When using **illustration** in paragraphs to develop an idea, provide concrete and specific examples to help clarify that idea for your readers.

In the following paragraph, the writer relies on examples to illustrate her point about the way old trading posts are nurtured and preserved in New Mexico and Utah.

> Other posts retain a dilapidation that seems equally nurtured—and as historic. The corrals at Salina Springs stand knock-kneed with the force of the sly, artistic wind. Near Little Black Spot Mountain, Pinon Post is a faded store that trades, nonetheless, with more than 150 weavers who bring in rugs for the wholesalers who come through. In Utah, the Oljeto Trading Post is a slow-motion collapse of mud and wood. Inside, the post assumes credibility with the now rare bullpen where customers stand in front of high counters and point to goods stacked precariously to the ceiling: canned food, medicine, a sewing machine, fan belts, bolts of cloth, videos, and tires. Another original bullpen is at the Hubbells Trading Post, a National Historic Site cleverly leased by the Park Service to an experienced trader.
>
> —Sharman Apt Russell, "Trading Posts"

Notice that the examples in Sharman Russell's paragraph are not merely decorative; they illustrate the idea announced in the first sentence (the topic sentence) of the paragraph. Although Russell uses a number of examples, you may often find that a single example, developed fully with explanation, can suffice. Whether you need to use one or several examples depends on the quality of your examples and on the way you present them—how clearly you use them to illustrate your idea. Think about your reader to judge sufficiency.

EXERCISE 5–12   **Writing Paragraphs Using Examples**
Write two paragraphs that include examples to illustrate some idea. For your first paragraph, use a single extended example. For your second paragraph, use three to five examples. Which paragraph do you prefer? Explain your answer.

3   Definition

When you use **definition,** you explain the meaning of a word or a concept in a variety of ways. You can identify the word or thing as a member of a class, thus categorizing it. (A bird, for example, is a warm-blooded, egg-laying creature that flies.) You can distinguish the word or thing from other members of its group by further specifying its unique characteristics. (The bird is also a feathered vertebrate.) And you can say what the word or thing is by saying what it is not. (A bird is not a mammal, nor is it an invertebrate.)

You can use definition to develop paragraphs, but when you define a concept, always identify and discuss its essential elements or characteristics. Consider here how Joan Didion uses definition to explain her ideas about self-respect.

To have that sense of one's intrinsic worth which constitutes self-respect is potentially to have everything: the ability to discriminate, to love and to remain indifferent. To lack it is to be locked within oneself, paradoxically incapable of either love or indifference. If we do not respect ourselves, we are on the one hand forced to despise those who have so few resources as to consort with us, so little perception as to remain blind to our fatal weaknesses. On the other, we are peculiarly in thrall to everyone we see, curiously determined to live out—since our self-image is untenable—their false notions of us. We flatter ourselves by thinking this compulsion to please others an attractive trait: a gist for imaginative empathy, evidence of our willingness to give. *Of course* I will play Francesca to your Paolo, Helen Keller to anyone's Annie Sullivan: no expectation is too misplaced, no role too ludicrous.

—Joan Didion, "On Self-Respect"

When you use definition to develop a paragraph, your task is not to quote the dictionary, not to give a terse definition; rather, it is to develop a definition of your own that in itself becomes an idea about the concept or the thing you are focusing on. Didion's idea about self-respect outgrows a single sentence; an idea evolves as she continues to define and explain just what she means by the term.

EXERCISE 5-13   Writing Paragraphs Using Definition

1. Write a paragraph in which you define an object by placing it in a class and distinguishing it from other members of the same class. Possible objects include a fork, a shovel, a pencil, a dollar, a dog, a computer, a guitar, an encyclopedia, a baseball, or a tree.

2. Write a paragraph in which you define a concept by identifying and briefly explaining its essential characteristics or qualities. Possible concepts include justice, courage, success, love, honesty, adversity, anger, or beauty.

4   Cause-and-effect analysis

Use **cause-and-effect analysis** to develop a paragraph when you want to explain how or why something happened the way it did (the causes) and the results or consequences of what happened (the effects). If you explain in a paragraph why you came to college and chose your present course of study, you would be considering the causes of your current situation. If you consider the consequences of your decision—that you are happy being away from home, that your courses are exciting, and that you wish you had more friends who shared your interests—you would be considering the effects of your actions. A single paragraph usually emphasizes either causes or effects, but inevitably the two are linked, as you will see in the following paragraph, which emphasizes causes.

For any trend, there are as many reasons as there are participants. This person runs to lower his blood pressure. That person runs to escape the telephone or a cranky spouse or a filthy household. Another person runs to avoid doing anything else, to dodge a decision about how to lead his life or a realization that his life is leading nowhere. Each of us has his carrot and stick. In my case, the stick is my slackening physical condition, which keeps me from beating opponents at tennis whom I overwhelmed two years ago. My carrot is to win.

—Carll Tucker, "Fear of Dearth"

The causes in this paragraph are here for a reason: they provide background for your understanding of the effect. Tucker runs. He has his reasons for running, just like those other "participants" he mentions. Cause and effect go together to develop Tucker's idea about motivation.

EXERCISE 5–14 Writing Paragraphs Using Causal Analysis

1. Write a paragraph analyzing the causes of a social or political problem. Then write a paragraph analyzing its effects.

2. In a pair of paragraphs, discuss the causes and probable effects of an important decision you have made or one you need to make.

5 Process analysis

Developing a paragraph using **process analysis** involves explaining how to do something step by step, or explaining how something works or how something happened. Process analysis essentially involves giving directions. Paragraphs developed by process analysis are usually arranged chronologically or spatially.

The following paragraph explains how Chicano literature changed. The paragraph is arranged in chronological order.

The early stages of Chicano literature were full of identity assertions: "I am Joaquin, lost in a world of confusion," or "I am a Quetzal who wakes up green with wings of gold, and cannot fly," or "I am the Aztec Prince and the Christian Christ," or "I do not ask for freedom—I *am* freedom." But Chicano literature has gone beyond its beginnings. It no longer simply asserts and defines an identity. It now paints its context and carries out its visions. The identities of crazy gypsy, Aztec Angel, Mud Coyote, and Crying Woman of the Night now go beyond their own definitions to live out their lives in the more fully developed mythological and social context of Chicano literature.

—Carmen Tafolla, "Chicano Literature: Beyond Beginnings"

In this paragraph, the idea that Chicano literature changed is reinforced by process development.

EXERCISE 5–15   Writing a Paragraph Using Process Analysis
Explain in a paragraph how something is made (bean bags, ice cream, pizza), how something works (a VCR, camera, pinball machine), how something is done (how birds build nests, how a certain sport is played, how photographs are developed, how an orchestra or band rehearses for a performance). In your paragraph, try to develop an idea as you account for the process.

6   Comparison and contrast

Comparison and contrast involve setting one thing off against another to gain a clearer picture of both. Comparison involves seeing similarities. We compare for many reasons: because our minds are built to see things in relation to one another, because we have been taught to do so, and because comparison works so well. We contrast to see differences more clearly. Comparison and contrast are natural ways to develop paragraphs and to help your reader understand your idea.

Here is a paragraph that uses comparison and contrast to develop an idea about how the different characteristics of American and Chinese homes point to differences in cultural outlooks.

Americans have a sense of space, not of place. Go to an American home in exurbia, and almost the first thing you do is drift toward the picture window. How curious that the first compliment you pay your host inside his house is to say how lovely it is outside his house! He is pleased that you should admire his vistas. The distant horizon is not merely a line separating earth from sky, it is a symbol of the future. The American is not rooted in his place, however lovely: his eyes are drawn by the expanding space to a point on the horizon, which is his future. By contrast, consider the traditional Chinese home. Blank walls enclose it. Step behind the spirit wall and you are in a courtyard with perhaps a miniature garden around a corner. Once inside his private compound you are wrapped in an ambiance of calm beauty, an ordered world of buildings, pavement, rock, and decorative vegetation. But you have no distant view: nowhere does space open out before you. Raw nature in such a home is experienced only as weather, and the only open space is the sky above. The Chinese is rooted in his place. When he has to leave, it is not for the promised land on the terrestrial horizon, but for another world altogether along the vertical, religious axis of his imagination.

—Yi-Fu Tuant, "American Space, Chinese Place"

In developing a paragraph using comparison and contrast, you can proceed in one of two ways. You can discuss the first element of the comparison in its entirety (in the preceding example, the American home) and then discuss the second element (the Chinese home), as Tuant does. Or you can take up each point of difference and compare and contrast each in turn, alternating as you develop the paragraph. John McPhee does this in the following paragraph about oranges.

An orange grown in Florida usually has a thin and tightly fitting skin, and is also heavy with juice. Californians say that if you want to eat a Florida orange you have to get into a bathtub first. California oranges are light in weight and have thick skins that break easily and come off in hunks. The flesh inside is marvelously sweet, and the segments almost separate themselves. In Florida, it is said that you can run over a California orange with a ten-ton truck and not even wet the pavement. The differences from which these hyperboles arise will prevail in the two states even if the type of orange is the same. In arid climates, like California's, oranges develop a thick albedo, which is the white part of the skin. Florida is one of the two or three most rained-upon states in the United States. California uses the Colorado River and similarly impressive sources to irrigate its oranges, but of course irrigation can only do so much. The annual difference in rainfall between the Florida and California orange-growing areas is one million one hundred and forty thousand gallons per acre. For years, California was the leading orange growing state, but Florida surpassed California in 1942, and grows three times as many oranges now. California oranges, for their part, can safely be called three times as beautiful.

—John McPhee, "Oranges"

McPhee uses this comparison and contrast of oranges grown in California and Florida to develop his idea about the effect of weather on the growth of oranges.

EXERCISE 5–16 Writing Paragraphs Using Comparison and Contrast

1. Develop an idea in a paragraph by comparing two things on the basis of common features. Stress the similarities. Possible topics include athletes and dancers, eating and learning, cooking and thinking.

2. Develop an idea in a paragraph by contrasting two things. Stress their differences. Possible topics include age and youth, training and education, the eating habits of dogs and cats.

7 Classification

Classification enables you to organize or order information that might otherwise confuse or overwhelm you or your audience. To *classify* means to group or categorize things according to their similarities. Classified ads organize goods for sale and services for hire. Each of us can be classified according to sex, race, religion, socioeconomic status, and age, among other things. Classifying involves sorting, distinguishing one thing from another. It results in clarity particularly when used to develop ideas in paragraphs.

In the following paragraph E. B. White uses classification to distinguish among three different New Yorks so that he can make an important point about the third New York.

There are roughly three New Yorks. There is, first, the New York of the man or woman who was born here, who takes the city for granted and accepts its size and its turbulence as natural and inevitable. Second, there is the New York of the commuter—the city that is devoured by locusts each day and spat out each night. Third, there is a New York of the person who was born somewhere else and came to New York in quest of something. Of these three trembling cities the greatest is the last—the city of final destination, the city that is a goal. It is this third city that accounts for New York's high-strung disposition, its poetical deportment, its dedication to the arts, and its incomparable achievements. Commuters give the city its tidal restlessness, natives give it solidity and continuity, but the settlers give it passion. And whether it in a farmer arriving from Italy to set up a small grocery store in a slum, or a young girl arriving from a small town in Mississippi to escape the indignity of being observed by her neighbors, or a boy arriving from the Corn Belt with a manuscript in his suitcase and a pain in his heart, it makes no difference: each embraces New York with the intense excitement of first love, each absorbs New York with the fresh eyes of an adventurer, each generates heat and light to dwarf the Consolidated Edison Company.

—E. B. White, "The Three New Yorks"

Classification, like the other techniques for paragraph development, is nothing more than a way of thinking, a way of analyzing and making sense of your evidence. In the preceding paragraph, White is not interested in the act of classifying for its own sake; he is interested in using classification so that you, his audience, can understand his idea about the different New Yorks and can see more clearly what he wants to say about those "settlers" who interest him so much. Classification serves him well, just as the climactic order of the paragraph does; they are means to an end—the clear presentation of an idea.

EXERCISE 5–17 Writing a Paragraph Using Classification
Classify three of the following: books, houses, ice cream, restaurants, sports fans, classical music, rock music. Then select one of those classifications that interests you most and develop an idea about it in a paragraph.

8 Division and analysis

Division and analysis involves taking something apart or breaking it down into component parts so that you can put it back together to understand its significance. Analysis also carries with it the obligation to make sense of those parts, to try to understand their relationship to one another.

The following paragraph uses division and analysis to point out gender bias in our language.

My first meaningful introduction to "the power of language" occurred at a rally for women's rights in Los Angeles that highlighted the not-so-subtle chauvinism in the English language. I was surprised to discover that the rally was not going to offer plans for the reintroduction of the Equal Rights Amendment or a call to elect more women to political office. Instead, the day's key speech was on gender-bias in the English language. When the rally began, the speaker at the podium read aloud the words on a sign above the podium: "Spell it with a *Y; WOMYN.*" Turning to the audience, she shouted, "And why not spell it with a *Y?* We must break away from the male bias in our language. So many of our words are based on a male model—*their, her, they, she* all have the word *he* in them; *son* is the base of *person; lad* is the base of *lady;* and *man* is the base of both *human* and *woman.* Now is the time for us to reclaim our language! We do not need *men* to define ourselves; we can stand on our own. That is why I say: Spell it with a *Y!"*

—Jessica Yellin, student

In this paragraph, dividing words into their component parts yields, through analysis, an idea about the bias that is built into the English language. When you use division and analysis, do so to reveal an idea, as Jessica Yellin did. Turn your ideas into effective paragraphs and essays.

EXERCISE 5–18 **Writing a Paragraph Using Division and Analysis**
Take some ordinary object—a bicycle, computer, telephone, or chair; or process—writing a paragraph, performing a laboratory experiment, or working out a math problem. Break that object down into its component parts, or consider the process in terms of its associated tasks, as a way of understanding the object or the process. Consider the implications of what you learned through division and analysis, and write a paragraph about your discovery.

9 Description and analogy

Description involves appealing to the senses of sight, taste, touch, and smell to convey an experience or a place. Reconsider McPhee's comparison-and-contrast paragraph about oranges (5e-6); almost every sentence in that paragraph describes something about oranges or the relationship between oranges and the weather. The paragraph also uses causal analysis; McPhee's idea has to do with the causal relationship between the weather and its effect on oranges. In White's paragraph about New York (5e-7), he describes three different New Yorks, so that classifying and describing go hand in hand in that paragraph.

Analogy is the comparison of one thing with another, dissimilar thing. Writers often use analogies and develop extended analogies so that readers can gain insight into an idea that is difficult to grasp. Although an entire paragraph might be built on an analogy, it is more common to see analogy used with other techniques to develop an idea.

Notice how the following paragraph develops an extended analogy between violinists and painters, but it also depends on description and process analysis to convey its idea.

Violinists use the bow in the same way painters use the paint brush. Violinists employ many different bowing techniques just as painters use a variety of brush strokes. The violinist may arrive at a passage in the music where a strong sustained sound is required. One of the most difficult techniques involves controlling the bow while pulling it slowly across the string. The violinist must maintain the friction of the bow on the string without producing unintentionally raucous sounds. The sound must not waver; it must be round, sustained, clear, and rich. Painters use a similar technique when they have to decide whether to use heavy or light strokes to produce a desired effect. The artist must know before putting brush to canvas what the end result will be. While painting, the artist visualizes the length and thickness of the stroke, and the resulting mark on the canvas corresponds to the texture of the violinist's sound. Both artists perfect these techniques of touch to enhance the effectiveness of their artistic performances.

—Karen DiYanni, student

EXERCISE 5–19   Writing a Paragraph Using Description and Analogy

1. Think of an unusual relationship between two dissimilar things and write a paragraph in which you develop the relationship, extending it whatever way you can. Use narration and description to help you develop that analogy.

2. Reread Loren Eiseley's paragraph in 5d-2. Identify and list the various organizational and developmental techniques that Eiseley uses in that paragraph. Write a paragraph explaining how Eiseley's use of analogy helps you understand his idea.

5f   Types and functions of paragraphs within an essay

Paragraphs have interesting relationships with one another, especially when they work together to build an essay. You already know that essays generally have three parts: beginnings, middles, and endings (see Chapters 6, 7, and 8). Each of those parts contains a varying number of paragraphs, depending on the essay's subject, its purpose, the complexity of its idea, and its overall length.

As a rule of thumb, a three- to four-page typed essay will contain one or two beginning paragraphs, three to five middle paragraphs, and one or two ending paragraphs. Each paragraph will contain between one hundred and two hundred words. A longer research essay will likely conform to these same proportions, but the length of the middle can vary considerably (see Chapter 44).

An essay, like a single paragraph, must be coherent and unified. The essay's components—words, sentences, and paragraphs—must fit together, and the essay itself must stay focused on a controlling idea or thesis. The accompanying chart outlines how each kind of paragraph helps create that unity and coherence.

Types of Paragraphs

- **Beginning paragraphs** start the essay. They create interest and introduce the idea.
- **Ending paragraphs** close the essay and pull its parts together to provide a final perspective on the idea.
- **Middle paragraphs** develop the idea. They can be either informational or transitional.

---

1 Developing beginning paragraphs

A **beginning**—sometimes called an **introduction**—performs important functions in an essay. It can consist of one or more paragraphs, depending on the length of the essay and the complexity of the idea. The paragraphs themselves can be brief (a couple of sentences), or they can be longer, as the following two introductions to essays illustrate.

> In the spring I was born naked. I was stuffed into a chamois cloth and presented to my mother.
>
> —China Forbes, student

> If reduced to its elements, the entire human body is worth approximately forty-seven dollars and twenty-three cents. We are primarily composed of hydrogen, oxygen, and carbon. The prices of these elements do not fluctuate on the common market, so only half of our elemental value is derived from traces of rare metals such as lanthanum that have poisoned our systems. In this respect, those who have died after smoking for several years or have been exposed to toxic waste and

mercury poisoning derive a final revenge by being worth perhaps a dollar or two more than those who die untainted. Unless a research laboratory wishes to reconstruct an entire skeleton, or, like Lenin, one is able to secure a permanent postmortem position, the value of human composition is embarrassingly low.

—Tracy Grikscheit, student

The beginning of an essay extends an invitation to readers and creates interest in what will follow in the middle of the essay. It also alerts readers to the essay's idea. The development of that idea is always the essay's central purpose. The beginning also states or implies how the essay will evolve or be organized, foreshadowing the whole essay—its subject, its idea, its development.

Guidelines for Writing Beginning Paragraphs

- Invite your readers into your essay with interesting stories, anecdotes, arresting details, a quotation, a question, or revealing background information.
- Be mindful of your audience. Tell them what they need to know to understand your idea.
- State your idea either explicitly or implicitly through hints and suggestions.
- Provide some indication of how the middle of the essay will develop the idea.
- Be confident about your idea. Avoid apologies for it or for not knowing enough about it.
- Organize your beginning in a familiar way, such as moving from a general discussion of an interesting subject to a specific idea about that subject.
- Use the techniques of narration, description, and illustration to develop your paragraph so that readers can better understand your idea.

EXERCISE 5–20   **Analyzing and Writing Beginnings**

1. As you read the following beginning from an exploratory essay, try to figure out the essay's idea. Then answer the questions that follow it.

I spy on my patients. Ought not a doctor to observe his patients by any means and from any stance, that he might the more fully assemble the evidence? So I stand in the doorways of hospital rooms and gaze. Oh, it is not all that furtive an act. Those in bed need only look up in order to discover me. But they never do.

—Richard Selzer, "Four Appointments with the Discus Thrower"

a. What can you infer about the "I" in this paragraph—about the narrator's profession and behavior? How does he feel about spying?
b. Considering your answers to the preceding questions and taking into account the title and the last two sentences of the beginning paragraph, what can you infer about the essay's idea? Explain your answer.

2. Read the following beginning from an analytical essay, and then answer the questions that follow it.

A short, delicate portrait of a patient—this is the first impression one has of Dr. Richard Selzer's essay "Four Appointments with the Discus Thrower." Selzer's persona (the "I" in his essay) is an inquisitive physician, looking in on his patient, who is a blind man lacking legs, seriously ill and about to die. The doctor describes his encounters with him before and after his death. This patient, known only as "Room 542," would be an ordinary, if unusually unfortunate, sufferer were it not for his odd habit of throwing his breakfast plate at the wall every morning.

Selzer is a subtle presence in this portrait; as in a story, his meaning isn't obvious.[. . .] His entrances into the essay's meaning are the doctor's words themselves, starting with his references to himself as a "spy"—a man "looking for secrets"—and the criminal undertone of the piece. It becomes clear that the doctor is commenting upon the crimes being committed against Room 542, the indignities Room 542 is enduring, and the strength of his character. But Room 542 is not, ultimately, the subject of the submerged meaning in the essay; the doctor is the subject. The doctor is judge, jury, and executioner in his essay; and he returns a verdict of guilty against himself.

—Brandt Kwiram, student

   a. Can you detect from Brandt Kwiram's beginning how he will develop his essay?

   b. Kwiram entitled his essay "The Patient Doctor." What does the title suggest to you about Brandt's idea—the claim that he makes in his essay?

  3. Reread one of your own essays. Revise your beginning based on what you now know about beginnings (see the checklists in 5f-1).

2   Developing middle paragraphs

Middle paragraphs, which appear in the body of an essay between the beginning and the ending, develop the essay's idea. There are two types of middle paragraphs: **informational paragraphs,** the most common, provide evidence and analysis necessary for understanding the essay's idea; **transitional paragraphs** serve as a bridge between informational paragraphs or between sections of informational paragraphs.

Using informational paragraphs

Informational paragraphs—also called topical or substantive paragraphs—do the major work of developing an essay's idea. Each informational paragraph develops an aspect of that idea. Each, therefore, has a narrower focus than the essay itself. Informational paragraphs must be viewed in relation to one another to understand an essay's idea.

Consider the informational paragraph on p. 123. As you read it, try to determine how well the paragraph follows the accompanying Guidelines for Writing Informational Paragraphs.

Computer Tip

Writing Multiple Versions

    Because editing an essay, paper, or report is easy on a computer—you can copy text, move it, and delete it with a mouseclick or a keystroke—it is a good idea to create more than one version of some parts of a piece of writing. You might write two or three different introductory paragraphs, for example, or a couple of conclusions, trying out differing ways of beginning and ending. This ease of editing gives you an opportunity to experiment with your writing. Take advantage of it.

Authenticity has many guises, each contributing something essential to our calm satisfaction with the truly genuine. Authenticity of *object* fascinates me most deeply because its pull is entirely abstract and conceptual. The art of replica making has reached such sophistication that only the most astute professional can now tell the difference between, say, a genuine dinosaur skeleton and a well-made cast. The real and the replica are effectively alike in all but our abstract knowledge of authenticity, yet we feel awe in the presence of bone once truly clothed in dinosaur flesh and mere interest in fiberglass of identical appearance.

—Stephen Jay Gould, "Counters and Cable Cars"

Gould's paragraph begins with the topic sentence, a claim about authenticity. In the second sentence, he narrows his interest from authenticity to "authenticity of *object*." He then provides contrasting evidence about "replica making" using one well-chosen example—a dinosaur skeleton—as evidence to illustrate and clarify his point about the power of an object that is

---

Guidelines for Writing Informational Paragraphs

- Use informational paragraphs to develop an idea.
- Convey your paragraph's idea implicitly or in a topic sentence. If using a topic sentence, you can place it anywhere in your paragraph, but remember not to rely on it exclusively to carry your idea.
- Use evidence in informational paragraphs to substantiate your idea and make your paragraphs convincing.
- Organize your paragraph to present your idea effectively (see 5d).
- Keep an eye on paragraph length. Limit your paragraphs to two hundred words to ensure that you do not lose track of your main idea.
- Be sure that a clear relationship exists between the idea in your informational paragraph and the essay's idea.
- To bring informational paragraphs to a close, consider restating the paragraph's idea and purpose in a fresh and interesting way. The last two or three sentences of a paragraph are often the most important.

authentic. Gould's final sentence repeats the paragraph's main idea in a fresh, interesting way, leaving you with a clear sense of what he thinks is the relationship between authenticity and awe, or what he calls in the first sentence, "our calm satisfaction with the truly genuine."

EXERCISE 5–21   Revising an Informational Paragraph
Select one of the essays you wrote for a course this semester. From the middle of that essay, choose an informational paragraph that you think is weak. Revise the paragraph using the Guidelines for Writing Informational Paragraphs (p. 123).

Using transitional paragraphs

Transitional paragraphs are bridge paragraphs that link or pull sections of an essay together to make it more coherent. These paragraphs often repeat or summarize information that has already appeared, or they point readers to the next part of an essay. In either case, transitional paragraphs provide clarification and focus.

Transitional paragraphs can be brief, consisting of one or a few sentences, or they can be as long as a typical informational paragraph. Whether long or short, transitional paragraphs serve to emphasize an idea, to make readers pause and think before proceeding to the next paragraph. They can alert readers to a significant shift in the development of the idea, or they can serve as a reminder of what the essay covered in a preceding paragraph. The accompanying chart provides guidelines for writing effective transitional paragraphs.

Guidelines for Writing Transitional Paragraphs

- Use transitional paragraphs to refer to what has come before—to summarize and clarify the idea from the previous paragraph or section of paragraphs.

- Use transitional paragraphs to point ahead, to anticipate and foreshadow an aspect of the idea that will be developed in the essay's middle.

- Use transitional paragraphs to simplify rather than complicate your idea.

As you read the following excerpt from the beginning of an essay by Ellen Goodman, try to identify the transitional paragraph.

There was a time in my life, I confess, when I thought that the only 1
inherent differences between men and women were the obvious ones.

In my callous youth, I scoffed at the mental gymnastics of sociobiolo- 2
gists who leaped to conclusions about men and women from long years
spent studying bugs. I suspected the motives of brain researchers who
split the world of the sexes into left and right hemispheres.

But now, in my midlife, I can no longer deny the evidence of my 3
senses or experiences.

Like virtually every woman in America who has spent time beside 4
a man behind a wheel, like every woman in America who has ever
been a lost passenger outward bound with a male driver, I know that
there is one way in which the male sex is innately different from the
female: Men are by their very nature congenitally unable to ask directions.

The historical record of their unwillingness was always clear. Con- 5
sider, for example, the valiant 600 cavalrymen who plunged into the Valley of Death . . . because they refused to ask if there wasn't some other
way around the cannons.

Consider the entire wagon train that drove into the Donner Pass . . . 6
because the wagon master wouldn't stop at the station marked Last Gas
before the Disaster.

Consider even my own childhood. My father—a man with a great 7
sense of humor and no sense of direction—constantly led us on what he
referred to as "scenic routes."

But for centuries we assumed that this refusal was a weird idiosyn- 8
crasy. We never dreamed that it came with the testosterone.

In recent years, I have from time to time found myself sitting beside 9
men who would not admit they were lost until I lit matches under their
fingertips in an attempt to read maps in a box canyon.

—Ellen Goodman, "In the Male Direction"

Goodman introduces her idea about men in the first four paragraphs. In the
next three paragraphs, she offers what she calls the "historical record"—her
account of men's follies, their failures. The transitional paragraph, her
eighth, points in two directions—back toward the idiosyncratic nature of
male habit that leads to costly blunders, and forward toward something in
the very nature of maleness. The word *testosterone* alerts you to the idea
Goodman will develop in the next section of her essay—the link between
blunders and testosterone. This pointing backward and forward character-

izes good transitional paragraphs and illustrates how they link ideas in sections of the middle.

EXERCISE 5–22 Writing a Transitional Paragraph
Select one of the essays you wrote for a course this semester. Reread the essay, looking for a place in the middle to insert a transitional paragraph that would clarify what you said and point to what follows. Write that paragraph.

3 Developing ending paragraphs

An **ending**—sometimes called a **conclusion**—has a close, functional relationship to a beginning. Together, beginnings and endings frame an essay; one leads into the essay, the other leads out of it. The ending also pulls all of the parts of the essay together, unifying the essay, and it reminds readers about how the idea or thesis was developed in the middle of the essay.

Perhaps the most important point to remember about an ending is its relationship to the rest of the essay. Because the ending of an essay depends on what comes before it, many of the details that appear in the ending point back into the essay, reminding readers of key aspects of the idea developed in the middle. Readers look for a final, fresh perspective on the idea and its development in the ending.

The chart on the opposite page, "Guidelines for Writing Ending Paragraphs," will help you regardless of what type of essay you are writing.

Computer Tip

Cutting Instead of Deleting
As you revise a piece of writing, you will replace sentences and paragraphs, often by simply deleting those you want to revise and replace. Sometimes, however, it is better to use your word processor's "cut" function, which preserves the text you want to revise and replace. The best way to do this is to cut and move the revised words, sentences, or paragraphs to the end of your draft. That way you can print them out later to see if there is anything you may want to reintroduce in what will eventually become your final version.

Guidelines for Writing Ending Paragraphs

- Remind readers about the essay's idea or thesis, but avoid merely restating what you said in your introduction. Provide a fresh perspective on your idea.
- Include details and phrases from the beginning and the middle that underscore key points. Use those details to remind the reader how you developed your idea, but avoid mere repetition.
- Remain focused on the idea you developed in the essay. Do not veer off in a new direction or present new evidence.
- If you call for a course of action, make sure it is reasonable and justified in terms of the evidence you presented.
- Avoid logical fallacies (see 7b-3).
- Avoid apology and bravado. Moderate, reasonable conclusions appeal to your readers' good judgment.
- Check to see that your ending is unified and coherent (see 5a–c). Also ensure that your ending makes the essay more coherent by pulling all of its parts together.

Ending and beginning paragraphs in essays

Endings for essays pull the entire essay together and make it coherent. Tim Burns's paragraph serves to illustrate an effective ending. Tim's analytical essay comparing Robert Lowell's poem "For the Union Dead" and the movie *Glory* ends this way.

"For the Union Dead" and *Glory* each represents Colonel Shaw in different but complementary ways. For Lowell, he is a static image, sitting atop his horse, waiting for the "blessed" bubble to break, waiting for things to change. Lowell hints at his stiffness, associates it with other New Englanders, and suggests to us through his images of destruction around Boston that we might take notice of Shaw and his men and take stock of ourselves. The movie lets us see the horse and the rider begin to move. The images become dynamic, and we have a chance to watch Shaw's transformation. He becomes a fierce, compassionate leader of his men. They follow him into battle, fighting for their freedom. But the movie does not leave us content with this heroic image of Shaw. It asks another question, a probing one, about the meaning of *glory*. As we look back on the movie's ending, we know that Shaw and his men may have died in vain, because when we look around us, we still see much of what Lowell saw in 1964. We see racial problems and strife. Not enough has been done. But we know, because of Lowell's images and those in the movie, that there is a better way. Shaw points us in the right direction.

—Tim Burns, student

Reading this ending paragraph independent of the essay, you cannot understand all of the essay's details. You do not know, for example, who Colonel Shaw is. You do not understand the reference to the "blessed" bubble. You have no sense of how *Glory* revealed Shaw's transformation into a "compassionate leader of his men." But you do gain a clear sense that Tim Burns's essay has revealed how Lowell's poem and the movie not only illuminate one another, but also offer a timeless message about racial strife in the United States. That point—Burns's thesis—stands on its own, but it grows out of those details that he reminds us about in this paragraph.

WWW
http://leo.stcloudstate.edu/ acadwrite/conclude.html
Offers strategies for writing conclusions.

If you read Burns's beginning paragraph, you can see how he provided essential background information about Colonel Shaw's command of black soldiers during the Civil War, about Lowell's poem, and about the movie *Glory*. This beginning paragraph also includes the thesis that Burns will develop in the middle of his essay.

Colonel Robert Gould Shaw knew what it meant to be noble and brave. Few white men in history have shown more courage and dedication in trying to give the black man his rightful place in America. Shaw did not put black men on a pedestal; he did not make speeches for them; he led them into combat while he faced much opposition for doing so. Prejudice was evident in the Northern army, and he had to overcome this prejudice just so that his black soldiers would have the right to fight for their own freedom. Shaw lost his life in the War between the States, and so did half of his regiment. History had largely forgotten him and his men until the poet Robert Lowell wrote "For the Union Dead" in 1964, about one hundred years after Shaw's men led their valiant charge against a Confederate fort. Then, in 1989, the movie *Glory* gave us another view of Colonel Shaw. Both the poem and the movie tell us what Shaw did during his time, but they seem to be showing us as well what we have not done in our time. These two works complement each other while presenting images of Shaw that remind us of the racial problems we face every day in America.

—Tim Burns, student

In the middle paragraphs, Burns develops his analysis by showing how Lowell's static images of Shaw come to life in the movie and by reminding us of our own failures in dealing with racial strife. The selected details in Burns's ending point back into his analysis. Whether in argument, analysis, or exploration, we need the middle paragraphs to understand all of the ending, and we need the ending to put the entire essay in perspective.

EXERCISE 5–23   Analyzing and Writing Endings

1. Read an analytical or argumentative essay from Chapter 7 or 8 (Ruth Chung's analytical essay in 8b or Matthew Weishar's argumentative essay in 7f). Explain how the essay's ending ties in with its beginning and middle.

2. Find an argumentative essay in a magazine. Analyze it and explain how well the writer relates the ending to the beginning and middle.

3. Select one of your own essays and rewrite the ending based on the Guidelines for Writing Ending Paragraphs in 5f-3.

6 *The Exploratory (Narrative) Essay*

The **exploratory essay** has an ambling, storytelling quality. Its tone suggests that you are inviting your reader to sit back and listen, that your idea will not unfold predictably but will follow the twists and turns of your mind playing over the evidence. The evidence is often a story of experience, but it could just as well be an allusion to or a story about a book you have read or a movie you have seen.

Although an exploratory essay has a beginning, a middle, and an ending, it offers, nevertheless, more organizational freedom than the argumentative essay. An exploratory essay can refer to almost anything that might cause your readers to pay attention—a painting, song, movie, poem, or book—as long as what you write about helps readers understand your main idea. Those surprising mental turns and the meaningful connections help generate reader interest just as they help clarify your idea.

Exploratory essayists ruminate, ponder ideas almost for the pleasure of the process, and move to the full expression of those ideas without insisting. They would not argue, for example, that final examinations be abolished and then offer three reasons—in three paragraphs—for doing so. A short, insistent argumentative essay can be effective, especially when those three reasons are sound and when the paragraphs develop cogent, supporting points. But that argumentative essay lacks the searching quality of the exploratory essay, which is more like an inquiry about an idea than a defense of it. The accompanying Features of the Exploratory Essay outlines the main characteristics of such an essay.

The *purposes* for writing exploratory essays vary, but primarily these essays give readers a chance to observe writers in the act of thinking about an idea and working it out, while they are presenting it. The exploratory essay fosters inquiry. Writers often use it as a way of trying to get at an idea that is not susceptible to rigorous proof; such ideas are, nevertheless, susceptible to rigorous analysis, and they are important. The two student writers whose work appears in this chapter are looking into the power of the imagination and the nature of learning. They have no interest in arguing a particu-

---

Features of the Exploratory Essay

- Develops an idea in an interesting, informal way.
- Permits the essayist to make far-reaching connections that clarify the idea.
- Encourages the use of experience and other texts as evidence.
- Encourages the essayist to use various kinds of evidence to add new dimensions to the idea, enriching it and making it more interesting as the essay evolves.
- Seems more like an inquiry into meaning than a proof.
- Has a beginning, a middle, and an ending.

lar point; instead, they want to explore an idea and reach a tentative conclusion large enough to account for their discoveries.

Audiences for exploratory essays usually consist of generalists (1d-1), but they are generalists who enjoy the art of playful, inquiring discourse, readers who are interested in elusive but important subjects that call on a writer to experiment and to make odd, but relevant, connections as a way of clarifying an idea. Specific audiences could range from a class of student writers to readers of familiar essays or academics assembled at a scholarly conference. Such readers have an interest in following how a well-informed writer plays seriously with a complex, compelling idea, using an essay form that can accommodate stories of experience as well as a whole array of other kinds of evidence.

6a   Exploring by connecting stories of experience

You may recall from Chapter 4 how Anna Norris connected stories about her photographs with written texts to find and develop an idea about the way meaning is affected by context (see 4c). By following Anna's example and Betsy Miller's complete essay (which we will refer to throughout the first part of this chapter), you can learn to connect your own memories of experience and begin to create your own exploratory essay. Writing this kind of essay involves more than connecting memories; but the process is no more complicated at the outset than telling an interesting story. Remember that one way to distinguish a storyteller from an essayist is the way they tell stories: a storyteller aims mainly to entertain; an essayist selects stories as evidence, using them to illustrate ideas as well as to entertain. Essayists make connections and discover relationships among their seemingly unrelated experiences, and in the process, they find meaning or significance in them. A story used effectively in an exploratory essay does just what data gathered from research does in an argumentative essay—it helps you develop your idea.

Although writers occasionally create an exploratory essay out of a single story, they more often connect two or more stories to illustrate their idea. Remember that a story is not an essay. Tacking a moral onto the end of a story does not create an exploratory essay; it creates a story with a moral tacked onto the end. As you study Betsy Miller's essay in the first section of this chapter, you will see how she links two and then three stories together, clarifying and enriching her idea as she develops it. In the second section

(6c), you will see Alexandra Johnes connect written texts and stories to develop an idea about learning.

By considering Miller's composing process as well as the distinguishing features of the essay she creates, you will learn how to apply the accompanying Guidelines for Developing an Exploratory Essay. You can, of course, create such an essay in other ways, but the composing process that led to Miller's essay encourages exploration. By examining her work, we can pinpoint the major features of the exploratory essay.

Guidelines for Developing an Exploratory Essay

- Recall an experience that continues to excite or haunt you. Re-create that experience in writing (see 6b).
- Think about what the experience means. Locate the **idea** in your story of experience (see 6b).
- Use collaboration to *develop* and *revise* your idea (see 6b-1).
- Use that experience and idea as a lodestone—a magnetic force—pulling in another experience related to the idea you discovered in the first experience (see 6b-2).
- Link your stories of experience. Include references to other texts that occur to you as you connect your stories and develop your ideas (see 6a and 6c).
- Write a beginning for your essay that will grab your readers' interest and introduce your idea. Add to your essay as you write and think of new evidence that can help you clarify your emerging idea (see 6b-5–6).
- Write an ending for your essay that further explains the idea (see 6b-6).
- Revise your essay, going back to clarify the meaning of your evidence so that your readers know enough to understand your idea.
- Select a short title to catch your readers' attention.

6b   Finding and developing an idea from a story

In her first-year college writing class, Betsy Miller was asked to write, in three typed pages or less, about an experience that still lingered in her memory, one that still clung to her imagination. She was asked to render that story so that her readers could *experience* it themselves, could know what it was like to have been there when it happened. Here is her first story.

Miller's first story

My two youngest brothers always get to open a few presents on Christmas Eve. Daniel, my youngest brother, celebrated his third Christmas this year. He joyfully pranced around the living room, surrounded by many gifts that most children his age, including Daniel, normally find fascinating. But only one present held Daniel's attention that evening: the Batman costume from Aunt Pat. Ever since he had unwrapped the gift and discovered what it was, he had dragged the box containing the costume around the living room, demanding that someone help him put it on. Finally, catching the attention of his mother, she helped Daniel, and he suddenly turned into Batman, running around the living room and shooting his family members with tiny plastic arrows from his knuckle gun. His glossy red hair poking out the sides, Daniel peered through the eyes of his Batman mask with a look of confidence and determination, ready to conquer any villains posing a potential threat to the successful completion of his mission, whatever it might be.

Tired of playing dead every time Daniel pegged me with one of his arrows, I began to read the box that had contained the Batman costume. A warning sign on its side caught my eye:

WARNING

Vest is not really bulletproof.

Cape will not enable user to fly.

I chuckled as I read the note of caution, then burst into laughter as I realized its absurdity. How could anyone think that a little piece of nylon could send them soaring into the air? My whole family joined me in laughter after I read the warning to them, as they too considered how silly it was. That is, everyone except Daniel. Although understanding the words I had said, he found no humor in them. Instead of joining in the laughter of the rest of his family, Daniel continued to prance about the room, completely absorbed in the fantasy of the world to which his Batman costume had flown him.

Each day, Daniel lives the excitement of a different world, one of which he is the sole creator. That night, Daniel was Batman. He ran about the room, stalking his prey and deftly conquering each one with his batlike agility--the thin, black cape streaming behind him. That night, there was no one in Daniel's world more powerful than he.

1   Using collaboration to find an idea

The students in Miller's composition class were organized into work groups whose purpose was to comment on one another's writing or to collaborate. Miller read her story to the other five members of her group, all of whom had written stories. Each student was to tell Miller what he or she thought the story was about and whether it contained an idea. Miller was to listen without comment to the group's responses, which follow.

I think the story is about how silly we are when we are young.

The story doesn't seem to be about being silly; it seems to be about Betsy's cruelty to her younger brother—the way we react to younger brothers and sisters when we get tired of playing the games they ask us to play. Then we say something to them to get even, and we hurt their feelings.

Well, I see all of that, but that last paragraph, that last part of the story, seems to be about Daniel and the power of his imagination. After all, Betsy tells us, "That night, Daniel was Batman."

Good point, but I think the story is really about the stupidity of warning labels. I read something the other day about those labels on mattresses and sofas, the ones you're not supposed to take off. You know, the ones that will get you fined. I see some of that absurdity in what Betsy tells us in her story.

At the end of the collaborative session, Miller and the other students were asked to think about their own stories, to reflect on their meaning, and to see if they could infer ideas from them. The session helped the students gain a clearer sense of what their stories were really about, or could be about if told in a slightly different way. For their next class, the students were asked to let the emerging idea serve as a lodestone to pull in a second story that could clarify, illustrate, and enrich the idea.

2   Writing and connecting to find out what you are thinking

Essayists must seek ways to help readers understand their ideas. No individual story tells us everything we need to know about the idea. Each story reveals something a little different; each has its part to play in the essay.

After thinking about her classmates' comments, Miller began writing her second story. She explored as she wrote, letting her two stories come together. She sensed that they were connected, and while she was drafting she wrote without worrying about what idea or ideas would bring them together in the essay. (See 4b and 4c for more on writing and connecting as ways of finding ideas.)

Daniel's cape was very much on Miller's mind as she wrote; in fact, she had decided to wear the cape herself, in an imaginary way, and to think also of her friend David decked out in his own cape while they played dodgeball. Her aim was to clarify her thoughts about the transforming power of imagination. Here is her second story.

Miller's second story

As David and I frolicked about the dodgeball court during recess in the third grade, there were no real Batman capes streaming behind us, but we soared just as high as Daniel did that Christmas Eve. We were completely absorbed in the thrill of competing against other dodgeball teams, focusing solely on our movements and the rules of the game. Nothing else in the whole world mattered to us on that wonderful afternoon except our game of dodgeball.

In my continuous quest to sharpen my dodgeball skills, I took it upon myself to ask David for some personal help in developing my ball-throwing technique. In his carefree manner, he remarked to me that it was all in the wrist and demonstrated exactly how he used his wrist to produce such power. In his blue and white school uniform, shirt untucked as usual, he smiled gleefully and hurled a ball across the court, hitting the wooden kick board on the opposite side with a resounding thud. Pleased by the fascination I showed toward his unique ability, he smiled, messed up my hair, and darted across the court to retrieve the ball and give me a try. Despite the simplicity and the clarity of his explanation, I never quite caught on to David's art of ball throwing, but I treasure my memory of him and me soaring, supported by our capes, together through our world of dodgeball.

A skiing accident over Christmas vacation took away David's ability to walk, ripping from him the cape that had allowed him to soar through his world of athletics, dominating every sport he undertook. Instead, he was forced to cope with life as a paraplegic during the prime of his athletic career. David's skiing accident forced him to picture himself in a wheelchair, a picture that he found too difficult to accept.

After losing his ability to fly in his world of athletics, the one he loved most, David was not able to climb back on the rest of his cape. He wheeled himself off a pier into Lake Washington this month, taking his life and the love of many with him.

3   Getting at the idea through creative thinking

Miller has still not found the precise leading idea that will hold her essay together, but she is getting closer. As E. B. White did in the paragraph you considered in Chapter 4, Miller is thinking as she writes. As she explores, she seems to be asking her readers to believe that the cape her little brother wore is a cape that all of us might want to keep wearing past childhood. She suggests that such a cape can empower everyone. But she also becomes keenly aware that such empowerment may not always sustain us. David, according to Miller's speculations, lost the cape we create in our imagination—his ability to fly. Nevertheless, Miller seems to be holding on to the idea that there is some life-sustaining power in it. She seems to believe that imagination itself can lift us above the mundane and the tragic. That idea evolved out of the writing and the connections she began to explore between the cape her brother wore on Christmas Eve and the capes she imagined she and her friend David had also worn on the dodgeball court.

These two writing activities—the recovery of a memory and the working out of its relationship to another memory—have led Miller closer to an idea. But even at this point in her drafting, she is still not ready to pin down the idea and limit it because she is not yet clear about all of its implications. Nevertheless, she is ready to try a beginning for her essay that may help her refine the idea even more.

4   Beginning the essay

The **beginning** of an essay—also known as the *introduction*—is an invitation to the reader. It not only guides the reader into the essay by alluding to the idea, but also makes the reader want to continue reading.

Because the beginning forecasts what will follow, it is difficult to say exactly *when* you should write it. If you have not begun to select and consolidate your evidence, whether that evidence consists of stories or research data, it makes little sense to try to write a beginning. First get a feel for the evidence. Write a bit of the middle, as Miller has done. Explore. Think and write concurrently about the evidence.

A good rule of thumb is to write a draft of your beginning only after you have begun to collect your evidence and to consider what you want to say about it. You can revise the beginning as you collect more evidence and refine your idea.

Your beginning should make it easy for the reader to understand your idea and how you will develop it. You need not say, "In this essay, I am going to develop the idea that imagination can empower us long past childhood, and I am going to develop that idea by telling you two or three stories so that you will be able to see what I mean." Most readers prefer something subtler—an inviting hint, perhaps. In the beginning of Miller's essay, which follows, she says, "But I still try to hold onto my cape." That tells her readers that she has not given up on the imagination's power to let her fly "high above my worlds." By placing that statement near the end of her introduction, Miller invites her readers to go on reading the rest of the essay, where they can discover why she continues to "hold onto" her cape. That statement also leads readers smoothly and logically into the middle.

Miller's beginning: First draft

I soar across the vast terrain of my world, a world about which I know everything there is to know, supported by my cape. My cape has several forms; it has accompanied me across many lands, each my own creation. It has brought me much comfort and pleasure throughout my life, instilling within me a great love for flying. My closest companion, it has always supported me in the past. But it is growing tired now, and I fear that someday it may no longer be able to take me flying across my worlds at my whim. The many forms of my cape are slowly being pulled out from under me, sending me tumbling down to the earth where I am confronted by a new world, one that is far more frightening, and intriguing, than the ones I have created for myself in the past. But I still try to hold onto my cape. Only my cape can take me flying high above my worlds, the ones about which I know everything there is to know.

In her beginning, Miller emphasizes the importance of the cape and her changing relationship to it. We sense that it is becoming more difficult for her to hold onto the simple idea that the cape empowers her. You know from Miller's two stories—the one about her younger brother and the other about David's accident—why she is having to rethink her idea. The cape did not do

---

Computer Tip

Saving Your Work

The single most important thing you can do when you write with a computer is to save your work often. In the event of a power failure or some other mishap that results in your computer shutting down, you will lose all work since your last save command. To protect yourself against the frustration of losing hours—or days—of work on a project, save at regular intervals. You can save every ten or twenty minutes, or you can save whenever you take a break or even pause to think or begin a new section of your paper.

---

for David what it did for her brother. Nevertheless, Miller continues to write about the power of the imagination. That idea is implicit in her beginning; she does not spell it out, but she hints at it. (Also see the revised version of Miller's beginning in 6b-5.)

5 Developing and revising the essay from the middle

An essay is a unified effort to express an idea, and its beginning and middle are dependent on one another. In the beginning, you give readers a sense of what your evidence means; in the **middle,** you present and evaluate that evidence, letting readers gain insight from your thoughts about what the evidence means.

When you write an exploratory essay and use stories as evidence, the stories themselves—if told effectively—illustrate something important about your idea. But often, no matter how well you tell the stories you link together, you need to add some *explanation* to make sure that your readers know what you know. Readers have to understand why you are telling the stories, what those stories have to do with your idea. The same is true when you present research data or other forms of evidence.

Revising the essay from the middle

After composing her middle and a draft of her beginning, Miller could very well decide to finish her essay using only the stories about David and

Daniel as evidence. She would need only to write an ending that in some fresh, informed way alludes to her idea and accounts for what her stories imply and what her exploration means. (Endings are discussed more fully in 6b-6.)

But Miller has not stopped thinking about her idea. Instead of being satisfied with the two stories, she continues to revise what she has already written, trying to clarify the relationship between her stories and her idea.

As she reads her draft and thinks about how to revise it, Miller is keenly aware of her readers. She tries to put herself in her readers' place and questions her own writing as if she is reading her draft for the first time, thinking of it impersonally and objectively. She asks herself these questions.

- What is each of my stories about?
- What does each story have to do with my idea?
- Is the relationship between the stories clear?
- Does the beginning both capture the essence of my stories and forecast my idea?

As you play the role of reader, you may find confusing sentences that need to be rewritten, and you may discover the need for more explanation at various points in the essay. You might also find that the need for more explanation leads to the need for more evidence—that is, for another story or for a different kind of evidence. That was Miller's experience, and you will no doubt find it to be the case when writing your own essays.

Computer Tip

Saving Early Drafts

When you are writing with a computer, you typically alter your draft as you go, without creating separate discrete versions. Sometimes, however, especially when working on long projects, it is advisable to save an early draft or two. You may wish to preserve some details of phrasing, some citations, or some idea or information from an early draft for use in your final version. Having it available in another file can come in handy.

Continuing the exploration

Revising led Miller to tell a third story in the middle of her essay. Her new story about fire fighting (pp. 142–143, paragraphs 6–7) helped clarify a notion that she only touched on in the story about her friend David—that the worlds of fantasy and reality sometimes clash violently. Miller's third story also led her to rewrite the beginning after her idea became clearer to her. Such revision is consistent with good writing practice. You will always make adjustments, writing and rewriting, as you go along.

Revising the beginning

After additional work on the middle, you will often revise the beginning, accounting more accurately for what readers should expect to find in the essay. Miller's readers—the members of her work group—gave her the following advice after reading her beginning: "Reconsider your beginning. See if you can become much less dependent on the word *cape*. Decode that word; help us understand what it stands for in your mind. Keep working to reveal your idea that is embedded in that word. You're onto something good!" Here is Miller's revised beginning.

Miller's revised beginning

Flying is a passion of mine. I have treasured its comfort ever since the first   1
time I soared above the imperfect world of reality in the land of my imagination, supported by the powerful, mysterious force of flight. The marvelous phenomenon of flight lifts me out of the present, carrying me to a world of my creation. And in transcending the constraints of time, my flights create a mockery of the incompleteness, the relentlessness of the world from which they snatch me. I do not remember where my first journey took me. I was so young that I do not remember the journey at all, only the wonderful feelings I found on my trip. I was comfortable, happy, optimistic, confident, powerful. And each time I fly, these feelings that I cherish come to me once again. I doubt that I have ever left the ground on any of my journeys; my flights are not of the physical sort. But they are very real in my mind. They are real in the way they inspire me to tackle the world of reality with a renewed enthusiasm, conquering its imperfections with the power inside me that I find on my adventures. My flights help change the way I picture my life; they help construct who I am.

EXERCISE 6–1   Close Reading and Writing

1. How has Miller's idea in the first beginning changed in the revised beginning? Write a paragraph about the differences. Cite specific evidence from Miller's two paragraphs to make your case more convincing.

2. Where in Miller's revised beginning do you find a hint about David's story? Cite the words or sentences that anticipate the dangers of flight. What can you infer about Miller's attitude toward such dangers? What is your evidence for that inference? Has Miller's attitude about such dangers changed from that expressed in the first version of the beginning? Explain your answer.

Returning to the middle

Let us go back to the middle of Miller's essay. In it, you will reencounter the stories about Daniel and David; you will also find the new story about fire fighting. As you read the middle, pay particular attention to the underlined sentences and phrases, which give you a sense of how Miller offers explanations along the way that tie her stories together and make her idea clearer. Here is the middle of Miller's essay, which she tentatively titled "Flying."

Miller's middle: Final draft

My two younger brothers always get to open a few presents on Christmas Eve. 2
Daniel, the youngest, celebrated his third Christmas this year. Convinced that the best gifts always come in large packages, he chose the presents he wished to open that evening solely on this condition. He was surrounded by stuffed animals, a race car track, a train set, and a few other gifts that, due to their size, made maneuvering about the living room a challenge. But only one present held Daniel's attention that evening: the Batman costume from Aunt Pat. Ever since he had unwrapped the gift and discovered what it was, he had dragged the box containing the costume around the room, demanding that someone help him put it on. Finally, receiving the needed help from his mother, Daniel turned into Batman, running around the living room and shooting his family members with tiny plastic arrows from his knuckle gun. His glossy red hair poking out the sides, Daniel peered through the eyes of his Batman mask with a look of confidence and determination, ready to conquer any villains posing a potential threat to the successful completion of his mission, whatever it might be.

Tired of playing dead every time Daniel pegged me with one of his arrows, I 3
began to read the box that had contained the Batman costume. A warning sign on
its side caught my eye:

WARNING

Vest is not really bulletproof.

Cape will not enable user to fly.

I chuckled as I read the note of caution, then burst into laughter as I realized its
absurdity. How could anyone think that a little piece of nylon could send them soaring into the air? My whole family joined me in laughter after I read the warning to
them, as they too considered how silly it was. That is, everyone except Daniel.
Although understanding the words I had said, he found no humor in them. Instead
of joining in the laughter of the rest of his family, Daniel continued to prance about
the room, completely absorbed in the fantasy of the world to which his Batman costume had flown him.

Each day, Daniel experiences the excitement of a different world, one where 4
he is the biggest, smartest, most powerful creature of all. That night, Daniel was
Batman. He ran about the room, stalking his prey and deftly conquering each one
with his batlike agility--the thin, black cape streaming behind him. That night,
there was no one in Daniel's world more powerful than he.

Many of my flights have placed me in the shoes of someone else, just as Daniel 5
became Batman that evening. Some of my favorite people to be when I was little
were cowboys, Olympic athletes, astronauts, singers, police officers--each unique
in a different way. The people in my adventures were quite varied. But they all had
something in common: they were all heroes of a sort. They were all good at something that, in pursuing their talent, brought them pleasure, confidence, success.
The person I liked to be the most was a firefighter. Conquering the powerful flames
that have so often destroyed beautiful monuments and taken away lives is a heroic
act that has always fascinated me. In my role as a firefighter, I concentrated my
actions on trying to defeat nature's attempt to create tragedy, to stop nature from
taking away its own creations.

Despite the remarkable capacity for imagination that most children have, pre- 6
tending to fight fires when I was a child was a challenge. Melinda Morbeck, my
childhood comrade, and I tried many approaches to creating a fire that appeared
convincing enough to warrant our battling against it, but rarely were we satisfied
with our attempts to create fictitious fires. Wrapped up in our fantasy of being fire's

archenemies, Melinda and I decided we were prepared to fight a real fire, so we torched one of the rhododendrons in my backyard. The powerful, destructive force of the fire took control and, before we even began to combat the flames, the fire had spread to the other rhododendrons and to the fence behind them. Within minutes, the scream of sirens announced the arrival of a fire truck, and real firefighters took over our unfinished mission. By the time they conquered all of the flames, all the rhododendrons were gone along with most of the picket fence surrounding the yard.

    During the following week, which Melinda and I spent in our rooms, I reflected on our brush with disaster--the violent collision of fantasy with reality. Our flight had taken us to a pleasant, fascinating world in which we were the heroes, the most powerful, skillful fighters of nature's wrath. But a vivid reminder of reality was displayed for us in the form of a very real fire, one that took over my backyard. Our flight took Melinda and me to a world of fantasy that, like all the worlds that can be reached by flying, is not totally separate from the one everyone shares. Fantasy cannot be entirely freed from the imperfect, unpredictable world of the present, a world in which I do not have total control over my future or my happiness. But I do have this control when I fly to my worlds, and the pleasant feelings I find there stay inside me when I am forced to return to the apathetic, uncontrollable world of reality.   7

    On a beautiful spring afternoon during my third-grade year, my friend David Ingham and I frolicked about the dodgeball court at our school, perfecting our roles as professional dodgeball players. Even though there were no real Batman capes streaming behind us, we soared just as high as Daniel did that Christmas Eve. We were completely absorbed in the thrill of competing against the other dodgeball team, focusing on our movements and the rules of the game. Nothing else in the whole world mattered to us on that wonderful afternoon except our game of dodgeball.   8

    In my quest to sharpen my dodgeball skills, I took it upon myself to ask David for some personal help in developing my ball-throwing technique. In his usual care-free manner, he remarked to me that it was all in the wrist and demonstrated exactly how he used his wrist to produce such power. In his blue and white school uniform, shirt untucked as usual, he smiled gleefully and hurled a ball across the court, slamming the wooden kick board on the opposite side. Pleased by the fascination I showed, David smiled, messed up my hair, and darted across the court to   9 retrieve the ball and give me a try. Despite the simplicity and the clarity of his explanation, I never quite caught on to David's art of ball throwing, but I treasure my memory of him and me flying together through our world of dodgeball.

But I am afraid my flights with David are over. A skiing accident over Christ-   10
mas vacation left him paralyzed from the waist down. The tragic intervention of reality took away his ability to soar through his world of athletics and dominating every sport he undertook. Instead, he was forced to cope with life as a paraplegic during the prime of his athletic career. David's skiing accident forced him to picture himself in a wheelchair, a picture that he found too difficult to accept. After losing his ability to fly in his world of athletics, the one he loved most, David chose to escape the cruel, apathetic world that had robbed him of his pathway to comfort, his source of happiness. David wheeled himself off a pier into Lake Washington this month, taking his life and the love of many with him.

But the direction of time is not all bad. Even though it prevents David from   11
coming back, it soothes me by pushing the horror, the terrible shock of his death farther and farther away from me as each day goes by. And when I think about David now, the joy we shared so often together is gradually overcoming my sorrow at this loss. The good feelings I have for him are stronger, more persevering, than the sad memory of his death. The passage of time has helped me focus on the joy we shared rather than on the tragic, inexplicable reality of his death. I could not fly through my worlds of comfort and happiness for a while after David died. But I have gradually regained my ability to soar into worlds that transcend reality and carry me for a brief time out of my constraining, unpredictable life. Each time I fly, I find comfort again. All the while, the sad memories of events in the past keep being pushed farther away from me, farther back in my memory until they are only shadows. Flying reminds me of my losses, but it helps me rediscover who I am. The worlds I create in my imagination restore my sanity, my stability, my identity.

EXERCISE 6–2   Understanding the Essay

Read Miller's beginning and middle twice and answer the following questions.

1. Reread Miller's beginning. How does she foreshadow what will follow in the middle? Link specific parts of the beginning to specific parts of the middle.

2. Identify the three stories Miller tells in the middle of her essay. How does each story contribute to her idea?

3. Paragraphs 7 and 11 contain a great deal of explanatory material (under-lined). In what ways does that material help you understand Betsy's idea? Write a paragraph or two to explain your answer.

4. In two or three sentences write what you think Betsy's idea turns out to be.

6 Ending the essay

The **ending** of an exploratory essay should take readers back to the beginning, reminding them in some way about the development of the idea. But the ending should not merely repeat what has already been said. It should sum up in a way that gives readers a fresh perspective on the idea.

In preparation for writing an ending, you should reread the entire essay and try to let that reading guide you as you attempt to capture the essence of it all. The ending is your last chance to make your reader see it your way.

The following paragraph is Miller's ending. The underlined portions reflect traces of her idea; they serve as reminders, stitching the parts of the essay together.

Miller's ending

Daniel, my younger brother, will be four years old this month. He will soon   12
embark on another year of his own soaring. One day, he will come to understand
that a little piece of nylon cannot support his weight in flight. But even then, he will
still be able to fly, as long as he holds on to the memory of its comfort. For now,
Daniel will find nothing funny in a warning label on the box of his Batman costume
trying to tell him that he cannot fly with his cape. Maybe the cape won't let him fly
across the living room for all to see. But who knows what Daniel can do in his
world?

Miller returns to her younger brother as a way of reminding readers about the childlike nature of flying. But she does much more: she reminds readers that the comfort people might derive from the kind of flying she is promot-ing depends on their ability to remember the comfort they got from such flights of fancy as children. It is that comfort that will sustain them later in life, long past their realization that "a little piece of nylon cannot support [their] weight in flight." In short, Miller repackages her idea in the ending and offers readers a new perspective on the idea.

The ending, like the beginning and the middle, is an integral part of the essay. Beginning, middle, and ending constitute a unified attempt to express an idea. The accompanying chart (Considering the Essay's Beginning, Middle, and Ending) will help you focus when you write your beginnings, middles, and endings for your essays.

EXERCISE 6–3   **Writing an Exploratory Essay**
Re-create a moment from memory—an experience—that still interests you, a moment that lingers in your imagination. Re-create that memory in the form of a story. (Aim for two or three typed pages, double-spaced.) Then follow Features of the Exploratory Essay (see p. 130) to create a four- to six-page exploratory essay in which you reveal what that story and others mean to you.

Considering the Essay's Beginning, Middle, and Ending

The Beginning

- Write the first draft of the beginning only after you have collected evidence and considered what you want to say about it—after you have a good sense of your essay's idea.

- Draw your reader into the essay with an anecdote (a brief, pointed story) that highlights your essay's idea.

- Be sure the beginning foreshadows the whole essay, but without revealing the details and surprises that follow.

The Middle

- Make the middle follow smoothly and logically from the beginning.

- Present your evidence and give your reader a sense of what it means.

- Explain the relationship between that evidence and your idea.

The Ending

- Capture the essence of what you have written.

- Sum up the idea in the ending by revealing a fresh perspective on your idea.

- Remind your reader of important aspects of your idea by drawing into the ending selected details that have appeared earlier.

6c   Connecting texts with stories of experience

As you learn to write more complex, and perhaps more interesting, exploratory essays, you will begin to move beyond your immediate experience to enrich the presentation of your idea. This section considers how Alexandra Johnes developed an idea about learning by combining stories of experience with other evidence—five published essays.

Johnes's initial work resembled that done by Betsy Miller (6b) in that she combined stories of experience as a way of finding and then developing an idea. The class was working on a common subject—education—and they read together a number of short exploratory essays, some by students, some by professional writers. You will see later how Johnes makes use of some of those essays.

1   Writing a letter as a way of enriching an idea

Reread the Guidelines for Developing an Exploratory Essay on p. 132 to refresh your memory about the process: developing a story of experience, questioning it to find an idea, and then combining it with other stories to clarify the idea. Johnes did all of those things before her teacher asked her to move beyond stories of experience to other kinds of evidence. The new, added requirement was to write a letter to a friend (not in her class), to make use of her initial stories in that letter, and to connect those stories with other kinds of evidence that might help the friend understand the idea about education that was beginning to take shape in her mind. Johnes and the other students were encouraged to give their imaginations free rein as they made meaningful connections during their letter writing (see 4c for more on connecting).

Here is an excerpt from the beginning of Johnes's letter in which she recalls a book she has read and links it with stories of experience as a way of investigating and enriching her idea about education:

Dear Eva,

     Have you read The Moviegoer by Walter Percy? I've been thinking a lot about the search lately, about what it means to be looking for something, to be looking for purpose.

     When I think back to my three years at M--, I think I'll always remember late night conversations the most, above and beyond any class discussion. I realized that among the mass of things I learned there, I learned the most from simply being part of the community.

The wonderful thing about college thus far has been that all of a sudden all those elements in life that were once considered distractions can be integrated into my education. For the first time what I'm thinking about doesn't seem so wholly at odds with what I'm studying.

But there's more to it than that. It's not all that simple. I guess maybe what I've been reveling in since I've been here is not so much college, per se, but rather growing up and having things fall into place, make sense.

Damian's older sister, Trisch, the one who's a professional ballroom dancer, has been a positive example for me. She was telling me that if her students found out how long she'd been studying ballroom, they'd think she was a fraud, since she only started ballroom in her senior year of college and was teaching less than a year later. But, because of her extensive background in both music and dance, she picked it up very quickly. Her being a ballroom dancer makes a lot of sense out of the pattern of her life. Perhaps when she started dancing or playing the cello, her friends and family were wondering what the point was, or why she was taking it so seriously, but now that she's a dance teacher, it would almost seem ridiculous if she hadn't done those things. See, I'm a firm believer that if you just keep following your heart, it will lead to a logical and happy place.

As for me, I thought about and studied a lot of different things when I was at M--, but they always seemed to be attached somehow to popular culture. When I studied feminism in my civil rights class, I wrote about the Wonderbra. I wrote about movies for the school newspaper. When I gave the Baccalaureate speech at graduation, I framed my speech around Susan Powter, the blonde, head-shaven woman who does the Stop The Insanity! infomercials. But the point isn't, yeah, I'm finally in college and can write about pop culture or yeah, I'm finally studying film. It's about having a certain cohesion to your life--but simply because it's cohesive doesn't mean it requires any less work.

I went to Las Vegas over Thanksgiving, and as a pop culture connoisseur, I was fascinated with the experience. However, it was not until I wrote an ethnography paper in class, and slaved and slaved over it, that I think I fully understood the experience and what it meant to me. I had to work my thoughts and work that essay. Simply because pop culture is something I think a lot about, or have a passion about, does not mean that I've figured it all out.

So that's what I'm trying to write to you about. I'm trying to write to you about working to figure things out, working to search for answers like Binx does in The Moviegoer, working to see and understand more clearly.

Johnes does not tell her friend much about the details of *The Moviegoer*; she doesn't need to. She tells her enough to let her know how the book was help-ing her explore her thoughts about education and learning. It provided another story or example for her, as Trisch's career had done. What she needed here was not to write a review about the book, but to let the evidence in the book serve as a springboard for thinking.

2   Multiplying the connections

As students moved from the ideas in the letter to their early drafts, they were encouraged to make other connections with the essays they were reading in class. Here is an early draft paragraph where Johnes tried to bring together several essays to make a point about the limitations of following only your passions when trying to learn. Notice how sketchy the connection is with the Ehrlich essay and with an essay by Jane Tompkins about Indians; they came to her while drafting. She will develop them in the final draft. You will see the paragraph in final form in the next section (6c-3):

And while this road [down which I followed my passions] did bear fruitful advantages, the greatest disadvantage was that I missed out on what I call "free learning," or learning without expectations. In Walker Percy's essay "The Loss of the Creature," Percy argues that a tourist can never really "see" the Grand Canyon as it really is, because his or her vision will be tainted by pre-existing expectations. Similarly, in --?-- essay "Indians, ---", in her desperate search for the most valid account of the history of the American Indians, she dismisses every one, ultimately not "seeing" any of them. And in Gretel Ehrlich's "Looking for a Lost Dog," Ehrlich. . . . In each case, the subject, in looking for something in particular (the Canyon as expected, the real history of the Indians), misses seeing the reality of what is right in front of them.

Just before this paragraph Johnes had made another sketchy note to herself about her reading. Remembering a student essay the class had read earlier, she wrote the author's name in brackets: [David Gray in here somewhere]. Let us see now how she developed that connection and how that connection established a context for the paragraph you have just read.

3 Developing the essay from the middle

Johnes's essay "Passionate Learning" suggests that school is a kind of game that students should enter into playfully and responsibly, but that even if they do, they will discover that following their passions may still not be satisfying enough. Here is a central section from the middle of her essay that lets you see her combining her analysis of David Gray's essay with stories of her own experience and with those other written texts she cited in her rough draft.

> In his essay "Dulcis Est Sapientia," David Gray points out that
>> the mind does not register, or does not make sense of, information where it is not accompanied by another factor, a will to understand. . . . By making sharp divisions in what knowledge we consider "useless" or "useful," we set up barriers, we put on intellectual blinders which keep us from steering off the familiar one-way track to understanding. (3)
>
> He suggests that while he is perfectly capable of learning Swahili, he would never be able to because it does not seem useful to him: "I can see no connection between Swahili and any other knowledge I have."
>
> Gray is pointing out that learning requires a will to learn, and that this will derives from the degree to which we can relate the prospective knowledge to knowledge we already have. He argues that "education should stress the context of ideas above the mere presentations of facts." He would have liked to use me as an example. My education history is a case in point. I only truly learned when I could connect my learning to myself, to my own personal agenda. However, where Gray would see my experience as cause to reorient the way education approaches students, I also see it as cause to reorient the way students approach education, and in the larger sense, to reorient the way people approach the world.
>
> Gray is pushing to make learning a more natural, and thus easier and more enticing, process for students. And while this goal is a valiant attempt to draw peo-

ple more into education, a much needed action, it also makes students lazy. Because, while we may be able to bundle education into a cuter and cuter package, we cannot do the same to our surrounding environment. Teachers can help students make connections, but once in the real world students must perform this task themselves. And this task does not come naturally; it requires work.

This revelation came to me recently when I found myself immersed in my passions but only understanding them minimally. Having followed my heart, I landed this fall at film school. In a directing class, my professor casually asked me what the theme was of one of my favorite scripts, and I found, much to my embarrassment, that I didn't quite know it exactly. In fact, I couldn't communicate very well at all what it was about, the script that I loved so much. I had eaten up its surface meaning. Unfortunately, and embarrassingly enough, this scenario seems to be part of a trend. I understand very little about those things which I am most passionate about. I am not very versed at putting my passions into words. This habit of mine is of particular concern in considering film as a medium of pop culture. Too often we absorb meanings of popular culture without ever knowing exactly what meanings we have absorbed.

Furthermore, only following my heart, only learning when I could relate new knowledge to previous knowledge, limited me from learning for learning's sake. In Walker Percy's essay "The Loss of the Creature," he argues that a tourist can never "see" the Grand Canyon as it really is because his or her vision will be tainted by preexisting expectations. Similarly, in Jane Tompkins's essay "Indians," Tompkins, in her desperate search for the most valid account of the history of the American Indians, dismisses every one, ultimately not "seeing" any of them. In "Looking for a Lost Dog," Gretel Ehrlich comes to realize that in her search for her dog, she misses experiencing her journey. In each case, the subject, in looking for something in particular (the Canyon as expected, the <u>real</u> history of the Indians, the dog), misses seeing what is there.

Similarly, in looking at new knowledge only as it related to old knowledge, I missed out on seeing the knowledge as it stood on its own. I saw it only as it related to my immediate state of mind, to my immediate place on my personal path. The same "familiar one-way track to understanding" that Gray wants to tap into locked me inside of it, blocking a clear view of the outside world. I evaluated all of new knowledge in terms of its usefulness to my understanding of myself. I saw each piece as a prospective answer to my personal pondering; if the piece did not offer some sort of resolution, I dismissed it as being irrelevant.

What I'm leading to is this: Life takes work.

There is more to this fine student essay about games and learning and passion. With her ending paragraph, Johnes managed to put all her ideas and evidence in perspective:

> To recognize that life takes work is to accept the rules of the game and thus, to have self-respect. As Joan Didion says, people with self-respect know the price of things. They
>
> > are willing to accept the risk that the Indians will be hostile, that the venture will go bankrupt, that the liaison may not turn out to be one in which every day is a holiday because you're married to me. They are willing to invest something of themselves; they may not play at all, but when they do play, they know the odds. (149)
>
> People who respect themselves "are willing to accept the risk" that the teacher might be wrong, that their hearts may take them in the wrong direction. "They are willing to invest something of themselves"; they may choose not to play the games at all, but when they do play, they play in full awareness of the rules. They know the odds. They know that it takes work to play well.

Johnes reminds you just how far you can take the exploratory essay. It can admit a variety of evidence—experience, books, essays, movies—and a host of ideas that are hard to get at but fun to think about. This form of the essay can treat serious subjects in an exploratory way and can lead to exciting discoveries. It lays the foundation for more formal writing by showing you how such writing must be grounded in expansive yet rigorous thinking.

EXERCISE 6–4   Writing an Exploratory Essay with Written Texts

Select an area of inquiry—education, seeing, some aspect of pop culture—and recall and re-create a moment from your own experience related to that area of inquiry. Then follow Guidelines for Developing an Exploratory Essay on p. 132 to create an exploratory essay of four to six pages in which you develop an idea related to your area of inquiry. Include in your essay two or three written texts that help you develop your idea.

7   The Argumentative (Persuasive) Essay

In an **argumentative essay** a writer tries to *persuade* readers to adopt his or her point of view about a given issue. The subject can range from local problems to national and international ones—from a local school district's busing plan, to a nation's educational goals, to international concerns about arms control.

A good, persuasive **argument** usually focuses on a controversial topic. You need not go far to find controversy; our diverse culture seems to thrive on it. Issues dealing with race, gender, war, drugs, technology, education, and leadership, for example, suggest controversies that seem never to be resolved. When you choose a topic to write about, or have one assigned by your instructor, you will investigate it, develop your ideas about it, and write an argumentative essay that presents and substantiates your point of view—the thesis that you will defend in a clearheaded and reasonable way.

As you begin thinking about your topic and considering the availability of evidence, you will investigate, asking questions and looking for answers. Your investigation might require you to conduct research in the library, to go out into the community to interview experts, to go into the field or the laboratory to conduct experiments, or simply to rely on your own experiences. Your investigation yields information that helps you reach a conclusion about your controversial topic. That conclusion is the leading idea that will become the thesis for your essay.

Given the nature of the topics that lend themselves to argument, your thesis will always be subject to further analysis; it will need thinking about again in light of changing conditions and the availability of new evidence. So you need not think that you will be developing the final and definitive answer to these long-standing controversies. Rather, you will present a clearheaded conclusion that takes into account the available evidence and contributes to the dialogue about the controversy.

Often, if you are writing an argumentative essay for a course, your instructor will specify the range and nature of your investigation. On other occasions, however, you will have to decide on your own what sources you need to consider so you can clarify your perspective on the controversy and develop and defend your thesis. This chapter will suggest how to develop a reasonable thesis and how to use evidence effectively when you write your essay. You will see how two students develop argumentative essays relying on rigorous thinking as well as written texts (7e and f). (Also see Part 8 for more detailed information on research.)

7a   Purpose and audience in argument

When you write an argumentative essay, your primary *purpose* is to present and defend your conclusion about a controversial issue so that you can influence change. That conclusion can lead to more controversy—on campus, in the local community, or in the nation—but it can also lead to social or institutional change. For example, you might try to persuade a community to change its voting habits. Or you might try to persuade an organization to change the way it makes decisions. You might even try to influence the critical reception of a new book through a persuasive argument about its value.

Arguments require an especially keen attentiveness to *audience* because your goal is to convince that audience of your conclusion; you do not want to invite your readers' opposition or hostility. However, the challenge is that not all audiences will agree with your

http://www.kcmetro.cc.
mo.us/longview/ctac/
flowpt1.htm
Presents guidance in writing argumentative essays.

point of view. To be persuasive, you need to show a real concern about how your readers might think about a given subject as well as how they might react to the way you think about that subject. You must consider conflicting points of view as you develop and present your own point of view. Remember that all audiences—whether hostile or friendly, whether you know them well or have no idea how to persuade them—respond to logic and reasonableness.

7b   Preparing to write a reasonable argument

Preparing to write an argument is a lot like preparing to write any other essay. However, written arguments do have some specific requirements. The accompanying chart, Features of the Argumentative Essay, lists the principles that apply to all good arguments. You can use the chart as a model in building an argument and as a checklist to test the effectiveness of your completed argument.

Features of the Argumentative Essay

- It conveys a reasonable conclusion—often called a *thesis* or a *claim*—about a controversial topic.
- It presents supporting evidence that is always incorporated, explained, and documented clearly and precisely.
- It considers and often presents the conflicting points of view about the controversy.
- It reflects thorough research and rigorous analysis.

---

1 Being logical and reasonable

Formal logic specifies guidelines for being reasonable, and you will benefit from keeping those guidelines in mind as you write. They will help you maintain a fair and reasonable argument, rather than an unbalanced, hotheaded, or fallacious one.

You are not expected to memorize these guidelines, but you should become familiar with them, and you should use them to help you evaluate your own arguments. Often, in collaboration, your classmates will help you spot problems in your writing that you may not be able to see.

This section will give you an overview of several aspects of logical thinking that will better inform those judgments that you and your classmates (and your larger audience) make about your arguments.

Inductive and deductive reasoning

When you reason *inductively*, you begin with particular instances: x, y, z, say; or a car wreck, a radio station, a gaggle of pedestrians, a busy intersection; or three different novels by three different writers. These grouped instances, or objects, seem to have nothing in common, but as you look at them, you begin to see relationships; you begin to interpret and bring them together, finally reaching a conclusion either about their relationship or something that their relationship has suggested to you. The conclusion that you reach is not forced; neither is it certain. Nevertheless, scientists and thinkers use this inductive form of reasoning to move to new places in thought. From the disparate pieces of evidence that you bring together, you draw a reasonable conclusion, accounting for their relationship as you see it.

Inductive reasoning is particularly useful when you try to determine causes of particular events or circumstances. You might identify a series of events as contributing causes of the Balkan War or the collapse of communist rule in eastern Europe. When you determine what you consider a primary cause, your conclusion will rarely be certain, but it must be reasonable in terms of the evidence. Because inductive thinking depends on probability and uncertainty, the connection between the evidence and conclusion is itself considered probable. Such conclusions turn out to be *probable, reliable,* or *unreliable,* rather than simply right or wrong.

The elements of inductive thinking are summarized in the accompanying chart.

Elements of Inductive Reasoning

- Begins with a specific observation
- Continues with additional specific observations
- Arrives at a general claim or a conclusion about the observations that is based on them and other available evidence
- Attributes causes to events or circumstances, resulting in a hypothesis that can be tested further
- Offers probability rather than certainty

When you begin to think *deductively,* you begin from a generalization—often from a conclusion that has been reached through an inductive process. Then you note something specific that applies to the generalization, and you reason from that relationship to a logical conclusion. If you reason according to the structural rules of deductive logic, your conclusion will be both valid (its structure conforms to the rules) and reliable (you are willing to act on the basis of its conclusion).

Deductive reasoning is syllogistic reasoning. A **syllogism** is an argument arranged in three parts: a major premise, a minor premise, and a conclusion. A *major premise* stipulates a general principle (e.g., that all spiders have eight legs), and a *minor premise* reflects a specific instance (e.g., that the creature crawling across your desk has six legs). Your *conclusion* that it is not a spider follows logically from these major and minor premises. Since these premises can be supported with relevant evidence, they can be considered reliable.

In many cases syllogistic reasoning depends on premises that are *assumptions* rather than facts. An assumption may or may not be based on evidence that makes it reliable. Consider the assumption behind the major premise in the following syllogism.

MAJOR PREMISE   Those who wear Gap clothes to school will be accepted by the school's most popular group. (Assumption)

MINOR PREMISE   Jose wears Gap clothes to school. (Fact)

CONCLUSION   Jose will be accepted by the school's most popular group.

When a premise is an assumption rather than a fact, you must be able to support the premise with considerable evidence. Because the major premise of this example rests on a shaky assumption (it cannot be supported with incontrovertible evidence), the argument is not necessarily reliable. In most instances, wearing Gap clothes (or any other brand or type of clothing) does not ensure automatic popularity. Since the assumption behind the major premise is unreliable, the argument based on it is not reliable. A premise is considered reliable when we are sufficiently convinced of its truth to act on it. The syllogism, however, is valid because validity concerns the syllogism's structure, which is sound; that is, if you accept the major premise, if the minor premise is also reliable, and the terms are properly distributed, then the conclusion follows logically.

Most arguments do not follow a formal syllogistic pattern. A newspaper editorial that supports the closing of military bases or a magazine column that argues for a student loan program run by the federal government would more than likely be presented with its major premise left unstated. An argument in which a premise is left unstated is an **enthymeme**. An enthymeme often appears as a conclusion supported by a single premise. Here is an example.

More than half of all varsity football players do not receive a diploma after studying six years at this university. We have to do something to improve that figure, or we should dismiss delinquent players.

Laid out in syllogistic form, the argument looks like this.

MAJOR PREMISE	(*unstated*) Students, including football players, should earn a diploma within six years or be dismissed.
MINOR PREMISE	More than half of all varsity football players do not receive diplomas within six years (but are still in school).
CONCLUSION	We have to improve players' academic performance or dismiss them.

You may agree or disagree about the reliability of the enthymeme's unstated premise. But the argument is easier to evaluate with the major premise stated. Be alert for arguments containing unstated premises; try to supply unstated premises so you can more easily assess their reliability. Remember, too, that an argument is only as strong as its premises. If an argument's premises are faulty, it can easily be refuted.

The accompanying chart outlines the elements of deductive reasoning.

Elements of Deductive Reasoning

Deductive Reasoning

- Begins with a general idea or major premise
- Continues with an additional minor premise applied to a particular case
- Concludes with a specific conclusion derived from the premise

Deductive Arguments

- Can be reliable or unreliable, depending on the reliability of the premises
- Can be valid or invalid, depending on the structure of their syllogisms
- When the premises are reliable, and the structure valid, deductive arguments provide certainty rather than probability

EXERCISE 7–1   **Analyzing Deductive Arguments**

Analyze the following deductive arguments. When necessary, supply the missing premises.

1. To improve the economy, the president should create public works projects and increase the number of available jobs.
2. I'm doing twice as much work today as I did ten years ago. I'd better slow down or I'll be endangering my health.
3. Students today do not read as much as they did in previous generations. How can we expect to have an enlightened citizenry unless they read more?
4. I think; therefore, I am.
5. She must be a good student since she is on the Dean's List.
6. Guns should be outlawed for civilians. The world has changed radically since the framers of the Bill of Rights included the right to bear arms.
7. Give me liberty or give me death.
8. When in Rome, do as the Romans do.
9. A political leader who cannot control his or her own family should not be given the responsibility of governing a state.
10. Alcoholic beverages destroy brain cells, so alcohol should be made illegal.

EXERCISE 7–2 **Constructing Arguments**
Construct a valid syllogism for each of the following minor premises. Example:

The New York Mets lost more games in 1993 than in any year since the first year of the franchise.

MAJOR PREMISE   Losing a large number of baseball games indicates that a team is in need of a major restructuring.

MINOR PREMISE   The New York Mets lost more games in 1993 than in any year since the first year of the franchise.

CONCLUSION   The New York Mets need a major restructuring.

1. Cigarette smoke is dangerous to the health of nonsmokers who breathe it.
2. Walking vigorously for twenty minutes a day provides excellent cardiovascular exercise.
3. Macy's reported substantial losses for the eight quarters of 1995 and 1996.
4. Speaking a foreign language can enhance one's pleasure when traveling abroad.
5. Interest rates have declined consistently in recent years.

Using inductive and deductive reasoning together

In practice, inductive and deductive reasoning work together and complement each other. Scientists, like other thinkers, use both inductive and deductive reasoning to construct arguments and reach conclusions. Consider the following account of the evolutionary connection between long-tongued moths and a species of orchid. In a story reported in the *New York Times*, Gene Kritzky, a scientist, hypothesized that a moth with a six-inch wingspan and a fifteen-inch tongue had to exist—even though there was no record of anyone ever having seen one. On the face of it, this may sound like an outrageous claim. But once you know that a type of orchid exists whose nectar lies fifteen inches deep into its flowery interior, then the existence of such a pollinating moth becomes more likely. The prediction becomes an even greater likelihood when you consider the following facts (Kritzky's evidence).

1. In 1862, Charles Darwin had made a similar prediction about the existence of a moth with a twelve-inch tongue, based on his discovery of a slightly smaller orchid (one with its nectar thirteen inches deep inside).

2. Darwin's orchid, like the one discussed in the *Times* article, was found in Madagascar.

3. Although the scientist who predicted the existence of this larger moth has not seen the larger orchid, someone else has seen and described it.

4. Both Darwin's orchid and this larger orchid cannot be pollinated by small insects that crawl into it, for the orchids are structured so that if the insects go too deeply in they can never get out.

5. Forty years after Darwin's prediction, the moth whose existence he had hypothesized was found.

Darwin arrived at his prediction that such a moth existed partly from his observation of the deep orchid and partly from his knowledge that no known creature could pollinate such a deep flower. He reasoned inductively from particular circumstances, but he also reasoned deductively from the scientific law of natural selection that he had formulated. Darwin reasoned that species develop and change to enhance their opportunities for continued successful existence. Since moths with slightly shorter tongues pollinate slightly smaller orchids, then according to the principle of natural selection, a longer-tongued species would evolve to pollinate the deeper flower.

To reach their hypotheses, both Darwin and Kritzky worked from an unstated assumption: that orchids are pollinated by insects. They also worked from the general law that stipulates how insects adapt to their environment. Thus, since Darwin's reasoning has been proven correct with regard to this kind of moth and this orchid species, and since more than likely the same principle applies to Kritzky's example, it will be only a matter of time before the longer-tongued moth is found.

2   Avoiding fallacies

A *fallacy* is an error. A logical fallacy represents an error or mistake in logic. These mistakes most often occur when writers fail to establish a clear relationship between the claims they are making and the evidence they present (or fail to present) to substantiate those claims. Often the errors are not immediately apparent because the warrants or premises that account for the relationship between evidence and claim are missing, unstated. When the errors are deliberate, something tricky may be going on: a fallacious argument constructed to conceal the weakness of its evidence or the shallowness of its claim. The following list of common fallacies should help you detect errors in logic in your own writing and in what you read.

Checklist of Common Logical Fallacies

- **Hasty generalization:** A conclusion based on insufficient evidence.
- **Stereotyping:** Assuming without sufficient evidence that members of a group think or behave alike.
- **Either-or thinking:** Limiting possible explanations to two.
- **Illogical causality:** Assuming that an event is caused by another simply because one event occurs after the other.
- **Non sequitur:** A statement that does not follow logically from another.
- **Begging the question:** Assuming as true what needs to be proven.
- **Circular reasoning:** Asserting the same point in different works.
- **Special pleading:** Arguing without considering opposing viewpoints.
- **Red herring:** Introducing an irrelevant or distracting consideration into an argument.

(continued)

- **Appeal to ignorance:** Assuming something is true because the contrary cannot be proven.
- **Playing prejudices:** Appealing to the prejudices of an audience.
- **Character attack:** Attacking a person's character rather than addressing the issue at hand.
- **False analogy:** Making an illogical connection based on irrelevant similarities.

Hasty generalization

A **hasty generalization** relies on inadequate evidence. Jumping to conclusions too quickly, before considering additional or alternative information, leads to hasty generalizations.

For our Victorian Novel course, we read ten enormous novels, including Dickens's *Bleak House* and Eliot's *Middlemarch,* which like the others are nearly a thousand pages. It seems as if all Victorian novels are that long.

Stereotyping

Stereotyping, a form of hasty generalization, involves making assumptions about things, places, or people based on insufficient evidence. For example, you might describe Los Angeles as crime ridden when many sections of Los Angeles are quite safe. Or you might assume that Italians are quick tempered, that women drive poorly, or that college professors are absentminded. These examples of stereotypical thinking make unwarranted assumptions about an entire group of people based on the characteristics of some. (See Chapter 26 on biased language.)

Either-or thinking

Sometimes called *false dilemma, **either-or** thinking* limits the solutions to a problem to two—either *A* or *B*. Other alternatives are ignored.

Either the Democrats band together now behind one of the declared candidates, or they will kill each other off politically and ensure an easy Republican victory in the next presidential election.

Either-or thinking is limiting. It oversimplifies complex issues, reducing them to extreme explanations that ignore viable alternatives.

Illogical causality

Illogical causality results from the assumption that because one event happens after another, the first causes the second. This is faulty cause-and-effect reasoning (see 3e), called *post hoc, ergo propter hoc* (Latin for "after this, therefore because of").

In 1991, under coach Bill Parcells, the New York Giants won their division, their league championship, and ultimately the Super Bowl. The following year, under Ray Handley, the Giants, with a mediocre 8 and 8 win–loss record, did not make it even to the first round of the playoffs. Handley must be a poor coach, one who is responsible for the Giants' slide into mediocrity.

Non Sequitur

Non sequitur is Latin for "it does not follow." A *non sequitur* is a conclusion that does not follow logically from an argument's premises—usually unstated.

I had worked hard during the entire term. I deserve an A for the course.

Here the unstated premise—"students who work hard all semester should get an A"—is probably unreliable.

Begging the question

To **beg the question** involves assuming the truth of an issue without providing evidence or arguments in its support.

Hondas are reliable because they are Japanese cars.

Circular reasoning

To engage in **circular reasoning** is to assert the same idea in different words, but without introducing evidence or reasons in support.

The growing popularity of aerobic exercise shows that people are becoming increasingly interested in aerobics.

Special pleading

In **special pleading** a speaker or writer presents a one-sided argument, completely ignoring contradictory information and opposing perspectives. Special pleaders present their case without indicating the existence of contrary evidence or the possibility of alternative views.

Doberman pinschers are a good breed of dog. They are alert, highly trainable, and elegant.

Red herring

Introducing a **red herring** into an argument deliberately sidetracks the discussion by bringing in an irrelevant matter.

"Officer, you shouldn't be giving me a ticket for illegal parking when criminals are roaming the streets at this very moment, killing people. The police ought to spend their time solving more important problems and preventing crimes instead of wasting it by harassing law-abiding citizens."

Appeal to ignorance

In an **appeal to ignorance** a speaker or writer argues that a situation is true merely because strong contrary evidence is lacking. Such an appeal assumes that a claim must be true simply because it cannot be disproved.

God must have created the world in six days because scientists can't prove that He didn't. In fact they can't prove that God does not exist, which means, of course, that He does.

Playing prejudices

This fallacy (often labeled *ad populum,* Latin for "to the people") appeals to people's emotion, to popular feeling, and to prejudice, rather than to reason.

In speaking to middle-class voters, a candidate for political office criticizes the incumbent on the basis of the incumbent's wealth, connections, and private school education, which she argues make her opponent insensitive to the needs and concerns of middle-class people like herself.

Character attacks

One of the most common fallacies, *ad hominem* (Latin for "to the man"), is an attack on an individual's character, attributing motives to that person that he or she may not possess. It is an attempt to discredit an idea by attacking the person presenting it rather than by addressing the issue at hand.

Senator Martino argues that we should attempt to control the budget deficit by cutting spending in the military and social services sectors. But the senator has had serious problems handling his personal credit. Why should we listen to his views on the nation's economic plan when he can't manage his personal finances?

False analogy

A **false analogy** misleads by comparing situations that are more unalike than similar. False analogies are also sometimes based on irrelevant similarities.

If we add proficiency in a foreign language to the graduation requirements, we will deter students from attending this university, just as we did when we added math and science requirements ten years ago.

EXERCISE 7–3 Identifying Fallacies

Identify the fallacies of reasoning in the following nine statements. Explain what, if anything, may be wrong or illogical in each statement.

1. If we don't do something about the problem of overpopulation soon, the planet simply will be unable to accommodate the spiraling increase in people with sufficient food or adequate living space.

2. Those who are ignorant of history are condemned to repeat it.

3. He is the best senatorial candidate: he is tall and good looking; he is an eloquent speaker; and he gets along well with his colleagues.

4. Something horrible must have happened to them. They would have called if they were going to be this late.

5. Joanne's intelligence is her outstanding quality. Even though she is attractive and socially graceful, her mental ability is her strongest asset.

6. People are not really free. They only think they are. Their lives are actually determined by forces that control them without their being aware of it. No one can prove that he or she is impervious to the multitude of influences that bombard us throughout our lives.

7. Astrologers must know what they're doing. My horoscope for the past week has been right on target.

8. If you don't buy this CD player now, it won't be here tomorrow. And besides, prices are expected to go up next week.

9. Students should grade themselves in their courses. After all, no one knows better than they do how hard they have worked and how much they have learned.

7c Developing a reasonable thesis

Let us move now to a series of practical considerations that will help you develop a more reasonable argument. Our most immediate concerns will be your tone, the nature and sufficiency of your evidence, the relationship between your evidence and your thesis, techniques for citing evidence, and, finally, development of a reasonable thesis.

1 Tone

Controversies often push writers and their opponents into extreme positions—my way is right, your way is wrong—when in fact a more reasonable solution lies between the extremes.

Audiences respond well if you adopt a fair-minded and reasonable (or moderate) tone in your arguments. Name-calling, pomposity, exaggeration, and anger work against you, as does the inadvertent use of fallacious reasoning (7b).

2 The nature and sufficiency of your evidence

Besides the rigorous, logical thinking that is so important to the development of your arguments, there are other clearly recognizable forms of evidence that writers use to support and substantiate those arguments.

Written sources

Most scholarly arguments depend on some form of written material as their primary form of evidence. Scholarly articles, newspaper reports, and essays are available in the library and on the Internet. As you read and evaluate such sources, you must be mindful of their objectivity. Be on the alert for bias and ensure that the person providing the information is indeed an expert in the field under consideration. Expert testimony—such as that given in courts of law and in scholarly articles—can help you establish the reasonableness of your thesis. Such testimony must be accurate, current, and free of bias.

Examples and illustrations

One or two well-chosen examples can clarify and illustrate your ideas. Examples are especially effective if you use them in combination with your written sources to create in your readers' mind a clear picture of what you mean. Later in this chapter, you will read an argument about medical marijuana in which a student writer tells a brief, effective story about a man who approaches him at a rally urging him to support the medical use of marijuana. From the student writer's point of view this man hurt the cause of medical marijuana because he appeared to be a drug user who was merely using a legitimate cause to support his illegitimate habit. The writer makes this cogent point through his example.

Statistics and factual information

Statistical and factual information tends to be persuasive, especially if you, as a writer, use your numbers and facts reasonably. Being reasonable with such evidence simply means that you do not try to make the data say more than it says, or suggests. Interpret it conservatively. If you have taken a survey, make sure that it represents accurately the population that you use it to represent. If you have administered a questionnaire, make sure that you interpret the answers fairly, that you do not misrepresent the information that you or others have gathered.

Sufficiency of evidence

There is no set answer to how much and what kind of evidence you must use to make your arguments persuasive. That is why it is so important for you to consider your audience, especially those who might disagree with you. As you hear (in your head or from your sources) what your opponents have to say about your chosen controversy, you will begin to imagine what it might take to change their minds or at the very least challenge their thinking. Your claims will have to be supported; you know that. And your argument will have to anticipate their objections, offering evidence that calls into question what they typically say about the controversy

3   Summarizing, paraphrasing, and quoting: techniques for citing selected evidence

The process of incorporating evidence always requires that you pare down the source—by selecting a passage, a phrase, or just a word that you will quote, or by distilling the essence of the source in the form of a summary or a paraphrase. Often, writers use a combination of these techniques.

When you *summarize* a source, you condense a fairly lengthy passage of text into a few sentences of your own words. A summary is always shorter than the original source; it strives to capture the essence of the source (see 2b-4 and 40b-1).

A *paraphrase* does the same thing as a summary but follows the structure of the original source—the particular order the writer uses to reach a conclusion, develop an idea, or create emphasis (see 40d-2).

When you *quote*, you record the writer's words verbatim and enclose them in quotation marks. The length of a quotation can vary from a single word to several paragraphs (see 40d-3).

These definitions, important as they are, do not suggest what you, as a writer, actually do with the material that you borrow from your sources. You select evidence—words, details, images—to help you clarify and strengthen your *thesis*, or leading idea.

http://www.wisc.edu/writing/Handbook/ Explains, through examples, how to introduce quotations, paraphrases, and summaries into research writing.

Being Aware of Readers' Expectations While Selecting Evidence from Sources

1. Begin with a clear sense of purpose: your main objective is the development of ideas within essays.

2. Explain the relationship between your selected evidence and your idea; neither evidence nor idea will stand on its own.

3. Subordinate to your own ideas whatever evidence you select from sources; keeping that subordination in mind reminds you of the importance of your own reflections.

4. *Avoid plagiarism* by keeping recorded reflections and evidence separate in your notes. (See 2b-1 and 2b-3 on reading and notetaking.) Identify both reflections and evidence during the entire process of developing your essay, beginning with your earliest forms of notetaking. (See 40d, i–j for more on preliminary notetaking and 41 for more on plagiarism.)

The development of that idea constitutes your primary work as an essayist, so borrowed source material should always be *subordinated* to your own ideas (see Chapter 4 for more on developing ideas).

Sources help you substantiate your ideas, but the selected evidence from those sources rarely stands on its own. You will have to *explain* its importance to your readers as you incorporate the evidence into your essays. That will be your most crucial work as a writer.

4   Building a relationship between evidence and thesis

As you consider your evidence and its relationship to your thesis, you can benefit from a systematic way of thinking about that relationship. Remember that the conclusion you draw from the evidence depends on your inferential skills—the skills that permit you to draw out the conclusion that makes sense of the evidence. That conclusion cannot be forced; it will probably not seem self-evident. As you look at the evidence (much of it conflicting) and try to reach a reasonable conclusion about it, you will have to give it considerable thought. As you continue to examine new evidence, your conclusion about the meaning of that evidence will continue to change until you have completed your research and examined all of your evidence. At that point you are ready to formulate the final thesis for your essay.

Stephen Toulmin

In *The Uses of Argument*, the philosopher Stephen Toulmin provides a relatively simple but logical and rigorous way for you to think about that important relationship between your evidence and the conclusion you draw from it. Toulmin does not give you a foolproof way of reaching a reasonable conclusion; no one can do that. But thinking the way he does will help you be more reasonable. Identifying three important elements that are common to most arguments—a claim, support, a warrant—Toulmin places heavy emphasis on the *claim* that an argument makes. In the language that we have been using in this handbook, a *claim* is nothing more than a thesis, or the lead idea you have formulated and that you want to defend. Toulmin identifies three types of claims: claims of fact, claims of value, and claims of policy. Support, or evidence, to substantiate these three different kinds of claims will vary according to the claim.

Claims of fact suggest the truth of some condition that can be substantiated but that requires considerable research to do so: *The apparent epidemic of drug sales in Washington Square Park is on a par with other epidemics during the last three decades.* Claims of fact such as this one about current drug sales and past epidemics require that you find existing evidence that can be verified but that may be very difficult to acquire. Even that verifiable evidence will need interpreting.

Claims of value express acceptance or denial of a standard of taste or morality: Good Morning, Vietnam *is the finest movie to come out of America's longest war.* A claim of value such as this one requires considerations of taste and morality; such considerations depend primarily on reasonableness and consensus about taste and morality rather than on verifiable, factual evidence.

Claims of policy assert that a particular policy or way of doing business should be adopted: *Curbing the drug epidemic in Washington Square Park requires more police patrols, more neighborhood effort, and increased support from local businesses.* Claims of policy require evidence that strongly suggests that the proposed policies have a reasonable chance of working; that they have worked elsewhere under similar circumstances.

You can see, however, that no matter how much evidence you accumulate to support these different kinds of claims, you can rarely build an absolutely airtight case. Your task is to be as reasonable as possible, not to be absolutely right. How convincing you are will depend on the quality of your evidence and the reasonable way you establish that relationship between the evidence and your thesis, between the support and the claim.

Warrants may, at first, be a little more difficult to detect and visualize than claims and support, but your understanding of them should help you write more convincing arguments. **Warrants,** in Toulmin's language, are "bridges" that establish connections between claims and support. They are essential to our understanding of the relationship between claim and support.

A warrant can be either implicit or explicit. When implicit, it resembles an enthymeme, a formal syllogistic argument in which one of the premises is missing; it is implied. Consider the claim of value that we mentioned earlier: Good Morning, Vietnam *is the finest movie to have come out of America's longest war.* That complicated claim requires two kinds of support: evidence that will allow us to understand that movie's value in terms of other fine movies to come out of the war; and evidence that will establish the meaning of *finest.* Against the latter claim, you might amass evidence to establish the movie's realistic portrayal of the unusual war. Your support could come from your own analysis of the movie, from your interviews with veterans who could comment on the movie's realism, and from your comparison of that movie with other war movies.

As sound as all of that evidence might be when you collect it and analyze it, the effectiveness of your argument will also depend on an unstated warrant that your reader will have to agree to accept: a war movie's ultimate value depends on its realistic portrayal of the war. If your reader does not accept that warrant, your argument will not be very persuasive. The

http://www.colostate.edu/ Depts/WritingCenter/ references/reading/ toulmin/page1.htm Uses the philosopher Stephen Toulmin's thinking model.

movie's portrayal of violence, human relationships, and human development under stress, or the haunting beauty of its images, might be much more important to some viewers than its realism. For those viewers, realism alone would not make the movie the finest of its kind, no matter how much support you might offer to substantiate your claim.

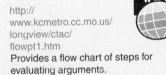

http:// www.kcmetro.cc.mo.us/ longview/ctac/ flowpt1.htm Provides a flow chart of steps for evaluating arguments.

If you think of your own arguments in terms of Toulmin's claim, support, and warrant, you can help yourself avoid common structural pitfalls: weak relationships between claim and support (thesis and evidence) and a failure to understand and account for the assumptions upon which your argument is based.

7d　Organizing and developing an argumentative essay

The Guidelines for Developing an Argumentative Essay on p. 172 take into account the necessary give and take between concerned interest groups. The guidelines also indicate that researching and writing lead to questions that in turn lead to more research and writing.

You can see, too, that your ability to detect the give and take between special-interest groups remains an important part of your researching and revising. In class, ask members of your work group or someone else to help you imagine the kind of opposition you will face from these special-interest groups. In doing this, you will know better how to take different viewpoints into account as you reach your conclusion and as you continue to refine your argument.

You need not follow the accompanying guidelines in sequence. Rather than providing a step-by-step system for developing an argument, they offer general considerations that will help you maintain focus. You will see in 7e and f how these guidelines helped two students create argumentative essays.

Guidelines for Developing an Argumentative Essay

- Select a controversial subject that interests you.
- Consider other points of view. Be fair to all sides of the argument during research by doing the following:
  - —As your evidence begins to lead you to a conclusion, search for contradictory evidence.
  - —Question your own evidence just as you question other investigators' conclusions.
  - —Avoid jumping to conclusions, and never be satisfied if your evidence leads to only one way of seeing your topic.
  - —Try to imagine how your audience will interpret your evidence. (See the Audience Checklist on p. 9 in 1d.)
  - —Let the principles of logic guide your effort (7b). Consider your argument in terms of Toulmin's claim, support, and warrant (7b-4).
- Based on the evidence you have gathered (from experience, reading, interviewing, and observing), formulate a tentative thesis, one that you will reconsider and modify as you do more reading, writing, and analysis.
- Consider what background information your audience will need to understand your point of view and the other points of view you will take into account. Make a tentative outline of how you think you will develop your argument (see 1f on organizing).
- Write a draft beginning, and go on to develop the middle of your essay. Write an ending.
- Ask your readers to resist your argument and to indicate weak spots. Also ask them to identify your thesis. (See 1h.)
- Revise your draft based on the feedback you receive.

7e Using experience and Internet sources as evidence in short essays

1 Editorials—Short argumentative essays

You will consider now a short argumentative essay that a student wrote as an assignment in a first-year writing course. Students were learning to write arguments in the form of editorials before they moved on to write longer, more complex arguments using written texts as their primary sources of evidence. Students were striving to write editorials that might be suitable for publication in a major newspaper.

Editorials (or op-ed pieces) are always controversial in nature and rely on the writer's experience and acquired expertise in a certain subject area. Editorials are usually limited in length (600–1200 words, depending on newspaper policy) and must necessarily rely on *rigorous thinking* as their most persuasive form of evidence. There is little room in an editorial for long citations from written texts. Writing editorials, therefore, provides an opportunity to practice logical thinking and efficient, spare use of written sources. Editorialists must be reasonable in their effort to persuade a skeptical reading audience of generalists. On the other hand, readers must be especially careful about considering what is left out of editorials—what has not been substantiated either with clear thinking or with convincing evidence.

As students prepared to write their own editorials, they studied both the form and general characteristics of published editorials. They first read and analyzed editorials that they selected from two or three of the nation's major newspapers (available on the Internet), paying particular attention to the way writers constructed their arguments and supported their ideas. Then they wrote a short letter to the editor of one of those newspapers about a selected editorial that had interested them. The letter was written in some critical and analytical way on the selected editorial—its development or its use of evidence. Completing these preliminary exercises, students learned that editorial writers, working under space constraints, cannot use lengthy quotations, that they must rely on their own rigorous thinking about the issue being considered, and they often must make assumptions about their readers, figuring out what must be rigorously explained and what can merely be claimed.

Finally, students wrote their own editorials. They were asked to select a controversial topic that not only interested them but also tapped into their experience. They were encouraged to think locally rather than globally—to look around them on campus to see what might need writing about or to look back on their experiences for a controversial issue worthy of analysis. The evidence for their argument would come from their own experience and investigation, newspaper or magazine articles they had read, and available Internet sources they considered reliable. But they knew that they would have to use written sources sparingly and effectively, that the weight of persuasion would come from clear, reasonable thinking.

2   A student essay

Consider now Christopher Christian's essay "Medical Marijuana." On your first reading, look for what you think is his leading idea, or thesis, and for the types of evidence that he uses to develop that thesis:

Last Friday, as I returned to my dorm after spending a long day at work, I   1
noticed a group of people on the sidewalk, holding up posters and chanting slogans. Coming closer, I saw that the signs they held up said, "Medical Marijuana Now!" I shrugged to myself; though I am not fervent on this issue, I do support the legalization of marijuana for certain medical conditions. I am a certified nursing assistant. I used to work on the medical/surgical/oncology floor at my hospital. About a third of my patients had cancer in some form, and I've seen what terminal illness looks like. I trust the doctors that take care of these patients to make medical decisions in the best interest of the patient. I see no reason why the public's opinion of a drug should control a licensed physician's ability to do what he feels is best for the patient.

Walking through the gauntlet of demonstrators, I realized that one, a   2
disheveled man who looked around forty, was approaching me. "Legalize Medical Marijuana!," he shouted at me, though he only stood an arm's length away. Not wanting to take the time to explain that I already supported medical marijuana, I chose instead to walk past this man and not take his pamphlet. A few seconds later, the protester yelled out after me, "You better hope you don't get cancer then!"

Last Tuesday, voters in four states and the District of Columbia had the oppor-   3
tunity to vote on a ballot initiative to legalize marijuana for medical conditions. The fact that the ballots passed in all four states is meaningless for now, as the federal

government has struck down similar laws in two other states. Both HIV and cancer patient advocacy groups have been fighting for legalization for some time. For people in end-stage AIDS, marijuana helps combat the nausea they feel and relieves some of the side effects caused by the powerful antiviral medications given to AIDS patients. Wasting, a sad but common result of AIDS, is also reduced with marijuana. Cancer patients have to deal with nausea from two sources--the chemotherapy they receive to fight their tumors and the morphine given to them for their pain. Marijuana could help patients in these two groups. These proposed laws would allow doctors to prescribe marijuana to AIDS and cancer patients that they believe would be helped by the drug.

    Unfortunately, many activist groups are fighting this proposal. Barry McCaffrey, the nation's drug czar, has said, "Let's have none of this malarkey on marijuana smoking by cunning groups working to legalize drugs. American medicine is the best in the world for pain management." That medical marijuana use would somehow enable the widespread legalization of drugs is a common attack on the proposed laws. In a recent Reuters article, Gilbert Gallegos, president of the Fraternal Order of Police, is quoted as saying, "Those who would surrender the war on drugs surrender our children to addiction, surrender our neighborhoods to crime, and surrender our streets to violence." In a recent open letter to the American public former presidents George Bush, Gerald Ford, and Jimmy Carter urged defeat of the medical marijuana propositions. When I was caring for terminally ill patients at my hospital, I saw no one protesting our doctors' judgments to prescribe morphine, or Vicodin, or Demerol to patients to relieve their pain. Yet many citizens in this country fear that, given the opportunity, our doctors will turn us all into potheads.   4

    The fear of medical marijuana, fueled by an imagined connection between medical and recreational drug use, is the greatest obstacle to allowing terminally ill AIDS and cancer patients this beneficial drug. This fear is only heightened when the proponents of medical marijuana act like children, shouting silly slogans at bystanders on the street. The protester who engaged me last Friday did not present our cause very well. I already supported medical marijuana, so his antics had no negative effect on me. Yet for those who are wavering on this issue, seeing the argument presented in that way will only convince them that the proponents of medical marijuana are merely using this issue as a stepping stone to recreational legalization.   5

What medical marijuana needs in order to become reality is calm, rational   6
debate firmly rooted in science and medicine. Those who support medical use of
marijuana should distance their arguments from those of various marijuana legalization groups to make this a discussion about terminally ill people and a physician-
prescribed medicine, not about a recreational drug. In an ideal world, a rational and
well-educated public would examine the scientific evidence about recreational
marijuana use and conclude that the laws against it cause more harm to users than
the drug itself. But since we don't live in this kind of world, we have to ask ourselves whose needs are more important: those who want to use marijuana recre-
ationally, whose battle for legalization will not be winnable anytime soon, or those
who seek to find relief from the suffering of terminal illness, whose cause could triumph with slightly more popular support.

3   Outlining—A way of understanding and evaluating arguments

Making an informal outline before you begin writing can sometimes help
you get started. But an outline after the fact of writing can also help you better
understand what you have written; a schematic representation sometimes
reveals flaws in logic or the need for clearer thinking and more evidence.

Our main concern here is to better understand Christian's argument.
Before turning to his thesis, however, let's outline the structure, or order, of
his thinking, paragraph by paragraph.

1 & 2   **Beginning:** Story + Christian's nursing credentials
3   **Middle:** Results of voting + complications with government
4   Opposing points of view + idea of fear
5   Fear associated with recreational use of marijuana and doctors' abuse
         when prescribing marijuana
6   **Ending:** Appeal for reason and distinction between uses of marijuana

With this structure in mind, reread the essay, looking for the connection
among the various parts of the essay (each of the paragraphs as well as the
beginning, middle, and ending) and for the overarching idea that holds the
essay together.

We know from the outset that Christian favors the use of medical marijuana; he tells us so in the first paragraph and repeats that fact throughout
the essay. We know too that he believes that doctors can be trusted to admin-

ister marijuana just as they would other pain-relieving drugs. But he does not belabor or support these claims with statistical evidence or examples— the first is a claim of fact; the second is a claim of value (whose unstated premise is that doctors are people who can be trusted to administer all medicine responsibly). His own argument takes as a given that marijuana can help cancer patients and AIDS patients, just as it takes as fact that doctors are competent to administer marijuana effectively and responsibly. Christian believes these two claims are true based on his own observations that were formed while working in the hospital.

Some readers may not believe these claims and will need more supporting evidence than Christian provides. Such evidence, as you will see, could indeed shore up what turns out to be his primary argument, but we do not need additional evidence to understand that argument—*the argument that fear of recreational marijuana and fear of doctors' ability to administer marijuana judiciously stand in the way of our reasonable consideration and support of the use of "medical marijuana."* Christian obviously believes that if we could get past those fears, reason would lead us all to support the use of marijuana for medical purposes.

Now let's look deeper into how this essay works. Consider again the various parts of the editorial, this time specifying just what Christian accomplishes in each part of the essay, along with a consideration of the nature of the evidence provided:

1–2   **Premise:** Marijuana, administered under doctor's supervision, produces positive results for AIDS and cancer patients.
Source: Personal experience/work.

3   **Premise:** Although voters in some recent elections have voted in favor of the medical use of marijuana, that will not ensure the legal use of the drug because the federal government has already struck down related laws in two states.
Sources: Newspapers and Internet.

4   **Premise:** There is considerable opposition to the medical use of marijuana by federal officials, police organizations, and former presidents.
Sources: Reuters (AP), Internet.
Premise: Fear (engendered by public officials and a general distrust of doctors) seems to be at the bottom of much opposition to the use of medical marijuana.

Sources: Christian's interpretations of his written sources, his own observations, and his own experiences as a hospital worker.

5   **Premise:** This fear of medical marijuana is exacerbated by the goofy behavior of some who support recreational use of marijuana and tie their claims to its medical benefits.

Source: Personal experience and observation.

6   **Thesis:** "What medical marijuana needs in order to become reality is calm, rational debate firmly rooted in science and medicine. Those who support medical use of marijuana should distance their arguments from those of various marijuana legalization groups to make this a discussion about terminally ill people and a physician-prescribed medicine, not about a recreational drug."

Sources: Reason.

EXERCISE 7–4   Analyzing

1. Make yet another schematic representation of this argument that puts the *thesis* at the top of the diagram and the various supporting propositions beneath it. Assess the adequacy of the evidence and the thinking associated with each of the supporting premises and look at the relationship between the premises and the argument. Then, make an informed judgment about whether you consider the premises *reliable* and whether you consider the overall argument *reliable* (see p. 156, for more on reliability). If you do not consider it reliable, tell how to make it so. If you do consider it reliable, explain why.

2. Choose one of those premises from your first exercise that you think could be strengthened with more evidence. Go to the Internet or the library to investigate that premise. See if you can bolster Christian's argument by providing a telling piece of evidence that will not change the overarching idea, or thesis. Or, develop a more *reliable* thesis of your own and show in outline form how you would develop and support it.

3. Rewrite the ending of the first paragraph to more accurately foreshadow the actual thesis of this argument. Do so in only one or two sentences.

4. Written sources (from the library or Internet) are usually identified and cited within the context of an editorial. How well does Christian adhere to such a policy, and how does his work affect your sense of the reliability of his argument? Explain.

7f   Using written sources and documentation as evidence in longer essays

You will consider now a process for developing an argumentative essay that makes effective use of written sources. For this essay the instructor did not require formal library research but encouraged students to make use of a small group of assigned essay readings. These readings allowed students to learn more about both the assigned topic and the use of such texts to develop an argumentative essay. The texts provided knowledge about the subject, helped students identify and understand a controversy related to that subject, gave them practice in reflecting about and incorporating such texts in their own essays, and eventually served as evidence in those essays.

You will see how one student followed this process and created an argumentative essay about effective leadership. Considering what he does will give you a clearer sense of how to develop your own argumentative essay, regardless of the subject or the assigned or selected texts. In a more formal research project, you will most likely choose a subject, select the texts, and then follow a procedure similar to that shown in this section. (See Chapters 39 and 40 for more on the research process.)

Matthew Weishar was in a first-year writing class tailored to students who were studying business and culture. During this course students wrote about social and ethical problems associated with business in corporate America. As one of the required assignments, Weishar's teacher asked all students to develop a four- to six-page argumentative essay about a controversial aspect of leadership and corporate management.

1   Background reading and preliminary exercises

Class members spent a few weeks reading, writing about, and discussing a number of articles and essays from the course syllabus that helped them learn about leadership. These written sources provided the foundation for all of the preliminary writing exercises and class discussions. However, students were free to use other texts, their own experiences, and the Internet to find relevant information that might help them better understand corporate leadership.

A preliminary exercise to discover an idea

The preliminary writing that led to the final essay was designed to help students discover and develop a controversial idea about corporate leadership. One of the early writing exercises asked students to read Martin Luther King, Jr.'s "Letter from a Birmingham Jail" and to think and write about King's leadership as revealed in that essay. They would have to read closely because the "Letter" was not explicitly about the nature of leadership. In order to infer the nature of King's leadership, they would have to read between the lines. Students were encouraged to conduct research on the Internet if they did not understand the context in which Dr. King wrote the letter following his arrest in Birmingham, Alabama, for marching against racial injustice.

From their careful reading of the "Letter," their Internet searches, and their collaboration in class, students discovered that King's writing of the letter was a thoughtful, courageous act, carried out under adverse conditions. The struggle for racial equality and fair treatment took place against police threats, violence, and strong social opposition from large segments of the Southern population.

> **WWW**
> http://www.seattletimes.com/
> mlk/index.html
> Provides general information about Dr. Martin Luther King, Jr.

In their writing exercise students were first asked to *reflect* on the nature of King's leadership (as they understood it from his "Letter") by connecting with other things they had read and learned. They were also asked to discern whether King's leadership might *suggest* principles that could apply to corporate leadership.

Here is the concluding paragraph of Weishar's first writing exercise— his final reflection—where he brings King and corporate leadership together:

The qualities that Dr. King displayed in his letter are quite similar to those necessary for a corporate leader. Corporate leaders must realize that their actions may have far-reaching consequences. When acting for the sake of the stockholders (those who have invested in the corporation), a leader must acknowledge the effect corporate decisions will have on the other stakeholders (those whose lives and communities may be inadvertently affected by corporate decisions). A leader's social responsibility extends further than the bottom-line profit. In addition leaders must take pride in their position as leaders, not simply because it is a leadership position but because they are honored to be at the head of a movement, or a company, which they believe in so strongly. In order for leaders to motivate those beneath them, they themselves must be motivated. Perhaps, of most importance, a corporate leader must realize that he or she is part of a company, just as Dr. King was of SCLC [Southern Christian Leadership Conference], and must put its interests ahead of his or her own.

You will observe later that neither Dr. King's "Letter" nor this passage from Weishar's reflections makes its way directly into Weishar's essay, but you will also see that Weishar's discoveries about *motivation* and *a leader's personal investment* in his work will inform his own ideas about leadership in the final essay. This writing exercise helped Weishar identify his own interest in particular aspects of leadership.

Ultimately, Weishar must decide what to put in and what to leave out of his essay. The preliminary exercises encourage thinking and give him a chance to practice reading and writing about potential sources, but that preliminary writing does not necessarily end up in the essay. It does, however, provide background information and give him a chance to practice using the assigned texts as he wishes.

A second exercise to discover a controversy

A second *writing exercise* asked students to read a chapter from Margaret J. Wheatley's *Leadership and the New Science* and to select a passage from that chapter that interested them. They were asked to imagine the organizational implications (the effect on an organization's effectiveness) of Wheatley's ideas about innovative leadership. To encourage students to make connections among their readings, Weishar's instructor also required them to reconsider and make use of two of three other essays they were reading about leadership—Lao-Tzu's "Thoughts from the Tao-te Ching," Machiavelli's "The Qualities of a Prince," and King's "Letter"—as they formulated their two-to-three-page (double-spaced) response about Wheatley.

Here are Weishar's reflections. He begins with a short quotation from Wheatley's book. This quotation (called an epigraph) is selected to generate curiosity and to point the reader toward the ideas that will be worked out in his response to the writing exercise. You can see that Weishar's reflective piece begins to take on the quality of a draft essay—there is controversy; there is an attempt on Weishar's part to make sense of the controversy; and there are written sources that he incorporates and uses to help him think about and question Wheatley, his principal source in this exercise. But this writing is not yet an essay; it is a reflective piece about Wheatley's ideas and their relationship to other ideas. In it, Weishar is searching for his own idea, letting his mind play over the sources.

Instructor's comments and questions appear in the margin of this reflective piece. They are there to help Weishar as he goes from this piece to his draft:

> The Potent force that shapes behavior in these fractal organizations, as in all natural systems, is the combination of simply expressed expectations of acceptable behavior and the freedom available to individuals to assert themselves in non-deterministic ways.
>
> —Margaret J. Wheatley

While many people believe that an organization must have some type of structured form to be effective, that is not always the case. As Margaret Wheatley tells us in Leadership and the New Science, it is not necessary for an organization to have a highly detailed system for its employees to follow. In fact, an organization may even wind up hurting itself by implementing such a system. 1

The only type of structuring which an organization truly needs is some basic guidelines. These guidelines will give employees a sense of what the organization's goals are and to what limits they may go to achieve them. Any further attempt to limit the realm of the employees' actions may be unnecessary and may inhibit new ideas. As long as the basic guidelines are clearly stated, there will be a natural tendency for the people within the organization to conform to its expectations. As Wheatley states in regard to a properly organized system, "The structure is capable of maintaining its overall shape and a large degree of independence from the environment because each part of the system is free to express itself within the context of that system." 2

Do you have any evidence/examples to support your claims about these guidelines? Other than Wheatley's word?

It is essential for a leader to allow freedom of expression within his organization. He is the leader and should not feel that he has to prove it. His purpose is not to dominate his subordinates, but to guide them. In "Thoughts from the Tao-te Ching," Lao-Tzu stresses the importance of simplicity in 3

Nice use of Lao-Tzu.

ruling. He suggests that the best ruler is one who does not make himself stand out. "The master doesn't try to be powerful; thus he is truly powerful." The leader must give his employees a chance to come up with their own ideas. He or she must be confident that the employees will not overstep their boundaries and must be optimistic that they may come up with a new concept or idea that will prove to be beneficial to the organization as a whole.

What if they do not come up with new concepts?

When you allow people a certain amount of freedom, you   4
must acknowledge that they may tend to drift in their own direction of thought. Occasionally, their thoughts and actions may not conform to those of the organization. Yet, the leader must not be quick to frown upon such thoughts. Eventually, the people will become accustomed to the organizational guidelines and will most likely adapt. As Wheatley states, "Fluctuations, randomness, and unpredictability at the local level, in the presence of guiding or self-referential principles, cohere over time into definite and predictable forms."

Under what circumstances will they adapt?

We must realize that there are exceptions to almost   5
every rule, and that applies here as well. There are certain people who are so caught up in their own ideas that they may forget that their primary obligation is to the organization. These people require more direction than basic guidelines. Machiavelli believed very strongly that people need to be ruled by a strong authority. He felt that a leader should constantly emphasize his power and guide the people. He did not believe that a ruler should give his subjects much freedom to come up with their own ideas because those ideas might be in conflict with his own, leading to confrontation and chaos.

Although an organization's well-being is not as important   6
as that of an entire land, it does not want to have too much dissension within its ranks. It is not necessary for the leader to enforce strict rules, but it is essential for him to make clear the basic guidelines which govern the organization. If employees do not think that they will be able to stay within the limits of those guidelines, they should not be part of the organization.

In general, the benefits of allowing a large degree of free-   7
dom within the organization with only simple levels of

instruction will most likely have positive effects on the organization, if it has any at all. It will allow people to express their own ideas and broaden the pathway for innovation. Any extreme behavior will most likely be short lived, for as Wheatley states, "The power of guiding principles or values . . . are strong enough influencers of behavior to shape every employee into a desired representative of the organization."

Clearly, Weishar has been influenced by Wheatley's ideas about organizational flexibility and minimalist guidelines, and we can see that he understands the complexity of those issues by the way he brings in Lao-Tzu to reinforce Wheatley's ideas and Machiavelli to question them. We can see too, because of these conflicting viewpoints about flexibility and control, that Weishar has found a *controversial* issue related to leadership (see 4d). He is interested in the extent to which the people in an organization should be controlled and in the working relationship between a leader and those being led. Working from this controversy, he may be able to develop a leading idea or thesis for his essay.

A third exercise to develop concrete evidence and avoid generalities

The third *writing exercise* anticipates common weaknesses in many argumentative essays: their lack of concreteness and specificity, their tendency to generality. The exercise addresses a specific weakness in Weishar's reflections about Wheatley (see the instructor's final comment). In this exercise, students were asked to ground their thinking—to make it more concrete—by relating their emerging ideas to a leadership/management story from their own experience, assigned written sources, or information found on the Internet. They were asked to look for a telling moment from the corporate world where leadership and management played a significant part so that they could analyze that story against the theoretical texts they had been reading about leadership. Students were cautioned not to fabricate the story but to reconstruct and summarize a real-world situation and to reflect about it.

Weishar's story about the Corning Corporation eventually became his essay's introduction. You will see it beginning on p. 187.

2   Using stories and written texts to build the argument

Weishar had already learned about the essential elements of an essay from his earlier work during the semester. Those reflective writing exercises that you have just read about suggest that he is comfortable with what he has learned about developing ideas: questioning sources, writing as a means of discovery, making connections among sources, and considering controversies (see 4a-d). He had already written essays that required him to organize his presentation into three major sections—beginning, middle, and ending—and to develop his ideas using sufficient evidence (stories, written texts, clear analytical thinking) to make them interesting and compelling.

After Weishar had completed the writing exercises, discussed them with other students in class, considered the additional feedback from his instructor, and reviewed in his mind the essential Guidelines for Developing an Argumentative Essay (see p. 172), he was ready to draft and begin to refine his essay. Here in the beginning of his essay, you can see how Weishar uses

Guidelines for Selecting Evidence from Sources

1. Select evidence that clarifies and strengthens your own ideas, without ignoring evidence that complicates or calls into question your analysis.

2. Remember that you always have choices to make about what to put in and what to leave out from your sources.

3. Summarize or paraphrase your source, or select telling words, phases, or images to incorporate into your own sentences. (See 40d for more on summarizing, paraphrasing, quoting, and reflecting.)

4. Develop a system for keeping up with your sources and what you are borrowing from them. (See 1e and 40d for more on notetaking, 7g and 41 on avoiding plagiarism.)

5. Keep in mind that you will be subordinating that evidence to your own ideas as you select evidence and prepare to write. The *quality* of the evidence and *what you think* about that evidence are more important than quantity.

the story about Corning from the third writing exercise to set up his argument. He uses the conventions of documentation here and in his final essay to identify within parentheses his sources. (See Chapter 43 for more on documentation.)

Weishar also follows the guidelines listed in the boxes on pages 185 and 186 for selecting and incorporating his written sources into the essay. You too should follow these guidelines to ensure that you quote accurately, establish clear relationships between your evidence and your thesis, document your sources, and avoid plagiarism.

These additional guidelines should help you as you *incorporate* selected evidence into your own essays.

Guidelines for Incorporating Selected Evidence

1. Always assume that your readers have not read your sources or shared your experiences, or that they do not know what it is that you want them to know about those sources.

2. Introduce your written or visual evidence to your readers by naming both the source (title) and the writer or artist who created it.

3. Cite sufficient evidence of written sources—in the form of summary, paraphrase, or quotation—so that your readers can easily grasp the sources' meaning and its importance. Aim always for the essential, avoiding long block quotations.

4. Distinguish your own thoughts and ideas from those in the sources that you cite. Pay particular attention to the way you move from a summarized source back to your own reflections.

5. Find words to describe visual sources that will permit your readers to see the source. Avoid cluttering details.

6. Shape your evidence for experiential sources (stories, anecdotes, tales) so that your readers see the relationship between evidence and idea.

7. Reflect on your selected evidence so that your readers can understand it outside the context of its original source and can also comprehend the relationship between evidence and idea. (See 40i for more on incorporating evidence into research essays.)

Weishar's beginning paragraphs

In 1993 Corning, a technology company headquartered in the foothills of   1
the Appalachian mountains, decided to re-engineer itself after its market value
plunged by a quarter late in the year ("Re-engineering" 437). That year Corning had
also suffered a $15.2 million loss. This loss occurred mainly because falling prices
were putting pressure on all of Corning's core businesses to reduce costs. Nevertheless, Corning knew something had to be done to turn the company around.

In the past, re-engineering had usually meant creating a drastic change within   2
the corporation. Most jobs were usually redesigned or eliminated completely. If
such a plan had been enacted by Corning, it could have had disastrous effects on
the town, since more than half of its inhabitants are employed by the firm. Fortunately, James Houghton, chairman of Corning at the time, made it clear that he
would not permit the re-engineering of the company if it meant severe consequences for the town (438). Instead, he learned from the mistakes of other companies. He researched why past attempts at re-engineering had failed and made
every attempt he could to ensure that it would not happen at Corning.

The key element in Corning's plan was that it allowed the workers to do their   3
own re-engineering. In January 1994 management asked a number of its key
employees to take on the task of redesigning the company from top to bottom. They
provided them with a building to work in and told them to divide themselves up
into teams to look at processes, such as manufacturing and innovation. Although
there were outside consultants, they stayed in the background, allowing the
employees to make the decisions. In addition, Corning made sure that these
employees had easy access to senior management, thus affirming management's
commitment (437-38).

The changes which they devised have helped greatly to improve the company.   4
Managers claim that they can make decisions quicker and estimate that this less
drastic form of re-engineering could produce $50-60 million in savings over the next
three years. Also, the number of levels between Mr. Houghton, the chairman, and
the shop floor, have been cut, allowing for a more direct line of communication
between the workers and management (439).

These first four paragraphs of Weishar's essay tell the story of Corning's
re-engineering, including the anticipated results of the changes. This story is
primarily a *summary* of a short case study Weishar had read about in another

of his courses (see 40d-1 for more on summarizing). Although we can infer what Weishar thinks about Corning's re-engineering effort from what he has chosen to include in his summary, he has not yet given us his own analysis of Corning's effort. He has not yet suggested why—for the purposes of his essay—he has begun his argument with this story. Here, in the final paragraph of Weishar's beginning, he analyzes and reflects on Corning's effort (see 40d-4, for more on reflecting) and gives readers an explicit sense of his leading idea—which will be his thesis for the argumentative essay:

Although there must be some type of structural, hierarchical system within every corporation, Corning's case illustrates the importance and benefits of instill-　5
ing flexibility in that system. By giving the employees the power to make decisions which would directly affect them (as well as the corporation itself), Corning avoided a massive restructuring effort that would have most likely resulted in unhappiness within its ranks. Although management controls the majority of the power in any corporation, it should refrain from using its authority in any case where the company is perfectly capable of running itself. A manager, like any leader, is responsible for setting the guidelines and goals by and for which his or her corporation should be run. Yet running the corporation should be a united effort by all of the employees to achieve desired goals in the quickest and most effective way they see possible.

Those last three sentences—beginning with "Although management controls"—constitute Weishar's leading idea for the essay. Keep them in mind as you look at how he goes on to develop that idea in the essay's middle. Recall his earlier writing exercises where his ideas about invested leadership and organizational flexibility began to play on his mind. In the last sentences, you can begin to see the influence of those early discoveries that Weishar made while completing the writing exercises (see 4b for more on writing to find an idea).

Weishar's middle paragraphs: Drafting and revising

While a CEO clearly holds the highest position on the corporate hierarchical ladder, it is crucial that he not use his position to isolate himself from those beneath　6
him on that ladder. It is more sensible for him to allow freedom of expression within his organization. He is the leader and should not feel that he has to prove it. His purpose is not to dominate his subordinates, but to direct them. In "Thoughts from the Tao-te Ching," Lao-Tzu stresses the importance of simplicity in ruling. He sug-

gests that the best ruler is one who does not make himself stand out. "The master doesn't try to be powerful; thus he is truly powerful" (24). A manager should not need to establish himself as an authority figure. His power is implied and therefore he need not constantly remind his employees that he is superior to them. If he does, there is a good chance that they will feel intimidated and be less prone to express their thoughts or ideas, out of fear that they will be in contradiction with his. The leader will find that it is more beneficial to give his employees a chance to come up with their own ideas. He should be confident that they will not overstep their boundaries, and be optimistic that they may come up with a new concept or idea that will improve the organization as a whole. In Corning's case, the employees' ideas helped save the company and remarkably improve its performance.

This first paragraph from the middle of Weishar's essay serves as a transition from the *beginning* (expanding and reinforcing the leading ideas), but it also introduces new textual evidence (Lao-Tzu) to reinforce the importance of a good relationship between a leader and those under him. Notice especially the last sentence of this first paragraph where Weishar goes back to the Corning story to begin to *weave* the middle and the beginning of the essay together. You will see him do more of this weaving later in the essay.

The story about Kroger that you will read in the next paragraph did not appear in Weishar's first draft, but after a conference with his instructor, Weishar realized that he was *still being too theoretical without providing sufficient concrete evidence.* Therefore, he summarizes and adds this new story to substantiate his ideas about flexibility, limited hierarchy, and effectiveness.

Another company, Kroger, which is the second largest grocery chain in the country, was able to avoid being taken over, in part, because of the thousands of   7 cost-saving ideas that its employees generated. Kroger was the target of two leveraged buyout attempts, which, if successful, could have put the company in tremendous debt and caused the termination of thousands of jobs. Yet, through the cooperative efforts of the managers and employees, the company was able to ward off the bidders, sacrificing a minimal number of jobs and incurring much less debt than it would have had the bidders been successful. With the help of the employees, the managers were able to structure a deal which enticed employees to increase their ownership of the company, while also increasing their participation in decision making, and together they were able to minimize downsizing to only a 10% cut of the company's total operations (Faludi 435-36).

   It is clear that Lao-Tzu's concept of "simplicity in ruling" can be very beneficial   8 to a company. As Margaret Wheatley tells us in her book Leadership and the New Science, it is not necessary for an organization to have a highly detailed system for its employees to follow (91-95). In fact, an organization may even wind up hurting itself by implementing such a program. She goes on to suggest that the only type of structuring which an organization truly needs is some basic guidelines. These guidelines give employees a sense of what the organization's goals are and to what limits employees may go to achieve them. Any further attempt to limit the realm of the employees' actions is generally unnecessary and may inhibit the development of new ideas.

   While Wheatley's strategy may seem good on a simplistic level, it lacks a cru-   9 cial element. It is not merely enough for a company to allow freedom of expression amongst its employees; it needs to encourage expression. Managers should open the lines of communication between themselves and their employees, letting them know that they not only allow employee input but also want it. In order for these exchanges to happen, both managers and employees must realize that it is okay to cross hierarchical boundaries. Just as an employee should not be the least bit hesitant to express his opinion on any aspect of the company and make suggestions for its improvement, a manager should not be hesitant to look to his employees for advice. After all, they are both working for a common cause--to see the company succeed.

   Look back at that last paragraph—Weishar's second paragraph devoted to Wheatley—and notice that at its very beginning, Weishar adds something to Wheatley's argument. He has discovered, by questioning Wheatley's thinking (see 4a), that she has overlooked an important concept. He wants to ensure that employees are encouraged to provide fresh ideas and notes that managers do not believe such ideas will just flow up the hierarchical ladder of their own accord.

EXERCISE 7–5   Reflecting

In paragraphs 7 and 8, Weishar is essentially *summarizing* two of his sources— one dealing with the Kroger story and the other dealing with Wheatley. In each instance, we can assume that he has distilled the essence of these sources without providing his own thoughts about them. In paragraph 9, he begins to be reflective, to let us see how he is thinking. Mark the place in the paragraph where you think the reflection begins and ends. Do you find his reflections effective? To what end? What would be the effect of eliminating Weishar's reflections from the paragraph?

Now, in this next paragraph Weishar turns his readers' attention to a concept of flexibility that you saw him dealing with in his preliminary writing exercises.

In order for there to be effective communication between both sides, the company must instill a certain degree of flexibility within its system. The day-to-day operations of a company should not be etched in stone. There is always a better way of doing something, and the company should never cease its efforts to improve itself. Wheatley suggests that as long as the basic guidelines are clearly stated, there will be a natural tendency for people within the organization to conform to its expectations. This will most likely hold true as long as both managers and employees realize that guidelines are not rules; or at least they shouldn't be. When developing an idea or a plan of action, the guidelines should definitely be considered, but they should not be the sole basis for thought. After all, sometimes the best ideas are the ones that seem the most outrageous.   10

Many people may feel that giving employees too much freedom within the context of company guidelines may be potentially hazardous to the company's success. Employees may spend too much time trying to be innovative and start to concentrate less on their current responsibilities. Yet, as business becomes increasingly global, and with that, more competitive, companies should always be looking to improve themselves to gain that extra edge over the competition. By encouraging employee input, managers take advantage of all of the resources available to them, and while doing so, better their relations with their employees. If employees feel that they are playing an integral role in the company's success, they will surely feel better about themselves and will most likely work more efficiently. As Wheatley states in regard to a properly organized system, "The structure is capable of maintaining its overall shape and a large degree of independence from the environment because each part of the system is free to express itself within the context of that system" (132). This theory has proven to be very accurate in practice. Corning allowed all parts of its company (system) to work together in a mutual effort to restructure itself, and found that it was very effective, greatly improving profits and employee morale.   11

In Kroger's case, management welcomed ideas from any of its employees about ways to avoid the takeover. The employees responded by coming up with ideas about how to cut costs to lessen the company's debt. They even agreed to have their own salaries cut so that there would be fewer layoffs. The employees' ideas were partly responsible for the survival and current success of the company. In both this case and Corning's, all parts of the "system" were free to express their ideas on the situation at hand, and ultimately, helped the company overcome its obstacles.

EXERCISE 7–6 Evaluating a Paragraph

1. In paragraph 11, how does Weishar anticipate and deal with his reader's objections?

2. Identify and write down from paragraph 11 what new twist Weishar adds to his network of ideas about leadership.

3. Name and list what you think Weishar does in paragraph 11 to *weave* the various parts of his essay's *beginning* and *middle* together.

4. Consider paragraph 11 in light of the paragraph definitions in 5f-2. Do you consider paragraph 11 an *informational* or a *transitional* paragraph? Or both? Explain. Could this paragraph serve as the *ending* for Weishar's essay? Explain.

Weishar's ending

Paragraphs 6–11 constitute the *middle* of his essay, the section where he develops and substantiates his idea using various written sources and his own clear-headed reflections. The next paragraph constitutes his *ending*, which should not only express his leading idea or thesis but also give us a fresh perspective on that idea as he leads us out of the essay while reminding us of crucial aspects of the work that he did in the middle of the essay. Here is Weishar's ending paragraph and the "Works Cited" list for his argumentative essay. (See Chapter 43 for more on documentation.)

The size of a corporation is not only an indication of its profits, but also of its   12
potential. As a company continues to grow and increase its number of employees it is, in effect, increasing its mental resources. Yet, it can only benefit from these resources if it allows them to be heard. For this to happen, the dividers that separate the managers from the employees must be eliminated. Both leaders and employees should step out of the corporate class system and realize that a corpora-

tion is a family, a large family, and that the family potential should be used to its advantage. Most people in the company want to see it succeed, and if management draws on the knowledge and ideas of thousands of employees, rather than just a select few, they stand a much better chance of succeeding.

Works Cited

Buchanan, Bruce S., Lamb, Robert B., and Smith, Roy C. Professional Responsibility: Markets, Ethics, and Law 1999-2000. 6th ed. Needham Heights: Pearson, 1999.

Faludi, Susan C. "Facing Raiders, Kroger Took Another Path." Buchanan, Lamb, and Smith 434-36.

Jacobus, Lee A. A World of Ideas: Essential Readings for College Writers. 5th ed. Boston: Bedford, 1998.

Lao-Tzu. "Thoughts from the Tao-te Ching." Jacobus 17-32.

Machiavelli, Niccolo. "The Qualities of the Prince." Jacobus 33-48.

"Re-engineering with Love." Buchanan, Lamb, and Smith 437-39.

Wheatley, Margaret J. Leadership and the New Science: Learning about Organization from an Orderly Universe. San Francisco: Berrett-Koehler, 1992.

In the last few sentences of the paragraph, Matthew creates an analogy between a corporation and a family as a way of highlighting the benefits that can be gained when family members are given an opportunity to have a say in the family. This new twist allows his readers to see his leading idea in a different light.

EXERCISE 7–7   **Evaluating an Ending**

1. In paragraph 12, does that new twist about the family clarify Weishar's leading idea for you, or does it confuse you? Explain.

2. Write down in your own words what you consider to be the leading idea (or thesis) of this essay.

3. Compare paragraphs 11 and 12 as possible endings for the essay. Which do you think is more effective? Explain in terms of the guidelines in 8f.

3   Outlining to see how you are thinking

Making an informal outline before you begin writing can sometimes help you get started (1f). However, as you have seen in this and preceding chapters, sometimes it is best just to start writing; you often do not know what you think about a subject until you begin writing about it. Once you have written a draft or a substantial number of sections, it will probably be helpful to create an outline of what you have written so that you can examine the structure of your thinking and your argument (see 7b).

An outline can reveal gaps in your thinking and organization; it can suggest interesting possibilities for revising and for filling in gaps in your thinking. (See 1f on outlining and mapping.)

Here is a brief outline of Weishar's work thus far.

Thesis: Contrary to common practice, corporations work best when they establish flexible work guidelines that create freedom and innovation in the workplace while encouraging employees to invest their full potential in the corporation's success.

First Premise: To ensure that a corporation is set up to receive ideas from its employees, the CEO should do everything possible to diminish hierarchical barriers.
Evidence: Lao-Tzu and Kroger story

Second Premise: Corporations do not need highly detailed systems to ensure productivity and efficiency; simple guidelines and diminished hierarchies work best.
Evidence: Wheatley

Third Premise: Guidelines and open communication are not sufficient by themselves; leaders must encourage through solicitation the free flow of ideas up the corporate ladder and around the workplace.
Evidence: Weishar's clear thinking

Fourth Premise: Effective communication depends on flexibility and freedom, constrained only by a necessity for employees to measure new ideas and innovations against the corporation's evolving guidelines.
Evidence: Weishar's clear thinking, Wheatley, Corning, and Kroger

This outline helps Weishar see that his two stories about Corning and Kroger ground and substantiate the theoretical ideas that he has borrowed and developed from Wheatley and Lao-Tzu. His essay does not simply repeat these sources, nor does it make one point and repeat it over and over through 11 paragraphs. Instead Weishar presents various aspects of his idea in different sections of the essay's *middle* and weaves those sections together as he goes along. Look back at each of the four premises to see how they differ from one another. Yet each is related to the larger idea he is developing.

Because the leading idea gets more interesting as the essay develops, you are more likely to keep reading. The movement from beginning to end is not static or simply repetitive; it is dynamic. Recall the way Weishar questions Wheatley's ideas in paragraph 8 of his essay; that questioning leads Weishar to give us more than Wheatley does. He borrows from Wheatley, but he adds to what he borrows. Throughout the essay, after Weishar introduces a source, you can see him thinking and reflecting about that source; he introduces it, explains it, and then relates it to his leading idea. Each source adds something slightly different to what he is telling us. Throughout the essay, Weishar goes back and forth, weaving sources together to form a whole. He begins with Corning, but he keeps referring back to that story as he does with Kroger and Wheatley. There is a pattern of variation and repetition that holds our interest.

From his outline, Weishar gets a clear glimpse of the way his mind has brought all of this material together; he can see the logical relationships among the parts of his essay. You can do the same with an outline of your drafts and final essay.

EXERCISE 7–8   **Questioning the Premises**

1. Consider each of Weishar's premises and reread his paragraphs. Group those paragraphs as you read, and list inclusive paragraph numbers beside each premise. List any questions you have about his premises and the evidence that he provides to support them. Think of your questions as a way of talking to Weishar, of giving him the advantage of better understanding his opposition.

2. Consider Weishar's argument about the importance of flexibility, diminished hierarchy, freedom of expression, and overall productivity in terms of Toulmin's claim, support, and warrant (7c-4). How does the argument measure up? Are there implied warrants about flexibility and productivity that remain unexamined? Or do you find Weishar's argument convincing, his support sufficient? Explain.

3. As you read each of Weishar's paragraphs, draw a line down the margin of his essay where you see him thinking and reflecting, where you see him adding value to his sources. Explain the effect on the essay if you eliminated all of those passages with a line beside them.

EXERCISE 7–9   Appraising Your Own Work

1. Create an outline for one of your own drafts. Identify the premise for each section of your essay as well as the evidence you include to substantiate each premise. Identify *gaps* in your presentation and consider ways of closing those gaps. Make notes to guide your future work.

2. Consider your argument in terms of Toulmin's claim, support, warrant. Are there any warrants that remain unsupported? Explain. Make notes.

3. Exchange drafts with a classmate and repeat requirements 1 and 2. Discuss your findings.

8   The Literary (Analytical) Essay

Writing essays about literature requires careful analysis as part of a critical reading of a literary work—a poem, play, story, novel, or essay, for example. To prepare for writing a literary analysis essay you can use the strategies you learned in Chapters 2 and 3, on critical reading and visual texts, respectively. You should also apply the writing skills you learned in working through Chapters 6 and 7 on exploratory and persuasive essays.

8a   Writing papers on literary works: The assignment

When writing a paper about a literary work, you should be clear about just what kind of essay or paper you want to write or have been assigned. There are various types of papers: a personal response (in which you express your feelings about a work), an analysis of an element or part of a work (a character analysis or an analysis of some other aspect of a work, such as its imagery or structure), an interpretation, a review, or an evaluation, to name several. You also should be clear about whether you need to consult secondary sources.

Primary sources include original works of writers and artists, original

http://vos.ucsb.edu
Provides an extensive list of resources in the humanities.

historical documents, data, and observations based on experiments and case studies. **Secondary sources** are interpretations and explanations of primary sources, often in the form of books and articles. In literature, for example, primary sources include poems, plays, novels, stories, and essays. In art, primary sources are paintings, drawings, etchings, engravings, sculptures, and works of architecture. Other primary sources in the arts include musical scores and the scripts of plays. The texts of Shakespeare's plays, for example, are primary sources, whereas interpretations of the plays constitute secondary sources. (For information on using primary and secondary sources, see 39c.) Check with your instructor if you have questions about the requirements of a writing assignment or about the use of primary and secondary sources.

1   Analyzing a poem

In literature courses you may be asked to analyze a poem as an exercise, a writing requirement, or as part of a longer assignment on a broader topic. We will illustrate one way to go about writing a brief analytical paper on a sonnet by Shakespeare. The focus is on the poem's images.

Here is the sonnet:

That time of year thou may'st in me behold
When yellow leaves, or none, or few, do hang
Upon those boughs which shake against the cold,
Bare ruined choirs where late the sweet birds sang.
In me thou see'st the twilight of such day
As after sunset fadeth in the west,
Which by-and-by black night doth take away,
Death's second self that seals up all in rest.
In me thou see'st the glowing of such fire
That on the ashes of his youth doth lie,
As the deathbed whereon it must expire,
Consumed with that which it was nourished by.
    This thou perceiv'st, which makes thy love more strong,
    To love that well which thou must leave ere long.

2   Making a list

One of the simplest ways to prepare yourself to write an analysis is to list items that relate to your topic—in this case the imagery of

Shakespeare's sonnet. The following list of details includes most of the poem's key images:

year	yellow leaves
few (leaves)	boughs which shake
cold	bare ruined choirs
sweet birds (song)	twilight . . . day
sunset (fading)	black night
glowing fire	ashes
deathbed	youth

Such a list can help you isolate and identify particular kinds of details. You might notice, for example, that the poem includes images of cold and warmth, of time and of death. It helps to group the images that focus on one aspect or element. This organization can help you focus your topic and see which of the images are central to the poem's meaning as you interpret it. Here is a list of images similar to the first, but this time with the images grouped according to their focus on either cold and warmth or time and death:

Cold/Warmth	**Time/Death**
cold	time of year
yellow leaves	bare ruined choirs
sweet birds (song)	twilight
sunset	west
black night	black night
glowing fire . . . ashes	youth
deathbed	deathbed
nourished	consumed

Notice, how as you begin to sort images, some images belong to both categories. Notice, too, how additional elements are added to this second, more organized list of details. The very act of focusing this way helps you begin to see better the way images work in the poem. But to bring this list of related images into even sharper focus, you need to make inferences about the meaning of the related images. The techniques of critical reading you learned in Chapter 2 are relevant here. And so are the strategies for preliminary writing, such as freewriting, that you learned in that chapter.

Here is a sample of freewriting about Shakespeare's sonnet that focuses on its images. The thoughts are somewhat disconnected, as typically occurs in freewriting. But as often also occurs in freewriting, a writer begins to ask questions and identify promising leads that can result in discovering an idea about the poem.

Freewriting Sample

That time of year--when leaves fall--autumn. Speaker compares self to season. Seasons of life--shift from day to night. Night or twilight = Fall? Day = Life; Night = Death. Fire = Life; Ashes = death. Fire consumes what it is nourished by? What's this?

Sonnet structure--4 + 4 + 4 + 2. Four line units. Meaning? Focus of each set of 4? Meaning of couplet? Last line: love what you will lose?

Fire and burning and going out. Day, twilight, night. Link between these? Repeats In me thou see'st. What does the speaker mean by this? That he is like the images he describes--day into night; fire into ashes? That he's dying? That someone else is dying? That he will leave life--or that someone he loves he will lose to death?

EXERCISE 8–1   **Freewriting**
Read the following poem carefully a few times. First, make a list of the images you observe. Second, put those images into at least two categories. Third, do a short ten-minute freewrite about you thinking about the poem. Ask yourself some questions. Speculate about possibilities for meaning. Identify words, phrases, and lines that puzzle you.

Those Winter Sundays
Robert Hayden

Sundays too my father got up early
and put his clothes on in the blueblack cold,
then with cracked hands that ached
from labor in the weekday weather made
banked fires blaze. No one ever thanked him.

I'd wake and hear the cold splintering, breaking.
When the rooms were warm, he'd call,
and slowly I would rise and dress,
fearing the chronic angers of that house,

Speaking indifferently to him,
who had driven out the cold

and polished my good shoes as well.
What did I know, what did I know
of love's austere and lonely offices?

3 Sample analysis of a poem

In moving from making a list, focusing on an aspect of a poem for analysis, and doing some freewriting about it to writing a more formal analysis requires mostly fine-tuning your thinking, deciding on how to organize your analysis, and refining your language. In the following sample analysis of the imagery in Shakespeare's sonnet, Michael Robertson focuses on how the images appeal to three senses: to sight, hearing, and touch. This becomes the basis for how the writer begins his analysis. But he organizes his analysis by picking up on something mentioned in the freewriting—the structure of the poem into three units of four lines each—three quatrains (though that technical term is not used in the sample analysis)—and a final, concluding couplet.

Notice how the writer does not simply list the images, but rather how he explains them. He explains how the images are related or linked in meaning, and how the images progress and build toward the idea and the feeling that Shakespeare conveys in the poem.

Sample Analysis: Shakespeare's Imagery in Sonnet 73

Perhaps the first thing to mention about the metaphorical language of the sonnet is that its central images appeal to three senses: sight, hearing, and touch. The images of the first four lines include appeals to each of these senses: we see the yellow leaves and bare branches; we feel the cold that shakes the boughs; we hear (in imagination) the singing birds of summer.

These images collectively become metaphors, ways of talking about one thing in terms of something else. Autumn, for example, is "that time of year" when leaves turn yellow and tree branches become bare of leaves. Shakespeare compares the barren branches to an empty choir loft because the chorus of singing birds has departed with the coming of colder weather. And because Shakespeare's speaker says that "you" (we) can behold autumn in him, we realize that he is talking about aging in terms of the seasons.

In lines 5-8 the metaphor of autumnal aging gives way to another: that of twilight ending the day. These lines describe the setting of the sun and the coming on of night. The emphasis here is on "black" night taking away the light of the sun; the sun's setting is seen as a dying of its light. The implied comparison of night with death is directly stated in line 8, where night is described as "death's second self." Like death, night "seals up all in rest." But while night's rest is temporary, the rest of death is final.

These metaphors of autumn and evening emphasize the way death comes on gradually. Autumn precedes winter and twilight precedes night just as illness precedes death. The poem's speaker knows he is in the autumn of his life, the twilight of his time. This metaphor is continued in a third image in lines 9-12 of the sonnet: the dying of the fire, which in its dying out of light and heat symbolizes the dying out of the speaker's life. In addition, the speaker's youth is compared with "ashes," which serve as the "deathbed" on which he will "expire."

Literally, these lines say that the fire will expire as it burns up the fuel that feeds it. In doing so, the fire glows with light and heat. The glowing fire then becomes a metaphor for the speaker's life, which is still "glowing," but which is beginning to die out as it consumes itself. Like the dying fire, the speaker's youth has turned to ashes. Also like the dying fire, the speaker's life is "consumed with that which it was nourished by." Literally, the fire consumes itself by burning up the logs that fuel it. The fire, like the speaker's life, in its very glowing burns towards its own extinction.

WRITING HINT   In any writing you do about literature and art, you will need to describe the work. In doing so you will use present tense, past tense, or both. In most instances, it is conventional to use present tense when describing literary works and works of art. Consider the following examples.

Vincent van Gogh's *The Starry Night* depicts a brilliantly lit night sky, in which stars *shine* with a burning light and the moon *glows* fiercely. [The verbs are all in the present tense because they describe the painting, which exists in a single time frame.]

In Robert Hayden's poem, "Those Winter Sundays," the speaker *reflects* on his father and *remembers* how much his father loved his family. [The verbs describing the speaker's actions are in the present tense; the verb describing the father (*loved*) is in the past—because the father's action is in the past, whereas the speaker's action occurs in the poem's present.]

(continued)

In his classic film *Battleship Potemkin,* the director, Sergei Eisenstein, *used* extreme close-up shots and other cinematic techniques such as montage to create startling visual effects. [The verb is in the past tense because the sentence describes the efforts of the director, not the work proper.]

EXERCISE 8–2   Annotating

Return to Robert Hayden's poem "Those Winter Sundays" on pages 199–200. Reread it and make some annotations, jotting some questions in the margins. Then look over your list of images and your freewriting about the poem to see what else you can add to them. Finally, convert your list and your freewriting into a 300–500-word analysis of Hayden's poem with a focus on its images. Remember to explain the significance of the images, and how the images convey the poem's meaning.

Like the exploratory and persuasive essays, the analytical essay has a beginning, a middle, and an ending. The analytical essay, however, is more direct than the exploratory essay. Its pace is brisker, its tone more businesslike and formal. The analytical essay is more of a presentation than an exploration. Instead of ambling along like a good story, it moves directly to the interpretive idea and the explanation of that idea. Your aim in an analytical essay is to convey what you learned through the analysis of a text.

The *purposes* for writing analytical essays vary, but primarily these essays give readers a chance to see the results of rigorous analytical work that you have done as part of the drafting. That work usually depends on the critical reading, questioning, and interpretation of a text, in this case, a literary work. The process of that reading, questioning, and interpreting is less evident in the analytical essay than in the exploratory essay, but the process

Features of the Analytical Essay

- Focuses on the writer's interpretation of a text—what it means and how it conveys meaning.
- Develops an idea about that interpretation in an interesting, formal way.
- Is more like a defense of the idea than an inquiry about it.
- Depends primarily on the text itself for evidence.
- Has a beginning, a middle, and an ending.

is reflected indirectly by the way you establish relationships between the text you have read and what you have to say about that text, between your evidence and your claim. The accompanying chart, Features of the Analytical Essay, outlines the main characteristics of the analytical essay.

A second chart, Analytical Methods and Objectives, outlines the principles of analysis and will help you stay focused on your analysis. (See also 2c and 2d on analysis and interpretation.) Let us turn to the tasks of analyzing and writing about the results of your analysis.

Analytical Methods and Objectives

- Think of the analytical process as an attempt to take a text apart so that you can bring it together again in your mind's eye.
- Read the text closely to see how it works and what you think it means. Notice details and their relationships.
- Work to discover and question the text's inherent ideas—what you think the text is about (see Chapters 2 and 3).
- If the text reminds you of other texts or ideas that you have read, analyze those texts and ideas.
- Your primary objectives are to understand the text being analyzed and to account for that understanding in an essay.

8b   Developing an analytical essay

Let us see how such an analysis might take place from start to finish—from analyzing a text to writing an essay about it. The analysis is of a written text, "Old Mrs. Grey," a brief essay written by Virginia Woolf. Ruth Chung, a student, selected the essay as her text for analysis because she found it interesting and intellectually challenging. Every time Chung read the essay and made discoveries about how it works, she became more interested in it. Each reading led Chung to more knowledge about the text and a clearer sense of its meaning.

When you are aiming to create an analytical essay, the process of reading is always followed by the process of writing. The processes of reading and writing inform and depend on one another. The Guidelines for Developing an Analytical Essay on p. 204 will help you create your own essay.

Guidelines for Developing an Analytical Essay

- Notice **details** within the text—a vivid image, phrase, word, anything that strikes you. Keep track of insights, connections, questions and observations in a reading journal or double-column notebook (see 1e-1 and 2b-3).

- Reflect on your questions and observations, and think about *how* the text works and *what* it means.

- Reread the text, considering your observations in relation to one another. Note the connections you find (see 4c).

- Select one detail from the text that interests you, and write a paragraph or two explaining what that detail has to do with the meaning of the text.

- Let the analysis of one selected detail lead you to analyzing other related details. These groupings or clusters of details often lead to deeper insight about a text.

- Collaborate and revise with your readers in mind. (See 1d on audience, 1h on collaboration, and 1g on revision.)

- Write a beginning for your essay that focuses readers' attention on your idea and the points that your analysis will reveal.

- Revise the middle—the analysis about detail and meaning as well as your interpretation—of the essay.

- Write an ending that offers a final perspective on your interpretation.

1   Reading Woolf's "Old Mrs. Grey"

Read Woolf's essay from start to finish, making notes of your own in the margins or in a reading journal. Later, you can compare your response with Chung's to see if you followed a similar process. Keep in mind that this is an essay you are reading, not a short story. Woolf makes her argument in subtle ways, using storytelling just as an exploratory essayist might and incorporating visual details, or images, to allow you to see part of what she conveys. As you read through Woolf's essay for the first time, place a check mark in the margin when some detail in the text seems vivid and interesting. Pay attention to the way Woolf repeats some of the details. Think about meaning as you read.

Old Mrs. Grey

Virginia Woolf

There are moments even in England, now, when even the busiest,   1
most contented suddenly let fall what they hold—it may be the week's
washing. Sheets and pajamas crumble and dissolve in their hands,
because, though they do not state this in so many words, it seems silly to
take the washing round to Mrs. Peel when out there over the fields over
the hills, there is no washing; no pinning of clotheslines; mangling and
ironing; no work at all, but boundless rest. Stainless and boundless rest;
space unlimited; untrodden grass; wild birds flying; hills whose smooth
uprise continues that wild flight.

Of all this however only seven foot by four could be seen from Mrs.   2
Grey's corner. That was the size of her front door which stood wide
open, though there was a fire burning on the grate. The fire looked like a
small spot of dusty light feebly trying to escape from the embarrassing
pressure of the pouring sunshine.

Mrs. Grey sat on a hard chair in the corner looking—but at what?   3
Apparently at nothing. She did not change the focus of her eyes when
visitors came. Her eyes had ceased to focus themselves; it may be that
they had lost the power. They were aged eyes, blue, unspectacled. They
could see, but without looking. She never used her eyes on anything
minute and difficult; merely upon faces, and dishes and fields. And now
at the age of ninety-two they saw nothing but a zigzag of pain wriggling
across the door, pain that twisted her legs as it wriggled; jerked her body
to and fro like a marionette. Her body was wrapped round the pain as a
damp sheet is folded over a wire. The wire was spasmodically jerked by
a cruel invisible hand. She flung out a foot, a hand. Then it stopped. She
sat still for a moment.

In that pause she saw herself in the past at ten, twenty, at twenty-five.   4
She was running in and out of a cottage with eleven brothers and sisters.
The line jerked. She was thrown forward in her chair.

"All dead. All dead," she mumbled. "My brothers and sisters. And   5
my husband gone. My daughter too. But I go on. Every morning I pray
God to let me pass."

The morning spread seven foot by four green and sunny. Like a fling   6
of grain the birds settled on the land. She was jerked again by another
tweak of the tormenting hand.

"I'm an ignorant old woman. I can't read or write, and every morning   7
when I crawls downstairs, I say I wish it were day. I'm only an ignorant
old woman. But I prays to God: O let me pass. I'm an ignorant old
woman—I can't read or write."

So when the colour went out of the doorway, she could not see the   8
other page which is then lit up; or hear the voices that have argued,
sung, talked for hundreds of years.

The jerked limbs were still again.   9

"The doctor comes every week. The parish doctor now. Since my   10
daughter went, we can't afford Dr. Nicholls. But he's a good man. He
says he wonders I don't go. He says my heart's nothing but wind and
water. Yet I don't seem able to die."

So we—humanity—insist that the body shall still cling to the wire. We   11
put out the eyes and the ears; but we pinion it there, with a bottle of
medicine, a cup of tea, a dying fire, like a rook on a barn door; but a rook
that still lives, even with a nail through it.

EXERCISE 8–3 Questioning the Essay
Reread Woolf's essay and devise your own questions about textual details. For
example, Chung wondered what Woolf meant by *our*—by humanity's—relationship to Mrs. Grey. In your reading journal, keep track of your questions and any
details from the text that help you respond to those questions (see 1e-1 on the
reading journal).

2 Questioning "Old Mrs. Grey"

During her second reading, Chung thought about the three-part structure of Woolf's essay—the beginning, middle, and ending that all essays
have. Chung was looking for suggestions in Woolf's first paragraph, her
beginning, that pointed to something in the middle of the essay (see 4a for
more on questioning). In more specific terms, Chung noticed in paragraph
1 that Woolf repeats the words *boundless rest* twice; she refers to *space unlimited* and *wild flight*. Chung saw traces of those images of freedom and
expansiveness in the rest of the essay, and she wanted to know what they
suggest about Mrs. Grey. She looked for references to freedom as she read
through the essay and noticed that although Woolf brings up the notion of
freedom, she also alludes to the notion of entrapment. Chung wondered

just what those details about freedom and entrapment reveal about Mrs. Grey's state of mind.

Chung also noticed that Woolf often compares two things as a way of revealing more about one of them. For example, in paragraph 3, Woolf compares Mrs. Grey's predicament to that of a marionette. Chung asked herself a series of questions about that comparison: Why does Woolf make that comparison? How does she use it and extend it within the essay? What does she gain by extending it beyond the paragraph where she first suggests it? What keeps jerking on those imaginary strings attached to Mrs. Grey? Are they really imaginary? Do we—humanity—have anything to do with the jerking?

Chung was struck by the images of flight and freedom that occur throughout the essay. She was particularly interested in the birds in paragraph 1 and the rook (the black bird) in paragraph 11. She wondered what those birds have to do with Mrs. Grey. Chung also noted Woolf's use of the light and fire in paragraph 2 and the many references to Mrs. Grey's eyes in paragraph 3. She wanted to see whether those details reappeared in other places within the essay.

The last paragraph seemed different from the rest of the essay. Chung reread the essay for details that might help her understand how Woolf's ending relates to what goes before it.

3 Analyzing textual details—The middle

As Chung reflected on her questions, she was struck by Mrs. Grey's desire to escape pain and suffering, and Woolf's use of certain details to highlight her suffering and longing. Chung's focusing question, the question that led her to consider the meaning of the entire essay, became: What is the relationship between these textual details about suffering and longing and Woolf's suggestion in the last paragraph about who causes the suffering? The answer to that question would more than likely become Chung's thesis—the idea she would explain and defend in an analytical essay.

Chung discovered that the details about suffering and longing fell naturally into groupings—details about the house, light, pain, mental anguish, and blame. She started to write the essay's middle to discover the relationships between the textual details in each of those groupings. Chung wrote first about how Woolf uses the house and landscape to convey Mrs. Grey's state of mind. Here is Chung's first middle paragraph.

Chung's first middle paragraph: An analysis of textual details

Throughout the essay, Woolf uses Mrs. Grey's house and the landscape outside 2 to describe the old woman's mental state. Woolf's description of the house and the rolling fields and hills seems to be just another picturesque view of England's countryside. From the context of Mrs. Grey's pain and her desire to die, however, the house, with its door wide open, may represent her body on the verge of death. The comparison may run still deeper. Woolf describes Mrs. Grey's mind as open and ready to be enveloped and swallowed by death's rays. It also follows that the image of the fields and hills, described as places of "stainless and boundless rest; space unlimited; untrodden grass; wild birds flying," comes to represent the pure, unblemished paradise, the haven from pain for which Mrs. Grey yearns. It could also simply be a representation of death, a state of being (or not being) that everyone must eventually face, a time when "even the busiest, most contented suddenly let fall what they hold."

In this paragraph, Chung is beginning to sort through the details she selected from the text. Notice that she sometimes provides a **summary** of (explains in her own words) what she observes in the text: "Woolf describes Mrs. Grey's mind as open and ready to be enveloped and swallowed by death's rays." At other times, Chung uses Woolf's words, placing them in quotation marks to indicate that they come directly from "Old Mrs. Grey." Chung combines summaries and quotations as she analyzes how Woolf uses the image of the house to represent Mrs. Grey's state of mind. As Chung continued to write and think about the textual details, she realized that Mrs. Grey was longing to die. She discovered that Woolf indicates that longing in her references to light. Chung continued her analysis, focusing on Woolf's use of light.

Chung's analysis of other textual details

Woolf further describes Mrs. Grey's longing for death using light as a symbol to 3 enhance our understanding of that longing. Through the seven-foot-by-four opening of Mrs. Grey's front door, sunshine pours in from the outside, putting "embarrassing pressure" on the fire burning in the grate, which appears "only as a small spot of dusty light feebly trying to escape." Here, the fire burning in the grate may represent the appeals and delights of life, which have become dreary to Mrs. Grey when compared to the lure of the afterlife, the sweet respite of death, as represented by the streaming sunshine from outside. Mrs. Grey is so enamored by the prospect of going to such a paradise of rest and relief that living for the present becomes pointless; it seems silly to do the week's wash "when out there over the fields over the hills, there is no washing; no pinning of clotheslines; mangling and ironing; no work at all."

The idea of a new life dawning is also represented by "morning spreading   4
seven foot by four green and sunny," which tries to infiltrate the house and beckons to Mrs. Grey through the front door. Mrs. Grey welcomes this light as much as she welcomes death, but the light has not yet been able to permeate the whole house. She has put so much hope into this state of rest that "when the colour went out of the doorway, she could not see the other page which is then lit up." This "other page" represents Mrs. Grey's present chapter of life, which has potential, even in her pain, to be enjoyable and fulfilling. But Mrs. Grey can see this life only as she sees the fire burning in the grate, which becomes dim in the light of her suffering and pain. She is so weary of her life that "her eyes had ceased to focus themselves . . . They could see but without looking." It isn't that she is physically blind, but that her pain is so great that it is all she can see. It could also be that nothing in her present life seems to be worth looking at because she cannot appreciate the little pleasures of life: "She had never used her eyes on anything minute and difficult; merely upon faces, and dishes and fields."

Chung brings textual details into her paragraph to help account for how Woolf uses those details in her essay. Throughout the three middle paragraphs, Chung remains focused on Mrs. Grey's longing for death, and she repeatedly demonstrates how the textual details substantiate her claim. Revealing that relationship between the textual details and the thesis is Chung's primary writing task, just as it will be yours when you write an analytical essay.

4   Collaborating to enrich the analysis

Although these are fine analytical paragraphs, Chung's work group had some questions about them. Students wanted to know more about the relationship between the textual details and Chung's idea about Mrs. Grey's longing for death. They were not so much interested in more details as they were in more analysis, more thinking.

As a way of illustrating how that kind of feedback from the work group can lead to revision and a richer analysis, let us look at a place in Chung's third paragraph that caught the work group's attention.

Here, the fire burning in the grate may represent the appeals and delights of life, which have become dreary to Mrs. Grey when compared to the lure of the afterlife, the sweet respite of death, as represented by the streaming sunshine from outside. Mrs. Grey is so enamored by the prospect of going to such a paradise of rest and relief that living for the present becomes pointless.

The first sentence in this excerpt is Chung's first interpretative leap in the paragraph, her first attempt to analyze and explain the textual details about light from Woolf's essay. When the members of the work group read that paragraph, they wanted to know more about what Chung meant in the sentence. They suggested that she separate that sentence from the one following it—creating blank space on the computer screen or page on which she was writing—and fill in the space with more analysis or explanation. Chung's revisions appear here underlined.

Chung's revision

Here, the fire burning in the grate may represent the appeals and delights of life, which have become dreary to Mrs. Grey when compared to the lure of the afterlife, the sweet respite of death, as represented by the streaming sunshine from outside. That sunshine is actually life-giving even though it is calling Mrs. Grey to death. Death, Woolf seems to be suggesting, is preferable to the life of pain that Mrs. Grey must endure. There is a sweeter, more peaceful life in death. The sunlight outside the door beckons, offering promise, relief, "stainless and boundless rest." Mrs. Grey is so enamored by the prospect of going to such a paradise of rest and relief that living for the present becomes pointless.

In her revision, note how Chung more fully explains the connections she sees within Woolf's essay.

EXERCISE 8–4 **Analyzing and Revising**

1. Look back through Chung's three middle analytical paragraphs and select a spot where you would like more explanation about one of her interpretative

sentences. Revise that section by filling in what you think Chung is suggesting. Add only your thoughts, not more textual detail.

2. Each of Chung's paragraphs ends with a quotation. Select one of those paragraphs and, after the quotation, add a sentence or two of explanation that helps readers see more clearly what you think the quotation means. Write your explanatory sentences in the context of what you think Chung is trying to say in the paragraph. In essence, help Chung complete her paragraph.

5 Writing the beginning

Chung's analysis of Woolf's essay leads her finally to a consideration of the intensity of Mrs. Grey's pain and weariness. After writing about the images of pain scattered throughout the essay, Chung turns to Woolf's last paragraph and her claim that humanity is responsible for prolonging Mrs. Grey's suffering. All of Chung's analysis (about the house, light, pain and mental anguish, and blame) becomes the middle of her essay. In the middle, Chung offers her interpretation of "Old Mrs. Grey," her idea about how the textual details of the essay suggest that Mrs. Grey would be better off dead and that humanity needlessly prolongs her suffering. That idea is the thesis of Chung's essay—the point she must defend.

Having written the middle of her essay, Chung is ready to write a beginning that will interest readers in her analysis of "Old Mrs. Grey" and, at the same time, suggest her thesis. Here is the draft of her beginning.

Chung's beginning

In her essay "Old Mrs. Grey," Virginia Woolf paints a picture of a ninety-two-year-old woman whose supreme desire is to die. There is no action or movement in this portrait; Mrs. Grey merely sits alone in a corner of her house. Woolf's short, page-long description not only depicts the sufferings of a single individual but of the old and the grey in general. And yet it is clear that the purpose of this piece is more than the extraction of sympathy. Woolf expresses her view that a life of such suffering is not worth living. She asserts that the physical and mental agonies of old age should not be prolonged on humanitarian grounds.

Chung's direct, succinct beginning orients readers; it gives them a sense of Woolf's essay and indicates what Chung thinks it means. Although Chung's introduction is good as is, she could improve it by giving her readers some clues about what the middle of her essay, where she substantiates her thesis about suffering and the reward of death, will contain. Readers usually like to know early on how textual details will contribute to their understanding of an essay's idea.

You can often convey how the textual details support your interpretation in a single thesis sentence such as: *Woolf does not make this assertion straight out; rather, she makes it through the suggestive details in her essay.* Chung could place that sentence at the end of her beginning paragraph, pointing the way to her own analysis of Woolf's use of suggestive details.

6 Writing the rest of the middle and the ending

The ending for an analytical essay, as for every essay, must account for what has gone on in the middle. It cannot, of course, rehash all of the detailed analysis, but it must represent the essence of that analysis and provide a fresh perspective—yours. Because the ending must express a full understanding of the middle, you should write it last or when you are almost finished with your analysis.

Drafting the middle

To understand Chung's ending, you need to see the rest of her analysis—the final three paragraphs of the middle. Here are paragraphs 5, 6, and 7 of the middle. They focus on the intensity of Mrs. Grey's pain. After writing and revising these middle paragraphs, Chung was able to move on to two drafts of an ending (as we will see later).

Chung's final three middle paragraphs

However, it is not fair to take Mrs. Grey's suffering lightly either, for she suffers 5 excruciating pain. Woolf compares her pain to a sadistic snake: "a zigzag of pain, wriggling across the door, pain that twisted her legs as it wriggled; jerked her body to and fro like a marionette." Woolf also speaks of a sharp, cutting pain by describing Mrs. Grey's body as being "wrapped around the pain as a damp sheet is folded over a wire . . . spasmodically jerked by a cruel invisible hand." The startling image of Mrs. Grey that these comparisons create, of her body writhing, twisting like a live wire, shows the sufferings the elderly must endure and explains Mrs. Grey's state of mind, her unexpected eagerness for death.

Woolf gives readers further insight into Mrs. Grey's mental anguish by taking   6
us into her mind as well as allowing us to hear what she has to say. Mrs. Grey looks
back to her active childhood, her entrance into the adult world, and the time spent
with her eleven brothers and sisters. But these memories can only bring her sorrow
and loneliness when she compares those times to the present. She is literally jerked
back to reality by a convulsion: "The line jerked. She was thrown forward in her
chair." Her old body is sick and deteriorating and all of her siblings have died; she
has even survived her husband and her children.

The tone of Mrs. Grey's voice as she mumbles is not bitter, for she has no   7
energy to complain. Woolf's fragmented sentences reflect Mrs. Grey's tiredness as
though she doesn't have even enough energy to speak: "'All dead. All dead . . . My
brothers and sisters. And my husband gone. My daughter too. But I go on.'" Her
words also have an almost Mother Goose-rhyme quality to them: "'I'm an ignorant
old woman. I can't read or write, and every morning when I crawls downstairs, I say
I wish it were day'" This suggests a regression into a childish state, or into senility,
but the words are coherent, expressing her feelings of debilitation and inadequacy.
While her words have no hint of bitterness in them, they evoke pity. Her daily sup-
plications to God--"'O let me pass'"--show how desperately she yearns to be
relieved of her suffering. The thought of Mrs. Grey crawling downstairs and falling
into bed by herself every day is especially poignant and helps readers understand
Mrs. Grey's fatigue and loneliness.

Drafting the ending

The first draft of Chung's ending is the weakest part of her essay. As you
will see, she has not completed her analysis. She tries to finish that analysis
and end her essay in the same paragraph. Avoid this common pitfall; essays
require a separate ending.

Read the following paragraph with this question in mind: How well
does Chung's ending account for the analysis presented in her essay?

Chung's ending: First draft

In the last paragraph of her essay, Woolf concludes by seeming to lay the blame   8
for Mrs. Grey's suffering on humanity, again using comparisons. She asserts that it
is the hand of humanity that jerks so cruelly on the wire of pain, that "puts out the
eyes and the ears," that "pinions" the bodies of the elderly on those wires of pain by

trying to keep them alive. The elderly are like tortured birds, pinned to a barn door, like "a rook that still lives, even with a nail through it." Woolf suggests that we, humanity, are responsible for prolonging their sufferings by caring for them and by trying to ameliorate their lives "with a bottle of medicine, a cup of tea, a dying fire." In a way, it seems as if Woolf is not really blaming humanity for the sufferings of the elderly but merely reprimanding us for not being aware of them. Or perhaps she is merely voicing her own ambivalence about the issue of euthanasia. And yet her strong language in the last paragraph and in other parts of the essay accuses us of being the active perpetrators of a crime, a crime that we could not help. If Woolf's intention for this essay was, indeed, to lay the blame on us for Mrs. Grey's pain, it is an invalid and unfair indictment, for Woolf demands that we be selfish and inhumane in order to be humane, to help the elderly by turning our backs on them. Woolf does not realize that even we, who accept the suffering of our parents and grandparents, accept it for our own futures as well as an immutable fact of life.

This is how Chung's instructor evaluated her ending: "Chung, you may have tried to do too much in this paragraph. You try to complete your analysis of 'Old Mrs. Grey'; you react to Woolf's idea about euthanasia and blame within the context of your own analysis; and, finally, you turn away from your focused analysis and judge Woolf's idea in an entirely new context." The final two sentences of Chung's ending provide the basis for another kind of essay, perhaps an exploration or an argument about who is to blame for the suffering of the older generation. Chung's essay is supposed to be about *how* Woolf develops her idea in "Old Mrs. Grey," not about the appropriateness or reliability of that idea. Remember always to stay focused on your thesis.

Consider Chung's revised ending. Her one long paragraph becomes two. The first of the revised paragraphs completes the analysis Chung was doing in the middle of her essay; the second revised paragraph constitutes the ending of her essay.

Chung's revised ending

In the last paragraph of her essay, Woolf concludes by laying blame for Mrs.   8
Grey's suffering on humanity. Again, she makes her point using comparisons. She asserts that it is the hand of humanity that jerks so cruelly on the wire of pain, that "puts out the eyes and the ears," that "pinions" the bodies of the elderly on those

wires by trying to keep them alive. The elderly are like tortured birds, pinned to a barn door, like "a rook that still lives, even with a nail through it." Woolf suggests that we, humanity, are responsible for prolonging their sufferings by caring for them and by trying to ameliorate their lives "with a bottle of medicine, a cup of tea, a dying fire." Our efforts to alleviate suffering inflict and prolong pain.

Perhaps Woolf is not really blaming humanity for the sufferings of the elderly but merely reprimanding all of us for being unaware of what we might be doing to cause such suffering. Perhaps she is merely voicing her own ambivalence about euthanasia. And yet her strong language in the last paragraph and her suggestive details throughout the essay suggest that Mrs. Grey is suffering unmercifully and that she longs to walk out that door of her house into those expansive fields to a new and deserved freedom. She longs to take flight, not to stay "pinioned" to a barn door. Woolf wants us to think about Mrs. Grey's pain and her desire, and she wants us to realize that our kindnesses toward the elderly may be misdirected. Woolf wants us to know that helping Mrs. Grey may very well mean helping her die.   9

EXERCISE 8–5   Analyzing the Revision

1. Are the two revised paragraphs more or less effective than the first draft of the ending (8b-6)? Explain your answer.

2. Now read Chung's entire essay (paragraphs 1–9). Assess how effectively Chung makes her case about the textual details and the idea she thinks Woolf is presenting. Annotate each paragraph, indicating where you think Chung does her analysis convincingly. When you think she needs to show either more thinking or more textual detail within the paragraph, mark those spots with the word *gap*. Bring your notes to class, where you should try to reach a consensus about the changes Chung might consider for her final version of the essay.

EXERCISE 8–6   Developing a Literary (Analytical) Essay

Select a text (a work of art, performance, or essay) and read or study it. You want to look into the way the text works. Make notes as you read or study. Write out questions as they come to you. As you look over your preliminary analysis, see if you can ask a focusing question—one that will take you to the heart of the text. Then, following the Guidelines for Developing an Analytical Essay on p. 204, write your own four- to six-page analytical essay about the text.

PART 3   GRAMMAR

9 *Basic Sentence Grammar*

A **sentence** is traditionally defined as a group of words that expresses a complete thought. The thought a sentence expresses involves a grammatical relationship established between a subject and a predicate. The **subject** indicates what the sentence is about—its central topic. The **predicate** indicates something about the subject; it makes a statement or asks a question about it. Notice the subjects (S) and predicates (P) in these sentences.

⌐S⌐ ⌐P⌐
Bees buzz.

⌐ S ⌐ ⌐——————— P ———————⌐
The rain fell heavily through the night.

⌐——————— S ———————⌐ ⌐ ⌐ ——————— P ———————⌐
The dense low-lying fog rolled across the meadow.

The chart on p. 218, The Parts of Speech, outlines the parts of speech and indicates where you can find comprehensive coverage of each item in the *Handbook.*

9a   Recognizing subjects and predicates

The subject of a sentence is always a noun, a pronoun, or a verb or clause that functions like a noun or pronoun. The predicate always contains a verb; often it also contains other words, such as prepositions, adjectives, adverbs, nouns, and pronouns.

http://
owl.english.purdue.edu/
writers/by-topic.html#parts
An overview of the parts of speech.

Consider the following examples.

SUBJECT	PREDICATE
Spiders	have eight legs.
The American Civil War	lasted from 1861 to 1865.
Many economists	predict a quick end to the recession.
Many older voters	reacted unenthusiastically to the tax hike.

The Parts of Speech

PART OF SPEECH	FUNCTION	EXAMPLE
Verb (See 10a)	Indicates action or state of being.	*spend, walk, see, care, be*
Noun (See 11a)	Names a person, place, thing, concept, or quality.	*John Smith, Pocahontas, home, child, coin, history, hope*
Pronoun (See 11b)	Takes the place of a noun.	*I, you, he, she, us, him, them, ours, who, anyone, myself, herself*
Adjective (See 12a)	Describes (modifies or qualifies) a noun or pronoun.	*hungry, rich, old, solid, desperate, neat*
Adverb (See 12a)	Describes a verb, adjective, or another adverb.	*often, quietly, cheerfully, nevertheless*
Preposition (See 13a)	Indicates the relationship between a noun or pronoun and another word in a sentence.	*into, from, to, with, above, at, behind, by, during*
Conjunction (See 13c)	Links or joins words, phrases, and clauses.	*and, but, or, after, until, therefore, however*
Interjection (See 13d)	Expresses surprise or emotion.	*Oh, Ah, Wow, Hey*

1 Subjects

The **simple subject** of a sentence is the single noun or pronoun that is its central subject. A simple subject appears most often as a single word, though it can also be a multiword proper noun such as *Golden Gate Bridge*. The **complete subject** of a sentence is the simple subject plus any additional modifying words or phrases. In the following example, the complete subject appears in italics and the simple subject is labeled SS.

┌─ SS ─┐
The majority of women painters from antiquity until the early twentieth century have suffered neglect if not outright dismissal.

Compound subjects identify two or more subjects used in a single sentence. A compound subject includes two or more simple subjects joined by a coordinating conjunction (*and, but, or, nor, for*) or by a correlative conjunction (*both . . . and, either . . . or, neither . . . nor, not only . . . but also*).

Mary Cassatt and Jean Renoir were two Impressionist painters who frequently painted scenes of women with children. *Neither Cassatt nor Renoir,* however, was considered as influential an Impressionist as Claude Monet.

2   Predicates

The **simple predicate** of a sentence is its verb. The **complete predicate** includes the verb plus its modifiers, complements, and object. Together the simple predicate and the complete predicate indicate something about the subject. In the following examples, the complete predicate appears in italics and the simple predicate is labeled SP.

┌─ SP ─┐
Our graduating class *used a Hawaiian theme for the senior prom.*

The simple predicate may include an auxiliary or helping verb along with the main verb. (See 10b on auxiliary verbs.)

┌─ SP ─┐
They *were awaiting his arrival.*

Compound predicates include two or more verbs that have the same subject. The verbs may be joined by either a coordinating conjunction (*and, but, or, nor, for*) or a correlative conjunction (*both . . . and, either . . . or, neither . . . nor, not only . . . but also*).

The performers *danced and sang* enthusiastically, though with little effect on the audience.

In some sentences, a compound predicate may be separated by other intervening words.

> Hurricane Andrew *reached* the southern coast of Florida at mid-morning *and battered* it mercilessly.

EXERCISE 9–1 Recognizing Subjects and Predicates
Identify the subjects and predicates in the following sentences. Underline the simple subject once and the simple predicate twice. Example:

> Charles Darwin published *The Origin of Species* in 1859.

1. Darwin acknowledged the provisional nature of evolution and affirmed the existence of natural selection.

2. Scientists regard debates on fundamental issues as a sign of intellectual health.

3. Evolutionary theory is now enjoying an upsurge of interest.

4. Creationists deny the premises of evolutionary theory.

5. Scientists continue to debate the validity of Darwin's theory.

9b Recognizing objects and complements

In addition to a subject and a predicate, a sentence may include other elements, such as the object of the verb and the subject or object complement.

1 Direct and indirect objects of verbs

The **object** of a sentence may be either a direct object or an indirect object. The direct and indirect objects of the verb form part of the complete predicate of a sentence.

A **direct object** is a noun or pronoun that receives the action of the verb in a sentence. Only transitive verbs (see 10d-2) can take objects.

> ┌— DO —┐
> The United Nations inspectors examined the weapons.

A direct object of a verb frequently answers the question *What?* or *Whom?* about the verb. (The inspectors examined *what?* The weapons.)

```
       ┌── DO ──┐
```
The new policy affected the students. [The new policy affected *whom?* The students.]

An **indirect object** of a transitive verb identifies the recipient to whom or for whom (or for what) the action of the verb is done.

```
      ┌ IO ┐ ┌ DO ┐
```
Bill sent Ingrid flowers.

```
                        ┌────────── IO ──────────┐
```
The president of the company gave her administrative staff

```
┌────────── DO ──────────┐
```
an inspiring motivational speech.

Direct and indirect objects can be simple, one-word objects or longer, more complete objects.

EXERCISE 9–2   Recognizing Direct and Indirect Objects of Verbs
Identify the direct and indirect objects of the verbs in the following sentences by underlining and labeling them DO or IO. Not all of the sentences will have both a direct and an indirect object. Example:

```
           ┌ IO ┐ ┌────── DO ──────┐
```
The college awarded <u>my uncle</u> an <u>honorary degree.</u>

1. Give me liberty or give me death.

2. The novelist George Eliot abandoned her work for several years.

3. The audience appreciated the performer's explanations.

4. I'll take a pastrami on rye and an Italian combo wedge with everything.

5. My grandmother sent my mother the traditional Egyptian engagement present of jewelry.

EXERCISE 9–3   Using Direct and Indirect Objects of Verbs in Writing
Write a paragraph in which at least three of your sentences contain an indirect object. You can choose your own topic or select one of these: something you own and value; something that annoys you; something you recently learned about; a news event; a historical event.

2   Objects of prepositions

An **object of a preposition** is usually a noun or pronoun that follows the preposition and completes its meaning. The object of a preposition is a part of the prepositional phrase of a sentence.

┌─OP─┐
Bill bought flowers for Ingrid.

The president gave an inspiring motivational speech to

┌──────OP──────┐
her administrative staff.

WRITING HINT   An indirect object (IO) always comes before a direct object (DO) in a sentence.

      IO   DO
      ┌┐ ┌──┐
They reserved us a table.

But the same meaning can usually be expressed in a prepositional phrase beginning with *to* or *for* and placed after the direct object.

             OP
     ┌DO┐   ┌┐
They reserved a table for us.

Notice how this change—from indirect object to object of a preposition—emphasizes the recipient (*us*) more than the direct object (*table*).

---

3   Complements

A **complement** is a word or group of words that completes the meaning of a subject or a direct object by renaming or describing it. It may be either a subject complement, which completes the meaning of a linking verb or an object complement, which completes the meaning of a transitive verb.

A **subject complement** (SC), which may be a noun or an adjective, follows a linking verb and identifies or describes the subject of the sentence.

SC (noun)　　　　　　　　　　　SC (adj.)

His sister is a newscaster.　　These muffins are delicious.

The most common linking verbs are the various forms of the verb *to be: am, is, are, was, were, has been, should be,* and so forth. Other common linking verbs include *appear, become, seem,* and, in some contexts, *feel, grow, look, taste, smell,* and *sound.*

His nephew *should be* a private investigator.

Your story *sounds* phony.

To distinguish between its two possible forms, a subject complement can also be called a **predicate noun** or a **predicate adjective.**

An **object complement** (OC), which can be a noun or an adjective, follows the direct object (DO) and renames or describes it.

　　　　　　　　　　OC (noun)
　　　┌─DO─┐ ┌──┐
The papers declared the play a hit.

　　　　　　　　　OC (adj.)
　　　┌─ DO─┐ ┌──┐
Wool socks will keep your feet warm.

EXERCISE 9–4　**Identifying Subject and Object Complements**

In the following sentences, underline and label the subject complements (SC) and object complements (OC). Example:

Her parents considered her a genius.

1. The rebels were experts in demolition.

2. The conclusion of the election was inevitable.

3. Home prices remained low, but only for a little while.

4. His intentions were hardly honorable.

5. Olympic officials declared the second-place runner the winner after disqualifying the reigning champion of the long-distance event.

Write a paragraph in which you employ subject and object complements.
You may choose your own topic or one of these: a favorite or difficult course;
a best friend; a book you read; a concert you attended; an idea that intrigues
you.

Recognizing and using phrases

A **phrase** is a group of related words that does not form a complete sentence. Phrases might lack a subject or a predicate or both. Typically, phrases
are embedded in sentences, adding information that clarifies, specifies, and
illuminates the point of a sentence. Phrases, then, serve as modifiers. They
also expand basic sentence patterns.

Consider the following example.

The next trout-fishing season will begin in early April.

The subject of this sentence is a noun phrase, *The next trout-fishing season*. The
predicate is a verb phrase, *will begin*. Concluding the sentence is a prepositional phrase, *in early April*. The prepositional phrase functions here as an
adverb, indicating when the season will begin.

1   Noun, verb, and prepositional phrases

Noun phrases

A **noun phrase** consists of a noun and its modifiers. A noun phrase can
function as a subject (S), object (O), or complement (C) in a sentence.

   ┌——S——┐   ┌——O——┐ ┌———O———┐
The Webers entertain *many guests* in *their spacious home.*

   ┌———S———┐   ┌——C——┐
Long cafeteria lines are *a familiar sight.*

Verb phrases

A **verb phrase** consists of a main verb and its auxiliary verbs. A verb
phrase functions as the predicate in a sentence or a clause.

He *could have done* worse.

If we *had known* earlier about the low cost of food and lodging, we *would have planned* to stay longer.

Prepositional phrases

A **prepositional phrase** consists of a preposition, its object, and any of the object's modifiers. A prepositional phrase can function as an adjective or an adverb.

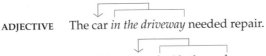

ADJECTIVE   The car *in the driveway* needed repair.

ADVERB   Tiger lilies grew *beside the road.*

On rare occasions, a prepositional phrase may function as the subject of a sentence.

Into the deepest part of the Ecuadorian jungle is the last place he had planned on going.

EXERCISE 9–6   **Practice with Prepositional Phrases**

Write a paragraph in which you use prepositional phrases in at least three sentences. Choose a topic of your own or one of these: a certain place (a campus hangout, your neighborhood), an object (a coin, photograph, tree, or flower) or a process (how to cook spaghetti, prepare for a hike, or teach someone to swim).

2   Verbal phrases

Verbal phrases consist of a verbal and related modifiers, objects, or complements. **Verbals** are verb forms that do not function as verbs in sentences; rather, they function as nouns or as modifiers, mostly as adjectives. As such, they cannot stand alone. The three types of verbals are participles, gerunds, and infinitives.

Participles functioning as adjectives:

They waited as the *chugging* train finally arrived.

We heard the *excited* tone in her voice.

Gerunds functioning as nouns:

Swimming is enjoying a resurgence of international interest.

Without soap there wasn't much sense in *showering*.

Infinitives functioning as nouns, adjectives, and adverbs:

NOUN   Her goal was *to excel.*

ADJECTIVE   We had plenty of time *to waste.*

ADVERB   The chef was eager *to cook.*

Participial phrases

A **participial phrase** consists of a present or past participle and accompanying modifiers, objects, or complements. Participial phrases function only as adjectives, modifying nouns, or pronouns.

The cat *crouching behind the sofa* is Garfield, not Dolce.

Having saved for a year, they set out to shop for furniture.

Gerund phrases

A **gerund phrase** consists of a gerund with related modifiers, objects, or complements. Gerund phrases always function as nouns, whether as a subject or subject complement, a direct or indirect object, or an object of a preposition.

SUBJECT   *Playing baseball professionally* has always been his dream.

DIRECT OBJECT   He enjoyed *eating home-cooked meals.*

OBJECT   They did not want him *driving after he veered off the road.*
COMPLEMENT

OBJECT OF   They were tired of *commuting two hundred miles a day.*
A PREPOSITION

Absolute phrases

An **absolute phrase** consists of a noun or pronoun and a participle or complement, along with any related modifiers or objects. Absolute phrases modify entire sentences rather than particular words in those sentences. An absolute phrase can appear in many places in a sentence, but it is always set off by commas.

Excitement over his girlfriend's return increasing by the minute, he found he could concentrate on little else.

The plane, *its engines thoroughly inspected,* was ready to take off.

The plane was ready to take off, *its engines having been thoroughly inspected.*

Infinitive phrases

An **infinitive phrase** consists of an infinitive with its related modifiers, objects, or complements. Infinitive phrases can function as nouns or as modifiers.

NOUN　　　*To give* is *to receive.*

ADJECTIVE　　College is a good place *to meet new friends.*

ADVERB　　　*To succeed in college,* read widely and reflectively.

EXERCISE 9–7　Using Verbal Phrases in Writing

Write a paragraph that includes at least three sentences with verbal phrases. Choose a topic of your own or one of these: why you like to travel, shop, play sports; how you learned to swim, ski, drive, play the guitar.

Appositive phrases

An appositive renames the word or words it follows. An **appositive phrase** is a noun phrase that renames the noun or pronoun it immediately follows. Appositive phrases are usually set off from the rest of the sentence by commas.

Toni Morrison, *author of several novels,* won the Nobel Prize for Literature.

The movie, *a fast-paced adventure story,* won rave reviews.

EXERCISE 9–8　Using Absolute Phrases in Writing

Combine the following pairs of sentences by converting the second sentence into an absolute phrase and attaching it effectively to the first sentence. Remember to use a comma (or commas) to set off the absolute phrase from the rest of the sentence. Example:

Our cat lay contentedly by the fire. Her tail moved from side to side like a metronome.

Our cat lay contentedly by the fire, her tail moving from side to side like a metronome.

1. Buildings crumbled along Market Street. Their foundations were damaged by the earthquake.

2. The game was officially halted in the fifth inning. The rain had persisted for over an hour.

3. There are remains of old Spanish forts everywhere. Their adobe walls are dissolving into dust.

4. We were now ready to talk business. The meal was finally finished.

5. Janetta sits at her desk. Her head is lowered over a pile of medieval art reproductions.

EXERCISE 9–9   **Using Appositives in Writing**
Combine the following sentence pairs by rewriting the second sentence in each pair as an appositive. Remember to set off the appositive phrases with commas if necessary. Example:

Bill watches television every night except Wednesday. Wednesday is his bowling night.

Bill watches television every night except Wednesday, *his bowling night.*

1. Black lung affects countless miners in Pennsylvania and West Virginia. Black lung is an incurable disease of the respiratory system.

2. Scientists have found the fossil of the oldest known vertebrate. The oldest known vertebrate is a jawless fish.

3. Brother Jim has been repeatedly denied a speaking permit by the university. Brother Jim is a preacher from Indiana.

4. Ben and Jerry are encouraging Americans to overeat for peace. Ben and Jerry are ice-cream makers who donate part of their profits to pacifist activities.

5. With the increased popularity of Caribbean cooking, plantains are replacing potatoes on American menus. Plantains are exotic bananas.

WRITING HINT   You can use phrases to expand and develop your sentences by emphasizing particular details and creating emphatic endings. Look at the following sentence, and notice how it changes as phrases are added to it.

The mare's restless shuffling kicks up dust, which catches the light as it floats down.

The mare's restless shuffling kicks up dust, which catches the light as it floats down *to stick on the horse's sweating flanks.*

The mare's restless shuffling *in the hay* kicks up dust, which catches the light as it floats down *to stick* in a gray film on the horse's sweating flanks.

In this last version, the emphasis remains the same, but the added phrases expand and enrich the sentence.

EXERCISE 9–10   Building Sentences with Phrases
Expand each of the following short sentences by adding phrases. Example:

A girl stands.

In a darkened hallway stands a girl *in a pink sweater.*

1. Her smile is a mask.
2. Her photograph caught my attention.
3. Perfection is what I strive for.
4. Reality slapped me across the face.
5. He knew now what he had to do.

9d   Recognizing and using clauses

A **clause** is a group of words that contains a subject and a predicate. An **independent clause** can stand alone as a sentence.

Rosa loves lasagne.

A **dependent clause** cannot stand alone because it begins with a subordinating conjunction or a relative pronoun.

Because Rosa loves lasagne

To form a complete sentence, a dependent clause must be joined to at least one independent clause.

Because Rosa loves lasagne, her mother makes it often.

1 Adjective clauses

An **adjective clause** modifies a noun or pronoun in another clause, although it usually appears immediately after the word it modifies. Adjective clauses are also typically introduced by a relative pronoun—*who, which, that, whose,* or *whom* (see 11b). When a dependent clause begins with one of these words, it can also be referred to as a **relative clause.**

Sappho is the ancient Greek poet *who lived on the island of Lesbos.*

Her poetry, *which exists mostly in fragments,* is lyrical, emotional, and erotic.

2 Adverb clauses

Adverb clauses modify verbs, adjectives, or other adverbs. They typically provide details about how, where, when, why, under what conditions, with what consequences, or to what extent an action occurs. They are introduced by subordinating conjunctions.

If you can make the first cut, you have a good chance to make the team.

His salary was increased *when the sales results were tabulated.*

WRITING HINT Although adverb clauses often occur at the beginnings of sentences, they can be used in other places as well. Changing the position of adverb clauses in your sentences is one way to avoid monotony. It is also a way to vary the emphasis and rhythm of your sentences. Consider the following examples.

The band members went out for pizza *after they finished performing.*

After they finished performing, the band members went out for pizza.

(continued)

Barbara McClintock continued her experiments with corn *even though her scientific work had long been ignored.*

Even though her scientific work had long been ignored, Barbara McClintock continued her experiments with corn.

3 Noun clauses

A **noun clause** can serve as a subject, an object, or a complement within a sentence. Noun clauses typically begin with a relative pronoun, such as *who, whom, whoever,* or *whomever,* or with a subordinating conjunction such as *when, where, whether, why, how, what,* or *whatever.*

SUBJECT	*That he complained* surprised me.
DIRECT OBJECT	Homer's *Odyssey* describes, in considerable detail, *how and why Odysseus' journey home from Troy took him ten years.*
SUBJECT COMPLEMENT	The administrative response to faculty demands for smaller classes was *that they were too costly.*
OBJECT OF A PREPOSITION	Don't listen to *what he says.*

EXERCISE 9–11 **Using Clauses in Writing**
Expand each of the following brief sentences by adding one or more dependent clauses. Example:

Only one person remained.

As the lights finally went out in the hall, only one person remained.

1. The old dog still barked loudly.
2. The church was being repaired.
3. They sat inside for more than two hours.
4. She always tried to look her best.
5. The sun shone through the branches of the newly planted cherry tree.

9e   Using the basic sentence patterns

You can use the basic grammatical elements described in 9a and 9b to construct many kinds of sentences. You can also combine and arrange the grammatical elements to create different types of sentences (see 9f).

The accompanying chart, Five Basic Sentence Patterns, outlines the simplest and most common sentence patterns. They form the core of all sentences in English. Every sentence you read and write will contain combinations of these sentence elements, but not always in the sequences illustrated in the chart.

Five Basic Sentence Patterns

1. Subject–Verb:

   ┌─S─┐ ┌─V─┐

   Whales swim.

2. Subject–Verb–Direct Object:

   ┌────S────┐ ┌V┐ ┌─DO─┐

   Some whales eat plankton.

3. Subject–Verb–Subject Complement:

   ┌───S───┐ ┌V┐ ┌─ SC ─┐

   All whales are mammals.

4. Subject–Verb–Indirect Object–Direct Object:

   ┌──────S──────┐ ┌V┐ ┌─IO─┐ ┌─DO─┐

   Breaching whales give viewers a thrill.

5. Subject–Verb–Direct Object–Object Complement:

   ┌──────S──────┐ ┌─V─┐ ┌─DO─┐ ┌──────OC──────┐

   Whale watchers consider whales the glory of creation.

EXERCISE 9–12   Using the Basic Sentence Patterns

In the following paragraph, label the sentences' subjects (S), verbs (V), subject complements (SC), direct objects (DO), indirect objects (IO), and object complements (OC) as appropriate. Then use the sentences as models for writing sentences of your own that incorporate subjects, verbs, subject complements, direct objects, indirect objects, and object complements.

Many readers enjoy a good detective story. Literary historians give Edgar Allan Poe credit for inventing the modern detective story. Poe's detective hero was a Frenchman. Poe named his detective C. Auguste Dupin. Dupin appeared in only three of Poe's stories. Dupin became the model for a long line of popular successors, including Sherlock Holmes.

9f   Using different types of sentences

Sentences can be classified by function; a sentence can, for example, make a statement, pose a question, give a command, or convey a strong emotion. They can also be classified by grammatical construction, such as simple, compound, complex, or compound-complex.

Computer Tip

Using Grammar Checkers

Grammar checkers can create as many problems as they help solve. They make mistakes as often as they show you how to correct them. If you use a grammar checker, consider its "corrections" as recommendations only—as suggestions for you to consider. Then check your *Handbook* or talk with a more grammatically knowledgeable classmate or your instructor.

---

1   Functional sentence types

A **declarative sentence** makes a statement. An **interrogative sentence** asks a question. An **imperative sentence** gives a command or makes a request. An **exclamatory sentence** expresses strong feeling.

DECLARATIVE	War reparations were required.
INTERROGATIVE	How effective were they?
IMPERATIVE	Consider what happened in their aftermath.
EXCLAMATORY	What a powerful speech that was!

Declarative sentences

Most of the sentences you write are declarative sentences; they describe, explain, analyze, or argue a position. Whether you are describing how to paint with watercolors, explaining how a free-market economy works, or arguing for the elimination of the death penalty, you rely heavily on declarative sentences. Such sentences make assertions, state facts, present opinions, offer evaluations, identify problems, and present solutions.

Interrogative sentences

Interrogative sentences can enhance writing by creating a personal tone—one that involves readers and stimulates them to think. The following passage blends interrogative sentences with declarative ones to develop an idea.

I am a clown and my makeup and mask are all that I am. My mask represents how far I will go to stay in character, to do what is expected of me. Like an artist perfecting her creation, I constantly check to see that I am doing what I should, what is expected, what my role requires. How long, I wonder, will I continue to wear this mask? Is it already too late for me to tear it off and become the person I want to be? My mask has grown almost too comfortable. I have become, it seems, too adept at performing the roles expected of me. Perhaps I will always remain a clown.

—Nancy McArthur, "Beyond the Smile of the Clown"

Imperative and exclamatory sentences

Imperative sentences can direct readers to consider a point or evaluate an idea. Too many imperative sentences, however, can create an insistent and overbearing tone.

Exclamatory sentences have their place in conversation, but outside of some kinds of descriptive and narrative writing, in which you may provide your reactions to an experience, you will rarely need them.

EXERCISE 9–13   **Identifying Functional Sentence Types**

Identify each of the following sentences as declarative, interrogative, imperative, or exclamatory.

1. What an unusual family they are!
2. Learn a foreign language now before it's too late.
3. To what extent has this experience been engaging?
4. Until the committee renders its decision, no further action can be taken.
5. Can health costs be limited by the strategies proposed?

2   Grammatical sentence types

Grammatically, sentences can be classified as simple, compound, complex, and compound-complex. This classification is based on the way sentences use dependent and independent clauses. A clause is a group of words with a subject and a predicate. An independent clause can stand alone as a sentence; a dependent clause cannot. (See 9d.)

Simple sentences

A **simple sentence** consists of a single independent clause without any dependent clauses.

You can see the mountain.

A sentence is classified simple even when it has a compound subject or predicate (or both) and includes modifying words and phrases.

You and your friends can see the mountain on your next trip.

You can see the mountain and climb to the top.

Compound sentences

A **compound sentence** consists of two or more independent clauses (IC) without any dependent clauses.

┌─────────────── IC ───────────────┐
Naomi and her sister, Ruth, once swam competitively;

┌──────── IC ────────┐
┌─┐   ┌────────────┐
now, *however*, they rarely swim at all.

Complex sentences

A **complex sentence** consists of a single independent clause (IC) with one or more dependent clauses (DC).

```
┌────────────────────── DC ──────────────────────────┐
When he heard that his brother had been wounded in the Civil War,
```

```
┌────────────────── IC ──────────────────────────────┐
Walt Whitman left home to find him and nurse him back to health.
```

```
┌─────────── IC ────────────┐ ┌────── DC ──────┐
Michael Jackson embarked on a music career when he was a child.
```

Compound-complex sentences

A **compound-complex sentence** consists of two or more independent clauses (IC) and at least one dependent clause (DC).

```
┌────────────────── IC ──────────────────┐ ┌────── DC ──────┐
Franz Schubert wrote his first song, "The Erlkönig," when he was eighteen,
```

```
┌────────── IC ──────────┐ ┌──── DC ────┐ ┌─── DC ───┐
and he continued to write songs until age thirty-one, when he died.
```

EXERCISE 9–14 Using Different Kinds of Sentences

The sentences in the following paragraph have been simplified. Revise the paragraph to add sentence variety by adding phrases and different kinds of clauses and by combining some of the sentences. Mix simple, compound, complex, and compound-complex sentences in the paragraph. Add or drop some words as necessary.

For a long time, psychologists have wondered about memories and what they are. They have also wondered where memories are stored in the human brain. Memory has been studied intensely. That's because it is the basis of human intelligence. According to one psychologist, memory is an umbrella term. It covers a whole range of processes. These occur in our brains. In particular, psychologists have identified two types of memory. One type is called declarative memory. It includes memories of facts. These include names, places, dates, even baseball scores. We use it to declare things. That's why it's called declarative. The other type of memory is called procedural. This type of memory is acquired by repetitive practice. It is also acquired by conditioning. It includes skills such as riding a bike or typing. We need both types of memory in our daily living. We need facts. We also use a variety of skills.

10 | *Verbs*

A **verb** is a part of the complete predicate that indicates an action (He *kissed* his mother), an occurrence (The responsibility *fell* on my shoulders), or a state of being (She *seems* tired). Different forms of a verb are used to indicate person, number, tense, voice, and mood. A verb's form also conveys information about the action within a sentence. The accompanying chart outlines some important characteristics conveyed by verbs.

Verb Characteristics		
Person	Indicates who or what experiences or performs the action—the person speaking, the person spoken to, or the person or thing spoken about.	**first person:** I *walk.* **second person:** You *walk.* **third person:** He/She/It *walks.*
Number	Specifies how many subjects experience or perform the action.	**singular:** It *walks.* **plural:** They *walk.*
Tense	Signals the time of the action. (See 10f–i.)	**past:** I *looked* out the window. **present:** I *look* out the window. **future:** I *will look* out the window.
Voice	Indicates whether the subject performs or receives the verb's action. (See 10j–k.)	**active voice:** The audience *watched* the performers. **passive voice:** The performers *were watched by* the audience.
Mood	Denotes the attitude expressed toward the verb.	**imperative:** *Listen* to me! **indicative:** You *are listening* to me. **subjunctive:** I wish you *would listen* to me.

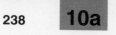

Verb Forms

10a Primary verb forms

All English verbs, with the exception of *be*, have five primary forms.

BASE FORM	PRESENT TENSE	PRESENT PARTICIPLE	PAST TENSE	PAST PARTICIPLE
look	looks	looking	looked	looked
walk	walks	walking	walked	walked
watch	watches	watching	watched	watched

The **base form** (or **simple form**) is the form cited in dictionaries. The base form is also used for the present tense when the subject of the verb is *I, you, we, they,* or a plural noun.

I *talk* and you *listen*.

Mom and Dad *argue* about politics.

The **present tense** (or **-s form**), which is produced by adding *-s* or *-es* to the base form, indicates action in the present when the subject is third-person singular (*he, she, it* or a singular noun).

He *smiles* and she *returns* his smile with one of her own.

USAGE NOTE   All singular nouns and many indefinite pronouns take verbs with the *-s* form in the present tense. (See 11a on nouns and 11b on indefinite pronouns.)

The judge clearly *believes* the defendant.

Everybody *wants* the deadline for the paper extended.

The **present participle** indicates continuing action. It is created by adding *-ing* to the base form of the verb. In order to function as the main verb in a sentence, a participle must be accompanied by a form of the verb *be*.

Mark *is anticipating* a good grade this semester.

They *were awaiting* instruction from the director.

When a present participle functions as the grammatical subject or object in a sentence, it is a **gerund** (see 9c-2).

Swimming is good exercise. [*Swimming* is the subject of the sentence.]

Karen enjoyed *fishing*. [*Fishing* is the direct object of *enjoyed*.]

Grammar and Writing

Using Strong Verbs

Improve your writing by focusing on verbs. Check your sequence of tenses for clarity and accuracy. Be sure verbs' moods carry the appropriate tenses.

Look over a recent piece of writing.

- Check for an overreliance on the verbs *be*, *do*, and *have*.
- Replace some of those with more interesting action verbs.
- Replace general verbs with more specific ones.
- Change some passive voice verbs to active voice alternatives.

EXAMPLES

               experienced   ate

On the first day of my trip I [had] a headache, but I [had] a big breakfast

                         ing

anyway before ~~I [had to]~~ meet my friends at our campsite.

Focus next on verb voice—active or passive voices. Change some of your passive voice verbs to active voice—especially those that use *is*, *was*, *are*, or *were*. Strive here, too, to choose specific concrete verbs.

PASSIVE VOICE   Many kinds of stories are included in the book, but the ones I am most interested in are about love.

ACTIVE VOICE   The book includes many kinds of stories, but those about love interest me most.

A present participle can also function as an adjective in a sentence.

> *Accepting* the award, the actor was clearly overjoyed. [*Accepting* modifies *actor*.]

> The defense furnished *supporting* evidence. [*Supporting* modifies *evidence*.]

The present participle does not change form to indicate person or number in a sentence.

The **past tense** usually indicates action that occurred in the past. A verb's past tense can almost always be recognized by its -*d* or -*ed* ending. The past tense does not change form to indicate person or number.

> They *persuaded* him to reconsider his opinion.

Some verbs form their past tense in other ways and are called **irregular verbs** (see 10c).

> His aunt and uncle *went* to Paris and *saw* the Eiffel Tower.

The **past participle** is identical to the past tense form of the verb, except in some irregular verbs (see 10c). Like the present participle, the past participle must be accompanied by a form of the verb *be* to function as the main verb in the sentence and does not change form to indicate person or number. The past participle is a part in the perfect verb tenses (see 10g) and the passive voice verbs (see 10k). It can also function as an adjective.

> Each *had waited* for the other to initiate the conversation. [past perfect tense]

> Nearly everyone *was helped* by the extra-credit question. [passive voice verb]

> Only occasionally will I eat an *overcooked* steak. [adjective]

USAGE NOTE   In speech the -*d* and -*ed* endings of past tense verbs are often dropped or given very little stress, as in *he asked me to leave* or *she composed a piece for the piano*. As a result, some people tend to forget these endings in writing.

In your writing, be sure to include the -*d* and -*ed* endings where they are needed, and avoid nonstandard forms of the past tense and the past participle.

EXERCISE 10–1   Selecting Standard Verb Forms

Revise the following sentences so that the verbs conform to standard English usage. Example:

Clarice ~~live~~ _lives_ in New Harmony, Indiana.

1. After the party is over, we walking directly home.
2. Children asking many questions that are difficult to answer.
3. We observe an accident on our way out of town.
4. Yesterday Darrell receive an important call from his advisor.
5. The coach knows that I am ill, but she still expect me to show up for practice.

10b   Auxiliary verb forms

Some verb forms do not make sense as main verbs of a sentence without the aid of an **auxiliary verb** (or a **helping verb**). The most common auxiliary verbs are _be, have,_ and _do._ (See the accompanying chart, Forms of _be, have,_ and _do._) The combination of an auxiliary verb with a main verb creates a **verb phrase** that typically indicates complete, continuing, or future action.

Forms of _be, have,_ and _do_

The verbs _be, have,_ and _do_ have irregular forms. If you are unfamiliar with their forms, you will need to memorize them.

BASE FORM	PRESENT TENSE	PRESENT PARTICIPLE	PAST TENSE	PAST PARTICIPLE
_be_	I _am_ he/she/it _is_ we/you/they _are_	_being_	I/he/she/it _was_ we/you/they _were_	_been_
have	I _have_ he/she/it _has_ we/you/they _have_	_having_	I _have_ he/she/it _had_ we/you/they _had_	_had_
_do_	I _do_ he/she/it _does_ we/you/they _do_	_doing_	_did_	_done_

VERB PHRASE
┌────┴────┐
AUXILIARY MAIN VERB
┌──────┐ ┌────┐

The movie *is being filmed* in downtown Boston. [continuing action]

VERB PHRASE   VERB PHRASE
┌────┴────┐   ┌────┴────┐
AUXILIARY MAIN VERB   AUXILIARY MAIN VERB
┌──┐ ┌────┐   ┌──┐ ┌────┐

I *have practiced* so that the magic trick *will succeed.*
[completed action/future action]

Verb phrases are also used for emphasis, for questions, and for negative statements.

But I *do recognize* the name of the Secretary of State. [emphasis]

Did you *visit* the acropolis? [question]

He *had* not *received* his magazine subscription as of last Wednesday. [negative]

USAGE NOTE   Some dialects use the base form *be* instead of *am, is,* or *are,* especially to express habitual or continued action. This usage is not standard, however, for college writing.

NONSTANDARD	He *be* the best player on the team.
STANDARD	He *is* the best player on the team.
NONSTANDARD	I *be* taking three math courses this year.
STANDARD	I *am* taking three math courses this year.

A **modal auxiliary verb** (such as *can, could, may, might, must, shall, should, will,* and *would*) combines with a main verb to form a verbal phrase. The modal auxiliary can refine the meaning of the main verb by indicating necessity, obligation, permission, possibility, and the like. Modal auxiliaries do not change form to indicate person or number and always combine with the base form of the main verb.

If she is to win the case, the defense lawyer *must undermine* the plaintiff's credibility. [necessity]

I really *should visit* my grandmother this weekend. [obligation]

You *may leave*. [permission]

If I *could manage* to get an interview, I know I *would prove* that I *could perform* the job. [possibility]

USAGE NOTE Use the conditional auxiliary *would* only in an independent clause, never in an *if* clause.

	INDEPENDENT CLAUSE	IF CLAUSE
NONSTANDARD	We *would* have helped if we *would have* known.	
STANDARD	We *would* have helped if we *had* known.	

WRITING HINT Modal auxiliaries can combine with other auxiliary verbs to form complicated verb phrases that require careful attention.

When *have* comes after a modal auxiliary, as in "I could have gone," the *could have* is pronounced with stress on *could* and no stress on *have*. Thus, in speech *could have* sounds like *could of* and is sometimes incorrectly written that way. Be sure to write *have*, not *of*, in sentences like these.

You *should have read* the directions more carefully.

It *would have saved* you considerable time and energy.

Also be careful when using *ought to*. It is awkward to use in the negative (with *not*). Combinations such as *shouldn't ought to* and *hadn't ought to* may be common in spoken English, but in writing *ought not to* is standard. You may want to use *should not* or *shouldn't* instead.

EXERCISE 10–2 **Using Auxiliary Verbs**

In the following sentences, fill in each of the blanks with an appropriate form of *be, have,* or *do*. Example:

Paul Simon's songs __have__ become classics.

1. Liz _____ cooking dinner for her friends tonight.

2. Last week, Cliff _____ promised us roasted leg of lamb.

3. How _____ he manage to scale the wall in five seconds?

4. I _____ hoping to see you before you left for Vermont.

5. He _____ tend to go on and on when he tells a good story.

10c Regular and irregular verbs

Regular verbs form the past tense and past participle by adding *-d* or *-ed* to the base form. The base form, past tense, and past participle are called the **principal parts** of the verb.

BASE FORM	PAST TENSE	PAST PARTICIPLE
call	called	called
follow	followed	followed
burn	burned	burned

The principal parts of **irregular verbs** do not follow the *-d* or *-ed* pattern in forming their past tense and past participle. Many irregular verbs form their principal parts by changing an internal vowel: *begin, began, begun; ring, rang, rung.*

http://
owl.english.purdue.edu/
writers/by-topic.html#parts
Offers broad coverage of verbs, including tense, voice, and mood.

Some irregular verbs do not change at all. Their base form is also used in the past tense and as the past participle: *bet, bet, bet; cost, cost, cost.* Some irregular verbs such as *go* and *am* change radically: *go, went, gone; am, was, been.* Learn these irregular verbs by memorizing their principal parts. Many of the most common irregular verbs appear in the chart on pp. 245–247.

EXERCISE 10–3 Using Irregular Verbs

For each irregular verb in parentheses, provide the appropriate past tense or past participle. Check the list of irregular verbs for any you are unsure about. Example:

Snow had *(fall)* __fallen__ throughout the night.

1. The population of California has *(grow)* _____ dramatically in the last decade.

2. After the phone had *(ring)* _____ a dozen times, he finally *(wake)* _____ up and answered it.

3. Annie Proulx has *(write)* _____ an award-winning novel called *The Shipping News.*

4. Bobby Bonilla *(swing)* _____ at a high fastball and *(drive)* _____ it over the center field fence.

5. When Pablo Morales *(swim)* _____ the hundred-meter butterfly at the Barcelona Olympics, he *(show)* _____ everyone that he *(can)* _____ still compete with the best swimmers in the world.

6. She *(ride)* _____ the horse with confidence and grace. It looked as if she had *(ride)* _____ all her life.

7. The cat has *(eat)* _____; I *(feed)* _____ it this morning.

8. The lawyers for the defense have *(prove)* _____ conclusively that their client could not have *(steal)* _____ the jewelry.

9. The tank had *(spring)* _____ a leak.

10. The book had been *(read)* _____ many times.

Common Irregular Verbs		
BASE FORM	**PAST TENSE**	**PAST PARTICIPLE**
arise	arose	arisen
awake	awoke	awaked *or* awoken
be	was	been
become	became	become
begin	began	begun
bite	bit	bitten
blow	blew	blown
break	broke	broken
bring	brought	brought
build	built	built
burn	burned *or* burnt	burned *or* burnt
burst	burst	burst
buy	bought	bought
can	could	could
catch	caught	caught

(continued)

BASE FORM	PAST TENSE	PAST PARTICIPLE
choose	chose	chosen
come	came	come
dig	dug	dug
dive	dived *or* dove	dived
do	did	done
draw	drew	drawn
drink	drank	drunk
drive	drove	driven
eat	ate	eaten
fall	fell	fallen
fight	fought	fought
fly	flew	flown
forget	forgot	forgotten *or* forgot
forgive	forgave	forgiven
get	got	gotten *or* got
give	gave	given
go	went	gone
grow	grew	grown
hang (suspend)	hung	hung
hang (execute)	hanged	hanged
have	had	had
hide	hid	hidden
know	knew	known
lay	laid	laid
lead	led	led
leave	left	left
lie	lay	lain
make	made	made
ride	rode	ridden
ring	rang	rung
rise	rose	risen
run	ran	run
see	saw	seen
set	set	set
shake	shook	shaken
shine (glow)	shone	shone
shine (polish)	shined	shined
shrink	shrank	shrunk
sing	sang	sung
sink	sank	sunk
sit	sat	sat
speak	spoke	spoken

(continued)

BASE FORM	PAST TENSE	PAST PARTICIPLE
spring	sprang	sprung
stand	stood	stood
steal	stole	stolen
stink	stank *or* stunk	stunk
swear	swore	sworn
swim	swam	swum
swing	swung	swung
take	took	taken
tear	tore	torn
think	thought	thought
throw	threw	thrown
wear	wore	worn
write	wrote	written

EXERCISE 10–4   **Using Irregular Verbs in Sentences**

Write two sentences for each of the following verbs. Use each verb first in the past tense and then as a past participle (with *have* or *had*). Example:

> *take:* I *took* the last seat. Michelle *had taken* the first one.

1. bring
2. choose
3. freeze
4. hide
5. ring
6. break
7. draw
8. forget
9. see
10. shake

10d   Other types of verbs

Two other important verb classifications are linking verbs and transitive verbs or intransitive verbs.

1   Linking verbs

A **linking verb** joins the subject of a sentence to a subject complement, which describes or renames the subject. Linking verbs usually describe states of being, not actions.

King Ferdinand *was* uncertain about Columbus's plan.

Queen Isabella *felt* confident about Columbus's chances of success.

In these examples the verbs (*was* and *felt*) link their subjects (*King Ferdinand, Queen Isabella*) to the subject complements (*uncertain, confident*).

Common linking verbs include all forms of the verb *be: am, is, are, was, were, be, being,* and *been.*

We *are* hungry but soon we *will be* famished.

I *am* unable to agree and she *is* unwilling to compromise.

Linking verbs often describe the senses. The sensory verbs include *look, sound, taste, smell,* and *feel.* They are almost always completed by adjectives that describe the subject of the sentence.

This food *smells* and *tastes* delicious.   The blanket *felt* soft.

Other common linking verbs convey a sense of existing or becoming, such as *appear, become, remain, seem, get,* and *grow.* These linking verbs are often completed by adjectives that describe the subject.

The grass *appears* brown and dead.   The congregation *remained* silent.

2   Transitive and intransitive verbs

A **transitive verb** transfers its action from a subject to a direct object. A transitive verb must have a direct object to complete its meaning.

She *bought* the car. [The meaning of the verb, *bought,* is completed by the direct object, *car.*]

An **intransitive verb** does not take a direct object.

He *blushes* easily. [The meaning of the verb, *blushes,* is complete in itself.]

Some verbs can be used both transitively (He *sees* his mistake) and intransitively (He *sees* poorly).

TRANSITIVE   Paul *speaks* German.

INTRANSITIVE   Paul *speaks* well.

3   Verbals

Verbals are verb forms that typically end in *-ing* or *-ed.* Verbals can function as nouns (*skiing* is fun) or as modifiers (the *stolen* goods, the desire *to succeed*).

A verbal cannot stand alone as the main verb in a sentence. *The clown smiling* and *the books read* are not complete sentences but sentence fragments (see 16a). A verbal must always be accompanied by an auxiliary verb when it serves as the predicate of a sentence.

Since verbals cannot stand alone as sentence predicates, they are called **nonfinite** (unfinished or incomplete) **verbs. Finite** (finished or complete) **verbs,** on the other hand, can serve as sentence predicates.

There are three kinds of verbals: participles, gerunds, and infinitives.

Participles function as adjectives. The present participle is the *-ing* form of a verb: *wishing, hearing, touching.* Although some verbs have irregular past participles (see 10c), the past participle of regular verbs is the *-d* or *-ed* form: *wished, heard, touched.*

He watched as the *falling* snow dropped quietly around him.

She noticed the *distracted* look on her father's face.

Gerunds, like the present participle, also end in *-ing.* Gerunds, however, function as nouns.

Hiking is very popular nowadays.   This restaurant prohibits *smoking.*

Infinitives can function as nouns, adjectives, or adverbs. An infinitive consists of the word *to* plus the main or base form of the verb.

NOUN   He wanted *to win.*

ADJECTIVE   She had no more money *to spend.*

ADVERB   The writer was ready *to revise.*

The three kinds of verbal phrases are participle phrases, gerund phrases, and infinitive phrases.

10e Using *sit/set, lie/lay,* and *rise/raise*

Three irregular verb pairs sometimes cause confusion: *sit* and *set; lie* and *lay;* and *rise* and *raise.* In order to distinguish between the pairs of words, you should think of them as either transitive verbs or intransitive verbs.

Sit is an intransitive verb and thus does not take an object. *Sit* means "to be seated." *Set* is a transitive verb and consequently takes an object. *Set* means "to put or place."

INTRANSITIVE	Our cat *sits* on the windowsill. [present tense of *sit*]
TRANSITIVE	He always *sets* his notes on the podium. [present tense of *set*]
INTRANSITIVE	They *sat* against the wall. [past tense of *sit*]
TRANSITIVE	The explanation *set* her mind at rest. [past tense of *set*]

Lie is an intransitive verb and means "to recline." *Lay* is a transitive verb meaning "to put or place."

INTRANSITIVE	I often *lie* down after dinner. [present tense of *lie*]
TRANSITIVE	She *lays* down the law in our house. [present tense of *lay*]
INTRANSITIVE	I *lay* down before dinner last night. [past tense of *lie*]
TRANSITIVE	She *laid* the tray on my lap. [past tense of *lay*]

Rise is an intransitive verb and means "to get up." *Raise* is a transitive verb meaning "to lift up."

| INTRANSITIVE | The foam was *rising* in the glass. [present participle of *rise*] |
| TRANSITIVE | They were *raising* their voices in celebration. [present participle of *raise*] |

Forms of *sit/set, lie/lay, rise/raise*

	BASE FORM	PRESENT TENSE	PRESENT PARTICIPLE	PAST TENSE	PAST PARTICIPLE
INTRANSITIVE	sit	sits	sitting	sat	sat
TRANSITIVE	set	sets	setting	set	set
INTRANSITIVE	lie	lies	lying	lay	lain
TRANSITIVE	lay	lays	laying	laid	laid
INTRANSITIVE	rise	rises	rising	rose	risen
TRANSITIVE	raise	raises	raising	raised	raised

EXERCISE 10–5   **Using *sit/set, lie/lay,* and *rise/raise***

Choose the appropriate verb for the context of the sentence. Example:

He (*rises/raises*) his hand in salute.

1. Mr. Anderson just (*lies/lays*) there staring at the wall.

2. After a while she (*rose/raised*) her head up and then (*set/sat*) on the edge of the bed.

3. (*Rise/Raise*) *High the Roofbeam, Carpenters* is the title of a book by J. D. Salinger.

4. Christians believe that Jesus (*rose/raised*) from the dead on the third day after his death.

5. He had (*laid/lain*) in the shade long enough. If his aunt saw him (*laying/lying*) there, she wouldn't like it. So he (*set/sat*) his drink aside and picked up the hedge clippers.

EXERCISE 10–6   Using *lie/lay, sit/set,* and *rise/raise* in Writing
Write a paragraph in which you use the present tense form of *lie/lay, sit/set,* and *rise/raise*. Then rewrite the paragraph changing all the verbs to past tense forms. Possible topics include getting up in the morning; going to bed at night; attending class during the day.

Verb Tenses

Tense indicates when the action of a verb occurs, whether in the past, present, or future.

PAST TENSE	She *wrote*.
PRESENT TENSE	She *writes*.
FUTURE TENSE	She *will write*.

These three tenses are called simple tenses to distinguish them from the perfect, progressive, and perfect progressive tenses. Perfect tenses indicate completed action: She *has written*. Progressive tenses indicate action occurring over time: She *is writing*. Perfect progressive tenses combine the sense of both continuity and completion: She *had been writing*.

Verb Tenses		
VERB TENSES	REGULAR VERB	IRREGULAR VERB
Simple present	He *cooks*	She *eats*
Simple past	He *cooked*	She *ate*
Simple future	He *will cook*	She *will eat*

(continued)

VERB TENSES	REGULAR VERB	IRREGULAR VERB
Present perfect	He *has cooked*	She *has eaten*
Past perfect	He *had cooked*	She *had eaten*
Future perfect	He *will have cooked*	She *will have eaten*
Present progressive	He *is cooking*	She *is eating*
Past progressive	He *was cooking*	She *was eating*
Future progressive	He *will be cooking*	She *will be eating*
Present perfect progressive	He *has been cooking*	She *has been eating*
Past perfect progressive	He *had been cooking*	She *had been eating*
Future perfect progressive	He *will have been cooking*	She *will have been eating*

Simple tenses

The **simple tenses** are the most familiar and the most frequently used in speech and writing. They refer to action in the basic time frames of past, present, and future. Singular and plural forms appear in the following examples.

1 Present tense

The **present tense** designates action occurring at the time of speaking or writing: *She lives in Toronto.* It is used to indicate habitual actions: *I exercise every morning.* It is also used to express general truths (*Time flies*) and scientific knowledge (*Light travels faster than sound*).

Forms of the simple present: He/She/It *works.* We *work.* You *work.*

In the present tense, the -*s* ending always appears on the third-person singular form.

Present tense also has some special uses:

* to indicate future time when used with time expressions:

  We *travel* to Italy next week.

  Michael *returns* in the morning.

* to describe works of literature and the arts:

  Hamlet *avoids* avenging his father's death for one reason.

2   Past tense

The **past tense** indicates action that occurred in the past and that does not extend into the present: *Bill <u>worked</u> on his history report for more than a month.*

Forms of the simple past: He/She/It *worked.* We *worked.* You *worked.*

In the past tense, the verb ending remains the same in all singular and plural forms.

3   Future tense

The **future tense** indicates action that has not yet begun: *Julia <u>will try</u> to get us all free tickets for the game.* Verbs in the simple future tense almost always contain the auxiliary verb *will.*

Forms of the simple future: He/She/It *will work.* We *will work.*

> USAGE NOTE   *Shall* sometimes replaces *will* in the first-person form to express determination or resolve: *I shall not fail; We shall overcome. Shall* is often used for first-person questions that request an opinion or seek consent. *Shall we see a movie this weekend? Shall we begin?* To use *will* in these cases would change the meaning considerably. In addition, *shall* appears frequently in commands (*Thou shall not kill*) and stipulations (*Skiers shall leave the slopes before dark*).

Perfect tenses

The **perfect tenses** express more complex time relationships than do the simple tenses. They generally indicate an action that has been completed before another action begins or an action finished by a specific time. Perfect tenses consist of a past participle preceded by the present, past, or future form of the auxiliary verb *have.*

1   Present perfect tense

The **present perfect tense** indicates that an action or its effects, begun in the past, either ended at some time in the past or continues into the present.

I *have enjoyed* many movies in recent years.

Forms of the present perfect (*have* or *has* + past participle): He/She/It *has worked*. We *have worked*. You *have worked*.

2 Past perfect tense

The **past perfect tense** designates an action that has been completed prior to another past action. It indicates a time further back in the past than the present perfect tense or the simple past tense.

He *had planned* to travel this summer until airfares skyrocketed.

Forms of the past perfect (*had* + past participle): He/She/It *had worked*. We *had worked*. You *had worked*.

3 Future perfect tense

The **future perfect tense** indicates that an action will be completed at some future time.

I *will have finished* reading *Emma* by the time of the final exam.

Forms of the future perfect (*will have* + past participle): He/She/It *will have worked*. We *will have worked*. You *will have worked*.

10h Progressive tenses

Progressive tenses indicate action that is continuing in the present, past, or future. They are constructed with a present participle (the *-ing* form) and the present, past, future, present perfect, past perfect, or future perfect form of the verb *be*.

Each of the six progressive tenses corresponds to one of the three simple and three perfect tenses.

1 Present progressive tense

The **present progressive tense** conveys a sense of ongoing action.

I *am requesting* financial aid for next year.

Forms of the present progressive (*am, is,* or *are* + present participle): He/She/It *is working*. We *are working*. You *are working*.

2   Past progressive tense

The **past progressive tense** conveys a continuing past action.

They *were driving* through the mountains when they heard the news.

Forms of the past progressive (*was* or *were* + present participle): He/She/It *was working.* We *were working.* You *were working.*

3   Future progressive tense

The **future progressive tense** suggests continuing action in the future.

They *will be trying* for the third time to make the Olympic bobsled team.

Forms of the future progressive (*will be* + present participle): He/She/It *will be working.* We *will be working.* You *will be working.*

4   Present perfect progressive tense

The **present perfect progressive tense** indicates an action that began in the past and continues into the present.

Christine *has been running* her own business for more than ten years.

Forms of the present perfect progressive (*have been* or *has been* + present participle): He/She/It *has been working.* We *have been working.* You *have been working.*

5   Past perfect progressive tense

The **past perfect progressive tense** suggests a continuing action that ended before another action.

They *had been sending* relief supplies to Sarajevo when the United Nations curtailed the shipments.

Forms of the past perfect progressive (*had been* + present participle): He/She/It *had been working.* We *had been working.* You *had been working.*

6   Future perfect progressive tense

The **future perfect progressive tense** indicates a continuing action that will end at a future time.

By the time she is twenty years old, she *will have been dancing* for more than three-quarters of her life.

Forms of the future perfect progressive (*will have been* + present participle): He/She/It *will have been working.* We *will have been working.* You *will have been working.*

EXERCISE 10–7 Using Verb Tenses

For each of the following sentences, provide the correct tense form for the verb in parentheses. Example:

When the night class ended, everyone (*head*) __headed__ for the parking lot.

1. Because of the heavy rains that (*fall*) _____ this past week, low-lying areas (*flood*) _____.

2. The demand for a good product or service (*increase*) _____ when the price is right.

3. If you begin work right after college, you (*work*) _____ for a quarter century by the time you (*be*) _____ in your mid-forties.

4. Once a book engages your attention, it (*become*) _____ difficult to put down.

5. Martin Luther King, Jr. (*preach*) _____ many memorable sermons and (*give*) _____ a number of historic speeches.

EXERCISE 10–8 Using Perfect and Progressive Verb Tense Forms

Write a paragraph in which you use perfect tense verbs and progressive tense verbs. Possible topics include a sport you watch or play; an activity you enjoy; an experience you had; an event from the news.

10i Verb tense sequences

Tense sequence refers to the relationship between the tense of a verb in an independent clause and the tense of a verb in a dependent clause. These verb tenses must follow patterns so that a passage is clear and makes sense. Consider the following examples.

When I *study,* I often *listen* to music. [Because the two actions occur simultaneously and because they are habitual acts, the verbs are both in the simple present tense.]

If I *get up* now, I *will have* time for breakfast. [The two acts occur in sequence, the first in the present and the second in the future; the verbs, thus, are in present and future tenses, respectively.]

Few people *know* what actually *happened*. [This sentence refers to the knowledge of the present about an event of the past.]

Few people *knew* what actually *happened*. [This sentence refers to what people knew at the time the event occurred rather than to what people know now.]

Here is an example in which the sequence of tenses is unclear and does not make sense.

Our friends *travel* often because they *enjoyed* it. [If the enjoying is past, then why do the friends still travel? The two actions are not sensibly related.]

Here are two better alternatives.

Our friends *travel* often because they *enjoy* going to new places.

Our friends *traveled* often because they *enjoyed* going to new places.

1   Infinitives and verb tense sequences

An infinitive in the present tense consists of *to* and the base form of the verb (*to discover, to ask*). Use the present tense infinitive to indicate a time equivalent to or a time later than that of the main verb.

EQUIVALENT TIME   He refuses *to vote* in the upcoming election. [His refusing and voting are both happening in the present.]

LATER TIME   They had planned *to attend* the party. [The planning occurred before the attending.]

An infinitive in the past tense consists of *to have* followed by the past participle of the verb (*to have worked, to have written*). Use past (or perfect) infinitives to indicate action earlier than that of the main verb.

They seem *to have gone* home early.

2   Participles and verb tense sequences

A **present participle** (the *-ing* form of the verb) shows action that occurs at the same time as that of the main verb, whatever the tense of the main verb.

Giving his students a second chance, the teacher *retested* them on the course work covered up to that point. [The teacher's giving occurs at the same time as the retesting.]

The **present perfect participle** (*having* + past participle) reflects action that occurs before that of the main verb.

Having convinced the jury, the defense lawyers rested their case. [The defense lawyers convince the jury, then rest their case.]

The **past participle** shows action that occurs before that of the main verb or at the same time as the main verb.

Convinced by the evidence the defense lawyers presented, the jury decided on a verdict of not guilty. [The jury is convinced before it decides.]

EXERCISE 10–9   Using Verb Tense Sequences
Examine the sequence of verb tense in each of the following sentences. Correct any verb tense sequences that are incorrect. Example:

<small>completes</small>
Gabriele will attend the party after she ~~will complete~~ her accounting problems.

1. Robert Redford directed his first movie after he had acted in many others.
2. Firefighters believe that to perform their work properly, they needed sufficient training and proper equipment.
3. Unprepared for the test's level of difficulty, the students decided to boycott it rather than take it.
4. Having worked hard all summer as a waiter at a steakhouse, he decided to take a long weekend trip with his friends before returning to college.
5. Unless both parties of the dispute begin to listen to one another seriously, the current unhappy state of affairs continues.

Voice

Voice refers to the relationship between the subject and the verb. If the subject performs the action, the verb is in the **active voice.** (Alice *opened* the bottle.) If the subject is acted upon, the verb is in the **passive voice.** (The bottle *was opened* by Alice.)

Active and Passive Voices

VERB TENSES	ACTIVE	PASSIVE
Present	She *invites* us.	She *is invited.*
Past	She *invited* us.	She *was invited.*
Future	She *will invite* us.	She *will be invited.*
Present perfect	She *has invited* us.	She *has been invited.*
Past perfect	She *had invited* us.	She *had been invited.*
Future perfect	She *will have invited* us.	She *will have been invited.*

 Uses of the active voice

Use the active voice when you want to emphasize who or what performed the action.

Michael *ate* the fudge royale ice cream.

Writers typically prefer the active voice because it makes for tighter, more vigorous prose. For example, consider the difference between the preceding active voice example and its passive voice counterpart.

The fudge royale ice cream *was eaten* by Michael.

The first sentence, written in the active voice, emphasizes Michael and what he did; the second sentence emphasizes ice cream and is longer than the first.

To invigorate your writing, use the active voice as much as possible. When you revise and edit your drafts, check for passive voice verbs you can rewrite in the active voice. You will not only strengthen your prose but reduce its wordiness as well.

10k **Uses of the passive voice**

The passive voice indicates that the grammatical subject of a sentence receives the action of the verb. It reverses the relationship between subject and verb established in the active voice. Verbs in the passive voice always include a form of the verb *be* immediately preceding the past participle of the main verb.

Use the passive voice when the performer of an action is either unknown or considered relatively unimportant.

The car radiator *was repaired* while its owner went to lunch.

The game *was played* outdoors under a sunny, cloudless sky.

The passive voice is sometimes used to avoid acknowledging responsibility.

It *was decided* that discounts would no longer be available. [Who decided?]

WRITING HINT   In situations where the event is more important than who or what caused it, the passive voice is especially useful. Descriptions of historical events and scientific developments, for example, often contain passive voice verbs. Notice how passive voice verbs enable the writer of the following passage to emphasize the historical importance of investment capital rather than the individuals involved in the events described.

Investment capital was used to finance development in the British Isles and abroad. In America, the Louisiana Purchase of 1803 was financed by two private London banks, Hope's and Baring's.

—Mark Girard, *Cities and People*

EXERCISE 10–10   **Identifying Active and Passive Voice Verbs**
In the following passage underline the active verbs <u>once</u> and the passive verbs <u>twice</u>.

The universe can be divided into an infinite number of "systems," which are nothing more than parcels of matter and energy. Each parcel, which can contain almost anything from a single spinning subatomic particle to an entire galaxy, is fair game for scientific study. Astronomers probe stars and the solar system. Chemists investigate systems containing carefully selected groups of atoms. Geologists study minerals or mountain ranges. Biologists examine complex systems called cells or ants or forests. Each system can be something you hold in your hand, like a rock, or it can be an integral part of something else, like your body's nervous system.

There are thousands of scientific subdisciplines, each with its own practitioners and jargon. These varied specialties differ primarily in the size and contents of the system under study. All systems, be they stars, bugs, or atoms, are governed by the same set of natural laws, but they are studied and described in very different ways.

—Robert M. Hazen and James Trefil, *Science Matters*

EXERCISE 10–11   **Using Active and Passive Voice Verbs**

Select a recent paper you wrote for one of your classes. Identify each verb in the paper as active or passive. Consider in each case whether you can tighten and strengthen your writing by converting some of the verbs in one voice into the other.

Mood

The **mood** of a verb refers to the writer's attitude toward what is being said or written. Verbs in the **indicative mood** state a fact, declare an opinion, or ask a question.

Columbus *is* generally *credited* with discovering America. [states a fact]

The contribution Columbus made to history *needs* reexamination. [declares an opinion]

Did Columbus *think* he had arrived in India, when he had actually landed in Central America? [asks a question]

Verbs in the **imperative mood** give directions or express requests or commands. Imperative verbs, which never change form, can appear without an explicit subject (*you* is understood as the subject).

Mr. James, please *give* this letter to Mrs. Jones.

Michael and Karen, *stop* that shouting right now!

Study the first four chapters for tomorrow's test.

Verbs in the **subjunctive mood** express wishes, stipulate demands or requirements, and make statements contrary to fact. They often appear in clauses introduced by *that* or *if*.

I wish that I *were* six feet two instead of five feet eight.

The course requires that a student *attend* class faithfully and *complete* written work on schedule.

Use the base form of the verb for the present tense of the subjunctive.

The first consideration is that the core curriculum *be* established.

The second concern is that it *remain* in place for at least five years.

In using the past tense of the subjunctive of *be,* use *were* for all subjects. (All other verbs are identical in the past indicative and past subjunctive.)

If I *were* you, I would accept the offer.

If we *were* not so comfortable, we might strive for more.

The subjunctive mood is also important for indirect discourse (see 15p). Use the subjunctive when making a strong suggestion or a recommendation.

The recommendation was that Jay apply for early admission.

Uses of the Subjunctive

1. When expressing a wish:

   I wish he *were* more upset by what has happened.

   Gwen sometimes wished that her friends *were* still unmarried.

2. When expressing a state contrary to fact in an *if* clause:

   If the new medication *were* to be proven safe, many of the restrictions governing its use would be lifted.

3. When using clauses beginning with *as if* and *as though:*

   The captain of the football team acted as if he were a hero.

4. When expressing a demand, request, or recommendation in clauses beginning with *that:*

   The preacher suggested that she *make* a generous contribution.

   The position requires that all candidates *be* college graduates.

The conditional

Although the conditional is not actually a mood of verbs, it is often confused with the subjunctive and thus deserves consideration along with the subjunctive mood.

Using conditional sentences

A **conditional** sentence does one of three things:

1. It indicates a relation between cause and effect.
2. It makes a prediction.
3. It speculates about what might occur.

Focusing on questions of truth, conditional sentences typically begin with *if* or an equivalent word, such as *when* or *unless*. Conditional sentences contain clauses that depend on one another, with the truth of one clause dependent on the truth of the other.

> *If you come home tomorrow, I will take you out to dinner.*

Notice that the conditional clause, introduced by *if,* is in the present tense. This is a simple statement of a possibility that could become a fact. The conditional differs from the subjunctive, which states a condition contrary to fact but is also often introduced by *if.*

> *If you were here now, I would take you out to dinner.*

Not all conditional sentences, however, begin with *if.* Some sentences that stress a factual relation between clauses begin with *when.*

When instructors *are* absent, they *request* substitutes.

This sentence suggests that when something happens (*instructors are absent*), something else happens (*they request substitutes*). In sentences that suggest a link between past events, use the past tense.

When instructors *were* absent, they *requested* substitutes.

EXERCISE 10–12   Using the Subjunctive
Revise the verbs in the following sentences that are not in the appropriate subjunctive form. Some sentences may be correct as written. Example:

>   *were*
> She moves as if she ~~was~~ a professional dancer.

1. If Dr. Shank was named to the committee, I would resign.
2. He treated her as if she was still a child.
3. The student senate recommended that the fees are lowered.
4. Thomas would give me his ticket if he were a true friend.
5. They proposed that David speaks on their behalf.

11 Nouns, Pronouns, and Case

11a Understanding nouns

A **noun** names a person (*singer, Whitney Houston*), place (*city, Miami*), thing (*car, Volvo*), concept (*justice*), or quality (*depth*). Nouns can be common or proper. **Common nouns** refer to classes—to any person, place, thing, concept, or general quality. **Proper nouns** name specific persons, places, things, concepts, or qualities.

COMMON NOUNS	PROPER NOUNS
judge	Ruth Bader Ginsberg
city	Indianapolis
dog	Fido
book	*Madame Bovary*
philosophy	Platonism

Nouns can also fall in a continuum of "abstract" or "concrete." **Abstract nouns** name concepts, ideas, or qualities—that is, things not experienced by the senses. An abstract noun is usually not preceded by an article (*a, an, the*) unless it is modified (see 15c). **Concrete nouns** refer to things we know through our senses of sight, hearing, touch, taste, or smell.

ABSTRACT NOUNS	CONCRETE NOUNS
happiness	smile
religion	priest
fertility	egg

Nouns can be either singular (naming one) or plural (naming more than one). Plurals are typically formed by adding -s or -es to the singular noun form: *flute/flutes; war/wars; potato/potatoes* (see 27d). Some nouns, however, have irregular plural forms: *mouse/mice; tooth/teeth*. Nouns derived from French, Greek, and Latin sometimes retain the plural of the original language: *alumnus/alumni; crisis/crises*.

Nouns can also be classified as count, mass, or collective. A **count noun** is a noun that can be counted and has a regular plural form: *book/books; brick/bricks*. A **mass noun** (sometimes called a **noncount noun**) is a noun that cannot be counted and, thus, cannot be made plural: *dust, news, health, peace, money, research, homework*. Qualifiers such as *some, much,* and *amount* often accompany mass nouns: *some dust, much news, an amount of money*. A **collective noun** names a group and usually keeps a singular form: *team, family, herd, school, crowd*.

Nouns are usually introduced by determiners. **Determiners** act like markers, or signals, that a noun will soon follow. A determiner limits the meaning of a noun and comes before any adjectives that describe the same noun. Although many words, including possessives, can act as determiners in a sentence, the most common by far are the **articles** *a, an,* and *the. The,* which introduces a particular noun, is a **definite article.** *A* and *an,* which introduce general nouns, are **indefinite articles.** The indefinite article *a* is used before words beginning with a consonant (*a minute, a new book*); *an* is used before words beginning with a vowel or an unpronounced *h* (*an old book, an hour*).

USAGE NOTE　When putting an indefinite article before a letter or a set of letters (such as an acronym or an abbreviation), choose *a* or *an* according to how the first letter is pronounced (not whether the letter itself is a consonant or a vowel).

a U.N. resolution (*U* is pronounced "yoo.")

an NRA member (*N* is pronounced "en.")

a CD player (*C* is pronounced "see.")

an F in math (*F* is pronounced "ef.")

Understanding pronouns

Pronouns take the place of nouns that precede or follow them in sentences. The noun that a pronoun refers to is called its **antecedent.**

The *doctor* would operate only if *she* had a good prognosis for success. [The antecedent of the pronoun *she* is the noun *doctor*.]

Pronouns are classified as personal, demonstrative, indefinite, relative, interrogative, reflexive, intensive, and reciprocal. Their forms and functions, with examples, are shown in the chart below, Pronouns.

Pronouns	
Type of pronoun	**Function**
PERSONAL I, me, my, mine we, us, our, ours you, your, yours he, she, it, him, her, his, hers, its they, them, their, theirs	Refer to people or things. *They* moved to a bigger apartment. *Theirs* is bigger than *ours*. I want *him* to find *us* a new apartment.
DEMONSTRATIVE this, that, these, those	Point to the nouns they replace. *These* are the freshest tomatoes.
INDEFINITE all, another, any, anybody, anyone, anything, both, each, either, everybody, everyone, everything, few, many, more, most, much, nobody, none, no one, nothing, one, several, some, somebody, someone, something	Refer to unspecified people or things, or to quantity. *Everyone* came, but hardly *anyone* ate. *No one* knows about *everything*. A *few* drank *some* wine.
RELATIVE that, what, whatever, which, whichever, who, whoever, whom, whomever, whose	Introduce clauses that modify nouns or pronouns. He is a speaker *whose* voice carries. *Whatever* you do, do not say *who* told you.
INTERROGATIVE what, whatever, which, whichever, who, whoever, whom, whomever, whose	Introduce questions. *Who* was there? *Which* route should we take?

(continued)

REFLEXIVE	Refer back to the subject of the clause
myself, yourself	in which they appear.
himself, herself	They surprised *themselves.*
itself, oneself	You have no one to blame but
ourselves, yourselves	*yourself.*
themselves	
INTENSIVE	Emphasize their antecedents.
(same as reflexives)	I will do it *myself.*
RECIPROCAL	Indicate mutuality or reciprocity.
each other, one another	They helped *one another.*

EXERCISE 11–1   **Identifying Pronouns**

In each of the following sentences, underline the pronoun once and its antecedent twice. Example:

Barry and Sylvia bought their tickets at the stadium.

1. Miguel will figure out a solution himself.

2. The audience that applauded the panelists also thanked them.

3. When the workers finished setting up for the carnival, they headed home.

4. Do you know who is responsible for granting waivers from required courses?

5. Until then, whatever you would like is fine with us.

 Understanding pronoun case forms

Pronouns change form to reflect their function in a sentence. The function of a pronoun, its role in a phrase or clause, is indicated by its **case.** Pronouns may appear in the subjective (or nominative), objective, or the possessive case (see the chart on p. 268, Pronoun Case).

http://www.edunet.com/
englinh/grammar/
pronoun.html
Provides a complete guide
to pronouns.

Pronoun Case			

Personal pronouns

Singular	SUBJECTIVE	OBJECTIVE	POSSESSIVE
First person	I	me	my, mine
Second person	you	you	your, yours
Third person	he, she, it	him, her, it	his, her, hers, its
Plural			
First person	we	us	our, ours
Second person	you	you	your, yours
Third person	they	them	their, theirs

Relative and interrogative pronouns

	SUBJECTIVE	OBJECTIVE	POSSESSIVE
	who	whom	whose
	whoever	whomever	

USAGE NOTE   Possessive personal pronouns never include an apostrophe. *Its* is a possessive pronoun. *It's* is a contraction of *it is* or *it has*. Similarly, *whose* is a possessive pronoun; *who's* is a contraction of *who is* or *who has*.

---

1   Subjective case forms

Use the **subjective case** form of a pronoun when it is the subject of a clause, a subject complement, or an appositive to a subject or a subject complement. (See 9a-1 for subjects, 9b-3 for complements, and 9c-2 for appositives.)

SUBJECT OF A CLAUSE

We can be either cooperative or confrontational.

SUBJECT COMPLEMENT

It is *they* who ought to be doing this work.

APPOSITIVES

Two players, *Carol* and *I,* represented the team.

USAGE NOTE   In conversation, you may sometimes use objective case forms of pronouns when formal written grammar requires subjective case forms. For example, in responding to a question such as "Are you Carmela Shiu?" you might answer, "Yes, that's *me*," rather than "Yes, that's *I*." *Me* sounds more natural because that form of the pronoun is used more often in speech. However, *I* is grammatically correct in this instance. In informal situations, you have considerable flexibility with this usage. In formal writing, however, use the grammatically correct case forms for all pronouns.

---

2   Objective case forms

Use the **objective case** form of a pronoun when it is the direct or indirect object of a verb or verbal, when it is the object of a preposition, or when it comes before an infinitive verb.

PRONOUN AS OBJECT OF A VERB OR VERBAL

When he handed *her* the flowers, she gave *him* a warm smile.

PRONOUN AS OBJECT OF A PREPOSITION

Everything was a joke to *them.*

PRONOUN BEFORE AN INFINITIVE

It was hard for *them* to hear the speech over the protesters' chants.

3   Possessive case forms

Use the **possessive case** form when a pronoun indicates ownership. Possessive pronouns can appear as adjective forms (*my, your, his, her, its, our, their*), which occur before nouns or gerunds; and as possessive forms (*mine, yours, his, hers, its, ours, theirs*), which replace possessive nouns.

In O. Henry's story "The Gift of the Magi," a young husband sells *his* watch to buy *his* wife a fancy comb to use on *her* abundant hair.

Ours is the hardest but most wonderful challenge of all.

WRITING HINT   In your writing, when a pronoun appears before a gerund (an *-ing* verbal used as a noun), use the possessive case: We have tasted *their* cooking. In this example, *cooking* is used as a noun and is the direct object of *have tasted*. If a pronoun appears before a participle, use the objective case: We have watched *them* cooking. In this second example, *cooking* is used as a participle to describe *them*.

EXERCISE 11–2   **Identifying the Case of Pronouns**
Identify the case of the pronouns in the following passage as subjective (S), objective (O), or Possessive (P).

When the committee members were interviewed after the hearings, *they* blamed each other for *their* embarrassing display of ineptitude, each insisting that *he* had performed admirably but that *his* committee colleagues had disgraced *themselves*. Those *who* saw the televised hearings can make up *their* own minds on the basis of what *they themselves* saw and heard.

EXERCISE 11–3   **Using Pronoun Case**
Fill in each blank with the appropriate form—subjective, objective, or possessive—of the pronoun in parentheses. Example:

The police officer gave (*he*) __him__ a stern warning.

1. Betty's friends urged (*she*) _____ to quit smoking.

2. His co-workers were angry at (*he*) _____ refusal to join the strike.

3. The first two contestants, Tonya Sanchez and (*I*) _____, were scheduled to appear at the same time.

4. The last piece of pizza is mine, not (*you*) _____.

5. This chair has one of (*it*) _____ legs missing.

11d   Using *who* and *whom*

Who and *whoever* are subjective forms used when the pronoun is the subject of a sentence or clause. *Whom* and *whomever* are objective forms used when the pronoun is the direct or indirect object of a verb or the object of a preposition.

Who gave me this paper? [*Who* is the subject of a sentence.]

Whom will the new tax plan benefit most? [*Whom* is the object of a verb.]

The coach praised *whoever* performed well in practice. [*Whoever* is the subject of a dependent clause.]

Give the letter to *whomever* it is addressed. [*Whomever* is the object of the preposition *to*.]

1   Using *who* and *whom* at the beginning of questions

You can decide whether to use *who* or *whom* at the beginning of a question simply by answering the question with a personal pronoun. If you can answer with a subjective case pronoun (*I, he, she, we, they*), use *who* in the question. If you can answer with an objective case pronoun (*me, him, her, us, them*), use *whom* instead.

http://www.uottawa.ca/ academic/arts/writcent/ hypergrammar/prntrcky.html Provides help with some of the trickier aspects of pronoun use.

Who was at the party? [*They* were at the party. Since *they* is a subjective case pronoun, *who* is the correct form.]

Whom do you believe? [I believe *her*. *Her* is objective case; therefore, *whom* is the correct form.]

USAGE NOTE   The distinction between *who* and *whom* at the beginning of questions applies to writing but not to speech. In everyday conversation (and in some kinds of informal writing), it is acceptable to use *who* at the beginning of questions such as "*Who* will I show it to?" and "*Who* did you bring?"

You can use the guidelines in the chart on p. 272 to help you decide whether to use *who* or *whom* in questions.

Deciding When to Use *who* or *whom* in Questions

1. Ask the question with both forms of the pronoun.

   Who/Whom deserves the biggest bonus?

   Who/Whom should we recommend for promotion?

2. Answer the question with a personal pronoun.

   She/Her deserves the biggest bonus. [Use the subjective personal pronoun.]

   We should recommend he/*him* for promotion. [Use the objective personal pronoun.]

3. Select *who* or *whom* based on the case indicated by the personal pronoun in your answer.

   Who deserves the biggest bonus? [Subjective case, *who,* is correct.]

   Whom should we recommend for promotion? [Objective case, *whom,* is correct.]

---

2   Using *who* and *whom* in dependent clauses

Use *who* or *whoever* if the pronoun functions as the subject of the clause. Use *whom* or *whomever* if the pronoun functions as an object within the clause. It makes no difference how the clause as a whole functions in the sentence; usage is determined by how the pronoun functions in its clause.

She was the candidate *whom* the electorate found most compelling. [*Whom* is the object of the verb *found.* The objective case pronoun is required even though the entire clause refers to the word *candidate,* itself a subject complement.]

Provide pencils and paper for *whoever* may need them. [*Whoever* is the subject of *may need.* The subjective case pronoun is required even though the entire clause is the object of the preposition *for.*]

You can use the accompanying chart to help you decide whether to use *who* or *whom* in dependent clauses.

Deciding When to Use *who* or *whom* in Dependent Clauses

1. Identify the dependent clause.

   Many voters did not know *(who/whom) the minor party candidates were.*

   Most voters, however, know *(who/whom) the major candidates represent.*

2. Separate the subordinate clause, convert it to a statement, and choose a personal pronoun that fits the statement.

   They/Them were the minor party candidates. [Use the subjective personal pronoun.]

   The major candidates represent they/*them*. [Use the objective personal pronoun.]

3. Select *who* or *whom* based on the case of the appropriate personal pronoun.

   Many voters did not know *who* the minor party candidates were. [Subjective case, *who*, is correct.]

   Most voters, however, know *whom* the major candidates represent. [Objective case, *whom*, is correct.]

EXERCISE 11–4   Deciding When to Use *who* and *whom*

For each of the following sentences, underline the correct relative pronoun for use in academic writing. Example:

From *who/whom* did you receive this advice?

1. *Whoever/Whomever* gets home first will have to walk the dog.

2. *Who/Whom* are you to talk like that to her?

3. Richard Nixon was a president *who/whom* was nearly impeached.

4. I want to work for *whoever/whomever* best appreciates my particular talents.

5. *Who/Whom* do you wish to consider for your advisor?

11e   Using personal pronouns with compound structures

For compound subjects and objects, use the personal pronoun you would use if the paired word and conjunction were not there. For compound subjects use *I/we/he/she/they*; for compound objects use *me/us/him/her/them*.

The accompanying chart lists guidelines for deciding whether to use a subjective or an objective pronoun in compound structures.

Deciding on Subjective or Objective Pronouns in Compound Structures

1. Separate each element of the compound structure.

   Bill and *she/her* attended the concert.

   Bill attended the concert.

   She attended the concert.

   I attended the concert with Amy and *he/him*.

   I attended the concert with Amy.

   I attended the concert with *him*.

2. Identify the case of the pronoun's function in the new sentence.

   She attended the concert. [*She* is the subject of *attended;* use the subjective.]

   I attended the concert with *him*. [*Him* is the object of *with;* use the objective case.]

3. Use the appropriate pronoun in the compound structure.

   Bill and *she* attended the concert.

   I attended the concert with Amy and *him*.

11f   Using personal pronouns with appositives

An **appositive** is a noun, noun phrase, or pronoun that renames the noun or pronoun it immediately follows. A pronoun appositive takes its case from the function of the noun it renames.

Three prominent defense attorneys—F. Lee Bailey, Roy Black, and *she*—boycotted the awards ceremony. [The appositive renames the subject, *attorneys,* so the pronoun is in the subjunctive case.]

The proposed wage increases, unfortunately, never included both groups of workers—the office staff and *us.* [The appositive renames *workers,* the object of the preposition *of,* so the pronoun is in the objective case.]

11g Using personal pronouns with elliptical constructions

An elliptical construction is one in which some words have been intentionally omitted, as in a comparison. When such an elliptical construction ends with a pronoun, mentally fill in the missing words of the construction to determine its grammatical function in the sentence. Once you know the pronoun's grammatical function, you can determine its case.

My father has considerably more mechanical aptitude than *I* [have]. [*I* is the subject of the implied verb *have.*]

Her sister is more artistic than *she* [is]. [*She* is the subject of the implied verb *is.*]

11h Using *we* and *us* with a noun

You may occasionally use the pronouns *we* or *us* before a noun to help establish the identity of the noun. If the noun is the subject or subject complement of a clause, use *we.*

We athletes should stick together. [*Athletes* is the subject of the sentence; the pronoun paired with it should be in the subjective case—*we.*]

If the noun is a direct object, an indirect object, or an object of a preposition, use *us.*

The administration never bothered to consult with *us* students. [*Students* is the object of *with;* the pronoun paired with *students* should be in the objective case—*us.*]

To decide whether to use *we* or *us* before a noun, mentally drop the noun and see if the pronoun itself should be in the subjective or the objective: *We should stick together; The administration never bothered to consult with us.*

11i   Using objective case forms with infinitives

Use objective case pronoun forms as both subject and object of an infinitive.

subject of infinitive   object of infinitive

They asked *her* to conduct the class.   She decided to reject *them*.

11j   Using possessive case forms with gerunds

Use the possessive case pronoun form immediately before a gerund. (A gerund is the *-ing* form of a verb used as a noun; e.g., *hiking* is exhilarating.)

gerund

They were disappointed with *his* cooking.

Before a participle (an *-ing* verb form used as an adjective), use an objective case form.

participle

I observed *them* kissing. (emphasis is on *them*)

To emphasize the action rather than those performing the action, use a possessive case pronoun form.

I observed *their* kissing. (emphasis is on *kissing*)

EXERCISE 11–5   Choosing the Appropriate Pronoun
Underline the appropriate pronoun in the following sentences. Example:

The possibility of *him/his* leaving never occurred to me.

1. It was unlike *they/them* not to call.
2. Leah reads novels more often than *I/me*.
3. The subject of *them/their* moviegoing never came up.
4. The government needs *we/us* taxpayers.
5. His father disapproved of *his/him* lifting weights.

12 Adjectives and Adverbs

Adjectives and adverbs are modifiers. They describe, limit, or qualify other words. You can use adjectives and adverbs to add detail to your writing and to make it more vivid.

12a Distinguishing between adjectives and adverbs

Adjectives modify nouns and pronouns. Adverbs modify verbs, adjectives, or other adverbs. In the following example, the adjective *fearful* modifies the noun *children* and the adverb *quietly* modifies the verb *entered*.

The *fearful* children entered the house *quietly*.

Here is another example with the adjectives italicized and adverbs in bold print.

I've come upon animals **suddenly before** and felt a *similar* tension, a *precipitate* heightening of the senses. And I have felt the *inexplicable* but **sharply** *boosted* intensity of a *wild* moment in the bush, where it is not until some minutes **later** that you discover the source of the electricity— the *warm* remains of a *grizzly* bear kill, or the **still** *moist* tracks of a wolverine.

—Barry Lopez, "The Stone Horse"

Adjectives answer the questions *which? how many?* or *what kind?*

The *yellow* crocuses were the *first* blooms of *last* spring. [which crocuses? *yellow*, which blooms? *first*; which spring? *last*]

Curious students are a joy to teach. [what kind of students? *curious*]

Some adjectives are formed by adding one of the following suffixes to nouns.

NOUN	SUFFIX	ADJECTIVE
charity	-able	charitable
style	-ish	stylish
dirt	-y	dirty
atom	-ic	atomic
season	-al	seasonal
pain	-less	painless
danger	-ous	dangerous
thought	-ful	thoughtful

Adjectives are also formed from verbs.

VERB	SUFFIX	ADJECTIVE
scare	-y	scary
hesitate	-ant	hesitant
notice	-able	noticeable
construct	-ive	constructive

However, many common adjectives have no identifying suffixes: *good, hot, little, young, fat.*

Participles and infinitives sometimes function as adjectives.

The *surprised* children looked at their *smiling* parents.

Philip had trouble deciding which car *to buy.*

Adjectives usually precede the nouns or pronouns they modify. Sometimes, however, they follow the words they modify.

The *beautiful ripe* fruit sat on the counter.

The fruit, *ripe* and *beautiful,* sat on the counter.

Adverbs answer the questions *when? how? how often?* or *where?*

I went to a Red Sox game *yesterday.*

We were *anxiously* awaiting the results of the final examination.

Karen sat *behind* me in chemistry class.

Adverbs are often formed by adding the suffix -*ly* to adjectives.

ADJECTIVE	ADVERB
glad	glad*ly*
careful	careful*ly*
unjust	unjust*ly*

But an -*ly* ending on a word does not necessarily identify it as an adverb. Some adjectives, such as *lonely* and *timely*, end in -*ly*, and some adverbs do not end in -*ly*: *here, there, now, often, seldom, never*.

Adverbs can either precede or follow the verbs, adjectives, or other adverbs they modify.

The waiter *carefully* set the dishes of steaming food on the table.

Although he worked *quickly*, he never rushed.

Adverbs can sometimes be shifted to the beginning or end of a sentence, depending on the rhythm or emphasis a writer wants to achieve.

Carefully, the waiter set the dishes on the table.

The waiter set the dishes on the table *carefully*.

EXERCISE 12–1   Identifying Adjectives and Adverbs
In the following paragraph, underline the adjectives once and the adverbs twice. Draw an arrow from each adjective to the word it modifies and from each adverb to the word, phrase, or clause it modifies. Example:

The snow fell swiftly in thick tufts, like new wool washed before the weaver spins it.

  She was an old woman now and her life had become a network of memories. The blankets her grandmother had woven so skillfully were neatly laid over the bedpost. Eagerly she anticipated the warmth of the woven woolen blanket. She remembered sleeping warmly on cold windy nights, wrapped in the carefully stitched quilts. Whenever a bird screeched raucously, she shivered violently. Eagerly she awaited the return of her ancestral artifacts.

Grammar and Writing

Managing Modifiers

Improve your writing by focusing on modifiers. Check a recent paper for modifiers.

- If you overuse modifiers, cut some of them.
- If you underuse modifiers, add a few.
- Check for correct usage of *good* and *well, bad* and *ill.*

Be aware of what modifiers contribute to your writing. Consider how modifiers clarify your thinking and convey your attitudes and feelings.

EXAMPLE

The [~~numerous~~] casualties extensive[ly] suffered by both sides in

the Civil War Battle of Gettysburg filled the battlefield with bodies

sprawled in [~~agonizingly awkward~~] *delete* contorted positions. The only

signs of life were supplied by *hordes of buzzing* flies around the *rigid* bodies.

EXERCISE 12–2   **Using Adjectives and Adverbs**

Transform the following words to adjectives; then transform the adjectives to adverbs. (You can consult a dictionary if necessary.) Finally, use the newly formed adjectives and adverbs in sentences. Example:

courage (*noun*); courageous (*adjective*); courageously (*adverb*)

Several *courageous* citizens identified the mobster in court.

They *courageously* stood up for my right to read whatever I want.

1. reason   2. help   3. act   4. fool   5. hero

12b Using adjectives with linking verbs

A modifier that follows a linking verb modifies the subject of the verb, and, therefore, is always an adjective. When adjectives follow linking verbs, they function as subject complements.

When functioning as linking verbs, sensory verbs are followed by nouns or adjectives, never by adverbs. When the verbs express action, however, they can be followed by adverbs.

The sauce *tasted* delicious. [linking verb with adjective]

The cook *tasted* the sauce regularly. [action verb with adverb]

12c Using adverbs with two forms

Some adverbs have two acceptable forms—a short and an -*ly* form. Sometimes the two forms have the same meaning; pairs such as *cheap/cheaply, deep/ deeply, loud/loudly, quick/quickly, sharp/ sharply,* and *slow/slowly,* for example, are interchangeable in informal conversation. But because the short form is informal, you will want to use the -*ly* form of the adverb in academic writing.

INFORMAL   Drive *slow* through the intersection.

FORMAL   She drove *slowly* through the intersection.

In other pairs, the short and the -*ly* forms of the adverb have different meanings. When using adverbs such as *high/highly, late/lately, near/nearly,* or *wrong/wrongly,* be sure not to confuse those meanings.

Lately, their attendance had improved, though earlier they had often come *late.* [*lately* means "recently"; *late* means "not on time"]

As they drew *near* the theater, they realized they had *nearly* forgotten to call home. [*near* means "close to"; *nearly* means "almost"]

EXERCISE 12–3 **Choosing Modifiers**

1. Underline the appropriate modifier—adjective or adverb—in each of the following sentences. Example:

Their _courageous/courageously_ action saved many lives.

  a. In the midst of storewide confusion, the salespeople remained _calm/calmly_.

  b. The snow began falling _light/lightly_ and then _steady/steadily_ intensified.

  c. Remember to drive _slow/slowly_ as you come through Devil's Pass.

2. In the following sentences, label the italicized _-ly_ words as adjectives [ADJ] or adverbs [ADV]. Examples:

> ADJ
>
> She played a _lively_ melody on the piano.

> ADV
>
> They went along _unwillingly_ with the plan.

  a. They were charged with _disorderly_ conduct.

  b. I _successfully_ completed my first year as an intern.

  c. Our accountant made a _costly_ mistake in our tax return.

EXERCISE 12–4   Using Adjectives and Adverbs in Writing

Write a descriptive paragraph of six to twelve sentences in which you use adjectives and adverbs to enhance your description. Choose adjectives and adverbs that help your readers imagine that they can see, hear, smell, taste, and feel what you are describing. Possible topics include your room; your neighborhood; a place on campus; a scene in nature; a concert; a scene from a movie.

12d   Using _good/well_ and _bad/badly_

Use the adjectives _good_ and _bad_ to modify nouns or pronouns: _a good time_; _a bad play_. To modify verbs, adjectives, or other adverbs, use _well_ and _badly_: _she speaks well_; _he hears badly_.

As adjectives, _good_ and _bad_ follow linking verbs.

> The turkey looks _good_.

> The chicken smells _bad_.

As adverbs, _badly_ and _well_ follow action verbs.

> They both behaved _badly_ throughout the proceedings.

> They skate _well_ enough to become professionals.

Well can be both an adjective and an adverb.

They looked *well* when we last saw them. [adjective meaning "healthy" and modifying *They*]

He performed *well* during the competition. [adverb meaning "effectively" and modifying *performed*]

EXERCISE 12–5   **Using *good/well* and *bad/badly* Correctly**
In the following sentences, correct the misuse of *good/well* or *bad/badly*. Some sentences may be correct as written. Example:

> *well*
> She no longer skates ~~good~~.

1. It was a good time; it was a bad time.
2. It did not go good; it did not go badly.
3. It could have gone better, but it was not badly.
4. They invested their money good, so good that they doubled their investment.
5. Good high school and college athletic prospects do not always turn out well as professionals.

12e   Using comparative and superlative forms

Adjectives and adverbs appear in three forms: **positive, comparative,** and **superlative.** The positive or simple form is the form most commonly used in speech and writing. The comparative and superlative forms of adjectives and adverbs are used to make comparisons.

POSITIVE	COMPARATIVE	SUPERLATIVE
hungry	hungrier	hungriest
small	smaller	smallest
useful	more useful	most useful
usefully	less usefully	least usefully

He was *hungry* at six o'clock, *hungrier* at eight, and *hungriest* at ten.

Although ours was a *useful* suggestion, Barbara's was even *more useful*, and Sharon's was the *most useful* of all.

Most one-syllable adjectives and many two-syllable adjectives add the suffixes -*er* and -*est* to form their comparative and superlative forms: *smooth/smoother/smoothest; tough/tougher/toughest.* All adjectives ending with -*ful,* such as *useful,* and all adjectives with three or more syllables add the words *more* and *most* before the positive to form the comparative and superlative: *momentous/more momentous/most momentous.* Most adverbs of two or more syllables and most adverbs ending with -*ly* add the words *more* and *most* before the positive to form the comparative and superlative. Adverbs and adjectives that show negative comparison use the words *less* and *least* before the positive form: *loudly/less loudly/least loudly.*

These general principles have some exceptions. For example, some adjectives use *more* in the comparative (*more severe; more remote*) but add -*est* in the superlative (*severest; remotest*).

Sometimes we use **incomplete comparisons** in speaking and writing, as in "the book was better" or "the service was worse." In the context of conversation it might be understood that the book was better than the movie or that the service was worse than the food. In academic writing, however, you need to provide sufficient context to make your comparisons clear. (See 21e.)

INCOMPLETE	Some believe that Einstein was the greatest.
COMPLETE	Some believe that Einstein was the greatest physicist in history.

Some adjectives and adverbs change form to indicate their comparative and superlative degrees. The chart on p. 285 lists these.

1 Distinguishing between comparatives and superlatives

Use the comparative forms of adjectives and adverbs to compare two things. Use their superlative forms to compare three or more.

ADJECTIVE—COMPARATIVE	Hebrew is a much *older* language than English.
ADJECTIVE—SUPERLATIVE	Chinese is one of the world's *oldest* languages.
ADVERB—COMPARATIVE	Juanita's approach will resolve the problem *more effectively* than Hwan's.
ADVERB—SUPERLATIVE	Hilda's solution will solve the problem *most effectively* of all.

Irregular Comparative and Superlative Forms of Adjectives and Adverbs

Adjectives

POSITIVE	COMPARATIVE	SUPERLATIVE
bad	worse	worst
good	better	best
ill	worse	worst
little	less	least
many	more	most
much	more	most
some	more	most

Adverbs

POSITIVE	COMPARATIVE	SUPERLATIVE
badly	worse	worst
ill	worse	worst
well	better	best

2 Checking for double or incomplete comparisons

A **double comparison** is a nonstandard form that uses two comparative adjectives when only one is necessary. Use only one form of the comparative, not both, to make a particular comparison; that is, use either -er or *more*, but do not use both together.

FAULTY   Mozart's symphonies are *more better* known and *more often* recorded than his string quartets.

REVISED   Mozart's symphonies are *better* known and *more frequently* recorded than his string quartets.

EXERCISE 12–6 Using Comparative and Superlative Forms

Choose between the comparative and superlative forms of the adjective or adverb pairs in the following sentences. Example:

It is <u>better/more better</u> to be cooperative than confrontational.

1. Of the three proposals, theirs was the *more/most* sensible.
2. Paris is the European city *more/most* often visited by Americans.
3. Which is the *larger/largest* of the mountains?
4. The fall of the Berlin Wall was the *more/most* stunning event of all.
5. They used to work out *more/most* regularly and with *greater/greatest* intensity than they do now.

EXERCISE 12–7   Using Comparative Forms of Adjectives and Adverbs in Writing
Write a paragraph in which you use the comparative and superlative forms of at least two adjectives and two adverbs. Include at least one adjective and adverb before the word(s) it modifies and at least one following the word(s) it modifies.

 Avoiding double negatives

A **double negative** is a nonstandard form using two negatives where only one is necessary. Although few speakers of English would misunderstand "I do not have no money," the statement is nonstandard because it contains two negatives and only one is necessary. The adverbs *barely*, *scarcely*, and *hardly* and the preposition *but* (meaning "except") are negative and should not be used with other negatives.

FAULTY   We couldn*'t hardly* see the band. Their music did*n't never* reach the back rows of the stadium.

REVISED   We *could hardly* see the band. Their music *never reached* the back rows of the stadium.

Although double negatives were once acceptable in English (Shakespeare used them for emphasis), using them in your writing may lead your readers to believe you are careless.

WRITING HINT   In standard written English, you can combine two negatives to make a positive understatement.

Her resignation was *not unexpected.*

He was *not displeased* with his performance.

You can use such double negatives as these when the alternative positive statement (*Her resignation was expected; He was pleased with his performance*) would be too strong.

12g   Avoiding overuse of nouns as modifiers

A noun can function as an adjective, modifying another noun.

    turkey dinner   night shift   mother figure   film critic

The meaning of such familiar terms is clear. Occasionally, however, a string of nouns used as adjectives either obscures meaning or becomes cumbersome; if this happens, you need to revise for economy and clarity.

> AWKWARD   To enhance company morale, management introduced a series of *employee relations communications strategies.*

> REVISED   To enhance company morale, management developed strategies to ensure communication between employees and supervisors.

EXERCISE 12–8   Using Irregular Adjectives and Adverbs

Make any necessary corrections to the irregular adjectives and adverbs in the following passage. Some sentences may be correct as written. Example:

                        well

Laurence Olivier performed very ~~good~~ in his Shakespearean roles.

    One of the best films I ever saw was Laurence Olivier's *Hamlet.* It was even more good than the very good version with Mel Gibson as Hamlet. Some other filmed versions of Shakespeare's play are not bad, but they are not as well as either Olivier's or Gibson's version. One of the worse Shakespearean characters Olivier ever portrayed was the bad king, Richard III. Of his many Shakespearean roles, Olivier's portrayal of Richard III contains perhaps his better Shakespearean acting. His portrayal does not compare badly with others', but his portrayal of King Lear in a later film, when Olivier was at the end of his career, is decidedly worst than his more youthful performances.

EXERCISE 12–9   Working with Nouns as Modifiers

Rewrite the following noun phrases to make their meanings clearer. Example:

annual human rights progress statements

annual statements on the progress of human rights

1. arms control impact statements
2. teacher education program analysis
3. a real estate law specialist
4. student dining hall policy committee meetings
5. English language deterioration concerns

12h Using possessive adjectives

Some possessive forms of personal pronouns also function as adjectives; they modify nouns and indicate ownership.

My idea might differ from yours. [*My* is a possessive adjective modifying the noun *idea*. *Yours* is a possessive pronoun.]

His goal was to become a millionaire by age thirty. [*His* is a possessive adjective modifying the noun *goal*.]

USAGE NOTE   In your writing take care to distinguish possessive adjectives from contractions and other words that are pronounced the same or similarly.

POSSESSIVE ADJECTIVE   The plan has *its* merits.

SOUND-ALIKE CONTRACTION   *It's* simple and workable.

EXERCISE 12–10   Working with Possessive Adjectives
Underline the correct word in each of the following sentences. Example:

They spend all *their/they're* time together.

1. The cat drank *its/it's* milk and washed *its/it's* paws.
2. We told him that *your/you're* daughter was in law school.
3. It is *your/you're* own fault if *your/you're* out of money.
4. Six members have paid their dues; *their/they're* the same people who do all the work.
5. *Its/It's* a nice jug, but *its/it's* handle is broken.

13 Prepositions, Conjunctions, and Interjections

13a   Recognizing prepositions

A **preposition** shows the relationship between a noun or a pronoun (the object of a preposition) and another word or group of words in a sentence. A word is a preposition only if it is followed by an object and modifiers to form a **prepositional phrase.** The word *in,* for example, can function both as a preposition and as an adverb.

We found the letters in the mailbox. [noun]

Letters of support have been pouring in. [adverb]

Prepositions can be used to indicate time, place, destination, possession, as well as other relationships among words in a sentence.

Common Prepositions

about	below	inside	since
above	beneath	into	through
across	beside	like	throughout
after	between	near	till
against	beyond	of	to
along	by	off	toward
among	down	on	under
around	during	onto	until
as	except	out	up
at	for	over	upon
before	from	past	with
behind	in	regarding	without

TIME	the lights came on *during* the intermission.
PLACE	the lamp stood *in* the corner *behind* the chair.
DESTINATION	they were heading *toward* the center of the city.
POSSESSION	that was the argument *of* the opposition.

The chart on page 289 lists the most common prepositions.

In addition to the common single-word prepositions, there is also a group of **compound prepositions** made up of two or more words. The accompanying chart lists some familiar compound prepositions.

Common Compound Prepositions

according to	by way of	in spite of
along with	due to	instead of
apart from	except for	in view of
aside from	in addition to	next to
as well as	in case of	on behalf of
because of	in front of	out of
by means of	in place of	with regard to

13b Using prepositions in writing

A preposition appears before its object—that is, the noun or pronoun it connects with another part of the sentence. The preposition, its object, and any related modifiers form a prepositional phrase. A prepositional phrase almost always functions as an adjective or an adverb in a sentence.

The girl dived *into* the pond. [preposition *into* + object of preposition *the pond* = prepositional phrase]

She wore a pink swimsuit *with* lavender stripes. [preposition *with* + object of preposition *lavender stripes* = prepositional phrase]

Prepositions are indispensable in writing, but take care not to overuse them. Some sentences can be improved by using adjectives, verbs, and gerunds instead of prepositional phrases.

WORDY	IMPROVED
He gave an explanation for his mistake.	He explained his mistake.
We began a period of study for the exam.	We began studying for the exam.

WRITING HINT   In speech, people sometimes use extra prepositions.

We met *up with* the director at noon.

Their garage is *out in back of* the house.

You can streamline your writing by eliminating such unnecessary prepositions.

We met the director at noon.

Their garage is behind [*or* in back of] the house.

WRITING HINT   Prepositions usually come before their objects. But in informal English, prepositions are sometimes placed after their objects. In conversation, these "deferred" prepositions frequently occur with questions, relative clauses, and passives.

Who are you talking *about?*

This book is the one that I'm interested *in.*

His problem has been taken care *of.*

In formal writing you should avoid putting prepositions at the end of a clause or sentence.

About whom are you talking?

This book is the one *in which* I'm interested.

We have taken care *of* his problem.

EXERCISE 13–1 Working with Prepositions in Your Own Writing
Refer to the preceding lists of prepositions. Compose a paragraph that includes at least five different prepositions.

13c Recognizing conjunctions

Conjunctions link words, phrases, and clauses to one another. The four types of conjunctions are: coordinating conjunctions, correlative conjunctions, subordinating conjunctions, and conjunctive adverbs. (See also 22a-1 and 22b-1.)

1 Coordinating conjunctions

Coordinating conjunctions connect parallel words, phrases, and independent clauses within a sentence. The accompanying chart identifies the coordinating conjunctions and their functions.

Coordinating Conjunctions		
CAUSE OR REASON	*for*	She ate, *for* she was hungry.
ADDITION	*and*	He listens to jazz *and* blues.
NEGATIVE CHOICE	*nor*	I didn't answer the door, *nor* did I peek out the window.
CONTRAST	*but*	The task was difficult *but* not impossible.
CHOICE	*or*	We will *or* we will not.
CONTRAST	*yet*	They were eager *yet* afraid.
RESULT	*so*	He wanted it, *so* he bought it.

CONNECTED VERBS	Maya Angelou might <u>sing</u> *or* <u>recite</u> her <u>poems</u> and <u>stories</u> in public.
CONNECTED PHRASES	Some poets' work was <u>neglected in their time</u> *yet* <u>revered in our own.</u>
CONNECTED CLAUSES	<u>Robert Frost wanted to achieve popularity as a poet,</u> *but* <u>he longed to be admired by the critics as well.</u>

An easy way to remember the coordinating conjunctions is with the mnemonic *FANBOYS*. In this aid to memory, each letter stands for a different conjunction: *for, and, nor, but, or, yet, so.*

2 Correlative conjunctions

Correlative conjunctions also connect words, phrases, and clauses that have parallel grammatical structures and that have equal emphasis. But as the accompanying chart shows, correlative conjunctions occur in pairs. (See 23b–2.)

Correlative Conjunctions		
both . . . and	not only . . . but also	neither . . . nor
either . . . or	whether . . . or	just as . . . so

Place each of the paired correlative conjunctions directly before the word, phrase, or clause it introduces.

He wanted *neither* to eat *nor* to sleep.

3 Subordinating conjunctions

Subordinating conjunctions introduce dependent (or subordinate) clauses and indicate the relationship of the dependent clause to the main clause of a sentence.

Even though the deadline for financial aid had passed, her parents decided to submit an application anyway.

This sentence could be written with the clauses in reverse order to increase sentence variety (see Chapter 24) or to change the emphasis within the sentence.

Her parents decided to submit an application *even though* the deadline for financial aid had passed.

The chart on p. 294 lists common subordinating conjunctions and their uses.

Common Subordinating Conjunctions

CAUSE	as, because, now that, since
COMPARISON	as if, than
CONDITION	if, if only, provided that, unless
CONTRAST	although, even if, even though, though
MANNER	as, as if
PLACE	where, wherever
PURPOSE	in order that, so that
TIME	after, before, until, when, whenever, while

4   Conjunctive adverbs

Conjunctive adverbs emphasize a close relationship in meaning between two independent or main clauses. They indicate a specific, logical connection between the ideas expressed in the two clauses they connect.

The books had not arrived; *however,* they were due within the week.

He was angry and upset; *moreover,* he was also terribly disappointed.

Conjunctive adverbs can appear in different places in a clause. Because they are adverbs, they can be shifted to create emphasis and provide variety.

Richard Cory had wealth, status, power, and good looks; *nevertheless,* he went home one night and put a bullet through his head.

Richard Cory had wealth, status, power, and good looks; he went home one night, *nevertheless,* and put a bullet through his head.

Common Conjunctive Adverbs

also	furthermore	likewise	otherwise
anyway	hence	meanwhile	similarly
certainly	however	moreover	still
consequently	incidentally	nevertheless	then
finally	indeed	next	therefore
further	instead	now	thus

WRITING HINT   Avoid beginning too many sentences or independent clauses with conjunctive adverbs. Positioning the conjunctive adverb further into the independent clause makes for smoother writing.

EXERCISE 13–2   Identifying Conjunctions

Identify the types of conjunctions in the following passage.

The concept of childhood, so vital to the traditional American way of life, is threatened with extinction in the society we have created. Today's child has become the unwilling, unintended victim of overwhelming stress—the stress borne of rapid, bewildering social change and constantly rising expectations. The contemporary parent dwells in a pressure-cooker of competing demands, transitions, role changes, personal and professional uncertainties, over which he or she exerts slight direction. We seek release from stress whenever we can, and usually the one sure ambit of our control is the home. Here, if nowhere else, we enjoy the fact (or illusion) of playing a determining role. If child-rearing necessarily entails stress, then by hurrying children to grow up, or by treating them as adults, we hope to remove a portion of our burden of worry and anxiety and to enlist our children's aid in carrying life's load. We do not mean our children harm in acting thus—on the contrary, as a society we have come to imagine that it is good for young people to mature rapidly. Yet we do our children harm when we hurry them through childhood.

—David Elkind, *The Hurried Child*

EXERCISE 13–3   Using Conjunctions

Write four sentences, each containing two independent clauses connected by one of the following words: *and, but, consequently, for, however, moreover, or, otherwise, then, yet.* Possible topics include watching television; preparing a meal; applying for a job; doing research; meeting someone new; making an important purchase.

Then rewrite your four sentences, using one independent clause and one dependent clause in each sentence. Use some of the subordinating conjunctions listed in the chart at the top of p. 294.

13d   Using interjections

Interjections are emphatic words or phrases that express surprise or emotion. They appear much more often in speech and dialogue than in expository writing, and they appear far less in formal and academic writing than in informal writing. They do not express a grammatical relation to other parts of a sentence; thus, they tend to stand alone as fragments.

Okay, already!   Help!   Wow!   Well!   What a night!

Wow! That was some dinner!

EXERCISE 13–4 Using Conjunctions

Write a paragraph in which you include three sentences using coordinating conjunctions and three more sentences using subordinating conjunctions. Then write a second paragraph in which you include three sentences using correlative conjunctions and three sentences using conjunctive adverbs.

14 *Maintaining Agreement*

In grammar there are two kinds of **agreement**. A subject and verb in a sentence must agree both in person (first person, second person, third person) and in number (singular or plural).

A professional tennis *tournament* usually *involves* six rounds of play. [third-person singular]

The seeded *players* sometimes *receive* a first-round bye. [third-person plural]

A pronoun must agree with its antecedent (the noun it refers to) in person, number, and gender (masculine, feminine, or neuter).

Our *parents* grow many kinds of vegetables in *their* garden.

Mom grows *her* Halloween pumpkins and *Dad* takes great pride in *his* meaty tomatoes.

Subject–Verb Agreement

14a   Making a verb agree with a third-person singular subject

Regular verbs take the same form in the first- and second-person singular, in the first- and second-person plural, and in the third-person plural. The only form that varies is the third-person singular form of the verb. (See 10c for more on regular and irregular verbs.)

	SINGULAR	PLURAL
FIRST PERSON	I think	We think
SECOND PERSON	You think	You think
THIRD PERSON	He/She/It thinks	They think

To make a present tense verb agree with a third-person singular subject, add -*s* or -*es* to the base form of the verb.

The instructor *believes* her students are well prepared for the final.

She *flosses* her teeth every day.

Two verbs—*have* and *be*—are exceptions to this rule. *Have* changes to *has* in the third-person singular of the present tense. *Be* changes to *is* in the third-person singular.

Nouns used as subjects are in the third person. To confirm that you are using the correct verb form with a noun subject, replace the noun with a third-person pronoun. If you can substitute *he, she,* or *it,* then you need the third-person singular form. If you can substitute *they,* use the third-person plural form.

Product endorsement (*generate* or *generates?*) even more income.

[It] *generates* even more income.

Five-set tennis matches (*last* or *lasts?*) more than three hours.

[They] *last* more than three hours.

Notice that the -*s* or -*es* ending on a noun indicates a plural noun, while the -*s* or -*es* ending on a verb designates a singular verb.

The movie *requires* sustained and careful attention. [singular subject; verb takes -s ending]

Both movies *require* sustained and careful attention. [plural subject; verb lacks -s ending]

USAGE NOTE   *Be* is the only verb that changes in number in the past tense. *Was* is used with first- and third-person singular subjects.

I *was* watching a team-tennis match on cable last night.

Pete Sampras *was* the only player I recognized.

Were is used with all plural subjects and with *you*.

The matches *were* long and drawn out.

You *were* always a fan of Andre Agassi, were you not?

EXERCISE 14–1   Working with Third-Person Subjects
Rewrite the following sentences, changing singular subjects to plural and plural subjects to singular. Then change the verbs to agree with their subjects. Example:

A video *game costs* one dollar for three minutes of play.

Video *games cost* one dollar for three minutes of play.

1. Archaeologists study buildings, tools, and other artifacts of ancient culture.
2. An adult student has extra responsibilities to cope with.
3. An anthropologist always looks for signs of social change and development.
4. A high cholesterol level increases the risk of heart attack.
5. Film critics spend a lot of time in the dark.

14b   Making separated subjects and verbs agree

Sometimes a subject and a verb are separated by words or phrases.

A box of oranges (*arrive* or *arrives?*) at the house once a month.

Low scores on the SAT may (*discourage* or *discourages?*) students from applying to certain colleges.

A box of oranges *arrives* at the house once a month.

Low scores on the S.A.T. may *discourage* students from applying to certain colleges.

> WRITING HINT   When using expressions such as *accompanied by, together with, in addition to, like,* and *as well as,* check your sentences carefully to maintain subject–verb agreement. Be sure your verb agrees with the subject of the sentence, not with the word closest to it.

The Dodger first baseman, along with most of his teammates, *refuses* to get his hair cut short.

The Eiffel Tower, like many famous monuments, *symbolizes* the city in which it is located.

EXERCISE 14–2   Maintaining Agreement between Subjects and Verbs
In each of the following sentences, underline the subject and then circle the verb that agrees with it. Example:

<u>One</u> of the many bird species *is/are* in danger of extinction.

1. Three of the four questions *is/are* challenging.
2. Bonsai trees *require/requires* careful pruning.
3. The participants in the ceremony *is/are* first-year college students.
4. Many movies made in the past year *contain/contains* violent scenes.
5. The music *was/were* composed by George Gershwin.

Making subject and verb agree with a compound subject

A **compound subject** is made up of two or more subjects joined by a conjunction. Compound subjects connected by *and* usually take a plural verb

Tom and Jerry *are* a famous pair of cartoon characters.

Liberty, equality, and fraternity *have* long *been valued.*

However, when parts of a compound subject function as a single unit or refer to the same person or thing, the subject is considered singular, and the verb should also be singular.

Ogilvy and Mather *is* known as a creative advertising agency.

Apple pie and ice cream *has been* a favorite American dessert for years.

When a compound subject is preceded by the adjective *each* or *every*, use a singular verb form.

Each sentence, phrase, and clause *needs* to be crafted with care.

Every candidate and criminal suspect *deserves* a fair hearing.

With compound subjects connected by *or, nor, either . . . or,* or *neither . . . nor,* the verb may be singular or plural. When both parts of the subject are singular, the verb is singular.

No food or drink *was* provided.

Neither the referee nor the tournament director *knows* when play will resume.

When both subjects are plural, the verb is plural.

Either the workers or the owners *will need* to make concessions.

But when one part of the subject is singular and the other is plural, the verb agrees with the subject closer to it.

To enroll, either junior standing or referrals from two faculty members *are* required.

WRITING HINT   If one of the subjects joined by *or* or *nor* is singular and one is plural, place the plural subject closest to the verb to avoid awkwardness.

AWKWARD   Either the committee members or the president *is* misinformed.

REVISED   Either the president or the committee members *are* misinformed.

(continued)

When the joined subjects are pronouns that take different verb forms, it is better to avoid having to make a choice. Rephrase the sentence.

AWKWARD   Neither you nor I (*am* or *are?*) ready for the test.

REPHRASED   Neither of us is ready for the test.

14d Making a verb agree with an indefinite pronoun subject

An **indefinite pronoun** is one that does not refer to a specific person or thing. Most indefinite pronouns take a singular verb. (The accompanying chart lists common indefinite pronouns that take singular verbs.)

Everybody *is* coming.

Everyone who can help with the preparations *should* arrive early.

Indefinite Pronouns Taking Singular Verb Forms

another	either	neither	other
anybody	everybody	nobody	somebody
anyone	everyone	no one	someone
anything	everything	nothing	something
each	much	one	

Some indefinite pronouns take plural verb forms: *both, few, many, others,* and *several.*

Both *were* destroyed by the 1966 flood in Venice.

Few, if any, *were* missed by the best students.

Still other indefinite pronouns can be either singular or plural, depending on the noun or pronoun they refer to: *all, any, enough, more, most, none,* and *some.*

SINGULAR   Some of the writing *is* excellent.

PLURAL   Some of the test questions *were* ambiguous.

14e   Making a verb agree with a collective noun subject

A **collective noun** names a group of people or things. They include such words as *group, class, team, committee, herd, crowd, number, audience,* and *family.* Because collective nouns describe a group that is considered a single unit, they usually take singular verbs.

The class *has performed* well throughout the term.

When emphasizing the individual members rather than the group as a whole, use a plural verb form.

The jury *are* expected to return to their homes upon completing their work on the case. [The individual jury members will return to their own homes.]

WRITING HINT   Since use of a plural verb with collective nouns such as *committee* and *jury* may sound incorrect, you can add a prepositional phrase or a plural word such as *members* after the collective noun:

The *committee members are* debating the proposal.

The *herd of cattle cross* the river.

USAGE NOTE   The collective noun *number* can take either a singular or plural verb. When used with the article *a,* its verb is plural.

A number of classical works *are* repeated every season in concerts throughout the world.

When used with the article *the,* its verb is singular.

The number of well-read teachers *is* diminishing every year.

EXERCISE 14–3   Checking for Subject–Verb Agreement

Revise the errors in subject–verb agreement in the following sentences.

1. Both first place and fourth place was won by runners from our team.

2. Neither the chief negotiator nor the strikers accepts the latest proposal.

3. Each of the employees have agreed to a pay cut.

4. The number of stores leaving the mall increase every month.

5. The faculty has not been able to decide among themselves.

  Making a verb agree with its subject rather than a complement

Be sure a linking verb agrees with its subject and not with a complement.

An important influence in politics today *is* minorities. [The verb, *is*, agrees with the singular subject *influence*, not with the plural complement *minorities*.]

However, if the parts in the last example were reversed, the verb would be the plural *are* rather than the singular *is*.

Minorities *are* an important influence in politics today. [The subject is now *minorities*, which takes the plural verb *are*.]

14g   **Making a verb agree with relative pronoun subjects**

When the relative pronoun *who, which,* or *that* acts as the subject of a dependent clause, the verb in the clause must agree in number with the pronoun's antecedent.

Success is the goal that *drives* many students to study hard. [*That* refers to *goal*, a singular noun, and takes the singular verb *drives*.]

Success, self-satisfaction, and a desire to please one's parents are elements that *motivate* students to perform their best. [*That* refers to *elements*, a plural noun, and takes the plural verb *motivate*.]

When the phrase *one of the* comes before the relative pronoun, you need to check the intended meaning of the sentence.

Cheryl is one of the team members who always *stay* late for extra practice. [Cheryl and some of her teammates stay late. *Who* refers to those who stay late for extra practice, and hence takes a plural verb.]

Cheryl is the only one of the team members who *comes* to practice an hour early. [Only one player comes early—Cheryl. The antecedent of *who* is *one*, which takes a singular verb.]

14h Making subject and verb agree in inverted sentences

In a sentence written with **inverted word order** (an inverted sentence), the subject follows the verb rather than precedes it. To maintain subject–verb agreement in inverted sentences, be sure that the verb agrees with the subject of the sentence, not with a nearby noun.

Beneath the papers *was* the address book she had been looking for. [The subject is *address book*, not *papers*.]

Among the junk collected for the tag sale *were* a grandfather clock and an antique chair. [The compound subject is *a grandfather clock and an antique chair*, not *junk* or *sale*.]

Inverted subject–verb order also occurs when sentences begin with *there* or *here*.

There *are* similarities between them. [The subject is *similarities*; the verb is plural.]

Here *is* the latest report on storm damage. [The subject is *report*; the verb is singular.]

Take particular care with the contractions *there's* and *here's*. Remember that the *'s* stands for *is*—a singular verb.

INCORRECT   *There's* still ten or twelve people without a ticket.

CORRECT   *There are* still ten or twelve people without a ticket.

EXERCISE 14–4 **Checking Subject–Verb Agreement**
Revise the errors in subject–verb agreement in the following sentences. Some sentences may be correct as written.

1. There was only ten minutes remaining in the game.
2. I paid the costs of shipping, which were minimal.
3. Here is some free tickets to the game.
4. The cultural achievements of ancient Greece is the subject of my report.
5. Sula is one of those people who thrives on competition.

14i Maintaining agreement with singular words that appear plural

Some nouns that look plural, such as *athletics, economics,* and *mumps,* are singular in meaning and take a singular verb.

Athletics *is* an important source of revenue at many universities.

Economics *predicts* the outcomes of some elections.

Mumps *is* essentially a childhood disease.

Some nouns that look plural, such as *politics* and *statistics,* may be used as either singular or plural nouns under certain circumstances.

SINGULAR   Politics *fascinates* me. [*politics* is a field of study or a set of ideas]

PLURAL   His politics *are* very different from mine. [*politics* refers to beliefs or views]

USAGE NOTE   The word *data,* the plural of *datum* (meaning "fact"), is often used as a singular noun. Scientists, for example, frequently think of data as a single collection of information rather than as individual facts. Although some writers and authorities retain the traditional use of *data* as a plural noun, others accept *data* in the singular as well.

SINGULAR   We cannot make a decision until all *the data has* arrived.

SINGULAR   Here *is the data* you need.

PLURAL   Our *data indicate* that it is time to make a change.

PLURAL   These *data strengthen* your argument.

When you think of data as a body of information, use the word with a singular verb form. When you think of data as a set of different facts, use it with a plural verb form.

14j Making verbs agree in titles and with words used as words

Titles of books, films, and other works take a singular verb—even when those titles appear plural or contain plural words.

"The American Geographies" *is* a wonderful essay written by Barry Lopez.

"Father and Son" *is* a poem by Stanley Kunitz.

http://webster.commnet.edu/
hp/pages/darling/
grammar/sv_agr.htm
Provides an explanation of
subject–verb agreement, with
quizzes and exercises.

In the same way, a word referred to as a word takes a singular verb form, even though the word may be plural.

The word "receivables" *is* used in business to mean an asset due to one business from another.

EXERCISE 14–5 Revising for Subject–Verb Agreement
Correct the errors in subject–verb agreement that you find in the following sentences.

1. Each of us were too tired to finish the race.

2. More upsetting than the things they said were the manner in which they said them.

3. John Steinbeck's novel *The Grapes of Wrath* describe the effects of the Depression on a single family.

4. There are no team members who does not deserve the coach's criticism.

5. Mathematics are not as popular a major as it once was.

EXERCISE 14–6 Reviewing Subject–Verb Agreement
In the following passage about television commercials, underline the correct verb in each italicized pair.

Television commercials (*is/are*) a form of religious literature. . . . I do not claim, for a start, that every television commercial (*has/have*) religious content. Just as in church the pastor will sometimes call the congregation's attention to nonecclesiastical matters, so there (*is/are*) television commercials that (*is/are*) entirely secular. Someone (*has/have*) something to sell; you are told what it is, where it can be obtained, and what it (*cost/costs*). Though these may be shrill and offensive, no doctrine (*is/are*) advanced and no theology invoked.

But the majority of important television commercials (*take/takes*) the form of religious parables organized around a coherent theology. Like all religious parables, they (*put/puts*) forward a concept of sin, intimations of the way to redemption, and a vision of Heaven. They also suggest what (*is/are*) the roots of evil and what (*is/are*) the obligations of the holy.

—Neil Postman, "The Parable of the Ring around the Collar"

Pronoun–Antecedent Agreement

To avoid repeating nouns in writing, you can use pronouns to stand in for them (see 11b). In doing so, you must be sure that each pronoun agrees with the noun it refers to (its **antecedent**). Pronouns and antecedents must agree in person, number, and gender. Consider the following examples.

The cab driver cut through the traffic as if *she* were slalom skiing. [*Driver* is the antecedent of *she*, which is third-person, singular, feminine.]

Although *they* were placed in a glass case, the awards meant little to him. [*Awards* is the antecedent of *they*, which is third-person, plural, neuter.]

14k Making a pronoun agree with an indefinite pronoun antecedent

An **indefinite pronoun,** such as *somebody* or *anything,* refers to an unspecified person or thing. Most indefinite pronouns are singular (see 14d for a list of indefinite pronouns).

SINGULAR   *Everybody has* his or her opinion.

SINGULAR   If *someone is* guilty, he or she should confess

WRITING HINT   It is becoming increasingly common to hear people say "Everybody has their opinion" and "If anyone is available, they will be called." In such instances plural personal pronouns (*their* and *they*) are

(continued)

matched with singular indefinite pronouns (*everybody* and *anyone*). However, in academic and professional writing, use a singular personal pronoun or rewrite to avoid the agreement problem altogether.

Everybody has *an* opinion. [*an* opinion, not *their* opinion]

If someone is guilty, *that person* should confess. [*that person* instead of *he* or *she*]

14l   Making a pronoun agree with a collective noun antecedent

When a collective noun such as *team* or *class* refers to the group as a unit, the collective noun takes a singular pronoun.

The class had to organize *its* own trip, without administrative assistance.

When a collective noun refers to the individual members of the group, it takes a plural pronoun.

The group decided to split up and go *their* own different ways.

14m   Making a pronoun agree with a compound antecedent

A **compound antecedent** has two antecedents joined by a conjunction. Compound antecedents can be either singular or plural. Those joined by *and* are plural and require a plural pronoun.

The man and his dog took *their* daily stroll through the park.

http://webster.commnet.edu/
hp/pages/darling/grammar/
pronouns.htm
Provides an explanation of
pronoun–antecedent agreement,
with quizzes and exercises.

When a compound antecedent is preceded by the word *each* or *every,* or if the sense of the compound is clearly singular—as when two words joined by *and* refer to a single person—use a singular pronoun.

Every college and university has *its* own identity.

Oedipus' wife and mother, Jocasta, killed *herself* when she realized who Oedipus was and what he had done.

For compound antecedents connected by *or, nor, either . . . or,* or *neither . . . nor,* the pronoun should agree with the nearer of the two antecedents.

Either the lead singer or the orchestra members must decide to follow *their* conductor's tempo directions.

WRITING HINT   If one of the antecedents is singular and the other plural, put the plural antecedent closer to the verb to avoid awkwardness.

> AWKWARD   *Neither* my friends *nor* my brother could stifle *his* laughter during the performance.

> REVISED   *Neither* my brother *nor* my friends could stifle *their* laughter during the performance.

USAGE NOTE   A third-person antecedent should not be referred to by *you.* This shift can occur when you forget that you are writing in the third person and begin to address the reader directly.

> INCONSISTENT   If a person wants to lose weight, *you* must exercise regularly.

> CONSISTENT   If a person wants to lose weight, *he or she* must exercise regularly.
>
> If people want to lose weight permanently, *they* must exercise regularly.
>
> A person who wants to lose weight must exercise regularly.

 Checking for gender-specific pronouns

Generic nouns and indefinite pronouns (such as *everyone* and *someone*) refer to both men and women, not to one sex or the other. Traditionally in English, when an indefinite pronoun or a generic noun served as the antecedent for a personal pronoun, that pronoun was the generic (or generalized) *he.*

Did anyone neglect to bring *his* money for the trip?

The person who organized this conference knew what *he* was doing.

Using the generic *he* in these examples, however, is sexist because it excludes women. The first example singles out males as most likely to forget their money. The second example assumes that the conference organizer must have been a male. The accompanying checklist details how you can avoid using sexist pronouns.

Avoiding Sexist Pronouns

To avoid sexism, use alternatives to the generic *he*.

1. Use masculine and feminine pronouns together.

    Has anyone forgotten *his or her* money for the trip?

    The person who organized this conference knew what *he or she* was doing.

    This option can create awkwardness when numerous references to *he or she* and *him or her* occur, so use it sparingly.

2. Construct sentences that avoid the problem of sexist pronoun usage. Instead of using a singular antecedent, use the plural.

    Did any *people* neglect to bring *their* money for the trip?

    The *organizers* of this conference knew what *they* were doing.

    Or rewrite the sentence to eliminate the second pronoun.

    Did anyone neglect to bring money for the trip?

    The person who organized this conference did an outstanding job.

EXERCISE 14–7 Maintaining Agreement between Pronouns and Antecedents
Revise the following sentences so that pronouns and their antecedents agree.

1. Every student is required to bring their registration cards to the first meeting of each class.

2. The jury announced their verdict.

3. Neither Yankees fans nor the team's administration was willing to support the proposed trade of Ken Griffey for Derek Jeter.

4. Anyone who wants to study abroad for a term should meet with their advisor to discuss the details.

5. Every flower and tree has their distinctive beauty.

EXERCISE 14–8   **Revising for Agreement**

Revise the following paragraph to eliminate problems in subject–verb agreement and in pronoun–antecedent agreement.

College students are not the only ones who experiences frustration in trying to write well. Almost every writer agonizes over some of their sentences when they know their work will be read by a critical audience. Writing well is a painful process. Sometimes it goes smoothly, but inevitably you come to the difficult passages. And even the smooth passages that seemed almost to compose itself needs revision after all. A student will have a healthier attitude toward their composition course if they understand that even the professional writer shares your feeling of agony as he tries to develop an extensive piece of writing for critical readers. Neither the first-year college student nor the professional writer escape the pain of writing.

15   *Grammar for ESL Writers*

If English is not your native language, you may find some of its features troublesome. This chapter provides practice in English grammatical structures that cause difficulty when English is a writer's second language (ESL).

15a   Distinguishing count nouns from noncount nouns

To use nouns and determiners correctly, you must first know whether a noun is a *count* or a *noncount* noun (sometimes called a *mass noun*).

A *count noun* refers to people, places, or things that are counted separately. Count nouns may be singular or plural. You may use a determiner such as *a* or *an* with a count noun.

Twenty-two *students* signed up for English 101.

One *student* never came to class. She was a transfer *student*.

A *noncount noun* is a noun that cannot be counted separately, such as *air*, *water*, and *wealth*. Noncount nouns do not have a plural form.

The *light* in the lecture hall was dim, and the *air* was pleasantly cool. Haroun had little *sleep* the night before.

Do not use *a* or *an* or a number before noncount nouns.

INCORRECT	We had *a rice* for dinner.
INCORRECT	We had *rices* for dinner.
REVISED	We had *rice* for dinner. *It* was delicious.

Words that indicate measures or portions can be used to show plural quantities of noncount nouns.

He ate *three bowls* of rice for dinner.

Please pick up *two pounds* of chicken at the supermarket.

The movers left *a few pieces* of furniture on the sidewalk.

Categories of Noncount Nouns

Groups of objects: homework, information, mail, news
Abstract words: courage, envy, health, time
Activities and sports: ballet, football, hockey, research, walking
Fields of study: anthropology, astronomy, engineering, photography
Foods: corn, fruit, lettuce, pasta, veal
Gases: air, nitrogen, oxygen, smog
Languages: Arabic, German, Japanese
Liquids: blood, coffee, gasoline, milk, tea
Materials: concrete, glass, iron, leather, polyester
Particles: pepper, rice, salt, sand
Weather: cold, ice, lightning, rain, sleet, snow, steam, sun

The distinction between count and noncount nouns differs from language to language. A noncount noun in English may well be a count noun in another language. The following English noncount nouns are count nouns in other languages. Take special care to use these nouns correctly.

http://leo.stcloudstate.edu/
grammar/countnon.html
Provides guidance in using
count and noncount nouns.
Designed for ESL writers.

advice	information	furniture	garbage	homework	housework
jewelry	luggage	mail	money	news	work

INCORRECT   Do you have enough *luggages* for your trip?

REVISED   Do you have enough *luggage* for your trip?

Some nouns can be either count or noncount, depending on the writer's intent. A few examples follow; you should note others as you encounter them.

NONCOUNT NOUNS	COUNT NOUNS
This *bread* is delicious. I ate three pieces.	The Italian bakery sells delicious *breads*. [kinds of bread]
This is strong *coffee*.	Stan bought five *coffees* to go. [five cups of coffee]
Lin has beautiful *hair*.	Investigators found two *hairs* at the crime scene. [individual hairs]
Sid has no *experience* as a teacher.	They had interesting *experiences* on their trip. [separate experiences]
We had hardly any free *time*.	Hsiao-mi took the test three *times*. [on three occasions]

EXERCISE 15–1   Working with Count and Noncount Nouns
Underline the correct use of the noun in the following sentences. Example:

Richard needs *information/informations* about computers.

1. Firefighters exhibit their *courage/courages* every time they answer an alarm.
2. The company thinks I have more than enough *experience/experiences* to qualify for the job.
3. We received some funny *advice/advices* last summer.
4. Over the weekend, my brother watched six full games of *football/footballs* on television.
5. Our history professor generously shared her *knowledge/knowledges* with us.

15b   Recognizing and using determiners

A **determiner** is a word or group of words that introduce a noun. Some determiners signal that a noun is to follow; other determiners indicate quantity. There are four types of determiners.

1. **Articles** indicate whether or not a noun refers to a specific person, place, or thing. The articles *a* and *an* are *indefinite articles* that refer to general nouns. The article *the* is a *definite article* that refers to specific nouns.

   We saw *a* movie last night. *The* movies of Charlie Chaplin are classics.

2. **Quantifiers** (such as *one, some,* and *a lot of*) indicate how much or how many of a noun.

   Several filmmakers from Taiwan have received the Palme d'Or award.

3. **Demonstratives** (*this, that, these,* and *those*) point to a noun and distinguish it from others.

   This picture is beautiful. *That* argument is insupportable.

4. **Possessive adjectives** (such as *my, your, his, hers,* and *its*) indicate ownership of a noun.

   My ideas differ from yours.

   Do not use more than one determiner with each noun.

   INCORRECT   *The my book* is over there.

   REVISED   *My book* is over there.

Use singular determiners with singular nouns and plural determiners with plural nouns.

   INCORRECT   Gretta read *a books* over the weekend.

   REVISED   Gretta read *a book* over the weekend.

   REVISED   Gretta read *several books* over the weekend.

15c Using the articles *a, an,* and *the* correctly

Many languages, including Russian and Japanese, do not have articles, words that identify specific or general references. English has two kinds of articles: the **indefinite articles** *a* and *an* and the **definite article** *the*. In deciding whether to use *a, an,* or *the*, you must first determine whether the noun is indefinite or definite. A noun is indefinite when neither the writer nor the reader has a specific person, place, or thing in mind.

Let's try to find *a parking place.* [any parking place, not a specific one]

Could we open *a window?* [any one of several windows]

I love *music.* [music in general]

A noun is **definite** when both the writer and the reader know which specific person, place, or thing it refers to.

Where is *the parking lot?* [a specific lot]

I opened *the window.* [the only window]

I love *the music* of the Jazz Age. [a particular style of music]

Next determine whether the noun is a noncount noun or a count noun (see 15a). Use the accompanying chart to decide how to assign articles to count and noncount nouns.

Choosing the Correct Article		
NOUN TYPE	**IF INDEFINITE**	**IF DEFINITE**
Singular count noun cat, hour	Use *a* or *an*	Use *the*
Plural count noun cats, hours	Use no article	Use *the*
Noncount beauty, time	Use no article	Use *the*

Using *a* or *an* with singular count nouns

Use *a* or *an* with every indefinite singular count noun.

INCORRECT   I wore *hat* today.

REVISED   I wore *a hat* today.

Every singular count noun must be preceded by a determiner. If the context does not require *a* or *an,* use another determiner.

http://leo.stcloudstate.edu/grammar/useartic.html
Offers guided practice in how to use articles and when they are unnecessary.

INCORRECT	We found *suitcase*.
REVISED	We found *a suitcase*.
	We found *the suitcase*.
	We found *our suitcase*.

WRITING HINT   Use *a* before a consonant sound. Use *an* before a vowel sound. Note that it is the initial sound, not whether the first letter is a consonant or a vowel, that determines whether *a* or *an* should be used.

a delicious meal; *a* history examination

a unique painting; *a* university [the *u* is pronounced like the consonant *y*]

an appetizer; *an* umbrella

an honest waiter; *an* hour later [the *h* is silent]

Using *the*

You can use the definite article *the* with all nouns—singular count nouns, plural count nouns, and noncount nouns.

When to Use the Definite Article *the*

- Use *the* when the noun has been mentioned previously. After the noun has been introduced, the reader knows which person, place, or thing it refers to.

  Early one morning, *a* child wandered into the Fifth Precinct station on Manhattan's Lower East Side. *The* child was shoeless and seemed to be lost. [*The child* was described in the preceding sentence.]

- Use *the* when the person, place, or thing is unique or generally known.

  The weather is getting stranger every year. [There is only one phenomenon we refer to as the weather.]

  I have never seen *the* Grand Canyon. [There is only one Grand Canyon.] Many immigrants pursue *the* American Dream. [The concept is generally known.]

(continued)

- Use *the* when the context makes it clear which person, place, or thing is being referred to.

    The sick baby is crying. [There is one sick baby.]

    The flowers on your desk are beautiful. [There is one arrangement of flowers on the desk.]

- Use *the* when a clause or an adjective limits the noun so that it is clear which one is being referred to.

    Schindler's List was the best movie I saw in 1993. [There can only be one *best* movie.]

You can use one *the* for two or more nouns joined by *and*.

   Dan circled *the* correct answer. [There is only one possible correct answer.]

   People congregated on *the* porch and deck.

   Insects flew amid *the* flowers, trees, and shrubs.

Using plural count and noncount nouns without an article

Do not use an article with plural count nouns or with noncount nouns when you make a generalization. A **generalization** is a statement based on or a conclusion derived from a limited number of examples.

INCORRECT	*The friends* are important.
REVISED	*Friends* are important.
INCORRECT	*The love* makes the world go around.
REVISED	*Love* makes the world go around.

> **USAGE NOTE** You will often come across generalizations with count nouns preceded by *a/an*, or *the* or even without an article.
>
> *A hamster* is a wonderful pet.
>
> *The hamster* is a wonderful pet.
>
> *Hamsters* are wonderful pets.

(continued)

There is no one rule for deciding how to phrase a generalization. However, you can avoid errors when you make generalizations with count nouns simply by using plural count nouns without an article.

INCORRECT GENERALIZATION   *The vegetable* is good for you.

INCORRECT GENERALIZATION   *A vegetable* is good for you.

REVISED   *Vegetables* are good for you.

Never use an article when you make a generalization with a noncount noun.

INCORRECT   Animals need *the oxygen* to survive.

REVISED   Animals need *oxygen* to survive.

WRITING HINT   You can often use indefinite plural count nouns and noncount nouns either without any determiner or with a quantifier.

Please buy *tomatoes* when you go to the store. [no determiner]

Please buy *some tomatoes* when you go to the store. [the quantifier *some*]

Water leaked all over the basement. [no determiner]

A lot of water leaked all over the basement. [the quantifier *a lot of*]

EXERCISE 15–2   Choosing the Correct Articles

Complete the following sentences using the noun or phrase in parentheses and, if needed, the articles *a, an,* or *the*. Example:

(*help*) __The help__ that you gave me was desperately needed.

1. (*children*) _____ sometimes require a lot of attention, and adults should realize this.

2. (*music*) I listen to _____ to relax.

3. (*best music*) _____ for relaxing is Keith Jarrett's.

4. (*advice*) She likes to give _____, but she does not like to receive it.

5. (*dog*) It is your turn to walk _____.

EXERCISE 15–3   **Working with Articles**

Correct improper use of articles in the following sentences, and supply missing articles as needed.

He had a nice apartment with many rooms, but everyone stayed in kitchen even though living room and a dining room were spacious and very inviting. His furniture was simple but functional. He had bought furniture from some friends, who lived in large house together but then had to move to small dorm rooms. When he invited friends over to his apartment, they stayed long and talked about many things such as why they came to America, what they wanted to do with their lives, and how they would make living. Some of friends wanted to make a lot of money and buy big house with pool and big yard. Others wanted to finish school so they could return to their home countries and work to improve conditions there.

15d   Choosing the correct quantifier for count and noncount nouns

Quantifiers such as *several* and *a little* are words and phrases that indicate the amount or quantity of a noun. They tell how much or how many.

a few teachers	*not many* books	*some* lunch
several new students	*a lot of* classrooms	*many* pieces

Some quantifiers can be used only with noncount nouns and others with only count nouns (see 15a). Still others can be used with both. Refer to the accompanying chart when choosing a quantifier.

Choosing the Correct Quantifier

QUANTIFIERS WITH COUNT NOUNS	QUANTIFIERS WITH NONCOUNT NOUNS	QUANTIFIERS WITH BOTH COUNT AND NONCOUNT	
a few dollars	*a little* money	*enough* jobs	*enough* work
too many problems	*too much* advice	*some* chairs	*some* furniture
forty minutes	*a great deal of* time	*a lot of* rings	*a lot of* jewelry
a number of bags	*a lot of* luggage	*any* minute	*any* time
several games	*little* time		
many tasks	*not much* energy		
a couple of sentences			

USAGE NOTE   Be aware of the difference between the quantifiers *a few* and *few*, and between *a little* and *little*. *Few* and *little* generally have a negative connotation. These words suggest "too few" or "too little."

He has only been here a week, but he has already made *a few* friends. [He has succeeded in making friends in a week.]

He has been here a year, but he still has *few* friends. [He has failed at making friends in a year.]

We had *a little* money to buy gifts. [We had money to buy some gifts.]

We had *little* money to buy gifts. [We did not have much money to buy gifts.]

WRITING HINT   Use the quantifier *any* with both noncount and count nouns in questions and negative sentences.

Do we have *any bread*?

We do not have *any bread*.

Are there *any tomatoes*?

I cannot find *any tomatoes*.

Use *how much* to ask about quantity with noncount nouns. Use *how many* to ask about quantity with count nouns.

How much bread do we need?

How many tomatoes should I buy?

15e   Using demonstratives correctly

Demonstratives are determiners that indicate the distance of a noun, in either space or time, from the speaker or writer. The demonstratives are *this, that, these,* and *those*. The following guidelines will help you use demonstratives correctly.

1. Use *this* and *these* to indicate that a noun is close to you in either space or time. Use *this* with noncount nouns and singular count nouns. Use *these* with plural count nouns.

INCORRECT	*These information* from the post office is very helpful.
CORRECT	*This information* from the post office is very helpful.
INCORRECT	*These bell* rings beautifully.
CORRECT	*This bell* rings beautifully.
INCORRECT	*This statistics* are inaccurate.
CORRECT	*These statistics* are inaccurate.

2. Use *that* and *those* to indicate that a noun is distant in either space or time. Use *that* with noncount nouns and singular count nouns. Use *those* with plural count nouns.

INCORRECT	*Those coffee* you made yesterday tasted delicious.
CORRECT	*That coffee* you made yesterday tasted delicious.
INCORRECT	*Those magazine* had an interesting article about the economy.
CORRECT	*That magazine* had an interesting article about the economy.
INCORRECT	In *that days* only men received an education.
CORRECT	In *those days* only men received an education.

EXERCISE 15–4   Choosing the Correct Demonstrative

Underline the correct demonstrative in each sentence. Example:

Nearly all the kids I taught were well behaved and smart. Why did *that/those* fact surprise my nonteaching friends?

1. Born in 1981, *those/that* students were heirs of the Reagan administration.

2. They had many gifts, and *these/those* gifts helped them survive the often cruel world of the Bronx.

3. My students all watched television because they had nothing else to do. I did not bother mentioning *this/that* problem to their parents.

4. One morning a student swallowed a penny. *That/Those* day there was no one on duty in the office.

5. The Teaching for America project was a stunning success its first year. *That/Those* same year, however, the program was abandoned.

15f   Using possessive forms of pronouns correctly

Possessive adjectives precede the nouns they modify and indicate ownership or a relationship. The possessive forms of pronouns substitute for noun phrases; they do not precede nouns. Use possessive adjectives, not possessive pronouns, to modify nouns. Although the forms of possessive adjectives are similar to those of possessive pronouns, their functions differ.

My ideas differ from *yours*. [*My*, a possessive adjective, modifies the noun *ideas*. *Yours*, a possessive pronoun, substitutes for the phrase *your ideas*.]

Her hobby is woodworking. *His* is gardening. [*Her*, a possessive adjective, modifies the noun *hobby*. *His*, a possessive pronoun, substitutes for the phrase *his hobby*.]

The possessive adjectives and possessive forms of the pronoun are listed in the accompanying chart.

Possessive Adjectives and Possessive Forms of Pronouns

POSSESSIVE ADJECTIVES	POSSESSIVE FORMS OF PRONOUNS
my, your, his, her, its, our, their	mine, yours, his, hers, its, ours, theirs
It was *my* idea.	The idea was *mine*.
It is *her* hat.	The hat is *hers*.
Our problems are minor.	The minor problems are *ours*.
That is *their* house.	That house is *theirs*.

Keep the following tips in mind when using possessive forms in your writing.

- Use the apostrophe to form the possessive of indefinite pronouns such as *one*, *anyone*, and *nobody*. (See 11b for more on indefinite pronouns, and 31a–1, 31b, and 31e on using apostrophes.)

  One's memory sometimes falters after the age of fifty.

  Diego is *everyone's* favorite uncle.

  You are *nobody's* fool.

- Use *whose* to ask about possession. You can use *whose* in a sentence with or without a noun. Do not confuse *whose* with *who's*, the contraction for *who is*.

INCORRECT   *Who's* idea was it?

REVISED   *Whose* idea was it?

- Do not use an apostrophe with possessive adjectives or possessive forms of pronouns.

Possessive adjectives

INCORRECT   The cat left *it's* dinner untouched.

REVISED   The cat left *its* dinner untouched.

Possessive pronouns

INCORRECT   That is not my telephone ringing; it is *your's*.

REVISED   That is not my telephone ringing; it is *yours*.

- Never write *its'*. There is no such form.

(For more on possessive forms of pronouns, see 11b–c.)

EXERCISE 15–5   **Working with Possessives**
Underline the correct possessive forms in the following sentences. Example:

Who's/Whose research paper is this?

1. That research paper is *mine/mines*, not *theirs/theirs'*.
2. The cat uses *its/it's* tongue to clean itself.
3. It was *nobodys/nobody's* fault.
4. *Ours/Ours'* was not the only complaint.
5. *Your/Yours* was the best response to that question.

15g   Using correct word order for adjectives and other noun modifiers

Use the chart on p. 324 to determine typical word order when you use two or more descriptive adjectives.

Noun modifiers other than adjectives typically occur in a particular order. Use the accompanying chart to help you determine the word order for noun modifiers, including adjectives.

Word Order of Adjectives and Other Noun Modifiers

1. **Determiner:** *a, an, the, these, those, your, their, Sue's, anyone's, many, a few, a little, some, too much, too many*

2. **Words indicating order or number:** *first, initial, second, next, final, last, one, twenty*

3. **Adjectives expressing opinion or judgment:** *easy, attractive, dedicated*

4. **Adjectives indicating size or length:** *small, large, tall, long, short*

5. **Adjectives indicating shape or width:** *round, square, circular, oval, wide*

6. **Adjectives indicating condition:** *broken, dilapidated, smooth-running*

7. **Adjectives indicating age:** *old, young, new, modern, antique*

8. **Adjectives indicating color:** *blue, green, yellow, aquamarine, amber*

9. **Adjectives indicating nationality or religion:** *Spanish, Chinese, Muslim*

10. **Adjectives indicating material:** *plastic, stone, wood*

11. **Nouns used as adjectives:** *dining room, student*

12. **The noun**

Examples:

    1   2   6   11   12
Those last warm summer nights in September remind me of my childhood.

  2   4   5   10   11   12
Six large oval mahogany kitchen tables were delivered to the wrong house.

    1   3   9   12
A number of remarkable Italian restaurants can be found in Boston's North End.

  1   12   1   3   7   8   12
My brother refurbished that sleek vintage green Mustang.

> **WRITING HINT** Avoid using a long string of adjectives with one noun.
>
> **AWKWARD** My cousin Hilda is a pretty, serious, lively, intelligent girl who is always ready to help out.
>
> **REVISED** My pretty cousin Hilda is a serious, intelligent girl who is lively and is always ready to help out.

Noun **modifiers** are words added to nouns to describe them and to make their meaning precise. In addition to adjectives (ADJ), noun modifiers include determiners, such as articles (AR), quantifiers (QUAN), demonstratives (DEM), and possessive forms of pronouns (PP).

┌PP┐   ┌ADJ┐
I remember her green summer dress.

QUAN ADJ   AR
There are some ripe peaches in the refrigerator.

AR   ADJ   ADJ
It was an interesting and stimulating idea.

AR QUAN ADJ   DEM
Yesterday was the first cold day we have had this winter.

No more than three noun modifiers are generally used with a noun. This section gives practice in the correct use of adjectives and participles used as adjectives.

> **USAGE NOTE** Adjectives always have the same form. They do not change to agree with the number or gender of the noun they modify.
>
> **INCORRECT** She wore a *red* dress and matching *reds* shoes.
>
> **REVISED** She wore a *red* dress and matching *red* shoes.

EXERCISE 15–6   Using the Correct Word Order for Adjectives
The adjectives in the left column modify the noun to their right, but they are not in the correct order. Rearrange the adjectives in proper order. Example:

serious/much   thought
much serious   thought

1. colorful/many/deep-sea   creatures
2. exciting/special/her   surprise
3. used/old/many   books
4. dining/wooden/room   table
5. corduroy/threadbare/green   pants

EXERCISE 15–7   Writing with Adjectives
Write about someone you know well in a paragraph or two. Include a description of the person's clothing or other belongings that characterize him or her. Use as many adjectives as you can. Ask your instructor or a native speaker in your class to check the word order of the adjectives you use.

 Distinguishing between present participle and past participle used as adjectives

Both the **present participle**, such as *irritating* and *pleasing*, and the **past participle**, such as *irritated* and *pleased*, can function as adjectives in a sentence. When used as adjectives present and past participles have very different meanings. Participles that describe feelings or states of mind can be troublesome for nonnative speakers, as the following examples illustrate.

INCORRECT   I was *embarrassing.*

REVISED   I was *embarrassed* by his behaviors. [the past participle used as an adjective]

REVISED   It was an *embarrassing* moment for me. [the present participle used as an adjective]

INCORRECT   It was an *interested* film.

REVISED   It was an *interesting* film. [the present participle used as an adjective]

REVISED   The *interested* audience did not speak during the showing of the film. [the past participle used as an adjective]

Keep the following in mind when you use participles as adjectives.

- Use present participles (*boring, intriguing, fascinating, exhilarating*) to describe people, places, or things that *cause* a feeling or state of mind:

  The book was *thrilling*. [The book caused this feeling.]

  New York is an *exhausting* city. [The place causes this feeling.]

- Use past participles (*bored, intrigued, fascinated, exhilarated*) to describe people, places, or things that *experience* that feeling:

  Kyung Hua is *fascinated* by English. [She experiences a feeling of fascination.]

  The tourists will be *exhausted* by noon. [They will experience exhaustion.]

- Take special care when using the following participles:

PRESENT PARTICIPLES	PAST PARTICIPLES
amazing	amazed
annoying	annoyed
boring	bored
depressing	depressed
exciting	excited
exhausting	exhausted
fascinating	fascinated
frightening	frightened
interesting	interested
satisfying	satisfied
surprising	surprised

INCORRECT   Kyung Hua was *surprising* by her parents' arrival.

REVISED   Kyung Hua was *surprised* by her parents' arrival.

INCORRECT   *The Grapes of Wrath* offers a *fascinated* view of life during the Great Depression.

REVISED   *The Grapes of Wrath* offers a *fascinating* view of life during the Great Depression.

EXERCISE 15–8 **Writing with Participles**

In two or three paragraphs, describe a movie you saw recently. Explain what it was like and how you felt about it. Use present and past participles to describe the movie and your reaction to it. Ask your teacher or a native speaker in your class to check the participles in your description.

15i   Learning the forms of *be*, *have*, and *do*

Although some languages, such as Russian and Japanese, do not use the verb *be*, the verbs *be*, *have*, and *do* are used frequently in English, both as main verbs and as auxiliary verbs. Since they are irregular, you must memorize their forms. Forms of *be* in particular should be carefully attended to.

Remember that all English sentences require a main verb. Do not omit the verb in a sentence that has a complement, a word that describes the subject. (See 10d-1 on linking verbs.)

| INCORRECT | He late. |
| REVISED | He *was* late. |

| INCORRECT | They never wrong about prices. |
| REVISED | They *are* never wrong about prices. |

Keep in mind the changes required for third-person singular forms of *be*, *have*, and *do*. Use the accompanying chart for reference.

Forms of *be*, *have*, and *do*				
BASE FORM	**PRESENT TENSE**	**PRESENT PARTICIPLE**	**PAST TENSE**	**PAST PARTICIPLE**
be	I *am* he/she/it *is* we/you/they *are*	*being*	I/he/she/it *was* we/you/they *were*	*been*
have	I *have* he/she/it *has* we/you/they *have*	*having*	I *have* he/she/it *had* we/you/they *had*	*had*
do	I *do* he/she/it *does* we/you/they *do*	*doing*	*did*	*done*

15j   Using the auxiliary verbs *be*, *have*, and *do* correctly

The **auxiliary verbs** (also called **helping verbs**) *be*, *have*, and *do* combine with a base form or a participle to create a verb phrase.

As a child I *was told* to study.

I *have learned* a lot about national politics this year.

I *do know* about the surprise party.

Progressive tenses, perfect tenses, the passive voice, negatives, and questions are all formed with auxiliaries. (For more on auxiliary verbs, see 11b.)

Progressive tenses

The **progressive tense** is used to indicate an action that continues in the past, the present, or the future. Use the appropriate form of *be* and the present participle to create the progressive tenses.

Remember the following points when you use the progressive tenses.

* The form of *be* must agree with the subject.

  INCORRECT   Bob *are going* to class even though he feels sick.

  REVISED   Bob *is going* to class even though he feels sick.

* Do not omit a form of *be* with the progressive tenses.

  INCORRECT   *We starting* a new school club.

  REVISED   *We are starting* a new school club.

Some verbs are used rarely in the progressive. They occur in the following categories. You must learn which verbs they are to use them correctly.

LINKING VERBS

be, become, exist, seem

VERBS THAT SHOW POSSESSION

belong, have, own, possess

VERBS THAT SHOW PERCEPTION

feel, hear, see, smell, taste

VERBS THAT SHOW FEELINGS, PREFERENCES, AND INTELLECTUAL STATES

believe, forget, hate, imagine, intend, know, like, love, need, pity, prefer, remember, suppose, understand, want, wish, wonder

INCORRECT   That book *is belonging* to Yokari.

CORRECT   That book *belongs* to Yokari.

Perfect tenses

The **perfect tense** is used to indicate an action that has been completed before another action begins, or an action finished by a specific time. Use the appropriate form of *have* and the past participle to create the perfect tenses.

Akiko *has visited* the United States three times. [This sentence uses the present perfect tense to indicate that her visits began and ended sometime in the past. In the present perfect, the past participle of the main verb follows the present of *have*.]

She *had wanted* to visit the Deep South last February, but visited Australia instead. [This sentence uses the past perfect tense to indicate that she wanted to travel to the Deep South sometime before she went to Australia. In the past perfect, the past participle of the main verb follows the past participle of *have*.]

Remember the following points when you use the perfect tenses.

- The form of *have* must agree with the subject.

INCORRECT   My brother *have seen* every Clint Eastwood movie.

CORRECT   My brother *has seen* every Clint Eastwood movie.

- Do not omit a form of *have* when you use the perfect tenses.

INCORRECT   Professor Lewis *gone* on sabbatical.

CORRECT   Professor Lewis *has gone* on sabbatical.

- Use the past participle of the main verb, not the past tense, to form the perfect tenses.

INCORRECT   Abdul and Sara *have ran* in the Boston marathon several times.

CORRECT   Abdul and Sara *have run* in the Boston marathon several times.

When you are not sure how to form the past participle, check your dictionary. If the past participle and the past tense have different forms, the dictionary will give both forms. Also consult the chart in 10c.

> **USAGE NOTE**   The present perfect tense after *since* requires a specific time. The present perfect after *for* requires a span of time.
>
> We have been visiting this campground *since 1989.*
>
> We have been visiting this campground *for ten years.*

Passive voice

In the **passive voice**, the grammatical subject of a sentence receives the action of the verb. Use the passive voice when the subject is unknown or considered relatively unimportant.

My brother *was elected* class president. [The emphasis in this sentence is on *My brother* rather than those who elected him.]

The passive voice combines the past tense of *be* and the past participle. Keep the following points in mind when you use the passive voice.

- The past participle never changes, but the auxiliary *be* must agree with the subject.

  INCORRECT   Many home-based businesses *was created* in the 1980s.

  CORRECT   Many home-based businesses *were created* in the 1980s. [The auxiliary *were* agrees with the plural subject *businesses.*]

- Use only transitive verbs in the passive voice. Transitive verbs, such as *kiss* and *hit,* are verbs that take a direct object.

  ACTIVE   Brazilians *speak* Portuguese.

  PASSIVE   Portuguese *is spoken* by Brazilians.

- Intransitive verbs, such as *smile* and *occur,* do not take an object. They cannot be used in the passive voice.

  INCORRECT   A strange thing *was happened* yesterday.

  REVISED   A strange thing *happened* yesterday.

> **USAGE NOTE**   Verbs using the word *get* are often heard in informal, spoken English. Such usage is correct. However, for more formal, written English, use the passive voice as described in this *Handbook*.
>
> **LESS FORMAL**   The bank robber *got arrested* yesterday.
>
> **MORE FORMAL**   The bank robber *was arrested* yesterday.

Negative sentences and questions

Negative sentences and many questions combine a form of *do* with the base form of a verb.

Please *do not forget* to turn off the air conditioner.

Did you *hear* what I said?

Keep the following points in mind when you use *do* in questions and in negative sentences.

- In questions place the *do* word first.
- Remember that the third-person singular in the present tense uses the form *does*.

  Does Jim often arrive late?

  No, but maybe he *does not* know about this meeting.

- Use the present tense form of the main verb after *do*.

  INCORRECT   *Did* you *saw* anything interesting?

  CORRECT   *Did* you *see* anything interesting?

EXERCISE 15–9   **Using *be*, *have*, and *do***

Complete the following sentences by adding the correct form of *be*, *have*, or *do*. Example:

Joel and Ethan Coen _____*are*_____ young, prize-winning filmmakers.

1. The brothers _____ a weird sense of humor, which characterizes their films.

2. In 1979, Ethan _____ working as a typist and Joel _____ editing horror films.

3. They started to talk about screenplays at that time, and they _____ worked together ever since.

4. Ethan _____ all the typing when they talk.

5. One of their films, *Barton Fink*, _____ awarded the Palme d'Or in 1991.

Recognizing and using modal auxiliaries

A **modal auxiliary** is an auxiliary verb that is used with a main verb to indicate necessity, obligation, permission, or possibility.

Wang *should wear* a suit to his interview tomorrow.

They *might offer* him the job.

Modals give information about the speaker or writer's attitude toward that verb. Modals have only one form. The accompanying chart indicates how to use modals.

Using Modals

MODAL	MEANING CONVEYED	EXAMPLE
can, could	ability	Carla *can* run five miles. I *could* run last year, but I *cannot* run today.
should	advisability	It is going to rain. You *should* take an umbrella.
must, have to	necessity	We *must* remember to go to the library. We *have to* return some books.
not	prohibition	You *must not* park in front of the police station.
must, must not	logical necessity	This letter *must* be from Svetlana. I know no one else in Moscow. The Smiths *must not* know our new telephone number.
will, would	intention	I think I *will* go to the movies tomorrow.
may, might, could	possibility	Fred is sick. He *may* or *may not* come to the meeting today.

Keep the following in mind when you use modals in your writing.

* Do not use the third-person singular -*s* ending with a modal.

INCORRECT   Glen *musts* register soon, or he will not get into the class.

CORRECT   Glen *must* register soon, or he will not get into the class.

* Always use the base form of the verb, not the infinitive or past tense, after a modal.

INCORRECT   Sid and Maria *could to speak* English last year.

INCORRECT   Sid and Maria *could spoke* English last year.

CORRECT   Sid and Maria *could speak* English last year.

* When the modal is followed by another auxiliary verb (*be, have,* or *do*), use the base form of the auxiliary verb. (See 15j for more on forms of *be, have,* and *do*.)

INCORRECT   The package *could not been delivered.*

REVISED   The package *could not be delivered.*

* Do not use more than one modal with any main verb. Use one of the following phrases as a substitute for the second modal.

MODAL	SUBSTITUTES
can	be able to
must	have to
should	supposed to, be obliged to

INCORRECT   Sylvia *might can* pass the history test this semester.

CORRECT   Sylvia *might be able to* pass the history test this semester.

* Use the perfect tense after *could, would,* and *should* to relate something that did not happen. Do not substitute *of* for *have* in this structure.

INCORRECT   I *could of* worked last summer, but I decided to attend summer school instead.

CORRECT   I *could have* worked last summer, but I decided to attend summer school instead.

EXERCISE 15–10   **Revising Errors with Modals**

Correct the errors involving modals in the following passage.

Great blue herons are beautiful birds that used to be hunted for their feathers. They could had become extinct, but they were saved at the last minute by conservation laws. Game wardens such as Arthur Knight of the Chesa-peake Bay area have protected them fiercely since then. Knight would has arrested his own brother for illegal hunting, say residents of his small town. Herons are fascinating birds for birdwatchers. An adult heron cans stand motionless while it watches for fish, and then can strikes with lightning speed. Young birds have a hard time learning this skill, however. Many would died of hunger without their parents' help. Besides fish, herons should also can able to find frogs and insects to supplement their diet. For that reason, they must to have a vital habitat.

—Adapted from Richard J. Dolesh, "The Great Blue Heron"

15l   Using gerunds and infinitives

Infinitives and **gerunds** are verbals—verb forms that function as nouns. An infinitive or a gerund can be used as a subject, an object, or a complement in a sentence. Take care to use the correct verb forms when using verbals as objects.

Attending college can be an exciting experience. [The gerund *attending* is the subject of the sentence.]

We enjoy *hearing* the lectures. [*Hearing* is the direct object of the verb *enjoy.*]

To see is *to believe.* [*To see* is subject of the sentence; *to believe* is the complement.]

Using infinitives as objects

Refer to the accompanying chart for guidelines on how to use infinitives as objects.

How to Use Infinitives as Objects

- Certain verbs are followed by an infinitive.

afford	consent	have	plan	swear
agree	decide	learn	pretend	threaten
arrange	deserve	manage	refuse	try
claim	fail	offer	seem	wait

(continued)

Some students *fail to balance* their academic and recreational activities.

Other students *learn not to be* outdone by those pressures.

Note that *not* precedes the infinitive in the negative form.

INCORRECT   Tsilya *wants going* to Europe this summer.

REVISED   Tsilya *wants to go* to Europe this summer.

- Some verbs are followed by a noun or pronoun and then the infinitive.

advise	command	force	order	teach
allow	convince	hire	persuade	tell
cause	encourage	instruct	remind	urge
challenge	forbid	invite	require	warn

The city *hired* an investigator *to find* the causes of the accident.

Jorge *persuaded* his employer *to give* him time off to attend classes.

- Other verbs may be followed either by a noun or pronoun and an infinitive, or directly by an infinitive.

allow	expect	help	want
ask	force	need	would like
cause	get	permit	

One student *asked to leave* the room.

The professor *asked* the disruptive student *to leave* the room.

The university *expects* Kara *to repeat* the course. She *expects to do* well.

- When the verbs *let*, *make*, and *have* mean *"allow," "cause,"* or *"require,"* they are followed by a noun or pronoun and the base form of a verb (the infinitive without *to*).

INCORRECT   Sue *has* her children *to read* or play games in the afternoon.

CORRECT   Sue *has* her children *read* or play games in the afternoon.

CORRECT   Sue *does not let* her children *play* video games.

CORRECT   Video games *make* her children *behave* aggressively.

Using gerunds as objects

Refer to the accompanying chart for guidelines on using gerunds as objects.

How to Use Gerunds as Objects

- Certain verbs are followed by gerunds.

admit	delay	imagine	practice	resist
allow	deny	keep	quit	risk
appreciate	discuss	mention	regret	stop
avoid	dislike	mind	remember	suggest
cannot help	enjoy	miss	report	tolerate
consider	finish	postpone	resent	understand

Sigeru Miyamoto *suggested changing* the nature of video games.

He *enjoyed creating* games with stories like fairy tales.

INCORRECT   Sal *denied to drink* before he drove his car that night.

REVISED   Sal *denied drinking* before he drove his car that night.

- Many verbs followed by gerunds may also include a possessive form indicating the person performing the action.

appreciate	deny	mention	regret	risk
cannot help	enjoy	mind	report	suggest
consider	forgive	postpone	resent	tolerate
delay	imagine	prevent	resist	understand

We *understand* your *wanting* to go right now.

The company *appreciated* Sam's *changing* his vacation schedule.

The letter didn't *mention* his *not being* able to attend the meeting.

- Remember that only gerunds may be the objects of prepositions. Many English phrases consist of a noun, a verb, or an adjective plus a preposition. Always use a gerund after one of the following phrases. However, this list is not complete. You should add to it as you encounter more such phrases.

(continued)

accuse someone of	be responsible for	fear of
apologize for	be tired of	interest in
approve of	be used to	look forward to
be afraid of	believe in	object to
be capable of	depend on	talk about
be interested in	dream of	think about

Greg *talks about changing* jobs, but he never does anything about it.

We would not *dream of leaving* without you.

Suwattana *is capable of handling* the project by herself.

Choosing an infinitive or a gerund

Some verbs may be followed by either a gerund or an infinitive. However, the meaning of the sentence may change depending on which form is used. See the accompanying chart for guidelines on working with verbs that take both infinitive and gerund objects.

Verbs Followed by Either Gerunds or Infinitives

- A few verbs may be followed by either an infinitive or a gerund with no change in meaning.

attempt	hate	omit
begin	like	prefer
continue	love	start

Keith *continued to apply* for student loans.

Keith *continued applying* for student loans.

Students *begin to look* for jobs before graduation.

Marcia *began looking* for work in May.

- Some verbs of perception (*hear, look at, notice, see, smell, watch*) may be followed by either the base form (the infinitive without *to*) or the gerund. However, the meaning changes slightly depending on which form you use.

Jake *saw* two men *rob* that house. [He watched the whole incident.]

Jake *saw* two men *robbing* that house. [The robbery was in progress when he noticed it.]

(continued)

- Some verbs change meaning depending on whether a gerund or infinitive object is used. These verbs are:

  forget   stop
  remember   try

  Notice the different meanings for the infinitive and gerund with these verbs.

  INFINITIVE   I *forgot to buy* groceries. [I forgot to buy them.]

  GERUND   I *forgot buying* groceries. [I forgot I had bought them.]

  INFINITIVE   I *remembered to meet* him after work. [I did not forget to meet him after work.]

  GERUND   I *remembered meeting* him in January. [I remember that I met him in January.]

  INFINITIVE   I *stopped to talk* to Myra. [I quit what I was doing to talk to Myra.]

  GERUND   I *stopped talking* to Myra. [I ended my conversation with Myra.]

  INFINITIVE   Please *try to open* the window. [Attempt to open the window.]

  GERUND   *Try opening* the window to cool off the room. [See if opening the window works to cool off the room.]

- When the verbs *allow* and *permit* do not have a noun or pronoun object, they are followed by a gerund. When they do have a noun or pronoun object, they are followed by an infinitive.

  WITHOUT NOUN OR PRONOUN OBJECT

  The city *does not allow parking* on certain streets.

  WITH NOUN OR PRONOUN OBJECT

  The police officer *did not allow Hassan to park* in front of the library.

EXERCISE 15–11   Choosing Gerunds and Infinitives

Underline the correct form of the object in the following sentences. Example:

Some people need *facing/to face* risks in order to feel good.

1. These people enjoy *participating/to participate* in sports such as hang gliding.
2. While most of us only think about *windsurfing/to windsurf*, the risk takers actually do it.
3. Shekeina Hale decided *finding/to find* a high-risk sport because she wanted a challenge.
4. A friend advised her *trying/to try* skydiving.
5. "At first I was terrified," she said. "But I stopped *being/to be* afraid after my first jump."

EXERCISE 15–12 Writing with Gerunds and Infinitives
In one or two paragraphs describe an important experience in your life. Use verbs followed by gerunds or infinitives. Ask your teacher or a native speaker to check your use of gerunds and infinitives.

15m Recognizing common phrasal verbs and correctly placing their objects

A **phrasal verb** is a verb phrase consisting of a verb and one or two prepositions or adverbs. (See also 9c, and 13a on prepositions, and Chapter 12 on adverbs.) Phrasal verbs often express an idiomatic, or nonliteral, meaning. That is, the complete phrasal verb has a different meaning from the meaning of each of its individual words. For example, when you use the two words *step* and *up* separately, they mean to take a step in a particular direction.

The lottery winner *stepped up* onto the stage to claim the prize.

However, the phrasal verb *to step up* means to increase, or to go faster.

Pat has decided *to step up* her training for the Olympics.

As you can see from the example of *step* + *up*, not every combination of verb plus preposition or adverb is a phrasal verb. However, you can test whether a combination is a phrasal verb by trying to substitute a similar verb in the phrase. If the phrase is a true phrasal verb, substitution is impossible.

POSSIBLE   The lottery winner *climbed up* onto the stage to claim the prize.

IMPOSSIBLE   Pat has decided *to climb up* her training for the Olympics.

Since many phrasal verbs are idiomatic, or nonliteral, you must be careful that they convey your intended meaning.

You should also check your understanding of the phrasal verbs in the accompanying chart by consulting your dictionary, by asking your instructor, or by asking a native speaker about the meaning.

Some Common Phrasal Verbs

INTRANSITIVE (DO NOT TAKE A DIRECT OBJECT)

act up	get on	run out
break down	give in	stay up
catch on	grow up	step in
cut in	hang on	wear off

TRANSITIVE (TAKE A DIRECT OBJECT)

call on	give up	take off
do over	*grow up*	tear down
figure out	hand in	throw away
get in	look up	turn on
get on	pay back	turn down
get over	*run into*	*watch out for*

Note: The verbs in italics are inseparable.

INFORMAL   After her arrest, Lisa stopped *hanging out* with drug dealers.

REVISED   After her arrest, Lisa stopped *associating* with drug dealers.

INFORMAL   The band was *turned on* by the prospect of going abroad.

REVISED   The band was *enthusiastic* at the prospect of going abroad.

Notice how in the last example, the preposition *at* replaces *by*. When you substitute a one-word alternative for an overly informal phrasal verb, you may need to make other minor adjustments in your sentence as well. (For more on using informal language in writing, see 26c.)

Like other verbs, phrasal verbs may be either intransitive or transitive. An **intransitive verb** (including an intransitive phrasal verb) does not take a direct object.

> We were encouraged to *hang on* to our goals. [*Our goals* is the object of the preposition *to*, not the phrasal verb *hang on*.]

A **transitive verb** (including a transitive phrasal verb) takes a direct object.

> They *picked out* some new clothes. [*Some new clothes* is the direct object of *picked out*.]

Transitive phrasal verbs may be *separable* or *inseparable*. Inseparable transitive phrasal verbs must always keep the verb and particle (a word such as *for, on,* or *up*) together. In using these verbs, you cannot place the object between the verb and the particle.

INCORRECT	The police are *looking* them *for*.
REVISED	The police are *looking for* them.

In using *separable transitive verbs*, you may place a noun object (NO) either after the verb and the particle or between the verb and the particle. But you cannot place the particle after additional words in the sentence. Notice how the separable transitive verb *look up* is used in the following example.

INCORRECT   Chris *looked* the word in the dictionary *up*. [The particle *up* does not come immediately after the noun object.]

REVISED   Chris *looked* the word *up* in a dictionary. [The particle *up* comes immediately after the noun object.]

REVISED   Chris *looked up* the word in a dictionary. [The parts of the phrasal verb are kept together, and precede the object.]

If the object is a pronoun, place it between the verb and the particle.

INCORRECT   Chris *looked up* it in a dictionary. [The pronoun *it* is placed
            after the particle.]

REVISED   Chris *looked* it *up* in a dictionary. [The pronoun *it* comes
            between the verb and the particle.]

EXERCISE 15–13   Working with Phrasal Verbs

Complete the following sentences using the phrasal verbs and objects in parentheses. Change verb tense when necessary, and place objects in their correct position. Example:

The overall project is complex, but we can (*break down/it*) into smaller parts.

We can *break it down* into smaller parts.

1. That math problem was not difficult. I (*figured out/it*) in just a few minutes.
2. The radio is loud. Could you (*turn down/it*), please?
3. Jerrilyn met an old friend today. She (*ran into/him*) on the bus.
4. Ned is in a bad mood because he is sick. It is difficult to (*get along with/him*)
   when he is like that.
5. This novel is fascinating. I cannot (*put down/it*).

`15n`   Using prepositions to express time, place, or motion

A **preposition** indicates the relationship between a noun or a pronoun
and another word or group of words in a sentence. The prepositions that can
be used to indicate relationships of time, place, and motion are sometimes
confused. Use the accompanying guidelines when using the prepositions to
indicate time, place, and motion in a sentence.

A Guide to Using Prepositions to Indicate Time, Place, or Motion

TIME

To indicate time, use the prepositions *in, on,* or *at.*

in the 1990s	*in* September	*in* a few minutes	*in* the morning
on Monday	*on* Labor Day		
at midnight	*at* 7:30 a.m.	*at* lunch time	

(continued)

PLACE
To indicate place, use the prepositions *in, on,* or *at.*

in Mexico City	*in* the shower	*in* my room	*in* Kansas
on the desk	*on* Mt. Hood	*on* the river	*on* a plane
at the movies	*at* the station	*at* the bookstore	*at* home

MOTION
To indicate motion, use the pronoun *into.*

into the night	*into* our house	*into* agreement	*into* a fight

EXERCISE 15–14 Using Appropriate Prepositions
Underline the correct preposition in each of the following sentences. Example:

I went to pick up my brother *in/on/at* the airport.

1. Three books were *in/on/at* the shelf.
2. I saw a cute puppy *in/on/at* the store window.
3. We noticed them as soon as they came *in/into* the room.
4. She lives *in/on/at* Main Street *in/on/at* Muncie, Indiana.
5. The public television station broadcast a moving documentary *in/on/at* Monday evening about veterans who served *in/on/at* Vietnam.

15o Placing adverbs

An **adverb** is a word that modifies a verb, an adjective, another adverb, or an entire sentence. Adverbs are used to indicate viewpoint, order, intensity, manner, place, or time. Adverbs can be placed at the beginning, in the middle, or at the end of a sentence. They can appear before or after a verb, or between an auxiliary verb and a main verb.

Quickly, they tried their key in the front door.

The coach has *never* given up on his team.

They skied down the icy slope *carefully.*

We *rarely* stay up late.

He looked *anxiously* in her direction.

Adverb Placement

- Adverbs conveying the writer's **viewpoint** should be placed at the beginning of the sentence.

  Fortunately, both sides came to an agreement and the strike ended.

  Surprisingly, she opted to visit her sister rather than her brother over vacation.

- Adverbs indicating **order** or **sequence** should be placed either at the beginning or at the end of the sentence.

  First, we will consider the causes of the war.

  We will examine justification for the war *last.*

- Adverbs indicating **intensity** should be placed immediately before the modified words.

  The decision *completely* surprised us.

  Their actions were *entirely* justified.

- Adverbs indicating **manner** can be placed immediately before the modified words or at the end of the sentence.

  The sleuth *silently* entered the room.

  The sleuth entered the room *silently.*

- Adverbs indicating location are usually placed at the end of the sentence.

  She planted snapdragons *here.*

  The hurricane uprooted trees *everywhere.*

- Adverbs indicating **time** are placed either at the beginning or at the end of a sentence. These adverbs always follow any adverbs that indicate manner and place.

  Yesterday, the baseball team won its first game.

  We completed our work *quickly.*

  It rained *hard here last* night.

An adverb cannot be placed between a verb (V) and its direct object (DO).

INCORRECT   We watched *silently* the rain.

REVISED   We watched the rain *silently*.

Use the chart on page 345 to help you decide on the placement of adverbs.

WRITING HINT   Place adverbs appearing in negative statements after the negative words.

Professor Josiah does not *always* return papers on time.

Our needs were not *adequately* provided for.

For questions, place the adverb some place after the subject of the sentence.

Will you *always* remember me?

Can you do this for me *now*?

EXERCISE 15–15   **Revising with Adverbs**

Rewrite the following sentences using the adverbs shown in parentheses. Example:

He did not see me or find out about my fear. (*luckily*)
Luckily, he did not see me or find out about my fear.

1. This is my first experience riding the New York subway and I am terrified. (*alone/completely*)
2. I need to go to the train station, but I am afraid I will get lost on my way. (*there*)
3. Before I left the apartment, I studied a subway map. (*carefully*)
4. I got on the wrong train and got lost. (*quickly*)
5. I got off the subway and took a taxi to the train station. (*miserably*)

EXERCISE 15–16   **Writing with Adverbs**
EXERCISE 15–16   **Writing with Adverbs**
In two to three paragraphs write about a time when you did something difficult. Use adverbs in your description. Ask your teacher, another student, or a native speaker to check the word order of the adverbs you use.

15p Changing forms with indirect discourse

Changes in word order and verb tenses often create problems when writers use indirect speech or indirect discourse. When you record a speaker's or another writer's words exactly, you use quotation marks around them (see Chapter 32). This is **direct discourse**. When you do not quote someone else's exact words but instead report what was said using **indirect discourse**, you do not use quotation marks.

DIRECT DISCOURSE	Meteorologist Kurt Manner said, "Weather patterns have changed all over the world."
INDIRECT DISCOURSE	Meteorologist Kurt Manner remarked that weather has changed all over the world.

When you convert direct discourse into indirect discourse, you should keep the accompanying guidelines in mind.

EXERCISE 15–17   **Recording Viewpoints Using Direct and Indirect Speech**
Interview several classmates about a topic in the news. Write two or three paragraphs in which you use both direct and indirect speech to report what they say.

Converting Direct Discourse to Indirect Discourse

- Change the simple present tense of direct discourse to the simple past tense.

DIRECT	He said, "Scientists *discover* traces of aluminum in the town's water supply."
INDIRECT	He said that they *discovered* aluminum in the town's water.

(continued)

- Change the present progressive tense of direct discourse to the past progressive.

  DIRECT   He said, "Scientists *are discovering* traces of aluminum in the town's water supply."

  INDIRECT He said that they *were discovering* aluminum in the town's water.

- Change the present perfect and the simple past of direct discourse to the past perfect.

  DIRECT   He said, "Scientists *have discovered* traces of aluminum in the town's water supply."

  INDIRECT He said that they *had discovered* aluminum in the town's water.

  (For more information on verb tenses, see 10f–i and 15h.)

- Change *will* to *would, may* to *might*, and *can* to *could*.

  DIRECT   He said, "Scientists *may discover* traces of aluminum in the town's water supply."

  INDIRECT He said that they *might discover* aluminum in the town's water.

- Change *have to* and *must* to *had to*.

  DIRECT   He said, "Scientists *must discover* traces of aluminum in the town's water supply."

  INDIRECT He said that they *had to discover* aluminum in the town's water.

- Report *yes/no* questions with the word *if* or *whether*. Use sentence word order, not question word order, with indirect questions. Do not use the words *do, does,* or *did* in an indirect question.

  DIRECT   He asked, "*Did* scientists discover traces of aluminum in the town's water supply?"

  INDIRECT He asked *if* they discovered aluminum in the town's water.

(continued)

- Report questions seeking information with *who, what, when, where, how,* or *why*.

  DIRECT   He asked, "*When* will scientists discover traces of aluminum in the town's water supply?"

  INDIRECT   He asked *when* they would discover aluminum in the town's water.

- Report invitations and commands with the infinitive.

  DIRECT   He said, "*Discover* traces of aluminum in the town's water supply."

  INDIRECT   He told them *to discover* aluminum in the town's water.

15q   Using verb tenses in conditional sentences

A conditional statement describes one event that must be true for another event to exist. A conditional sentence usually contains two clauses, an independent clause and a dependent clause (see 9d). The dependent clause in a conditional sentence typically begins with a word such as *if, when, whenever,* or *unless*.

┌ DEPENDENT CLAUSE ┐ ┌────── INDEPENDENT CLAUSE ──────┐
Unless he arrives soon, we will have to leave without him.

When you write conditional sentences that include more than one clause, you must pay attention to the sequence of tenses you use in the independent and dependent clauses. Use the chart on pp. 350–351 to help you decide which tenses to use when describing real or unreal conditions in the past, present, or future.

Sentences with the verbs *hope* and *wish* are like conditional sentences. They too are used to write about uncertain situations.

I hope I can pass that test. [I might or might not be able to pass it.]

I wish I could pass that test. [I probably cannot pass it.]

Follow these guidelines for using verb tenses with *hope* and *wish*.

- Use the past tense to express a wish about the present or future.

  I wish I *knew* the answer. [I do not know the answer.]

  I wish I *were* going with you tomorrow. [I am not going with you tomorrow.]

- Use the past perfect to express a wish about the past.

  Jana wishes she *had stayed* in school. [She did not stay in school.]

  Veronica wishes she *had* not *bought* that new car. [She did buy that new car.]

- Use the present or future tense to express hopes.

  I hope you *have* a great time on your vacation.

  I hope I *will be* able to find a job after I graduate.

Guidelines for Using Verb Tenses in Conditional Sentences

- **Sentences that express real, factual conditions.**

  If the moon is full, the ocean tide runs high.

  In these sentences, the conditions stated in both the dependent and the independent clauses actually exist or did exist. Use the same tense in both clauses.

  INDEPENDENT CLAUSE   DEPENDENT CLAUSE

  Carlos bit his fingernails whenever he got nervous.

- **Sentences that express future real conditions.**

  If we leave now, we will get to the theater on time.

  These sentences predict situations that are likely to occur. Use the words *will*, *may*, *can*, *should*, or *might* followed by the base form of the verb in the independent clause; use the words *if* or *unless* plus a present tense verb in the dependent clause.

  INDEPENDENT   DEPENDENT
     CLAUSE   CLAUSE

  We will go to the party unless it snows.

- **Sentences that express present and future unreal conditions.**

  (continued)

If we won the lottery, we would be rich.

These sentences tell about unlikely or untrue situations in the present or future. Use the words *would*, *could*, or *might* followed by the base form of the verb in the independent clause; use the word *if* plus the past tense of the verb in the dependent clause.

INDEPENDENT CLAUSE   DEPENDENT CLAUSE

Nagash would study French if he had more time.

- **Sentences that express unreal conditions.**

If you had filled the gas tank yesterday, we would not have run out of gas.

These sentences tell about situations that failed to occur in the past. Use *would have*, *could have*, or *might have* followed by the past participle of the verb in the independent clause; use *if* plus the past perfect tense of the verb in the dependent clause.

INDEPENDENT CLAUSE   DEPENDENT CLAUSE

If I had taken one more course, I would have earned a minor in philosophy.

EXERCISE 15–18   **Writing with the Words *hope* and *wish***

Write three sentences for each of the following:

1. Describe what you hope will happen when you graduate from school.

2. Tell about something you wish were true about your life right now.

3. Write about something you wish had or had not happened in the past.

PART 4

Clear and Effective Sentences

16 *Sentence Fragments*

A **sentence fragment** is a group of words that is punctuated as a sentence (beginning with a capital letter and ending with end punctuation) but is not grammatically complete. A sentence fragment may lack a subject or a finite verb, or both. A **finite verb** is the main, complete verb of a clause; it changes form to indicate tense, person, number, voice, and mood. A **nonfinite verb** (a verbal) does not change form or show tense; it needs an auxiliary verb to change form and act as the main verb of a sentence.

| FINITE VERB | Drew *works* on his paper. |
| NONFINITE VERB | Jennifer was *working* on her paper. |

A sentence fragment might also be a dependent clause that is not joined to an independent clause. (See 9d for more on identifying dependent and independent clauses.)

16a   Correcting sentence fragments

Fragments can be corrected simply by supplying the missing sentence part: the subject, verb, or independent clause.

| FRAGMENT | Gave the band the support it had been hoping for. [Subject is missing: Who or what gave the band that support?] |
| REVISED | *Two well-attended performances* gave the band the support it had been hoping for. |

FRAGMENT   Two well-attended performances. [Verb is missing: What is being said about those performances?]

REVISED   Two well-attended performances *gave the band the support it had been hoping for.*

FRAGMENT   Because the two performances were well attended. [An independent clause to complete the idea initiated by *because* is missing: What happened as a result of those performances?]

REVISED   Because the two performances were well attended, *the band got the support it had been hoping for.*

As you can see from the following example, there are several ways to correct a sentence fragment.

FRAGMENT   The wind shrieking through the hills.

REVISED   The wind *was shrieking* through the hills. [auxiliary verb added to verbal]

REVISED   The wind *shrieked* through the hills. [verbal changed to finite verb]

REVISED   *We listened to* the wind shrieking through the hills. [independent clause added to dependent clause]

REVISED   The wind, shrieking through the hills, *frightened the animals.* [verb, *frightened,* and direct object, *the animals,* added]

Sometimes the best way to correct a sentence fragment is to combine the fragment with the sentence preceding or following it.

FRAGMENTS Jimmy Santiago Baca was born in 1952 in Santa Fe, New Mexico. And has lived as well in North Carolina, California, and Arizona. He makes his home on a small farm. Where he lives with his wife and children. Outside Albuquerque.

REVISED   Jimmy Santiago Baca was born in 1952 in Santa Fe, New Mexico, and has lived as well in North Carolina, California, and Arizona. He makes his home on a small farm, where he lives with his wife and children outside Albuquerque.

Use the accompanying chart to help you find fragments.

Checking for Sentence Fragments

- **Locate the subject.** If a sentence has neither an explicit nor an implied subject, it is a fragment (see 9a).
- **Locate the verb.** If a sentence does not have a verb, or if it has a verbal without an auxiliary verb, it is a fragment (see 9c-2).
- **Look for subordinate conjunctions at the beginning of clauses.** A sentence must have at least one independent clause, a clause that has a subject and a main verb and that does not begin with a subordinating conjunction (see 13c-3).
- **Look for relative pronouns at the beginning of clauses.** If a relative pronoun introduces a clause, it is not a sentence. (Questions may begin with interrogative pronouns [11b], some of which are the same as relative pronouns, but those questions are still complete sentences: *Who won the game? Which team did you root for?*)

EXERCISE 16–1 Identifying and Correcting Sentence Fragments

Identify the sentence fragments in the following list and explain how you can correct each one. Example:

To the lighthouse.

Add an independent clause: *They planned a trip* to the lighthouse.

1. With only the funds from last year's collection.
2. Learning a foreign language.
3. Cruising the streets late at night in a new sports car.
4. Who was promoted during the company's days of expansion.
5. Throughout Africa and perhaps throughout Asia as well.

16b   Revising phrase fragments

Phrases (groups of related words that lack a subject or a finite verb) function as verbs, prepositions, nouns, or appositives. Sometimes verbal phrases, prepositional phrases, noun phrases, or appositive phrases are used, incorrectly, as complete sentences. A phrase misused as a sentence is called a phrase fragment.

1   Verbal phrase fragments

A *verbal phrase* consists of a verbal (an infinitive, a present or past participle, or a gerund) and any related objects or modifiers (see 9c-2). A verbal phrase fragment lacks a finite verb and sometimes a subject. Fragments consisting of verbal phrases can either be combined with a related independent clause or be converted to independent clauses.

FRAGMENT   The Clinton welfare plan was designed to accomplish a number of goals. Including putting more people to work.

REVISED   The Clinton welfare plan was designed to accomplish a number of goals, *including putting more people to work.* [The fragment is combined with a related independent clause.]

2   Prepositional phrase fragments

A *prepositional phrase* consists of a preposition, its object, and any object modifiers. Prepositional phrase fragments have neither subjects nor finite verbs. Revise a prepositional phrase by combining it with a related independent clause.

FRAGMENT   The Clinton welfare plan required an increase in taxes. For the middle class.

REVISED   The Clinton welfare plan required an increase in taxes *for the middle class.*

3   Noun phrase fragments

A *noun phrase* consists of a noun and its modifiers (see 9c-1). Noun phrase fragments do not have finite verbs. Revise a noun phrase fragment by combining it with a related independent clause.

FRAGMENT   Various new therapies for the common cold. They created hope that a cure was likely to be found soon.

REVISED   *Various new therapies for the common cold created* hope that a cure was likely to be found soon.

Grammar and Writing

Avoiding Sentence Fragments

Apply your knowledge of sentence fragments to a recent piece of your writing. Use the chart on p. 355 for guidance.

- Check that your sentences include a subject and verb.
- Check that -*ing* verbs are accompanied by an auxiliary verb.
- Read your writing aloud and listen for complete sentences.
- Attend to where your voice drops (at a period) and consider whether what is punctuated as a sentence includes a subject and verb.

EXAMPLE

When Karen was three years old. She began to play the violin.

When Karen was three years old, she began to play the violin.

---

4   Appositive phrase fragments

Appositives are nouns, pronouns, or noun phrases that rename other nouns (see 9c-2). An appositive cannot stand alone as a sentence and is best revised by combining it into the independent clause it refers to.

FRAGMENT   One of the people I remember fondly from high school is the baseball coach, John Ramos. A gentle man who knew the game well.

REVISED   One of the people I remember fondly from high school is the baseball coach, John Ramos, *a gentle man who knew the game well.*

EXERCISE 16–2   **Working with Phrase Fragments**

Change the following phrase fragments into independent clauses. Then add whatever elements are necessary to make the sentences complete. Example:

Jane owns a convertible. One of the fastest cars in town.

Jane owns one of the fastest cars in town, a convertible.

1. We used to have fun in that convertible. Cruising up and down Lincoln Avenue.
2. Jane would drive us all over town. Without a care in the world.
3. The other day she drove her convertible into another car. A dark blue sedan with a broken headlight.
4. The black-and-white patrol car at the curb. The officer approached her.
5. I left the scene of the accident. To find the driver of the abandoned car.

16c Revising compound predicate fragments

Compound predicates consist of two or more verbs and their objects (see 9a-2). A compound predicate fragment results when one predicate is set off in a separate sentence without its subject. Correct a compound predicate fragment by combining it with the related independent clause.

FRAGMENT   They put the difficult year behind them. And looked to the future.

REVISED   They put the difficult year behind them *and looked to the future.*

EXERCISE 16–3   **Revising Phrase Fragments and Compound Predicate Fragments**
Revise the fragments in the following paragraph by combining each with an independent clause or by rewriting it as a separate sentence. Example:

He heard the ice breaking. All around the lake.

All around the lake he heard the ice breaking.

The student council president proposed numerous arguments. In favor of abolishing grades. He presented his arguments without fanfare. Assuming that they would not spur much real discussion. His main argument. It persuaded the administration to agree to a trial term. As an experiment. Hoping to emphasize learning for its own sake. A few faculty members began meeting. To develop new courses and teaching strategies.

16d Revising dependent clause fragments

Dependent clauses begin with either a subordinating conjunction (such as *if, when, after, unless*) or a relative pronoun (*who, which, that*). Although dependent clauses have both a subject and a verb, they cannot stand alone as sentences. A dependent clause requires an independent clause to complete its meaning (see 9d); otherwise, it is a dependent clause fragment.

http://leo.stcloudstate.edu/
punct/fragmentcauses.html
Identifies the causes of
sentence fragments and
suggests strategies to repair them.

    Revise a dependent clause fragment by combining it with an independent clause either before or after the fragment. Or convert the dependent clause fragment into an independent clause.

> **FRAGMENT**   Much of the country watched. As the Dallas Cowboys won the Super Bowl.
>
> **REVISED**   Much of the country watched *as the Dallas Cowboys won the Super Bowl.*

EXERCISE 16–4   **Revising Dependent Clause Fragments**
For each of the following items, identify the dependent clause fragment as (DC) and the complete sentence as (C). Then revise each fragment to make it part of the complete sentence.

1. They hoped to win the lottery. Which would solve their financial problems.

2. I really did not know what to think. Whether to believe them or not.

3. The executive left for the airport. As soon as the meeting was over.

4. Whoever hoped to complete the program requirements with distinction. Would have to do it within the allotted time.

5. The birds flew from the cherry tree to the oak in the rock garden. Then over to their nest in a plant hanging on our porch.

17   *Comma Splices and Fused Sentences*

A **comma splice** is a sentence error in which two independent clauses are incorrectly separated by a comma instead of a period. A **fused sentence** is an error in which two sentences are run together without a punctuation mark between them. Comma splices and fused sentences are types of **run-on sentences** because they run together sentences that should be separated.

COMMA SPLICE	Beethoven was not born deaf, he lost his hearing gradually.
REVISED	Beethoven was not born *deaf. He* lost his hearing gradually.
FUSED SENTENCE	Beethoven was not born deaf he lost his hearing gradually.
REVISED	Beethoven was not born *deaf; he* lost his hearing gradually.

The accompanying chart outlines the various ways to correct comma splices and fused sentences.

Ways to Eliminate Comma Splices and Fused Sentences

- Divide independent clauses into separate sentences (17a).
- Join clauses with a semicolon (17b).
- Join clauses with a semicolon and a conjunctive adverb (17c).
- Join clauses with a comma and a coordinating conjunction (17d).
- Combine clauses into a single independent clause (17e).
- Convert one of the two clauses into a dependent clause (17f).

USAGE NOTE   Separate independent clauses with a colon instead of a semicolon or a period when the second clause explains or summarizes the first one (see 30f).

> The Fifth Amendment is, of course, a wise section of the Constitution: you cannot be forced to incriminate yourself.
>
> —Lillian Hellman

Separate independent clauses with a semicolon rather than a period when the second clause is closely related to the first, especially when the latter clause contrasts or shares the form of the first.

> Before 8000 BC wheat was not the luxuriant plant it is today; it was merely one of many wild grasses that spread throughout the Middle East.
>
> —Jacob Bronowski

17a   Dividing clauses into separate sentences

Often the most convenient way to revise comma splices and fused sentences is to put a period after each independent clause.

COMMA SPLICE	Mickey Mouse is among the most popular American cartoon characters, he is often accompanied by his companion Goofy.
FUSED SENTENCE	Mickey Mouse is among the most popular American cartoon characters he is often accompanied by his companion Goofy.
REVISED	Mickey Mouse is among the most popular American cartoon *characters. He* is often accompanied by his companion Goofy.

17b   Joining clauses with a semicolon

When the ideas in two independent clauses are closely related and equally important, join them with a semicolon (see 30a).

COMMA SPLICE	Supermarket tomatoes often taste bland, homegrown garden tomatoes are juicier and sweeter.
FUSED SENTENCE	Supermarket tomatoes often taste bland homegrown garden tomatoes are juicier and sweeter.
REVISED	Supermarket tomatoes often taste bland; homegrown garden tomatoes are juicier and sweeter.

In this example, the second independent clause elaborates on the first statement by providing a contrast. Use a semicolon when an idea developed in one clause is expanded in another.

EXERCISE 17 1   **Identifying Comma Splices and Fused Sentences**
In the following sentences, circle where any comma splices begin and underline the points at which two sentences are fused. Then revise the sentence. Example:

The plums were delicious⊙they were sweet and cold.

The plums were delicious: they were sweet and cold.

1. The art of photography developed in the nineteenth century it is continually being perfected.
2. Some states have passed laws banning smoking in public places, soon others will follow.
3. The store ran a special on dairy items butter, milk, and cheese were being sold at bargain prices.
4. Whenever I feel overwhelmed with work, I stop for a while I try to relax and collect myself to return to the task at hand.
5. Some say that youth is wasted on the young, I cannot agree, however.

17c Joining clauses with a semicolon and a conjunctive adverb

COMMA SPLICE   The project will take a long time to complete, therefore, we should begin work on it now.

REVISED   The project will take a long time to *complete; therefore,* we should begin work on it now.

FUSED SENTENCE   The ideas of cultural anthropologists were neglected for years lately however their ideas have become increasingly influential.

REVISED   The ideas of cultural anthropologists were neglected for *years; lately, however,* their ideas have become increasingly influential.

Conjunctive adverbs can be placed in different positions in a sentence. (See 13c-4 for a list of common conjunctive adverbs and 30b for additional advice about using them in your writing.)

WRITING HINT   Conjunctive adverbs tend to increase the formality of writing. Conjunctive adverbs create a less conversational tone than that achieved by using coordinating conjunctions. Remember also that using too many conjunctive adverbs can slow your sentences down because the semicolons signal longer pauses than commas. (See Chapter 30 for more on semicolons.)

She did not plan to major in *economics, but* she did.

She did not plan to major in *economics; however,* she did.

17d Joining clauses with a comma and a coordinating conjunction

To link closely related independent clauses of equal importance, use a comma followed by a coordinating conjunction (*and, but, or, nor, for, so, yet*).

* Use *but* or *yet* to indicate contrast or opposition.

  He wanted to go, *but* he could not.

* Use *so* or *for* to introduce an explanation.

  They were only a few miles from their destination, *so* they kept on walking.

* Use *and* to indicate the addition of two or more things.

  They went out to dinner, *and* they went to a movie.

* Use *or* to indicate alternatives.

  They could go to the concert, *or* they could stay home and listen to it on the radio.

In the following examples, note that the comma splice and fused sentence errors are corrected by adding a comma and a coordinating conjunction.

COMMA SPLICE   We could have ordered pasta and garlic bread, we could have selected something from the budget menu.

REVISED   We could have ordered pasta and garlic *bread, or* we could have selected something from the budget menu.

FUSED SENTENCE   I finally found the book it was not what I expected.

REVISED   I finally found the *book, but* it was not what I expected.

EXERCISE 17–2 **Revising Comma Splices and Fused Sentences**

Using a semicolon, conjunctive adverb, or coordinating conjunction, correct the following comma splices and fused sentences. Revise each sentence error in two different ways. Example:

His was the most moving speech hers was the least.

His was the most moving *speech, and* hers was the least.

His was the most moving *speech; hers* was the least.

1. It was one of the team's best games of the season they played with conviction and authority.
2. The truth sometimes may be hard to acknowledge, it is necessary if improvement is to follow.
3. I usually love pizza for dinner, I had it for lunch.
4. The hummingbird may be hardly bigger than a bumblebee it is really a bird, not an insect.
5. Ask not what your country can do for you ask what you can do for your country.

17e   Converting two clauses into a single independent clause

Sometimes the two clauses of a comma splice or fused sentence are best revised by combining them into a single independent clause.

COMMA SPLICE   Medical knowledge was in its infancy during the Civil War, little was known about the causes of infection.

FUSED SENTENCE   Medical knowledge was in its infancy during the Civil War little was known about the causes of infection.

REVISED   *Medical knowledge about the causes of infection* was in its infancy during the Civil War.

The revision is more precise; it identifies exactly what kind of medical knowledge was in its infancy. The revised sentence is also more succinct.

17f   Converting one of two independent clauses into a dependent clause

When the idea in one independent clause is more important than the idea in the other, the less important clause can be made dependent by introducing it with a subordinating conjunction (such as *because* or *although*). (See 13c-3 for a list of common subordinating conjunctions.)

COMMA SPLICE   Television news shows are largely entertainment, they should be clearly identified as such.

FUSED SENTENCE   Television news shows are largely entertainment they should be clearly identified as such.

REVISED   *Because* television news shows are largely entertainment, they should be clearly identified as such.

EXERCISE 17–3   Rewriting Comma Splices and Fused Sentences
Correct the following comma splices and fused sentences by combining the two independent clauses into a single sentence. Example:

People are often willing to give advice, they are less inclined to take it.

People are often willing to give advice *but are* less inclined to take it.

1. Jerome circled the block several times, he was searching for a parking space.
2. We left right after the game, we went to get a pizza.
3. You have no basis for a lawsuit you have no witnesses.

Correct the following comma splices and fused sentences by changing one of the two independent clauses into a dependent clause. Example:

We had to stop finally, we were so exhausted.

We were *so exhausted that we* finally had to stop.

4. I had a good record my first season I never had another one as good.
5. We went home there was nothing else to do.
6. She was crossing the street, she lost the heel of her right shoe.

Checking for Comma Splices and Fused Sentences

- Put brackets around each independent clause in your drafts.
- Underline the words that link the independent clauses.
- Circle the punctuation marks that separate the independent clauses.
- If you identify independent clauses with only a comma between them, you have found a comma splice.
- If you identify independent clauses with no punctuation and no words between them, you have found a fused sentence.
- If you identify independent clauses linked by a conjunctive adverb (such as *however* or *therefore*), check for appropriate punctuation: a semicolon between the independent clauses or a comma following the conjunctive adverb.

EXERCISE 17–4 Correcting Comma Splices and Fused Sentences

Correct the comma splices and fused sentences in the following paragraph two different ways, using a coordinating conjunction, a conjunctive adverb, or a subordinating conjunction. Note the logical relationship between the two clauses you are joining, and choose a connector that clarifies that relationship. Example:

Ralph is always bragging, no one seems to mind. [comma splice]

Ralph is always *bragging, but* no one seems to mind. [add a coordinating conjunction]

Ralph is always *bragging; however,* no one seems to mind. [add a conjunctive adverb]

Even though Ralph is always bragging, no one seems to mind. [add a subordinating conjunction]

Ralph has a good friend, Ed Norton, he does not always appreciate Ed. Ralph's wife, Alice, is patient with his far-fetched schemes, she loses her temper from time to time. Ralph is a very large man he is basically gentle and sweet. Ralph is a bus driver he has been a bus driver for quite a few years he will more than likely remain a bus driver all his working days.

18 *Misplaced, Interrupting, and Dangling Modifiers*

A **modifier** is a word or a phrase that functions as an adjective or adverb to limit or to qualify the meaning of another word, phrase, or clause in a sentence. Make sure that modifiers point clearly to the words, phrases, or clauses they modify. If the connection between a modifier and the word or words they modify is unclear, your readers will be confused. The guidelines in the accompanying chart can help you revise misplaced, interrupting, or dangling modifiers.

Revising Misplaced, Interrupting, and Dangling Modifiers

- Connect misplaced modifying words, phrases, or clauses with the word(s) they modify (18a–c).
- Recast squinting modifiers so they refer to only one word or group of words (18d).
- Bring together interrupting modifiers that are split off from the word(s) they modify (18e–h).
- Correct dangling modifiers by making sure they logically modify some word or sentence element (18i–j).

Misplaced Modifiers

A **misplaced modifier** is a modifier that is positioned in a sentence so that it is unclear which word, clause, or phrase is modified. Often, a modifier is misplaced when it can modify more than one word, clause, or phrase in a sentence.

18a Revising misplaced words

One type of misplaced modifier is the awkward placement of a single word, usually an adverb (see 12a).

| CONFUSING | Andrew watched the snow fall excitedly. |
| REVISED | Andrew excitedly watched the snow fall. |

Limiting modifiers, such as *almost, even, hardly, just, merely, nearly, only, scarcely,* and *simply,* restrict the meaning of the word or phrase that immediately follows it. Make certain that the modifier is placed correctly.

| CONFUSING | The office only is open in the afternoon. [Does *only* modify the noun *office,* or the prepositional phrase *in the afternoon?*] |
| CLEAR | *Only* the office is open in the afternoon. [Everything else is closed in the afternoon.] |

CLEAR   The office is open *only* in the afternoon. [The office is never open in the morning.]

Notice how changing the placement of *nearly* in the following sentences changes the meaning.

Nearly all of the one hundred people who attended the lecture were from the neighborhood.

All of the *nearly* one hundred people who attended the lecture were from the neighborhood.

EXERCISE 18–1   Placing Limiting Modifiers

For each of the following limiting modifiers, write two sentences, placing the modifier in a different position in each sentence to change its meaning. Example:

   only   You can *only* look at the car.
             Only you can look at the car.

1. almost
2. even
3. hardly
4. just
5. simply

18b   Revising misplaced phrases

The guidelines for revising misplaced words also apply to misplaced phrases. Place phrases as close as possible to the words they modify. This guideline is especially important for placing prepositional phrases in sentences (see 9c-1).

Prepositional phrases should be placed directly before or immediately after the words they modify. Notice how a misplaced prepositional phrase causes confusion in the following example.

CONFUSING   Ann was unhappy that she failed to win first place by a large margin. [Did Ann win first place by a small margin, or did she fail to win first place?]

REVISED   Ann was unhappy that she failed *by a large margin* to win first place.

1 **Misplaced participial phrases**

Misplaced participial phrases (see 9c-2) can cause confusion. The solution is to place participial phrases directly before or immediately after the words they modify.

CONFUSING   Stretching across the yard, I saw a clothesline. [It is unlikely that the speaker was stretching across the yard.]

REVISED   I saw a clothesline *stretching across the yard.*

WRITING HINT   If possible, place phrases that modify nouns immediately after the words they modify.

MISPLACED   He needed a car for his trip with automatic transmission.

IMPROVED   He needed a car *with automatic transmission* for his trip.

USAGE NOTE   Although phrases that modify nouns should immediately follow the words they modify, phrases used as adverbs can often be placed at different points within a sentence. An adverb phrase can be placed within a sentence near the word it modifies (usually the verb).

The Bulldogs lost in the first round to their cross-town rivals.

The same phrase can also be placed at the beginning or the end of the sentence:

In the first round, the Bulldogs lost to their cross-town rivals.

The Bulldogs lost to their cross-town rivals *in the first round.*

18c Revising misplaced clauses

The guidelines for revising misplaced words and phrases also apply to misplaced clauses. Remember to keep dependent clause modifiers as near as possible to the words they modify.

CONFUSING   Professor Ricks taught a seminar on contemporary American films that the students enjoyed. [What did the students enjoy, the seminar or the films?]

REVISED   *The students enjoyed* Professor Ricks's seminar on contemporary American films.

EXERCISE 18–2 Revising Misplaced Word, Phrase, and Clause Modifiers

Revise the following sentences to eliminate the awkwardness and confusion caused by misplaced modifiers. Example:

Strung along the path through the park, the people saw brightly colored Japanese lanterns.

The people saw brightly colored Japanese lanterns *strung along the path through the park.*

1. The president of the Czech Republic was comfortably able to speak in front of his political opponents.
2. Rolling dangerously near the edge of the cliff, the driver stopped the car.
3. The swimmers crouched ignoring the cheers on their blocks.
4. My parents showed the new car to me sitting in the garage.
5. There are many autographs of athletes on the walls who have eaten at Malcolm's diner.

18d Revising squinting modifiers

A **squinting modifier** is a type of misplaced modifier that confuses the meaning of a sentence because it appears to modify the words that come both before and after it. Revise squinting modifiers by moving them to their correct position, where they refer clearly to only one word or sentence element.

SQUINTING   The man who spoke quickly ran out of breath. [Did the man speak quickly, or did that man quickly run out of breath?]

REVISED   The man who *quickly* spoke ran out of breath.

REVISED   The man who spoke ran *quickly* out of breath.

EXERCISE 18–3 Revising Squinting Modifiers

Rewrite each sentence two times to eliminate the squinting modifiers. Example:

SQUINTING   Going for a long walk often relaxes her.

REVISED   A long walk *often* relaxes her.

REVISED   To relax, she *often* goes for a long walk.

1. The position he expected to get finally was eliminated.
2. The mayor announced when he completed his trip he would schedule a news conference.
3. Students who cheat on exams often escape detection.
4. Writing teachers tell students when they are older they will appreciate the course.
5. She awoke suddenly getting out from beneath the covers.

Interrupting Modifiers

Interrupting modifiers are modifiers whose placement causes confusion in sentences. Interrupting modifiers disrupt the continuity of thought in a sentence and can make it difficult to understand the meaning of a sentence. Avoid letting modifiers separate verbs and subjects, separate verbs and direct objects, split infinitives, or separate parts of a verb phrase.

18e   Revising lengthy modifiers that separate a verb from its subject

Phrases and clauses that come between a subject and verb can be awkward or confusing.

AWKWARD   The concert, because it snowed heavily all day, was canceled.

REVISED   Because it snowed heavily all day, *the concert was canceled.*

18f   Revising modifiers that separate a verb from its direct object or a subject complement

Sentences in which direct objects and subject complements follow immediately after the verb are clear and easy to read. Avoid using modifiers to separate a verb from its object.

AWKWARD   Dan Marino threw, during his best season as the Miami Dolphins quarterback, forty-eight touchdown passes. [The verb is separated from the object.]

REVISED   During his best season as the Miami Dolphins quarterback, Dan Marino *threw forty-eight touchdown passes.* [The object directly follows the verb.]

18g Revising modifiers that split an infinitive

Because the infinitive form of a verb is a two-word unit, splitting that unit with words or phrases can create a confusing sentence. Avoid placing an adverbial modifier between *to* and the verb of an infinitive.

http://www.uottawa.ca/
academic/arts/writecent/
hypergrammar/
msplmod.html
Provides examples of how misplaced modifiers cause writing confusion.

AWKWARD   President Lincoln expected the North to quickly and decisively win the war.

REVISED   President Lincoln expected the North *to win* the war quickly and decisively.

Occasionally, however, splitting an infinitive is less awkward than not splitting it. In such cases, you should probably choose to rewrite the sentence so that it does not include an infinitive.

AWKWARD   Community college enrollment is expected to more than double in the next decade.

REVISED   More than double the current community college enrollment is expected in the next decade.

But sometimes the split infinitive is the best choice for effectively conveying a meaning if the modifier is limited to one word.

We need *to carefully weigh* expected benefits against unexpected losses.

18h Revising modifiers that separate parts of a verb phrase

A verb phrase consists of a main verb along with one or more auxiliary verbs: *will go, were being seen* (see 5f-2). A single adverb or two consecutive adverbs can usually be inserted into a verb phrase without causing confusion or awkwardness. But in all other cases avoid splitting parts of a verb phrase.

ACCEPTABLE   They *had* only rarely *eaten* vegetarian dishes. [Two one-word adverbs break up the verb phrase *had eaten*.]

AWKWARD   Many television viewers will, when it is time for a commercial, change channels or get something to eat.

REVISED   When it is time for a commercial, many television viewers *will change* channels or get something to eat.

EXERCISE 18–4   Revising Interrupting Modifiers

Revise each of the following sentences to eliminate the interrupting modifiers. Example:

The recent graduate wanted to eventually attend graduate school.

The recent graduate wanted *eventually to attend* graduate school.

1. Political protests began to, among youth, be popular during the Vietnam War.

2. Most adolescents have by the time they are eighteen years old become physically mature.

3. The school senate finally passed, in response to pressure from administrative lobbyists, a resolution banning smoking on campus.

4. The organizers of the carnival expect to if they can recoup their investment.

5. Many great composers were by the time some of their best works were performed no longer alive.

Dangling Modifiers

A **dangling modifier** is a word, phrase, or clause that does not modify any element in a sentence. A dangling modifier often seems to refer to something that is implied in the sentence. Readers try to correct a dangling modifier, often to humorous effect, by having it modify the closest word in the sentence. *Singing sweetly, the baby stopped crying.*

18i   Revising dangling word and phrase modifiers

Dangling word modifiers are often adverbs. To revise a dangling word modifier, add the word or words for the modifier to modify.

DANGLING   Courageously, the suspect was apprehended. [It is unlikely that the suspect is courageous.]

REVISED   *Courageously, the officer apprehended the suspect.*

Dangling participial phrases and prepositional phrases are best revised either by adding the word or words for the modifier to modify, or by changing the modifier into a phrase or a clause that clearly modifies another part of the sentence.

DANGLING   Singing for his supper, Mark and Heidi giggled. [Did Mark and Heidi sing for his supper?]

REVISED   Singing for his supper, *Fred made* Mark and Heidi giggle.

REVISED   *As he sang for his supper,* Fred made Mark and Heidi giggle.

18j   Revising dangling elliptical clauses

An **elliptical clause** is a dependent clause that lacks all or part of the subject or predicate. To revise a dangling elliptical clause, include the words implied by the clause.

DANGLING   While brewing, Kristie can determine how fresh the coffee is.

REVISED   *While the coffee is brewing,* Kristie can determine how fresh it is.

EXERCISE 18–5   Revising Dangling Modifiers

Revise each of the following sentences to correct the dangling modifiers. Example:

Having missed classes for a month, my grades were in jeopardy.

Because I missed classes for a month, my grades were in jeopardy.

1. Flying over Detroit, the Canadian border appeared part of the city.
2. Thinking about the day's events, the ringing phone startled her.
3. When driving along Lake Shore Drive, the sun shone brightly on the lake.
4. To protest the increase in tuition, administrative offices were occupied by student groups.
5. To become a doctor, four years of postgraduate study must be completed, medical boards must be passed, and a residency completed.

EXERCISE 18–6   **Revising Misplaced, Interrupting, and Dangling Modifiers**
Revise the following sentences to eliminate the misplaced, interrupting, and dangling modifiers. Example:

> Soaring high in the sky, they saw two eagles.
>
> They saw two eagles soaring high in the sky.

1. Instead of going to the movies with friends, exams kept me home studying.
2. After studying the entire afternoon, it was too late to go to the museum.
3. To be successful in college, the system must be understood by students.
4. With a long list of written requirements, I was not sure I would be able to do the work for the course.
5. Before attending the lecture, dinner would have to be eaten.

EXERCISE 18–7   **Revising Misplaced, Interrupting, and Dangling Modifiers**
Revise the sentences in the following paragraph to eliminate the misplaced, interrupting, and dangling modifiers. Example:

> Soaring high in the sky, they saw two eagles.
>
> They saw two eagles soaring high in the sky.

> Instead of going to an afternoon movie with friends, exams kept them home studying. After studying the entire afternoon and evening, it became too late to go at all. Studying more often makes a difference. To be successful on an exam and in a course, the instructor's system must be understood by students. Before taking the exam the next morning, breakfast would have to be eaten. Acing the exam, their instructor would be pleased with their progress.

19   *Avoiding Shifts and Maintaining Consistency*

A **shift** is an abrupt change from one verb tense, mood, or voice to another, or from one pronoun person or number to another, that results in confusing writing. The chart on p. 376 identifies the types of unnecessary shifts that can cause confusion.

Unnecessary Shifts

- Shifts in pronoun person and number (19a)
- Shifts in verb tenses (19b)
- Shifts in mood (19c)
- Shifts in voice (19d)
- Shifts between direct and indirect quotations (19e)
- Shifts in diction and tone (19f)

19a Maintaining consistency of person and number

Avoid unnecessary shifts among first-person pronouns (*I, we*), second-person pronouns (*you*), and third-person pronouns (*he, she, it, one, they*).

INCONSISTENT	When *one* travels abroad, *you* should take traveler's checks instead of cash. [shift from third-person pronoun to second person]
REVISED	When *you* travel abroad, *you* should take traveler's checks instead of cash.

Also avoid shifts between singular and plural nouns and pronouns (shifts in number).

INCONSISTENT	*Jen and Lily* drank *her* iced teas.
REVISED	*Jen and Lily* drank *their* iced teas.

Sometimes, however, your meaning will clearly warrant such a shift.

Jen and Lily swam in *his* Olympic-size pool.

Shifts in number often involve inaccurate agreement between pronouns and their antecedents.

INCONSISTENT	When teachers assign *a reading,* they should discuss *them.*
REVISED	When teachers assign *a reading,* they should discuss *it.*

EXERCISE 19–1   **Avoiding Shifts in Pronoun Person and Number**
Underline the unnecessary shifts in person and number in the following sentences. Then rewrite each sentence to eliminate the shift. Example:

Studies have shown that <u>one</u> is subject to increased risk for heart attack if <u>you</u> lead a sedentary life.

Studies have shown that *people* are subject to increased risk for heart attack if *they* lead sedentary *lives*.

1. When one visits Gettysburg, you should be sure to walk over to Cemetery Ridge and look for Little Round Top.

2. A person likes to feel that they are appreciated.

3. All the speakers invited to the conference had a good reputation in the field.

4. If a person travels abroad they will encounter different customs.

5. Many secretaries are poorly paid, even though a secretary does important work.

19b   Maintaining consistency in verb tenses

A verb tense establishes the time of the action of a piece of writing. A change in tense indicates a change in time. Shifting between different tenses unnecessarily or illogically can confuse and distract readers.

INCONSISTENT	The committee meeting *began* when the chair *calls* the members to order. [confusing shift from past tense to present tense]
REVISED	The committee meeting *began* when the chair *called* the members to order. [past tense]

Sometimes more than one verb tense is used in a sentence, paragraph, or essay when the meaning calls for such a shift. (See 10f–i for more on sequence of tenses in verb usage.)

EXERCISE 19–2   Avoiding Shifts in Verb Tenses

Underline the unnecessary or illogical verb tense shifts in the following sentences. Then rewrite each sentence to eliminate the shift. (Some sentences may be correct as written.) Example:

The authority of the president <u>is being</u> questioned. A good example <u>was</u> the committee's vote to censure him.

The authority of the president *is being* questioned. A good example *is* the committee's vote to censure him.

1. Smoke billowed from the windows as people run in every direction.

2. If I find the money, I will return it.

3. Once upon a time, there is a family of bears that lived in the forest.

4. The requirements for graduation will be changed next year. The change will have affected only next year's first-year college students; it does not affect students already matriculated.

5. Given the strength and amount of the evidence, it was hard to believe that it takes the jury members so long to have made up their minds.

EXERCISE 19–3 Shifting Tenses Logically

Think of something important in your life that has changed—a situation, an opinion, or a relationship, for example. What caused the change? Was it for the better? Write a paragraph in which you explain what changed. Use the past tense to describe how things were before the change and the present tense to describe how things are today.

19c Maintaining consistency in mood

Always avoid shifts from one verb mood to another. Verbs in the indicative mood make statements and ask questions. (*She swims well. Are they home?*) Verbs in the imperative mood give commands and offer advice. (*Close the window. Try this on for size.*) Verbs in the subjunctive mood express wishes, conditions, or statements contrary to fact. (*If only they were here.*)

INCONSISTENT   *Drive* slowly on snowy roads and you *should keep* the car in lower gears than usual. [shift from imperative to indicative]

REVISED   *Drive* slowly on snowy roads and *keep* the car in lower gears than usual.

19d Maintaining consistency in voice

Avoid shifting unnecessarily between the active voice (*They bought their tickets early*) and the passive voice (*Their tickets were bought early*). Subjects with active voice verbs initiate action; subjects with passive voice verbs receive action.

INCONSISTENT   The Japanese army *was being fought* in the Pacific Ocean while the Allies *defeated* the German army at Normandy.

REVISED   The Japanese army *fought* in the Pacific Ocean while the Allies *defeated* the German army at Normandy.

However, a shift between the active and passive voice is occasionally both logical and necessary to maintain focus on a subject.

The campaign workers *labored* tirelessly for their candidate and *were rewarded* with her election. [The shift from the active to passive voice keeps the focus on the original subject—*campaign workers.*]

EXERCISE 19–4   **Avoiding Shifts in Mood and Voice**
Underline the unnecessary mood and voice shifts in the following sentences. Then rewrite each sentence to eliminate the shift. Example:

Jodie <u>requested</u> a raise and asked <u>that she be</u> transferred.

Jodie *requested* a raise and *asked* for a transfer.

1. Even though I enjoy seafood, a steak is enjoyed even more.

2. The coach demanded an explanation and that she was given an apology.

3. If the test were too easy, it is not a challenge.

4. Remember to proofread your paper and you should submit it on time as well.

5. Although concert violinists often play violins made by Antonio Stradivari, those instruments are rarely owned by the musicians.

 19e   Avoiding shifts between direct and indirect quotations

Direct quotations, also called direct discourse, reproduce someone else's exact words. When you use direct discourse, place the quoted words within quotation marks.

Indirect quotations, or indirect discourse, report or summarize what someone else has said or written without repeating the same words (see 15p).

Shifting between direct and indirect discourse within the same sentence can result in confusing sentences. Avoid such shifts in your essays, especially in research essays, where you are most likely to incorporate quotations from secondary sources.

INCONSISTENT	Stephen Jay Gould has said that "evolution is a theory" and he has also argued that it is a fact. [shift from direct to indirect discourse]
REVISED	Stephen Jay Gould has argued that evolution is both a fact and a theory. [indirect discourse]

WRITING HINT   The differences between direct and indirect discourse usually involve tense and person. Ordinarily, the verbs in an indirect quotation are in the same tense as the main verb (MV).

$$\lceil MV \rceil$$
Charmaine *asked* us where Allen *was.*

In a direct quotation the verbs are in the tense that the speaker actually used.

Charmaine *asked* us, "Where *is* Allen?"

EXERCISE 19–5   **Maintaining Consistency in Direct and Indirect Discourse**
Write two sentences for each of the following quotations, one using direct discourse and the other indirect discourse. Maintain consistency in verb tense in each sentence. Example:

"I regret I have only one life to lose for my country."   —*Nathan Hale*

DIRECT	Nathan Hale once announced: "I regret I have only one life to lose for my country."
INDIRECT	Historians have described Nathan Hale as a quintessential patriot because he once said he regretted he had only one life to lose for his country.

1. "Societies need to have one illness which becomes identified with evil, and attaches blame to its 'victims.'"   —*Susan Sontag*

2. "Those who are ignorant of history are condemned to repeat it."
   —*George Santayana*

3. "The prejudice against color, of which we hear so much, is no stronger than that against sex." —*Elizabeth Cady Stanton*

4. "Nothing in life is to be feared. It is only to be understood." —*Marie Curie*

5. "Science without religion is lame; religion without science is blind." —*Albert Einstein*

19f Maintaining consistency in diction and tone

Diction refers to a writer's word choice. Strive for consistency in diction by using the same level of language throughout a piece of writing. If you are using formal language, for example, you should avoid contractions (*you're, it's*), colloquialisms, and slang expressions (see 26c).

INCONSISTENT	The significance of Columbus's voyages continues to be debated, sparked by celebrations of the five hundredth anniversary of the discovery of America. *Some scholars are out to trash Columbus's cultural contribution.* [The italicized sentence should be made consistent with the level of diction of the other sentences.]
REVISED	The significance of Columbus's voyages continues to be debated, sparked by celebrations of the five hundredth anniversary of the discovery of America. *Some scholars argue for a revisionist interpretation of Columbus's cultural contribution.*

Tone refers to the writer's attitude toward the subject. It is conveyed by a writer's choice of words, by the length and complexity of sentences, and by the selection of details. Tone, like diction, can be technical, formal, informal, or colloquial. (For examples of varied tones, see 1d-3.)

Unless you want to vary your tone or to achieve some intentional effect or purpose (e.g., for comic effect or to shock readers), avoid shifting your tone in a piece of writing.

EXERCISE 19–6 Avoiding Unnecessary Shifts and Inconsistencies
Revise the following paragraph to eliminate unnecessary shifts and inconsistencies—in pronoun person and number, in verb tense, in voice and mood, in direct and indirect discourse, and in diction and tone.

The conventional definition of a classic is a work that has withstood the test of time. One proponent of this definition is the eighteenth-century writer Samuel Johnson, who in his *Preface to Shakespeare,* suggested that regarding works of genius, "of which the excellence is not absolute and definite, but gradual and comparative . . . no other test can be applied than length of duration and continuance of esteem." Johnson's definition is really great because it suggests that a work that continues to engage readers in different times can be considered somehow extra special. They have that extra kick that grabs your attention. But you should be able to tell if a work were to become a classic long before it is judged to have become one.

20 *Pronoun Reference*

A **pronoun** replaces a noun in a sentence. Substituting pronouns in place of nouns enables writers to avoid using the same word repeatedly and to add variety to a sentence. For example, instead of writing *Carl rejoined the team when Carl recovered from Carl's injury,* you would write *Carl rejoined the team when he recovered from his injury.*

When you write with pronouns, you need to make certain that the pronoun's **antecedent,** the noun that the pronoun refers to, is clear. A pronoun that can refer to two antecedents makes for a confusing sentence: *Emily told*

Revising Ambiguous Pronoun Reference

- Make each pronoun refer to a single antecedent (20a).
- Keep pronouns and antecedents close together (20b).
- Check uses of *this, that, which,* and *it* for clarity (20c-1).
- Avoid the indefinite use of *it, they,* and *you* (20c-2).
- Use *who, which,* and *that* with appropriate antecedents (20c-3).
- Avoid using adjectives or possessives as antecedents (20c-4).

Beth she won the prize. (Did Emily or Beth win the prize?) *The family agreed on the distribution of the inheritance, but it would take time.* (Does *it* refer to the family, the distribution, or the inheritance?) The accompanying chart provides advice for revising unclear pronoun reference.

20a   Making sure a pronoun refers to a single antecedent

Make sure that pronouns in your writing clearly refer to only one antecedent. For example, the sentence *Grace told Diane she was not going* is not clear because the pronoun *she* could refer to either Grace or Diane. The sentence should be revised so that the pronoun refers to only one antecedent—either Grace or Diane. If the reference cannot be made clear, the sentence should be rewritten without the pronoun.

http://www.uottawa.ca/
academic/arts/writcent/
hypergrammar/pronref.html
Covers a wide range of issues
relating to pronoun
reference.

REVISIONS   Grace told Diane to forget about going.

Grace said that Diane was not going.

Grace said to Diane, "I am not going."

WRITING HINT   When you write sentences that report what someone has said, and especially sentences using such verbs as *said* and *told*, use direct rather than indirect quotation (see 19e).

CONFUSING   Ozzie told Izzie that he was upset.

CLEAR   Ozzie told Izzie, "I am upset."

CLEAR   Ozzie said, "I am upset."

20b   Keeping pronouns and antecedents close together

Placing a pronoun too far from its antecedent can confuse readers.

CONFUSING   I. M. Pei is a world-renowned architect who designed *the pyramid addition* to the Louvre Museum. The John Fitzgerald Kennedy Library in Boston, the John Hancock Building also in

Boston, and the Johnson Museum of Art at Cornell University are other buildings designed by Pei. Many critics call *it* a controversial yet aesthetically pleasing sight. [The antecedent of the pronoun *it* is *the pyramid addition*, but several nouns appear between the antecedent and the pronoun, making that connection unclear.]

To avoid confusion caused by remote pronoun reference, keep pronouns and antecedents as close together as possible. You may have to repeat the noun or use a synonym to make the reference clear.

REVISED   I. M. Pei is a world-renowned architect who designed *the pyramid addition* to the Louvre Museum. Many critics call *it* a controversial yet aesthetically pleasing sight. The John Fitzgerald Kennedy Library in Boston, the John Hancock Building also in Boston, and the Johnson Museum of Art at Cornell University are other buildings designed by Pei.

EXERCISE 20–1   Clarifying Ambiguous and Remote Pronoun Reference
Revise the following sentences to eliminate all unclear pronoun references. Make sure that all pronouns refer to only a single antecedent and are placed close to their antecedent. Example:

When you meet the officials at the Olympic games, you will be impressed by them.

You will be impressed by the officials at the Olympic games.

1. My grandparents grew up in different parts of Italy. My grandmother came from Parma, a city in northern Italy, near the French border. My grandfather was born and raised in Palermo, in Sicily. They could not have been more different.

2. The British shaped many aspects of the culture of the Indian subcontinent, including education and governmental institutions. They had little effect on their religion, however.

3. There is a difference between the athletes of today and those of a generation ago. Most of them are bigger, stronger, and faster.

4. Halley's comet, which is due to appear again in 2061, is named after Edmund Halley, the astronomer who first plotted its orbit. Although extensive records document the existence of other comets, his is the most famous.

5. A few years after American Express bought the Shearson investment company, it was sold.

20c   Clarifying confusing references with particular pronouns

A few pronouns may cause special problems: *this, that, which, it; it, you, they;* and *who, which, that.* When you edit your work, always check to make sure you have used these words clearly.

1   Using *this, that, which,* and *it*

Sometimes writers use *this, that, which,* or *it* to refer to an idea or circumstance described in a previous clause, sentence, or paragraph. But using the words *this, that, which,* and *it* in writing to refer to ideas or circumstances can more often than not be vague and confuse readers. Restrict such broad use of these words to informal conversation: *At least I was on time, which is more than I can say for you.*

CONFUSING	Light can be explained as either a series of particles or a series of waves. The particle theory envisions light as composed of discrete, individual bits of light. The wave theory describes light as larger units, whose behavior differs from that of particles. *This* was not understood before the early twentieth century. [What was not understood? The particle theory? The wave theory? Both points?]
REVISED	Light can be explained as either a series of particles or a series of waves. The particle theory envisions light as composed of discrete, individual bits of light. The wave theory describes light as larger units, whose behavior differs from that of particles. *The differences between these theories were not well* understood before the early twentieth century.
CONFUSING	Contrary to the beliefs of his contemporaries, Galileo theorized that the earth revolved around the sun. *That* earned him a severe reprimand from the Catholic Church. [There is no explicit antecedent for *that.*]

REVISED   Contrary to the beliefs of his contemporaries, Galileo
theorized that the earth revolved around the sun. *Galileo's
refusal to alter this belief* earned him a severe reprimand from
the Catholic Church.

WRITING HINT   One way to avoid vague usage of *this* is to develop the
habit of following *this* with a noun. Ask yourself the question: This *what?*
Your answer—this *theory,* this *refusal,* this *change,* this *analysis,* and so on—
will help you choose an appropriate noun. (Of course, you could also use
plural forms where appropriate: these *theories,* these *changes,* these *analyses.*)

2   Avoiding indefinite use of *it, they,* and *you*

In everyday conversation, people use *it, they,* and *you* indefinitely.

It said in the news that the refugee situation is worsening.

They say that New York City is a great place for the wealthy to live.

You know who your real friends are when adversity strikes.

These uses, however, are too informal for academic writing. To avoid ambiguity in your writing, use *you* to refer only to "you, the reader," and use *it*
and *they* to refer only to clear antecedents.

INFORMAL   In the introduction, *it* explains the author's thesis.

FORMAL   The introduction explains the author's thesis.

INFORMAL   Automobile advertisements often try to make *you* associate
cars with power.

FORMAL   Automobile advertisements often suggestively associate cars
with power.

EXERCISE 20–2   **Avoiding Broad and Indefinite Pronoun Reference**
Revise the following paragraph to eliminate broad use of *this, that, which,* and *it,*
and to clarify indefinite pronoun references of *it, they,* and *you.*

In Jane Austen's *Emma,* the title character is an intelligent young woman
who thinks she knows more about men than she actually does. This gets her
into trouble because she makes mistakes and misjudgments about a number

of different men. One of them is critical, which almost leads her to turn bitterly against a very good and kindhearted man. That is what the novel emphasizes, and this is what later helps her to see it, which you understand before she does.

3   Using *who, which,* and *that* with appropriate antecedents

Always be sure to use the relative pronouns *who, which,* and *that* appropriately. Use *who* to refer to people or animals with names.

Bill Moyers, *who* was once Lyndon B. Johnson's press secretary, is now a regular political commentator for PBS.

You would enjoy our cat, Dolce, *who* entertains us regularly.

Use *which* or *that* to refer to things, ideas, unnamed animals, and anonymous or collective references to people.

The Appalachians, *which* are among the most accessible of mountains, are also among the most beautiful.

The novel *that* received the National Book Award was relatively unknown.

This world is a comedy to those *that* think, a tragedy to those *that* feel.

—Horace Walpole

4   Avoiding pronouns with adjectives and possessives as antecedents

Pronouns cannot refer to adjectives and possessives as antecedents. Since a pronoun can only stand in for a noun, only nouns can function as the antecedents of pronouns.

CONFUSING   Throughout Walt Whitman's work, *he* celebrates the American land and its people. [There is no noun antecedent to which *he* can refer.]

REVISED   *Throughout his work, Walt Whitman* celebrates the American land and its people.

REVISED   *Walt Whitman's work* consistently celebrates the American land and its people.

The accompanying chart suggests ways to check your use of pronouns for accuracy.

Checking Pronoun Reference

- Does each pronoun clearly refer to only one antecedent? Are the antecedents nouns, not adjectives or possessives?
- Do intervening nouns make the references unclear? Do you need to repeat a noun or use a synonym?
- Are the antecedents of *this, that, which,* and *it* clear and precise? Do you follow every *this* with a noun?
- Do the pronouns *it, they,* and *you* have definite antecedents? If *you* is used, does it clearly refer to the reader?
- Are the antecedents for *who, which,* and *that* appropriate?

EXERCISE 20–3 **Establishing Clear and Appropriate Pronoun Reference**

Revise the following sentences to correct unclear or inappropriate pronoun references. (Some sentences may be correct as written.) Example:

In the Swiss Alps they use carefully trained St. Bernards for rescue missions.

Ski patrols in the Swiss Alps use carefully trained St. Bernards for rescue missions.

1. Recent research suggests that the damaging effects of multiple sclerosis can be dramatically reduced.

2. In the U.S. senatorial races of 1992, six women were elected, which is three times as many female senators as served before the election.

3. University policy disallows reimbursements of even partial tuition after the start of the term, which angers many students and their parents.

4. After Matthew and Andrea discussed the value of a college degree with their teachers, they saw the educational system differently.

5. Not enough jurors are skeptical of expert witnesses, the testimony of which is sometimes not reliable.

EXERCISE 20–4 **Revising for Clear Pronoun Reference**

Revise the following paragraph to eliminate vague and unclear pronoun references.

In the seventeenth century they used punctuation far more casually than we do today. The abundance of punctuation marks and their sometimes strange placement have been blamed on the printers, who were often illiterate and served by apprentices, which knew even less about it. Scholars have surmised that they tossed in punctuation simply to fill in spaces in the lines of print they set. But could they have randomly placed it in a text and have it still appear readable? They may have left them out now and then because of laziness, but you should not blame them for the lack of consistency in Elizabethan punctuation.

21 *Mixed and Incomplete Sentences*

To keep your meaning clear, avoid writing mixed and incomplete sentences by ensuring that the parts of your sentences fit together logically and grammatically, and that they include complete, rather than partial, grammatical structures.

Causes of Mixed and Incomplete Sentences

- Incompatible grammatical patterns (21a)
- Faulty predication (21b)
- Confusing elliptical constructions (21c)
- Missing words (21d)
- Incomplete comparisons (21e)

Mixed Sentences

A **mixed sentence** results when incompatible grammatical structures are combined or when an illogical relationship between subject and predicate creates confusion in meaning.

21a Revising mixed sentences with incompatible grammatical patterns

A mixed sentence will often begin with one grammatical pattern and switch to another, incompatible one. Consider this example.

MIXED   After hearing so many conflicting views was the reason we became confused.

Often no single type of revision of a mixed sentence is better than any other. Thus, you should revise mixed sentences in ways that fit the context of your writing. Create a clear subject predicate relationship when revising mixed sentences. The following revisions share a clear and logical relationship between subject and predicate.

REVISED   After hearing so many conflicting views, we became confused. [Eliminating *was the reason* establishes an independent clause, now modified logically by the introductory phrase.]

REVISED   Hearing so many conflicting views confused us. [Eliminating the preposition *after* allows the gerund phrase *hearing so many conflicting views* to function as subject.]

REVISED   The many conflicting views confused us.

WRITING HINT   Mixed sentences sometimes result from the careless use of an introductory phrase or clause. Remember that adverb clauses and prepositional phrases are modifiers; they cannot function as the subject of a sentence.

MIXED   In walking briskly for twenty minutes is an effective aerobic exercise. [*Walking* is the object of *in*, not the subject of *is*.]

REVISED   In walking briskly for twenty minutes, you perform an effective aerobic exercise.

MIXED	Because of his courage and honesty made Arthur Ashe an important spokesperson for AIDS awareness. [The dependent clause *Because of his courage and honesty* cannot function as the subject of *made*.]
REVISED	His courage and honesty made Arthur Ashe an important spokesperson for AIDS awareness.

21b Revising mixed sentences with faulty predication

When the subject and predicate do not make sense together, the result is an illogical relationship known as **faulty predication.** Faulty predication often occurs with the verb *be.*

FAULTY	The *purpose* of the presidential debates *was intended* to give the public a better understanding of the issues. [The subject, *purpose*, is illogically linked with the predicate, *was intended.* Since *purpose* suggests an intention, the predicate, *was intended*, is redundant.]
REVISED	The purpose of the presidential debates *was* to give the public a better understanding of the issues.

1 *When* and *where* used with *be*

One common type of faulty predication results from using the adverbs *when* or *where* after the verb *be.* Avoid using *is when* or *is where* to define or explain a term or an idea.

FAULTY	A debate *is when* opposing viewpoints are presented. [*When* indicates a time; it cannot be used to define or modify *debate.*]
REVISED	In a debate, opposing viewpoints are presented.
REVISED	A debate involves the presentation of opposing viewpoints.

2 *The reason . . . is because*

Faulty predication also results from using the construction *the reason . . . is because.* Use either *reason* or *because* in providing explanations, but not both words together. Using *reason* and *because* together is redundant.

FAULTY   *The reason* Tim whistles during exams *is because* he is nervous.

REVISED   *The reason Tim whistles during exams is that he is nervous.*

REVISED   Tim whistles during exams *because* he is nervous.

USAGE NOTE   Although you often hear or use *is when, is where,* and *the reason is because* in everyday conversation, this phrasing is not acceptable in standard written English. And *be* is not the only verb that can lead to clumsy and inconsistent predication. You should check all of your sentences for faulty predication.

FAULTY   The history of preventive dentistry reduced the dental treatment costs. [*Preventive dentistry,* not its history, reduced treatment costs.]

REVISED   *Preventive dentistry reduced* the cost of dental treatment.

EXERCISE 21–1 **Revising Mixed Sentences**

Revise the following sentences to eliminate mixed grammatical constructions and faulty predication. (More than one revision is possible.) Example:

A sentence fragment is leaving out a subject or a verb.

A sentence fragment is a group of words that lacks a subject or a verb.

1. When the Berlin Wall was torn down was a turning point in the demise of communism in Eastern Europe.

2. Racial discrimination is when a person is treated unfairly based on the color of his or her skin.

3. The reason cattle ranchers are concerned is because of the drought.

4. In Cooperstown, New York, is where they have the Baseball Hall of Fame.

5. Because typhoons destroy so much so fast is why they are dangerous.

EXERCISE 21–2 **Working with Predication**

Complete each of the following sentences in a clear and logical way. Example:

By working two jobs

By working two jobs *she hoped to pay off her student loans.*

1. When children are punished for no reason
2. Maturity is
3. By registering early
4. The use of sun blockers is
5. The reason we left early

Incomplete Sentences

An **incomplete sentence** results from leaving out essential words, phrases, or clauses. Sentence fragments, the most serious kind of incomplete sentence, have no subject or predicate (see Chapter 16). But a sentence can also be incomplete because the writer has omitted a word or a phrase necessary for the sentence to be clear.

21c Revising confusing elliptical constructions

An **elliptical construction** is a compound structure in which words are left out or implied rather than directly stated. Writers and speakers use elliptical constructions to streamline their discourse, to avoid repetition, and to emphasize points. In the following example, four words (*of a book should*) have been omitted from the sentence. Their appearance in brackets indicates that they are implied and need not be included for the sentence to make sense.

The beginning of a book should capture the reader's interest and the ending [*of a book should*] leave the reader with something to think about.

When you write with elliptical constructions, be sure that the omitted words match the words that have not been omitted (that is, that they are parallel). For example, if you leave out a phrase in the second part of a compound structure, it should be the same as the phrase that you used in the first part. Similarly, a verb or an auxiliary omitted in the second part of a compound should be parallel to the verb in the first part.

The Russian skaters finished first and the Americans [*finished*] second.

In the accident the driver was killed but the passenger [*was*] only injured.

Notice the confusion that results when the elliptical structure does not maintain a parallel structure.

FAULTY   The first part of the test *requires* quick thinking and fast writing, the other two more sustained analysis and interpretation. [The first subject, *first part*, is singular and takes a singular verb; the second subject, *the other two*, is plural and should take a plural verb.]

REVISED   The first part of the test *requires* quick thinking and fast writing; the last two sections *require* more sustained analysis and interpretation.

REVISED   The first part of the test requires quick thinking and fast writing, the last [*requires*] more sustained analysis and interpretation.

21d Revising sentences to include missing words

It is not uncommon for writers to leave out words by mistake (especially articles, pronouns, and prepositions) in the haste of composition. Proofread your writing carefully to look for these unintended omissions.

In the following example the meaning is obscured by omitting *that*. The incomplete sentence requires revision to clarify the ambiguities.

FAULTY   Max and Al heard many songs from the 1960s had become familiar to the next generation. [The sentence is unclear about whether 1960s songs became familiar to the next generation or whether Max and Al listened to 1960s songs that had become familiar to the next generation.]

REVISED   Max and Al heard *that* many songs from the 1960s had become familiar to the next generation.

Many English idioms involve phrasal verbs whose meaning changes with the addition of different prepositions. The phrasal *give in*, for example, means something different from *give out, give up*, or *give away*. Often, prepositions that function as part of an idiomatic phrase are omitted in elliptical constructions. Be especially careful when using this kind of elliptical construction that the prepositions are identical.

Ellen both believed and participated *in* the seance. [The phrasals in the elliptical construction are *believed in* and *participated in*.]

If the prepositions are not identical, both must appear in the sentence so that each idiomatic phrase maintains its meaning.

FAULTY   The tribe not only believed but also lived *by* these traditions.

REVISED   The tribe not only believed *in* but also lived *by* these traditions.

21e Revising incomplete comparisons

When you use comparisons in your writing, be sure that they are complete, clear, and logically consistent. Comparisons are statements that express a relation between two or more things, as in *Bicycles are a more suitable form of transportation than cars around campus,* or *Her motorcycle is a more expensive model than his.* (See 12e on comparative forms of adjectives and adverbs.)

To be complete, a comparison must express the relation or connection between the items compared with sufficient precision and fullness to ensure clarity.

INCOMPLETE   Peg's dedication was greater. [Greater than whose or what?]

REVISED   Peg's dedication was greater *than ours.*

A clear comparison avoids ambiguity and cannot be understood in more than one way. If a comparison is ambiguous, it must be revised to convey only one meaning.

UNCLEAR   The study session helped Rose more than her roommate. [Did the session help her more than it helped her roommate or more than her roommate helped her?]

CLEAR   The study session helped Rose more than her roommate *did.*

To be logically consistent, a comparison must make sense. The words in one part of the comparison must not contradict those in the other part.

ILLOGICAL   Oliver Stone's films are as timely as Spike Lee. [It is illogical to compare a person's work with a person.]

LOGICAL   Oliver Stone's films are as timely as *Spike Lee's.*

EXERCISE 21–3   **Revising Incomplete Sentences**

Revise the following sentences to eliminate confusing elliptical constructions or unclear, inconsistent, or incomplete comparisons. Some sentences may be correct as written. Example:

The employees feared their boss would reject their request.

The employees *feared that* their boss would reject their request.

1. Bureaucrats are often more concerned with filling out forms than problems.

2. The French drink more wine than people in Italy.

3. Sandy and Drew had a special interest and feeling for Renaissance architecture.

4. Modern scientists have a better understanding of the medical value of leeches than before.

5. Few people stop to consider the word *woman* derives from *man*.

EXERCISE 21–4   **Revising Mixed or Incomplete Sentences**

In the following paragraph fix those sentences that are mixed or incomplete.

Adrienne Rich is not just one of America's best feminist poets or one of America's best woman poets, she is one of America's best poets. Her most [exemplary] poems are read not because they are supposed to be good for us but because they are good, and in some cases (which is all any poet can ask for), they are [very] good. She is a serious writer and [an] important [one] and her prose [book] on the institution of mother-hood is a serious and important book.

—Adapted from Margaret Atwood, "Adrienne Rich: Of Woman Born"

22 *Writing Coordinate and Subordinate Sentences*

Use **coordination** to emphasize that certain ideas and actions are equally important.

WORDS   They walked and *talked.*

PHRASES   The movie's violent scenes occurred *in the beginning* and *at the end.*

CLAUSES   *They considered going to a movie,* but *they went to the mall* instead.

Use **subordination** to distinguish a main idea or action from less important ones.

Although the movie's violent scenes occurred in the beginning and at the end, the violence was neither excessive nor protracted. [When the violence occurs is less important than its intensity and duration.]

After considering going to a movie, they went to the mall instead. [Going to the mall is emphasized over going to the movies.]

22a   Using coordination to relate equal ideas

1   Writing sentences with coordination

When you want to express a relationship between ideas of equal importance, you could write two separate sentences: *The Civil War began in 1861. It ended in 1865.* You could also combine the two sentences into one using a coordinating conjunction—*and, but, or, nor, for, so, yet* (see 13c-1).

The Civil War began in 1861, *and* it ended in 1865.

When using coordinate structures, be sure the coordinating conjunctions you use are logically appropriate.

EQUIVALENCE   They found jobs, *and* they acquired independence.

CONTRAST   There is authority in the classroom, *but* it does not belong to the teacher.

ALTERNATIVES   Economic conditions must improve quickly, *or* political chaos will ensue.

CONSEQUENCE   It was a dreary, rainy day, *so* we remained indoors.

WRITING HINT   When you join two independent clauses with a coordinating conjunction, be sure to use a comma before the conjunction. However, when the independent clauses are short, you may choose to omit the comma.

It was dark *and* it was cold.

You do not need a comma between two coordinate words, phrases, or dependent clauses.

He enjoys apple pie *but* not cherry pie.

They have traveled in Europe *and* in Asia.

You might also write coordinate structures without a conjunction. Coordination is indicated by a semicolon between two independent clauses, especially those parallel in structure (see 23c and 30a).

She liked lasagna and garlic bread; he preferred lighter fare.

When you use a semicolon to join coordinate clauses, you will sometimes want to use a conjunctive adverb, such as *however, therefore,* or *moreover,* along with appropriate punctuation (see 30b).

Thoreau grew the food he ate at Walden Pond; *however,* on Sundays he went to a friend's house for dinner.

You can also create coordinate structures by using the correlative conjunctions *either . . . or, neither . . . nor, both . . . and,* and *not only . . . but also* in the sentence (see 13c-2).

You will need to sell *either* your car *or* your motorcycle.

Human behavior can be *neither* predicted *nor* controlled.

USAGE NOTE   When you use *not only . . . but also,* be certain that the correlative conjunction coordinates grammatically related elements within the sentence.

Not only Bosnia-Herzegovina *but also* Kosovo was rocked by ethnic strife.

The school administrators *not only* underestimated the drop in enrollment, *but also* failed to plan for the expected drop in funding.

Both . . . and is not used to coordinate independent clauses; it is used only to connect elements within a sentence.

Both coffee *and* tea contain a lot of caffeine.

WRITING HINT   Coordination is especially useful in revising your writing. If you find that a draft sounds choppy and disconnected, using coordinate conjunctions and conjunctive adverbs to link related ideas can clarify your writing and enhance its fluency. Consider how coordination improves the following passage.

WITHOUT COORDINATION

I know very little about laboratory science. I have the impression that conclusions are supposed to be logical. From a given set of circumstances a predictable result should follow.

WITH COORDINATION

I know very little about laboratory science, *but* I have the impression that conclusions are supposed to be logical; *that is,* from a given set of circumstances a predictable result should follow.

—Barbara Tuchman, "Is History a Guide to the Future?"

Tuchman's coordinate structures are clearer and more readable than the uncoordinated sentences of the first version. Tuchman's paragraph is also less choppy, and the relationships among its equal ideas are clearer.

2   Avoiding excessive or illogical coordination

Coordination can be overused. In the following example, excessive coordination results in monotonous and stilted writing.

EXCESSIVE COORDINATION

Eating fast food is now a common experience for many people, *and* this is the case in many countries around the world. The food is not especially good, *but* it isn't too bad either, *and* you get used to it. The food is not especially tasty *nor* is it healthy. Some people defend the taste, however.

REVISED

Eating fast food is now a common experience for many people *not only* in the United States *but also* in other countries. Though *neither* particularly tasty *nor* especially healthy, the fast food served at such places has its defenders.

The revised version more accurately expresses the relationship among its ideas. The revision also offers relief from the monotony of the first version's repeated coordinate structures.

Illogical coordination occurs when the ideas in two connected clauses are unrelated or when the coordinating word expresses an inaccurate relationship between the ideas.

Checking Coordination in Your Writing

- Locate coordinate conjunctions: *and, but, or, nor, for, so,* and *yet.* Check to see that the conjunction linking independent clauses is appropriate and logical.
- Check for excessive coordination. Consider revising to subordinate some of your coordinate structures (see 22b). Or consider replacing some coordinate conjunctions with conjunctive adverbs. You may want to rewrite the independent clauses as complete sentences.
- Check for independent clauses joined only by a semicolon. Consider whether the ideas on both sides of the semicolon are equally important.

ILLOGICAL   Mozart was a brilliant composer, *and* he was a crass man. [The two ideas may be true, but they are not logically connected or equally important and therefore should not coordinate.]

REVISED   Mozart, though a crass man, was a brilliant composer.

The chart on page 400 offers advice for analyzing the coordinate structures in your writing.

EXERCISE 22–1   Combining Sentences to Coordinate Related Ideas

Combine the following short sentences into longer ones that better coordinate related ideas. Supply a logically appropriate coordinating conjunction, correlative conjunction, or conjunctive adverb. Or simply link the clauses with a semicolon. Write two versions for each combination. Example:

Why Houdini made his escapes can be explained. How he made some of them remains a mystery.

Why Houdini made his escapes can be explained, *but* how he made some of them remains a mystery.

1. Humans have highly developed senses of touch and taste. They cannot rival dogs for hearing and smell.

2. It was the best of vacations. It was the worst of vacations.

3. It was not what the ravens did that intrigued the researcher. It was the way they did it that amazed him.

EXERCISE 22–2   Revising to Eliminate Excessive or Illogical Coordination

Revise the following sentences to eliminate excessive or illogical coordination. Example:

He was losing his hair and his eyesight remained good.

He was losing his hair, *but* his eyesight remained good.

1. The snow was only an inch deep, and it was melting quickly, and there was a lot more snow in the forecast, but it could create rush-hour traffic problems.

2. They never did get to go on a honeymoon. And they decided to take a special trip on their fifth anniversary.

3. The pond was filled with fish, and they were jumping to the surface at the food thrown to them by the campers, and then the children ran out of food, but the fish continued to jump, and then finally they stopped, and the surface of the pond was calm.

22b   Using subordination to distinguish main ideas

1   Writing sentences with subordination

Subordination is a writing technique that distinguishes the main idea in a sentence from qualifying or expanding ideas.

Mr. Kaspar was a gifted master carpenter who loved to grow vegetables, especially squash, peppers, and tomatoes.

This sentence emphasizes Mr. Kaspar's carpentry ability while relegating the less important information about his gardening hobby to a dependent clause. To emphasize Mr. Kaspar's gardening talents, the sentence could be rewritten to subordinate his ability as a carpenter.

Mr. Kaspar, *who was a gifted master carpenter,* loved to grow vegetables, especially squash, peppers, and tomatoes.

Although he was a gifted master carpenter, Mr. Kaspar loved to grow vegetables, especially squash, peppers, and tomatoes.

The technique of subordination offers you options in your writing. You choose how to use it to add detail. You decide what to emphasize in your sentences.

> WRITING HINT   Usually, the independent clause in a sentence receives the greatest emphasis. But in short sentences and in those in which the dependent and independent clauses are similar in length, either clause may appear more emphatic.
>
> No one will race unless there is another entry.

Subordination has other uses as well. Use subordination to combine short sentences that have implied relationships. It signals logical relationships among facts and details, typically with the subordinating conjunctions *unless, if, after,* and *because* (see 13c-3).

When the first simple flower bloomed on some raw upland late in the Dinosaur Age, it was wind pollinated, just like its early pine-cone relatives. It was a very inconspicuous flower *because* it had not yet evolved the idea of using the surer attraction of birds and insects to achieve the transportation of pollen.

—Loren Eiseley, "How Flowers Changed the World"

WRITING HINT   Subordination is a good technique to use when developing details of cause, condition, time, location, choice, and purpose.

- To show **cause** or to explain why, use *because* or *since.*

  Because snow was forecast, they decided not to hike up the mountain that day.

- To indicate a **condition,** use *even if, provided, since,* or *unless.*

  Unless the Democrats and the Republicans can learn to live together peacefully, they are in for a stormy future.

- To establish **time,** use *as soon as, after, before, since, when, whenever, while,* or *until.*

  LeeAnn did not choose a graduate program *until* she received several acceptances.

- To indicate **location,** use *where* or *wherever.*

  The candidate attracts a crowd *wherever* he goes.

- To indicate **choice,** use *rather than* or *whether.*

  Whether I go on the foreign exchange trip or not, I will have enjoyed dreaming about it.

- To show **purpose,** use *that, in order that,* or *so that.*

  His friends helped him finish the yard work *so that* he could join them for a card game.

EXERCISE 22–3   **Combining Sentences to Subordinate Related Ideas**

Combine each of the following sets of short sentences into a longer sentence. Use subordinate structures to signal the relationship among details or ideas. Example:

We opened the front door. A bird flew from the nest. It had built a nest in a plant that hung from our porch roof.

When we opened the front door, a bird flew from the nest it had built in a plant that hung from our porch roof.

1. I was reaching over the counter for a chocolate layer cake. I noticed a banana chocolate cream pie. I decided to buy both.

2. *In Country* is a novel by Bobbie Ann Mason. It is about a young American girl coming to terms with the Vietnam War. It is a moving book.

3. The tennis team had performed well all season. The team members were invited to a postseason tournament. They performed well in the tournament. They made it to the semifinals.

2   Avoiding excessive subordination

In an effort to avoid excessive coordination or to keep from writing too many short, choppy sentences, writers sometimes use too many dependent clauses. The result is excessive subordination. Revise by writing shorter, clearer, and more emphatic sentences.

EXCESSIVE SUBORDINATION

Because the owners of Ben and Jerry's, which is located in Vermont, were concerned that small dairy farms that were family run were going out of business, they made a commitment to buying only dairy products from Vermont rather than dairy products from large western dairy farms even though buying products from the family-run farms was more expensive.

REVISED

The owners of Ben and Jerry's, which is located in Vermont, were concerned that small, family-run dairy farms were going out of business. They therefore made a commitment to buying only local dairy products rather than less expensive dairy products from large western dairy farms. [Note that the revision is two sentences long and that several subordinating phrases have been changed to one- or two-word adjectives.]

3   Avoiding illogical subordination

Illogical subordination occurs when the most important idea or information is placed in a dependent clause, or when the subordinating conjunction inaccurately identifies the relationship between the clauses.

ILLOGICAL   Isadora Duncan died in 1927, *even though* she greatly influenced modern dance.

The idea in the subordinating clause is more important than that in the independent clause.

REVISED   *Even though* she died in 1927, Isadora Duncan greatly influenced modern dance.

The accompanying chart provides guidance for using subordinate structures.

Checking Subordination in Your Writing

- Underline the subordinate structures in each of your sentences.
- Check to see that the most important idea appears in the main or independent clause and that related details appear in the subordinate structures.
- For clauses introduced by subordinating conjunctions, consider alternative placement in the sentence—with corresponding shifts of emphasis.
- Check for sentences that include strings of subordinate clauses. Consider whether the main idea of the sentence is sufficiently clear and emphatic.
- Check for logical relationships between clauses by examining the meaning of the subordinating conjunctions you use.

EXERCISE 22–4   **Eliminating Illogical and Excessive Subordination**

Revise the following sentences to eliminate illogical or excessive subordination. Example:

The president's budget would not be passed although a compromise could be reached.

The president's budget would not be passed *unless* a compromise could be reached.

1. Beethoven lost his hearing even though he continued to compose music.
2. Old homes are common in New England even though they are often painted white.
3. When the results are finally tabulated, each side is convinced that its candidate will be victorious, though there are some skeptics on each side who believe no such thing, for they expect defeat not victory, but they are prepared for that disappointment.

EXERCISE 22–5   Revising with Coordination and Subordination
The following passage consists of simple sentences. Use coordination and subordination to emphasize main ideas and express logical relationships.

> Photographs furnish evidence. An event seems proven when a photograph of it exists. A photograph passes for proof that a particular event occurred. The picture may distort the reality. It may approximate what occurred. It may capture only a small part of it. It does capture something like what actually happened, what was. A photograph is selective. What it selects is a slice of the actual. Photographs certify experience.

23   *Using Parallelism in Sentences*

Parallelism in writing involves using a similar grammatical form for two or more coordinate elements. Parallel structure expresses a close connection or contrast between sentence elements, whether they are words, phrases, or clauses. Parallelism tightens writing by making it balanced and rhythmical. The parallel structure in the following sentence has been aligned for visual clarity.

> On coming to a new place, my father would *take a pinch of dirt,*
> *sprinkle it in his palm,*
> *sniff it,*
> *stir it with a blunt finger,*
> then *rake it on his tongue,* tasting.
>
> —Scott Russell Sanders

The accompanying chart identifies how parallelism can help you improve your writing.

Uses of Parallelism

- To coordinate elements in a series (23a)
- To pair ideas (23b)
- To enhance coherence (23c)

23a Using parallelism to coordinate elements in a series

All items listed in a series—whether single words, phrases, or clauses—need to be written in parallel grammatical structures.

NOUNS   Among the necessities of life are *food, clothing,* and *shelter.*

VERBS   The boat *yawed, jibed,* and *veered* perilously close to the rocks.

PHRASES   Aaron and Elaine could not decide whether to spend their vacation *at the shore* or *in the mountains.*

CLAUSES   Tell me *where you went, what you saw,* and *why you returned* early.

Presenting parallel elements in nonparallel grammatical form upsets the reader's expectations, frequently creating awkwardness and confusion.

NONPARALLEL   The vacation package included *food, lodging, recreation,* and *having entrance fees paid for.* [The first three items included in the series are nouns, the last is a participial phrase.]

REVISED   The vacation package included *food, lodging, recreation,* and *entrance fees.* [All four items are nouns.]

23b Using parallelism with pairs

One of the more common uses of parallelism in writing is to pair two ideas. When you want to compare or contrast ideas, use a coordinate conjunction, a correlative conjunction, or the subordinate conjunction *as* or *than,* to connect the ideas, and state the ideas in parallel grammatical form.

A sentence that includes two clauses in a grammatically parallel structure is called a **balanced sentence.** In a balanced sentence, the two clauses are closely paired so that the meaning of each clause is reflected off the other.

Buddies seek approval but friends seek acceptance.

—Ellen Goodman

There is a time for joy; there is a time for sorrow.

Balanced sentences create a memorable pairing and can be both emphatic and humorous, as the following example illustrates.

This man, I thought had been a Lord among wits; but, I find, he is only a wit among Lords!

—Samuel Johnson

1 Parallelism with coordinate conjunctions

Use similar grammatical structures when connecting sentence elements with a coordinating conjunction—*and, but, or, nor, for, so, yet.*

Life is ten percent what you make it and ninety percent how you take it.

—Irving Berlin

When sentence elements joined by a coordinating conjunction are not parallel, the relationship between them may not be evident.

NONPARALLEL   The film was *terrifying* and *with a lot of suspense.*

REVISED   The film was *terrifying* and *suspenseful.*

2 Parallelism with correlative conjunctions

Use parallel forms with correlative conjunctions, such as *either . . . or, neither . . . nor, both . . . and,* and *not only . . . but also.* The grammatical structure following the first part of the correlative conjunction should be identical to that following the second part (see 13c-2).

Deborah Tannen's book not only *states* that men and women have different ways of communicating, but also *explains* these differences.

NONPARALLEL   He writes neither *checks* nor *uses a credit card.* [A noun follows *neither,* but a verb phrase follows *nor.*]

REVISED   He neither *writes checks* nor *uses a credit card.*

3 **Parallelism with the subordinate conjunctions *than* and *as***

In using *than* and *as* when connecting ideas, be sure to use a similar grammatical structure in both parts of your comparison or contrast.

As my opponent's score rose, my spirits declined.

It is not greedy to enjoy a good dinner, any more than it is greedy to enjoy a good concert.

—G. K. Chesterton

NONPARALLEL   Many recent college graduates have chosen *to become doctors* rather than *studying law or business.*

REVISED   Many recent college graduates have chosen to become *doctors* rather than *lawyers or business executives.*

USAGE NOTE   In short sentences, you can sometimes omit prepositions, articles, and subordinating conjunctions that are repeated in a parallel series. But sometimes including these elements may make the parallelism clearer and more effective.

Olga told me that I had insulted Kit, [*that*] he was angry, and [*that*] he expected an apology.

(See 25a-2 for more on deliberate repetition.)

EXERCISE 23–1   **Identifying Parallelism**
Underline the parallel elements in the following sentences. Example:

He neither <u>confirmed</u> nor <u>denied</u> the allegation.

1. "It was the arrival of this fly that convinced me beyond any doubt that everything was as it always had been, that the years were a mirage, and that there had been no years."   —*E. B. White*

2. "Some books are to be tasted, others to be swallowed, and some few to be chewed and digested."   —*Francis Bacon*

3. "This freedom, like all freedoms, has its dangers and its responsibilities."   —*James Baldwin*

4. "In some ways writing is the act of saying *I*, of imposing oneself upon other people, of saying listen to me, see it my way, change your mind."
   —*Joan Didion*

5. "Persons attempting to find a motive in this narrative will be prosecuted; persons attempting to find a moral in it will be banished; persons attempting to find a plot in it will be shot." —*Mark Twain*

EXERCISE 23–2 **Imitating Parallelism**

Select any three sentences from Exercise 23–1 and write new sentences that imitate the parallel structures. Example:

> This freedom, like all freedoms, has its dangers and its responsibilities.
> —James Baldwin

> This political idea, like all political ideas, has its advocates and its critics.

23c Using parallelism to enhance coherence

Parallelism emphasizes the connections among related elements in sentences and paragraphs. This emphasis on connections results in coherence because readers can readily see how sentence elements are related.

Parallelism within sentences is illustrated in the following example. As you read the paragraph, identify mentally how the parallel elements structure and clarify the writers' point.

> Like cultural literacy, scientific literacy does not refer to detailed, specialized knowledge—the sort of things an expert would know. When you come across a term like "superconductor" in a newspaper article, it is enough to know that it refers to a material that conducts electricity without loss, that the main impediment to the widespread use of superconductors is that they operate only at very low temperatures, and that finding ways to remove this impediment is a major research goal in materials science today.
> —Robert M. Hazen and James Trefil, *Science Matters*

Parallelism among sentences is useful to enhance the connections among related ideas within a paragraph. Consider how parallel structure connects related ideas in the following example.

The Middle Ages of Europe were a continuation and a formation. They were a continuation of old Rome in race, language, institutions, law, literature, and the arts. They were also a continuation of cultures independent of Rome.

Grammar and Writing

Using Parallelism

Parallel grammatical structures make your writing easier to follow. They help you achieve clarity and emphasis.

- Use parallel structures for items in a series, for comparisons and contrasts.
- Employ parallelism in your longer and more complex sentences.
- Use similar grammatical structures in different sentences.

EXAMPLE

Read not to contradict and confute;
    nor to believe   and take for granted;
    nor to find talk and discourse;
    but to weigh   and consider.
              —Francis Bacon

The accompanying chart will help you check for parallelism in your writing.

Checking for Parallelism

- Check places where you list items in a series. Be sure you use a parallel grammatical structure for all items.
- Check places where you use coordinate and correlative conjunctions. Consider whether your grammatical structures are similar before and after each conjunction.
- Check places where you use *than* and *as*. Look to see that you have used similar grammatical structures for both parts of any comparisons or contrasts.

> WRITING HINT   You can use parallelism to emphasize an idea or to build a sentence or paragraph toward a climax. Consider the following example.
>
> I lived it over and over again, the way one relives an automobile accident after it has happened and one finds oneself alone and safe. I could not get over two facts, both equally difficult for the imagination to grasp, and one was that I could have been murdered. But the other was that I had been ready to commit murder. I saw nothing very clearly but I did see this: that my life, my *real* life, was in danger, and not from anything other people might do but from the hatred I carried in my own heart.
>
> —James Baldwin, "Notes of a Native Son"

EXERCISE 23–3   Revising for Parallelism

Revise the following paragraph to express coordinate ideas in parallel form.

Many word processors will work together with other programs that check your spelling and they find typographical errors. These programs read through your essay and pointing out every word they do not recognize. Each program has a dictionary, or word list, and when a word in your essay is flagged, that means it is not in the program's dictionary. You have a choice of moving on or you can correct the error. Some programs will even suggest a spelling: if you wrote *spagetti,* the program will display the word *spaghetti,* ask if that is what you mean, and you can substitute the correct form.

24 *Achieving Sentence Variety*

Sentence variety involves using different kinds of sentence structures throughout a piece of writing for stylistic effect. A lack of variety in writing by beginning too many sentences the same way or using sentences of a similar type or length makes for monotonous writing and tedious reading. Varying your sentences in the ways outlined in the accompanying chart can make your writing more interesting.

Ways to Achieve Sentence Variety

- Mix long, short, and medium-length sentences (24a).
- Begin sentences in different ways: with transitions, with phrases and clauses, with subjects (24b).
- Vary sentence types by including occasional questions, commands, and exclamations (24c).
- Vary sentence structure by blending simple, compound, and complex sentences. Use both periodic and cumulative sentences (24c).

24a   Varying sentence length

Varying sentence length makes for better writing, partly because sentences of different lengths do different jobs. Short sentences emphasize ideas. Long sentences tend to elaborate, to explain, or to define ideas. Sentence variety also contributes to the movement or flow of prose, partly through the emphasis created with short sentences, partly through the rhythms created in longer, more complex ones.

Too many short sentences in succession can create a jarring uniformity and a choppy rhythm. A series of short sentences also fails to highlight the relative level of importance among major and minor points.

UNVARIED SHORT SENTENCES

Once Thoreau had to spend a night in jail. He did not pay his poll tax. He wanted to protest against a U.S. government policy. The government had a policy toward Mexico that Thoreau disapproved of. His friend Emerson came to the jail. He bailed Thoreau out. Before he did he asked Thoreau why he was behind bars. Thoreau responded by asking Emerson why he was not.

REVISED FOR VARIETY

Thoreau once had to spend a night in jail for refusing to pay his poll tax. Thoreau objected to the tax on the grounds that it supported U.S. policy toward Mexico, a policy Thoreau strongly disapproved of. When his friend Emerson came to bail him out of jail and asked Thoreau why he was in jail, Thoreau responded by asking Emerson why he was not.

Computer Tip

Using a Style Checker

Style checkers tend to be more useful than grammar checkers. A style checker can point out features of your writing that you may not have noticed. You might use many long or short sentences, for example, or rely heavily on clichés, passive voice verbs, repeated words or phrases, or the verb *be*. A style checker can highlight such patterns of language use, and you can decide what to do about them.

Long sentences are necessary to explain complex relationships among ideas, but too many long sentences make it difficult to find the important points embedded within strings of clauses.

UNVARIED LONG SENTENCES

In the notebooks in which I recorded my months of Soviet research, I listed several dozen basic categories of human experience with which to organize my themes: friendship, family, childhood, heroism, education, sex, marriage, religion. I realized upon finishing my list that one fundamental category, love, was missing from it, and this was not an oversight, [for] throughout my time in the Soviet Union, I barely, if ever, heard one mention of the word *lyubov*—"love" in its romantic sense. It confirmed my suspicion that love in the Soviet Union is a luxury, an accessory, but hardly the prerequisite for marriage or happiness that it is in Western Europe or the United States.

DU PLESSIX GRAY'S VERSION

In the notebooks in which I recorded my months of Soviet research, I listed several dozen basic categories of human experience with which to organize my themes: friendship, family, childhood, heroism, education, sex, marriage, religion. I realized upon finishing my list that one fundamental category was missing from it: love.

It was not an oversight. Throughout my time in the Soviet Union, I barely, if ever, heard one mention of the word *lyubov*—"love" in its romantic sense. It confirmed my suspicion that love in the Soviet Union is a luxury, an accessory, but hardly the prerequisite for marriage or happiness that it is in Western Europe or the United States.

—Francine du Plessix Gray, *Soviet Women*

Alternating between short and long sentences will enable you to use the short sentences to emphasize important points, while retaining longer ones to express more complex relations among ideas. Notice how the following paragraph mixes sentences of varying lengths.

I still shy away from nightclubs, from bars, from parties where the solvent is alcohol. My friends puzzle over this, but it is no more peculiar than for a man to shy away from the lions' den after seeing his father torn apart. I took my own first drink at the age of twenty-one, half a glass of burgundy. I knew the odds of my becoming an alcoholic were four times higher than for the children of nonalcoholic fathers. So I sipped warily.

—Scott Russell Sanders, "Under the Influence"

Placing a short sentence at the end of a paragraph is one way to achieve sentence variety and emphasis. But you can also achieve emphasis by placing a short sentence first. Sanders uses this technique at the beginning of "Under the Influence."

My father drank. He drank as a gut-punched boxer gasps for breath, as a starving dog gobbles food—compulsively, secretly, in pain and trembling.

A short sentence can also be effective in the middle of a paragraph, especially as a transition between main ideas. The following paragraph from "Under the Influence" illustrates this effect.

The secret bores under the skin, gets in the blood, into the bone, and stays there. Long after you have supposedly been cured of malaria, the fever can flare up, the tremors can shake you. So it is with the fevers of shame. You swallow the bitter quinine of knowledge, and you learn to feel pity and compassion toward the drinker. Yet the shame lingers and, because of it, anger.

Use the checklist on p. 416 to help you avoid the tedium of too many sentences of similar length.

Checking for Varied Sentence Length

- Count the words in each sentence.
- If many sentences are the same length (within five words), rewrite some to vary their lengths.
- Look at strings of short sentences to see if they should be combined to express more clearly the relationship between their ideas.
- Look at your longest sentences to see if any contain more than a single idea. Consider splitting such sentences to better emphasize their different ideas.

EXERCISE 24–1   **Varying Sentence Length**

Revise the following passage to vary sentence length.

Alice Walker's "Everyday Use" is about two sisters who are raised together in the South. Their mother is a poor, uneducated black woman who has worked hard to support her daughters. Each daughter has developed a different idea of what her future will be. Dee is the older and is determined to break away from her life of poverty and traditionalism. Her sister, Maggie, chooses to remain with their mother and follow a more traditional lifestyle.

EXERCISE 24–2   **Revising Your Writing to Vary Sentence Length**

Examine one of the papers you recently wrote for a course. Revise it to achieve better variety in sentence length.

 24b   Varying sentence openings

Varying the types of sentence openings you use is as important as varying the length of your sentences in terms of creating emphasis and interesting rhythms.

UNVARIED SENTENCE OPENING

Spring is a welcome season in regions with varying climates. It is most appreciated after long cold winters when the ice and snow have lingered. The arrival of spring brings hope and joy. Spring is a time for trees to bud and flowers to bloom, for ice and snow to melt away in the warmth of the sun. It is the season of sport and activity.

VARIED SENTENCE OPENING

Spring is a welcome season in regions with varying climates. Most appreciated after long cold winters when ice and snow have lingered, the arrival of spring brings hope and joy. In spring, trees bud and flowers bloom. Ice and snow melt away in the warmth of the sun. In addition, spring is the season of sport and activity.

1 Using transitions to create sentence variety

Transitions, whether words or phrases, explicitly link one sentence or paragraph with another. Words indicating time, such as *now, then,* and *later,* serve as transitional links, or bridges, between sentences describing a series of events.

The students were playing catch, tossing frisbees, or just sitting in the quad, soaking up the April sun. *Later,* they said, they would do their homework.

Phrases such as *on the other hand, in spite of,* and *on the contrary* explicitly indicate a contrast between what has come before and what comes after.

http://leo.stcloudstate.edu/style/sentencesv.html
Provides help with sentence combining for greater fluency and sentence variety. Emphasizes coordination and subordination.

On the one hand, the arrival of April means warmer temperatures and more sunshine. *On the other hand,* it also means tax day and tornado watches.

(For more on transitional words and phrases see 5c-3.)

WRITING HINT Adverbs sometimes make effective sentence openers. Using them occasionally can make your sentence openings more interesting.

Eventually the snow melted and the plants began to emerge.

Rarely did we come close to resolving our differences.

2   Using phrases and clauses to create variety

To avoid beginning all sentences with a simple subject or a transition, begin some sentences with dependent clauses (see 9d).

Although spring is a welcome season in regions with varying climates, it is most appreciated following a long cold winter, one accompanied by abundant ice and snow.

While the lecturer droned on, students in the back row slept soundly.

Beginning some sentences with phrases is another way to achieve sentence variety. Use prepositional phrases (9c-1) and verbal phrases—including participial, infinitive, and absolute phrases (9c-2)—as introductory phrases.

PREPOSITIONAL PHRASES

In spring crowds fill the streets and the parks.

During warm spring afternoons, offices empty as workers find places to sit in the sun and enjoy their lunch.

VERBAL PHRASES

Caught up in the general optimism brought on by the arrival of spring, people tend to be friendlier and happier. [participial phrase]

To take advantage of the warm sun and the cool breeze, we took our papers and moved out to the deck to finish our work. [infinitive phrase]

WRITING HINT   One of the quickest ways to check sentence openings for variety is to circle the first two or three words of each of your sentences. You will see quickly whether you repeatedly begin sentences with the same part of speech. You may find that you begin every sentence with a noun, pronoun, or adjective, or that you repeatedly begin sentences with coordinating conjunctions (13c-1), subordinating conjunctions (13c-3), or conjunctive adverbs (13c-4). Whatever pattern you find, use the techniques described in this chapter as guides for revision.

EXERCISE 24–3   Practicing Ways to Vary Sentence Openings

Combine each of the following pairs of sentences into a single sentence using different kinds of openings. Omit and change words as needed. Experiment with different versions to come up with the most effective opener. Example:

> I finally learned to operate my VCR. It was quite a difficult process.
>
> *With some difficulty,* I finally learned to operate my VCR.

1. I read the instruction manual carefully. I hoped to learn how to program the timer on my VCR.

2. A friend who knows about computers came to my rescue. She did so just before I gave up entirely.

3. Learning to record was still not easy. It was not easy even with help.

4. I can set the machine to record a day in advance. This is a great convenience.

5. I seldom go out to the movies anymore. I have now learned to use my VCR.

EXERCISE 24–4   Writing to Ensure Varied Sentence Openings

Write a paragraph of six to ten sentences in length about the highlights of spring, summer, winter, or fall. Be sure to vary your sentence openings.

24c Varying sentence types

You can use different sentence types to achieve a varied and interesting writing style. You can also vary sentences within paragraphs according to their rhetorical effects. Rhetorical variety can, in fact, be one of the most effective ways to add variety to a sentence. Rhetorically, sentences can be classified as cumulative or periodic.

1 Cumulative sentences

A **cumulative sentence** states the main idea in the independent clause first and includes any modifying phrases later. Cumulative sentences get longer by accumulating details, adding modifying phrases and clauses to follow the main idea. These sentences are useful when you want to identify the main point of a sentence right away.

I have grown fond of semicolons in recent years. The semicolon tells you that there is still some question about the preceding full sentence; something needs to be added; it reminds you sometimes of the Greek usage. It is almost always a greater pleasure to come across a semicolon than a period. The period tells you that that is that; if you didn't get all the meaning you wanted or expected, anyway you got all the writer intended to parcel out and now you have to move along. But with a semicolon there you get a pleasant little feeling of expectancy; there is more to come; read on; it will get clearer.

—Lewis Thomas, "Notes on Punctuation"

2 Periodic sentences

A **periodic sentence** delays the main idea of the sentence to the end of the sentence, in part to build suspense. Notice how the following sentence uses this strategy of the periodic sentence to build to a climactic end.

Where justice is denied, where poverty is enforced, where ignorance prevails and where any one class is made to feel that society is in an organized conspiracy to oppress, rob and degrade them, neither persons nor property will be safe.

—Frederick Douglass

EXERCISE 24–5   Writing Cumulative and Periodic Sentences
Rewrite the following paragraph first with cumulative sentences and then with periodic sentences.

These men work with animals, not machines or numbers. They live outside in landscapes of torrential beauty. They are confined to a place and a routine embellished with awesome variables. They go to the mountains as if on a pilgrimage to find out what makes a herd of elk tick. Their strength is also a softness. Their toughness is a rare delicacy.

EXERCISE 24–6   Revising for Sentence Variety
Revise the following paragraph to vary the lengths, openings, and types of its sentences.

Norma Jean wants to change her life or at least her lifestyle. She has become an avid weight lifter and health nut. She is now taking an English class at the community college. Leroy gets defensive about this, feeling his English may not be up to par for her. Leroy had been working, and he was constantly on the road. He never really knew what his wife was doing. He did know that she was there when he came home, and she had a wonderful meal prepared. Leroy is home all the time now. He sees less and less of Norma Jean. She may be trying to avoid him. She is also trying to improve herself physically and mentally. This seems admirable.

Achieving Emphasis and Conciseness

Two aspects of effective writing reinforce one another: emphasis and conciseness. Emphasis involves stressing key words and ideas; conciseness involves expressing ideas directly and succinctly. Conciseness leads to emphasis; emphasis results from conciseness.

25a   Writing with emphasis

Good writing is emphatic writing. When you write with **emphasis**, your sentences stress your most important words, phrases, and ideas. You can write emphatic sentences by following the advice in the accompanying chart.

Ways to Write with Emphasis

- Use parallel structures (25a-1).
- Use short sentences with longer ones (25a-2).
- Repeat important words, phrases, and clauses (25a-2).
- Place the most important words and ideas last or first in sentences (25a-3).
- Invert, or reverse, normal word order (25a-3).
- Use an occasional short paragraph (25a-4).

---

1   Achieving emphasis with parallel structures

Parallelism is a writing strategy that uses similar grammatical structures to coordinate words, phrases, or clauses both within and between sentences.

PARALLEL WORDS   They were *tired, cold,* and *hungry.*

PARALLEL PHRASES   *With laughter, with tears,* and *with unease,* the mother was reunited with her estranged daughter.

PARALLEL CLAUSES   *Until the day of justice dawns, until the moment our bonds are cut,* we shall not be free.

Use parallel structures emphatically by placing them in order of least to most important, as the following passage illustrates.

It was a feeling of closeness. It was something strange. It was as though there were only we two in the world. It was as though I had been jerked suddenly out of myself, out of my world of the schoolboy, out of a world in which I was ashamed of my father.

—Sherwood Anderson, "Discovery of a Father"

2   Achieving emphasis with short sentences and repetition

Short sentences can be emphatic when they are used in contrast to a series of longer sentences. Short sentences can also carry emphasis related to their placement.

In the following passage, a short sentence follows two longer ones. Note how the final sentence is emphatic because it stands in contrast to the preceding sentences.

Victory would mean peace forced upon the loser, a victor's terms imposed upon the vanquished. It would be accepted in humiliation, under duress, at an intolerable sacrifice, and would leave a sting, a resentment, a bitter memory upon which terms of peace would rest, not permanently, but only as upon quicksand. Only a peace between equals can last.

—Woodrow Wilson

Words repeated within a sentence can have an emphatic effect. Note how Alice Walker uses repetition in the following passage.

> But add to all of these things the one thing that seems to me second to none in importance: He gave us back our heritage. He gave us back our homeland; the bones and dust of our ancestors, who may now sleep within our caring and our hearing. He gave us the blueness of the Georgia sky in autumn as in summer. . . . He gave us continuity of place, without which community is ephemeral. He gave us home.
>
> —Alice Walker, "Choice: A Tribute to Dr. Martin Luther King, Jr."

3 Achieving emphasis by placing important elements in key positions

Placing the most important words of a sentence last achieves an emphatic effect.

To become finalists the gymnasts need strength, grace, and discipline.

Placing *discipline* last in this sentence implicitly suggests that it is the most important quality in the list.

Another way to emphasize an idea is to place it at the beginning of a sentence or paragraph. This arrangement is a bit less emphatic than the end-of-sentence (or paragraph) placement.

EMPHATIC   Discipline and desire are the qualities that make good athletes great.

MORE EMPHATIC   The qualities that make good athletes great are discipline and desire.

EXERCISE 25–1   **Recognizing Techniques of Emphasis**

Identify the techniques of emphasis used in the following passage.

People have been reading the Bible for nearly two thousand years. They have taken it literally, figuratively, or symbolically. They have regarded it as divinely dictated, revealed, or inspired, or as a human creation. They have acquired more copies of it than of any other book. It is quoted (and misquoted) more often than other books. It is called a great work of literature, the first work of history. It is at the heart of Christianity and

Judaism. Ministers, priests, and rabbis preach it. Scholars spend their lives studying and teaching it in universities and seminaries. People read it, study it, admire it, disdain it, write about it, argue about it, and love it. People have lived by it and died by it. And we do not know who wrote it.

—Richard Elliott Friedman, *Who Wrote the Bible?*

EXERCISE 25–2   Writing with Emphasis

Write two sentences for each phrase listed here. In the first sentence, place the phrase in an emphatic position; in the second, put it in a less emphatic position. Example:

every day
Every day we went swimming at the lake. [emphatic]
We went swimming every day at the lake. [less emphatic]

1. in a few days

2. without hesitation

3. as soon as you can

4. carelessly

5. grinning from ear to ear

Inverting a sentence involves reversing the normal sentence pattern by putting some part of the predicate before the subject. The inverted sentence pattern looks like this.

object (or complement) → verb → subject

STANDARD   A small red fox occasionally appeared in the far corner of the yard.

INVERTED   In the far corner of the yard, there occasionally appeared a small red fox.

The inverted sentence keeps the reader waiting to find out what will happen in that corner of the yard and thereby creates suspense which, in turn, creates emphasis.

4   Achieving emphasis with short paragraphs

Just as using an occasional short sentence within a paragraph can emphasize an idea, so too can a short paragraph. In the following example, a student begins with a paragraph of average length and then sets off a short paragraph for emphasis.

> As the older class lines up in front of the younger, one of the fourth graders catches sight of the first-grade Asian-American girl sitting with her classmates. He begins to pick on her, bowing deeply at the waist with his hands clasped together as if in prayer. He is singsonging, "Ah-so, Ah-so." An expression of sheer pleasure illuminates his face, and a smile spreads across his mouth. He continues his revelry until he gets his food and sits down with his friends.
> And what of the girl? What becomes of her?
> She is digesting what she will later recognize as the first racial slur she has ever experienced. Presently she does not know this.
>
> —Suyin So, "Grotesques"

The short paragraph in this example also uses interrogative sentences to achieve emphasis. Like inverted sentences and short paragraphs, however, interrogative sentences are emphatic only when they are used sparingly and skillfully. The same is true of sentence fragments used intentionally for emphasis.

EXERCISE 25–3   **Writing with Emphasis**
Write a paragraph in which you use at least four of the six techniques for achieving emphasis discussed in 25a. (See the chart on p. 421.) You may choose a topic of your own or one of these: a family member, a friend, a valued possession, an experience, an ambition, a newsworthy event.

25b   Writing with conciseness

Readers expect writers to get to the point directly and succinctly, to write with **conciseness.** Yet concise writing involves much more than banging out one short sentence after another; it involves avoiding unnecessary words and using precise grammatical constructions. Consider the following wordy passage and its more concise revision.

WORDY   In order to reach a fair decision for the issue at hand, it would be necessary for the members of the committee involved with the decision to hear the testimony of a number of different people.

CONCISE   To decide the issue fairly, the committee needs to interview a number of people.

To write concisely, avoid using words and phrases that could be expressed in fewer words. To write sentences concisely, follow the guidelines in the accompanying chart.

Ways to Write More Concisely

- Eliminate unnecessary intensifiers (25b-1).
- Replace wordy phrases (25b-2).
- Avoid negations (25b-3).
- Eliminate redundancy (25b-4).
- Avoid overuse of the verb *be* (25b-5).
- Prefer verbs to nouns (25b-6).
- Prefer the active to the passive voice (25b-7).
- Avoid the overuse of prepositions and prepositional phrases (25b-8).

---

1   Eliminate unnecessary intensifiers

An **intensifier** is a word (typically an adjective or adverb) that emphasizes the word it modifies. Some intensifiers, such as *very* and *really*, are usually unnecessary or could be more precisely worded. For example, to say that an eventuality is *very likely possible* is to say that it is *probable.* To say that you are *very, very tired* is to say that you are *exhausted.* If something makes you *really happy,* it may make you *ecstatic* or *excited* or simply *happy.* Intensifiers in such cases often add nothing but verbiage.

Overused intensifiers defeat their purpose; too many uses of *very* and *really* diminish the power of the words they modify. If your words are too weak to stand alone, perhaps you should choose more precise words instead.

Grammar and Writing

Achieving Emphasis and Conciseness

Techniques of emphasis, like seasonings for food, are best used sparingly. Less, sometimes, can be more.

(continued)

Keep the following points in mind:

- Emphasis and conciseness enhance each other.
- Conciseness leads to emphasis.
- Emphasis and conciseness go hand in hand.

EXAMPLE

People **negotiate** with each other every day, even when they don't think of themselves as doing so. You **negotiate** *with your spouse* about where to go for dinner and *with your child* about when the lights go out. You **negotiate** *the price of a new car, the salary and responsibilities* for a new job, *the criteria for determining* who deserves special recognition. **Negotiation is** a basic means of getting what you want from others. **It is** back-and-forth communication designed to reach an agreement.

2 Replace wordy phrases

Wordy phrases use more words than necessary to convey meaning or to make a point. To streamline your writing, replace wordy phrases with precise words where possible. Here is a list of wordy phrases and their more concise alternatives.

WORDY	CONCISE
at the present moment	now
due to the fact that	because
in this day and age	today
for the most part	mostly
in order to	to
give consideration to	consider
I am of the opinion that	I think
in view of the fact that	since
a large number of	many
make contact with	contact
persons of the Catholic faith	Catholics
sufficient amount of	enough

WORDY	CONCISE
ideas of a serious nature	serious ideas
in light of the fact that	since
regardless of the fact that	although
for the purpose of	to
in close proximity to	near
aware of the fact that	know
in the event that	if
in the final analysis	finally
has the capacity for	can

Wordy phrases often contain buzzwords—words that sound important but that express little real meaning. Buzzwords can be nouns (e.g., *area, factor, sort, thing*), adjectives (*interesting, significant, weird*), or adverbs (*absolutely, awfully, basically, quite*).

WORDY   Those types of basically complicated questions are the sort of ones that most often appear on the final.

CONCISE   *Complicated questions* often appear on the final.

CONCISE   *That type of complicated question* often appears on the final.

3   Avoid negating words

To reduce wordiness, you may want to eliminate negating words (i.e., words that negate a positive word or phrase), such as *no* and *not*.

WORDY   I *do not approve* of the administration's response to the student protests.

CONCISE   I *disapprove* of the administration's response to the student protests.

WORDY   He is *not feeling well.*

CONCISE   He is *ill.*

But remember that sometimes you may want to maintain that emphasis on the negative that this structure offers.

4   Eliminate redundancy

Redundancy is the needless repetition of words, phrases, sentences, paragraphs, or ideas. Redundant expressions add nothing to what has already been said. Redundancy comes in three forms: redundant word pairs, redundant modifiers, and redundant categories.

Redundant word pairs

REDUNDANT   *Each and every* one of us won a prize.

REVISED   *Each* of us won a prize.

Redundant modifiers

REDUNDANT   Our *future hope* was for a chance to travel around the world.

REVISED   Our *hope* was for a chance to travel around the world.

Redundant categories

REDUNDANT   A book *blue in color* was left on the desk.

REVISED   A *blue* book was left on the desk.

Redundancies are easy to overlook in writing because they are so commonly used. Advertisers offer "free gifts," and they boast of "billions and billions sold." Weather reporters describe the temperature as "minus five degrees below zero." Sportscasters describe a college athlete as having a "fine future ahead of her." Journalists report that a pair of convicts "successfully escaped" and that "foreign imports" threaten "our country's internal economy."

Here is a list of some additional redundancies to avoid.

REDUNDANCIES

basic fundamentals	important essentials
circle around	join together
component parts	past history
continue on	positive benefits
cooperate together	refer back
crisis situation	repeat again
expensive in price	true facts

Make sure you look for redundancy in your writing and rewrite those passages more concisely.

EXERCISE 25–4 **Recognizing Redundancies**

The following exercises can help you become more aware of the types of redundancies to avoid in your writing.

1. Watch a television news broadcast from beginning to end. List the redundancies you hear.

2. Watch a television comedy or drama. List the redundancies you hear.

3. Choose five advertisements from a popular magazine. List the redundancies you find.

5   Avoid excessive use of the verb *be*

The verb *be* expresses relations between things and is both a linking verb and an auxiliary verb (see 10b). Excessive use of *be* in its most common forms—*is* and *was, are* and *were*—often makes writing static, bland, and flat.

EXCESSIVE USE OF *BE*	It *is* sometimes the case that students *are* absent from class when an assignment *is* due.
REVISED	Students sometimes miss class when assignments are due.

USAGE NOTE   The forms of the verb *be* are useful and necessary, especially as auxiliaries (see 10b). You will need to use varying forms of *be* often. Notice any opportunities to substitute active verbs when forms of *be* proliferate in your prose.

Using too many sentences that begin with the expletive *It is, There is,* or *There are* can weaken your writing. These introductory words delay the real subject to the middle of the sentence, both making the reader wait to know the subject and putting the subject in a less emphatic position than at the beginning of the sentence. To delay the subject to create suspense or emphasis (see 24c), keep the expletive. Revise to eliminate it.

WEAK	*It is* essential for news anchors today to have a full head of hair.
REVISED	News anchors today must have a full head of hair.
WEAK	*There is* a new Whoopi Goldberg movie *that* is much better than her last one.
REVISED	The new Whoopi Goldberg movie is much better than her last one.

USAGE NOTE   Although expletives can be wordy and roundabout, sometimes they are the best way to express a thought or provide emphasis.

There is no excuse for missing the appointment.

It was the worst mistake *that* I ever made.

6   Prefer verbs to nouns

The tendency to use nouns rather than verbs to carry a sentence's meaning is called **nominalization.** It results when a verb form is changed to a noun: the verb *instruct* becomes the noun *instruction.* Nominalization tends to make writing abstract. It also reduces its energy and liveliness.

NOMINALIZATION   It is our *expectation* that we will receive an answer soon.

REVISED   We *expect* to receive an answer soon.

WRITING HINT   Be aware of the weak verbs that typically accompany nominalizations. The verbs *make, take,* and *give,* for example, frequently lead to nominalization.

We will *make a recommendation.* [We will *recommend.*]

She will *give a ruling* on the issue. [She will *rule* on the issue.]

EXERCISE 25–5   **Revising Nominalizations**
Rewrite the following sentences to eliminate nominalization. Example:

The board's *discussion* concerned a tuition increase.

The board *discussed* a tuition increase.

1. The intention is to increase support staff salaries.
2. The senators have no expectation that the governor will consider their request.
3. The governor's refusal of the request is a certainty.
4. The appearance of the union representative before the board was on July 30.
5. The union's assessment of the salary problem was correct.

7   Use the active rather than the passive voice

Using too many passive voice verbs contributes to wordiness. As a general guideline, use the active voice most of the time and the passive voice only when you do not want the agent of the verb to be the subject of the sentence.

Passive constructions can be more than just wordy. Sometimes writers and speakers use them to conceal important information from audiences.

EVASIVE   It has been decided that a decision about increasing tuition will be postponed until all relevant data have been reviewed.

REVISED   The Board of Trustees decided to postpone its decision about increasing tuition until it has reviewed all relevant data.

USAGE NOTE   Do not avoid the passive altogether. At times it is necessary and effective, as the following examples illustrate.

The streets of Paris *are laid out* in a circular pattern.

Walt Whitman's brother *was wounded* during the Civil War.

EXERCISE 25–6   **Evaluating Your Writing for Wordiness**
Go through one of the papers you recently wrote and edit it for passive voice constructions, excessive use of *be,* and excessive nominalization.

8   Avoid the excessive use of prepositional phrases

Used skillfully, prepositions clarify meaning and enhance the beauty and power of writing. Used excessively, however, prepositions contribute to wordiness.

WORDY   In the presence of so many temptations in such alluring guises, it is no wonder that people without strong convictions of morality and a confident sense of their own self-worth find themselves responding in a highly engaged manner to the promises of gratification, happiness, and pleasure that temptations of such power hold out to them.

REVISED   Given so many alluring temptations, people without strong moral convictions and a sense of self-worth readily respond to the powerfully attractive rewards such temptations promise.

EXERCISE 25–7   Revising for Conciseness

Revise the following wordy paragraph to make it more concise. Pay particular attention to unnecessary words, passive voice constructions, and excessive use of expletives, prepositions, and forms of *be*.

There are many reasons why it is dangerous for college students to accept the barrage of credit-card offers that will be made available to them, beginning as early as their first year in college. The most obvious reason, of course, is that most students will be tempted to use the cards to purchase things that they need, perhaps including their books and clothes, even food—although many will not be in a very good position for the money to be paid when due to the credit-card company or bank that was the primary issuer of the card. Although it is certainly very important that young adult males and females learn to make good use of credit that is made available to them, it is simply unwise for many to try to learn the use of credit while they are students and not members of the workforce.

EXERCISE 25–8   Reducing Wordiness in Your Writing

Go through one of the papers you wrote recently and eliminate the various types of wordiness discussed in 25b. Use the strategies described in this chapter to guide your revision.

26 *Using Appropriate Words*

To communicate effectively as a writer, you need to understand the connotative, or associative, meanings of words as well as their denotative, or dictionary, meanings. You also need to distinguish among abstract words and concrete words, among general words and specific words, and among formal words and informal words. This chapter discusses these and other distinctions between words as well as various ways you can use words to suit your purpose and audience. The accompanying chart identifies key characteris-tics of words that all writers need to understand in order to choose words appropriately.

Characteristics of Words

- Denotation and connotation (26a)
- General and specific words (26b)
- Abstract and concrete words (26b)
- Formal and informal language (26c)
- Jargon (26d)
- Archaisms, neologisms, and acronyms (26e)
- Regionalisms and dialect expressions (26f)
- Euphemisms (26g)
- Clichés (26h)
- Similes and metaphors (26i)

26a   Understanding denotation and connotation

Denotation is a word's literal meaning; **connotation** is a word's associations along with its literal meaning. Denotations tend to be neutral and objective. Connotations are subjective and personal, frequently involving feelings and suggesting concrete images.

Consider the word *dictator*. The denotative meaning of *dictator* is "a person exercising absolute power, especially one who assumes absolute control without the free consent of the people." In reading or hearing that word, however, you may conjure up connotative images of a specific individual as well as the purges, executions, and oppression that dictator engaged in. More than likely these connotations are negative because dictators, historically, have been ruthless tyrants. The images you associate with the word *dictator* will be influenced partly by your previous knowledge and by your personal experience.

Words such as *dictator* and *mother* have strong connotations, whereas words such as *metaphalanges* and *sodium bicarbonate* typically have weak connotations, largely because the meanings of such scientific terms are limited almost exclusively to their denotations. These technical words lack the personal response and emotional power of more connotatively charged words. The technical terms convey more precise information than does the familiar term; the familiar term conjures up immediate images and feelings that the technical terms do not.

EXERCISE 26–1   **Determining a Word's Connotations**
Identify as many connotations as possible for each of the following words. Which words have the fewest connotations for you? Why?

1. skeleton
2. eagle
3. silk
4. hydrogen sulfate
5. green
6. bed
7. black hole
8. lottery
9. food
10. electromagnetic field

EXERCISE 26–2   **Determining Positive and Negative Connotations**
Put each of the following sets of words on a continuum, showing how they range from negative to positive connotations. Example:

```
negative _____neutral_____ positive
   |            |             |            |            |
pigheaded   stubborn    unyielding   determined   principled
```

1. shy, bashful, reticent, timid, reserved, withdrawn

2. famous, renowned, celebrated, well-known, notorious, infamous

3. miserly, stingy, parsimonious, frugal, economical, mercenary, cheap

4. difficult, arduous, challenging, demanding, exacting

5. courage, bravery, fearlessness, valor, fortitude

EXERCISE 26–3   Using Historical Perspective to Determine Connotations
The war fought in the United States between 1861 and 1865 is typically referred to as the Civil War, but it has been identified in other ways. Which of the following terms favor the North, which favor the South, and which seem neutral?

1. The American Civil War

2. The War between the States

3. The War of the Rebellion

4. The War for the Union

5. The War for Southern Independence

6. The War of Secession

7. The Yankee Invasion

8. The War of the North and South

9. The War of Northern Aggression

10. The Second American Revolution

26b   Using general and specific, abstract and concrete words

General words identify broad categories (*country, president, books*); **specific words** identify individual people or objects (*Thailand, president of the AFL-CIO, dictionaries*). **Abstract words** identify ideas and ideals that cannot be perceived by the senses (*education, generosity, fatherhood*); **concrete words** identify something tangible to the senses (*rose, stone, tomato*). Good writing uses words from both ends of the spectrum, from abstract and general words to concrete and specific ones. Abstract and general terms represent ideas, explain attitudes, and explore relationships such as contingency (if something will happen), causality (why it occurs), and priority (what is first in time or importance). Concrete and specific words clarify and illustrate general ideas and abstract concepts.

GENERAL/ABSTRACT   Technology revolutionized communication in the 1990s.

SPECIFIC/CONCRETE   The invention of cellular phones made mobile phone conversations possible.

GENERAL/ABSTRACT   Industrialists with cellular phones have meetings from their cars.

SPECIFIC/CONCRETE   Donald Trump has probably made business deals from the back seat of his limousine.

GENERAL   The storm caused serious damage throughout the region. It was one of the worst ever to hit the area.

SPECIFIC   The hurricane caused extensive destruction in three northern counties. Hundred-mile-an-hour winds toppled trees, blew roofs off houses, and upended cars, trucks, even small planes. Torrential rains swept across the state, swelling creeks and rivers until they flooded homes and offices, washing away coastline houses, creating rivers in what had been walkable streets.

EXERCISE 26–4 Expanding General Statements with Concrete Details

Expand each of the following sentences with specific and concrete words. Example:

Transportation in Holland is excellent.

Holland has the densest rail network in the world. Trains link all major cities and nearly all towns and villages. The trains consistently run on time, and they run so frequently that thirty minutes is the average span between trains departing for any particular destination.

1. Social policy must be a top priority of the administration.

2. The show included many different types of cars.

3. After being accused of a crime he did not commit, he began to wonder about his future.

4. The food was abundant and delicious.

5. Standards of permissible violence in the films of the 1990s differed from the standards of the past.

EXERCISE 26–5   Revising for Concreteness and Specificity

Rewrite the following sentences to make them more concrete and specific. Example:

Our cat's behavior amused us.

Our cat's habit of nibbling at our toes made us giggle.

1. Protect yourself and your passengers while you are driving.

2. A mosquito's feeding habits are repulsive.

3. Avoid certain foods to keep your weight down.

4. For dessert we had pie, fruit, and ice cream.

5. The visitors' conduct displeased their hosts.

26c   Using formal and informal language

Formal language represents the standard or level of discourse suitable for academic and business writing. The tone of formal language is usually serious without being stuffy or pretentious. It is also not especially intimate or personal. **Informal language,** by contrast, is more conversational; it establishes a closer relationship between writer and audience. In using informal language, you may address the reader personally as *you.* And you can refer to yourself as *I,* something you usually avoid in more formal writing.

> http://www.uottawa.ca/ academic/arts/writcenter/ hypergrammar/diction.html
> Provides a linked discussion of clichés, connotation, and other aspects of diction.

The formality or informality of language is relative, a matter of degree. Much writing, for example, is neither exclusively formal nor completely informal. You should avoid extreme informality in your academic and professional writing, striving for a tone appropriate to your subject and audience.

Keep in mind that highly formal language is traditionally reserved for ceremonial occasions, such as the inauguration of a president or a traditional wedding. Highly informal language is used within small groups, among family and friends, for example, who may even invent their own words, especially slang and jargon.

1 Colloquialisms

Colloquialisms are informal expressions appropriate to ordinary spoken language but not to written language. The expressions *hang out with* and *get even with* are considered colloquial. These expressions may be appropriate for casual conversation but should be avoided in academic writing. To raise the level of formality suitable for professional and academic writing, you would instead use the standard English words *spend time with* or *retaliate*.

Colloquialisms also include clipped forms of words, such as *dorm* for *dormitory*, *prof* for *professor*, or *vet* for *veterinarian*. Clipped word forms are appropriate only when you want to create a conversational tone. Notice the difference in level of formality in the following examples.

STANDARD	Students who live in the *dormitories* have more opportunities to meet with their *professors* than students who commute.
CONVERSATIONAL	Students who live in the *dorms* have more opportunities to meet with their *profs* than students who commute.
INFORMAL	*Dorm* students have more chances than commuters to meet with their *profs*.

2 Slang

Informal language also includes **slang,** a vocabulary of playful but typically short-lived words and phrases that deliberately displace standard language, sometimes with vividness and irreverence. Most slang words go out of fashion in a few years, though some become part of the commonly used vocabulary of English. Slang words such as *far out* and *grind* are no longer current, having been displaced by *awesome* and *geek,* respectively. Whereas a previous generation of students *cut* classes, the current generation *blows them off*. Most likely, current slang terms will, before long, be replaced with others invented by a new generation of speakers and writers.

WRITING HINT   Avoid mixing slang or colloquial language with more formal discourse. Check your academic writing for any excessively informal words or phrases. Similarly, check for excessive formality in your informal writing. Strive to keep the level of formality consistent in each piece of writing.

EXERCISE 26–6   Revising for Different Levels of Formality
Write five sentences that use slang terms you are familiar with. Then rewrite the sentences using standard words and phrases that convey the same meaning.

 26d   Avoiding jargon

Jargon is the specialized or technical language of a trade, profession, or other group. For those who understand it, jargon is a kind of shorthand that makes lengthy explanations unnecessary. At its best, jargon is precise and efficient. Lawyers, for example, use the word *tort* to refer to any wrongful act, other than a breach of contract, for which the wronged party is entitled to seek compensation. Doctors use the term *cholecystitis* to indicate an inflammation of the gallbladder.

Among members of specialized groups, jargon is an effective and useful communication tool. For communicating with those outside the group, however, jargon can confuse and needlessly complicate a subject. While doctors easily understand *viral rhinorrhea* (the common cold) and may prescribe a *salicylate* (aspirin) to alleviate its symptoms, most patients would not know those terms. Using jargon with an audience unfamiliar with its meanings can result in confusion and misunderstanding.

Technical words sometimes carry both a standard and a specialized meaning. Computer language, for example, has absorbed a number of words from standard English and given them specialized meanings within its jargon. Here are just a few of them: *bit, boot, crash, disk, hacker, memory, mouse,* and *virus.* Using such computer jargon with a specialized audience can enhance communication as well as identify you as someone with knowledge of computers. But using these words with their specialized meanings in non-computer contexts and with those outside a group of computer users can result in confusion.

EXERCISE 26–7   Using Jargon and Slang

1. Think of some group or team you belong to or a hobby or leisure activity you pursue. Make a list of its specialized words and meanings (whether or not they can be found in a dictionary).

2. Create a dialogue in which two people are speaking the special language of their shared interest.

26e   Using archaisms, neologisms, and acronyms

Archaisms are words or expressions that were once common but are no longer current. Archaisms such as *beweep* ("weep"), *quoth* ("said"), and *bethink* ("to think upon") are listed in dictionaries because they are found in older literary works and historical documents. It is useful to know such words because as a reader you will better understand literature that includes them. However, you should avoid them in your own academic writing.

Neologisms are newly created words that have not come into common usage and are not recorded in dictionaries. The word *brunch* was once a neologism but has now come into established usage, as have the words *gridlock, telemarketing, makeover,* and *surrogate mother.* Other recent additions include *infomercial, sound bite, liposuction,* and *slam dunk.* Until newly minted words make repeated appearances in print, however, avoid using them in academic writing.

One form of neologism you can use in all types of writing is the **acronym.** An acronym is an abbreviation that comes to have the familiarity and currency of an ordinary word. Examples of acronyms include NAFTA (North American Free Trade Agreement), MADD (Mothers against Drunk Driving), RAM (random access memory). Remember not to use periods following the letters of an acronym.

There are two issues to keep in mind when you use acronyms. The first occurs with former acronyms, such as *radar.* Although *radar* was originally an acronym for the sequence of words *radio detection and ranging,* it is now a word that is written in lowercase letters, unlike *NATO* and *AIDS.* Be sure to check your dictionary if you are uncertain about how to spell or use an acronym or initialism. The second complication occurs with clipped forms, such as *sitcom* for *situation comedy.* In such cases, the acronym is composed of shortened forms of words rather than of the first letters of the words in sequence. Notice that these abbreviated words combine to form a new word, a kind of neologism, and as such are written in lowercase letters.

WRITING HINT   In using acronyms in writing, you can either spell out the words the acronym represents when you first use it and then use the acronym for each subsequent appearance, or you can use the acronym from the start and include at its first appearance a parenthetical explanation—as with "ROM (read only memory)."

EXERCISE 26–8   Discovering Archaisms, Creating Neologisms

1. Read the first act of any play by Shakespeare, and find three archaisms.
2. Create three neologisms for a sport, discipline, or area you know well.

EXERCISE 26–9   Understanding Acronyms

Find out what the following acronyms mean.

1. NOW
2. snafu
3. UNESCO (or Unesco)
4. laser
5. OPEC

26f   Understanding regionalisms and dialect expressions

Pronunciation and accents vary in different parts of the United States and in different parts of the world where English is used. Differences also occur in diction, or word choice. As a reader, you will find that understanding the meaning of regional variations in language and dialect expressions can aid your comprehension. As a writer, you can use your awareness of the regional and dialect expressions in your geographic region to select appropriate language for different audiences and occasions.

1   Regionalisms

Regionalisms are expressions distinctive to a particular area or region. The northerner's *pail* is the southerner's *bucket;* a Northeast *bag* is a Midwest *sack.* In Chicago *pop* is something to drink rather than something to eat (an ice cream or ice pop), as a New Yorker would have it. In Appalachia, a Ph.D. is a *teacher-doctor* and a cemetery is a *burial ground.* In certain parts of the South you will hear *reckon* in place of *guess* (*I reckon I'll get on my way*) and *right* for *very* (*I'm right sorry about that*). Although they occur unconsciously in conversation, such regional expressions should be used in writing only when you wish to achieve a particular rhetorical purpose, such as to establish a regional identity or to convey the spirit of a place.

The same is true of regional expressions that extend beyond national borders. In reading you would understand that a Scottish *loch* is a lake, a South African *dorp* is a village, Jamaican *dunny* is money, and European *football* is American soccer. In writing or speaking to a British audience about cars and driving, you would use their terms (*boot* for trunk, *bonnet* for hood, *lorry* for truck, *roundabout* for traffic circle). You would make such linguistic choices primarily to be understood. But you might also do so out of courtesy, or to demonstrate your familiarity with the local or national idiom, or to establish common ground with your audience.

2　Dialect expressions

Dialect is language that uses regional variations in grammar, vocabulary, and spelling. The study of regional dialects, *dialectology*, democratizes linguistic differences, acknowledging all dialects as inherently valuable. Every dialect of English is an authentic and legitimate subsystem of the language with an inherent logic governing it.

Each of us speaks or writes a particular dialect of English, one that expresses our racial and ethnic identity as well as our regional identity. The varieties of English spoken throughout the United States and around the world testify to the richness of the language and to its diversity. Each dialect is a systematic form of the language governed by a grammar and by standards informing its choices of words and expressions. Like other language systems, dialects of English change over time with old expressions dropping out and new ones added.

Dialects of different population groups show consistent patterns of usage in speech and writing. Within the context of their dialect systems, these language variations can be logically and rhetorically effective. Dialect expressions, however, may create problems in communication when the audience extends beyond the specific dialect language community. In those instances, writers and speakers need to consider the efficacy of various linguistic choices. When dialect expressions impede communication, they should be omitted. When they enhance group cohesion or establish group identity, they may be freely used.

five of the following words. Explain what your dictionary reveals about
~~cial~~ acceptability. Identify contexts in which you would use or avoid each

~~am~~	6. menfolk
~~ky~~	7. hoagie
3. soul food	8. reckon
4. lingo	9. howdy
5. hillbilly	10. fink

26g   Avoiding euphemisms

A **euphemism** is an inoffensive term used as a substitute for a more
direct and possibly offensive one. Funeral directors, for example, use the
euphemism *slumber room* to describe the place where a corpse has been laid
out. Because the word *corpse* strongly connotes death, *the deceased* often replaces it. Euphemisms are often used to spare people's feelings and to be
polite. You will rely on euphemisms from time to time in your everyday experience when you judge that circumstances warrant avoiding harsh or overly
direct words. In academic writing, however, you should avoid euphemisms
and instead express yourself as directly and honestly as you can.

EUPHEMISM   Downsizing the employee base became necessary to maintain the profitability of the organization.

REVISED   Laying off employees became necessary to maintain the
profitability of the organization.

Euphemisms are common in political discourse, where they typically
result in evasiveness. George Orwell perhaps put it best when he suggested
that political language consists "largely of euphemism, question-begging and
sheer cloudy vagueness." Orwell's examples are compelling and relevant.

Defenceless villages are bombarded from the air, the inhabitants driven
out into the countryside, the cattle machine-gunned, the huts set on fire
with incendiary bullets: this is called *pacification*. Millions of peasants are

robbed of their farms and sent trudging along the roads with no more than they can carry: this is called *transfer of population* or *rectification of frontiers*. People are imprisoned for years without trial, or shot in the back of the neck or sent to die of scurvy in Arctic lumber camps: this is called *elimination of unreliable elements*. Such phraseology is needed if one wants to name things without calling up mental pictures of them.

—George Orwell, "Politics and the English Language"

EXERCISE 26–11 **Playing with Euphemism**

1. Euphemize the following words and phrases.

   a. garbage collector   c. hung over   e. pain   g. riot
   b. to get fired   d. pregnancy   f. toilet   h. steal

2. De-euphemize the following words and phrases.

   a. relocation center   d. adult entertainment
   b. underachiever   e. intelligence gathering
   c. supervisory personnel   f. ethnic cleansing

26h   Avoiding clichés

Clichés are expressions that have been overused and have become trite. If you hear someone say that a situation is "sad but . . ." you know that the next word will be *true,* as in the cliché "sad but true." You can probably fill in the blanks on many of the following: *cut and _____; beck and _____; a new lease on _____; between a rock and a _____. You get the _____.* Clichés are so familiar that in hearing or reading them you can easily predict what is to come, and nearly always accurately. As a result, the freshness and surprise that characterize effective writing are lost.

EXERCISE 26–12 **Rewriting Stale Clichés**
Choose three clichés from the following list and write either comic variations or fresh versions. You can change a word, phrase, or the entire expression to bring the cliché back to life. Examples:

   sadder but wiser
   sadder but kinder

   hit below the belt
   hit below the belly button

1. absence makes the heart grow fonder
2. thrown off the track
3. tried and true
4. the not-too-distant future
5. add insult to injury

6. know the score
7. sell like hotcakes
8. green with envy
9. hot and heavy
10. dressed to kill

26i   Using figurative language

Language can be classified as either literal or figurative. When we speak or write *literally,* we mean exactly what each word conveys; when we use **figurative language,** however, we mean something other than the literal meaning of the words. Literally, telling someone "go jump in a lake" means telling that person to go for a swim. Figuratively, the expression means something closer to "Go away" or "I do not want to consider what you have to say." Two frequently used figures of speech are especially important for reading and writing: metaphor and simile.

1   Metaphor

A **metaphor** is an expression that compares two seemingly dissimilar things. The heart of metaphor is resemblance, in which one thing is described in terms of another. Metaphors make connections between apparently unrelated things, often with the power of surprise.

More than 2,300 years ago Aristotle defined metaphor as "an intuitive perception of the similarity in dissimilars." He also suggested that to be a "master of metaphor" is the greatest of a writer's achievements. In our own century, Robert Frost has echoed Aristotle by suggesting that metaphor is central to poetry. Frost was a master of metaphor in his poetry and prose as well as in his conversation, which he seasoned liberally with metaphor. For example, Frost was fond of saying that writing free verse (poetry without a strict pattern of rhythm or rhyme) is like playing tennis without a net.

Metaphor is not used only by poets. You use metaphor in your daily conversation, especially when you describe your feelings or explain events and circumstances to people who did not experience them. Using metaphor is natural, even inescapable. It is so common, in fact, that some comparisons (called *dead metaphors*) have become so familiar we hardly notice them as metaphors at all. We refer, for example, to the *legs* of a table, the *eye* of a needle, the *arms* of a chair, the *head* of an organization. We describe people who are tense as *on edge*, people who are detached as *distant*. With metaphor, *it was very painful* can become *it was the lash of a whip upon my flesh*.

In writing with metaphors, be careful not to create a **mixed metaphor**, a metaphor involving an inconsistent comparison. Mixed metaphors can often lead to unintentional humor.

MIXED	Paul and Mary's argument was a battle that blazed with anger. [The metaphors of war and light are mixed.]
REVISED	Paul and Mary's argument was a fight with well-defined battle lines.

As readers, we can better understand what writers mean when we interpret their metaphors. As writers, we can more richly convey our meaning through the use of metaphor because we can create unexpected, interesting connections.

Checking Your Diction

Use the following questions to check your choice of words.

- Consider the positive and negative connotations of your words.
- Clarify and illustrate generalities and abstractions with specific examples and concrete details.
- Suit your level of formality to your audience and purpose. Eliminate slang or colloquialisms.
- Eliminate or define jargon, unless you are writing for an audience of specialists.
- Be sure the meanings of neologisms or acronyms are clear to your audience.
- Revise to eliminate euphemisms or archaisms.
- Unless they are appropriate for the audience and occasion, revise regional or dialect expressions.
- Rephrase to eliminate clichés.
- Check for mixed metaphors, and revise any that you find.

2   Simile

When a metaphorical connection is made explicitly by means of the words *like*, *as*, or *as though*, the comparison is called a **simile**. *Karen dances like an angel* is a simile; *Karen is an angel* is a metaphor. The difference between the two types of figurative language involves more than the word *like:* the comparison in the simile is more restrictive than it is in the metaphor. That is, Karen's angelic qualities are extensive in the metaphor—she has many angelic qualities. In the simile, however, she only dances like an angel.

> WRITING HINT   Do not be afraid to use similes and metaphors in your writing. But be careful about mixing metaphors and lapsing into cliché or trite comparisons (see 26h). To improve your ability to use metaphor and simile, attend to how good writers use them.

EXERCISE 26–13   Identifying and Evaluating Similes and Metaphors

Underline the metaphors and similes in the following passages. Explain what is being compared and comment on the effectiveness of each comparison.

1. What happens to a dream deferred?
   Does it dry up like a raisin in the sun?
   > —Langston Hughes

2. Life's but a walking shadow, a poor player
   That struts and frets his hour upon the stage
   And then is heard no more. It is a tale
   Told by an idiot, full of sound and fury,
   Signifying nothing.
   > —William Shakespeare

EXERCISE 26–14   Revising Mixed Metaphors

Revise any mixed metaphors you find in the following sentences to make the metaphors and similes consistent. Example:

His actions sowed the seeds of confusion, resulting in a rising tide of criticism.

His actions resulted in a rising tide of criticism.

1. Difficulties emerged like mosquitoes from a stagnant pool, creating thorny problems for all involved.

2. The howling wind bent the branches, which tilted gracefully like dancers swaying to a tune.

3. The book was filled with brilliant insights that continued to buzz in her mind.

4. His ideas, rooted in a strong belief in tolerance and understanding, left a trail of believers in their wake.

5. He had to get off the fence and take the plunge.

EXERCISE 26–15　Identifying and Understanding Similes and Metaphors

Identify the similes or metaphors in the following paragraph. Explain how they help convey the writer's idea.

But at that moment I glanced round at the crowd that had followed me. It was an immense crowd, two thousand at the least and growing every minute. It blocked the road for a long distance on either side. I looked at the sea of yellow faces above the garish clothes—faces all happy and excited over this bit of fun, all certain that the elephant was going to be shot. They were watching me as they would watch a conjurer about to perform a trick. They did not like me, but with the magical rifle in my hands I was momentarily worth watching. And suddenly I realized that I should have to shoot the elephant after all. The people expected it of me and I had got to do it; I could feel their two thousand wills pressing me forward, irresistibly. And it was at this moment, as I stood there with the rifle in my hands, that I first grasped the hollowness, the futility of the white man's dominion in the East. Here was I, the white man with his gun, standing in front of the unarmed native crowd—seemingly the leading actor of the piece; but in reality I was only an absurd puppet pushed to and fro by the will of those yellow faces behind. I perceived in this moment that when the white man turns tyrant it is his own freedom that he destroys. He becomes a sort of hollow, posing dummy, the conventionalized figure of a sahib. For it is the condition of his rule that he shall spend his life in trying to impress the "natives," and so in every crisis he has got to do what the "natives" expect of him. He wears a mask, and his face grows to fit it. I had got to shoot the elephant. I had committed myself to doing it when I sent for the rifle. A sahib has got to act like a sahib; he has got to appear resolute, to know his own mind and do definite things. To come all that way, rifle in hand, with two thousand people marching at my heels, and then to trail feebly away, having done nothing—no, that was impossible. The crowd would laugh at me. And my whole life, every white man's life in the East, was one long struggle not to be laughed at.

—George Orwell, "Shooting an Elephant"

26j   Avoiding racially and ethnically biased language

One aim of writing is to communicate clearly so your readers will understand your ideas. Another is to write persuasively so they will accept and perhaps come to share your views. A form of language that interferes with both of these aims is **biased language,** which disparages, stereotypes, or patronizes others. Biased language almost always reflects negative assumptions about race, ethnicity, sex, age, social class, religion, physical or mental characteristics, geographical area, or sexual orientation. Biased language should be avoided because it almost always offends people.

The language of racial and ethnic prejudice reflects generalizations that unfairly stereotype all members of a particular racial or ethnic group. Not all African American males want to be professional basketball players, nor do all white Anglo-Saxon Protestant youths attend prep schools. Not all Japanese are expert in the martial arts, and not all Asian Americans are mathematical whizzes. When **stereotypes,** or assumptions about members of a group, persist, they perpetuate the idea that all members of a group share qualities or behaviors that may or may not apply to a few.

One adverse consequence of racially and ethnically biased language, then, is its stereotypical straitjacketing. Stereotyping is inaccurate, simplistic, and unfair. It suggests notions that do not accurately reflect the diverse beliefs, attitudes, and behaviors of the many people it lumps together. In its excessive generalization, biased or prejudiced language is simpleminded. It is also unfair toward the many who do not exhibit the characteristics presumed by the stereotype.

Biased language insults the person or group to which it is applied. In denegrating others, biased language creates division and separation. In using biased language about races and ethnic or cultural groups, speakers and writers risk alienating members of those groups, thus undermining the communication and shared understanding language should promote.

In referring to race and ethnicity, take pains to choose your language carefully, so as not to offend those you might hope to persuade. Use the terms preferred by particular groups for identifying themselves. If you are unsure how to refer to a group or to any of your acquaintances, you should ask—if you can. As you read newspapers and magazines and watch films and television, notice changes in preferred terminology for racial and ethnic groups.

INSTEAD OF	USE
Afro American	African American or Black
Indian	Native American
Eskimo	Inuit
Oriental	Asian American

26k Avoiding sexually biased language

Sexually biased language, or **sexist language,** ignores or minimizes the contributions of one gender, while emphasizing and giving credit to those of the other. Historically, the roles played by men are more likely to be glorified than those played by women. Writers who wish to avoid perpetuating sexist ideas must consciously use inclusive language. For example, when referring to an unknown person or to people in general, avoid using such words as *man* and *mankind,* which exclude half the human race; use instead more inclusive terms such as *human being(s), humanity, people, persons,* and *individual(s).*

Since sexual bias pervades our language, you need to be vigilant to catch and revise instances of it in writing. When Neil Armstrong first walked on the moon, he was referred to as the first *man* on the moon (not the first *human, individual,* or *person* there). Armstrong's carefully chosen words uttered as he walked on the moon were: "That's one small step for [a] man, one giant leap for mankind." This was acceptable usage in 1969, and most people did not take offense at Armstrong's use of *mankind* instead of *humankind* or *the human race.* Over thirty years later, however, people have become far more sensitive to the gender exclusion implicit in such a choice of words.

1   Sexist pronouns

Perhaps the most challenging problem for writers using inclusive language occurs with pronouns. To avoid sexist writing, do not use masculine pronouns when referring to someone who might be either male or female. And avoid using the generic *he*—letting *he* refer to a person of either sex. Revise the sentences using plural forms to be more inclusive.

SEXIST   A professor knows *he* is responsible for keeping *his* office hours.

REVISED   Professors know *they* are responsible for keeping *their* office hours.

SEXIST   Every kindergarten teacher has *her* own techniques for motivating young children.

REVISED   Kindergarten teachers have different techniques for motivating young children.

Especially troublesome are indefinite pronouns, such as *everybody, anyone,* and *everyone.* Consider the sentence *Everyone has his own ideas about the issue.* Grammatically, indefinite pronouns are singular and thus must take singular pronouns. However, in the previous example, the singular pronoun *he* excludes women. To be more inclusive, you can write *his or her: Everyone has his or her own ideas about the issue.* Although more inclusive, this solution can become cumbersome when you need many references to *she and he, him and her,* and *his and her* in a piece of writing. A better solution is to revise indefinite pronouns to make them plural: *People have their own ideas about the issue.* Or you can eliminate the pronoun altogether: *People have different ideas about the issue.*

2   Occupational stereotypes

Another area to look out for sexist language is that of occupational stereotypes. Do not assume, for example, that all grade school teachers are women, that all surgeons are men, or that secretaries and nurses are always women. And be careful to avoid using such words as *fireman* and *policeman* when *fire fighters* and *police officers* are more inclusive and equally effective terms. As in other instances of gender-specific language, only mention an individual's gender when it is relevant.

INSTEAD OF	CONSIDER USING
anchorman	anchor
businessman	business executive; manager
chairman	chair
cleaning lady	housecleaner
clergyman	priest; rabbi; minister
congressman	legislator; member of Congress
fireman	fire fighter
foreman	supervisor
insurance man	insurance agent
mailman	letter carrier; mail carrier; postal worker
policeman	police officer
salesman	sales representative
stewardess	flight attendant
weatherman	weather reporter; meteorologist
workman	worker

Sexually biased language is fairly easy to revise. Use the accompanying guidelines to keep your language free of sexist bias.

Ways to Avoid Sexist Language

- Avoid using the word *man* or *men* to refer to both women and men. Also avoid words containing those terms, such as *man-made* (use *synthetic* instead).

SEXIST	It is time for all good *men* to stand up and be counted.
REVISED	It is time for all good *people* to stand up and be counted.
SEXIST	The *congressmen* should vote against the proposal.
REVISED	The *legislators* should vote against the proposal.

- Avoid "feminine" suffixes such as -*ess* and -*ette*.

SEXIST	Rita Dove is a prominent American *poetess*.
REVISED	Rita Dove is a prominent American *poet*.

(continued)

- Use parallel terms when referring to members of both sexes. Do not always put the male term first as if it were the more important.

> **SEXIST**   Dr. Noel Rogers and Linda Rogers have been *man and wife* for ten years.
>
> **REVISED**   Noel and Linda Rogers have been *husband and wife* for ten years.

Instead of *men and ladies,* say *ladies and gentlemen* or *men and women.*

- Use plural forms instead of singular masculine forms.

> **SEXIST**   *A doctor* must work as an intern and resident before *he* can be licensed to practice medicine independently.
>
> **REVISED**   *Doctors* must work as interns and residents before *they* can be licensed to practice medicine independently.

- Eliminate the pronouns entirely.

> **REVISED**   *A doctor* must work as an intern and resident before *being* licensed to practice medicine independently.

- Avoid using gender terms unnecessarily, as with *male nurse* or *female lawyer.*

> **SEXIST**   The *male nurse* was represented by three *women lawyers.*
>
> **REVISED**   The *nurse* was represented by three *lawyers.*

- Avoid using language that patronizes either sex.

> **SEXIST**   His response to a crisis is *womanish.*
>
> **REVISED**   His response to a crisis is *ineffectual.*

EXERCISE 26–16   Eliminating Sexist Language

Consider how the following sentences may reveal gender bias. Revise to eliminate the bias.

1. Take the car to your mechanic and ask him to check the gas manifold.
2. The material in that shirt is completely man-made.
3. A secretary should always be ready to do her boss's bidding, even if she finds him pushy and arrogant.

4. We will need all the manpower we can get.

5. If you have a complaint about the food, make sure to tell your waitress.

EXERCISE 26–17   Thinking about Stereotypes in Advertisements
Look at advertisements in a popular magazine. Identify words, phrases, and situations that seem stereotypically feminine or masculine. Consider whether the illustrations convey these stereotypes as well.

26l   Avoiding other kinds of biased language

Racial, ethnic, and gender bias are not the only biases language can convey. Other forms include expressions that show insensitivity toward age, social class, religion, geographical location, physical and mental qualities, and sexual orientation. In using any of these characterizing terms, be careful that your language does not offend.

1   Age

Certain words referring to a person's age may be taken as disparaging, even when you have no intention of being so. A young person may resent being called an *adolescent*, a *kid*, or even a *teenager*, while an older person may prefer not to be described as *a senior* or *elderly*. Moreover, referring to an individual as an *old woman* or *a man who looks good for his age* may seem simply descriptive, but may be taken as unflattering and, indeed, unnecessary to the context. *Old woman* carries with it suggestions of wrinkles and sagging skin. A man who *looks good for his age* implies that the man looks physically fit only if his age is considered. Use age descriptors carefully, with sensitivity, and only as necessary.

2   Social class

When describing social class, avoid terms that patronize or demean a group of people, and do not use social class to build an argument or pigeonhole members of a group. Avoid disparaging terms such as *redneck, white trash,* and *wealthy snob.* Remember that your readers may come from across the social spectrum and take care to avoid negative and unfairly biased class terms.

3   Religion

Although most words used to designate religious groups do not convey bias (Protestant, Muslim, Christian, Jew, Buddhist), refer to religion reasonably and fairly, regardless of your own beliefs. Avoid assuming that your religious preferences or beliefs are the norm. Avoid generalizing about the religious beliefs of others. When referring to religious figures, beliefs, or events, keep your language free of judgmental words. Avoid overgeneralization by implying, for example, that all Catholics have big families, that all Protestants can quote Scripture, or that all Muslims wear turbans and speak Arabic.

4   Geographical area

People from one region or section of a country sometimes consider those from other parts of the country less sophisticated, less advanced, or less capable than they are. Some city dwellers think of their rural counterparts as naive country *hicks*. The insult is reversed with the country dweller's view of the urban inhabitant as a *city slicker*, someone not to be trusted. Even when geographical references are not directly patronizing or denigrating, they may convey ignorance in their simplistic or overly general ideas. Not all New Yorkers are rude, for example, nor do they all live fast-paced lives. Southerners do not all speak with a drawl, nor are they all hospitable. Californians are not all sun worshipers and surf lovers, nor are all Midwesterners untutored farmhands.

5   Sexual orientation

In the same way you avoid denigrating language in referring to people's race, ethnicity, age, social class, or other characteristics, be careful when making references to sexual orientation. Do not assume that your readers share your sexual orientation any more than they may share your political views or religious beliefs. Be as unbiased toward different sexual orientations as you are toward behaviors resulting from different social backgrounds or cultural traditions. Avoid referring to a person's sexual orientation if such a reference would be gratuitous and irrelevant. In discussing the acting career of Rock Hudson, for example, you would avoid mentioning his homosexuality—unless it was directly relevant to your point.

> WRITING HINT   In general, avoid labeling people as *victims*—as *AIDS victims, cancer victims*, or *victims of Down's syndrome*, for example. Instead refer to them as people—people with AIDS, individuals with cancer, or people with Down's syndrome. Give the person priority over the illness or physical or mental condition.

EXERCISE 26–18   Becoming Aware of Biased Language
Find a newspaper or magazine article or advertisement that exhibits sexist bias. Find another that exhibits one of the other biases discussed in this chapter. Explain which words and phrases may be considered offensive and why.

EXERCISE 26–19   Revising Biased Language
Revise the language of the item you located for Exercise 26–18 to eliminate the bias.

EXERCISE 26–20   Examining Biased Language
Explain the purpose of the biased language included in the following paragraph.

> I grew up in a town where some people were referred to as "Dagos" and "Wops" while others were called "Ricans" and "Spics." These terms reflected bias, of course. But they also revealed a kind of simple ignorance of the "other," of those who looked different and talked differently, and whose customs and culture were not like those who were neither Italians nor Puerto Ricans. It is a shameful reality of contemporary life that dismissive racist terms and ethnic slurs continue to be used, though less publicly than a generation or even a decade ago.

27   *Improving Your Spelling*

English spelling can be troublesome, mostly because English is a complex language that derives from a variety of other languages, based on different sound systems. In addition, spelling certain English words correctly is challenging because words with similar sounds may be spelled differently. The *ee* sound in *beef*, for example, appears in words with many varied spellings: *be, sea, key, esprit, belief, conceit, people, eon, these.*

Even though numerous inconsistencies plague English spelling, most English words are spelled the way they sound. The exceptions do not diminish the usefulness of rules for spelling. This chapter covers both the rules and practical hints that will help you improve your spelling.

27a Using word meanings to aid spelling

English spelling depends heavily on the connection between words and their meanings. You should consider spelling, then, in relation to vocabulary and *etymology*, or word origins. To improve your spelling while increasing your vocabulary, learn the meanings of words in clusters to discover the relationships among words and to connect the spelling of words with their meanings.

If you know, for example, that the word *copyright* has something to do with the right of legal protection for creative work, you will not misspell it as *copywrite*, even though you may also know that a person who works for an advertising agency writing copy for ads is a *copywriter*. The difference in spelling reflects a very real difference in meaning. The similar sound of the words is not nearly as important as their significant difference in sense.

27b Recognizing homonyms

Homonyms are words that sound alike but are spelled differently and have different meanings: *bored/board; horse/hoarse; cite/sight/site; plane/plain; night/knight; rain/rein/reign.* For these and many other words identical or similar in sound (*advice/advise; allusion/illusion*) you cannot use pronunciation as a guide to spelling.

The chart on p. 460 identifies some homonyms that appear frequently in writing and can create spelling confusion. Always check your use of such homonyms carefully. Although not especially difficult to spell, they are easy to confuse.

Frequently Confused Homonyms			
its	(possessive form of *it*)	to	(toward)
it's	(contraction of *it is*)	too	(also; very)
		two	(number after one)
their	(possessive form of *they*)		
they're	(contraction of *they are*)	whose	(possessive form of *who*)
there	(in that place)	who's	(contraction of *who is*)
than	(as compared with)	your	(possessive form of *you*)
then	(at that time; therefore)	you're	(contraction of *you are*)

1   Recognizing homonyms with more than one form

Homonyms sometimes appear as a single word and sometimes as more than one word. Be sure to choose the homonym form that conveys your meaning. If you are unsure what a particular form of a homonym means, check your dictionary. Here are some homonyms whose different forms occasionally cause confusion.

They *always* [invariably] approach problems in *all ways* [every way] before deciding which solution is the best.

Every day [each day] you go to class, you wear *everyday* [usual] clothes.

I *may be* [might be] late, but then *maybe* [perhaps] I will be early.

They were not *altogether* [entirely] sure that gathering people *all together* [in a group] was the best way to discuss the issue.

By the time I had my paper *all ready* [completely finished], the deadline had *already* [before] passed.

Other variable-form homonyms include the following.

anybody [anyone]; *any body* [any single person]

anymore [ever]; *any more* [more of something]

sometimes [occasionally]; *some times* [certain times]

somebody [someone]; *some body* [some individual person]

> **WRITING HINT**   Remember to spell *cannot* as one word, and *a lot* and *all right* as two words.
>
>   Be sure that the spelling of homonyms reflects the meaning you wish to convey.

EXERCISE 27–1   Choosing the Appropriate Homonym

For each of the following sentences, underline the appropriate homonym. Example:

> Never <u>lose</u>/loose <u>sight</u>/cite of your goal.

1. When *your/you're* finished, put *your/you're* papers over *there/their/they're*.
2. Please *accept/except* our *advice/advise*.
3. This is the *principal/principle affect/effect* of the *scene/seen*.
4. *Who's/Whose* to say *weather/whether* it was a better film *then/than* her last?
5. My *patience/patients* should have long *passed/past*.

27c   Applying common spelling rules

1   Distinguishing between *ie* and *ei*

    You probably know the *ie/ei* rule: "*i* before *e* except after *c*, or when sounded like 'ay,' as in *neighbor* or *weigh*." This rule yields the following spellings.

http://www.qconline.com/ myword/perfectc.html
Looks at the limitations of computer spell-checkers and offers advice about using them.

    i **before** *e:* belief, field, grief, hygiene, pier, relieve

    but *e* **before** *i* **after** *c:* ceiling, conceit, conceive, deceive, receive, perceive

    ei **pronounced "ay":** beige, eight, freight, sleigh, vein, weight

    But the *ie/ei* rule does not always hold true. **Some exceptions to the *ie/ei* rule:** *caffeine, conscience, either, financier, foreign, forfeit, leisure, seize, sovereign, species, their, weird.* Also notice that adding a *t* to the word *sleigh,* for example, yields the word *sleight,* which looks similar to *sleigh* but is pronounced differently. (*Sleight* rhymes with *right,* not with *hate.*)

2   Dropping or retaining the final *e*

In adding suffixes to words ending in a silent *e,* drop the *e* when the suffix begins with a vowel.

explor[e] + ation = exploration   requir[e] + ing = requiring
forc[e] + ible   = forcible

EXCEPTIONS   To avoid homonym confusion, use *dyeing* (staining with a color) and *singeing* (to burn slightly).

dye + ing   = dyeing [not *dying,* present participle of *die*]
singe + ing = singeing [not *singing,* present participle of *sing*]

To keep the sound of *c* or *g* soft in certain words, note the following.

notice + able   = noticeable
courage + ous = courageous

Retain the silent *e* if the suffix begins with a consonant.

require + ment = requirement   care + ful = careful
state + ly   = stately

EXCEPTIONS   argu[e] + ment   = argument
judg[e] + ment   = judgment
acknowledg[e] + ment = acknowledgment
aw[e] + ful   = awful
tru[e] + ly   = truly
whol[e] + ly   = wholly
nin[e] + th   = ninth

3   Spelling words ending in *-cede, -ceed, -sede*

With the exception of *supersede,* all words ending in a suffix pronounced "seed" end either in *-cede* or in *-ceed.* Only three words end in *-ceed: exceed, proceed,* and *succeed.* All others end in *-cede:* such as *intercede, precede, secede, concede, recede.*

4   Distinguishing *-ally* from *-ly*

Use the suffix *-ally* for words ending in *-ic.*

logic + ally = logically
magic + ally = magically

EXCEPTION   publicly (not publically)

Use the suffix *-ly* instead of *-ally* for words that do not end in *-ic*.

slow + ly   = slowly
haphazard + ly = haphazardly

EXERCISE 27–2   Spelling by the Rules
Identify the correctly spelled words and use each one in a sentence.

1. fatally/fataly
2. tragicly/tragically
3. uncharacteristicly/uncharacteristically
4. initially/initialally
5. wholely/wholly/wholy

6. adviseable/advisable
7. deceitful/decietful
8. heinous/hienous
9. grievous/greivous
10. hygeine/hygiene

5   Retaining the final *y* or changing it to *i*

To add a suffix to words that end in *y*, change the *y* to *i* when the letter before the *y* is a consonant.

beauty + ful = beautiful
merry + ly   = merrily
spy + ed   = spied

defy + ance   = defiance
forty + eth   = fortieth
happy + ness = happiness

EXCEPTIONS   Keep the *y* before the suffix *-ing*.

hurry + ing = hurrying
cry + ing   = crying

bully + ing   = bullying
purify + ing = purifying

Retain the *y* in some one-syllable words.

wry + ly   = wryly
dry + ness = dryness

fry + er = fryer

When a word ends in *y* preceded by a vowel, keep the *y* when adding a suffix.

employ + er   = employer
disobey + ed = disobeyed

deploy + ment = deployment

Also, proper names retain the *y* and simply add the suffix.

June and James P. Grundy = the Grundys
Candy + esque = Candyesque

Spelling Words with *y* or *i*
Identify the correctly spelled word in each of the following pairs.

1. gayly/gaily
2. dayly/daily
3. lonelyer/lonelier
4. fancyful/fanciful
5. supplyed/supplied
6. hurryed/hurried
7. dressyer/dressier
8. dryness/driness
9. complyance/compliance
10. fussyly/fussily

6 Doubling consonants

Adding a prefix or a suffix to an existing word sometimes results in a doubled consonant. The following guidelines will help you know when to double a consonant.

Doubling consonants when adding prefixes

In adding a prefix that ends in a consonant to a word that begins with one, combine the two consonants.

mis + spell = misspell
under + rated = underrated

If the word begins with a vowel, combine the prefix and the word.

mis + appropriate = misappropriate
de + emphasize = deemphasize

Sometimes, you need to make a slight adjustment in the prefix when you combine it with words that begin with a consonant. For example, if you combine the prefix *in* (meaning "not") with the following words, you need to adjust the prefix to double the initial consonant of the root word.

(in) im + mobile = immobile
(in) il + legible = illegible
(in) ir + relevant = irrelevant

The technical term for this prefix change is *assimilation*. This same process occurs with other prefixes, such as *con* (meaning "with"): *collect, correlate, commiserate*. Other examples include *accept (ad + cept)* and *eccentric (ex + centric)*.

Doubling the final consonant when adding suffixes

For one-syllable words that end in a consonant, double the final consonant when you add a suffix.

hop + ing = hopping
flop + y   = floppy
scar + ed = scarred

For two-syllable words, double the consonant when the accent falls on the second syllable.

control´ + able = controllable   concur´ + ed = concurred
begin´ + ing   = beginning

EXCEPTIONS
Words ending in *d* and *y* never double the consonant.

reward + ed = rewarded   dismay + ing = dismaying
rotund + ity = rotundity   decay + ed   = decayed

When not to double the final consonant when adding suffixes

Do not double the consonant when the accent falls on the first syllable of a multisyllable word.

pro´fit + able = profitable   tar´get + ed   = targeted
hap´pen + ing = happening   con´fident + ly = confidently
ben´efit + ed   = benefited

Do not double the consonant when the suffix begins with a consonant.

equip + ment = equipment
adroit + ness = adroitness

Do not double the consonant when the final consonant is preceded by more than one vowel or by another consonant.

sweep + ing = sweeping   light + ly = lightly
blurt + ed   = blurted

Do not double the consonant when a word's accent changes with the addition of the suffix.

refer´ + ence = ref´erence

EXERCISE 27–4   Deciding When to Double Consonants

Add suffixes and prefixes to the following words, and decide whether or not to double the consonant.

1. merit + orious
2. worship + ing
3. confer + ing
4. toboggan + ing
5. noncommit + al

6. dis + qualified
7. mis + spent
8. re + apportioned
9. pre + programmed
10. re + entry

27d   Forming plurals

1   Regular plurals

The most common way to form the plural of nouns is to add -s.

boy/boys   marble/marbles   auction/auctions

However, words ending in s, sh, z, x, or ch form their plurals by adding -es.

pass/passes   wish/wishes   buzz/buzzes
ax/axes   church/churches   fax/faxes

For words ending in o, add either -s or -es. If the final o is preceded by a vowel, add -s. If the final o is preceded by a consonant, add -es.

patio/patios   tomato/tomatoes

EXCEPTIONS

piano/pianos   pro/pros
memo/memos   solo/solos

For words ending in y, change the y to i and add -es—but only when the y is preceded by a consonant.

history/histories   eulogy/eulogies   ally/allies

When the *y* is preceded by a vowel, retain the *y* and add *-s*.

attorney/attorneys   toy/toys   alley/alleys

EXCEPTION

Proper names: There are three *Harrys* in the class.

For most words that end in *-f* or *-fe*, change the *-f* or *-fe* to *v* and add *-es*.

shelf/shelves   yourself/yourselves   wife/wives

EXCEPTIONS

roof/roofs   dwarf/dwarfs or dwarves
safe/safes   hoof/hoofs or hooves
                    scarf/scarfs or scarves

2   Irregular plurals

For irregular plurals and words that use the same form in both the singular and the plural, become familiar with the appropriate forms.

man/men   locus/loci   deer/deer
woman/women   alga/algae   sheep/sheep
child/children   basis/bases   moose/moose
foot/feet   alumna/alumnae   series/series
tooth/teeth   alumnus/alumni   species/species

3   Plurals of compound nouns

Form the plural of compound nouns written as one word by making the last part of the word plural.

streetcar/streetcars   bloodhound/bloodhounds
briefcase/briefcases   bookshelf/bookshelves

Compound words that are separated or hyphenated form plurals by making the most important part of the compound plural.

sister-in-law/sisters-in-law
lieutenant governor/lieutenant governors
leap year/leap years

EXERCISE 27–5   Spelling Plural Nouns
Form the plural of each of the following nouns.

1. mother-in-law   4. criterion   7. fish   9. crutch
2. bride-to-be   5. cupful   8. speech   10. turkey
3. cash   6. fox

27e   Spelling words with unstressed vowels and consonants

Although it is not a letter of the alphabet, the **schwa** is the most common sound in the English language. This sound is considered an unstressed vowel—an "uh" sound we make in many of the words we speak. Pronounce the following words and listen for the unstressed vowel.

acad[*e*]my   emph[*a*]sis   mir[*a*]cle
hist[*o*]ry   wom[*a*]n   sent[*e*]nce
hum[*a*]n   comp[*e*]tent

The schwa is designated by an upside-down *e* (ə). You can find the schwa in the pronunciation key of your dictionary.

It is not always easy to remember whether *definate* or *definite* is the correct spelling; whether *grammer* should be spelled *grammar* or which of *demacratic, demecratic,* or *democratic* is correct. To spell these words and others with an unstressed vowel or schwa, think of a related word in which the vowel is stressed. Let us take *dem[ ]cratic* as an example. How do you know that the unstressed vowel should be *o* rather than *i* or *e*? Because in all likelihood you know that a related word, *democracy,* is spelled with an *o*. Likewise, you know that the word *hist[ ]ry* is spelled *history* and not *histery* because you know the related words *historian* and *historical,* in which the vowel *o* is stressed and easy to hear.

Here is a brief list of words with silent consonants.

aisle   indict   pneumonia
climb   knee   surprise
column   knight   thumb
foreign   paradigm   Wednesday

EXERCISE 27–6   **Spelling Using the Schwa**

For each of the following words, supply the missing vowel without checking the dictionary. Then compare your guess with the dictionary.

1. affirm_tive	6. rep_tition	11. auth_r	16. pres_dent
2. exist_nce	7. sed_tive	12. conserv_tory	17. narr_tive
3. friv_lous	8. gramm_r	13. med_cine	18. comp_rable
4. prec_dent	9. defin_te	14. hyp_crisy	19. not_riety
5. nutr_tive	10. ill_strate	15. monot_nous	20. des_lation

 27f   Spelling words with the hyphen

Some compound words are spelled as single words *(birdsong)*, some are written as two words *(ice cream)*, and some are joined with a hyphen *(walk-on)*. When you are unsure of how to spell compound words, consult an up-to-date dictionary. Words such as *figurehead* and *benchmark,* now single words, were formerly hyphenated. The accompanying chart offers guidelines as to when you should use a hyphen to join compound words.

When to Hyphenate Compound Words

- When two or more words serve as a single modifier before a noun:

    He is a *well-respected* dancer.

    We filed an *out-of-state* tax return.

- But not when the modifier occurs after the noun:

    As a dancer, he is *well respected.*

- When a compound adjective appears as part of a series:

    They were due in at either *eight-* or *nine-o'clock.*

- With fractions:

    one-fourth

- With whole numbers between *twenty-one* and *ninety-nine.*

(continued)

- With coined compounds (words not ordinarily linked):

    She gave me an *over-the-shoulder* smile.

- When attaching prefixes to words beginning with a capital letter:

    They were accused of being *un-American.*

    It was to be a conference on *non-Eurocentric* issues.

- When attaching suffixes to capital letters:

    the *A*-train

EXERCISE 27–7   Spelling Compound Words

Add hyphens only when appropriate in the following compound words. Use a dictionary to check your work.

1. home run hitter   4. U turn
2. dust buster   5. governor elect
3. fifty five

Computer Tip

Using a Spell Checker

Always use your spell checker before printing out a final version of your work. You'll often be surprised how many words contain typos even when you know the correct spelling. And spell checkers can identify the correct spelling of some words you might be unsure about. But be aware of the limitations of this computerized writing tool. Spell checkers are limited to the words in their dictionaries. If you are spelling incorrectly words that are not included in those dictionaries, you (and the spell checker) will not be aware of it. Also, spell checkers will not help you if you have written "their" when you mean "there" or "they're," which you will probably spell correctly in all of these forms. You'll need to proofread for spelling by eye as well as by using your spell checker.

28 *End Punctuation*

The period, question mark, and exclamation point indicate where one sentence ends and another begins. All three marks are thus considered **end punctuation** (or terminal punctuation) marks. More often than not you will punctuate the end of a sentence with a period, but you have some choice between using a period, a question mark, or an exclamation point.

28a   Using the period

Use a period (.) to end a sentence that makes a statement or gives a mild command.

STATEMENTS	The day was unlike any she had ever experienced.
	These are the times that try our souls.
MILD COMMANDS	Let your imagination soar.
	Give me my arrows of desire.

Use a period for an indirect question, which implies a question rather than asks it directly.

INDIRECT QUESTION	I have often wondered why some people learn languages easily.
INDIRECT QUESTION	Students often ask what it takes to earn an *A*.

Most abbreviations take periods. Note, however, that the abbreviations in the last two columns of the following list may be written with or without periods. Whichever style you adopt, make sure you use it consistently. If you are not sure how to punctuate an abbreviation, look it up in your dictionary.

Mr.	i.e.	B.A. (or BA)	A.D. (or AD)
Mrs.	e.g.	M.A. (or MA)	B.C.E. (or BCE)
Ms.	etc.	Ph.D. (or PhD)	U.S.S.R. (or USSR)
Rev.	a.m.	M.D. (or MD)	U.K. (or UK)
Dr.	p.m.	J.D. (or JD)	U.S.A. (or USA)

USAGE NOTE   Strictly speaking, *Ms.* is not an abbreviation. Some authorities, therefore, advocate that *Ms* be written without a period. However, we use a period for the following reasons: (1) *Ms.* is modeled on the abbreviations *Mr.* and *Mrs.*; (2) the name of an influential magazine carries the title *Ms.* Readers will expect a period after the abbreviation *Ms.* (Do not confuse this abbreviation with the lowercased one for a manuscript—*ms.*)

Do not include periods when using the postal abbreviations for states.

FL   TN   CA

However, you can write either Washington, DC, or Washington, D.C.

Do not use a period when abbreviating names of organizations, companies, and agencies: *NAACP* (National Association for the Advancement of Colored People), *EPA* (Environmental Protection Agency), *CNN* (Cable News Network). **Acronyms**—abbreviations that are also pronounced as words—omit the period: *AIDS* (acquired immune deficiency syndrome), *NASA* (National Aeronautics and Space Administration), *NOW* (National Organization for Women). (See Chapter 36 for more on abbreviations.)

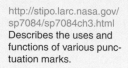

http://stipo.larc.nasa.gov/sp7084/sp7084ch3.html Describes the uses and functions of various punctuation marks.

EXERCISE 28–1   **Using Periods in Abbreviations**
In each of the following sentences, insert periods in the abbreviations only where appropriate. Some sentences may be correct. Example:

Mr Julio Rodriguez received an MBA.

Mr. Julio Rodriguez received an M.B.A. (or MBA.)

1. OU has many students studying for their MA.

2. Some 1990 graduates earned both an Ed.D and a PhD.

3. Senator Smith has an L.LD.

4. The APA held its annual meeting in Brooklyn, NY.

5. I.B.M. is the familiar abbreviation for International Business Machines.

28b   Using the question mark

The question mark (?) is used most often after direct questions. Direct questions often begin with an interrogative word (*who, what, when, why, how*); they usually involve inverted word order.

When is the question mark used?

Where have all the flowers gone?

It is drizzling, is it not?

Do you understand this rule?

Indirect questions are followed by a period rather than a question mark: *I often wondered when a question mark should be used.* The word order in an indirect quotation is not inverted.

We never did find out where all the flowers went.

WRITING HINT   You may use question marks within sentences to indicate questions in a series.

> I had trouble resolving a number of questions: who would come on the trip? what would our itinerary be? how long would we remain abroad?

You can also punctuate such questions as complete independent sentences.

> I had trouble resolving a number of questions. Who would come on the trip? What would our itinerary be? How long would we remain abroad?

Both methods are grammatically correct. Notice, however, that the single-sentence version creates a more swiftly moving sentence. Using capital letters to begin new sentences slows down the pace. Use the method that best serves your purpose for writing.

The question mark can also be used to express uncertainty about a date, number, or word.

Geoffrey Chaucer, 1343(?)–1400, author of the *Canterbury Tales*, held a number of court appointments, including collector of taxes.

Do not use a question mark to indicate uncertainty about an event.

INCORRECT   It will snow (?) over the weekend.

CORRECT   It might snow over the weekend.

In punctuating questions that include quotations, place the question mark before the closing quotation marks when the question is part of the quotation. Do not use a comma or period after a question mark.

FAULTY   The most frequently asked question is "When are we paid?".

REVISED   The most frequently asked question is "When are we paid?"

When the question is not part of the quotation, however, place the question mark after the closing quotation marks.

Who was it that said, "Cut these words and they bleed"?

Do you agree that "it takes a thief to catch a thief"?

(For more on punctuating questions with quotation marks, see 32i-3.)

EXERCISE 28–2   Using the Question Mark

Revise the following sentences by adding or deleting question marks, or by substituting other punctuation marks as appropriate. (Not all sentences are incorrect.) Example:

He asked his sister, "Why do you spend so long in the bathroom."

He asked his sister, "Why do you spend so long in the bathroom?"

1. The coach asked, "Who missed the practice."
2. Is it true that the proposal will save the company money.
3. "May I use this?," asked Priscilla.
4. They all looked at me and asked me why I had come.
5. Some questions remained: Who would go, when would they leave, and how long would they be gone.

28c　Using the exclamation point

Use the exclamation point (!) to indicate surprise or strong emotion. You can also use the exclamation point to give a command.

Help!　　What a gifted comedian she is!

Oh no!　　On your marks! Get set! Go!

Do not use a period or a comma after an exclamation point in direct quotation.

FAULTY　　He exclaimed, "I can't believe what I'm hearing!".

REVISED　　He exclaimed, "I can't believe what I'm hearing!"

Exclamations are more likely to occur in speech, where we can use our voices to indicate the emotion. They usually do not work as well in writing. Use exclamation points sparingly in academic writing, for they can be distracting. They also tend to exaggerate the importance of a point by calling too much attention to it. (Exclamation points shout!)

Overreliance on the exclamation point results, ironically, in a lack of emphasis. To create emphasis, choose your words carefully (see Chapter 26) and construct your sentences to highlight important points (see 25a). As Lewis Thomas once noted, "If a sentence really has something of importance to say, something quite remarkable, it doesn't need a mark to point it out."

EXERCISE 28–3　Revising Direct and Indirect Questions

Convert the following direct questions to indirect questions and the indirect questions to direct ones. Example:

He asked whether we had a good time.

He asked, "Did you have a good time?"

1. They asked whether justice had been done.
2. Is it always necessary to end a sentence with a mark of end punctuation?
3. Was it a good idea or a bad one?
4. What an extraordinary acrobat!
5. Will you please hurry up!

EXERCISE 28–4   Deciding on Terminal Punctuation

Insert the correct end punctuation mark in each of the following statements.

1. You were the only one to receive a perfect score
2. Will you please, please, please, please stop talking
3. The answer to the question is not easily found
4. Do you agree that "It's not over till it's over"
5. Was it U. S. Grant or W. T. Sherman who said "War is hell"

EXERCISE 28–5   Using End Punctuation and Capitalization

Add punctuation and capital letters where necessary.

What is the potency of Ellis Island for someone like me—an American obviously, but one who has always felt that the country really belonged to the early settlers, that as J F Powers wrote in *Morte D'Urban*, it had been "handed down to them by the Pilgrims George Washington and others, and that they were taking a risk in letting you live in it" I have never been the victim of overt discrimination; nothing I have wanted has been denied me because of the accidents of blood but I suppose it is part of being an American to be engaged in a somewhat tiresome but always self-absorbing process of national definition. And in this process I have found in traveling to Ellis Island an important piece of evidence that could remind me I was right to feel my differentness something had happened to my people on that island a result of the eternal wrongheadedness of American protectionism and the predictabilities of simple greed. I came to the island, too, so I could tell the ghosts that I was one of them, and that I honored them—their stoicism and their innocence, the fear that turned them inward, and their pride. I wanted to tell them that I liked them better than I did the Americans who made them pass through the Great Hall, and stole their names, and chalked their weaknesses in public on their clothing.

—Mary Gordon, "Ellis Island"

29   *Commas*

Unlike end punctuation (see Chapter 28), commas (,) slow down a sentence rather than end it. One function of the comma, then, is to direct the rhythm of the sentence. Writers use commas to pace their writing, to enable readers to feel its pulse, to suggest when they can pause. In fact, commas can be heard as slight pauses in a sentence.

Commas also help writers make their meaning clear. To some extent commas help guide a reader's understanding, in part by separating the grammatical parts of sentences from each other. Clauses or phrases, for example, can be set off from the rest of a sentence with commas. The accompanying chart identifies the uses of the comma covered in this chapter.

Uses of the Comma

- To separate main clauses linked by a coordinating conjunction (29a)
- To separate introductory words and phrases from the main clause of a sentence (29b)
- To set off nonrestrictive elements (29c)
- To separate items in a series (29d)
- To separate coordinate adjectives (29e)
- To set off transitional and parenthetical elements (29f)
- To set off absolute phrases (29g)
- To set off contrasting elements, *yes* and *no*, direct address, and tag questions (29h)
- To set off dates, addresses, places, titles, and numbers (29i)
- To set off quotations (29j)
- To aid comprehension (29k)

29a Use a comma before a coordinating conjunction that links independent clauses

Use a comma to separate two independent clauses when the second clause is preceded by a coordinating conjunction (*and, but, or, nor, for, so, yet*). An independent clause includes a subject and predicate but no introductory subordinating conjunction (see 9d). The comma signals the end of one independent thought and the beginning of the next.

She encouraged him, *and* her support gave him the impetus to continue.

It was not the best of possible outcomes, *but* it was not the worst.

The flowers must be watered this weekend, *or* they will die.

The forces of repression have reasserted themselves, *yet* the people's thirst for freedom has not been quenched.

> **USAGE NOTE**   Although a comma usually precedes a coordinating conjunction that joins independent clauses, use a semicolon to join long clauses that contain internal commas. (See Chapter 30.)
>
> > People around the country, though generally satisfied with the verdict, were disappointed with the punishment the judge meted out; *yet* they did not erupt into violence, remaining calm and orderly instead, throughout the long holiday weekend.

You can omit the comma before the coordinating conjunction when the clauses are short and closely related in meaning.

My heart leapt up and I ran to her.

I played well but I could not win.

Always use a comma if a sentence would be confusing without it.

> **CONFUSING**   Watson had to be prepared for Holmes had many questions.
>
> **REVISED**   Watson had to be prepared, for Holmes had many questions.

Always use a comma and a coordinating conjunction between independent clauses. Using only a comma results in a comma splice, a type of run-on sentence error (see 17d).

EXERCISE 29–1   Punctuating Linked Independent Clauses

Add commas or coordinating conjunctions where necessary in the following sentences. Example:

We would have gone home for the reunion but we had to work.

We would have gone home for the reunion, but we had to work.

1. They circled the arena three times and they ran as if possessed.
2. I found the videocassette of the concert and I also found a good audiotape.
3. Changes would have to be made in the way the vote was to be recorded or the results of the balloting could not be considered reliable.

4. Some say that college athletic scholarships should be abolished but others argue for continuing to provide them.

5. Skiers should use only reliable equipment and they should be sure to keep it in good condition.

29b Use a comma to set off introductory elements

Use a comma to follow an introductory word, expression, phrase, or clause. Introductory elements include adverbs (12a); conjunctive adverbs (13c-4); transitional expressions (29f); adverb clauses (9d); and participles, infinitives, and various kinds of phrases (9c).

Fortunately, the rain stopped and the tennis match began. [adverb]

Moreover, it was a very lucrative offer. [conjunctive adverb]

On the other hand, you may be right. [transitional expression]

After suffering through an uneventful opening week, the play became the most popular of the season. [adverb clause]

Overjoyed, he leaped into the air. [participle]

In a reversal of opinion, the chair voted for the plan. [prepositional phrase]

Her decision made, Joy dropped the letter in the mailbox. [absolute phrase]

Carrying his new fishing rod, Juan headed for the lake. [participial phrase]

To justify his decisions, the president went on national TV. [infinitive phrase]

The participial and infinitive phrases in the preceding examples are used as modifiers. When they are used as subjects, however, these and other verbals are not followed by a comma.

Carrying his new fishing rod was a proud moment for Juan.

To justify his decisions is the president's first responsibility.

You may omit the comma after short introductory elements if doing so does not cause confusion.

CLEAR	By the end of the term you should have written six essays.
CLEAR	After class we should meet for lunch.
CONFUSING	By thirty-five careers of professional ballplayers are often over.
REVISED	By thirty-five, careers of professional ballplayers are often over.

EXERCISE 29–2   Punctuating Introductory Elements

Insert commas after the introductory elements where necessary in the following sentences. Example:

After the Oscars had been awarded ticket sales of the winning films increased dramatically.

After the Oscars had been awarded, ticket sales of the winning films increased dramatically.

1. Clearly this would not be an easy task.
2. Bodies tensed for the jolt the wrestlers collided.
3. As with other college applications this one required a personal statement.
4. Unless you have decided on a career you should consider majoring in liberal arts or in one of the sciences.
5. To prepare for an exam you should devise a series of study strategies.

29c   Use commas to set off nonrestrictive elements

Words, phrases, and clauses that constitute **restrictive elements** of a sentence limit the meaning of the words they modify and are not set off from the main clause of the sentence with commas. **Nonrestrictive elements,** which do not limit the meaning of the words they modify, are set off from the main clause of a sentence with commas.

RESTRICTIVE	Professional athletes *who perform exceptionally* deserve their high salaries.
NONRESTRICTIVE	Bobby Bonds, *who led the league in home runs and batting average,* deserves his high salary.

In the first example, the clause *who perform exceptionally* is essential to the meaning of the sentence since it modifies, or restricts, *professional athletes.* The modifying clause is thus not set off by commas. In the second example, the clause *who led the league in home runs and batting average* does not limit the noun it modifies, *Bobby Bonds.* Instead, it provides additional information about him. It is therefore nonrestrictive and is set off with commas. Restrictive elements, especially clauses and participial phrases, usually identify the noun they modify: *who perform exceptionally* identifies which athletes deserve high salaries. The clause modifying the noun *Bobby Bonds* does not identify or restrict the noun to a greater degree.

Sometimes a modifying element can be interpreted as either restrictive or nonrestrictive. Your use of commas, or no commas, will tell the reader what you intend. Consider how the punctuation changes the meaning of the following sentence.

The houses, needing a coat of paint, were given one.

The houses needing a coat of paint were given one.

The first sentence suggests that all the houses needed a coat of paint. The second sentence implies that only some houses needed a coat of paint.

WRITING HINT   You can decide whether to set off an element with commas by imagining your sentence without the words in question. If the words can be deleted without altering the meaning of the sentence or without confusing its meaning, they are nonrestrictive and should be set off with commas. If they cannot be deleted without altering sentence meaning, they are restrictive and should not be set off with commas.

The major computer manufacturers, which have been battling for control of the U.S. market, have begun a series of joint ventures. [The clause *which have been battling for control of the U.S. market* adds incidental information about the major computer manufacturers but does not identify them. Removing the clause would not change the basic meaning of the sentence; the clause is nonrestrictive.]

(continued)

The companies that stand to lose the most are manufacturers of software. [The clause *that stand to lose the most* defines which companies are being talked about. Removing the clause would make the sentence almost meaningless; the clause is therefore restrictive and should not be separated by commas.]

1   Nonrestrictive adjective and adverb clauses

A clause that functions as an adjective or an adverb in a sentence can be either restrictive or nonrestrictive. Only nonrestrictive clauses are set off with commas.

NONRESTRICTIVE CLAUSES

The American political system, *although it has faults,* remains one of the finest in the world. [The clause is not necessary to the meaning of the independent clause and is therefore nonrestrictive.]

I borrow books from my local public library, *which has a splendid collection of material on animals.* [The clause is not essential to the meaning of the independent clause and is thus set off with a comma.]

RESTRICTIVE CLAUSES

They visited a place *where their ancestors first settled in America.* [The clause restricts the meaning of *a place.* Without the clause the reader does not know which place was visited.]

Every approach *that the group thought reasonable* was tried. [The clause restricts the meaning of *Every approach.* Dropping the clause would change the meaning of the sentence.]

WRITING HINT   When you write sentences that include relative clauses, use *that* only for restrictive clauses. Some writers use *which* for both restrictive and nonrestrictive clauses, although many prefer to use *which* only for nonrestrictive clauses.

2   Nonrestrictive phrases

Both participial and prepositional phrases can be either restrictive or nonrestrictive, though prepositional phrases are usually used restrictively.

NONRESTRICTIVE PHRASES

Nicole and Pierre, *pleased with their first game,* decided to play another.

Marilyn Monroe, *even with all the adulation she received,* was unhappy.

RESTRICTIVE PHRASES

Money received *as a gift* is not as special as money earned.

The tray *for the dessert* is on the top shelf.

3   Nonrestrictive appositives

An **appositive** is a noun or noun substitute that replaces another noun or noun substitute by renaming it. Those appositives that are nonessential to the meaning of what they rename are set off with commas.

NONRESTRICTIVE APPOSITIVES

Raymond Carver, *one of contemporary America's best short-story writers,* never published a novel.

Michelangelo's *David, a sculpture carved from an enormous block of Carrera marble,* is approximately eighteen feet high.

Restrictive appositives are usually proper nouns of one or two words. A restrictive appositive usually comes right after a common noun and identifies which person, place, or thing is being described.

RESTRICTIVE APPOSITIVES

The American writer *Ernest Hemingway* once remarked that all of modern American literature derived from Mark Twain's *The Adventures of Huckleberry Finn.* [*Ernest Hemingway* identifies which American writer made the remark.]

Michael Jackson's album *Thriller* remains his best seller. [*Thriller* identifies which album.]

EXERCISE 29–3　**Punctuating with Nonrestrictive Elements**

Identify the restrictive and nonrestrictive clauses, phrases, and appositives in the following sentences. Add commas to set off the nonrestrictive elements where necessary. Example:

> Marie Curie a French scientist discovered radium.
>
> Marie Curie, a French scientist, discovered radium.

1. The enormous oak with the diseased branch was scheduled for surgery.
2. Fileting is a technique that eliminates the bones from meat and fish.
3. Rudy is looking forward to the day when he can retire.
4. The finest American red wines are made from the cabernet grape which grows well in California.
5. The Colorado Rockies a Denver franchise are a recent addition to baseball's National League.

29d　Use commas between items in a series

Use commas to separate items in a series of three or more words, phrases, or clauses.

> He didn't know whether the car was a Ford, a Buick, or a Chevrolet.
>
> To read, to write, to think—all are necessary for academic success.

USAGE NOTE　Some writers, particularly journalists, omit the comma before the next-to-last item in a series (the one before the coordinating conjunction).

> Gertie ordered tomato juice, pancakes and coffee with cream.

However, in academic and other writing, the final comma in a series helps keep the meaning clear.

> UNCLEAR　　Gertie ordered tomato juice, pancakes, bacon and eggs and coffee with cream. [Did she order four or five items?]
>
> CLEAR　　　Gertie ordered tomato juice, pancakes, bacon and eggs, and coffee with cream.

In a moment, without haste, but against his better judgment, he made the desperate leap.

If the time is right, if the place seems suitable, and if the occasion warrants it, make your move.

When one or more items in a series contains commas, separate the items with semicolons rather than with commas (see 30c).

We brought an apple pie; lemonade; and red, white, and blue streamers to the party.

29e   Use commas to separate coordinate adjectives

In using **coordinate adjectives** (two adjectives that modify the same noun or pronoun) separate them with a coordinating conjunction or with commas.

Beds of colorful and long-stemmed flowers adorned the yard.

Beds of colorful, long-stemmed flowers adorned the yard.

Do not, however, use both a comma and a coordinate conjunction to separate coordinate adjectives.

INCORRECT   Beds of colorful, and long-stemmed flowers adorned the yard.

In cases where the adjectives are *cumulative* rather than coordinate, do not use commas. Adjectives are *cumulative* when the one nearer the noun is more closely related to the noun in meaning.

COORDINATE   The job required careful, patient, methodical work. [Each adjective individually modifies the noun *work*.]

COORDINATE   The warm, quiet, fragrant evening put me to sleep. [Each adjective independently modifies the noun *evening*.]

CUMULATIVE   The dark blue fabric appealed to them. [No comma is needed because *dark* modifies *blue* and *blue* modifies *fabric*.]

CUMULATIVE   When she travels, she likes to read fast-paced science fiction novels. [The compound adjective *fast-paced* modifies *science fiction*, and *science fiction* modifies *novels*.]

To check whether you should use commas between adjectives, try putting the word *and* between them or rearranging the order of the adjectives. If you can do either of these things, you need commas between the adjectives.

Consider the previous examples and apply these tests.

EXAMPLE   The dark blue fabric appealed to them.

TEST I   The dark and blue fabric appealed to them. [Adding *and* confuses the meaning; the adjectives are cumulative.]

TEST II   The blue dark fabric appealed to them. [Putting *blue* before *dark* is confusing; *dark blue* makes more sense.]

These tests are not always reliable. (See Chapter 12 for more on adjectives.)

EXERCISE 29–4   **Punctuating Items in a Series**
Add or delete commas as necessary in the following sentences. Example:

> Their favorite pastimes were reading exercising and eating out.
>
> Their favorite pastimes were reading, exercising, and eating out.

1. The party was long loud and enjoyable.
2. Their goals were modest: to win a few games and to have some fun.
3. He was fashionably dressed in a double-breasted pin-striped suit, a starched pure white shirt with a colorful paisley tie and elegant black calfskin loafers.
4. The teachers assigned read and graded the many required papers.
5. We went to the hardware store for paint spackle rollers tray liners and brushes.

29f   Use commas to set off transitional and parenthetical expressions

Transitional expressions include conjunctive adverbs (such as *therefore* and *however*) and other words and expressions used to join sentence elements. **Parenthetical expressions** add supplementary information or digressions and are not essential to the grammatical structure of the sentence. Both transitional and parenthetical expressions are set off from the main clause of the sentence with commas.

It was, in fact, an amazing discovery.

On the other hand, it should not have been so surprising.

Recent studies have suggested that diets that include red wine, surprisingly, and cheese, even more surprisingly, lower one's risk of heart disease.

29g Use commas to set off absolute phrases

An **absolute phrase** modifies an entire independent clause, rather than a particular word or group of words in the clause. An absolute phrase usually consists of a participle and its subject. Absolute phrases may occur anywhere in a sentence. Wherever they occur, they are always set off by commas.

The game being over, the fans headed for the exit ramps.

Her boyfriend, his ardor cooled by her icy demeanor, sat meekly in the rear.

EXERCISE 29–5 Punctuating Transitional and Parenthetical Expressions and Absolute Phrases

Insert commas where necessary in the following sentences. Example:

We went along though with some reservations with the plan.

We went along, though with some reservations, with the plan.

1. Stocks having plunged sharply investors waited cautiously before buying.
2. In the meantime preparations were being made for an offensive.
3. It was furthermore a time of great hope.
4. Their work done it was time to relax.
5. This period of change however also remained a time of continuity.

29h Use commas to set off contrasting elements, *yes* and *no*, direct address, and tag questions

Commas are used to set off contrasting elements, the words *yes* and *no*, expressions of direct address, and tag questions (short questions "tagged on" to statements you make in expressions of direct address).

CONTRASTING ELEMENTS

The boys were willing to work, though not all day long.

The children, not the adults, had the best roles.

YES AND *NO*

Yes, I do want to go to Martha's Vineyard.

No, that will not be an acceptable form of payment.

DIRECT ADDRESS

Friends, Romans, countrymen, lend me your ears.

Please hear me out, Howard.

TAG QUESTIONS

It was not a good movie, was it?

You don't have any aspirin, do you?

EXERCISE 29–6 Punctuating Contrasting Elements, *yes* and *no*, Direct Address, and Tag Questions

Insert commas where necessary in the following sentences. Example:

No it was not the best solution was it Bill?

No, it was not the best solution, was it, Bill?

1. We have to consider the long-range consequences not just the immediate payoff.

2. We were never really in the game were we?

3. Yes indeed this is the way a trip should go.

4. The world has become on the other hand a global village.

5. Do you really think Kim that this is the right decision?

29i   Use commas with dates, addresses, place names, numbers, and titles

Use commas with dates, addresses, place names, and numbers. Use commas to separate personal and professional titles from the name before them.

Dates

Use a comma to separate the day of the month from the year. Also put a comma after the year, unless the year ends the sentence.

The book was published on August 30, 1999, though not released until January 1, 2000.

When dates appear in inverted order, as they often do in British usage, commas are unnecessary. Commas are not needed when a date contains only a month and year.

The book was published on 30 August 1999 and released four months later.

The United States entered the war in December 1941.

Addresses and place names

Use a comma after each part of a place name when written out in a sentence, but do not use a comma directly before or immediately after a ZIP code.

Dover, New Jersey, bears little resemblance to Dover, Delaware.

The address is Mr. D's Music Store, 14 Main Street, Columbus, Ohio 12345.

Numbers

Use commas in numbers of four or more digits.

The book has 3,662 pages.

More than 50,000 fans attended last night's free concert in the park.

Do not use a comma in a date, within street numbers, in telephone numbers, in Social Security numbers, or in ZIP codes.

We have finally arrived at the year 2000.

Our previous address was 3119 Poe St., Berkeley, California 90123.

Please call me at 329-555-6572.

Titles

Use a comma between a name and a title that follows the name. Also use a comma to separate a title from whatever follows it in a sentence. Note that the final period in a title is included before the comma.

Lucia Hernandez, PhD, is the youngest economist on the faculty.

Richard Kim, Jr., has been elected mayor.

EXERCISE 29–7 Punctuating Dates, Addresses, Place Names, Titles, and Numbers
Insert commas where needed in the following sentences. Example:

It is difficult to find a new car that costs less than $10000.

It is difficult to find a new car that costs less than *$10,000.*

1. Philip Weber MD is a graduate of Brown Medical School.

2. The town's population has gone over the 25000 mark.

3. Please send your remittance to 23875 Kissena Boulevard Flushing New York 01234.

4. The referendum was held in April 1999 and new elections were to follow on January 15 2000.

5. Participants are expected from Brussels Belgium and Anchorage Alaska.

 **29j** Use commas with quotations

Use commas to set off quotations from introductory words and from words that identify the source of the quotation. Always place commas before the quotation marks (see 32i–1).

Of Montaigne's essays Emerson said, "Cut these words and they bleed."

"Much madness is divinest sense," wrote Emily Dickinson in one of her best-known poems.

Do not use commas when explanatory words follow a quotation that ends in a question mark or an exclamation point (see 32i–3).

"How could this have happened?" she wondered.

"What an outrageous idea!" he exclaimed.

Commas are also unnecessary following a verb or when quotations are introduced by *that*.

Leo Tolstoy's novel *Anna Karenina* begins "All happy families are alike, but each unhappy family is unhappy in its own way."

John Donne wrote that "no man is an island."

When using an indirect quotation, one that does not repeat a speaker's exact words, do not use a comma.

> Olive Schreiner declared that if women ran governments, wars would be eliminated.

> Montaigne says that he knows no one as well as he knows himself.

EXERCISE 29–8　Using Commas with Quotations

Insert or delete commas as needed in the following sentences. Example:

> Who said "Boredom is the root of all evil"?

> Who said, "Boredom is the root of all evil"?

1. Einstein once remarked "God does not play dice with the universe."
2. What do you think Portia means when she says that "The quality of mercy is not strained"?
3. "The world will little note, nor long remember, what we say here" said Abraham Lincoln in his Gettysburg Address.
4. "Where can I find the registrar's office?", she inquired.
5. Jason asked if we wanted to go to the lake with him.

29k　Use commas to aid comprehension

You may need to use a comma for no other reason than to prevent confusion or misunderstanding.

CONFUSING	Before the game finished the players were celebrating.
REVISED	Before the game finished, the players were celebrating.
CONFUSING	Of twenty five experienced difficulty solving the problem.
REVISED	Of twenty, five experienced difficulty solving the problem.

EXERCISE 29–9　Using Commas to Avoid Confusion

Insert commas where needed in the following sentences. Example:

> For Gloria Joan was a role model.

> For Gloria, Joan was a role model.

1. Unlike Harvard Yale requires no expository writing course.
2. For many flowers are nothing more than pollen sources.

3. Even when they are tired bus drivers need to remain alert and courteous.

4. Those who can do.

5. In grade school subjects are required.

EXERCISE 29–10 Using Commas to Alter Meaning

Explain how the meaning of the following sentences is changed when the commas are deleted.

1. Harold saw Tanya when he arrived, and blushed.

2. The book includes comments from writers Al Hart and Jim Seal, bartenders, and former alcoholics.

3. No, stopping is advised.

4. The Browns' daughter, Janice, majored in engineering.

5. The film was shown in places such as Phoenix and Sacramento, little towns, and villages.

29I   Avoid using unnecessary commas

Commas used unnecessarily can distract or confuse readers. They can also inhibit fluency in writing.

1   Omit commas between subjects and verbs, verbs and objects or complements, and prepositions and their objects

Needless commas cause confusion and disrupt the flow of the sentence.

INCORRECT	The jubilant crowd, welcomed the victorious home team. [comma separates subject and verb]
REVISED	The jubilant crowd welcomed the victorious home team.
INCORRECT	We had decided, to agree on the plan despite our reservations about, one of its major objectives. [comma separates verb and object; comma separates preposition and object]
REVISED	We had decided to agree on the plan despite our reservations about one of its major objectives.

2   Omit commas around restrictive elements

Do not use commas to set off elements that restrict or limit the meaning of the words they refer to (see 29c).

INCORRECT	Jane Austen's novel, *Pride and Prejudice,* is a classic. [The commas suggest, incorrectly, that Austen wrote only one novel.]
REVISED	Jane Austen's novel *Pride and Prejudice* is a classic.
INCORRECT	The props, that the director used, were clever.
REVISED	The props that the director used were clever.
INCORRECT	The prohibition, against smoking, is strictly enforced.
REVISED	The prohibition against smoking is strictly enforced.

3   Omit commas in compound constructions

Do not use a comma before or after a coordinating conjunction that joins two words, phrases, or clauses of a compound construction.

INCORRECT	We should eat quickly, and get ready to leave.
REVISED	We should eat quickly and get ready to leave. [compound verb]
INCORRECT	We saw the bikers race down the hill, and around the pond.
REVISED	We saw the bikers race down the hill and around the pond. [compound prepositional phrases]
INCORRECT	They want an increase in course offerings, and a decrease in class size.
REVISED	They want an increase in course offerings and a decrease in class size. [compound direct objects]

4   Omit commas before the first and last items in a series

Although you need commas between the items in a series, you do not need them before the first and last items.

INCORRECT	The film included, action, sentiment, and humor.
REVISED	The film included action, sentiment, and humor.

INCORRECT	Swimming, tennis, and cycling, were their favorite sports.
REVISED	Swimming, tennis, and cycling were their favorite sports.

Always check your sentences for missing or unnecessary commas. You can use the accompanying checklist to familiarize yourself with the most frequent uses of the comma.

Using Commas

- Use commas to separate independent clauses in compound sentences (29a).

  We may be too tired to study, but we are not too tired to go dancing.
- Place commas after introductory elements (29b).

  In fact, there was no rain that summer.
- Place commas before and after nonrestrictive elements (29c).

  The entire cast, including the children, performed magnificently.
- Use commas between items in a series (29d).

  He spoke of blood, sweat, and tears.
- Use commas with transitional and parenthetical expressions (29f).

  However, the Romans excelled equally in civil engineering.

  The winner, as some expected, was Bill Clinton.
- Use commas to separate quotations from their identifying phrases (34j).

  "No one," he advised, "should underestimate the power of an opponent."

EXERCISE 29–11 Omitting Needless Commas

Eliminate unnecessary commas from the following sentences. Example:

The quilt, that lay on the antique bed, was made by her grandmother.

The quilt that lay on the antique bed was made by her grandmother.

1. At the beginning, and the end of the race a gong is sounded.
2. They said, that there would be plenty of opportunity for advancement.
3. Shakespeare's play, *Hamlet,* is his most famous.
4. The study showed, that some diets can be harmful to one's health.
5. The cross-country skier took long, smooth, strides over the snow.

EXERCISE 29–12   Using Commas

Insert commas where appropriate in the following passage.

> The commas are the most useful and usable of all the stops. It is highly important to put them in place as you go along. If you try to come back after doing a paragraph and stick them in the various spots that tempt you you will discover that they tend to swarm like minnows into all sorts of crevices whose existence you hadn't realized and before you know it the whole long sentence becomes immobilized and lashed up squirming in commas. Better to use them sparingly and with affection precisely when the need for each one arises nicely by itself.
>
> —Lewis Thomas, "Notes on Punctuation"

EXERCISE 29–13   Checking for Commas

Review one of your papers for its use of commas. Use the charts at the beginning and end of this chapter for guidance. Be alert for both missing commas and for unnecessary commas.

30   *Semicolons and Colons*

It is important to learn to distinguish between the semicolon and the colon. Use the *semicolon* to indicate a stop; use the *colon* to signal an addition or to create a sense of expectation.

In some cases both marks of punctuation may be grammatically correct or rhetorically effective. It will be up to you to choose the effect you wish to create with a colon or semicolon.

> We wanted to visit our friends; bad weather, however, forced us to postpone our plans.

> We hoped to see our friends soon: our plans were to visit them the very next day.

Refer to the chart on p. 496 for a summary of when to use a semicolon and colon.

Using the Semicolon and the Colon

Semicolon

- To signal a close link between the ideas in independent clauses (30a–b)
- To separate clauses linked by a conjunctive adverb (30b)
- To separate independent clauses that contain commas (30c)
- To separate long items in a series (30d)

Colon

- To introduce a statement that summarizes, amplifies, or explains a statement made in an independent clause (30f)
- To introduce a list (30g)
- To introduce a long or a formal quotation (30h)
- To introduce appositives (30i)
- To separate a book's title from its subtitle (30j)
- To follow the salutation of a letter (30j)
- To follow the headings in a memo (30j)
- To separate hours from minutes (30j)

Semicolons

Semicolons (;) are used to separate sentence elements, usually independent clauses; they are also used to separate items in a series when those items contain commas; and they are used between clauses linked with a conjunctive adverb. The pause indicated by a semicolon is shorter than a period's full stop but longer than the breathing space of a comma.

30a Use semicolons to signal a close relationship between independent clauses

When you write sentences with closely related independent clauses, use a semicolon between them to signal that relationship. In the following example, the relationship is close because the second clause explains the first.

I refused the prize; I thought the contest rules were unfair.

You may write sentences in which one clause restates another or in which an independent clause expands on or contrasts another. You may use a semicolon instead of a comma and conjunction when the phrasing in the clauses is balanced.

RESTATEMENT   The semicolon indicates something more is coming; the sentence is not yet finished.

EXPANSION   To earn an A in a lab science course, you have to pay the price; that price typically includes many hours performing laboratory experiments.

CONTRAST   The Red Sox have strong pitching and weak hitting; the Mariners have strong hitting and weak pitching.

BALANCE   If you can begin to work on a difficult project, you can build momentum to continue it; if you can sustain your momentum, you will be likely to complete it.

The following example includes two additional clauses that expand the initial independent clause.

> She had come in steerage; she knew not a word of English when she stepped off the horsecar into Madison Street; she was one of the innumerable unsleeping aliens.
>
> —Cynthia Ozick, "The Question of Our Speech"

WRITING HINT   A comma can be used between short independent clauses not joined by a coordinating conjunction. But a semicolon is also correct.

His round face was mournful, his shoulders slumped, his belly sagged.
—Tom Wicker, *A Time to Die*

The train gathered speed; the brakes squeaked; it lurched and stopped.
—Paul Theroux, *The Great Railway Bazaar*

Use a comma to balance clauses that make a comparison.

The more they earned, the less they saved.

The sooner we start, the better we will feel.

30b **Use semicolons between independent clauses linked with a conjunctive adverb or a transitional phrase**

Independent clauses joined by conjunctive adverbs (see 13c–4), such as *however, therefore,* or *moreover,* require a semicolon between them.

They expected the concert to be boring; *however,* they found it completely engaging.

I have been overcharged for these items; *therefore,* I am entitled to a refund.

They will be here on time; *moreover,* they will arrive ready to work.

A semicolon is also required between independent clauses that are linked by a transitional phrase, such as *after all, as a result, at any rate, even so, for example, in fact,* or *on the other hand.*

The president's approval rating dropped ten points; *as a result,* the White House stepped up its media blitz.

The birthrate on soap operas is eight times higher than the U.S. birthrate; *in fact,* it's higher than the birthrate of any developing nation in the world.

WRITING HINT   Be careful not to punctuate conjunctive adverbs and transitional phrases that come at the beginning of independent clauses with a comma before and after. Use commas before and after conjunctive adverbs and transitional phrases only when they occur later in the clause.

They expected the concert to be boring; they found it, *however,* completely engaging.

I have been overcharged for these items; I am entitled, *therefore,* to a refund.

30c Use semicolons to separate long and complex independent clauses and those that contain commas

The use of semicolons makes the long sentence in the following example easy to follow. The ideas are closely related and therefore belong in one sentence; however, the clauses are long and somewhat complicated.

> He was not a young man when we were growing up and he had already suffered many kinds of ruin; in his outrageously demanding and protective way he loved his children, who were black like him, and menaced like him; and all these things sometimes showed in his face when he tried, never to my knowledge with much success, to establish contact with any of us.
>
> —James Baldwin, "Notes of a Native Son"

30d Use semicolons to separate items in a series

You most often separate items in a series with commas (see 29d). However, when the items contain commas or other punctuation, using semicolons to separate them will make your sentences clearer to readers.

> The course objectives included understanding the beliefs of Confucianism, Buddhism, Islam, Judaism, and Christianity; appreciating the cultural values, attitudes, and assumptions associated with those beliefs; and recognizing the diverse ways the world's peoples acknowledge the divine.

Notice that all elements of the series are separated by semicolons even though the last one contains no commas. If any element of a series includes commas within it, all elements of that series must be separated by semicolons.

> As an English major you can expect to read works of many different genres; to write different kinds of papers, including critical analyses and research essays based on your reading; and to present oral reports.

<table>
<tr><td>**30e**</td><td>Avoid semicolon errors</td></tr>
</table>

1   Do not use semicolons to separate an independent clause from a phrase or from a dependent clause

INCORRECT	The birds built a nest; which was protected by the roof.
REVISED	The birds built *a nest, which* was protected by the roof.
INCORRECT	In a corner of the yard, far from the house; grew an oak sapling the children planted.
REVISED	In a corner of the yard, far from the *house, grew* an oak sapling the children planted.

2   Do not use semicolons to introduce a list or a series

Use a colon to introduce a series (see 30g).

| INCORRECT | The documentary described five kinds of intelligence; analytical, social, physical, verbal, and mathematical. |
| REVISED | The documentary described five kinds of intelligence: analytical, social, physical, verbal, and mathematical. |

3   Do not overuse semicolons

Too many semicolons can distract and confuse readers by contributing to choppy and unclear writing.

| OVERUSED | Their trip to Europe included visits to Paris, France; Rome, Italy; Madrid, Spain; and Berlin, Germany; their trip gave them a chance to make many new acquaintances and experience different customs; it also stimulated their interest in learning more about the countries they visited; in fact, upon returning they enrolled in courses in European languages and history. |
| REVISED | Their trip to Europe included visits to Paris, Rome, Madrid, and Berlin. The trip gave them a chance to make many new acquaintances and experience different customs. It stimulated their interest in learning more about the countries they visited; |

in fact, upon returning they enrolled in courses in European languages and history.

Notice how the revised version replaces some semicolons with periods, thus creating separate sentences. You should revise overuse of the semicolon in this way.

EXERCISE 30–1   Punctuating Independent Clauses with the Semicolon

Insert semicolons where necessary in the following paragraph. Example:

A few companies did well most others did not.

A few companies did well; most others did not.

Many small computer companies have been going out of business they are simply unable to survive the drastic price wars. The companies that have survived so far make a superior product they also offer outstanding service. Some of these companies, such as Dell and Compaq, have grown considerably since they started they offer an array of products and services that surpasses those of former industry giants such as IBM. What is happening in the computer industry is similar to what happened in the airline industry a few powerful companies are driving out competition from smaller and less financially secure operations. The short-term consequence is lower prices for consumers the long-term consequence will almost certainly be a price escalation.

EXERCISE 30–2   Using the Semicolon to Separate Clauses Linked with Conjunctive Adverbs

Insert a semicolon where needed in the following sentences. Also insert appropriate commas to set off the conjunctive adverbs. Example:

I did not buy the car instead I leased it.

I did not buy the *car; instead,* I leased it.

1. We knew the lines for the free meals would be long therefore we arrived hours before the food was distributed.

2. The excursion fare was well below the normal price it was not as low as the special weekend fare however.

3. Preparing for the Olympics brought residents of Atlanta together moreover their preparations helped them appreciate their city.

4. They had no desire to go out in the heavy rainstorm nevertheless they felt obliged to fulfill their promise to attend a party with friends.

5. It was a splendid meal indeed it was perhaps the best I have ever had.

EXERCISE 30–3　Punctuating Correctly with Semicolons
Revise the following sentences to correct any misuses of the semicolon. Example:

As far as we could see; nothing would be done now.

As far as we could *see, nothing* would be done now.

1. There were two matters to consider; the cost of the program and its likelihood of success.

2. From among the many suggestions made by workers; management selected two for immediate implementation.

3. Throughout its history; Poland has had to resist aggressors.

4. Four automakers were involved in deliberations; regarding import quotas.

5. Political relations between the United States and Vietnam have a long history; the administrations of FDR, Truman, Eisenhower, JFK, and LBJ had dealings with Vietnam; moreover, the legacy of Vietnam has involved intricate negotiations for subsequent administrations, especially those of Richard Nixon and Jimmy Carter; however, the Reagan, Bush, and Clinton administrations have not been exempt.

Colons

The **colon** (:) is used to introduce statements that recapitulate, summarize, or explain an independent clause. Colons are also used to introduce a list, a quotation, or an appositive. In addition, writers use colons between the titles and subtitles of books; between numbers indicating minutes, hours, and seconds; and in the salutation of a business letter (see 47a).

30f　Use colons to introduce a statement that qualifies a statement in an independent clause

Use colons to introduce summary, amplifying, and explanatory material in a sentence.

She was certain she would win: the stars had indicated it, and she had dreamt about it every night for a week.

It had been a typical day on the job: he set up his waiter station, served throngs of customers, and cleaned up before heading home, exhausted, at midnight.

When an independent clause follows a colon, it is generally not capitalized (see 34a). However, you may use a capital letter to emphasize the importance of the second statement.

http://leo.stcloudstate.edu/
punct/colon.html
Explains the role of the
colon, and offers an extensive
discussion of its uses.

The Economy has only one credo: Anyone can play who's willing to play.

—Fanny Howe, "The Plot Sickens"

30g Use colons to introduce a list

Use a colon to introduce a list only when the words before the colon make up an independent clause.

These are the requirements for the course: faithful attendance, active participation, and timely submission of assignments.

When we cleaned the attic we accumulated a collection of forgotten goods: a prewar sewing machine, broken toys, a bag of marbles, a pile of bottle caps, and a shoe box full of baseball cards.

30h Use colons to introduce long or formal quotations

To introduce a long or formal quotation, or to introduce a quotation formally, use a colon before the quotation.

This is the opening sentence of the story: "It was lunchtime and they were all sitting under the dining tent pretending that nothing had happened."

Whenever a colon follows quoted material, place the colon after the closing quotation marks.

These are the opening words of Sylvia Plath's poem "Mirror": "I am silver and exact. I have no preconceptions."

30i　Use colons to introduce delayed appositives

You can achieve a dramatic stylized effect by using the colon to introduce a delayed appositive.

He wanted only one thing from her: money.

She wanted only one thing before she left: her mother's forgiveness.

30j　Use colons in salutations, memo headings, hours/minutes, titles/subtitles

Use the colon to follow the salutation of a formal letter, to follow the headings in a memo, to separate hours from minutes, and to separate the title of a book from its subtitle.

FORMAL LETTER	Dear Professor Funk:
MEMO HEADINGS	To: Madalyn Stone From: Tony English Re: Sales Estimates
HOURS/MINUTES	6:45 p.m.
TITLE/SUBTITLE	*Emily Dickinson: A Critical Introduction*

30k　Avoid misuse of the colon

Be careful not to misuse the colon. A colon can only follow an independent clause in the situation described in 30i. Do not use a colon after an incomplete sentence or partial statement.

INCORRECT	We bought: milk, bread, cheese, and ice cream.
REVISED	We bought milk, bread, cheese, and ice cream.

A colon is not used after words such as *including* and *such as*.

INCORRECT	This *Handbook* discusses punctuation marks such as: the comma, the colon, and the semicolon.

REVISED	This *Handbook* discusses punctuation marks such as the comma, the colon, and the semicolon.

Do not use a colon after a verb.

INCORRECT	The most important statistic for a pitcher in baseball is: earned run average.
REVISED	The most important statistic for a pitcher in baseball is earned run average.

EXERCISE 30–4   Using the Colon

Insert colons where necessary or delete them where unnecessary. Example:

> Remember one thing above all, look ahead, not back.

> Remember one thing above all: look ahead, not back.

1. The title of this important book is *Foods; Their History and Uses.*
2. Dear Senator Inouye,
3. Three things were necessary for survival food, water, and shelter.
4. We will always remember our first date. We got a flat tire and ran out of gas.
5. The opening words of the poem are: "Once upon a midnight dreary."

EXERCISE 30–5   Writing with the Colon

Write three sentences using colons. Imitate sentences in this chapter, if you wish.

EXERCISE 30–6   Using Colons and Semicolons

Punctuate the following sentence pairs by replacing the period after the first sentence with a colon or semicolon. Explain your choices. Example:

> We felt exhilarated. Our proposal had been entirely accepted.

> We felt exhilarated: our proposal had been entirely accepted. [replace period with colon, since second clause explains first]

1. The sight held awesome wonders. Power, beauty, grace, and violence.
2. We won first prize in the drawing. The new red Miata was ours.
3. Some were satisfied. Others were not.

4. In Rome and Florence, Italians lunch on McDonald's hamburgers. In Boston and New York, Americans often lunch on pasta.

5. Faulkner's prose is copious, sensuous, and sonorous. Hemingway's writing is spare, taut, and generally stripped of ornamentation.

31 *The Apostrophe*

The **apostrophe's** (') primary use is to indicate possession. In nouns, possession is shown either by a phrase beginning with the word *of* (*the sins of the father*) or with an apostrophe and an *-s* ending (*the Smith's house, the day's work*).

The apostrophe is also used to form the plurals of letters (*dot your* i*'s*), numbers (two 5's for a 10), and symbols (&'s). And the apostrophe is used in contractions to show the omission of a letter or number (*it's* for it is; *a '91 Chevy*).

31a Use apostrophes to form the possessive case of nouns and indefinite pronouns

The possessive case indicates ownership or possession (see 11c).

1 Singular nouns or indefinite pronouns

Add an apostrophe and *-s* to form the possessive case of singular nouns or indefinite pronouns.

Georgia O'Keeffe's paintings of flowers are among her most beautiful.

It was really *nobody's* fault.

2 Singular nouns ending in *-s*

For a singular noun ending in *-s,* most writers add *-'s* to show possession.

The expert *witness's* testimony seemed convincing.

Yeats's book *Collected Poems* was first published by Macmillan in 1939.

3   Plural nouns

Indicate the possessive case of plural nouns by adding an apostrophe and *-s* for words not ending in *-s*.

> http://www.ex.ac.uk/ ~SEGLea/psy6002/ apostrophes.html
> Offers a quick overview of correct use of the apostrophe.

The *children's* books of E. B. White have become classics of our literature.

The Feminine Mystique by Betty Friedan helped launch the *women's* movement.

For plural nouns ending in *-s*, add only the apostrophe.

The three defense *witnesses'* testimony held up well under cross-examination.

The *girls'* clothing section is on the second floor.

4   Compound words and phrases

Add an apostrophe and *-s* to the last word in compound words and phrases.

My *father-in-law's* trips to Italy, France, and Ireland have provided some of his most memorable dining experiences.

William Carpenter II's office is at 50 Ridge Street.

It was *nobody else's* affair.

5   Joint possession for two or more nouns

Add an apostrophe and *-s* to the last noun when two or more nouns are joined by *and* to show joint possession.

David and Hilda's new condominium has been tastefully furnished. [David and Hilda own the condominium jointly.]

Laurel and Hardy's comedy routines illustrate classic slapstick. [Laurel and Hardy perform as a team.]

6   Individual possession for two or more nouns

Add an apostrophe and *-s* to each noun when two or more nouns are joined by *and* to show individual possession.

Lee's and Kai's offices are equipped with computers and telephones. [Lee and Kai have separate offices similarly equipped.]

The administration's and the faculty's positions on the issue began to coalesce. [The two different positions started to come together.]

EXERCISE 31–1   Using Apostrophes with Singular and Plural Noun Possessives

Insert an apostrophe or an *-s* where necessary to form the correct possessive case of the words in parentheses. Example:

It had to be (somebody) coat.

It had to be somebody's coat.

1. The (president) proposals were modified by Congress.

2. It was one of (Vince Gill) best vocal performances.

3. Students sometimes disregard their (teachers) advice.

4. (Andrew and Miguel) grades were the two highest in the class.

5. We could not decide whether to eat at (D.J. or Sabatino).

31b   Do not use an apostrophe to form the possessives of personal pronouns and adjectives

Possessive pronouns (see 11c–3) and possessive adjectives (see 12h) do not use apostrophes. Be careful not to confuse possessive pronouns and possessive adjectives with contractions (see 31c).

Pronoun	Possessive Forms	
he	his	[*not* his']
she	her, hers	[*not* her's, hers']
it	its	[*not* it's, its']
we	our, ours	[*not* our's, ours']
you	your, yours	[*not* your's, yours']
they	their, theirs	[*not* their's, theirs']
who	whose	[*not* who's, whos']

Be especially careful to distinguish between *its,* the possessive form, and *it's,* a contraction meaning *it is* or *it has.* Similarly, distinguish between *whose,* the possessive form, and *who's,* a contraction for *who is.*

FAULTY   The bank is currently reviewing *it's* mortgage lending policy.

REVISED   The bank is currently reviewing *its* mortgage lending policy.

FAULTY   The team, *who's* owner is out of town, won three straight games.

REVISED   The team, *whose* owner is out of town, won three straight games.

EXERCISE 31–2   **Selecting the Correct Form of Possessive Pronouns and Possessive Adjectives**

Underline the appropriate possessive form in each of the following sentences. Example:

The book was his, not (*hers*/*her's*).

1. The fault was (*yours*/*yours'*) entirely.
2. I could not decide (*whose*/*who's*) argument was more persuasive.
3. (*Its*/*It's*) owner will turn up eventually.
4. (*Theirs'*/*Theirs*) was not the only valuable suggestion.
5. (*His'*/*His*) time will come.

31c   Use the apostrophe in contractions and to indicate missing letters, numbers, or words

A **contraction** is a shortened form of a word or a group of words. Contractions are two-word combinations that use apostrophes to signal that letters have been omitted from one of the words. Although contractions are common in speaking and informal writing, you should avoid them in academic writing—except in cases when you wish to establish a less formal tone. Consider your audience, your purpose, and your writing occasion before deciding whether to use contractions.

The accompanying chart lists the most frequently used contractions.

Common Contractions			
ORIGINAL	**CONTRACTION**	**ORIGINAL**	**CONTRACTION**
cannot	can't	let us	let's
could not	couldn't	she is, she has	she's
did not	didn't	should not	shouldn't
do not	don't	they are	they're
he is, he has	he's	was not	wasn't
has not	hasn't	we are	we're
have not	haven't	who is, who has	who's
I am	I'm	will not	won't
I would	I'd	would not	wouldn't
it is	it's	you are	you're

Contractions are also used to indicate omissions of letters and numbers in some common phrases.

five of the clock   five o'clock
class of 1999   class of '99

EXERCISE 31–3   **Using the Apostrophe with Contractions**

Spell out the words for each contraction in the following sentences. Example:

I would've come if only I'd known.

I would *have* come if only I *had* known.

1. It's only one of many topics we need to discuss.

2. There wasn't a single example to illustrate their idea.

3. Do you really believe she doesn't care?

4. If they won't come, then we'll have to go without them.

5. Let's see what we can do about it tomorrow.

WRITING HINT   You can use the apostrophe to reflect dialect speech patterns when writing fiction, poetry, essays, or drama. Notice how the apostrophes in the following poem convey the way the speaker, a mother, talks to her son.

> Life for me ain't been no crystal stair. . . .
> But . . . I'se been a-climbin' on,
> And reachin' landin's,
> And turnin' corners,
> And sometimes goin' in the dark.
> Where there ain't been no light.
> So boy, don't you turn back.
> Don't you set down on the steps
> 'Cause you finds it's kinder hard.
>
> —Langston Hughes, "Mother to Son"

31d Use the apostrophe to form the plural of letters, numbers, symbols, and words used as words

My handwriting is hard to decipher because I rarely cross my *t*'s, and my *a*'s sometimes look like *o*'s.

The *1590's* can be designated the decade of the English sonnet, the *1950's* the decade of the folk song.

There were many ***'s scattered throughout the document.

There are no *if's*, *and's*, or *but's* about it.

Be aware that you can form the plural of years and symbols with or without the apostrophe: 1990's, 1990s; #'s, #s. However, use whichever style you choose consistently.

31e Avoid using the apostrophe incorrectly

Be careful not to insert apostrophes where they do not belong. The list on p. 512 details the common apostrophe errors and how to correct them.

Revising Apostrophe Errors

Do not use an apostrophe with present tense verbs.

INCORRECT	Stress increases' a person's susceptibility to illness.
REVISED	Stress increases a person's susceptibility to illness.

Do not use an apostrophe to make a nonpossessive noun plural.

INCORRECT	Research studies' have repeatedly demonstrated a link between stress and the onset of illness.
REVISED	Research studies have repeatedly demonstrated a link between stress and the onset of illness.

Do not use an apostrophe before -*s* when indicating the plural possessive of a noun. Use an -*s* followed by an apostrophe for plural possessives.

INCORRECT	The general public continues to follow researcher's efforts to further investigate this link.
REVISED	The general public continues to follow researchers' efforts to further investigate this link.

EXERCISE 31–4 Using Apostrophes in Plurals
Use the plural of each of the following in a complete sentence.

1. i
2. z
3. if
4. but
5. 1980 (the decade)

EXERCISE 31–5 Using the Apostrophe to Indicate Possession
Change each phrase in parentheses to a possessive noun. Example:

The films (of Peter Greenaway) are bizarre.

Peter Greenaway's films are bizarre.

1. The attitude (of the participants) bordered on hostility.
2. The goal (of the team) was to win 75 percent of its games.

3. The causes (of the war) should be considered in light of the previous political and economic circumstances (of the century).

4. The power (of the god) was believed to be such that neither sun nor stars would shine without his assistance.

5. The vacations (of the Webers and the Hammonds) were both disrupted by the political instability in Greece.

EXERCISE 31–6   Revising Apostrophe Errors

Supply all missing apostrophes in the following passage.

> Shoppings function as a form of therapy is widely appreciated. You dont really need, lets say, another sweater. You need the feeling of power that comes with buying or not buying it. You need the feeling that someone wants something you have even if its just your money. To get the benefit of shopping, you neednt actually purchase the sweater, any more than you have to marry every man you flirt with. . . .
>
> But even shopping for blue jeans at Bobs Surplus on Main Street—no frills, bare bones shopping—is an event in the life of the spirit. Once again I have to come to terms with the fact that I will never look good in Levis. Much as I want to be mainstream, I never will be.
>
> —Phyllis Rose, "Shopping and Other Spiritual Adventures in America Today"

32   *Quotation Marks*

Quotation marks, used in pairs (" ") at the beginning and end of a quotation, and used singly (' ') in quotes within quotes, tell your audience that certain words have been borrowed from another source. For example, *Abraham Lincoln once said that "a house divided against itself cannot stand."* Quotation marks also set off titles, definitions, and words used in certain ways (e.g., to indicate irony). For advice on how to use quotation marks with other punctuation, refer to the section listed in the chart on p. 514. See also 40i on using quotations in research writing.

Directory for Using Quotation Marks with Other Punctuation

- With commas (29j)
- With brackets (33c-2)
- With ellipses (33d)
- With capital letters (34b)
- With semicolons and colons (32i-2)
- With question marks, exclamation points, and dashes (32i-3)

32a   Use quotation marks for direct quotations

Direct quotations record the exact words of a source, whether those words are spoken or written. It is important to record the quotation verbatim, exactly as it appears in the original source.

Do not use quotation marks for indirect quotations, those that do not record the exact words of a source.

INDIRECT   The coach said that she would accept no excuse for sloppy play.

DIRECT   The coach said, "I will accept no excuse for sloppy play."

32b   Use single quotation marks for quotes within quotes

When quoting a source directly, place the quotation inside double quotation marks.

> Albert Einstein once said, "Imagination is more important than knowledge."

Single quotation marks are used when you enclose one quotation within another. Double quotation marks appear at the opening and closing of a quotation, but any quotes within quotes take single quotation marks.

In one of his essays, Russell Baker humorously remarks, "I know what 'the price has been adjusted' means in New Age Babble. It means 'price is going up.'"

> USAGE NOTE   British practice in handling quotation marks is the opposite of the American convention. Single quotes are used for normally quoted material and double quotation marks for quotes within quotes.

32c   Set off lengthy quoted passages

For quoted passages that exceed four typed lines in your paper, begin a new line and indent ten spaces from the left margin for each line of the quotation. This format, called block quotation, does not require quotation marks because the blocked passage is set off visually from the rest of your text.

In Culture and Truth, Renato Rosaldo explains why the topic of culture is so important to Americans today:

> These days questions of culture seem to touch a nerve because they quite quickly become anguished questions of identity. Academic debates about multicultural education similarly slip effortlessly into the animating ideological conflicts of this multicultural nation. How can the United States both respect diversity and find unity?

(For more on using block quotations, see Chapter 40 on research.)

32d   Use quotation marks with poetry

Quote poetry as you would prose. Separate the lines of poetry with slashes. Include a space before and after each slash.

The dramatist Lorraine Hansberry derived the title of her best-known play, *A Raisin in the Sun*, from a poem by Langston Hughes. In "Dream Deferred" Hughes asks, "What happens to a dream deferred? / Does it dry up / like a raisin in the sun?"

When your poetry quotation exceeds three lines, indent the lines of the poem ten spaces from the left margin of your text. Reproduce the formatting of the poem as closely as possible. Do not use quotation marks around the block quotation.

> In one of his most engaging poems, "Waiting Table," Kraft Rompf describes how waiters will do whatever is necessary for a tip from their customers.
>
> > But for a
> > tip—for a tip, for a tip
> > I would work so very, very
> > hard, and so gladly let
> > them shine into my soul,
> > and bow to them and laugh
> > with them and sing. I would
> > gladly give them everything.

32e Use quotation marks for dialogue

When you quote conversations or dialogue, enclose the words of each speaker in double quotation marks. Indicate changes in speaker by beginning a new paragraph. This will make it easier for your readers to follow the dialogue.

> "Will you have lime juice or lemon squash?" Macomber asked.
> "I'll have a gimlet," Robert Wilson told him.
> "I'll have a gimlet too. I need something," Macomber's wife said.
>
> —Ernest Hemingway, "The Short Happy Life of Francis Macomber"

WRITING HINT When writing essays based on personal experience, try to include some dialogue, which you can set off with quotation marks. Using direct speech, or dialogue, in your narrative essays brings readers more immediately into the scene or situation you are describing.

32f Use quotation marks to enclose titles and definitions

When referring to titles of short poems, short stories, articles, essays, songs, sections or chapters of books, or episodes of television and radio programs, enclose the titles in quotation marks.

At nineteen Adrienne Rich wrote the poem "Aunt Jennifer's Tigers."

Katherine Anne Porter's short story "Rope" describes a married couple's escalating argument and its eventual resolution.

Both *Business Week* and *Time* once ran articles entitled "The Mommy Track."

George Orwell's "Politics and the English Language" is one of the most frequently reprinted twentieth-century essays.

"Mrs. Robinson" was one of Simon and Garfunkel's most popular songs.

The best-known chapter in Loren Eiseley's *The Immense Journey* is entitled "How Flowers Changed the World."

For the titles of longer works, such as long poems, plays, and novels, use italics (or underlining) rather than quotation marks (see 35a on italics).

Definitions can be set off with quotation marks, though underlining or italicizing them is more common. Italicize the original language and use quotation marks for the translation.

The Italian words *la dolce vita* can be translated *"the sweet life."*

32g   Use quotation marks for words used in special ways

Use quotation marks for words used ironically.

My growing brother's "little lunch" consisted of an eight-ounce steak, two baked potatoes, a half-gallon of milk, and a quart of ice cream.

Use quotation marks around any invented words.

Nobody can apply for a job these days—or interface with a personnel recruiter in the hopes of impacting on his bottom line—without a degree in "bizbuzz," the jargon that prioritizes the career path of the rising young ballpark figurer.

—William Safire, "Bizbuzz"

Words referred to as words can be italicized (underlined) or placed within quotation marks. Whichever method you choose, use it consistently.

INCONSISTENT	The words imply and infer are frequently confused. So are "affect" and "effect."
CONSISTENT	The words "imply" and "infer" are frequently confused. So are "affect" and "effect."

32h   Avoid common misuses of quotation marks

Avoid using quotation marks merely to emphasize particular words or phrases. Also, do not use quotation marks around slang or other forms of colloquial language (see 26c). In both cases, the quotation marks call undue attention to words, which can be better emphasized by careful word choice and effective word order.

MISUSED	Theirs was not the most "exciting" of relationships, but at least it was "stable."
REVISED	Theirs was not the most exciting of relationships, but at least it was stable.
MISUSED	Every October I go to Vermont to see the "totally awesome" foliage.
REVISED	Every October I go to Vermont to see the spectacular foliage.

32i   Follow established conventions for using quotation marks with other punctuation

You will often need to use quotation marks with other punctuation marks. The following guidelines explain how to use quotation marks with periods, commas, semicolons, colons, question marks, exclamation points, and dashes.

1   Periods and commas

Periods and commas usually appear immediately before closing quotation marks.

"It was not the first time this happened," she said. "Nor will it be the last."

For sentences that end with a parenthetical citation of a source (e.g., a page number or an author and page number), place the period after the citation. (For more information on punctuating parenthetical citations, bibliographies, and Works Cited lists, see Chapters 43 and 44 on research writing.)

INCORRECT	In his book *The Great War and Modern Memory*, Paul Fussell describes the German trenches as "efficient, clean, pedantic, and permanent." (45)

INCORRECT	In his book *The Great War and Modern Memory*, Paul Fussell describes the German trenches as "efficient, clean, pedantic, and permanent." (45).
REVISED	In his book *The Great War and Modern Memory*, Paul Fussell describes the German trenches as "efficient, clean, pedantic, and permanent" (45).

2 Semicolons and colons

Semicolons and colons appear immediately after closing quotation marks.

Some thought it necessary to engage in what George Orwell describes as "doublespeak"; most, however, saw no reason for it.

George Orwell coined the term "doublespeak": language used hypocritically to give a false impression, usually an opposite impression of what is true.

> USAGE NOTE   Unlike American conventions, British publications place colons and semicolons before the closing quotation marks rather than after.

3 Question marks, exclamation points, and dashes

If a question mark, exclamation point, or dash is part of the quotation, place it before closing quotation marks. If a mark of punctuation is not part of the quotation, place it after closing quotation marks.

PART OF QUOTATION

"Did you call?" he asked.

"Leave him alone!" we shouted.

"If you do, I'll—" she warned.

NOT PART OF QUOTATION

Do you remember the story "The Most Dangerous Game"?

I loved the *Seinfeld* episode "The Raincoat"!

"Get with it"—that's an expression I just can't stand.

EXERCISE 32–1   Using Quotation Marks

Supply quotation marks where they are needed in the following sentences. Example:

> Willa Cather's short story Paul's Case is one of her finest works.

> Willa Cather's short story "Paul's Case" is one of her finest works.

1. The last lines of Shakespeare's Sonnet 29 are For thy sweet love rememb'red such wealth brings, / That then I scorn to change my state with kings.

2. Franz Schubert's song The Trout is based on a poem by Heinrich Heine.

3. Smith and Moore acknowledged that a cure for cancer may never be found.

4. Suarez and O'Rourke write, even under the best of circumstances a relatively high rate of recidivism exists.

5. The words amount and number are sometimes confused with each other.

EXERCISE 32–2   Revising Use of Quotation Marks

Revise each of the following sentences to supply missing quotation marks, eliminate unnecessary ones, or move those incorrectly placed. Example:

> "In the last episode of *Dallas*", the instructor remarked, "we can see the major themes of the show reflected".

> "In the last episode of *Dallas*," the instructor remarked, "we can see the major themes of the show reflected."

1. You could hear the fear in his voice when he asked, How is she?

2. What is the final word in Walt Whitman's "When I Heard the Learn'd Astronomer?"

3. How many times have you been told to "stop and smell the roses?"

4. The title of the popular '60s "hit" song is "Where Have All the Flowers Gone?".

5. In her article The End of Reading, Melinda Melendez argues that "visual" and "oral" literacy have already replaced the "printed" word.

EXERCISE 32–3   Supplying Marks of Punctuation

Revise the following sentences by inserting commas, periods, question marks, exclamation points, colons, and semicolons where they belong. Example:

"It was not the time for it" he said.

"It was not the time for it," he said.

1. "Please be ready on cue with your lines" said the director.

2. Who has the line "If that's how you feel, it's time I left"

3. It was Annie Dillard, not Joan Didion, who wrote "Living Like Weasels"

4. What year did Robert Frost write "The Road Not Taken"

5. Did Lewis Thomas write an essay called "On Punctuation"

The accompanying chart summarizes the rules for using quotation marks in writing.

Using Quotation Marks

Use quotation marks
- For direct quotations and for quotes within quotes
- For titles of short works
- For dialogue and definitions
- For words used ironically

Place quotation marks
- After periods and commas
- Before semicolons and colons
- After question marks, exclamation points, and dashes that are part of the quotation
- Before question marks, exclamation points, and dashes that are not part of the quotation

Do *not* use quotation marks
- For indirect quotations
- For titles of long works
- For words you want to emphasize
- For long block quotations (five or more prose lines; four or more poetry lines)

Note: For guidance on using quotations in your writing, see the following sections of the *Handbook:*

• Quotations versus summaries and paraphrases (40d-1–3)
• Introducing quotations into your writing (40d-5 and 40i-1)
• Citing sources for quotations (40j and 43a)
• Avoiding plagiarism when you include quotations (40j)

EXERCISE 32–4   Using Quotation Marks
Add quotation marks where necessary.

It is a complex fate to be an American, Henry James observed, and the principal discovery an American writer makes in Europe is just how complex this fate is. America's history, her aspirations, her peculiar triumphs, her even more peculiar defeats, and her position in the world—yesterday and today—are all so profoundly and stubbornly unique that the very word America remains a new almost completely undefined, and extremely controversial proper noun. No one in the world seems to know exactly what it describes, not even we motley millions who call ourselves Americans.

—James Baldwin, "The Discovery of What It Means to Be An American"

33   *Other Punctuation Marks*

Like the punctuation marks discussed in Chapters 28–32, those explained in this chapter—dashes, parentheses, brackets, ellipses, and slashes—help writers express their meaning clearly and emphatically. Using these punctuation marks effectively will also help you vary the tone of your writing.

33a   Using the dash

The **dash** (—), whether used singly or in pairs, allows you to interrupt a sentence to insert nonessential information. Although dashes can appear anywhere in a sentence, pairs of dashes often occur near the middle and single dashes at the end of sentences.

PAIR OF DASHES   Television brought the Vietnam War—mostly its daily battles and body counts—into our living rooms.

SINGLE DASH   I was enthralled with the skeletal models of the two biggest dinosaurs—the brontosaurus and the diplodocus.

With most typewriters and word processors you make a dash by combining two unspaced hyphens (--). Do not put a space before, between, or after the hyphens. Many word processing programs automatically convert this to an em dash.

1   Use dashes to insert an interrupting comment

Use dashes to insert an interrupting comment, whether for illustration, explanation, or emphasis.

ILLUSTRATION

I remember a day in class when he leaned far forward in his characteristic pose—the pose of a man about to impart a secret—and croaked, "If you don't know how to pronounce a word, say it loud!"

—E. B. White, "Will Strunk"

EXPLANATION

It is a serious matter to shoot a working elephant—it is comparable to destroying a huge and costly piece of machinery—and obviously one ought not to do it if it can possibly be avoided.

—George Orwell, "Shooting an Elephant"

Computer Tip

Using Dashes

Most recent word processing programs allow you to use different kinds of dashes. A dash, as you may know, is not a hyphen (-). The shorter type of dash, which is wider than a hyphen, is called an en dash because it is approximately the width of the letter N. The longer em dash is the width of the letter M. Use an en dash for a span, as between times: 11:00–12:15; use an em dash for a parenthetical comment—like this one—when you write.

EMPHASIS

During the "working" day, she labored beside—not behind—my father in the fields.

—Alice Walker, *In Search of Our Mothers' Gardens*

2 Use dashes to indicate a shift in tone, a hesitation in speech, or a break in thought

SHIFT IN TONE

The engaged girls—how many of them there seem to be!—flash their rings and tangle their ankles in their long New Look skirts.

—Cynthia Ozick, "Washington Square, 1946"

HESITATION IN SPEECH

"Don't—don't go," he pleaded.

BREAK IN THOUGHT

She began to see a way out, but then—nothing.

3 Use dashes to introduce or comment on a list

INTRODUCING A LIST

He loved everything about his room—the quiet space, the way light filtered through its tiny windows, the memorabilia on the walls.

COMMENTING ON A LIST

Honesty, decency, integrity, generosity—these were the ideals by which she desired to live.

4 Use dashes to set off parenthetical expressions within parenthetical expressions

The architecture of Versailles, Louis XIV's resplendent "country" palace—originally a hunting lodge—and primary seat of the royal court, provided every luxury except plumbing.

A colon can also be used to insert an explanation or introduce a list. But the dash is less formal than the colon (see 30g). The dash marks a sharp, pronounced break in the continuity of a sentence. Use dashes sparingly in academic writing, since heavy use of dashes can create fragmented writing that is difficult to read.

EXERCISE 33–1   Using Dashes

Put dashes where they belong in the following sentences. Some sentences may be correct as written. Example:

> I will arrive at least I will try to arrive before noon.
>
> I will arrive—*at least I will try to arrive*—before noon.

1. My attendance at meals may be somewhat haphazard for six months or so I will not adhere to any kind of schedule.

2. Though the emphasis was on exercise hiking, swimming, running we had plenty of time to relax.

3. The army doctors would put a strap around your head, clamp some sort of instrument over your eyes, and then stick a hose into your ear and pump cold water into your ear canal.

4. I took to calling at Clay's every few days it is simply a pleasant place to be.

5. It was to be honest a complete fiasco.

EXERCISE 33–2   Writing with Dashes

Use dashes to combine each pair of sentences into a single, concise sentence. You may need to add, drop, or change some words. Example:

> Reena decided to quit her job and look for a better one. It was a brave decision.
>
> Reena decided to quit her job—*a brave decision*—and look for a better one.

1. It rained all night at Seven Islands but the rain tapered off in the early morning to drizzle and mist. It rained heavily and steadily.

2. Darwin was far from being an atheist, but he was deeply puzzled by this enormous multiplicity of forms. He had, after all, taken a degree in divinity from Cambridge.

3. All of the committees went to work immediately on the project. The committees were finance, program, and local arrangements.

4. The faculty, the students, the staff were all opposed. They were opposed to the provost's decision to curtail library hours.

5. Both the streets and the lanes were paved with the same material. They were paved with tough black mud in wet times, deep dust in dry.

EXERCISE 33–3   Writing Sentences with Dashes

Write five sentences of your own that contain dashes. Include at least two sentences with pairs of dashes. You can, if you wish, use example sentences from 33a as models for your sentences.

EXERCISE 33–4   Using Dashes

Punctuate the following passage using dashes where necessary.

> Her day began before sunup, and did not end until late at night. There was never a moment for her to sit down, undisturbed, to unravel her own private thoughts; never a time from interruption by work or the noisy inquiries of her children. And yet, it is to my mother and all our mothers who were not famous that I went in search of the secret of what has fed that muzzled and often mutilated, but vibrant, creative spirit that the black woman has inherited, and that pops out in wild and unlikely places to this day.
>
> —Alice Walker, "In Search of Our Mothers' Gardens"

33b   Using parentheses

Parentheses ( ) typically enclose words, phrases, and clauses of secondary importance to a sentence. They are also used to enclose numbers and letters used in lists. Parentheses are often used with other punctuation, including periods, commas, question marks, and exclamation points.

1   Use parentheses to enclose nonessential explanatory information

Nonessential explanatory information may amplify, specify, exemplify, or otherwise expand what precedes it.

AMPLIFY

The author's first novel (written on a summer fishing trip in Vermont) was excessively self-indulgent and almost entirely autobiographical.

SPECIFY

Beethoven's middle period (1800–15) is the source of many of his most famous and most moving works, including the Razumovsky Quartets (opus 59) and the fifth and sixth symphonies (opus 67 and opus 68, respectively).

EXEMPLIFY

Although other books had occasioned court battles (*Ulysses,* for example), Lawrence's *Lady Chatterly's Lover* achieved the greatest notoriety.

2   Use parentheses to enclose numbers and letters within lists

We can isolate four major areas for investigation: (1) social; (2) economic; (3) political; (4) environmental.

Parentheses can also be used to restate a spelled-out number, as is often done in business and legal writing; to enclose a date, especially when identifying the year of a work's publication or first performance; and to enclose a parenthetical citation (see Chapters 43 and 44).

The bill is due in nineteen (19) days.

Kate Chopin's *The Awakening* (1904) was one of the first feminist novels.

Socrates has been considered both Plato's teacher and his nemesis (Vlastos 24).

3   Use parentheses carefully with other punctuation

Periods

Place a period inside a closing parenthesis when the material inside the parentheses is a complete sentence and when the parenthetical sentence is not enclosed within another complete sentence. (When a complete sentence is enclosed within another complete sentence, do not use a period.) When the material inside the parentheses is not a complete sentence, place the period outside the closing parenthesis. For additional information on end punctuation (including punctuating with periods), see Chapter 28.

Commas

A comma may come after the closing parenthesis, but not before the opening parenthesis.

Even though it did not attain television's highest ratings for a sitcom's final episode (*M*A*S*H* achieved that distinction), the final episode of *Cheers* was watched by millions.

Question marks and exclamation points

Place question marks and exclamation points before the closing parenthesis if the material in parentheses is a question or an exclamation.

We tried to recall the mathematical formulas (but how could we possibly remember them all?) as we prepared to answer the test questions.

Our laughter (so deep was our joy!) turned to tears.

Quotation marks

If all of the words requiring quotation marks occur within parentheses, place the quotation marks within the parentheses as well.

Richard Selzer wrote an essay ("The Masked Marvel") about a famous wrestler who later became one of Selzer's medical patients.

Be careful not to overuse parentheses because, like dashes, parentheses can break up the continuity of your writing.

WRITING HINT   The choice of commas, dashes, or parentheses depends on how you want to be understood. Prefer commas most of the time, use dashes to signal a striking interruption, and use parentheses to enclose information that is more a helpful courtesy than an essential part of your message. But in many instances, commas, dashes, and parentheses are interchangeable. The choice of one or the other necessarily will change the emphasis of a statement, but no one choice will be more correct than another.

Choosing Dashes, Parentheses, or Commas

Dashes, parentheses, and commas can all be used to set off nonessential information, including parenthetical expressions. Ordinarily, dashes are the most emphatic way to set off such expressions and parentheses the least emphatic. The following considers a sentence from Alice Walker's "In Search of Our Mothers' Gardens," first as she wrote it—with dashes—then with parentheses and commas in their place.

(continued)

- **Dashes** initially create a strong pause and heavy emphasis (33a).

  They dreamed dreams that no one knew—not even themselves, in any coherent fashion—and saw visions no one could understand.

- **Parentheses** downplay the interrupting effect of the parenthetical information, giving it the character of an aside (33b).

  They dreamed dreams that no one knew (not even themselves, in any coherent fashion) and saw visions no one could understand.

- **Commas** simply include the parenthetical information. Commas are the least interruptive way to include parenthetical information (29f).

  They dreamed dreams that no one knew, not even themselves, in any coherent fashion, and saw visions no one could understand.

Avoid using more than one set of dashes or parentheses in a single sentence—though you may try including one set of each (along with a set of commas) in a single sentence.

For lunch try a fruit salad—say, cottage cheese, grapes, bananas, orange sections, and strawberries (you can substitute melon balls if you're prone to hives)—and see how satisfying it can be.

—Claire Cook, *Line by Line*

EXERCISE 33–5   Practice with Parentheses

Add any parentheses that would be either helpful or necessary in the following sentences. Example:

Clearly not a historic occasion or even an event of much significance, it was fun, nonetheless.

Clearly not a historic occasion (*or even an event of much significance*), it was fun, nonetheless.

1. They learned that many creative artists, directors and choreographers, for example, had been invited to participate in the conference.

2. An astonishing variety of items, power tools, underwear, office furniture, buttons, even bicycles, could be ordered from the Sears catalog.

3. Some of the possibilities included: 1 a sales tax, 2 a sin tax, 3 a value-added tax, and 4 an increased income tax.

4. Claude Raines once starred in an unusual film *The Invisible Man,* based on the H. G. Wells novel.

5. The most vocal of the protesters were those from Mothers against Drunk Driving MADD.

EXERCISE 33–6 Selecting Dashes or Parentheses

Replace commas in the following sentences with dashes or parentheses where appropriate.

1. The Reagan proposal was, not surprisingly, extremely favorable to business.

2. He had long suspected that the three candidates, LaRue, Johnson, and Hirsch, might split the vote and imperil a woman's chance to win the election.

3. The Central Park concert, already interrupted twice by rain, was postponed indefinitely.

4. Many instructors believe in the efficacy of freewriting, a kind of informal, exploratory writing, as a way to help students discover what they think.

5. Some outstanding actors, Robert Redford and Paul Newman among them, have shared star billing in at least one film.

33c Using brackets

Brackets [ ] enclose parenthetical elements already within parentheses—they are parentheses within parentheses. Brackets are also used around words inserted within a quotation.

1 Use brackets to enclose parenthetical material within parentheses

The overwhelming concern (at least according to EPA [Environmental Protection Agency] officials) was that the oil spill be contained.

As an introduction to the subject (Freud's psychological theories [especially his dream theory] and other influential ideas), Calvin Hall's *A Primer of Freudian Psychology* is compact and useful.

2   Use brackets to enclose words inserted into quotations

To have a direct quote make logical or grammatical sense, you some-times need to replace words in the quote. Indicate this replacement by putting brackets around the new word.

According to Ortega, "[Suarez] possessed [charisma] to an extraordinary degree."

As Allen Waters has noted, "Without question, the most valuable player in the history of the franchise [the New York Yankees] has been Babe Ruth."

Use the word *sic* (which means "thus") in brackets generally to indi-cate an error in punctuation, spelling, grammar, or usage in the quoted passage. *Sic* tells the reader that the error is in the original and is not your mistake.

E. T. Smith writes, "Only two American families have contributed more than one U.S. President: the Adams and Rosevelt [sic] families."

EXERCISE 33–7   **Using Brackets**
Insert into the parenthetical passages you created in Exercise 33–5 an occasional clarifying word or detail. Put the words or details in brackets.

EXERCISE 33–8   **Using Brackets for Clarification**
Assume you are quoting the following statement and want to clarify the scien-tific terms for your readers. Use brackets to add the information that the Meso-zoic era occurred about 180 million years ago, the Miocene epoch about 25 mil-lion years ago.

Dinosaurs lived during the Mesozoic era. Dinotheres lived during the Miocene epoch and, like the dinosaurs, are now extinct.

33d   Using ellipses

Ellipses, three equally spaced periods (. . .), usually signify that words have been omitted from a direct quotation. They may also indicate a pause or hesitation the same way a dash does (see 33a).

1 Use ellipses to indicate pause or hesitation

PAUSE   What I'm looking for is . . .another chance.

HESITATION   And the winner of this year's award for best picture . . . is . . .
              Schindler's List.

2 Use ellipses with quotations

When you incorporate directly quoted material into an essay, you may occasionally want to use only a portion of a passage. If the part you want to quote includes words from different sections of the passage, but not the entire passage, you must indicate the omitted words with ellipses.

When an ellipsis falls within a sentence, each of the three periods is preceded and followed by a space. You can use more than a single ellipsis in a passage.

ORIGINAL TEXT

Literacy is not merely the capacity to understand the conceptual content of writings and utterances, but the ability to participate fully in a set of social and intellectual practices. It is not passive but active, not imitative but creative, for participation in the speaking and writing of language is participation in the activities it makes possible.

—James Boyd White, "Literacy and the Law"

OMISSION OF WORDS IN THE MIDDLE OF A SENTENCE

As James Boyd White suggests, "Literacy is . . . the ability to participate fully in a set of social and intellectual practices."

OMISSION OF WORDS FROM DIFFERENT SENTENCES

"Literacy," writes James Boyd White, "is . . . the ability to participate fully in a set of social and intellectual practices. . . . It is . . . active . . . creative . . . participation in the speaking and writing of language."

When an ellipsis coincides with the end of your sentence, use the ellipses followed by the end of sentence punctuation.

OMISSION OF WORDS AT THE END OF A SENTENCE

James Boyd White writes, "Literacy is not merely the capacity to understand the conceptual content of writings and utterances . . ."

Whenever ellipsis marks occur after a grammatically complete sentence, include this fourth period without any space before it. The closing quotation marks come after the end punctuation (see 32i).

But if your quotation includes a parenthetical reference to a source, you must place the end punctuation after the parenthetical source citation.

> James Boyd White writes, "Literacy is not merely the capacity to understand the conceptual content of writings and utterances . . ." (23).

(See 32h–i for more on punctuating quotations, and Chapter 43 for more on punctuating source citations.)

With quotations of more than a single sentence, an ellipsis in the middle can signal the omission of various amounts of text.

ORIGINAL

It would be hard to overestimate the importance of the icon for Muscovite culture. Each icon reminded man of God's continuing involvement in human affairs. Its truth could be immediately apprehended even by those incapable of reading or reflection. It offered not a message for thought but an illustration for reassurance of God's power in and over history for men who might otherwise have been completely mired in adversity and despair.

—James H. Billington, *The Icon and the Axe: An Interpretive History of Russian Culture*

QUOTATION OMITTING A SENTENCE

In explaining the pervasive significance of religious icons in Russian culture, James H. Billington notes, "It would be hard to overestimate the importance of the icon for Muscovite culture. . . . Its truth could be immediately apprehended even by those incapable of reading or reflection" (35).

QUOTATION WITH AN OMISSION FROM THE MIDDLE OF ONE SENTENCE TO THE END OF ANOTHER

In explaining the pervasive significance of religious icons in Russian culture, James H. Billington notes, "It would be hard to overestimate the importance of the icon. . . . Its truth could be immediately apprehended even by those incapable of reading or reflection" (35).

QUOTATION WITH AN OMISSION FROM THE MIDDLE OF ONE SENTENCE TO THE MIDDLE OF ANOTHER

In explaining the pervasive significance of religious icons in Russian culture, James H. Billington notes that icons were a sign "of God's continuing involvement. . . . an illustration for reassurance of God's power in and over history" (35).

Omission of words and phrases from quotations of poetry is treated the same way as prose—with three periods within brackets.

ORIGINAL

Whose woods these are I think I know.
His house is in the village though;
He will not see me stopping here
To watch his woods fill up with snow.

QUOTATION WITH AN ELLIPSIS AT THE END

Robert Frost's "Stopping By Woods" begins with just a hint of trespassing:
Whose woods these are I think I know.
His house is in the village though;
He will not see me stopping here
To watch his woods. . . . (1–4)

To omit a line or more in the middle of a poetry quotation set off from the text, provide a line of spaced periods.

QUOTATION OMITTING A LINE OR MORE IN THE MIDDLE

Robert Frost's "Stopping By Woods" begins with just a hint of trespassing:

Whose woods these are I think I know.

. . . .
He will not see me stopping here
To watch his woods fill up with snow. (1, 3–4)

EXERCISE 33–9   Using Ellipses

Condense the following by including ellipses to indicate deleted words, phrases, and sentences. Write your own summary of the following passage. In your summary, quote some of Ehrlich's phrases and sentences, but leave out some words, and indicate those omissions with ellipses.

A Cowboy is someone who loves his work. Since the hours are long—ten to fifteen hours a day—and the pay is $30 he has to. What's required of him is an odd mixture of physical vigor and maternalism. His part of the beef-raising industry is to birth and nurture calves and take care of their mothers. For the most part his work is done on horseback and in a lifetime he sees and comes to know more animals than people. The iconic myth surrounding him is built on American notions of heroism: the index of a man's value as measured in physical courage. Such ideas have perverted manliness into a self-absorbed race for cheap thrills. In a rancher's world, courage has less to do with facing danger than with acting spontaneously—usually on behalf of an animal or another rider.

—Gretel Ehrlich, "About Men"

33e   Using slashes

The **slash** is a diagonal line also called a *virgule* or *solidus* (/). Slashes are used to indicate line divisions in poems quoted within a text (see 32d), to separate terms, to separate the parts of a fraction, and to separate parts of shorthand dates.

INDICATING LINE DIVISIONS IN POETRY

The last lines of the poem convey the speaker's sense of regret: "What did I know, what did I know / Of love's austere and lonely offices?" (See also 32d on quoting poetry.)

There is a space before and after the slash only in quotations of poetry.

SEPARATING ALTERNATIVES

It was one of those either/or situations.

He took the course with a pass/fail option.

SEPARATING PARTS OF FRACTIONS

They began swimming when they were only 2 1/2 years old. (See 37a–b for advice on spelling out numbers.)

SEPARATING MONTH, YEAR, AND DAY IN SHORTHAND DATES

May 27, 1997

5/27/97

EXERCISE 33–10   Using Brackets, Slashes, Ellipses, Parentheses, and Dashes
Use the punctuation marks discussed in this chapter as needed in the following sentences. Example:

> The night of April 20, 1995, was if I remember correctly the night of a severe storm.

> The night of April 20, 1995, was *(if I remember correctly)* the night of a severe storm.

1. Consider the last two lines of Shakespeare's Sonnet 138: "Therefore I lie with her, and she with me, And in our faults by lies we flattered be."
2. According to one source, "John Fitgerald Kenedy sic was groomed for politics from the day he was born."
3. In 1861 a quick succession of events sparked by the attack on Fort Sumter a military stronghold in South Carolina led to the outbreak of civil war in the United States.
4. Those who market books not just those who write them argue that publicity is crucial to a book's success if it is to have any success at all.
5. Our many hours spent cleaning the attic or should I say the oven nearly sent us to the hospital.

EXERCISE 33–11   Using Varied Punctuation Marks in Writing
Write an eight- to twelve-sentence paragraph in which you use the following punctuation marks at least once: dash (or dashes), parentheses, brackets, ellipses, and slashes.

34 *Capitals*

The most important function of capital (or uppercase) letters in writing is to signal the beginning of a sentence. Without capital letters as indicators of sentence boundaries, you would have a difficult time making sense of what you read because sentences would run into one another. Capital letters are also used for the first letter in quotations and lines of poetry, for proper nouns and adjectives, for certain words in titles, and for the letters *I* and *O*. However, because the conventions of using capitals are changing, you should consult a new or recently revised dictionary when you are unsure about an accepted form.

34a   Capitalizing the first word of a sentence

Capitalize the first word of a sentence.

This is the most rigorous course I have ever taken. Can you help me?

A number of capitalizing situations require the writer to choose a particular style and then stick with it.

Capitals with a series of questions

When you write a series of questions, you may or may not use capitals for the first word of each question. But be consistent with the style you choose.

Which problem should the administration tackle first? The budget deficit? Education? Health care?

Which problem should the administration tackle first? the budget deficit? education? health care?

Capitals with sentences following colons

When using colons in writing, you may or may not use capitals for the first letter that follows the colon. But be consistent with the style you choose.

She welcomed the opportunity to perform: It meant a lot to her.

She welcomed the opportunity to perform: it meant a lot to her.

Capitals with parentheses and dashes

A complete, separate sentence within parentheses should begin with a capital letter.

Cause of death has an important effect: degenerative disease often entails a substantial diminution of brain size. (This effect is separate from the decrease attributed to age alone.)

Do not use capitals when incorporating a parenthetical independent clause within a sentence—whether you set it off with parentheses or with dashes.

The true beauty of nature is her amplitude; she exists neither for nor because of us, and possesses a staying power that all our nuclear arsenals cannot threaten (much as we can easily destroy our puny selves).

—Stephen Jay Gould, *Bully for Brontosaurus*

They assume—this is the orthodox assumption of the industrial economy—that the only help worth giving is not given at all, but sold.

—Wendell Berry, "Feminism, the Body and the Machine"

34b   Capitalizing the first word of a quotation

In using quotations, capitalize the first word of full-sentence quotations, except when the quote is introduced by the word "that."

The motto "Live free or die" appears on New Hampshire license plates.

Kwame said to Abdullah, "The next time you need help, ask for it."

Is it true that "it's better to be a live dog than a dead lion"?

You may need to adjust sentences with quotations to indicate any capitalization changes you make. See also 28b.

Embedded quotations

Do not capitalize quotations incorporated into the body of one of your sentences, even if the original quotation begins with a capital. Instead, use brackets to indicate how the quotation's first letter has been altered.

ORIGINAL QUOTATION

"Only a mediocre person is always at his best."

EMBEDDED QUOTATION

W. Somerset Maugham once remarked that "[o]nly a mediocre person is always at his best."

Interrupted quotations

When you break up a sentence from a quotation with words of your own, do not capitalize the word that begins the second part of the quotation sentence. Capitalize the first part if it is capitalized in the original.

ORIGINAL QUOTATION

"I have nothing to declare but my genius."

INTERRUPTED QUOTATION

"I have nothing to declare," Oscar Wilde told U.S. custom officials, "but my genius."

34c   Capitalizing the first letter in a line of poetry

Traditionally, poets capitalize the first letter of each line of a poem. Some poets, however, do not observe this convention. If you write poetry, you have the option of capitalizing or not capitalizing the first word of each line. In quoting poetry, capitalize the lines exactly as the poet does.

> Between my finger and my thumb,
> The squat pen rests.
> I'll dig with it.
>
> —Seamus Heaney, "Digging"

> If when my wife is sleeping
> and the baby and Kathleen
> are sleeping
>
> —William Carlos Williams, "Danse Russe"

34d   Capitalizing proper nouns and adjectives

Use capitals for **proper nouns** (names of specific people, places, and things [see 11a]): *Lisette, Paris,* the *Eiffel Tower.* Use capitals for **proper adjectives** (adjectives formed from proper nouns): a *Parisian* cafe. Do not capitalize articles (*a, an, the*) accompanying proper nouns or proper adjectives. (Also note that some people such as poet e. e. cummings and musician k. d. lang do not use capital letters in their names.)

When proper nouns are used in a common or everyday context, they are not capitalized.

Would you like ketchup with your *french* fries?

Be aware that writers may capitalize nouns and pronouns unconventionally. Emily Dickinson did so routinely, mostly for emphasis.

We grow accustomed to the Dark—
When Light is put away—

Advertisers often capitalize unconventionally: "Narcisse for the Bath and Body"; "Visit our Infiniti showroom for a Guest Drive." Similarly, corporations refer to the *Board of Trustees* and university administrations to the *Faculty*, the *College*, or the *University*.

When you use a common noun as an integral part of a proper name—*college*, for example, as in *Boston College*—capitalize the common noun. Words such as *street, river, county, prize*, and *award* are capitalized only when they become part of a specific (proper) term: *Basin Street*, the *Mississippi River, Dade County, Pulitzer Prize, Academy Award*. The accompanying chart provides additional guidance on capitalization.

Commonly Capitalized Words

NAMES OF PEOPLE

Booker T. Washington	Helen Keller
Pythagorean theorem	Shakespearean sonnet
Steffi Graf	Arthur Ashe

NAMES OF PLACES AND GEOGRAPHICAL REGIONS

Africa	Indian Ocean
Tibet	Mount Rainier
Indianapolis	Connecticut Avenue

NAMES OF STRUCTURES AND MONUMENTS

the Washington Monument	the Golden Gate Bridge
the Sears Tower	the Lincoln Tunnel

(continued)

DAYS OF THE WEEK, MONTHS, AND HOLIDAYS

Monday night football	Sunday brunch
an October day	April showers
Canada Day celebrations	Memorial Day parade

HISTORICAL EVENTS, PERIODS, MOVEMENTS

the Boer War	the Inquisition
Modernist writers	the Stone Age
the Fabulous Fifties	the Baroque Era

NAMES OF ORGANIZATIONS, INSTITUTIONS, AND BUSINESSES

International Business Systems	the Democratic Party (*or* party)
the Boy Scouts of America	Daughters of the American Revolution
Dell Computer Corporation	the Colorado State Legislature

ABBREVIATIONS AND ACRONYMS

SAT	NATO	NBC	TV
AFL-CIO	NAACP	YWCA	VCR

RELIGIONS AND RELIGIOUS TERMS

Muslims; Islam	Allah; Muhammad; the Koran
Christians; Christianity	Jesus; the Christ; the New Testament
Buddhists; Buddhism	Buddha; the Enlightened One
Jews; Judaism	Moses; the Bible; the Hebrew Scriptures

ETHNIC GROUPS, NATIONALITIES, AND LANGUAGES

Latino/Latina	Arabic
Italian American	Chinese philosophy
African American	Thai cuisine

TRADE NAMES

Nike	Wrangler's
Sony	Kleenex
Wheaties	Jeep

(*continued*)

COMPOUND WORDS

Native-American artifacts
Mexican-Indian foods
Asian-American communities

ACADEMIC INSTITUTIONS AND COURSES

Pace University   Spelman College
Anthropology 200   our History 101 teacher

---

1   Capitalize titles of individuals

Capitalize titles when used before a proper name. Do not capitalize titles that follow a proper name or titles used alone.

Justice Scalia	Antonin Scalia, a Supreme Court justice
Governor Christine Todd Whitman	Christine Todd Whitman, governor of New Jersey
Professor Howard Livingston	Howard Livingston, an English professor
Doctor Maria Velásquez	Maria Velásquez, a local doctor

2   Capitalize academic institutions and courses

Capitalize the names of specific schools, departments, and courses. Do not capitalize common nouns for institutions or areas of study.

University of Michigan	a Michigan university
Economics Department	an economics major
Biology 101	an introductory biology course

34e   Capitalizing the titles and subtitles of works

Capitalize the first word, the last word, and all words in between (except articles, prepositions, and conjunctions) for titles and subtitles of works.

In Search of Our Mothers' Gardens (book)
Across the River and into the Trees (book)
Landscape with the Fall of Icarus (painting)
The Marriage of Figaro (opera)
The Day after the Bomb (movie)
Poe's Narrators: A Study (report)
"Living Like Weasels" (essay)
"I Stand Here Ironing" (short story)
"To Helen" (poem)
"The River Merchant's Wife: A Letter" (poem)

34f   Capitalizing *I* and *O*

Capitalize the personal pronoun *I* (except in quoting literary works that use the lowercase form). Capitalize the interjection *O* (an old form for the more modern, "oh"). Capitalize *oh* only when it begins a sentence.

Do you realize that I have been studying for three hours straight?

Hear our prayer, O Lord.

"Oh, we are in for it now," we said.

There were oh, so many books to read.

34g   Avoiding the misuse of capitals

1   Do not capitalize words designating family relationships

Use capitals with words designating family relationships only when they are used as names or titles, or in combination with proper names. However, when you substitute a word indicating a family relationship for a name, or use such a word as part of a name, capitalize it.

When he was a boy, *Father* became a good auto mechanic.

When he was a boy, *my father* became a good auto mechanic.

It was a pleasure to visit *Uncle Andy* and *Aunt Marge*.

It was a pleasure to visit *our uncle* and *aunt*.

2   Do not capitalize words denoting seasons or parts of the year

summer vacation   fall term
winter quarters   spring weather
autumn leaves   sophomore year

3   Do not capitalize words for compass directions except when designating a specific geographic area

We headed south first, then west.

The Northeast was hard hit by the economic slump of the 1990s.

> WRITING HINT   When referring to words in a foreign language, such as Italian, French, or Spanish, be careful to respect its rules of capitalization, which may differ from those in English. For example, the names of the seasons and the days of the week, which begin with capital letters in English, begin with lowercase letters in many other languages, including those named above.

EXERCISE 34–1   Supplying Capital Letters

Restore the following passage to its original form by inserting capitalization where it is needed. Also eliminate any unnecessary use of capital letters.

to be married in las vegas, clark county, nevada, a bride must swear that she is eighteen or has parental permission and a bridegroom that he is twenty-one or has parental permission. someone must put up five dollars for the license (on sundays and holidays, fifteen dollars. the clark county courthouse issues marriage licenses at any time of the day or night except between noon and one in the afternoon, between eight and nine in the evening, and between four and five in the morning.) nothing else is required. the state of nevada, alone among these united states, demands neither a premarital blood test nor a waiting period before or after the issuance of a marriage license. driving across the mojave from los angeles, one sees the signs way out on the desert, looming up from that moonscape of rattlesnakes and mesquite, even before the las vegas lights appear like a mirage on the horizon: "getting married? free license information first strip exit." perhaps the las vegas wedding industry achieved its peak operational efficiency between 9:00 p.m. and midnight of august 26, 1965, an otherwise unremarkable thursday which happened to be, by presidential order, the last day on which anyone could improve his draft status merely by getting married. one hundred and seventy-one couples were pronounced Man and Wife in the name of clark county and the state of nevada that night, sixty-seven of them by a single justice of the peace, mr. james a. brennan. mr. brennan did one wedding at the dunes and the other sixty-six in his office, and charged each couple eight dollars. one bride lent her veil to six others. "I got it down from five to three minutes," mr. brennan said later of his feat. "I could've married them *en masse,* but they're people, not cattle. people expect more when they get married."

—Joan Didion, "Marrying Absurd"

EXERCISE 34–2   **Observing Unconventional Capitals**
Collect samples of unconventional uses of capitalization from a newspaper, a magazine, and a literary work. Bring the samples to class and be prepared to explain the effects of any unusual capitalization you find.

35   *Italics*

Italic type is a style of printing *in which the letters are slanted to the right.* Italic type is used for certain kinds of material such as book titles, for words requiring special distinction, and for emphasis. Many computers and printers can reproduce italic type. If you do not have printer capability for italics, use underlining in its place.

35a   Using italics for titles

Use italics to indicate the titles of long or complete works such as novels (see the chart on p. 546). Note that the Modern Language Association suggests neither capitalizing nor italicizing any articles that precede the names of magazines or newspapers (the *Atlantic Monthly,* the *New York Times*). Titles of shorter works, such as poems and essays, and titles of sections of works, such as chapters, are set off with quotation marks (see 32f).

Titles to Italicize (or Underline)	
BOOKS	
Pride and Prejudice	*Plagues and Peoples*
FILMS	
Casablanca	*The Talented Mr. Ripley*
PLAYS	
A Doll House	*The Glass Menagerie*
LONG POEMS	
The Prelude	*Paradise Lost*
NEWSPAPERS	
the *Atlanta Constitution*	the *Los Angeles Times*
MAGAZINES	
Newsweek	*Science News*
PAMPHLETS	
Dangerous Drugs	*Wines of California*
WORKS OF VISUAL ART	
van Gogh's *The Starry Night*	Kahlo's *Self-Portrait with Monkeys*
MUSICAL WORKS	
Tchaikovsky's *Nutcracker*	Mozart's *Don Giovanni*
TELEVISION AND RADIO PROGRAMS	
Prime Time Live	*All Things Considered*

(continued)

RECORDINGS

Bruce Springsteen's *Born to Run*   Whitney Houston's *Bodyguard*

JOURNALS

Nursing Review   *Journal of Economics*

PUBLISHED SPEECHES

Lincoln's *Gettysburg Address*   King's *I Have a Dream* speech

EXCEPTIONS

Titles of sacred works and their parts as well as public documents do not take italics.

the Bible   the Bill of Rights
the New Testament   the U.S. Constitution
the Koran   the Magna Carta

35b   Using italics for words, letters, numbers, and phrases used as words

The word *groovy* has dropped out of current usage.

The letter *y* is not part of the Italian alphabet.

Robert Parish wore the number *00* when he played for the Boston Celtics.

Who coined the phrase *over the hill*?

You may use quotation marks instead of italics in these situations (see 32g). Whichever style you choose, be sure to use it consistently.

Italics may also be used to highlight words being defined.

The researchers were looking for *microcytes*, abnormally small red blood cells, often associated with anemia.

35c   Using italics for foreign words and phrases

English has acquired many words from foreign languages (see 31a). Many of these words are now part of the English language and should not be italicized: spaghetti (Italian), chef (French), kindergarten (German), mesa (Spanish). To find out whether a word or expression is considered foreign, look it up in a dictionary. If it does not appear in your dictionary, you should italicize it.

The famous opening movement of Beethoven's Fifth Symphony is marked *allegro non ma troppo* (fast, but not too fast).

The common sunflower, *Helianthus annuus,* has a tall coarse stem and large, yellow-rayed flower heads that produce edible seeds rich in oil.

35d   Using italics for the names of trains, ships, aircraft, and spacecraft

Although you should italicize the names of specific trains, ships, aircraft, and spacecraft, do not italicize general types and classes of these vehicles.

We took Amtrak's *Empire Builder* to Seattle.

We rode the Metroliner between Boston and Washington.

TRAINS

the *Orient Express*   the *Silver Streak*

SHIPS

the *Nina*   *USS Constitution*

AIRCRAFT AND SPACECRAFT

the *Spirit of St. Louis*   the space shuttle *Endeavor*

35e   Using italics for emphasis

Although you can use italics for emphasis, do so only sparingly to avoid a tone of insistent exaggeration. Writing becomes more effective when emphasis is created through conciseness, careful word choice, and well-constructed sentences (see 25a and 26b).

I wanted to find out in what way the *specialness* of my experience could be made to connect me with other people instead of dividing me from them.

—James Baldwin

"Mommy, there's a *world* in your eye."

—Alice Walker

And above all I did not wish to be *trivial*; I did not wish to be embarrassing.

—Mary Gordon

> **WRITING HINT**   Be aware of the visual effect of italics when you write. Italic type can be used to highlight key terms or concepts. It can also be used for heads and subheads in longer papers and reports. For more on the appearance of your written and printed work, consult Chapter 45.

EXERCISE 35–1   Using Italics

In the following sentences, add italics where necessary by underlining. Indicate unnecessary italics by circling the incorrectly italicized words. Example:

(The)*New York Times* has a long tradition of distinguished sports writing.

The *New York Times* has a long tradition of distinguished sports writing.

1. Although one of Mary Cassatt's most consistent subjects in her art was family life, paintings like The Bath and The Family avoid sentimentality.

2. Brancusi and Rodin, among other sculptors, have rendered people *kissing*.

3. Among the *ships* that made the *voyage* was the Cristofero Colombo.

4. Thor Heyerdahl's book Kon-Tiki describes his sailing adventures on a raft he built and sailed in the South Seas to Easter Island, in Polynesia.

5. Disparate accounts of the event were presented in *the Washington Post*, the San Francisco *Chronicle*, and the Minneapolis *Star*.

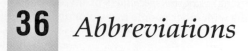 36 *Abbreviations*

Abbreviations serve as a form of shorthand. They enable writers to replace long names and titles with simple, brief sets of letters. A convenience, abbreviations can help writing and reading become more efficient.

The guidelines for using abbreviations outlined in this chapter pertain to nontechnical academic writing and most other writing geared toward a general audience. Technical writing typically includes more numerous and varied abbreviations. (For information concerning abbreviations in documenting source citations in the humanities and sciences, see Chapters 43 and 44.)

Abbreviating personal and professional titles and academic degrees

Some personal and professional titles and some academic degrees are abbreviated when placed before or after a name.

Mr. Magnus Larsen	Mrs. Bizet
Ms. Anne Fujiyoshi	Dr. Weber *or* Kaare Weber, MD
St. Joan of Arc	Carolyn Smith, PhD
Robert M. Chang, Jr.	Archangelo Narazitti, LLD

> **USAGE NOTE**   In sentences, the abbreviations for junior (Jr.) and senior (Sr.) are set off with commas.
>
> > Like his son Martin Luther King, Jr., Martin Luther King, Sr., was a distinguished preacher.

Other titles, including religious, military, academic, and governmental titles, should not be abbreviated in academic writing (*President Nelson Mandela,* not Pres. Nelson Mandela). In nonacademic writing you may abbreviate titles before a full name, but you should spell them out when they appear before a surname only.

Rev. John Kauta	Reverend Kauta
Gen. Andrew Jackson	General Jackson
Prof. Elaine Showalter	Professor Showalter
Sen. Barbara Boxer	Senator Boxer

Abbreviate academic degrees when used alone. Do not, however, abbreviate personal or professional titles used alone.

ACCEPTABLE   He received his EdD the same year his sister received her PhD.

UNACCEPTABLE   She had a reputation as a tough prof.

REVISED   She had a reputation as a tough professor.

Be careful not to abbreviate a single title twice with a person's name. Use an abbreviated title before *or* after the name, but not in both places.

UNACCEPTABLE   Dr. Amelia Sternheim, MD

ACCEPTABLE   Dr. Amelia Sternheim

ACCEPTABLE   Amelia Sternheim, MD

However, you can use two abbreviations for two different titles.

Prof. Peter Edelson, Esq.

36b   Using familiar acronyms and abbreviations

Acronyms are abbreviations that are pronounced as words, such as *NATO* (North Atlantic Treaty Organization) and *MADD* (Mothers against Drunk Driving). Abbreviations not pronounced as words are sometimes called **initial abbreviations** or **initialisms** (to emphasize that each letter is sounded). Examples include *IBM* (International Business Machines) and *NBC* (National Broadcasting Company). Usually, initial abbreviations use all capital letters. Sometimes, however, they may be written with only the first letter capitalized: *Unesco, Nabisco,* and *Nimby,* for example. (See 28a for information on punctuating acronyms and abbreviations.)

If you use a term that has an abbreviated form only once in an essay or a report, spell it out. However, when a term appears often in a report, or when you write for an informed audience, use the abbreviation. Spell out the full term on first use, note the abbreviation in parentheses, and use the abbreviation thereafter.

The Modern Language Association (MLA) has published a guide for writers that contains detailed guidelines on issues of manuscript style for papers in the humanities. The MLA has entitled the book *MLA Handbook for Writers of Research Papers,* Sixth Edition. Writers of papers and articles in the social sciences should consult the publication of the American Psychological Association (APA). The APA guide, which can be found in most libraries, is entitled *Publication Manual of the American Psychological Association,* Fifth Edition.

36c   Using the abbreviations *a.m., p.m., B.C. (BC), A.D. (AD),* and symbols

Using *a.m.* and *p.m.*

The abbreviations *a.m.* and *p.m.* should be used only with exact times.

Class begins at *11:15 a.m.* and ends at *1:15 p.m.,* exactly two hours later.

The notation *a.m.* abbreviates the Latin *ante meridiem,* meaning "before noon"; *p.m.* abbreviates the Latin *post meridiem,* meaning "after noon."

USAGE NOTE   The abbreviations *a.m.* and *p.m.* should be used only with numbers, never with the words *morning, evening,* and *night.*

INCORRECT	We met at 7:30 p.m. in the evening.
REVISED	We met at 7:30 p.m.
REVISED	We met at seven-thirty in the evening.

Using *B.C. (BC)* and *A.D. (AD)*

In abbreviations for years, place *BC* ("before Christ") or *BCE* (before the common era") after the year: *500 BC; 5000 BCE* Place *AD (anno Domini—* "the year of the Lord") before the year: *AD 1066;* and *CE* ("common era") after the year: *2000 CE* Note that you should use these abbreviations only when your readers may be confused about the time period you are referring to: *The Hopewell culture flourished in what is now the Midwest of the United States from 100 BC to 550 AD.*

Using symbols ($, %, @, #, &, +, −, =)

Symbols, such as $, %, @, #, &, +, −, and =, are spelled out except in technical discussions that refer to numbers and symbols frequently. As a general rule, avoid using symbols in academic papers, except in graphs and tables.

INAPPROPRIATE	Nearly 100% of those applying are accepted.
REVISED	Nearly 100 percent of those applying are accepted.

It is acceptable, however, to use the dollar sign before certain figures: *$10 million.*

The university's fund-raising goal is $10 million.

In writing scientific and business reports that require many numbers and symbols, using the symbols (rather than words) will make your writing easier to understand. Let the nature of your writing task, your audience, and your purpose influence your decision about using such symbols. And remember to use the style you choose consistently.

36d Using Latin abbreviations for documentation

In general, avoid using the following Latin abbreviations except when citing sources in a research paper or when making a parenthetical point.

ABBREVIATION	MEANING
i.e.	that is (*id est*)
e.g.	for example (*exempli gratia*)
etc.	and so forth (*et cetera*)
cf.	compare (*confer*)
et al.	and others (*et alia*)
N.B.	note well (*nota bene*)

WRITING HINT Avoid ending a sentence with an abbreviation. A sentence that ends with *etc.,* for example, gives readers the impression that you ran out of examples or did not bother to provide specifics.

INAPPROPRIATE	Some companies provide extensive benefits for their employees; e.g., they offer health and dental plans, vacation time, stock options, etc.
REVISED	Some companies provide extensive benefits for their employees; for example, they offer health and dental plans, vacation time, stock options, and the like.

36e   Using other types of abbreviations

Given names and academic courses

INCORRECT	Chas. is taking Robt. Mitchell's advanced chem. course.
REVISED	*Charles* is taking *Robert* Mitchell's advanced *chemistry* course.

Months, days, and holidays

INCORRECT	Did Jan. 17, 1993, fall on a Tues.?
REVISED	Did *January* 17, 1993, fall on a *Tuesday*?
INCORRECT	New Yr's Eve is my favorite holiday.
REVISED	New *Year's* Eve is my favorite holiday.

Geographical designations

INCORRECT	They drove from Nashville, TN to Miami, FL.
REVISED	They drove from Nashville, *Tennessee,* to Miami, *Florida.*

Exceptions include *Washington, D.C.,* and *U.S.* (the latter can serve as an adjective but not as a noun).

U.S. involvement in Vietnam was a hotly contested issue in the 1960s.

Many immigrants who visit Washington, *D.C.,* come away with a sense of pride in the United States. [*United States* as noun]

Units of measurement

Avoid abbreviating units of measurement, except in technical writing.

INCORRECT	Mary is five ft., two in. tall.
REVISED	Mary is five *feet,* two *inches* tall.

Exceptions include *mph* (miles per hour), *rpm* (revolutions per minute), and *cps* (cycles per second).

We were traveling at 70 mph when the police pulled us over.

Do not abbreviate parts of a company's name (e.g., *Inc., Bros.,* or *Co.*) unless the abbreviation is part of the actual name. Use the ampersand (&) only when it is part of the company's name.

Company names

INCORRECT	Sears, Roebuck and Co. opened a store next to the A and P.
REVISED	Sears, Roebuck *& Company* opened a store next to the *A&P.*

36f Using abbreviations for reference information

Although it is conventional to abbreviate such words as *editor* (*ed.*), *page* and *pages* (*p.* and *pp.*), *chapter* (*ch.*), and *volume* (*vol.*) in citing sources, do not use such abbreviations in the body of a paper.

INCORRECT	The preface to the 1855 ed. of Whitman's *Leaves of Grass* is often reprinted with the last edition (the 1892 or deathbed ed.) of this revolutionary book of poems.
REVISED	The preface to the 1855 edition of Whitman's *Leaves of Grass* is often reprinted with the last edition (the 1892 or deathbed edition) of this revolutionary book of poems.

Abbreviations Checklist

Check your writing for incorrect or inappropriate use of abbreviations. Consult the appropriate sections in this chapter for advice about using the following types of abbreviations.

- Personal and professional titles such as *Ms.* and *Dr.* (36a)
- Academic degrees such as *B.S. [or BS], M.A. [or MA],* and *Ph.D. [or PhD]* (36a)
- Acronyms such as *OPEC* and *NATO* (36b)
- Times, years, and symbols such as *7:15 a.m., 500 BC,* and *$1,500* (36c)
- Latin abbreviations such as *etc.* and *e.g.* (36d)

(continued)

- Given names and academic courses (36e)
- Months, days, and holidays (36e)
- Geographical designations such as *NJ* and *Calif.* (36e)
- Units of measurement such as *mph* and *rpm* (36e)
- Company names such as *A&P* (36e)
- Reference information such as *p.*, *vol.*, and *ed.* (36f)

EXERCISE 36–1 Using Abbreviations

Revise the following sentences to provide abbreviations where they are acceptable in academic writing. Also eliminate any inappropriate abbreviations. Example:

> The pres. vetoed the bill, even though it had been approved by 75% of the senators who voted.

> The *president* vetoed the bill, even though it had been approved by 75 *percent* of the senators who voted.

1. Of the many summer courses offered, Expository Writing and Economics were among the most heavily subscribed. Expos and Econ have long been popular with visiting students.

2. Of the many titles she could have used, Eliz. Bennet, Esq., opted for the one that meant the most to her: Dr.

3. To get the best possible mpg, try to keep the engine at around 2,200 rpm when you are doing fifty-five mph.

4. Although more than seventy % of the students at OU are female, only one-third of the faculty and none of the sr. administrators are women.

5. The morning bio and chem sections are already fully enrolled.

EXERCISE 36–2 Clarifying Abbreviations

Revise the following paragraph's abbreviations for greater ease of comprehension.

> The NAACP has long been an important organization in American political and social life. The National Association for the Advancement of Colored People, however, has recently considered changing its name, since the term "Colored" is no longer commonly used to refer to people of African-American descent.

37 *Numbers*

When you use numbers in writing, you will sometimes spell them out and other times write them as numerals. In scientific and technical writing, numbers are usually written as figures. However, in nontechnical writing geared toward a general audience, numbers are usually spelled out according to the conventions outlined in this chapter.

37a Spelling out numbers of one or two words

In a nontechnical piece of writing that uses numbers, if you can spell out a number in one or two words, do so.

The twenty-five members of the class were all present for the party.

A hyphenated number, as in the preceding example, is considered one word. (See 38b–3 for more on using hyphens with compound numbers.)
Use figures for numbers that cannot be spelled out in one or two words.

She needed another 122 votes to win the election.

When a sentence contains some numbers that should be spelled out and others that should be written as figures, make sure to use one convention consistently.

INCONSISTENT   Our cruise was a short one hundred miles; other vacation-
                ers elected longer trips—up to 475 miles.

CONSISTENT   Our cruise was a short 100 miles; other vacationers elected
                longer trips—up to 475 miles.

37b Spelling out numbers at the beginning of a sentence

Always spell out numbers that begin a sentence. However, sentences that begin with spelled-out numbers of more than two words can be awkward and difficult to read. In that case, revise the sentence to begin with another word.

INCORRECT	100,000 or more marchers demonstrated at the rally.
REVISED	More than 100,000 marchers demonstrated at the rally.
AWKWARD	One hundred fifty-seven million dollars was the selling price of the two companies combined.
REVISED	The selling price of the two companies combined was $157 million.

WRITING HINT   When you use more than one number to modify a noun, spell out the first number or the shorter of the two numbers to avoid confusion: *six 8-inch slats, 300 one-gallon containers.*

37c   Using figures according to convention

Although convention generally requires that most numbers of one or two words be spelled out, there are many exceptions. As the accompanying chart shows, figures are always used for days and years; pages, chapters, and volume numbers of books; acts, scenes, and lines of plays; decimals, fractions, ratios, and percentages; temperatures; addresses; scores and statistics; exact amounts of money; and the time of day.

Guidelines for Using Figures

DAYS AND YEARS

February 15, 1945	February 1945	A.D. [*or* AD] 700	the 1990s
15 February 1945	June 3rd	406 B.C. [*or* BC]	1980–88

Note: Reserve the use of ordinal numbers expressed as figures (*1st, 2nd, 3rd*) for dates without the year. In other instances, spell out ordinal numbers (*first, second, third*).

PAGES, CHAPTERS, VOLUMES

page 49	chapter 15
pages 135–47	volume 2

(continued)

ACTS, SCENES, LINES

> *Othello*, act 5, scene 1, lines 1–12 [*or Othello*, 5.1.1–12]

DECIMALS, FRACTIONS, RATIOS, AND PERCENTAGES

> 37.5   3/4   4:1 [*or* four to one]   [52% *or* 52 percent]

TEMPERATURES

> 721 °F   10 °C

ADDRESSES

> 244 Orchard St., Apt. 3K
> Aberdeen, NJ 07654

SCORES AND STATISTICS

> a combined SAT score of 1200
> a margin of 2 to 1

AMOUNTS OF MONEY

> $3.75 $2.16 million   75¢

Exceptions: Round dollar or cent amounts of two or three words may be spelled out: *twenty-five dollars, fifty cents.*

TIME OF DAY

> 7 a.m.   2:45 p.m.   1640 hours

Exceptions: When expressing time without *a.m.* or *p.m.*, spell out the numbers: *seven in the morning, seven-thirty in the evening* (not *7 in the morning* or *7:30 in the evening*). When using *o'clock* to indicate time, express the number in words: *three o'clock* (not *3 o'clock*).

EXERCISE 37–1   Using Numbers

Revise the following sentences so that the numbers are expressed as numerals or words according to the conventions outlined in this chapter. Example:

The Battle of Gettysburg began on July 1st, 1863.

The Battle of Gettysburg began on *July 1*, 1863.

1. Hamlet's famous soliloquy that begins "To be or not to be" can be found near the beginning of the third act. To be precise, it occurs at lines 55–89 of the first scene of act three.

2. Our biology text was published in nineteen seventy-five.

3. His birthday, April first, is often cause for practical jokes as well as for celebration. His brother, born on January 1, considers himself luckier since he can be considered a New Year's baby rather than an April fool.

4. The board measured ten ft. three and one-half in. by one ft. one in.

5. 200 people attended the meeting.

EXERCISE 37–2   Using Numbers

Revise the following paragraph to express numbers as numerals or words appropriately.

> On December 5th, 1985, a cold snowy day that registered zero °F, J. D. Spencer, a halfback for the Los Angeles Raiders, carried the ball for two hundred sixty-nine and a half yards. This impressive record of running yardage was complemented by a 3:2 ratio of yards from pass receptions. Spencer began the game at 4 o'clock in the afternoon and finished 3 hours later, at 7:09 in the evening, to be exact. His feat was broadcast over channel seven on television and on the radio station six hundred sixty AM, WFAN. You can find these statistics in the imaginary volume of *Great Sports Stats for the Nineteen Eighties* on page one thousand two hundred and fifty-nine.

38 *Hyphens*

Hyphenation occurs most often for the simple reason that a word is too long to fit at the end of a line of type. In such cases the writer divides the word, putting part of the word at the end of one line and the remainder of the word at the beginning of the next line. Writers also use hyphens to join words or parts of words, as in *go-between* and *knick-knack*. Do not confuse a **hyphen** (-) with a dash (—), which is made by combining two hyphens (see 33a).

38a Use hyphens to divide words at the end of a line

When you must divide a word at the end of a typewritten line, be sure to divide it between syllables and to place the hyphen immediately after the first part of the divided word. The word *intricate,* for example, which contains three syllables (*in•tri•cate*), can be divided after *in-* or after *intri-*. Dictionaries indicate syllabication for all words; to be sure your word divisions are correct, check a reliable dictionary.

In addition, follow the conventions described in the accompanying chart on dividing words at the end of a typewritten line.

Conventions for Dividing Words at the End of a Line

- Do not divide one-syllable words, even long ones such as *thought* and *health.*
- Although the first letter of a word may comprise a syllable, do not leave one letter on a line. Leave at least two letters on each line when dividing a word.

INCORRECT	Guard against infection by applying an i-odine ointment to the wound.
REVISED	Guard against infection by applying an io-dine ointment to the wound.

- Do not divide abbreviations, contractions, or numbers. *U.S.A., couldn't,* and *50,000* should not be hyphenated.
- Do not hyphenate names of people and places. Neither *Thomas Jefferson* nor his home, *Monticello,* can be hyphenated.
- Only divide words between syllables. You cannot hyphenate the word *recess,* for example, as *rec-ess* but only as *re-cess.*
- Divide compound words only between the words that form the compound. Split the word *homecoming,* for example, across two lines as *home-coming,* not as *ho-mecoming* or *homecom-ing.*
- Divide words according to their prefixes and suffixes. Divide *subordinate* after the prefix (*sub-ordinate*) and the word *fairly* before the suffix (*fair-ly*).
- Remember to attach the hyphen to the part of the word on the first line and not to the part of the word that begins the next line.

EXERCISE 38–1   Deciding Where to Hyphenate Words

Divide each of the following words into syllables. Then place a hyphen after each syllable that can be left at the end of a line.

1. contract   5. swimming   8. synonymous

2. slurpy   6. certitude   9. hardworking

3. laudable   7. didn't   10. meaty

4. introverted

38b   Use hyphens with compound words

Compound words consist of two or more words joined together as a single word. Some are written as one word, others as hyphenated words, and still others as separate words without hyphens.

ONE WORD	skyline, scarecrow, outlaw
HYPHENATED	brother-in-law, cross-examination, nation-state
SEPARATE	junior high, energy guide, ice cream

1   Hyphens with compound adjectives

Use a hyphen for **compound adjectives**—two or more adjectives that function as a unit to modify a noun or pronoun—when the adjective precedes the noun or pronoun. When the compound adjective follows the noun or pronoun, however, do not hyphenate.

Pete Sampras is a world-renowned tennis star.

Pete Sampras is world renowned as a tennis star.

Do not use a hyphen when part of the compound adjective ends in *-ly.*

The surprisingly short concert disappointed the audience.

2   Hyphens with coined compounds

A **coined compound** connects words not ordinarily linked or hyphenated. Use coined compounds sparingly in formal and academic writing; reserve them to create an informal tone.

They were in a let-it-all-hang-out frame of mind.

3 Hyphens with fractions and compound numbers

Use a hyphen when spelling out fractions to connect the numerator and denominator.

The cake was one-quarter finished before dinner even began.

The strip of wood was three-eighths of an inch wide.

Also use a hyphen to spell out whole numbers from twenty-one through ninety-nine, even when those numbers are part of larger numbers.

one thousand thirty-five

eighty thousand six hundred fifty-two

Usually compound numbers are expressed as figures (see 37a).

4 Hyphens in a series

Use a hyphen for a series of compound words built on the same base. Be sure to leave a space after the first word.

First- and second-generation immigrants composed the class.

> WRITING HINT It is sometimes difficult to determine when to hyphenate a compound word. Conventions shift rapidly and are unpredictable. Even compound words that begin with the same word are treated differently: *breakthrough, break dance, break-in*. And although many words pass through successive stages—from two words (*base ball*) to a hyphenated form (*baseball*) to a single word (*baseball*)—some remain at the first or second stage. Consult your dictionary for help with hyphenating compound words. (See also 27f on spelling hyphenated words.)

38c Using hyphens with prefixes and suffixes

Prefixes are generally combined with word stems without hyphens: *pre*fatory, *inter*view, *dis*belief, *non*compliant, *re*elect. In cases where the prefix precedes a capital letter or when a capital letter is combined with a word, separate the two with a hyphen: anti-American, pre-Columbian, H-bomb.

Certain prefixes, such as *all-*, *self-*, *quasi-*, and *ex-* (to mean "formerly"), normally take a hyphen when combined with words: *all-*encompassing, *self-*denial, *ex-*player, *quasi-*convincing.

Very few suffixes take a hyphen. Two of these are *-elect* and *-some*, as in governor-*elect* and twenty-*some*.

Using Hyphens with Prefixes

- Use hyphens when using the prefixes *all-*, *ex-*, *quasi-*, and *self-*.

    all-important, ex-wife, quasi-independent, self-reliant

- Use a hyphen when the base word is a proper noun, a number, or a capitalized word.

    pro-European, post-1990, mid-August

- Use a hyphen when the base word is a compound.

    anti-abortion rally, ex-governor

- Use a hyphen with two or more prefixes for a base word.

    pro- and anti-war demonstrations

- Use a hyphen to prevent confusion in meaning between two similar words. Distinguish *recall* (a recollection), for example, from *re-call* (to call back).

- Use a hyphen to prevent confusion that could result from combinations of vowels and consonants (e.g., double *i*'s or consonants) in such words as *anti-intellectual* and *non-native*. But note that some prefixes, especially those with double vowels, do not use the hyphen: *reentry, cooperation, coordination, nonexistent.* Check your dictionary when in doubt.

WRITING HINT   Do not capitalize words containing the prefix *ex-* and the suffix *-elect*, even in titles with proper names.

INCORRECT	Ex-Mayor Bradley
REVISED	ex-Mayor Bradley
INCORRECT	Governor-Elect Ramirez
REVISED	Governor-elect Ramirez

EXERCISE 38–2   Using the Dictionary to Check Hyphenation

Consult your dictionary to see how to hyphenate the following words.

1. scofflaw

2. ringmaster

3. oil slick

4. head start

5. interdependent

6. reevaluate

7. aftermath

8. preprogrammed

9. retrograde

10. profeminist

EXERCISE 38–3   Using Hyphens

Supply missing hyphens in the following passage.

How they did it—those millions of black women . . . —brings me to the title of this essay, "In Search of Our Mothers' Gardens," which is a personal account that is yet shared, in its theme and its meaning, by all of us. I found, while thinking about the far reaching world of the creative black woman, that often the truest answer to a question that really matters can be found very close.

In the late 1920s my mother ran away from home to marry my father. Marriage, if not running away, was expected of seventeen year old girls. By the time she was twenty, she had two children and was pregnant with a third. Five children later, I was born. And this is how I came to know my mother: she seemed a large, soft, loving eyed woman who was rarely impatient in our home.

—Alice Walker, "In Search of Our Mothers' Gardens"

39 *Understanding Research*

Doing research is not a new experience. Every time you solve a problem, you follow a familiar process. Structured research has much in common with that problem-solving process.

Directed research is the formal research you will do to accumulate evidence and develop a thesis on an assigned or selected research topic. Eventually, you will present and defend that thesis—your reasoned conclusion about the accumulated evidence—in a research essay.

Directed research often begins as you read your required course materials and come upon a topic that intrigues you. Your quest to find out more about this topic can involve such diverse activities as conducting experiments, administering surveys, and undertaking field research; but most often, your search takes you into the library. It may also lead you to the Internet and to the World Wide Web. These information systems connect you to a wide array of computer networks and resources that give you immediate access to information that can supplement your library's collection. Once in the library or on the Internet, you can locate books, journals, magazines, newspapers, and other sources that contain additional information on the subject you have chosen or been assigned. This process, which begins with your interest in a particular topic, leads to your acquiring more knowledge about it, forming a thesis about it, and finally writing a research essay on it.

To look upon research as a tedious or boring trip to the library where you do no more than select sources, go back to your room to read, fill out index cards, organize evidence, and write a report of your findings is to overlook the potential for excitement at discovering your own idea about a topic and communicating that idea to your audience. As a researcher, you seek out and find answers to questions. You experience the pleasure of learning new things and enrich your understanding of your topic. Along the way, you should acquire a sense of what it is like to be a productive scholar and an accomplished problem solver.

39a Getting ready to do research writing

The research process includes both directed research and writing the research essay (see Chapter 40). Like the writing process we explored earlier in the *Handbook* (see Chapter 1), the research process follows a recursive path that moves back and forth from researching to writing and from writing to researching.

http://
www.researchpaper.com
Offers a good starting point
for beginning the research
process.

This chapter will help you make sense of your research assignment and will show you how to select an appropriate topic. You will also learn how to use library resources and do field research to compile a collection of sources on your topic for use in a research essay. In addition, this chapter, as well as Chapters 40 and 44, will follow Ericka Kostka's research process so that you can see how research is done.

1 Understand the assignment

Whatever research assignment you are given, carefully consider any written guidelines or your instructor's advice about the assignment. Analyze the assignment by breaking down and sorting the individual tasks. Consider the purpose and audience, length requirements, and the due date and any interim deadlines (e.g., for completing preliminary research, for submitting a tentative thesis, and for handing in drafts).

The assignment given to Ericka Kostka, whose research essay appears in Chapter 44, specified the following requirements.

Investigate an issue that has far-reaching social and ethical consequences, and write an essay of six to twelve pages for a general audience, using primarily secondary sources. Your research essay should present and defend your point of view about the issue. You have four weeks to complete the assignment.

2   Think about purpose and audience

Your overarching purpose for doing research will always be to become knowledgeable about a given topic so that you can develop a thesis about it and write a research essay. And, within your essay, your purpose may be to provide information or to persuade readers of your point of view. But when you read your assignment, look carefully for other implied purposes so that you know what your instructor expects in response to the assignment. Make sure, for example, that you understand the key terms that specify your assignment: *analyze, explain, argue, survey, compare or contrast, explore, persuade.* Each of those terms indicates a particular way of approaching your topic. If you have any doubts about what you are being asked to do, discuss the assignment with your instructor.

Once you have established your purpose, consider your potential audience. Your audience will likely be your instructor, but the assignment or the topic itself may specify or suggest a wider audience. You need to know whether you will be writing for a general audience of interested readers or whether you will be addressing an audience of specialists. You should think about whether your audience will be friendly or hostile and what opinions and attitudes that audience might hold. In addition, give some thought to the response you hope to elicit from your audience. (See 1d for more details on audience and purpose.)

3   Devise a schedule and pace yourself

It is often difficult to know at the outset how long it will take to complete your research and your writing. The recursive process of going back and forth from research to writing should continue until you can develop and defend your thesis. Often, your instructor will help you limit the scope of your research by specifying a deadline, a required length for the final essay, and the approximate number of sources that you should consult. You may also be told the types of sources to consult; generally you will have to consult a mix of primary and secondary sources (39c).

The amount of time you spend on research and writing will depend on your efficiency in locating sources in the library and on the Internet, as well as on your effectiveness as a critical reader and as a writer.

This chapter and the others in Part Eight will help you learn the essential skills that will make you an effective research writer. A useful beginning step is to develop a workable schedule for your research project. The accompanying overview chart will give you a sense of what is involved in a research project (see the sections cited in parentheses for detailed information on each task). Use this overview to plan a strategy for researching and writing that will enable you to complete your project within the allotted time frame. You can make notations about your schedule as well as about your topic and your reading in a *reading* or *research journal* (see 1e-1–2).

Scheduling your research project will be much easier after your first visit to the library. Once you begin to assemble your working bibliography (see 39g), start reading, and restrict your topic, you will have a clearer sense of your topic, and you will be able to judge better your own speed for performing these various tasks. You will be able to pace yourself.

If you are required to conduct field research—surveys, interviews, experiments (see 39f)—be aware that your project can take more time because you may need to supplement the field research with directed library research. In addition, field research can be time consuming. You may need to mail away surveys and wait for the replies; you will then have to factor in time for sorting the data that are returned to you. You may also need to schedule interviews in advance or repeat experiments over time. Consider these variables, plan carefully, and structure your schedule accordingly.

Schedule and Overview of the Research Process

DUE	DO PRELIMINARY RESEARCH
_____	1. Understand the nature of the assignment (39a-1), consider purpose and audience (39a-2), and devise a schedule (39a-3).
_____	2. Select a topic that interests you (39b).
_____	3. Do preliminary research to get background information (39d).
_____	4. Compile a working bibliography containing each useful source you encounter (39g).
_____	5. Based on what you learned from your initial foray in the library, restrict your topic (40a).

(continued)

EXTEND THE RESEARCH

_____ 6. Do more research on your restricted topic and evaluate the sources in your working bibliography (44a–b).

_____ 7. Read your sources critically and evaluate their effectiveness in light of your topic and purpose (40c).

_____ 8. Take accurate notes on helpful sources. Use summaries, paraphrases, and quotations, as appropriate (40d). Be careful to avoid plagiarism (41c).

_____ 9. Devise a focusing question to help guide your research. That focusing question will develop into your thesis (40e).

_____ 10. Reflect on your sources and notes to help spark your creativity, make connections, and generate ideas (40d-4).

_____ 11. Consider whether to do field research (39f).

PLAN, WRITE, RESEARCH SOME MORE, AND REVISE

_____ 12. Begin developing an informal outline of your essay indicating how you might organize and present the defense of your thesis. Revise this plan as you do additional research (40g).

_____ 13. Consider your audience and purpose (40f).

_____ 14. Draft your essay (40h).

_____ 15. Incorporate evidence from your note cards to support and develop your thesis (40i).

_____ 16. Determine the required documentation style and be sure to document all of your sources properly (Chapter 43) both in the text (43a and 43d) and at the end of the paper in a list of Works Cited (43c) or a References list (43f).

_____ 17. Revise the essay. Consult with your instructor and collaborate with your classmates to help with your revisions. Do additional research if necessary (40j).

_____ 18. Prepare the final manuscript (40k).

_____ 19. Submit the final essay.

39b Selecting your topic

Whether you are choosing from a list provided by your instructor or selecting your own, you should try to work with a topic that interests you and that you care about. It makes little difference whether you know a great deal about the topic; at the outset, interest is paramount.

Try thinking about what you have been studying in the course to get ideas. Go back to your reading journal or your personal journal and see what questions you recorded about the course, looking for the material that really sparked your interest. Do some reading; skim, preview, or reread your text-books for the course; look at magazines, journals, encyclopedias, or other reference books (see 39d-2). Try various techniques for generating ideas, such as freewriting (2b-2), annotating (2b-1), questioning (4a and 8a-3), and listing details and observations (8b-1) to get your creative juices flowing. Also consider what you would like to know more about, and make a list of two or three topics for investigation. Let those topics be the subject of your initial search in the library (39d).

Ericka Kostka, for example, selected the gray wolf as a topic for research in her Social and Ethical Issues writing course. When her instructor asked students to select a topic that had far-reaching social consequences, Kostka recalled her interest in the gray wolf that had arisen a few years earlier during a visit to Yellowstone National Park. What she learned there sparked her interest in unnatural ecological imbalances. She wanted to pursue the topic and the gray wolf in a research essay. The following statement reflects Kostka's early interest in the demise of the gray wolf and her concern about the feasibility of bringing wolves back to the park.

I was one of the 215,000 people who trooped through the "Wolves and Humans" informational slide show at Yellowstone. It was here that I heard the chilling howl of the gray wolf that communicates something about which humans can only speculate. I saw the wolf as the hunted when I heard of its systematic decimation at the beginning of the century. I saw the wolf as the hunter when I heard of its place as the premier predator of the park's hooved animals. Having confirmed this faithful representation of the duality of the gray wolf's history in Yellowstone, I wanted to come to my own conclusions about the restoration of the gray wolf population in the park.

As you can see, Kostka had a personal interest in her research. She had been affected by what she saw and heard earlier on that trip to the park. When she began her research, that personal interest propelled but did not limit her. She knew that she had to move beyond her personal experience to *investigate* the problem so that she could think more rigorously about it. In addition, she had to reach her own conclusion about how to solve the gray wolf problem. These two tasks—investigating the topic thoroughly and reaching a conclusion about it—are fundamental in the research process. The tasks will likely lead you, as they led Kostka, to the library.

Try to get feedback from your instructor before becoming too involved in researching and writing about a topic. You will want to determine whether your topic will interest others, whether there are adequate resources in your library or in your community to enable you to proceed, and whether the topic can be completed in the allotted time. Your instructor may have helpful hints on these matters. Often, as a starting point for discussion, instructors will require a brief statement about your planned topic.

39c   Using primary and secondary sources

In your research, you will likely be consulting both primary and secondary sources. *Primary sources* are firsthand accounts: historical documents, interviews, surveys, experiments, diaries, journals, letters, books, articles, eyewitness accounts of an event, or a writer's original work (a novel, poem, short story, or essay)—any source that you can examine directly as raw evidence, as if you are the first to look at it.

Secondary sources are materials written about primary sources. Secondary sources include analyses of raw evidence by scholars, experts in a field, or other researchers. Secondary sources also include critical writing that expresses an opinion, draws conclusions, or explains an issue or circumstance. You can find secondary sources in the form of books, pamphlets, reviews, articles, and essays.

When you read or examine primary sources, you do all of the analytical work. Yours will be a fresh look at the source, free of the bias of other researchers. That freedom to interpret can be exciting, but it can also be a bit intimidating. Secondary sources can help you analyze the primary sources because in them you will find interpretations, ways of looking at the raw evidence. But be aware that secondary sources can bias the way you look at raw material. When you turn to secondary sources, look for insight but not for an answer. Only you can come up with the thesis or the solution to the problem you are investigating.

Most of your research will involve consulting both primary and secondary sources. Let your purpose and assignment determine the types of sources you consult in your research. In her research, Kostka consulted secondary sources because she was not able to conduct field research.

39d Discovering the library's resources

The library contains a wealth of information that will be a great help to you as a researcher. Whether you are beginning to do background reading to find a topic, looking for information to help you focus your topic, or preparing to investigate your topic in depth, the library is the place to go.

Before Ericka Kostka went to the library, she considered limiting her investigation to the wolf problem in Yellowstone. But because she did not yet know enough about the problem to decide how to restrict her topic (see 40a), she decided instead to keep an open mind. She needed more information. Once in the library, Kostka had a more immediate problem than the gray wolf controversy; she had to find her way around and learn to use the library's resources efficiently.

To be an efficient researcher, it helps to have some kind of research strategy. Begin by learning the physical layout of the library and the organization of the book stacks; familiarize yourself with the available reference guides and the library's card and online catalogs. Your research will go more smoothly if you identify keywords related to your topic (see 39e-2 on keyword searches). *Keywords* consist of synonyms or other words that capture a part of what the topic is about. They will help you as you search through the library's catalogs. Kostka's list of keywords included *wolf, wolf restoration, animal repopulation,* and *endangered species.*

Once you are oriented in the library, devise a plan of action. Try to be systematic in your research (e.g., find all the sources you can about one particular keyword at a time), but also realize that research is a process of discovery. Allow yourself to find the unexpected and to pursue interesting sidetracks up to a point; but try to stay organized and focused on your topic. Kostka found many intriguing subjects listed when she searched for her keyword *wolf.* But had she become too involved in tracing interesting topics such as the importance of wolves in the folklore of many cultures, she would have lost valuable time and shifted her focus.

1   Getting oriented in the library

Your first stop in the library should be the circulation or information desk. The library staff will answer your questions and provide information about the library's floor plan, its resources, and its computers. The floor plan shows you where the books are shelved. A map also shows you the location of the reference room, where you can begin your general research; the periodical room, where you can find the most recent copies of magazines, newspapers, and journals; and the storage area for other periodicals, including those on microfilm and microfiche. Larger libraries may have a computer resource room and many other specialized areas where you can find collections of books, journals, and indexes related to specific academic disciplines; your library may also have different reference centers for science, humanities, social sciences, and government documents. Once you know what resources the library contains and where to find them, you are ready to start your preliminary research.

If you feel overwhelmed or confused while doing research, or if you just have a simple question, take advantage of one of the most helpful resources a library has to offer: its staff and, in particular, the reference librarian. Reference librarians are familiar with all of the library's holdings and are experts in retrieving information.

Computer Tip

Accessing the Library Online

You can now do much of your researching online. Most university libraries and many public libraries now have online Web access to Internet research sources, CD and other databases, as well as online subscriptions to both popular and scholarly journals. Some of these tools allow you only to gather information about titles, authors, and publication information, while others allow you to retrieve either an abstract or the full text of an article. Consult a reference librarian for information about the electronic sources available.

2   Using reference books

The library's reference room is perhaps the most important room in the library for a researcher. There you will find encyclopedias, dictionaries, indexes, abstracts, bibliographies, and so forth. These reference books do not circulate; they are always in the reference room, and a librarian is usually there to offer assistance. But remember that these reference materials merely point you toward other sources—books, periodicals, other indexes, other bibliographies—that will help with your research. You cannot finish your research in the reference room.

Use reference materials to decide if a particular topic interests you or to get a general sense of the issues and controversies that surround your topic. These references are not difficult to use, but they differ slightly from each other. Always look in the front of each reference work for information about how to use it.

All of the printed indexes and guides in the following discussion should be in the reference room. Many reference works are also available on CD; these disks give you immediate access to computer-based sources ranging from dictionaries to periodical indexes. You will have to consult the floor plan to locate your library's card catalog, online catalog, CD, and other computer resources.

Guides to reference books

Two important general guides organize and list reference books by fields and provide useful summaries.

Balay, Robert, ed. *Guide to Reference Books.* 11th ed. Chicago: ALA, 1996.

Walford's Guide to Reference Material. 8th ed. London: Library Association, 1999.

These general guides lead you quickly to other reference books that can help you locate sources for your essay.

General and specialized encyclopedias

General encyclopedias provide good background information on a wide range of topics. Short articles can help you identify areas of scholarly debate associated with your subject. A short bibliography of related sources often appears at the end of these articles.

Specialized encyclopedias provide longer and more detailed articles about topics, often by specialists in a particular field. They may also provide more bibliographic information than you find in general encyclopedias. Consult a reference librarian for specialized encyclopedias on your topic or in your discipline.

Remember, encyclopedias, like all reference materials, enable you to familiarize yourself with your topic. They cannot be your main source of information. They provide a starting point.

GENERAL ENCYCLOPEDIAS

Academic American Encyclopedia. Rev. ed. Danbury, CT: Grolier, 1998.

Collier's Encyclopedia. 24 volumes. General coverage of a wide range of topics. Designed for high school and college use.

Encyberpedia: The Living Encyclopedia from Cyberspace.
<http://www.encyberpedia.com/ency.htm>.

Encyclopaedia Britannica. 32 volumes. Consists of four parts: the *Micropaedia,* containing short factual articles; the *Macropaedia,* containing longer entries with depth of coverage; a 2-volume index; and the *Propaedia,* outlining the information contained in the other volumes.

Encyclopedia Americana. 30 volumes. Strong in science and technology.

The New Columbia Encyclopedia. 1 volume. General encyclopedia.

Random House Encyclopedia. 1 volume. General encyclopedia.

For her preliminary research, Ericka Kostka consulted both the *Encyclopedia Americana* and the *Encyclopaedia Britannica;* each helped her get a better sense of the gray wolf problem. In the *Americana* Kostka found not only general information about the wolf's physical characteristics, but also information about the wolf's eating habits. They reminded her of what she had learned at Yellowstone about the wolf as hunter and as hunted. Kostka also found the short bibliography (shown on p. 578) at the end of the encyclopedia article.

Bibliography
Davidson, Max, *The Wolf* (Merrimack 1984).
Fox, Michael W., *Behavior of Wolves, Dogs, and Related
    Canids* (1971; reprint, Krieger 1984).
Klinghammer, Erich, *The Behavior and Ecology of Wolves*
    (Garland 1979).
Mech, L. David, *The Wolf: The Ecology and Behavior of an
    Endangered Species* (Univ. of Minn. Press 1981).
Pimlott, Douglas H., ed., *Wolves* (Unipub 1975).
Simon, Noel, *Wolves* (Biblio. Dist. 1985).

Because the *Britannica* contains both short, factual articles and long, narrative articles, Kostka decided to look first in the index for an overview of the topical coverage. She looked under *wolves* and found nothing; under *wolf*, she found the following entries.

wolf **12:***726:2b*
    major ref. in Mammals **23:**414:1a
    ancestry of dog **4:**149:2a; **17:**444:1b
    effect of predators on biosphere
        14:1032:1b
    for a list of related subjects see
        PROPAEDIA: Section 313

She checked each entry listed. In the first article, she read that the gray wolf "performs an important natural function in controlling the number of large herbivores and in weeding out those less fit for survival." The article—on the effect of predators on the biosphere—also provided additional information about the natural selection problem.

Because Kostka was doing general reading and was not yet ready to restrict her topic, she was writing informal notes in her reading journal about the ideas that came to her. She made a note about the wolf as the hunter and the hunted and began to wonder who—conservationists or the landowners—might be right about the wolf. She knew that it would take more research to find out, and she had other sources to consult in the reference room.

Biographical reference books

Biographical sources provide information about the lives of famous people. They often include pictures, bibliographies, and historical information associated with the people whose lives are highlighted.

American Men and Women of Science

American Women Writers

Contemporary Authors

Contemporary Dramatists

Contemporary Novelists

Contemporary Poets

Current Biography

Dictionary of American Biography, plus supplements

Dictionary of American Scholars

Dictionary of National Biography, 1882–1900 plus supplements

International Who's Who

Notable American Women

Who's Who in America

Who's Who of American Women

Who's Who in Government

World Authors

Specialized bibliographies

It is standard practice in scholarly writing to include at the end of books or chapters and at the end of articles a list of the sources that the writer consulted or cited. Those lists, or bibliographies, often include sources that you will also want to consult. You saw such a listing for the encyclopedia article that Ericka read.

But other more specialized and comprehensive bibliographies are available. These bibliographies list important articles and books related to specific fields of study. They are excellent starting points for focused research because they are more detailed and technical than the bibliographies you will find in general reference books.

Annual Bibliography of English Language and Literature

Bibliographic Index

Bibliographical Guide to the History of Indian-White Relations in the United States

Bibliographies in American History

Bibliography of North America

Essay and General Literature Index

Foreign Affairs Bibliography

Goldentree Bibliographies in Language and Literature

International Bibliography of the Social Sciences
International Bibliography of Sociology
MLA International Bibliography of Books and Articles on the Modern Languages and Literatures
New Cambridge Bibliography of English Literature
Science and Engineering Literature
Social Work Education: A Bibliography
The Year's Work in English Studies

Dictionaries

Unabridged and specialized dictionaries offer authoritative information on language beyond what you can find in a standard college or abridged dictionary. Unabridged dictionaries provide a wide range of meanings for words, some historical information about the derivation of words, and information about usage, among other things.

UNABRIDGED DICTIONARIES

American Heritage Dictionary of the English Language. 4th ed. Boston: Houghton, 2000.
Funk and Wagnall's New Standard Dictionary of the English Language
Oxford English Dictionary
Random House Dictionary of the English Language
Webster's Dictionary and Roget's Thesaurus. <http://www.refdesk.com>.
Merriam-Webster's Collegiate Dictionary. 10th ed. Springfield, MA: Merriam, 2001.

SPECIALIZED DICTIONARIES

Follett, Wilson. *Modern American Usage.* Ed. Jacques Barzun.
Fowler, H. W. *Dictionary of Modern English Usage.*
Onions, Charles T., et al., eds. *The Oxford Dictionary of English Etymology.*
Partridge, Eric. *A Dictionary of Slang and Unconventional English.* 8th ed. Ed. Paul Beale.
Webster's New Dictionary of Synonyms.

Atlases and gazetteers

An atlas is a collection of maps; a gazetteer is a dictionary of places. Look to these sources for geographical data.

Columbia Lippincott Gazetteer of the World

Cosmopolitan World Atlas

Encyclopaedia Britannica World Atlas International

Goode's World Atlas

National Atlas of the United States

National Geographic Atlas of the World

The New York Times Atlas of the World

Webster's New Geographical Dictionary

Almanacs and yearbooks

Almanacs and yearbooks provide statistics and other factual information, often on current events. These reference sources are compiled annually.

Americana Annual

Annual Register of World Events

Facts on File

Guinness Book of World Records

The World Almanac and Book of Facts

Book indexes

Book indexes can help you locate books when you do not have complete bibliographic information about a book or when you have an author's name and want to know if that author has published relevant books on your topic. The indexes are listed by author, subject, and title and are available online (O) or on CD, as indicated.

Books in Print (O, CD)

Cumulative Book Index (CD)

Paperbound Books in Print (CD)

3   Using periodicals

Periodicals include magazines (published weekly or monthly), journals (usually published quarterly), and newspapers. In magazines and newspapers you will find general information to help with your research. Occasionally you will also find highly specialized articles on a subject. Rely on magazines and newspapers as important sources for your preliminary research. They will contain current events and up-to-date information that you may not be able to find in books.

Journals almost always pertain to a particular academic field and contain specialized information and critical articles related to that field. Journals not only provide important information but also offer critical analyses of that information. Thus, journal articles help you attain perspective on your topic. To find articles in magazines, journals, and newspapers, you need to search the periodical indexes and computer databases in your library (see 39d–e).

During your research, you are likely to find periodicals stored on one of three types of *microform: microfilm* (film on a reel—usually 35mm), *microfiche* (a flat sheet of film), and *microprint* (a reduced image printed on an opaque white card). Microform condenses printed material and saves valuable storage space in libraries. Because you cannot read microform with the naked eye, you will have to use one of the library's reading machines; they magnify the material and often allow you to print copies of selected pages. Fees for copying vary. Remember that the periodical you need is most likely on microform. When you do not find it in the periodical reading room or on the shelves with other bound periodicals, always check microform.

Periodical indexes

Periodical indexes will direct you to articles in periodicals. These indexes are not difficult to use, but they do vary widely in content, format, and organization. Look in the front of the index for a list of the abbreviations used as well as guidelines for using the index. A number of different indexes are available, each covering a select group of periodicals. Check the beginning of the index or volume to determine which periodicals it lists.

Also be sure to check whether your library has the periodicals you want to consult. The *serials catalog,* which you can find in the periodical reading room, or the online catalog will inform you of your library's periodical holdings; these catalogs should also tell you whether the periodicals can be found on microform or in their original printed form. You will likely find current issues in the library's periodical room, but back issues may be stored elsewhere. When looking for periodicals, you can save time by asking the librarians for assistance.

Printed indexes are being replaced by the library's online catalog of holdings. Even if your library has printed indexes or a serials catalog, try the online catalog first. Check the printed indexes, usually located in the periodical reading room, if you do not find what you want on the online catalog.

Many libraries offer CD computer database versions of periodical indexes. Check with your reference librarian for information about what systems are available in your library and how to use them. (For more on using databases, see 39e-3.)

General periodical indexes

General indexes for periodicals list articles from newspapers and general-interest magazines. These periodicals can provide current sources on your topic. However, these general-interest sources may not provide sufficient coverage.

ERIC (Education Resources Information Center). An educational database containing full-text articles and abstracts.

FirstSearch. Specialized databases that include library collections and journal articles.

InfoTrac. A computerized index to more than one thousand periodicals, available on CD. A single disk covers three years, and coverage—including law, business management, technology, social sciences, and humanities—begins in 1982 or later. InfoTrac includes the *General Periodicals Index, Magazine Index Plus, National Newspaper Index,* and *Academic Index.*

Magazine Index. This monthly index covers more than one thousand magazines. Available on microfilm, online through DIALOG and Bibliographic Retrieval Service (BRS), and InfoTrac.

ProQuest. A database of periodical articles. Through ProQuest you may find other databases on biology, nursing, and psychology.

National Newspaper Index. Indexes major newspapers, including the *Christian Science Monitor,* the *Los Angeles Times,* the *New York Times,* the *Wall Street Journal,* and the *Washington Post.* Available in print, on microfilm, and online through DIALOG and BRS.

New York Times Index. Indexes the most complete national newspaper and provides important summaries of longer news items. Useful for dating events. Arranges stories chronologically under subject heading. Published every two weeks, with annual consolidations. Available online and on CD.

Poole's Index to Periodical Literature. Indexes periodicals from 1802 to 1906.

Popular Periodicals Index. A subject index for popular periodicals not listed in other indexes, especially the *Readers' Guide.*

Readers' Guide to Periodical Literature. Indexes general-interest periodicals from 1900 to the present. This indispensable guide for over 200 publications—appearing semimonthly with quarterly and annual consolidations—helps you investigate political trends, current social issues, recent scientific discoveries, and important cultural events. Entries are arranged by author and subject. It is also available online and on CD.

Wall Street Journal Index. Indexes the newspaper and *Barrons.* Available on CD.

Kostka went to the *New York Times Index* for more information on how to approach the gray wolf problem. In the consolidated index for 1985–1989, she found numerous entries under *wolves,* including the following, which seemed important to her.

WOLVES. See also
Hunting and Trapping, **1985:** F 20, Mr 26, **1989:** D 5
Oil (Petroleum) and Gasoline, **1988:** My 11
Parks and Other Recreation Areas, **1985:** F 18
  US Fish and Wildlife Service reviews National Park Service proposal to reintroduce 30 breeding pairs of timber wolves to Yellowstone National Park, move opposed by Wyoming Congressional delegation and Idaho Cattleman's Association (S), Je 3,III,4:6 (1986)
  Twelve wolves from the Rocky Mountains in the Canadian province of Alberta settled in Glacier National Park, Montana, where they spent the winter hunting deer and elk; map (M), Je 29,I,22:1 (1986)
  William E Schmidt article on plan by US Fish and Wildlife Service to repopulate Alligator River National Wildlife Refuge in North Carolina with red wolves; illustration; map (M), N 13,I,22:3 (1986)
  British Columbia campaign to kill wolves, which includes shooting of wolves from helicopters, stirs opposition, most of

it from Project Wolf, headed by Paul Watson; opponents
fear extinction of wolf and charge that scientific rationale
for kill program is flawed; proponents argue that failure to
thin out wolves will exacerbate decline in prey population;
photo (M), Mr 3,III,3:1 (1987)
    Federal Fish and Wildlife Service plan to reintroduce grey
wolves in Yellowstone National Park is thwarted by
resistance of sheep and cattle ranchers; service is
proceeding with plans to release red wolves, which are even
scarcer, in Alligator River National Wildlife Refuge in
North Carolina (S), My 17,I,53:2 (1987)

Kostka then consulted four entries from the 1985 *Readers' Guide:* one on
Yellowstone; three on problems related to wolves elsewhere.

Wolves
        See also
        Coyotes
Crying wolf in Yellowstone. S. Begley. *Newsweek* 106:74
        D 16 '85
FCC stops Alaska's aerial wolf hunt [use of radio telemetry]
        Sci News 127:57 Ja 26 '85
How delicate is the balance of nature? [study of wolf
        control in Minnesota] L. D. Mech. il *Natl Wildl* 23:54–9
        F/Mr '85
Revered and reviled. Minnesota's wolves are in trouble
        again. D. Nevin. il *Smithsonian* 15:78–87 Ja '85

Specialized periodical indexes

Specialized periodical indexes list articles from scholarly journals, usually related to a particular academic discipline; these indexes help you
research your topic in depth. Ask a reference librarian for help in using these
indexes, many of which are available online (O) or on CD, as indicated.

Applied Science and Technology Index (O, CD)

Art Index (O, CD)

Biography Index (O, CD)

Biological and Agricultural Index (CD)

Business Periodicals Index (O, CD)

Computer Literature Index

Current Index to Journals in Education (O, CD)

ERIC (Education Resources Information Center)

Essay and General Literature Index

General Science Index (O, CD)   A cumulative subject index for periodicals, arranged in alphabetical order, that contains a separate listing of citations to book reviews. Subject fields include astronomy, atmospheric science, biology, chemistry, mathematics, microbiology, and zoology.

Humanities Index (O, CD)

Index to U.S. Government Periodicals (O, CD)

Music Index (CD)

Philosopher's Index (O, CD)

PsycLIT (O, CD)   Compiled by the American Psychological Association and made available online and through several CD vendors, this database contains citations and abstracts to over 1,300 periodicals in psychology and the behavioral sciences as well as to book chapters and book records.

Public Affairs Information Service (O, CD)

Social Sciences Index (O, CD)

Technical Book Review Index

Vertical File Index (O)

Kostka consulted the *General Science Index* and found twelve entries under *wolves*, including the following.

Waiting for wolves to howl in Yellowstone. T. Williams.
  il *Audubon* 92:32-4+ N '90
Who's afraid of the big bad wolf? L. D. Mech. il *Audubon*
  92:82-5 Mr '90
Wolves from the north. F. Hoke. *Environment* 32:23-4
  Je '90
Wolves vs. dogs. F. Graham, Jr. *Audubon* 92:18+ N
  '90
Yellowstone lets the wolf through the door. C. Joyce.
  New Sci 126:21 Je 2 '90
                    Food and feeding
Validation of estimating food intake in gray wolves
  by ^{22}Na turnover. G. D. Delgiudice and others. bibl
  il *J Wildl Manage* 55:59–71 Ja '91

Kostka then found thirty-one entries listed under *wolves* in the *PsycLIT* index, including the following.

TI   DOCUMENT TITLE: The public and the timber wolf in Minnesota.
AU   AUTHOR(S): Kellert, -Stephen-R.
IN   INSTITUTIONAL AFFILIATION OF FIRST AUTHOR: Yale U, School of Forestry &
Environmental Studies, New Haven, CT, US
JN   JOURNAL NAME: Anthrozoos; 1987 Fal Vol 1(2) 100–109
IS   ISSN: 08927936
LA   LANGUAGE: English
PY   PUBLICATION YEAR: 1987
AB   ABSTRACT: Reviews the results of a study of public attitudes, knowledge,
behaviors, and symbolic perceptions of the timber wolf in Minnesota. Data were
obtained from telephone interviews with urban and northern counties residents in
Minnesota, including deer hunters, livestock farmers, and trappers. Limited factual
knowledge of the timber wolf was found among the general public, although
considerably greater knowledge was found among trappers and, to a lesser degree,
hunters. Most Ss, except farmers, viewed the wolf in favorable and positive terms.
(PsycLIT Database Copyright 1989 American Psychological Assn, all rights reserved)
KP   KEY PHRASE: public attitudes & knowledge & behaviors & perceptions of timber wolf;
farmers & hunters & trappers & general public
DE   DESCRIPTORS: PUBLIC-OPINION; KNOWLEDGE-LEVEL; BEHAVIOR-; SOCIAL-PERCEPTION;
ANIMAL-ETHOLOGY; ADULTHOOD-; WOLVES-
CC   CLASSIFICATION CODE(S): 3120; 2440; 31; 24
PO   POPULATION: Animal
UC   UPDATE CODE: 8904
AN   PSYC ABS. VOL. AND ABS. NO.: 76-11819
JC   JOURNAL CODE: 3155

Kostka's use of periodical indexes

The *New York Times Index* gave Ericka Kostka a clear sense that the wolf
problem was not confined to Yellowstone National Park, and it became clear
to her that she would eventually have to limit her research to a particular
area. From these index entries about Yellowstone, she could also see that
there had been vigorous opposition to bringing wolves back into the park.
This information contrasted with what she had read earlier in the encyclopedia article, which described how wolves stabilize populations in some herds
and thereby help balance the ecosystem. She noted these facts in her reading
journal and photocopied the page from the *New York Times Index* so that
when she was ready, she could locate and read these articles to provide background information. Kostka was already compiling a working bibliography
(see 39g)—a preliminary list of books and articles that she might use in her
essay and that she would read to help her limit her topic (see 40a).

Kostka also checked the *Readers' Guide to Periodical Literature* and the
General Science Index. Her instructor advised her to look at several of the
yearly volumes in the *Readers' Guide* to get a sense of whether there was continuing interest in her topic. She consulted each of the annual indexes from
1985 to 1996 and found numerous entries under *wolves* for each of those years.

Because Kostka found so many articles on her topic in the *Readers' Guide* and the *General Science Index,* she began to feel confident, even before consulting the sources themselves, that she could find enough information about the wolf problem in Yellowstone to write a good research essay. Nevertheless, she still kept an open mind about whether to limit her research and just how to limit it.

Abstracts and citation indexes

Abstracts provide summaries of articles or books in designated fields of study that can help you gauge the usefulness of particular sources. The title of the abstract suggests the nature and extent of the coverage. Many journals print an abstract with each article, and collections of abstracts are published regularly. *Citation indexes* allow you to track what has been written about an article or book so that you can see how articles comment on one another. Many citation indexes and abstracts are available online.

ABSTRACTS

Biological Abstracts

Chemical Abstracts

Communications Abstracts

Dissertation Abstracts International

Ecology Abstracts

Historical Abstracts

Physics Abstracts

Psychological Abstracts

Science Citation Index

Sociological Abstracts

Social Sciences Citation Index

CITATION INDEXES

Arts and Humanities Citation Index

Science Citation Index

Social Sciences Citation Index

4 Using the library's special resources

In addition to books, journals, magazines, and newspapers, libraries often have other resources that can support your research and provide important information. Usually a librarian will be available to help you with these resources.

- **Art collections.** Drawings, engravings, paintings, photographs, and 35mm slides.

- **Audio collections and listening areas.** Music, readings, speeches, radio dramas, and documentaries recorded on audiocassettes, compact discs, and records—as well as listening areas equipped with cassette decks, turntables, and compact disc players.

- **Government documents.** U.S. government reports, catalogs, pamphlets, hearings, newsletters, and other documents. The *United States Government Publications Index* and *Monthly Catalogue of United States Government Publications,* available online and on CD, will help you identify sources.

- **Interlibrary loans.** Librarians can often borrow books for you through interlibrary loans. Such loans take time to arrange, but they can bring you books and periodicals that your library does not have in its collection.

- **Computer center.** Usually contains software for a wide range of applications including word processing, spreadsheet, and database management packages, as well as computers for students and faculty to use.

- **Special collections.** Manuscripts, memorabilia, rare books, and other archival materials.

- **Video collections.** Filmstrips, slides, and videocassettes.

39e Searching for sources in the library and on computers

The computer has transformed the process of searching for sources. A search that in recent times was conducted from print indexes or card catalogs is now done almost entirely from a keyboard.

1   Using the library catalog

The *library catalog* lists all of a library's holdings, including books, periodicals, cassettes, films, and microforms. In the past, all libraries used a card catalog system to record their holdings. However, most libraries have transferred the record of their holdings to an online catalog or a microfiche catalog. The online system enables researchers to use public computer terminals to search quickly and efficiently for information.

All library catalogs list holdings alphabetically three ways: by author, by title, and by subject. In addition, all catalog entries include a call number that will help you locate books on the shelves. The call numbers appear in the library catalogs and on the spine of the books. Be sure to copy the correct numbers before going to get the books. The books are shelved according to these call numbers. The librarian can recall books that have been checked out or retrieve a book from the special storage area. Recalling a book that has been checked out takes time, so plan accordingly. If your library has closed stacks and you cannot take the books from the shelves, you must fill out a slip with the call number, present it at the circulation desk, and wait for the book to be brought to you.

The call number system used by most academic libraries is the Library of Congress System. Its call numbers begin with letters: *A* for general works, *B* for philosophy, *C* and *D* for history, and so forth. Some libraries use the older Dewey Decimal System. Its call numbers begin with three digits, 000 to 999. Each number indicates a category of information: 300–399 for social sciences, 500–599 for natural science, 800–899 for literature, and so forth. Some libraries use both systems to classify books.

When you do a library search, consult the *Library of Congress Subject Headings* (LCSH), a three-volume reference book that lists all of the subject headings used to classify books. You can find the LCSH in the reference room or near the catalog in libraries that use the Library of Congress call number system. LCSH will help you locate books by subject. It will also help you select keywords for use in your other computer searches.

Using keywords that are closely related to your subject will help make you a more efficient researcher. A precise subject heading or keyword will clearly identify your topic and direct you to relevant sources. Broad subject headings may lead you to thousands of entries that will overwhelm you and may not be relevant to your search. The LCSH, in fact, can help you find keywords that might not occur to you on your own. Ericka Kostka, for example, found these other subject headings under the entry *wolves: Canis lupus, Gray Wolves, Timber Wolves, Canis, Wolves—extermination, Wolves—Control,* and *Folklore.* She also found the Library of Congress call numbers associated with these general categories: *wolves, control,* and *folklore.*

You are likely to have better luck with subject searches using the online catalog or CDs because the computer can search quickly and extensively.

Using the online catalog

The online catalog gives you rapid access to the same kind of information that you find in the card catalog. But note that the two catalogs do not necessarily contain the same listings. Sometimes only part of a library's holdings are online. Also, books and other materials acquired before the switch to a computerized system may not be listed in the online catalog, and more current books may not appear in the card catalog. It is a good idea to check both catalogs when you are looking for a particular book or are doing extensive searches. A librarian can tell you how the two catalogs differ at your library.

Many libraries are connected through nationwide computer networks to other libraries' catalogs and to the Online Computer Library Center (OCLC) that links libraries across the country. Smaller, local networks connect affiliated colleges, universities, museums, and institutes that have agreed to pool their research resources. These computer networks are particularly useful for verifying bibliographic citations and for helping you find books that are not in your school's library. You can request materials from other libraries through the interlibrary loan service provided by your reference librarian.

The first time you use an online catalog, ask a librarian for assistance, or read the library's printed instructions for using the online system. See the next section on performing keyword searches.

If you search for a book in the computer catalog by author or title, you will get individual entries such as the following, which Kostka found.

Location:	BOB-Stacks QL737.C22M4
Author:	Mech, L. David,
Title:	The wolf: the ecology and behavior of an endangered species, by L. David Mech.
Publisher:	Garden City, N.Y., Published for the American Museum of Natural History by the Natural History Press [1970] xx, 384 p. illus., maps. 24 cm.

Sample Online Catalog Entry, Author

If you search the online system for books by subject, you will see a list such as the following one on the screen. When you type one of the numbers from this list and press the *Enter* key, the computer will give you a full citation for the book.

This subject: Wolves.   has   11 citations
                                                                 in entire catalog

Ref#	Author	Title	Date
1	Barry, Scott.	The kingdom of wolves /	1979
2	Eckels, Richard Preston, 1909–	Greek wolf-lore . . .	1937
3	Fiennes, Richard.	The order of wolves /	1976
4	Fox, Michael W., 1937–	The soul of the wolf /	1980
5	Gesell, Arnold Lucius, 1880–196>	Wolf child and human child; being a>	1941
6	Lopez, Barry Holstun, 1945–	Of wolves and men /	1978
7	Mech, L. David.	The wolf: the ecology and behavior >	1970
8	Miller, Gerrit Smith, 1869–1923>	The names of the large wolves of no>	1912
9	Peters, Roger.	Dance of the wolves /	1985
10	Rutter, Russell J.	The world of the wolf ,	1968
11	Zimen, Erik, 1941–	The wolf : his place in the natural>	1981

Type a number to see associated information.

Sample Online Catalog Entry, Subject

2   Performing keyword searches

Keyword searches, which take advantage of the computer's speed and its ability to search across the entire catalog, are especially useful when you are searching by subject rather than by title or author. The keyword search matches words or terms that you select with words or terms in the catalog or another database. Instructions for doing keyword searches will be available on the computer's screen when you select a search function or in printed handouts available at the computer terminals.

You should do a keyword search when you do not know exact titles, subject headings, or the author's full name; the search will help you locate a particular source when you do not have enough information to call it directly to the screen. But you can also use a keyword search to control the way the computer scans the catalog. In essence, you can modify the search to meet your own needs by combining keywords with special symbols that are explained in the instructions. The process is simple. Follow the instructions, and do not be afraid to experiment.

When Kostka did her computer search, she decided to see what she could find by doing a keyword search using the words *gray wolf*. She had no success. Then she tried the word *wolves* and found twenty-five items, many of them very general and irrelevant.

To narrow the search, Kostka decided to use the special search function that allowed her to combine keywords and special symbols to find more specific references. She chose the words *wolves* and *Yellowstone* as her keywords and then used a designated connecting symbol (/) between the words (*wolves/Yellowstone*), thereby limiting the search to only those sources that contained both of her keywords. Her search yielded no titles. After scanning the twenty-five titles that she had obtained with the word *wolves*, Kostka realized that she would have to do most of her research from periodicals, rather than from books.

Kostka's instructor had no objection to the types of sources she used in her research. However, you should always check with your instructor to ensure that you are using the required balance of primary and secondary source materials, books, and periodicals.

3   Using computerized databases

Most libraries have access to large online database networks. These databases store vast amounts of specialized information about books and periodicals, and their listings give you more information than you can get from single library catalogs. Specifically, databases can provide (1) a list of sources related to your topic, (2) abstracts or brief summaries of sources, and (3) the full text of a source that may not be available in your library.

The most widely used database services in academic libraries are the Bibliographic Retrieval Service (BRS) and DIALOG, systems that provide access to hundreds of databases and over a million sources of information. The Research Libraries Information Network (RLIN) also provides a bibliographic database (BIB) and access to Anthropological Literature, Avery Index to Architectural Periodicals, Hispanic American Periodicals Index, Handbook of Latin American Studies, History of Science & Technology database, Inside Information (from the ten thousand most requested journals at the British Library's Document Supplement Centre), Public Affairs Information Service, and Periodical Abstracts. RLIN is an online database with

Computer Tip

Using Bookmarks

A convenient way to save time when doing research online is to "bookmark" or check off a source you would like to look at more closely later. A bookmark highlights a URL so you don't have to copy it down, character by character, yourself. After you have scanned through a range of sources and bookmarked likely candidates for your research, you return to your list and click on the bookmarked entries to actually look into them. Later, your bookmarks can serve as a URL Works Cited list.

millions of bibliographic records for books, journals, archival materials, and videos. These items are owned and cataloged by over 100 major research libraries that are members of the Research Libraries Group (RLG). Ask a librarian for help with these online database networks; the librarian will advise you about the feasibility of doing a database search for your particular topic.

You can also access many of these databases from your computer at home if it is Internet-ready. Often you have to pay a fee to subscribe to these networks, but more and more colleges and universities are giving students access to their mainframe computer systems and to the Internet (see Chapter 42 for more on the Internet and the World Wide Web). Check with your academic computing facilities and with the reference librarians for information about accessing these services.

Online services give you immediate access to *Newspaper Abstracts, Periodical Abstracts,* the *New York Times Index,* and the *MLA International Bibliography,* among others. For recent additions to online databases check *Ulrich's International Periodicals Directory.*

As helpful as database searches can be, they sometimes yield an overwhelming amount of information. Thus, the keywords you select for conducting a database search, whether authors, titles, or words related to your subject, should be very specific so that the database does not give you too many sources. Specificity will help make your search manageable. Try consulting the thesaurus of *descriptors* (keywords) found in most databases to help you limit your search, or brainstorm with your reference librarian for terms most likely to yield useful sources.

Ericka Kostka consulted Periodical Abstracts (providing abstracts and indexing to articles from over 1,600 general reference publications as well as the most recent six months of the *New York Times* and *Wall Street Journal*). Her search using the keyword *wolves* yielded ninety-three possible sources; eight of those looked promising because they were about problems associated with the wolf as an endangered species.

Kostka used the same keywords, *wolves* and *Yellowstone*, to discover much new and old material through advanced search techniques that are built into most search programs. These advanced techniques (often called *Boolean search techniques*) allow you to choose whether to search for each of your keywords separately (*wolves* OR *Yellowstone*) or to combine them as a way of limiting your search so that you find only sources containing both terms (*wolves* AND *Yellowstone*), or to combine some terms and exclude others (*wolves* AND *Yellowstone* NOT *Idaho*). The precise techniques for initiating these combinations vary from program to program.

Use these same Boolean techniques for Internet searches. You can find detailed instruction for Internet research in Chapter 42, including Internet resources on the gray wolf controversy.

39f   Doing field research

Based on your audience, purpose, and course requirements, you may find it necessary to gather your evidence for your research paper outside the library by doing *field research*—conducting interviews, collecting information through surveys, and making direct observations. Field research is a fairly common part of research projects in the social sciences, the natural sciences, and business.

As a field researcher seeking raw evidence, you are responsible for determining where to find the information, how to gather it, and from whom to get it.

1   Conducting Interviews

Interviewing involves asking questions of people so that you can collect information about your topic. When you find it necessary to conduct interviews, think about who can help you. Do you need to question experts or a sample of people in your community? You must also devise your questions in advance and prepare a realistic schedule for your interviews. Whether you are talking to a leading scientist or a randomly chosen motorist at a congested intersection, you are taking busy, committed people away from their lives and work; you owe them the courtesy of being efficient and considerate. Most of what you do in interviews is dictated by common sense, but the accompanying chart lists practical tips that will help you plan and conduct your work.

Tips for Conducting Successful Interviews

- Generate your questions carefully (see 4a on questioning); be precise and thorough. You are not likely to be granted follow-up interviews. Keep in mind three important principles as you draw up your questions.

  1. Ask for facts. "How many wolves have you observed in the park over the last decade?" "How many wolves have wandered out of the park's boundaries and attacked sheep?" Such questions lead to straightforward and informative answers, but they also lead to other questions, to interpretations, and to important digressions.

  2. Ask for an interpretation of the facts. "What do you think about the current debate over reintroducing the wolf into wilderness preserves?" "You said there have been four wolf attacks on sheep in the last decade. What do you make of those attacks?" Interpretative or open-ended questions take longer to answer. Factor in time for such answers.

  3. Ask for an expert opinion, as appropriate. Expert witnesses know a great deal about the topic and can give you considerable information, perhaps far more than you need. Be prepared to keep your questions and the interview focused.

- Establish a set time frame for the interviews. You will probably have no more than an hour to conduct the complete interview; plan accordingly.

- Set up your interviews in advance. It is always a good idea to make an appointment and to ask for permission if you expect to use a tape recorder or a video camera.

- Practice your interviewing technique with a friend. Develop the art of listening. Learn to ask your questions as the opportunity arises. Be flexible. Take a minute near the end of your practice interview to review your list of questions to see that you have asked them all.

(continued)

- On the day before the interview, call to confirm the appointment. Check all of your equipment. If you are using audiovisual equipment, purchase extra batteries and tapes, and gather together pencils and pens, a notebook, and your final list of questions.
- Dress appropriately, considering where the interview will be conducted.
- Arrive a few minutes early; respect the time limits of the interview; enjoy the occasion to talk with an expert or eyewitness; take adequate notes to ensure that you have a record of the interview; and at the end of the interview thank the person. A follow-up thank-you note is also a good idea.

2   Conducting surveys

Conducting surveys requires the same kind of careful planning that interviews do. In fact, a series of interviews could be the basis for your survey. But surveys can also take the form of questionnaires distributed through the mail or handed out in one of your classes, at your dormitory, or in your community.

Whatever your purpose, whether you are trying to find out about corporate decision-making procedures or the voting patterns of college students, you will have to make a special effort to design an appropriate questionnaire. Because you are not likely to have the opportunity to talk with questionnaire respondents, you should create a questionnaire that is carefully tailored to your needs.

Drawing up an effective questionnaire is demanding work, requiring not only knowledge of the commonsense guidelines associated with interviewing, but also special planning and a good deal of legwork. The accompanying chart outlines guidelines for designing and administering questionnaires.

How to Design and Administer Questionnaires

- Devise questions that are easy to tabulate. Fact questions and questions that ask for responses on a scale from 1 to 5 will make your analysis of the data easier. If you ask open-ended questions, make them precise and limit the amount of space for answers.

(continued)

- Consider using a computer to help you tabulate the results of your questionnaire. Ask your instructor for guidance or check with your computer center about programs that tally data.

- Think about your respondents. Settle on a representative sample that will provide reliable and adequate coverage of the population you are surveying. Consider how many questionnaires you can expect to have returned to you.

- Get expert advice. After you know what you are looking for and who your target audience will be, consult someone who does research for a living (such as a mathematics, social science, or psychology professor on your campus). Ask for advice about sample size. Before you interview the expert, consult the interviewing guidelines in this chapter. Also do some background reading on sampling techniques.

- Ask a friend to help you test your questions. Or let your instructor review your draft questionnaire. Based on the input you receive, revise the questions. Always aim for objective questions.

- Make your questionnaire easy to use. Type it up, leaving adequate space for responses. Be sure your questions are easy to understand. Deliver or mail the questionnaire directly to the respondents. Designate a convenient collection point or provide a stamped, addressed envelope. Specify a desired return time. Decide whether you will follow up with those who do not return the survey (of course, follow-up is impossible if the survey is anonymous).

3 Observing

Collecting data, or evidence, through observation can lead you to a neighborhood mall, where you might sit in the optical shop observing customer behavior, or into the wilderness, where you might track wolves. Whatever your project, you will be observing for the primary purpose of collecting evidence that will help you solve your research problem or confirm or refute your hypotheses.

Before heading out into the field to observe, devise an observation plan. Careful planning is just as important to successful observing as it is for effective interviewing and surveying. Think about what your assignment and goals are. What do you want to know? If you are trying to find out what hours an optical shop should remain open to maximize profits and customer satisfaction, you might have to experiment with observing during different hours of operation to get a better sense of customer needs. You might also benefit from combining observation with interviews and questionnaires to get a more comprehensive picture of customer needs. You will also need to think about observing customers long enough to find out whether there are consistent patterns. However basic or complicated your means of observation, it is necessary to plan carefully and well in advance.

Also realize that you need to keep some distance from what you are observing; it is important to be objective and to avoid introducing bias into your findings. Just as you avoid devising survey questionnaires that lead respondents to a particular, preferred reply, as an observer you need to keep professional distance and avoid either projecting your own ideas onto what you are seeing or altering your surroundings in any way.

You also need a system for recording what you observe. You might have to rely on special equipment such as a video camera or tape recorder. When observing, you should always take notes and make sketches in field notebooks, recording details of what happened, what did not happen, and what mistakes and discoveries you made. Question your evidence and make connections (see 4a on questioning, and 4c on connecting). Consider working with a partner so you can compare observations. Review the accompanying observation checklist before you get started.

Checklist for Observing

- Prepare well in advance and plan carefully. Decide how and when to observe in light of your purpose.
- Record what you observe as you observe it. Use a field notebook to take notes or make sketches, but also use electronic equipment, such as a video camera and tape recorder, when useful and feasible.
- Keep your observations and your reflections separate so that you will be able to distinguish the evidence from what you thought about it.
- Be objective. Avoid introducing bias into your results.
- Try to work with a partner to compare results and thereby minimize error.

39g Compiling a working bibliography

A *working bibliography* is the list of books, articles, and all other sources that you compile as you do your research. As you do preliminary research with reference books, periodical indexes, library catalogs, and databases, prepare source cards for any and all sources that look worthwhile. The sources you put in the working bibliography are there tentatively, however. After you consult the listed sources and evaluate them, you may discover they are not helpful (see 40b–c on evaluating and reading sources); if so, you can then remove the source from your list.

Eventually, after you have evaluated and selected sources and started writing your essay, what remains in your working bibliography will become your Works Cited list (if MLA style), or your References list (if APA style) (see 43c and 43f).

Ericka Kostka began her research by reading from encyclopedias; one of those encyclopedia articles included a brief but promising bibliography at its end, so she photocopied it for her working bibliography. But when Kostka consulted the *New York Times Index* and then the *Readers' Guide to Periodical Literature*, she found so many promising sources that listing and photocopying became inefficient. At that point, she began to prepare source cards (also called bibliography cards) for each of the useful-looking sources she encountered. Examples of her source cards follow.

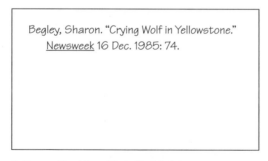

Begley, Sharon. "Crying Wolf in Yellowstone."
<u>Newsweek</u> 16 Dec. 1985: 74.

A Source Card for a Periodical Article

After Kostka finished preparing her source cards from the *Readers' Guide,* and before she located the sources, she consulted the library's card and online catalogs to make sure she had not overlooked obvious sources associated with the gray wolf problem. She also consulted abstracts and citations. She drew up source cards for all of the sources that looked promising, including the source card on the opposite page, for a book.

```
    Lopez, Barry H. Of Wolves and Men.    QL
        New York: Scribner's, 1987.        737.C22
                                           L66
```

A Source Card for a Book

Kostka was careful to include on each source card the information she would need both to locate the source in the library and to prepare her Works Cited list.

Kostka's instructor asked students to use the Modern Language Association (MLA) documentation style, commonly used in humanities courses. Be sure to check with your instructor about the required documentation style for your project before proceeding with your research or devising source cards. (See Chapter 43 on documentation styles, including MLA.) Use the appropriate one as you compile your working bibliography. That way you will have all the information you need to help you find the sources and the information will be in the appropriate format for preparing your Works Cited list.

The chart, on p. 602, Information to Record in a Working Bibliography, outlines the information you should include on source cards.

To prepare your working bibliography, use 3 × 5-inch index cards, one for each source. Using cards gives you great flexibility for arranging the cards either alphabetically by author or by type of source. If you would prefer not to work with index cards, use notebook paper or a computer. If you do work on a computer, look into the various functions of your software that can help you compile lists or format your sources.

Directed research in the library and field research are necessary parts of the research process. In Chapter 40 you will learn how to evaluate the sources and evidence you accumulated in your research. You will also learn how to take notes and write the research essay. Inevitably, writing the essay will take you back to the library; as you write your essay, you will discover the need for additional research.

Information to Record in a Working Bibliography

BOOKS

Library call number
Author's name
Editor's name (if any)
Translator's name (if any)
Full title, including subtitle
Place of publication
Publisher
Date of publication
Other: volume number, edition, page numbers for relevant sections or chapters

PERIODICAL ARTICLES

Author's name
Full title of article, including subtitle
Full title of periodical
Volume number and issue number (if any)
Date of issue
Page numbers for the entire article

SOURCES FROM INDEXES

Name of the index so you can return to it if necessary
Call number
Any other information to help identify and locate the source in the library

ELECTRONIC SOURCES—INTERNET COMPUTER SERVICES, CD-ROM

Author's name
Title of document
Information about print publication (if any): title of source publication, date of printing, volume, and page numbers
Information about electronic publication: title of source, editor, version, date of publication or last update, and sponsor name
Access information (for online resources only): date of access and network address (URL)

NONPRINT SOURCES

Note where you found the information
List it in the specified documentation style and format on your source card

40 *Writing the Research Essay*

In this chapter you will see how the evidence collected from research can be used to develop an essay. You will learn how to restrict a topic, evaluate sources, take notes, and then how to plan, organize, draft, and revise a research essay. To illustrate the research process, we will continue to follow the work of one student, Ericka Kostka, to see how she researched her topic (the fate of the gray wolf) and wrote an essay to defend a thesis. (Kostka's full essay appears in Chapter 44.)

40a   Restricting your topic

Once you settle on a topic that interests you and compile a working bibliography (see 39b, g), you are ready to start thinking about the potential sources you have compiled. You are also ready to begin reading those sources to expand your knowledge of your topic. Instead of locating and reading all the sources you can find on a very general or broad topic, you rein yourself in and do thorough research on a specific topic. Topic restriction will save you valuable research time; it will also give you the opportunity to delve into a particular area and become an expert on it.

To restrict your topic adequately, follow the advice in the guidelines on p. 604. Admittedly, restricting a topic is not always easy. At the outset, when you consider a topic like Kostka's, the possibilities may seem endless: "Should I try to account for the extermination of wolves all across North America? Should I try to focus on stockgrowers' opposition to wolves in Wyoming and Minnesota, or should I try to figure out why Alaska is allowing hunters to kill wolves at a time when the park service in Wyoming has reintroduced the wolf population in Yellowstone?" Reaching a decision about just where to focus your research depends on your being knowledgeable about your topic and the availability of sources. Consult with your instructor if you have difficulty restricting your topic.

Guidelines for Restricting a Topic

- Become knowledgeable about your unrestricted topic by doing preliminary research. You might read encyclopedia articles or other reference books and consult representative sources from your working bibliography. Always avoid restricting when you have too little information.

- As you gather background information about your topic, try to identify a problem or controversial issue about which experts or special-interest groups disagree. When you find controversy, you can be sure you are on to a topic worth pursuing. Where there is controversy, there is a problem to solve and an opportunity to interpret—for you to make your own sense of an issue, to explain or find a solution (see 4d and 2d on controversies and interpretation).

- Limit the scope of your investigation. For example, you might focus on only one geographical area, such as gray wolves in Yellowstone National Park. Or you could study only one aspect of the topic, such as tracking wolves with radio-transmitter collars as opposed to the broader topic of tracking wolves. Perhaps you could limit the time frame of your research, considering only the efforts made during the last five years to introduce wolves into sanctuaries, for example. Or you might use a combination of these methods.

- Be sure that your research can provide sufficient sources on the topic and that all the material you need will be accessible. Also consider whether you will have adequate time to work with the materials and complete the assignment. Be sure, too, that your evidence is sufficient for you to develop a reasonable and objective thesis (see 40e).

Let's look at how Kostka restricted her topic. As outlined in Chapter 39, Kostka was interested in wolves when she began her research. She had first been introduced to wolf recovery during a visit to Yellowstone, but she had no specific knowledge of the issue. By doing some preliminary research, Kostka found ample background information on wolves in two encyclopedia articles and from the listing of periodical articles that she found in the *New York Times Index*, the *Readers' Guide to Periodical Literature*, and the *General Science Index* (see 39d). She discovered a long-standing debate between environmentalists who wish to protect wolves and stockgrowers who view protected wolves as an inevitable threat to their livestock.

Kostka's first visit to the library had taken less than two hours. She spent most of the time in the reference room consulting periodical indexes, abstracts, and the online catalog. She found more than twenty sources for her working bibliography; each of these sources looked promising.

As she scanned her working bibliography and thought about the potential sources listed there, Kostka saw that the issue extended far beyond the boundaries of Yellowstone. The presence of the gray wolf was a problem in several states including Wisconsin, Minnesota, and Wyoming. But she could see from the titles of recent articles that a great deal of attention was being given to the wolf problem at Yellowstone. Restricting her topic to that particular area seemed reasonable, and, based on her preliminary research, she was sure she would be able to find sufficient information about wolves in Yellowstone.

But Kostka's instructor had cautioned the class against restricting the topic based on too little information, so before settling on her topic, Kostka decided to read two of the periodical articles from her working bibliography—a general article on wolves in North America by Diane Edwards in *Science News,* and a specific article on wolves at Yellowstone by Ted Williams in *Audubon*—to get a clearer sense of the controversy between environmentalists and stockgrowers. These articles gave Kostka much more detailed information than did the encyclopedias and confirmed the wisdom of restricting her research to the wolf problem at Yellowstone. In particular, Diane Edwards gave Kostka a clear sense that the problem in North America was too broad to deal with in a six- to twelve-page research essay.

40b   Evaluating the usefulness of sources

Evaluating sources involves a preliminary assessment or scanning of the sources in your working bibliography and then a more thorough and critical reading of the sources themselves (see 40c). Both steps will help you determine the usefulness of sources.

As soon as you restrict your topic, evaluate the usefulness of the sources in your working bibliography. Scan the bibliography for sources that seem to have nothing to do with the newly restricted topic and weed them out. Check titles to determine relevance, but be aware that titles can be misleading. Place any pulled source cards in a separate "dead" file; do not throw them away because you may need to go back to them later to consult a source you initially deemed unusable.

Kostka started weeding sources as soon as she restricted her topic to the wolf problem in Yellowstone. All the sources that dealt with the wolf in other geographical areas, with the selected killing of wolves in Alaska, or with the introduction of wolves into Minnesota and North Carolina, were relegated to a separate file.

After you have scanned the source cards, go to the Internet or library, locate the sources remaining in your working bibliography, and scan them. You should not be reading the sources closely or taking detailed notes at

---

Guidelines for Evaluating the Usefulness of Sources

- Consider the relevance of the source to your restricted topic.

- Consider whether the source is too general or specific for your research needs.

- Check the date of publication. Is the source current? Will current sources serve your purpose, or would older sources be more appropriate?

- Look at the author's credentials to establish whether he or she is an authority on the topic. You can also check to see what other experts have written about the author. Consult a biographical reference book or index for more information.

- Ascertain the author's point of view on the topic and whether that point of view seems reasonable. Consider the author's tone and intended audience.

- Do a preliminary source evaluation. Scan the table of contents, the preface, the index, the title, notes about the author, subheadings, available abstracts, the afterword, and the listed sources. Once you have eliminated sources that are obviously irrelevant, do a more thorough evaluation of the remaining sources.

- Be sure to record connections you make while scanning or reading. Note these connections and any other ideas about your sources in a reading journal (1e-1), in a double-column notebook (2b-3), or on note cards (40d). For any notes you take, keep track of your sources to avoid unintentional plagiarism (Chapter 41).

- Scan electronic sources that you have downloaded and deemed reliable. (See Chapter 42 for more on evaluation of electronic sources.) After you judge electronic sources reliable, evaluate their usefulness as you would for any other sources.

this point, but browsing, skimming, investigating research possibilities. Read the table of contents, preface, first few paragraphs, abstract, or headings within a source. The guidelines on the previous page will help you with this initial assessment of sources. Once you have done this preliminary evaluation, you can start reading whatever sources remain to evaluate them more closely.

40c   Reading sources critically

Once you have done a preliminary assessment of sources, you can begin a more thorough evaluation that involves reading the sources that remain in your working bibliography. You will want to read those sources carefully and critically.

To read critically, keep the guidelines in the chart on p. 608 in mind. (Also see Chapter 2 on critical reading.) You will also find that as you read your sources and become more knowledgeable about your topic, you will be able to focus your research and restrict your topic even more.

As you read and evaluate your sources, you will get a clear sense of the different points of view on your topic and of the arguments offered in support of those viewpoints. You will also start to evaluate the substance of the arguments you encounter—identifying strengths, weaknesses, and gaps in each. (See Chapter 2 on critical reading.)

http://www.library.cornell.edu/
okuref/research/skill26.htm
Offers guidance for evaluating sources critically.

To help keep yourself on track, it is a good idea to develop a focusing question from your restricted topic. You will seek to answer that focusing question as you read and do subsequent research. In addition, the question will give direction to your research; it will help you know just what to look for as you continue reading and evaluating.

As Ericka Kostka read her sources, she pinpointed five special-interest groups, each with its own perspective on the wolf population controversy: (1) the National Park Service; (2) environmentalists and wolf experts; (3) the Wyoming Stockgrowers' Association; (4) the National Wool Growers Association; and (5) politicians from bordering states. As she learned more, Kostka

---

Guidelines for Reading Sources Critically

- Read with an open mind. Be receptive to different points of view and do not take sides—read objectively. Try to distinguish facts from emotional appeals or theories about those facts.

- Question what you are reading. Ask yourself many questions. (See the questioning guidelines in 4a.)

  > What do I notice as I read? What patterns do I see emerging? How do I feel about what I am reading? What is the writer's main idea? How well does the evidence (facts, anecdotes, examples) support the idea?

- Let your reading lead you to other sources. The reference lists at the end of books and articles can alert you to other sources.

- Write as you read. Take notes (see 40d) that can be incorporated into your essay. These notes can also include your comments and reflections about that evidence.

- Think about the relevance and reliability of your sources using the evaluation guidelines in 40b. Continue to weed out unusable sources.

---

was able to develop a focusing question about her restricted topic, the wolf population problem in Yellowstone. This focusing question directed her inquiry.

> To what extent does it seem reasonable, given all of those conflicting interests, to make an effort to maintain the restored wolf population in Yellowstone?

The best focusing questions are like Kostka's: specific, straightforward, and manageable. They require more than a simple *yes* or *no* response; they encourage thinking about what you are reading and researching. They also require you to be analytical, reasonable, and objective—to weigh various points of view against one another so you can decide where you stand on your topic or issue.

Once you have settled on a focusing question, you will also be able to consider your sources objectively—to look carefully at the facts and distinguish facts from emotional appeals. For example, Kostka had no doubt that stockgrowers who lose cattle and sheep to wolves would be emotional about their losses and that their arguments would reflect their emotions. She knew, too, that some environmentalists might overstate their case in favor of the wolf. But with her focusing question in mind, she was able to consider those emotionally charged defenses without being swayed or biased. She focused on weighing what she read against the real threat to the wolf population.

A good focusing question should also lead you to more questions and eventually to a reasonable and objective thesis (see 40e) that explains the accumulated evidence. Kostka's focusing question spurred her to ask herself these questions as she read each source. You can ask yourself these or similar questions as you read and evaluate your sources and work your way to a reasonable thesis.

- What does this source reveal about the special-interest group's argument— its main points, its evidence, its underlying concerns?

- In what ways does this information about a particular group contribute to my understanding of the larger problem?

- Does the evidence in the source seem logical and convincing?

- What has the source failed to consider?

- Can I detect any bias in the source?

- Is the writer aligned exclusively with a special-interest group, or are other points of view considered?

- Do I find myself resisting the information in the source? How exactly do my findings differ from those of this writer?

40d   Taking notes

As you critically read sources and determine their usefulness, you will want to take notes. Thorough and accurate note taking during research will help you once you start writing the research essay and when you need to acknowledge your sources.

The notes you take will serve two purposes. They will help you learn about your topic; the writing you do will clarify what you are reading and will help you organize your thoughts about it. In addition, the notes you take as you read and evaluate sources may eventually become the evidence you incorporate into your essay to help readers understand your thesis. You will eventually have to decide what to include and what to leave out of your essay based on audience considerations and your purpose (see 40f and 40i).

As you take notes, always try to distill your sources into a form you can use later in your essay, such as a summary (40d-1), a paraphrase (40d-2), a

---

Guidelines for Note Taking

- At the top of each 4 × 6-inch index card, notebook page, or computerized note entry, include the author's last name, an abbreviated form of the title, and inclusive page numbers for the material you include from the source. There is no need to include full bibliographic information, such as publication date, since you will have recorded that in your working bibliography (see 39g).

- Provide a subject or category heading at the top of each card, identifying in two or three words the main subject or idea of the notes. This heading will help you later when you organize your notes.

- Use a separate card for each fact or idea that you take from a source. If you put several ideas or notes on a single card, it will be difficult to arrange your notes when you organize them in preparation for writing the essay.

- Clearly identify the type of note on the card. If you quote verbatim from a source, use quotation marks at the beginning and at the end of the quotation. If you summarize, label the notes as a summary or signal the summary with an S at the beginning and at the end; if you paraphrase, label the notes as a paraphrase or signal the paraphrase with a P at the beginning and at the end. Use double slash marks (//), a different color ink, or some other signal to distinguish clearly your own comments from source material.

- Cross-reference connections that occur to you as you read your sources.

- Check the accuracy of your notes before you put the source aside. Have you quoted accurately? Are all of your facts, numbers, and other data correct? Did you include the correct page numbers for the material in your notes? If your note includes material that extends for more than one page in a source, indicate the page break in your notes by putting the page number in brackets: [223]. Then record inclusive page numbers at the end of the note: 222–23. This way, if you decide to use only part of the note in your essay, you will know the exact page for the material without having to consult the original source again.

- Be careful not to plagiarize—to take someone else's words or ideas, organizational patterns, or computer programs without giving proper credit.

direct quotation (40d-3), reflections on what you are reading (40d-4), or a combination of these (40d-5). Your notes should always be carefully and accurately recorded. If your notes include accurate and complete information, you will not have to waste valuable time later going back to the original sources to clarify confusing entries or to fill in gaps. In addition, it is crucial that you clearly distinguish your reflections from the ideas and words of the sources themselves. Taking careful notes will help you avoid accidental plagiarism (see Chapter 41).

Note taking is not a mechanical process of copying from your sources to your note cards. You should be doing a great deal of thinking and reflecting (40d-4) as you read and take notes. As you read and think about your sources, try to make connections between ideas. When you come across a word, a phrase, or an idea in one source that reminds you of something in another, record that connection; it could turn out to be important when you start organizing your notes and writing your essay. Develop a system of cross-referencing that will permit you to keep track of the connections you make as you proceed with your research.

Although there is no single, correct way to take notes, most researchers find that 4 × 6-inch index cards provide enough space for detailed notes and complement the system of using 3 × 5-inch index cards for your working bibliography (making it easy to distinguish source cards from note cards). Some researchers, however, prefer using a notebook or computer when taking notes. The accompanying guidelines will help you as you take notes, no matter what system you use.

1 Summarizing

When you write a **summary,** you condense a fairly lengthy passage of text into a few sentences of your own words. A summary is always shorter than the original source. It captures the essence of the source, the writer's main idea(s); it also enables a reader unfamiliar with the source to understand the idea.

As you summarize, remember three things: (1) You may eventually use the summarized material in your own essay, so begin to think of what your reader needs to know to understand your summary. Let the reader's needs guide you as you decide how much detail to include. (2) Even though you are summarizing someone else's work in your own words, the idea and the information belong to the other writer, not to you. If you use that summarized material in your essay, you must give the author credit for it (see Chapters 41 and 43). (3) Remain true to the author's intended meaning. When you select a passage from a source that you want to summarize, or when you choose to summarize a complete source (such as an article or an essay), follow the Guidelines for Summarizing, on the opposite page.

Ericka Kostka relied a great deal on summary as she read, evaluated, and took notes from her sources. Three paragraphs from a journal article gave her important information about the way political influence caused the Park Service at Yellowstone to curtail its educational program on wolves.

ORIGINAL SOURCE

The message from "the environmental President" to the Park Service was clear. And it encouraged other messages: "I demand that the department disavow itself of this lobbying effort," brayed Wyoming Senator Malcolm Wallop to Interior Secretary Manuel Lunjan when he discovered that the Park Service was sending out educational wolf packets containing natural history of the sort that Wallop doesn't believe. Montana Representative Pat Williams went further, still, questioning "the appropriateness of providing the public with *information* [my emphasis], about wolf reintroduction." Similar complaints were voiced by Senator Burns and Congressman Marlenee.

Patiently, the Park Service noted that the Endangered Species Act requires it to use "all methods and procedures necessary" to restore the wolf—in this case, dispelling precisely the sort of mythology that western ranchers and politicians clutch to their breasts. And it noted that its own management policies require it to "identify and promote" the conservation of endangered species.

At the same time, however, the Park Service backed off. It agreed not to mail out its educational packets (which had run out anyway). It temporarily canceled an immensely popular wolf-restoration slide show. It stopped writing about wolf reintroduction in the park newspaper. And it prohibited Defenders of Wildlife from selling pro-wolf-restoration posters at park visitor centers.

—Ted Williams, "Waiting for Wolves to Howl in Yellowstone"

Guidelines for Summarizing

- Read the source, looking for the writer's main idea.
- As you read, note keywords, striking images, and important sentences.
- In your own words, write down the main idea of the passage.
- Test your summary of the main idea during a second reading. Carefully check the summary against the passage itself. Make sure you have captured the essence of the passage.
- A summary is a substantially shortened version of the source but includes sufficient information so that your reader can understand the source.
- If you decide to incorporate a few of the writer's keywords or phrases into your summary, be sure to enclose them in quotation marks and record the page numbers in parentheses right after the closing quotation marks.
- Be sure you have an entry in your working bibliography for the source.
- Follow the Guidelines for Note Taking on p. 610 as you prepare your summary.

Kostka completed several note cards as she read Williams's article. The accompanying card contains her summary of the three paragraphs and her reflections.

Williams 38   Politics

     S / According to Williams, political pressure has hindered the park's educational programs on the issue of wolf recovery. / S

     // Williams does a good job in this fairly long section on politics. Besides the three paragraphs on p. 38, he also lets us see in an earlier section how political pressure leads to commissioned studies that slow down decision making. S / Williams argues that these studies take time, relieve pressure on the Park Service to get the job done, and also satisfy scientists who get paid to do them. Everyone benefits from not getting the job done. (p. 38) / S. In this other section of the essay, Williams shows how complicated and messy this political business can get. // See Diane Edwards for more on wolf politics.

Note Card with Summary, Reflection, and Connection

Notice how Kostka summarizes the essence of Williams's argument and reduces three paragraphs to one sentence, in her own words (see the first sentence identified by the S/). On that same note card, Kostka chooses to reflect and refer to an earlier, related section in Williams's article. Within her reflections, she summarizes the earlier section. Because she clearly distinguishes between her notes and reflections and labels her note cards properly, Kostka will be able to work with these notes easily.

2 Paraphrasing

When you **paraphrase,** you aim to convey in your own words the essence of the source and a sense of its structure—the ordered way in which

---

Guidelines for Paraphrasing

- Read the source, looking for the writer's main idea.
- Write down, in your own words and using your own sentence structure, what you think the main idea is. Order your paraphrase just as the original source is ordered; include appropriate details.
- Check your paraphrase against the source. Make sure that you have captured the essence of the source and that your wording differs significantly from the wording in the original source.
- Include sufficient information in your paraphrase so that your reader can understand the source.
- Avoid plagiarism (see Chapter 41) by giving credit to the author of the paraphrased material. Note source page numbers. If you include important terms and phrases from the source, put those words in quotation marks.
- Reflect on the source but be sure to separate your reflections and paraphrase.
- Be sure you have an entry in your working bibliography for the source.
- Follow the Guidelines for Note Taking (see p. 610) as you prepare your paraphrase.

the writer reaches a conclusion, develops an idea, or creates emphasis. A paraphrase follows the structure of the original source more closely and may include more details than a summary. Paraphrases may be as long as or longer than the original source. If the writer's structure is as important as the idea itself, paraphrase the selection rather than summarize. If the development of the idea is more important than the author's wording, paraphrase rather than quote.

Because you follow the original source closely in a paraphrase and may include considerable detail from it, you must be especially careful not to use keywords and phrases from the source unless you enclose them in quotation marks. As a general rule, write the entire paraphrase in your own words, quoting only when the words of the source are essential to preserve meaning. As you paraphrase, follow the guidelines on page 614.

Kostka was especially interested in the last of Williams's three paragraphs about the effects of politics on the Park Service's information program (see 40d-1). She believed the order in Williams's paragraph created emphasis, so she decided to paraphrase that paragraph. Notice how Kostka's wording and sentence structure differ from the original but retain the same order of information.

Williams 38   Effects of Politics

P / As a result of political opposition, the Park Service stopped mailing educational material about wolves, canceled its slide show on the wolf, stopped writing about restoring the wolf population, and prohibited selling wolf posters in the park. / P

// This is the essence of Williams's case about the effects of politics on the educational program. He makes this case convincingly, citing considerable details. No hesitation on my part to accept these conclusions. //

Note Card with Paraphrase and Reflection

3 Quoting

When you use a **quotation,** you record the writer's words verbatim and enclose them in quotation marks. When you quote, record a writer's exact words, being careful to preserve the punctuation marks, capitalization, and spelling in the original. If you make any alterations to the quoted passage, do so carefully and sparingly. To add words, substitute words, or provide explanations within the quoted passage, put those additions in brackets (see 33c-2). If you delete words or phrases, indicate these deletions with an ellipsis within brackets (see 33d). If the writer has made a mistake within the quoted material, you can, if you choose, indicate that mistake by placing the Latin word *sic* (meaning "thus") within brackets immediately after the error. As with paraphrases and summaries, when quoting, always give credit to the writer by documenting what you quote (see Chapter 43 on documentation). (Also see Chapter 32 on quotation marks.)

Several reasons to quote rather than summarize or paraphrase are outlined in the chart on p. 617. Always quote sparingly and in the situations described in the chart. (Also see 40i-1.)

As Kostka evaluated Williams's article about the gray wolf in Yellowstone, she was struck by the politicians' language as they voiced opposition to the reintroduction of wolves into the park. She saw immediately that their own words undercut the effectiveness of their arguments. She decided to record some of those voices from Williams's article in note cards, anticipating that she could use the quotations later in her essay (see 40i).

Williams (36)   Politicians
                                                                against Wolves

"Wyoming Senator Alan Simpson has asserted that wolves eat people. Montana Senator Conrad Burns predicts that if wolves are returned to Yellowstone, 'there'll be a dead child within a year.' [. . .] Simpson's office now claims he really didn't say 'wolves eat things human and alive' (although he did)" (36).

// 2d Simpson response came after he was questioned about his earlier statement. Williams has summarized Simpson in the first sentence and quoted him in the third. //

Note Card with Quotations and Reflection

Guidelines for Quoting

You should quote:

- When the writer's words are so cogent and memorable that summarizing or paraphrasing would undercut their effectiveness or alter their meaning
- When you believe the writer's words will lend authority to what you have to say and will be more persuasive than your summary or paraphrase of those words
- When you want to take exception to what a writer has said
- When you want to comment on a writer's words as a way of expressing your own position or idea (40d-4)
- When you want to let a speaker's own words expose the weakness of his or her argument
- When you want to cite statistical information from the source

---

4   Reflecting

Reflecting on your sources is an important part of the process of taking useful notes. When you reflect, you enter into a conversation with the source you are reading; you think carefully about the source, trying to make connections with other sources, to relate ideas that come to mind, to clarify and gain insight. Learn to listen to these thoughts. In doing so you become an active, critical reader who hears a text and your mind's reaction to it. (See also Chapter 2 on reading.)

Noting your reflections on sources will prove beneficial when the time comes to organize and write your research essay. From those reflections in your notes or in your reading journal, you can find ideas and discover patterns and additional connections. Your research essay will not merely be a compilation of the ideas of other writers and researchers; it will contain what you think about your sources. Maintaining a record of your reflections as you take notes will help you make sense of your research; it will help you make the leap from the ideas and words of others to your own ideas on your topic.

When you record your reflections in your notes, be sure always to distinguish them from the information you take directly from the sources in the form of summaries, paraphrases, or quotations. Always take care to avoid plagiarism.

5   Combining summary, paraphrase, quotation, and reflection

Often, you will combine summary, paraphrase, quotation, and reflection on the same note card. Combining gives you the flexibility to adapt the source material to your own needs and to make it easier to maintain your own style and voice in your essay. Ensure that combining does not become the occasion for carelessness. Be exact when you use a source verbatim; enclose the borrowed words in quotation marks. When you summarize and paraphrase, make sure you do not inadvertently borrow keywords and phrases from the source without enclosing them in quotation marks.

Ericka uses a combination of summary, quotation, and reflection on a note card that captures the essence of the continuing debate between stockgrowers and biologists over the reintroduction of wolves into Yellowstone.

ORIGINAL SOURCE

The Montana Stock Growers Association, for example, predicts that the wolves will wander outside the parks and, in Montana alone, would kill up to 1,000 livestock a year.

   Biologists with the National Park Service disagree. In a study delivered last week, they found no scientific grounds for refusing to bring the wolves back. The study argues that wolves will kill few livestock and will thin herds of elk that have grown too large to be sustained in protected areas.

—Christopher Joyce, "Yellowstone Lets the Wolf through the Door"

See Kostka's note card on p. 619.

Researchers often photocopy source material when time is limited. Coin-operated photocopy machines are usually available in the library's reference room. If you make photocopies, be careful not to consider the copies your own notes or your own thinking about a source. Be sure to record all of the information you will need to prepare note cards and your list of sources (see 43c and 43f).

Joyce 21   Debate

S / In a recent article in the <u>New Scientist</u>, Christopher Joyce reports on the continuing debate between stockgrowers and biologists over the reintroduction of wolves into Yellowstone. Biologists claim there are "no scientific grounds" for stockgrowers' prediction that stray wolves will "kill up to 1,000 livestock a year" in Montana. / S

// This is yet another variation on the debate between stockgrowers and environmentalists. Here, the biologists' claims are based on a study; the stockgrowers' are not. // Cross-reference: see note cards for Diane Edwards and Ted Williams for more on the debate.

Note Card Combining Summary, Quotation, and Reflection

40e   Developing a reasonable thesis

You read and evaluate sources and take notes from them in order to collect enough information about your topic so that you can develop a reasonable thesis about it. As you develop that thesis, you will use the information recorded in your notes or in your reading journal to help you support, illustrate, and account for your thesis. Your notes—whether summary, paraphrase, quotation, or reflection—will become the evidence you incorporate and cite in your essay. (See also 40i for more on incorporating evidence.)

An effective thesis is a reasonable one. It emerges from a careful consideration of your focusing question and the conflicting points of view on your topic. As your own position within a controversy begins to emerge, always test the reasonableness of your thesis by asking yourself how other researchers and writers might react to your thesis. Use the questions in the chart on p. 620 to test the reasonableness of your thesis.

If you have read or listened to those who have entered the debate about your subject, you will likely have the knowledge and background to anticipate objections and counter them. Ignoring other points of view can only weaken your argument. That kind of single-mindedness makes your thesis seem unreasonable. (See 7b for more on developing a reasonable thesis.)

Guidelines for Gauging the Reasonableness of Your Thesis

- Is my thesis based on the investigative work I have done?
- Is my thesis focused?
- Is my thesis objective, fair, and deliberate, taking into consideration all sides of the issue?
- Have I avoided a heated, two-sided debate or a simple declaration that invites resistance?
- Have I let my readers know that I have considered and anticipated the responses of those who might disagree with me?
- Have I been thorough in my research or do I need to do more research on my topic to get a fuller picture of other points of view?

When Kostka finished evaluating all of her sources and began to think about writing her essay, she saw quite clearly that the five special-interest groups she had been considering fell into two general categories: the stock-growers (and their constituents) and the environmentalists (and theirs). After researching, taking notes, and then writing in her journal about these two groups and their various arguments for and against the wolf, Kostka began to see that there might be a way for the wolf population to be restored and protected in Yellowstone and for the stockgrowers also to be protected. She wanted to offer reasonable alternatives to the stockgrowers; otherwise, she knew she would be unable to convince them to keep the wolf in the park.

Rarely will you settle on a thesis on your first attempt at devising one. As you write, think, and do additional research, you make discoveries about your topic that will inevitably lead you to modify your thesis. Many writers, in fact, begin by devising a working thesis to guide the organization and writing of their first draft. Kostka devised a working thesis that was modified as she started writing and discovered gaps in her argument.

Kostka's working thesis

Because evidence strongly indicates that wolf populations are important to the predator-prey balance in Yellowstone and because that repopulation can be viable for both the gray wolf and its opponents, I believe we should reverse the one-sided concessions forced upon a now endangered population by supporting the program to restore the wolves in the park, and by keeping their endangered classification until the population is restored.

This working thesis was not an idea Kostka brought to the assignment. It evolved through learning and writing, as she considered conflicting points of view, reflected about them, and questioned them. For a clear sense of this evolutionary process, reread the sections on Kostka's selection of a topic (39b), her restriction of the topic (40a), and her focusing question. (Also see Chapter 4 on developing a thesis.)

 40f   Considering your audience

Once you have developed a working thesis, you will have to figure out how to communicate that thesis to your readers. To do that, try to answer the following three questions.

1. What evidence should I include in my essay?
2. How do I present the evidence to my readers so that they will understand it?
3. How do I order the evidence for my readers?

The following general advice should help you as you try to answer these questions with regard to your particular essay.

1. Select the evidence that will, in your mind, help your audience see what you want them to see.
2. Present your evidence with adequate explanation—provide enough background information, draw inferences, form conclusions about the connections you jotted down in your notes or journal, clarify the relationship between your evidence and your ideas. Do not throw raw evidence at your readers; interpret it for them. And be sure to be clear and objective.
3. Order or arrange your evidence in a way that will make it easy for your audience to follow your reasoning (see 40g).

Research essays that are also arguments require an especially keen attentiveness to audience because your goal is to convince that audience of your conclusion without inviting opposition or hostility. To be persuasive, you must show a real concern for what your readers might think about a given subject and how they might react to the way you think about that subject (refer to 1d for more on considering audience). Most audiences—whether hostile or friendly, whether you know them well or have no idea how to persuade them to adopt your point of view—will respond to logic and reasonableness. The rules of formal logic will help you ensure that your argument is fair and reasonable rather than unbalanced, hotheaded, or fallacious (see Chapter 3 on logical thinking).

 40g Organizing your essay

Once you have compiled notes and reflections on your sources, you are ready to start writing. But because writing research essays tends to be a fairly long and complicated process, it is a good idea to organize your notes and your thoughts first.

There is no single right way to order your research; always work with your audience in mind, thinking of what readers need to know to understand your thesis. Grouping your notes by subject headings and outlining are two useful strategies for organizing.

1 Organizing your notes

If you are careful to label each note with a subject heading in the upper right corner (see 40d), you will have an easier time organizing your notes. Those subject headings can also lead you to ideas about how to structure your essay and to make connections that you missed while reading your sources. You might also notice gaps in your research. Essentially, these subject headings—whether on note cards, pieces of paper, or a computer file—will help you analyze your notes, group related information together, and see how all your information might be ordered within the essay.

The following general subject headings helped Kostka organize her note cards and ultimately revealed the key to her essay's organization: politicians' concerns, legal background for extermination, bad wolf folklore, environmentalists' concerns, radio tracking, stockgrowers' concerns, public concerns, and Park Service's concerns. As Kostka evaluated her notes, she saw that they fell logically into categories that represented the special-interest groups.

Kostka had also cross-referenced her sources as she read and evaluated them (see 40d), and those cross-references helped her get organized, kept her thinking about the interrelationships of her sources, and made her mindful about the way special-interest groups responded to one another. She could see the weaknesses in the arguments of some sources—what the various groups failed to say as they responded to the wolf population problem.

2   Outlining

Outlines are useful organizational devices. As explained in Chapter 1, an outline is a visual representation of how you expect to organize your essay. You will find that an outline will help you map out in your mind just how you will present your argument to convince your audience of the reasonableness of your thesis.

Your outline will also help you assess the effectiveness of your organization. It can show you whether you need to reorganize, provide more details, offer more explanation, or do more research. Be prepared to revise your outline as you learn and write and perhaps shift your focus.

Kostka's informal outline guided her as she began to draft her essay and incorporate information from her note cards.

Kostka's informal outline

1--Background on Extermination of Wolves
    Legal Basis--the Law
    Bad Wolf Folklore
    Real Threats
2--The Wolf as Endangered Species
    Yellowstone, Prime Territory for Wolves
    Restoring Ecological Balance, Starvation versus Predation
3--Stockgrowers' Continuing Opposition
4--Concessions and Restitution for Damage
    Radio Tracking
    Monetary Compensation
5--Retaining Endangered Classification
6--Public Support

Notice how the subject headings from Kostka's notes have been ordered in her outline. Kostka is beginning to use her notes to build an argument that will support her working thesis favoring the reintroduction of the wolf into Yellowstone. She does not yet know how reasonable that argument will sound once she writes it down and tries to defend it. Much will depend on her ability to offer sound, reasonable explanations of the evidence she found during her research.

Kostka constructed a formal sentence outline after she wrote her first draft. She used that formal outline to check the logical relationships among the various sections of her essay and to reveal any gaps that required further research or explanation. Kostka's final outline appears in Chapter 44.

40h   Drafting your essay

Beginning a research essay can be easier if you organize your note cards and prepare an informal outline before you start drafting the essay. Organizing will help you see how your evidence and your supporting ideas work together and whether you have gathered enough evidence to make your ideas clear and compelling to your reader. Organizing will also help you determine what you want to say and where you might want to begin writing.

Begin writing wherever you feel most comfortable. It might seem logical to begin at the beginning, but doing so is not always advantageous. The beginning—or introduction—should interest your readers in your topic, give them a clear sense of your entire argument, and suggest how you will present your case. But you may not have all of that worked out as you begin drafting, so it might be wise to start writing the middle of your essay—the argument itself. You can write your beginning (and your ending) after you have worked out the details of the argument. (See Chapter 7 for more on writing an argumentative essay.)

Let your notes, your outline, your working thesis, and your sense of audience help direct you as you draft. Be aware that drafting can often reveal gaps in your knowledge and a need for more research about a particular supporting idea. When you discover such gaps, you need not stop writing altogether. You can skip over the troubling section of your essay until you have time to return to the library and consult additional sources.

Keep in mind that you will be writing multiple drafts of your essay. Rarely do writers get the words right the first time. Allow yourself the freedom to draft and to discover ideas as you write. Be open to new ideas that may emerge and to new research you may encounter as you write.

Also, provide citations for your sources (see Chapter 43) as you incorporate them into your draft. Providing citations as you write will ensure accuracy and help you avoid inadvertent plagiarism. It will also save you time when you prepare the final draft because you will not have to go back and sort through your notes to locate sources.

Kostka had a fairly clear sense of how she wanted to develop her argument. At the outset, she wanted to work out some of the more difficult sections in the middle of the essay. She began by following her informal outline. After drafting the first section on the extermination of wolves in Yellowstone, she decided to skip the next main section on the wolf as an endangered species (she anticipated this to be a relatively straightforward section) and turn to the stockgrowers' opposition. Understanding her major opponents would help her develop what she considered the most crucial part of her argument: that the stockgrowers should receive specific concessions and restitution when wolves wandered out of the park and killed stock. There was no doubt that wolves would cross boundaries; the question was what to do about it. With the opposition from stockgrowers and politicians in mind, Kostka thought she could do a better job of presenting the ecological claims that favored reintroduction of the wolf into Yellowstone. As she drafted the paragraphs in the middle of her essay, Kostka also incorporated information from her note cards into those paragraphs and documented that information using her working bibliography. (See Chapter 7 for more on drafting. See also the accompanying annotations to Kostka's complete essay in Chapter 44 to see how she developed her essay.)

40i Incorporating evidence

As you begin incorporating evidence from your note cards into draft paragraphs, remember that your task is to use your evidence to develop your thesis and supporting ideas. Work at showing your readers how the evidence is related to the idea you are developing.

Incorporating evidence involves integrating or weaving your summaries, paraphrases, quotations, and reflections into the essay while maintaining your own authority and voice. You will want to interpret your evidence, analyze it, make connections from it, and draw inferences from it for your audience. Subject headings and cross-references on your note cards will help you remain organized during this process. When incorporating evidence, be sure that your words and ideas, rather than those of your sources, dominate the essay. Use your sources to explain, justify, and support your own ideas.

One way to maintain your own authority and voice as you incorporate evidence into the essay is to search your research journal and reflections in your notes for your own ideas about the evidence. Let your ideas guide you. Be especially careful to separate your own thoughts from those of your sources. Doing so will also help ensure that you do not plagiarize. The tips in the accompanying chart will keep you on track as you incorporate evidence into your essay.

Guidelines for Incorporating Evidence

- Clearly introduce and conclude each summary, paraphrase, or quotation in such a way that readers know where it begins and ends.

- Ensure that the incorporated material blends smoothly into your sentences and paragraphs (see 40i-1). Avoid shifts in verb tense or awkward phrasing that would contrast sharply with the incorporated evidence, making your sentences difficult to read and understand.

- Provide a parenthetical citation within the essay to document the source of your evidence and avoid plagiarism. That in-text citation will correspond to the source list at the end of the essay (see Chapter 43).

- Explain the incorporated evidence so that readers can understand how the evidence relates to a paragraph's main idea and, when appropriate, to your thesis (see 40i-2).

---

1 Integrating source material

When you put information from your notes into your paragraphs, introduce that material by identifying the author or title of the source. You can also identify the author's special credentials if you are appealing to his or her authority to help you establish your claim.

At the end of each summary, paraphrase, or quotation, cite information about the source in parentheses. Parenthetical information normally includes the author's last name (unless you have already cited the name in your paragraph) and relevant page numbers. The title (or a shortened version of it) can also appear as a part of the parenthetical citation when more than one work by that author appears in your list of sources, or when you do not know the author. This parenthetical information signals for your readers the end of the incorporated material. (See Chapter 43 for more precise information on citing references.)

You will also want to integrate your sources so they blend smoothly into your paragraphs. Avoid awkward phrasing or indiscriminate shifts in verb tense that might distract the reader from your idea. To avoid such problems, be sure the tense of your verbs matches or is compatible with the tense of the verbs in the borrowed passage.

AWKWARD

Wildlife biologist John Weaver has made the observation that wolves would be released in Yellowstone wearing radio collars that "may be equipped with remote-controlled tranquilizing darts, a new device that could greatly facilitate the capture of problem animals" (qtd. in Cauble 29).

REVISED

Wildlife biologist John Weaver observed that wolves will be released in Yellowstone wearing radio collars that "may be equipped with remote-controlled tranquilizing darts, a new device that could greatly facilitate the capture of problem animals" (qtd. in Cauble 29).

Always consider reducing quoted material to the words you consider most essential. The fewer quoted words, the less difficult the integration.

When you introduce quotations, pay particular attention to your selection of verbs. Write in the active voice. Your verb choice can convey directly and clearly your attitude about the subject. Verb choice can also suggest your own evaluation of the writer and the source material. In Kostka's revised opening sentences, she chooses the neutral verb *observed*. Had she chosen the disparaging verb *belittle*, she would have conveyed Weaver in a different sense: "Wildlife biologist John Weaver belittled the fact that wolves will be released in Yellowstone wearing radio collars. . . ." These are some of the effective verbs that you can use to introduce quotations: *comments, explains, observes, says, suggests, alleges, claims, grants, condemns, deplores.* The verbs in this list move from neutrality toward judgment. Choose a verb that accurately represents both the writer's attitude and your evaluation.

Integrating a paraphrase or summary

You will often use a paraphrase or a summary in your essays to help illustrate or substantiate your idea. In the following example you can see how Kostka paraphrased one of her sources and used it in a draft paragraph.

She paraphrased in this case because she wanted to present the information in the same order she found it in the source, and she wanted to include more detail than she could in a summary. Notice how she uses her own words throughout the paraphrase.

ORIGINAL SOURCE

At the same time, however, the Park Service backed off. It agreed not to mail out its educational packets (which had run out anyway). It temporarily canceled an immensely popular wolf-restoration slide show. It stopped writing about wolf reintroduction in the park newspaper. And it prohibited Defenders of Wildlife from selling pro-wolf-restoration posters at park visitor centers.

—Ted Williams, "Waiting for Wolves to Howl in Yellowstone"

KOSTKA'S PARAGRAPH

Yellowstone should uphold the interests of the wild, not those of the prevailing political view. But the park buckled under pressure. According to Ted Williams, the park not only stopped mailing educational material, it also canceled its slide show on the wolf, stopped writing about restoring the wolf population, and prohibited the sale of wolf posters at the park (38).

Integrating parts of quotations

Brief quotations—words or phrases—can be incorporated into your sentences by enclosing the words in quotation marks and ensuring that you blend in the quotation so that your sentence is easy to read and understand.

In the following paragraph, Kostka decided to quote only the factual information she found in Diane Edwards's article on reintroducing wolves to Yellowstone. Notice how Kostka introduced the quoted material by including Edwards's name and the title of the periodical in her paragraph.

ORIGINAL SOURCE

Biologists, who seek an "ecological wholeness" in the natural preserve by reintroducing the missing wolf, say they have set a goal of 10 breeding pairs (only one pair of wolves in a pack of 3 to 25 produces offspring).

—Diane D. Edwards, "Recall the Wild Wolf"

KOSTKA'S PARAGRAPH

I believe that a compensation program similar to that used in Minnesota is a more direct and consistent way to deal with the slight economic loss that may affect western sheep and cattle growers as a result of wolf recovery than allowing ranchers to kill an endangered species. Diane Edwards, writing for Science News, reports that biologists "have set a goal of 10 breeding pairs" producing offspring for three consecutive years (379). Declassification must only be allowed after the recovery goal has been reached and the gray wolf is no longer considered to be on the verge of extinction.

Integrating long quotations

Occasionally you will want to incorporate a lengthy quotation into your essay. Formatting these *block quotations* is determined by the conventions set forth in the documentation style you are using. Set off quotations of more than four typed lines (according to MLA) or forty words (according to APA) from the rest of your paragraph by indenting each line of the block quotation ten spaces (MLA) or five spaces (APA). (See Chapter 43 on documentation as well as Chapter 32 on the mechanics of using quotation marks, especially 32c on block quotations.)

Here is an example of one of Kostka's block quotations integrated into a paragraph of her essay and documented according to MLA requirements.

Collaring wolves will allow that this federal control over nuisance animals can be effectively exercised. Wildlife biologist John Weaver made this observation:

> Each wolf released in Yellowstone would be wearing a radio collar, enabling researchers to keep tabs on its wanderings. The collars may be equipped with remote-controlled tranquilizing darts, a new device that could greatly facilitate the capture of problem animals. (qtd. in Cauble 29)

Under this proposal, wolves would be subject to reasonable federal control, rather than to the vengeance of ranchers whose hatred for them tends to be deeply rooted.

Like other incorporated material, block quotations should be introduced to ensure that they fit in with the rest of the paragraph and should include parenthetical documentation. Notice that Kostka's block quotation does not include quotation marks and that the parenthetical citation falls after the concluding punctuation—according to MLA style.

Use block quotations sparingly. Too many of them interrupt the rhythm of your paragraphs and suggest that you are doing little thinking. If you find yourself relying on too many block quotations, try to glean the essence of those long quotations; either summarize or paraphrase the essential information and quote only the words or phrases that you need to make your point.

If you are in any way altering a quotation—adding, deleting, or noting an error in the original—as you integrate it, be sure to use brackets, ellipses, and the Latin word *sic* properly. (See 40d-3, as well as 33c on brackets and 33d on ellipses.)

2   Reflecting on integrated source material

Remember that you incorporate information from sources to help clarify and substantiate your ideas. In addition to introducing source material so that it flows well, documenting it, and making sure that your reader knows where it begins and ends, you should also offer your reflections on it as a way of linking the source material with your ideas. In the following paragraph from her essay, Kostka links her sources—in this case, two quotations—with her argument that the wolf population should be maintained in Yellowstone. The underscored sentences highlight her reflections.

> Political figures opposing park education programs find them to be biased because accurate information and evidence on the subject support repopulation. These officials, with an eye to special-interest groups, would prefer the public to be exposed to the unsupported rhetoric that they offer as testimony on the wolf, testimony such as Montana Representative Ron Marlenee's declaration that wolves are "cockroaches" (qtd. in Williams 36). Despite a lack of any evidence to support his claim, Wyoming Senator Alan Simpson "has asserted that wolves eat people" (Williams 36). Given the prevalence of misinformation about the wolf, even among elected officials, it is especially critical that the National Park Service adhere to its educational efforts so that the public can make informed judgments on the issue.

Kostka's reflections will help her readers understand the idea in the paragraph as well as the idea behind the essay itself (her thesis). In addition, Kostka cites the source of the two quotations, avoiding plagiarism by keeping her reflections separate from the source material. (See Chapter 41 for a full account of how to avoid plagiarism.)

40j   Revising your research essay and collaborating

Writers inevitably go through several drafts of a research essay. As you draft and reread your work, you revise. **Revising** is re-seeing what you have written, considering it with an eye to whether you have done what you set out to do and whether your audience will understand you. As you revise, you will also want to consider how you have used your evidence and whether all parts of the essay—beginning, middle, and ending—come together and work toward communicating your thesis. Based on your assessment of your accomplishments, you rewrite and revise. The basic guidelines for revising covered in 1g will serve you well as you reread the draft of your research essay looking for ways to improve it. The strategies of distancing yourself from your work, reading and rereading, and seeking objective opinions and advice are especially valuable.

Try to find a collaborator to help you spot problems and confirm your accomplishments. If you give your draft to a fellow student or talk about it with your instructor, you are likely to get additional insight about the effectiveness of your essay along with ideas for revision. (See 1h on collaboration.)

Ericka Kostka went through numerous drafts and revised often as she reread and reevaluated her work. She filled in the gaps that she and her collaborators identified in the first draft and improved the way she incorporated evidence into her paragraphs. She also added a final section to her essay that gave her readers a sense of initial public support for the wolf reintroduction problem at Yellowstone. The suggestion to do that came from a classmate during a collaborative workshop, and it strengthened her argument and essay.

You may be wondering how, then, do you know when to stop drafting and revising? There is no conclusive answer to that question, but when you can say "yes" to the following questions, you have likely reached a final draft that is ready to be edited, proofed, and prepared for submission (40k).

1. Can my readers follow my train of thought?
2. Have I made my point clearly and convincingly?
3. Have I included sufficient evidence to illustrate what I mean and to be convincing?

4. Have I acknowledged my sources properly?
5. Am I satisfied with what I have written?

In addition, reconsider your draft in light of the accompanying checklist on rethinking and revising the research essay.

Rethinking and Revising Your Research Essay

- **Reconsider what you set out to do.** Have you solved the problem you set out to solve; namely, have you resolved the controversy to your satisfaction? If your purpose was to inform or explain, have you done so? Have you interpreted the evidence, formulated a thesis, and presented an explanation and defense of that thesis that seems reasonable to you?

- **Consider your accomplishments in light of what others have said about your essay.** Take all of the feedback that you may have received during collaborative workshops and private consultations with friends, classmates, and your instructor. Consider all of their suggestions in light of what you are trying to do. Revise your essay and your thesis if necessary.

- **Fill in the gaps.** After you have considered your own assessment of the draft and input from your collaborators, do additional research if you need more evidence. Perhaps consult discarded working bibliography cards. You might also just resume drafting, adding more reflections to clarify the relationship between your evidence and ideas.

- **Consider the structure of your draft by writing a formal outline.** After you fill in the gaps and complete other revisions, develop a formal sentence outline as a way of verifying for yourself the logical relationships among the sections of your essay (see 1f-1 on outlining). Consider moving parts of your essay around to make the essay more convincing; refine your explanations of the evidence.

- **Check the accuracy of all incorporated evidence.** Check summaries, paraphrases, and quotations against your note cards. Make sure that the source material you are using is accurate and that you have documented each citation. Return to the original source if you are in doubt—never be sloppy.

- **Create a title.** Devise a title that will catch the reader's interest and convey a sense of your essay and your point of view.

- **Consider the way the beginning, middle, and ending work together to make your essay more effective.** If you spot problems, revise and then reread the essay.

40k   Preparing the final manuscript

After you have completed drafting and revising your essay, prepare an alphabetical list of all of the sources that you cited in your essay. This list will be entitled "Works Cited" in MLA style (see 43c) or "References" in APA style (see 43f).

You also must prepare a final copy of the manuscript, making it as clean, neat, and near perfect as possible. As you prepare this final copy, check for errors in grammar, usage, spelling, punctuation, and mechanics as well as the physical layout of the essay. Edit and proofread carefully using the guidelines in 1i. You can see two complete student research essays, one formatted in MLA style and one in APA style, in Chapter 44.

Attention to detail and presentation will pay off. Your readers will find your essay pleasurable and will not be distracted from the essay by careless mistakes. You can be confident that you will benefit from what Roy Reed, a distinguished journalist, calls "putting the final shine on the piece."

41 *Avoiding Plagiarism*

Plagiarism is a strange-sounding word that, according to the *Shorter Oxford English Dictionary*, derives from the Latin *plagiarius* (kidnapper, literary thief) and the French *plagium* (man-stealing, kidnapping). These two related words suggest the serious transgression that characterizes the work of the plagiarist: theft, stealing. To plagiarize is to steal, to take from someone else (from a source other than yourself) what is not yours to take *unless you acknowledge the taking*.

You are often required to build your own work on the work that others have done before you, just as professional scholars do. Giving credit to someone who has helped you is expected. Not to give credit is to plagiarize, to steal. Plagiarizing is to present the following as your own:

- A phrase, sentence, or passage from another writer's work without using quotation marks

- A summarized or paraphrased passage from another writer's work without acknowledging the borrowing

- Facts, ideas, or written text gathered or downloaded from the Internet and presented as your own
- Another student's work with your name on it
- A purchased paper or "research" from a term-paper mill or agency that creates papers for a fee and submitting it as your own work

Other related forms of academic fraud include:

- "Collaborating" between two or more students who then submit the same paper under their individual names
- Submitting the same paper for two or more courses without the knowledge and the expressed permission of all teachers involved
- Giving permission to another student to use your work for a class

When you, as a writer, make use of someone else's work, you must acknowledge that work whether it be a printed text (book, essay, newspaper article, song), a text taken from the Internet (written or visual), a piece of artwork in the public domain, or the results of a laboratory experiment or a survey. Specifically, you must acknowledge borrowed information and ideas as well as the organizational patterns that writers use to defend their ideas.

It follows that you must keep track of your own thoughts and the thoughts of others as you do your research and take notes so that when you begin to blend your ideas with what you have borrowed from others, you know when and how to signal the shift from borrowed material to your own thoughts and ideas, or vice versa. To signal such shifts you must learn the technique for incorporating borrowed evidence (see 40d for guidelines on note-taking techniques and 40i on incorporation of evidence) and be ever-mindful of your obligation to acknowledge the work of others (see 41d).

Because plagiarism—whether intentional or not—is a form of theft, the consequences of plagiarism are serious. Scholarly dishonesty usually results in course failure and sometimes dismissal from college, depending on the seriousness of the offense.

41a   Knowing what sources to acknowledge

To avoid plagiarizing material, it helps to know what sources require acknowledgment and what sources do not. The following specific guidelines will help direct you.

1 Source materials requiring acknowledgment

The following materials must always be properly acknowledged if you are to avoid plagiarism.

- **Someone else's words.** When you use someone else's words verbatim, you must enclose those words in quotation marks and acknowledge the source from which they were taken. Someone else's words can take the form of complete sentences or paragraphs, or they can be individual keywords or phrases integrated into one of your own sentences, paraphrases, or summaries.

- **Someone else's ideas, organizational patterns, or facts.** When you use someone else's ideas—whether unsubstantiated opinions or well-developed assertions—you must acknowledge the source. Someone else's ideas can take a number of forms: if you incorporate the words or ideas of an interviewee or if you develop your entire essay in response to someone else's thesis, you must acknowledge that the material is not yours. If you develop or order your ideas in the same way that your source did, even if you use your own words, you must acknowledge the source. In addition, when you use facts—whether statistics, graphs, illustrations, or tables—that constitute the work or findings of a particular individual rather than the widely known data in a field, you must acknowledge the source.

- **Help provided by others.** Credit anyone who helps you develop an idea, conduct a survey, or organize your essay. An acknowledgment page can follow the title page, or acknowledgments can be given in explanatory or content notes (see 43b and 43e).

- **Material taken from the Internet.** You must acknowledge all material taken from the Internet whether that material is attributed to a particular author or whether it appears to be anonymous. (See the guidelines on p. 636 pertaining to *common knowledge.* Do not assume that all material appearing on the Internet is common knowledge.)

2 Source materials not requiring acknowledgment

The following types of source materials need not be acknowledged.

- **Results of your own field research.** If you conduct surveys, use questionnaires, conduct laboratory experiments, or record personal observations in your journal, you can explain and claim credit for that work in your essay (see the sample student essays in Chapter 44, for example). However, always acknowledge anyone else who may have contributed to the research.

- **Common knowledge.** Information that is widely known or circulated in a field is known as common knowledge. Consider historical dates, the standard definitions of words, and information that is known to everyone who has basic knowledge about a given field of study or a particular problem as common knowledge. That Sigmund Freud and Carl Jung advanced early theories about the analysis of dreams need not be acknowledged; nor need knowledge that on January 27, 1973, the peace accord ending the conflict in Vietnam was signed. A good test for common knowledge is whether you find information repeated from article to article (especially in encyclopedias and other general information sources) without acknowledgment. If you are in doubt about whether material from a source constitutes common knowledge, acknowledge the source to be safe.

41b The most common pitfalls for the plagiarist

The most common kind of plagiarism results from carelessness. When writers try to build an entire essay from a patchwork of passages selected from sources, mixing summary, paraphrase, and quotation together indiscriminately—doing little of their own thinking—there is a good chance that the ideas and words of others will make their way into the final essay without proper acknowledgment. Often an inexperienced writer gets lost in the presentation of evidence and fails to acknowledge the sources, or he or she forgets to make clear the difference between borrowed material and original, reflective work.

Sometimes, the plagiarism occurs because the writer is not careful enough when taking notes, and the material from note cards begins to seem to the writer like his or her own work. Ownership is lost in the translation from original source to note cards to the student's essay. Students accidentally omit quotation marks when quoting directly, or they inadvertently reproduce the structure of an argument from a source, or they summarize or paraphrase the source without signaling the beginning and end of the borrowed material and without actually acknowledging where the material has come from.

Less frequent, but prevalent, is the deliberate plagiarism that occurs when writers intentionally leave off quotation marks, purchase a completed paper from an agency that specializes in feeding off the needs of college and university students, or leave out the source of information to mislead readers into thinking that the incorporated material actually belongs to the writer rather than to someone else.

Remember that plagiarism is plagiarism whether the act is intentional or not and that the consequences are always serious.

41c   Being alert for plagiarism in your writing

The most important thing you can do to avoid plagiarism is to exercise care when you take notes and then again when you incorporate source material from your notes into your essay. The techniques outlined in sections 40d and 40i will help you by keeping you mindful of the difference between your own thoughts and the source material.

A more general and more important way to avoid plagiarism is to have ideas of your own. Interpret the evidence, make inferences from it, and analyze

---

Guidelines for Avoiding Plagiarism

- Develop ideas of your own, always keeping them distinct from the ideas you find in sources.

- If you quote verbatim from a source, use quotation marks. Be sure your summaries and paraphrases are in your own words and that you signal the beginning and end of such summarizing or paraphrasing. Careful note taking will help.

- Integrate source material carefully. (Follow the Guidelines for Incorporating Evidence on p. 626.)

- Be sure that your voice predominates in your essay. Remember, you are the thinker and writer. You use sources to help clarify and substantiate your ideas and thesis and to lend authority to your argument. Never simply compile a report about someone else's research and ideas unless you have been specifically instructed to do only that.

- Be sure that you have adequate parenthetical citations and that each citation corresponds to the list of sources at the end of the essay (see Chapter 43).

it to discover your own ideas. Then, when you write your essay, use the evidence to support your ideas, acknowledging it properly, as you move beyond the analysis found in your sources to your own thinking.

As you conduct research, take notes, and write your essay, always distinguish your ideas from the ideas you find in your sources; separate the evidence you produce through independent field research from the evidence you borrow from sources. Acknowledge whatever is not yours.

The difference between plagiarism and being honest is also a practical matter that comes down to mechanics, to the way you incorporate borrowed evidence into your essay. The most obvious kind of plagiarism results from failure to cite the source of borrowed information either in the text of your paragraph or in parentheses, at the appropriate place in your paragraph.

Plagiarism that does not seem deliberate is nevertheless serious. It often results from using phrases from a source without giving credit for those borrowed forms of expression, even though the writer gives credit for the ideas.

ORIGINAL SOURCE

At the same time, however, the Park Service backed off. It agreed not to mail out its educational packets (which had run out anyway). It temporarily canceled an immensely popular wolf-restoration slide show. It stopped writing about wolf reintroduction in the park newspaper. And it prohibited Defenders of Wildlife from selling pro-wolf-restoration posters at park visitor centers.

—Ted Williams, "Waiting for Wolves to Howl in Yellowstone"

PLAGIARISM

Yellowstone should uphold the interests of the wild, not those of the prevailing political view. But the park buckled under pressure. According to Ted Williams, the park stopped mailing its educational packets, canceled a popular wolf-restoration slide show, stopped writing about wolf reintroduction, and prohibited selling pro-wolf-restoration posters at park visitor centers (38).

In this paragraph, acknowledgment is given to Williams for the information, but not for the borrowed language. Such plagiarism usually results from sloppy note taking or from rushing through research. To correct this plagiarized paragraph, the writer should revise by summarizing or paraphrasing all of the borrowed material or by putting borrowed phrasing in quotation marks.

41d Guidelines for selecting and incorporating evidence—A recapitulation

The following guidelines should help you as you read and select evidence from your own sources. The varied examples will suggest to you several ways that you might do your own work. Incorporating evidence seamlessly into your essays will require diligence, but that hard work will reward your readers. By removing the clutter from your paragraphs and by careful selection and citation of evidence (*accompanied by reflection*) you will make it easier for your readers to follow your thinking and understand your ideas. First, study the guidelines for selection of evidence.

Guidelines for Selecting Evidence from Sources

1. Select evidence that clarifies and strengthens your own ideas, without ignoring evidence that complicates or calls into question your analysis.

2. Remember that you always have choices to make about what to put in and what to leave out from your sources.

3. Summarize or paraphrase your source, or select telling words, phrases, or images to incorporate into your own sentences. (See 40d for more on summarizing, paraphrasing, quoting, and reflecting.)

4. Develop a system for keeping up with your sources and what you are borrowing from them. (See 1e and 40d for more on note taking.)

5. Keep in mind that you will be subordinating that evidence to your own ideas as you select evidence and prepare to write. The *quality* of the evidence and *what you think* about that evidence are more important than quantity.

These additional guidelines should help you as you *incorporate* selected evidence into your own essays.

Guidelines for Incorporating Selected Evidence

1. Always assume that your readers have not read your sources or shared your experiences, or that they do not know what it is that you want them to know about those sources.

2. Introduce your written or visual evidence to your readers by naming both the source (title) and the writer or artist who created it.

3. Cite sufficient evidence for written sources—in the form of summary, paraphrase, or quotation—so that your readers can easily grasp the sources' meaning and its importance. Aim always for the essential, avoiding long block quotations.

4. Distinguish your own thoughts and ideas from those in the sources that you cite. Pay particular attention to the way you move from a summarized source back to your own reflections.

5. Find words to describe visual sources that will permit your readers to *see* the source. Avoid cluttering details.

6. Shape your evidence for experiential sources (stories, anecdotes, tales) so that your readers see the relationship between evidence and idea.

7. Reflect on your selected evidence so that your readers can understand it outside the context of its original source and can also comprehend the relationship between evidence and idea. (See 40i for more on incorporating evidence into research essays.)

8. Document your sources!

41e   Documentation

In Chapter 43 you will find detailed instructions about how to use the MLA system of documentation, along with several other systems, including APA and CSE. These various systems are associated with scholarly work done in particular academic disciplines: Modern Language Association (MLA), American Psychological Association (APA), and Council of Science Editors (CSE; formerly CBE, for Council of Biology Editors).

42   *Using the Internet for Research*

The Internet is a vast computer network that can give you access to current events and national news; world news; ongoing research in almost every field; topics of cultural, scientific, and educational interest; library holdings; bibliographies; even conversations among researchers and special-interest groups. This network also allows you to communicate via e-mail with other people.

The Internet connects you to the World Wide Web (abbreviated as WWW, or the Web), a system of linked documents that are placed on the network. These documents, each of which is located on a *Web page,* contain information that can supplement and enhance your research, giving you immediate access to library holdings, computer databases, and Web sites. Individual Web pages may be linked to other pages at a given *site*—locations where information is stored—on the WWW, or they may be linked to other pages at different sites.

At first it seems overwhelming to visualize exactly where all that information is on the Web and how it is organized. Its sheer volume might make you wonder why you should bother searching the Web. You might well imagine that the information is in the library. But much of the information on the Web is not in your library.

The Internet gives you access to a great deal of information that is more current than what is available in printed texts. For example, the Web can give you access to conversations that researchers in almost every field of knowledge are having with one another. It also provides speed and flexibility, allowing you to search many databases, even other libraries' collections, and to conduct these searches in ways that will expedite your research. You can search sources covering several years (often eight to ten) at once, and you can print or download citations, abstracts, and sometimes the complete text of scholarly articles without leaving your room.

Features of Internet research worth noting

This chapter's examination of the kinds of sources available on the Web suggests several important features of Internet research:

1. You can find important information quickly.

2. The search engines limit the search and give you sources that are likely to yield additional information.

3. You can conduct these preliminary searches and evaluate the sources either from the annotated lists provided by the search engines or by quick visits to the sites.

4. Supplemental research in the library may be necessary to confirm or deny the worth of sources that have yet to be subjected to rigorous review and analysis.

42a Accessing the Internet and navigating with a browser

You normally gain access to the Internet either through a *modem* that connects your computer to a telephone line or a *local area network* (LAN), which provides even faster service than a modem. To gain Internet access through one of these connecting devices, you will need an account with a school or institution, or with an Internet service provider such as America Online, Prodigy, or the Microsoft Network. Some dormitories have wired terminals that provide direct access to your school's computer system and to the Internet. Check with the academic computing facilities at your college or university to find out what you need to do to open your own account and gain access to the system.

If you do not have a computer, check with your library's staff. Often the library will have computers that will give you direct access to the Internet. All you have to do is sit in front of the computer, follow either the printed instructions or those on-screen, and begin searching. Librarians should be able to direct you to these computers and to those members of the staff who can help you use them. Computers are also available in Internet cafes.

Navigating the Web

The distinctive navigating features of the Web are tied to *hypertext* links—electronic pathways within a Web page, from Web page to Web page, or from Web site to Web site. These links often appear underlined in color or as a "button" device on your computer screen. When you point to these hypertext links with your mouse, the pointer on the screen indicates that you have pointed to a link that can take you to another site and more information. To move from one link to another location or another Web site, you only need point and click. Moving from link to link is called *browsing the Web*.

When you open a *browser* application—either Netscape Navigator or Microsoft Internet Explorer—you get a framework page with a small window showing the currently active location or Internet address. This window lets you type in addresses using a convention known as the *Domain Name System* (see the box, p. 645). In addition, the browser's icons and menus provide tools that allow you to move forward or backward through a series of sites you have browsed, or to print a page or capture an image currently displayed. Your browser also lets you save and re-use addresses for Web sites you wish to revisit, simply by selecting the "bookmark" or "favorites" function and then clicking to add the site to your inventory. Later you can find your site quickly by pulling down the Bookmarks or Favorites menu and clicking on the item. The browser also provides ways for you to select or download the entire contents of a Web page for storage in your computer files. (See the Computer Tip below and Tips about Downloading and Printing on p. 655.) These functions can be critical to your documentation process, helping you retrieve documents and keep track of key source addresses. (See 40d for more on note taking, and Chapter 43 on documenting sources.)

Using a search engine

The first screen you see when you open a browser is usually ISP's home page, sometimes customized to contain a variety of information. The home page is likely to show an additional window for scanning the Internet using a *search engine,* a special software device that does an automatic search for sites when you ask for information. Among the most common and most powerful of these search engines are Google, AltaVista, Yahoo!, InfoSeek, and Eureka!,

---

Computer Tip

Saving an Image from the Internet

You can copy images from the Internet onto your computer and use them privately or for restricted viewing in your class. (Often the images you wish to copy are protected by copyright and cannot be reproduced for wider distribution.) Right-click your mouse button over the image, select SAVE IMAGE AS on the pop-up menu, and give the image a name. Choose a directory or folder on your drive or disk where you want to store the image.

but new engines appear frequently. (See the box on pp. 646–647 describing features of various search engines.) A search engine may let you choose from a hierarchy of topics to find what you want, but most also allow you to use a system of keywords similar to that used for an online library catalog (see 42b-2). A word search will give you, almost instantaneously, a list of promising sites related to the keywords you selected. From this list of sites, you can click and choose as you wish, moving from one site of information to another, gaining access to thousands of documents while sitting at your personal computer or one of your school's terminals (see 42c on evaluating Internet sources).

Guidelines for Internet Searches

- Link your computer to the Internet and open your browser.
- From the browser's home page, go to the search box (or follow the browser's procedure for selecting a particular search engine).
- Enter the keywords needed for your search (see 39e-2–3).
- When the search engine shows a list of its "top" 10 to 25 sites, survey the list to identify the most promising. Click on these. (The engine may give you more sites [lower in its hierarchy] that are worth pursuing.)
- When a site you visit gives you links or references to others that are related, click on the hyperlinks provided (or make a copy of the addresses if there are no direct links).
- After skimming the site you visit, you may decide to print or download its pages for late examination. Note the size and downloading time of the document to be sure it is worthwhile. Also record or store the address and references from the source for later documentation or a return access (see Chapter 40).
- If you are not satisfied with the first search results, you can (a) try new search words or Boolean combinations (see 39e-2–3); (b) try a different search engine on your browser; (c) enter an exact copy of any related addresses that seemed promising in an earlier search in the browser's address box.
- Do not be afraid to experiment. Retracing your steps on the browser's *back* button or its *home* button may let you pursue another line of inquiry.

As you conduct your searches, follow the procedures in the accompanying chart.

Remember that the browser and the search engine will select sites on the basis of the keywords you enter to limit and refine your searches. You can find more about the search criteria by clicking information buttons on the home page for the browser or the search engine. You can modify the search (including the way keywords are combined) by following onscreen instructions or the suggestions in 42b. You can also expand your search by selecting a different search engine. If you want to designate a different search engine when your home page has no button, you can enter a complete Internet address in the address window.

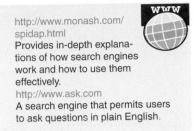

http://www.monash.com/spidap.html
Provides in-depth explanations of how search engines work and how to use them effectively.
http://www.ask.com
A search engine that permits users to ask questions in plain English.

Computer Tip

Using the Domain Name System

- To access a domain on the Internet:

  Type the technical designation by which the domain is to be accessed (usually *http*, or *hypertext transfer protocol*), followed by the characters *://* followed by the domain name. Example: http://webcrawler.com. This entire string is known as the URL (*universal resource locator* or the Internet address).

- Consult directories on the Internet, a list provided by search engines from a keyword search, or a printed directory for Internet addresses.

Even during your initial Internet searches, it would be wise to download or copy lists provided by your search engines; the lists contain a great deal of useful information about links, and change often.

A list of well-known search engines with an indication of their key features appears on p. 646.

Internet Search Engines

AltaVista
http://altavista.com

Very complete and fast search. *Keyword and Boolean searching.* (See 42b-3.)

Excite
http://www.excite.com

Easy search of Web pages, reviews, and news groups. *Subject area, keyword, and Boolean searching.*

Google
http://www.google.com

Very thorough, fast searches. *Accepts words, sentences, and does Boolean searches easily.*

Hotbot
http://hotbot.com

Fast, easy search with many options. E-mail, message boards, chat rooms, home pages. *Subject area, keyword, and Boolean searching.*

InfoSeek
http://infoseek.go.com

Searches Web pages, Usenet news groups, FTP and Gopher sites. *Subject area and keyword searching. No Boolean searching.*

Lycos
http://www.lycos.com

One of the largest URL catalogs. *Subject area, keyword, and Boolean searching.*

ProFusion
http://www.profusion.com

Searches multiple engines simultaneously. *Keyword and Boolean searching.*

(continued)

WebCrawler
http://webcrawler.com/info.wbcrwl

Fast and complete search engine. Includes newsgroups and e-mail. *Subject area, keyword, and Boolean searching.*

Yahoo!
http://www.yahoo.com

Includes news, e-mail, and chat rooms. *Subject area and keyword searching. No Boolean searching.*

42b Narrowing and refining your search

Because there is so much information on the Web, you will almost certainly need to limit your searches so that you are only identifying information that is directly related to your research area. There are three primary ways to facilitate and narrow your searches: subject area, keyword, and Boolean searches.

1 Subject area searches

You can look for Web sites according to subject areas in many of the search engines (see the listing above), pursuing subjects arranged in a hierarchy that allows you to narrow your search by topic and subtopic. Because each search engine develops its own list of topical sites based on editorial judgment and experience, search engines can vary widely in both the number and quality of sites offered for selection by subject area. One of the most comprehensive subject listings for Web sites is offered by Yahoo! However, Google, HotBot, InfoSeek, and Lycos have extensive lists as well.

When Ericka Kostka needed some information about the gray wolf reintroduction program in Yellowstone, she looked at the Yahoo! site which contained broad subject areas, such as "Arts & Humanities," "Business & Money," "Health," "Reference," and "Science"—the last of which offered a subtopic of "Animals." Clicking on this subtopic allowed her to find and click again on a subtopic of "Wildlife," a page with 413 topics and special descriptive site listings, many with links to other wildlife sites. On this page

---

Computer Tip

Using the Internet to Find a Topic

You can pursue a topic that interests you by using a search engine such as Excite or InfoSeek, which has subject areas or categories arranged hierarchically. First, find categories that seem relevant to your area of interest or your topic. Within a broad area such as *politics*, for example, you might find the topic *government*, and within that area, *elections*. As you follow the subject tree into more specific topics, jot down other related topics that might be either interesting to you or relevant to your assignment.

Kostka decided to pursue the topic "Endangered Species," with 75 sites listed, and while a click to that page did not reveal a separate category for wolves, she found several sites with further links on endangered species, and three sites with relevant government documents.

When Kostka went through a similar range of hierarchical topics on the HotBot search engine, she found a useful topic, "Environmental Monitoring," where she was able to receive a number of "Site Recommendations" that would provide detailed information about this subject. With such sequences of subject searching, Kostka was able to move quickly from general to more restricted and specific topics.

Another useful resource for pursuing subjects and subtopics is the *Library of Congress Subject Headings* (LCSH) reference, a three-volume book that lists all of the subject headings used to classify library books (see 39e-1–2 on library catalogs and keyword searches). Using the key terms from this listing, Kostka was able to pursue some relevant subject topics by means of a keyword search.

http://www.lib.berkeley.edu/
TeachingLib/Guides/
Internet/FindInfo.html
Offers valuable guidance
on searching the Internet.

2   Keyword searches

After you have selected keywords that are closely related to your chosen area of research, you are ready for additional searching on the Web. Enter your keywords in the window of the search engine, much as you would for an online library catalog (see 39e-2). The search engine will give you a list of *hits*, each of which serves as a hyper-text link to a source of information.

http://www.infotoday.com/
databases.shtml
Provides tips for doing more advanced Internet searches.

Before searching, consult the home page of the search engine for advance search procedures or for drop-down windows that allow you to customize your search. Also consult the engine's *Help* screen. Unless you restrict searches, you may find more information than you can reasonably consider. A recent search for *gray wolf Yellowstone,* using Google, yielded 13,800 Web pages. A more restricted search (gray wolf Yellowstone 2000–2003) on the same search engine yielded 82 Web pages. Restricting your topic will help you consolidate your search and expedite your effort to sort and evaluate the information.

3   Boolean searches

Boolean searching allows you to use simple operators to restrict your searches. The most common operators are AND, OR, and NOT. These opera-tors work essentially the same way on the Internet as they do when you search the library's online system (see 39e-2). However, every search engine has different configurations, requiring that you pay particular attention to minor differences in the way you specify the kind of search you want to con-duct and the manner in which you enter the operators.

The underlying principles for Boolean searches remain constant.

- AND (&) limits your search by combining terms: *gray* AND *wolf.* This designation ensures that you get sources related only to *gray wolf* (both terms combined). The search would be limited to sources that contain both keywords.

- OR (/) expands the search to include any source with either keyword: *wolf* OR *Yellowstone.* Both keywords would be included in the search

- AND NOT (!) limits the search by excluding one term: *wolf* AND NOT *Yell-owstone.* This designation would include all wolves except those associated with Yellowstone.

Always enter Boolean operators in CAPS, with a space between keywords and operators. If the designation is highly complex, use parentheses: (*gray*

AND *wolf* AND *Yellowstone*) AND (NOT *red* AND *wolf*). Boolean searches can use abbreviations: *wolf* & *Yellowstone*.

Some search engines do not recognize Boolean operators, but permit you to limit searches in other ways. On the home page of the search engine, in a drop-down window, you may find the term *exact phrase*. If you select that option, the search engine will look for the entire keyword phrase just as you have entered it into the engine's window: *gray wolf*, or perhaps *Yellowstone Park*. If there is no such choice, you may achieve the same effect by placing the keyword phrase in quotation marks: *"gray wolf"* or *"Yellowstone Park."* These variations and options will more than likely be explained on the search engine's *Help* screen. If not, experiment.

On pages 660–661 are excerpts from the extensive sources uncovered by two search engines in Ericka Kostka's research for her paper on the introduction of gray wolves into Yellowstone Park. When different search engines are used for the same request, even with the same Boolean operators in the keywords, the results are different. Kostka's search results varied depending on the search engine and the terms used. In the example, the results from WebCrawler differed considerably from those obtained from AltaVista. Note also that the entries in the AltaVista results provided dates for the time of most recent posting for its sites—a feature that allowed this search engine to restrict results by time of posting. Many of the entries on these two lists contained links to other sites, which led to further links and additional sources. A subsequent search on Google produced more than 50 pages of electronic links to possible sources. Clearly, searching with two or more engines pays off with more choices. The number of sources to be discovered on the Web is significantly greater than were found in a new search of RLIN, which had only 40 print sources related to the Yellowstone project (39e-3). While this large number shows the value of doing electronic searches, the sheer volume of sources also suggests the need to select and evaluate them carefully (see 42c).

4   Using other online resources

Online libraries

Many libraries, both public and academic, make information about their collections available online. However, access to a particular library's holdings is often restricted to library members or to students and faculty of that college or university. Even virtual libraries do not make all of their collections available to those who visit the site. You can generally see the library's online catalog of its collections, and sometimes you can access the library's research databases, where you can find abstracts of scholarly journal articles. But often you cannot print out full-text copies of articles.

Often the fastest and most reliable way of obtaining research information is through your own library's databases, if they are available through a Web site. As a student, you will usually be able to access databases that are not available to others, as well as many other databases on the Web. Many libraries also provide quick-reference information sheets for students and faculty that explain the latest searching techniques. Even if your library does not have a Web site, visiting other Web sites could give you the information about selected sources that you will need when checking your own library's online catalog. If sources are not available within your library, you can request an interlibrary loan to obtain necessary research material (see 39d-4 on interlibrary loans).

One of the simplest ways to determine whether another library's collection is available is to search LibCat, a direct link to information about public, private, and virtual libraries around the world. You can enter over 1,000 academic and public libraries' collections on the Web.

Here are a number of sites that can help you with your library and reference searches:

Internet Reference Sites	
AskERIC http://ericir.syr.edu	Educational database
Internet Public Library http://www.ipl.org	Experimental reference library: virtual
LibCat http://208.249.120.62/ lc/lca.cfm	Information about and quick online libraries
Refdesk http://www.refdesk.com	General reference site
Reference Collection http://www.lib.uci.edu/ rraz/genref.html	General reference resources, University California–Irvine

Online periodicals

Many periodicals are now available online so that you can print or download full articles with complete text. If you do not know the URL for a particular newspaper or periodical, you may be able to find it using your search engine. Web sites and search engine home pages will also link you to newspapers, magazines, and other periodicals. Here are some useful periodical sites:

CNN.Com
http://www.cnn.com

Electronic Library
http://www.elibrary.com

RocketNews
http://rocketnews.com

New York Times
http://www.nytimes.com

Time/Warner Publications
http://pathfinder.com

Wall Street Journal
http://interactive.wsj.com/public/us

Online government documents

The federal government maintains many sites that you can consult for your research. Each of these major sites provides countless other links to additional information.

Bureau of the Census
http://www.census.gov

Bureau of Justice Statistics
http://www.ojp.usdoj.gov/bjs

Department of Education
http://www.ed.gov

Fish & Wildlife Service
http://www.fws.gov

Library of Congress
http://lcweb.loc.gov

National Institutes of Health
http://www.nih.gov

National Library of Medicine
http://www.nlm.nih.gov

NASA
http://www.nasa.gov

Statistical Abstract of the U.S. (Uncle Sam's Reference Shelf)
http://www.census.gov/statab

Thomas (Congressional Legislation)
http://thomas.loc.gov

White House
http://www.whitehouse.gov

Usenet discussion groups

Often, researchers communicate through Usenet discussion groups (newsgroups) and discussion lists, (listservs). These are the electronic equivalents of open bulletin boards on which to post views and exchange ideas. Newsgroups and listservs are available to anyone. Their entries appear in a series, in the order they are posted, with replies and further comments following in a sequence known as a "thread." Comments usually are identified with the screen names of participants, and while serious researchers usually identify themselves to promote responsible exchanges, others may choose to remain anonymous. A thread of Usenet exchanges can allow careful and considerate participants to have a useful exchange of information and ideas.

Researchers also exchange ideas by means of a listserv, a forum that functions as a subscription list of people of similar interests who wish to receive communications in the form of e-mail. After signing up as subscribers on the list, listserv members regularly receive e-mail communications as posted from other members, or they may post the list with messages of their own. You can learn about the topics and subscription lists that are available on the Web, as well as addresses for other forms of electronic communication, by consulting <http://www.liszt.com> and following the instructions on the site. To subscribe to a list, you send an e-mail message to the address name of the listserv you want, leaving the subject line blank. Using a minimum of terms with no punctuation (except any "dots" and slashes in the address), type the word "subscribe" followed by the name of the list address, followed by your first and last name as the subscriber. A message subscribing to a group for information on oceanography would read: *subscribe ufsiu.uc.be ErickaKostka.*

Usenet and listserv messages can be posted at any time according to the user's convenience—a process known as asynchronous communication. Other Internet channels allow synchronous or real-time instant exchanges for users logged onto a system simultaneously. Perhaps the best-known syn-
chronous channel of this type is the
"chat room."

All electronic communication, both
asynchronous Usenets and listservs as

http://www.albion.com/
netiquette/
Offers advice on socially
acceptable Web etiquette.

well as synchronous sessions, require participants to observe the same con-
ventions of responsible exchange known as "netiquette" that apply to e-mail and all electronic communications.

42c   Evaluating Internet sources

1   General precautions

The biggest problem you face as you confront this vast array of informa-
tion on the Web is how to evaluate it, how to judge its reliability. Because the information is often new and has not been processed and subjected to the scrutiny of rigorous scholarly review, you must be careful about using it uncritically; it is often not as reliable as the information you find in printed sources in the library. Remember this: *Anyone can post information on the Internet.* This means that researchers on the Web must be especially concerned with reliability and evaluation of sources.

The second problem with the Web is its inherent seductiveness; it can eat
away your time. The ease with which
you can move from site to site around
the country and around the world
(and the slow loading time on some
equipment) can draw you into hours
of browsing when your time could
be better spent elsewhere—conducting
research in the library or writing your
research essay. You must be a strict

http://www2.widener.edu/
Wolfgram-Memorial-
Library/webevaluation/
webeval.htm
Provides a collection of materials to
assist in evaluating both print and
electronic sources.

manager of your time when you search the Web, or searching will steal time and energy needed for writing.

When conducting research, go to the Web for specific purposes, find your sources, and either download them onto your computer (store them on your hard disk or on a floppy) or print them. (See the box for tips about downloading.) Do some serious evaluating before you decide to copy, and pay particular attention to document length. You can often find book-length documents on the Web.

Tips about Downloading and Printing

- Download and store material on your computer to save time and money; you generally pay a monthly fee.

- Download electronic documents as plain text (rather than storing them with various Internet codes). Your computer should give you choices about the way you want to save the information when you click "Save as" under "Edit."

- Store electronic documents in a designated folder in your computer or on a floppy disk so that you can find them easily. Evaluate the documents later.

- After evaluating the documents, print only the portions that you need for future reference.

- Always keep up with where you found the material on the Internet because you will have to document electronic sources if you use them in your research essay. You may not be able to go back to the Internet at a later date and find the documents. (See 43c and 43f-4 for more on documenting electronic sources.)

---

2   Evaluating electronic sources

The reliability of the information you find on the Web will vary from document to document, so you must apply sound judgment as you evaluate each of your electronic sources, just as you would the print sources you find in the library. However, you can be fairly confident that the print sources have gone through review processes, that they have been judged by other scholars, and that the editorial and production process that resulted in the published book contributed to its reliability. This is especially true of books published by university presses and articles in scholarly journals where there has usually been a rigorous review and evaluation process.

Evaluating Web site documents

A good rule of thumb to apply when you are evaluating documents has to do with *reliability*. A source can be considered reliable when you and your audience are sufficiently convinced of its truth or value to act on it. Because we know that credibility, truth, or value can be relative (different people looking at the same piece of information may see its value quite differently), you must be very careful to consider viewpoints other than your own when judging a document's reliability. Never assume that the information is reliable just because it convinces you at the moment you read it. Check it against other information that you find in your research; check it, too, against the demands of special-interest groups who have a vested interest in your topic but may not agree with your point of view (see 1d and 40e-f for more on special-interest groups). Finally, consider what your collective audience might think of the reliability of that information if you use it as evidence in your research essay. Would that audience be likely to act on (or assent to) that information?

Consider the following excerpts from two different Web pages that focus on the introduction of gray wolves into Yellowstone. Two special-interest groups are represented here, the National Wildlife Federation (favoring wolf introduction) and the American Farm Bureau Federation (opposing wolf introduction). You can expect to find each presentation to favor its particular agenda; special-interest groups will always argue in their own behalf. You must always look for the loopholes or openings in the arguments that seem to leave out important information or that raise questions in your mind.

American Farm Bureau Federation (Statement issued by Richard L. Krause of the AFBF) <http://powayusd.sdcoe.k12.ca.us/mtr/Krause.htm>

The gray wolf as a species is not in danger of becoming extinct. There are approximately 70,000 gray wolves in Canada, another 15,000 in Alaska, and yet another 2,500+ in Minnesota, Wisconsin and Michigan. In addition, there are close to 100 wolves already in Montana, Idaho, Wyoming.

The introduction program was not done to save the gray wolf. Since the gray wolf population does not need protection, this program also was not done for any of the reasons that are listed in Endangered Species

Act. Rather, it was done to artificially increase the number of wolves already existing in these three states.

The following are reasonable questions for you, as a researcher, to ask about the claims made in these two paragraphs:

- What is the source of the statistics in the first paragraph? Do those numbers (should they prove to be correct estimates) signify that the gray wolf is not an "endangered species" according to the Endangered Species Act?
- What does the Endangered Species Act say?
- Were there other reasons for introducing gray wolves into Yellowstone besides those listed or implied by Mr. Krause?

National Wildlife Federation
<http://nwf.org/endangered/news/wolfpr.html>

The long-delayed **reintroduction of the Gray Wolf** to the Greater Yellowstone ecosystem is a timely demonstration of **a flexible and effective implementation of the Endangered Species Act,** according to Tom Dougherty, Western Regional Staff Director for the National Wildlife Federation, America's largest conservation education organization. . . .

"The National Wildlife Federation has been working for more than a decade to bring the wolf back to its natural home," said Dougherty. "**The Greater Yellowstone ecosystem is incomplete without the gray wolf.** It needs this keystone species to function naturally and in balance."

"Contrary to the way it is now being portrayed by the far right-wing in Congress, reintroduction demonstrates that the **Endangered Species Act has plenty of room** to negotiate environmental and community concerns," Dougherty commented. "It was common-sense conservation that allowed the compromise of returning the wolves as an experimental population, and the National Wildlife Federation is proud to point to this incredible biological and social success story."

http://www.tiac.or.th/
Discusses the skills necessary for making intelligent judgments about the value of Internet sources.

Additional questions and concerns for further research:

- What does Mr. Dougherty mean by "flexible and effective implementation"?

- Does Yellowstone need wolves to balance the ecosystem, considering the available evidence about predator-prey imbalances?

- What does Mr. Dougherty mean by "common-sense conservation" and the notion of "compromise"? Does that suggest a willingness to compromise with the opponents?

EXERCISE 42–1　Considering Balance and Reliability of Particular Web Sites
To gain additional insight into the question of special-interest group bias, locate both of these sites on the Internet and consider the entire presentation at each site.

1. Which site seems to be the least biased, overall? How can you tell?

2. To what extent are you willing to act on the information given by these two sites? Would you use the evidence provided by either site? Under what conditions? Explain.

Keep in mind our earlier note of caution: anyone can enter information on the Web. Pay attention to the site where the information is posted. Be extremely wary of anonymous documents. When you can return to a particular Web site that is well established and that continues to post relevant information about your topic, you can begin to have confidence that the information posted there is more reliable than information that has been posted on a new discussion site. But all information needs to be re-evaluated continually against what you are learning from other sources, both electronic and print. Be rigorous in your scrutiny, and question what you read (see 4a for more on questioning). Guidelines for determining the reliability of online sources are summarized in the accompanying chart.

Questioning and Evaluating Electronic Sources

- Always be concerned about the document's *reliability*—its credibility and value to your research audience.

- What would various special-interest groups think about the reliability of the information obtained from the Web? Can the information be verified?

- Does the discussion group or the listserv seem reliable? What do conversations with members reveal about their seriousness, their credentials, and their biases?

(continued)

- How do the electronic sources measure up to the print sources in terms of reliability and currency?
- Is the electronic source anonymous, or did it come from a particular person at an established, reliable site?
- Am I sufficiently convinced of the value of the source to cite it in my research essay?

Evaluating the gray wolf controversy online

A quick evaluation of the search engine results from Kostka's wolf project (pp. 660–661) suggests that both the ecologists' special interests and those of the ranchers and stockgrowers are represented, with the ecologists having more entries. Nevertheless, if you read the sources with an open, questioning mind, they suggest a great deal about the many sides of the gray wolf controversy. Many of the sources related to the ecologists' special interests present a clear, often unbiased, account of information not necessarily favorable to their cause.

It is relatively easy to make a quick appraisal of the worth and objectivity of individual sources when you visit their respective Web pages. Those initial pages tell a great deal about the coverage that you can expect at that site. And there are interesting surprises for student researchers looking for new topics related to the reintroduction of wolves.

The Internet research from these two initial lists should be followed up with library research. Government documents, newspapers, reports of the Montana Stockgrowers' Association and the Farm Bureau, court decisions, and information about wolf packs and pack distribution both inside and outside Yellowstone would help complete the picture of what has happened since the wolves were reintroduced and what controversies still need to be resolved in this age-old struggle between man and nature.

Evaluating Usenets and other discussion channels

When you are connected to a discussion group of any kind (42b-4), the credibility of the members is a critical issue. Is it a discussion group whose members have academic credentials and who seem to be conducting scientific investigations with as little bias as possible, or are the members part of a group bound together by a passionate interest in the subject that could bias

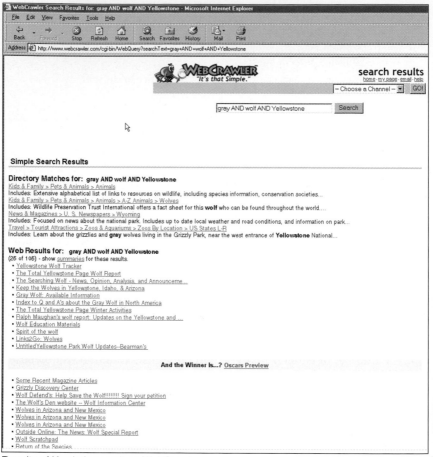

Results of Kostka's search on WebCrawler

their exchange and their selection and presentation of information? You may need to eavesdrop on discussions over a period of time (often called *lurking*) to be able to discern what you need to know about credentials and biases. Always try to consult more than one source. When possible, always check electronic sources against print sources in your library.

Results of Kostka's search on AltaVista

Do not hesitate to enter into discussions with the participants of discussion groups or listservs via e-mail. Ask probing questions; keep track of those conversations. You might want to save and document the conversations as well as the posted information. Such conversations could be conducted just like an interview (see 39f-1 for more on interviewing techniques). Conversations could take place over several weeks as you are conducting research. As you begin to know more about your subject, you can return to an earlier conversation with someone in a discussion group or on a listserv and ask more informed questions about your topic.

43 *Documenting Sources*

In writing a research essay you use facts and opinions from outside sources as evidence to support your ideas. You have an obligation to document the source of this cited material, whether you use the actual language of the source or restate it in your own words.

Established conventions for documenting sources vary from one academic discipline to another. The Modern Language Association (MLA) style of documentation is preferred in literature and languages. For papers in the social sciences the American Psychological Association (APA) style is preferred, whereas papers in history, philosophy, economics, political science, and business disciplines are formatted in the Chicago Manual of Style (CMS) system. The Council of Science Editors (CSE) recommends varying documentation styles for different natural sciences. This chapter covers MLA and APA styles of documentation and briefly illustrates the CMS and other CSE documentation systems. If you are in doubt about which style to use, check with your instructor.

Whatever style of documentation you use, be certain to format your citations consistently within that style. You will need to acknowledge your sources in two ways: (1) with in-text, parenthetical citations (see 43a and 43d); (2) with a list of sources at the end of your paper (see 43c and 43f). In-text, or parenthetical, citations identify the specific page of a source for a quotation, an idea, a fact, an interpretation, or another type of reference. Parenthetical citations provide readers with an immediate indication of what material you borrowed. For more detailed information about a paper's sources, readers can consult the list of sources at the end of the paper. There they will find complete bibliographical data about the source.

MLA Documentation Style

The method of documentation described and illustrated in this section is recommended by the Modern Language Association in its *MLA Handbook for Writers of Research Papers* (6th ed. New York: MLA, 2003). MLA documentation style is used both in student papers and in scholarly articles in literature and languages. Consult the accompanying chart that lists MLA forms for an overview of the types of citations described in this section. Do not be intimidated by the number of citation samples. Mastering the basic citation forms for books and periodicals will give you the formula from which any citation can be derived.

http://www.mla.org/
set_stl.htm
Provides guidelines for documenting electronic sources in MLA style.

Directory of MLA Sample Entries

In-text, Parenthetical Citations (see 43a)

1. Author not named in text, 666
2. Author named in text, 666
3. Entire work, 667
4. Work with two or three authors, 667
5. Work with more than three authors, 667
6. Multivolume work, 667
7. Anonymous work, 668
8. Corporate author, 668
9. Indirect citation, 668
10. Literary work, 668
11. Author of two or more cited works, 669
12. Authors with the same last name, 669
13. Two or more sources in a single citation, 669
14. Nonprint source, 669

(continued)

(continued)

43a MLA style for in-text, parenthetical citations

MLA style uses two methods for citing borrowed material within the text: (1) The author and page number of the source are identified immediately following the borrowed material. (2) The author is identified in the text and the page reference is given immediately following the borrowed material.

In-text citations guide readers to the appropriate source in the Works Cited list where readers can get the bibliographic information they need to locate the material within a particular source.

Use the following guidelines when writing with parenthetical citations.

- Keep the citations concise, but provide all necessary information.
- Use an author's last name in the first and subsequent in-text citations. Use an author's first initial and last name if two authors in the Works Cited list share the same last name.
- Punctuate and format the parenthetical citations in the following manner.
  1. Place the parenthetical citation either at the end of the sentence or at a natural pause within the sentence. In either case, the citation should follow, as closely as possible, the material it refers to.
  2. If the citation is placed immediately following a quotation, place the citation after the closing quotation marks.
  3. Place any punctuation marks in the text immediately following the closing parenthesis of the citation.
  4. In block quotations, place the parenthetical citation following the final punctuation mark of the quotation.
  5. Include a page reference for the borrowed material.

1.   Author not named in text

When the author is not named in the text, place that author's last name and the page reference in parentheses, at a point where the citation does not interrupt the flow of your writing. Do not use a comma or the abbreviations *p.* or *pp.* within the parentheses.

Hawthorne's son Julian recalled that his father read novels for relaxation, but that he seriously <u>studied</u> popular newspapers and magazines (Reynolds 114).

2.   Author named in text

If the author is identified in the text, cite only the page number in parentheses.

Herzog notes that there are more protests against experiments on domestic animals like dogs and cats than against research involving animals like snakes (349).

3. Entire work

When citing an entire work such as a complete article or book rather than a particular passage within the work, do not refer to the work within a parenthetical citation. The source must be cited in the Works Cited list.

Bennett and Ames survey the use and abuse of alcohol in various cultures.

4. Work with two or three authors

Include the last name of each author in the text or in a citation.

Lichtenstein and Danker have noted that beginning in 1974, the New Orleans Center for the Creative Arts (NOCCA) has produced successful performers such as Wynton Marsalis and Harry Connick, Jr. (284).

Classroom research can be done most effectively when one becomes a "participant observer" (Cohn, Kottkamp, and Provenzo 89-91).

5. Work with more than three authors

When citing a work with four or more authors, either list the last name of each author or list the author whose name appears first on the title page, followed by *et al.* (meaning "and others").

A pregnant adolescent "experiences restricted social relationships and less positive interactions with both friends and family" and so is subject to severe emotional stress (Passino et al. 118).

6. Multivolume work

Cite the author, volume number, and page reference (Hamilton 26: 293). Separate the volume number and the page reference by a colon followed by one space. Do not use the words *volume* or *pages* or the abbreviations *vol.* or *p.* when referring to passages within a volume. An arabic number to the left of the colon identifies the volume and a number to the right of the colon indicates the page number(s).

Alexander Hamilton may have foreseen the fatal result of his duel with Aaron Burr because on 4 July 1804 he wrote to his wife: "Fly to the bosom of your God and be comforted" (26: 293).

To refer to an entire volume of a multivolume work, follow the author's name with a comma and the abbreviation *vol.* (Hamilton, vol. 3). Do not abbreviate *volume* when using the word in text: "In volume 3, Hamilton mentions . . ."

7. Anonymous work

Cite an anonymous work by its title, which may be shortened to a key defining word or phrase (as is the article "Democracy and Mega-Scandal" in the following example).

The truth about the Contras, 3, Star Wars, and other controversies will probably never be known ("Democracy" 6-8).

8. Corporate author

It is best to cite the name of a corporate, or collective, author in the text rather than in a long parenthetical reference.

A 1990 report by the State Board of Education of New York urges curricular revisions that emphasize multiculturalism (2-4).

9. Indirect citation

When quoting from an indirect or secondary source (such as an author's report of someone else's statement), use the abbreviation *qtd. in* (meaning "quoted in") and then cite the source. Always identify the original writer or speaker in the text or citation.

Robert Coughlan wrote that Faulkner "acts like a farmer who had studied Plato and looks like a river gambler" (qtd. in Blotner 2: 1468).

10. Literary work

Give the page number(s) from the edition of the work that is being cited. Because some literary works exist in many different editions, it is helpful to follow the page numbers with a semicolon and appropriate abbreviations for major divisions of the work (210; ch. 15) or (5; act 1). For a poem, cite line number(s) and in your first reference use the word *line(s)*.

For verse plays, do not use page numbers. Give the act, scene, and line numbers separated by periods.

Hamlet's last words are "the rest is silence" (5.2.247).

11. Author of two or more cited works

To distinguish among multiple works by an author, include the title or a shortened title in an in-text phrase or in a parenthetical citation.

Kingston describes how she had to learn the appropriate cultural behavior for a Chinese-American female (Woman 35-40).

In this example, *Woman* is an abbreviated form of Maxine Hong Kingston's book entitled *The Woman Warrior.*

12. Authors with the same last name

When two or more authors cited in a paper have the same last name, include the author's first name in a brief in-text phrase or in a parenthetical citation. To distinguish Larry L. King from Martin Luther King, Jr., for example, do the following.

In his essay "American Redneck," Larry L. King describes his early manhood.

Do the same for parenthetical citations.

"American Redneck" (L. King) describes a young writer's experiences.

13. Two or more sources in a single citation

In referring to more than one source in parentheses, include information for both sources, separated by semicolons.

Recent interpretations of Shakespeare's The Tempest consider the play's racist implications (Takaki 52; Greenblatt 121).

14. Nonprint source

Provide enough information for readers to locate the source in the Works Cited list.

The TV series The Civil War includes a moving letter written by Sullivan Ballou to his wife shortly before his death.

43b   MLA style for explanatory and reference notes

1   Explanatory notes

Explanatory notes are used for incidental comments or for information that does not relate directly to an essay's thesis or idea and that would be disruptive if placed in the body of the paper. Explanatory notes can be used to clarify, illustrate, or further explain an idea; to provide definitions; or to identify individuals and events. Avoid overusing explanatory notes because they can distract from the main text of the essay.

Use a superscript arabic number immediately after the term or passage to be expanded on. That number corresponds to a list of notes placed at the end of the paper (endnotes). Head this separate page "Notes" and place it immediately before the Works Cited list. (The corresponding list of notes could be placed at the bottom of the typewritten page and called footnotes.)

To format the notes, indent five spaces and place the superscript number followed by one space and the explanatory note. Double-space the notes and arrange them in numerical order.

TEXT WITH SUPERSCRIPT

The Volstead Act provided for enforcement of the Eighteenth Amendment by empowering federal agents to prosecute bootleggers and other violators.[1]

EXPLANATORY NOTE

[1]The law, passed in 1919, was named for its sponsor, Andrew Joseph Volstead, congressman from Minnesota.

2   Reference notes

Reference notes direct readers to additional sources and often to another section of an essay. References that support an essay's ideas usually include the word *see,* and those that contradict an essay's ideas include the word *compare.* A source named in a reference note should be included in the Works Cited list. These notes are formatted like explanatory notes.

TEXT WITH SUPERSCRIPT

Mark Twain was convinced that the novels of Sir Walter Scott had infected the South with false romantic notions.[2]

REFERENCE NOTE: BOOK

[2]For a full account of Twain's opinion of Scott, see Krause 145-49.

REFERENCE NOTE: PERIODICAL

[3]A contrasting view is provided by Jonelson 54.

If your instructor prefers that you use a note format to present citations in your paper, an alternative to MLA style offered by the *MLA Handbook,* sixth edition, uses the following note style to provide complete documentation. A Works Cited page is not needed if complete bibliographic information is provided in these notes.

The format for notes differs from the format for items in a Works Cited list. There is no brief introductory phrase introducing a citation in a Works Cited list, and the publication information is organized slightly differently.

A reference note that refers to a book should follow these formatting conventions.

- Indent the first line of the reference note one-half inch or five spaces. Any subsequent lines of the note do not indent.
- Include the author's name exactly as it appears on the book's title page.
- Separate the author from the title with a comma.
- Place the publication information after the title and in parentheses. Begin with the city of publication followed by a colon and one space before listing the publisher and the year of publication separated by a comma.
- Place the page number(s) outside the closing parenthesis and do not put a comma or period between them.

To format a reference note for an article in a scholarly journal, follow these guidelines.

- Indent the first line of the reference note one-half inch or five spaces. Any subsequent lines of the note do not indent.

- Include the author's name exactly as it appears in the article, followed by a comma and a space.
- Place the full title of the article within quotation marks. Place a comma before the closing quotation mark.
- List the full name of the publication (without including initial articles).
- Provide the volume and date of publication and page number(s) as necessary.

43c   MLA style for the Works Cited list

All the sources cited in a paper should be listed at the end of the paper. This separate listing is called the "Works Cited" list. A concluding list of sources that were examined but not cited in a paper is called a "Works Consulted" list. In a typical research paper a single listing of Works Cited is all that is required.

Following the last page of the paper and any concluding notes, begin the list with the title "Works Cited" without quotation marks or underlining, centered, and an inch from the top of the page. The Works Cited list is paginated as the rest of the paper. Double-space between the title and the first entry.

Arrange the citation entries in alphabetical order by authors' last names. If a source is anonymous, alphabetize it by the first major word in its title (not *a, an,* or *the*). Begin each entry flush with the left margin, but indent all subsequent lines of the entry one-half inch (or five typed spaces). Double-space within and between entries. Sample Works Cited entries for books, periodicals, and other sources follow.

1   Books

A standard MLA entry for a book consists of three elements: author, title, and publication information. These three elements are separated from one another by a period and one space. The entry concludes with a period.

┌──── author ────┐   ┌──── title ────┐ ┌──── subtitle ────┐

Benton, Janetta Rebold.   The Medieval Menagerie: Animals in the Art of the

                                                         one space

indent | Middle Ages.   New York: Abbeville, 1992.
5 spaces |
                      └──────────────────┘ publication information

Computer Tip

Avoid Right-Side Justification

If you use a word processor to prepare your Works Cited list, turn off the right-side justification to avoid disrupting your spacing and your placement of punctuation marks. In fact, it is a good idea to avoid using right-side justification throughout your research papers since your text will include citations within parentheses and other documentation details, all of which must follow precise spacing requirements.

Keep the following guidelines in mind when preparing book entries for the Works Cited list.

1. **Author:** An author's name (exactly as it appears on the title page) should appear last name first, followed by a comma, then by the first and middle names or initials. Put a period after the author's name.

2. **Title:** Copy the title and subtitle (if any) from the title page, not from the cover or spine of the book. Underline the title and capitalize all major words (see 34e on capitalizing titles). Separate the main title from the subtitle with a colon. Put a period after the title and subtitle.

3. **Publication information:** Copy the publication information (the city of publication, the publisher, and the year of publication) from the title and copyright pages. If more than one city is listed on the title page, cite the first one only. If the name of the city is not well known or if it is confusing, include a state or country abbreviation following a comma. Put a colon and one space after the city of publication before the publisher's name. Abbreviate or shorten names of publishers by dropping articles and words such as *Press* and abbreviations such as *Co.* ("Bantam Books, Inc." becomes "Bantam"), using only the last names of persons ("Charles Scribner's Sons" becomes "Scribner's"), and by using only the first in a string of last names ("Harcourt Brace Jovanovich, Inc." becomes "Harcourt"). Abbreviate "University Press" so that it reads "UP." If the publisher is an imprint of another publisher (as Belknap Press is an imprint of Harvard University Press), include both publisher names separated by a hyphen ("Belknap-Harvard UP") in the Works Cited list. The publisher's name is followed by a comma, one space, and the most recent year of publication.

Computer Tip

Using Citation Formatting Software

You can use such software as Daedalus and BiblioCite to create standardized, perfectly formatted "Works Cited" or "References" pages for your research papers. All you have to do is type in author, title, and publication data. Be sure, however, that any such program you use is current. If not, you'll have to do some editing and entering of formats on your own, especially for Internet sources.

---

1. Book with one author

Benton, Janetta Rebold. The Medieval Menagerie: Animals in the Art of the Middle Ages. New York: Abbeville, 1992.

2. Book with two or three authors

List the authors' names as they appear on the title page. Invert the name of the first author only. Separate the authors' names from one another with commas.

Lichtenstein, Grace, and Laura Danker. Musical Gumbo: The Music of New Orleans. New York: Norton, 1993.

McCrum, William, William Cran, and Robert MacNeil. The Story of English. New York: Viking, 1986.

3. Book with more than three authors

List only the first author (last name first) followed by a comma and the Latin abbreviation *et al.* ("and others").

Bendure, Glenda, et al. Scandinavian and Baltic Europe on a Shoestring. Berkeley: Lonely Planet, 1993.

4. Book with an anonymous author

Begin the entry with the title. Alphabetize the entry using the first main word in the title (not *a, an,* or *the*). Do not use the word *anonymous* in the entry.

The World Almanac and Book of Facts. New York: NEA, 1983.

5. Book with an author and an editor

Begin the entry with the author's name. Place the editor's name after the title, introducing it with *Ed.* ("edited by").

Orwell, George. Orwell: The War Commentaries. Ed. W. J. West. New York: Pantheon, 1985.

If, however, the in-text citations generally refer to the editor, begin the entry with the editor's name.

West, W. J., ed. Orwell: The War Commentaries. By George Orwell. New York: Pantheon, 1985.

6. Book with an editor

In general, treat the editor(s) as you would an author.

Bennett, Linda A., and Genevieve M. Ames, eds. The American Experience with
Alcohol: Contrasting Cultural Perspectives. New York: Plenum, 1985.

7. Selection from an anthology

Include the author and the title of the selection, followed by the title of the anthology, its editor, the publication information, and inclusive page numbers. Put the selection title within quotation marks, but underline it if the work was originally published as a book.

Chrisman, Noel J. "Alcoholism: Illness or Disease?" The American Experience with
Alcohol: Contrasting Cultural Perspectives. Ed. Linda A. Bennett and
Genevieve M. Ames. New York: Plenum, 1985. 7-21.

8. Two or more selections from an anthology

Cite each selection by cross-referencing it to the anthology within the Works Cited list. Be sure to include the editor(s) and inclusive page numbers in the selection citations.

Bennett, Linda A., and Genevieve M. Ames, eds. The American Experience with
Alcohol: Contrasting Cultural Perspectives. New York: Plenum, 1985.

Freund, Paul J. "Polish-American Drinking: Continuity and Change." Bennett and
Ames 77-92.

Stivers, Richard. "Historical Meanings of Irish-American Drinking." Bennett and Ames 109-29.

9. Book with a corporate author

When a corporation, committee, or other group is listed as the author on the title page, cite it as you would a person. If the same group published the book, abbreviate words in the publisher listing.

National Geographic Society. Discovering Britain and Ireland. Washington: Natl. Geog. Soc., 1985.

10. Book in a series

Provide the name of the series and the series number (if there is one), immediately after the title. The name of the series is neither in quotation marks nor underlined. The publication information follows the series information.

Gannon, Susan R., and Ruth Anne Thompson. Mary Mapes Dodge. Twayne's United States Authors Ser. 604. New York: Twayne-Macmillan, 1993.

11. Book with a title within the title

If a book title contains a title normally enclosed in quotation marks, keep the quotation marks. If a book title contains a title normally underlined, the shorter title is not underlined.

McCarthy, Patrick A., ed. Critical Essays on James Joyce's Finnegan's Wake. New York: Hall, 1992.

Renza, Louis A. "A White Heron" and the Question of Minor Literature. Madison: U of Wisconsin P, 1984.

12. Two or more books by the same author

Cite the name of the author in the first entry only. In subsequent entries by that same individual author or group of authors, use three hyphens followed with a period in place of the author's name. List the works alphabetically by the first major word in the title (not *a, an,* or *the*).

Woodward, C. Vann. The Future of the Past. New York: Oxford UP, 1989.

---. Origins of the New South. 1951. Baton Rouge: Louisiana State UP, 1971.

---. Reunion and Reaction. Boston: Little, 1966.

13. Multivolume book

If two or more volumes of a multivolume book are used, list the total number of volumes immediately after the title.

Malone, Dumas. Jefferson and His Time. 6 vols. Boston: Little, 1943-77.

When only one volume of a multivolume work is used, give the volume number after the title and include the total number of volumes in the work at the end of the entry. When the volume has its own title, include that title after the author's name and before the publication information. Follow with the volume number and the title of the complete work. Conclude with the total number of volumes followed by the inclusive publication dates for the work.

Blotner, Joseph. Faulkner: A Biography. Vol. 1. New York: Random, 1974. 2 vols.

Malone, Dumas. The Sage of Monticello. Boston: Little, 1977. Vol. 6 of Jefferson and
    His Time. 6 vols. 1943-77.

14. Translation

Begin the entry with the author's name followed by the title; then give the translator's name, introduced by *Trans.* ("translated by"). If the translated work also has an editor, give the names in the order they appear on the title page.

Wilhelm, Richard. Confucius and Confucianism. Trans. George H. Danton and
    Annina Periam Danton. New York: Harcourt, 1931.

If the in-text citations generally refer to the translator's work or commentary, place the translator's name first.

Danton, George H., and Annina Periam Danton, trans. Confucius and
    Confucianism. By Richard Wilhelm. New York: Harcourt, 1931.

15. Revised edition

If an edition other than the first is specified on the title page of a book, include that information in the Works Cited entry. Use the abbreviation *Rev. ed.* if the title page lists the book as a "Revised edition."

Holloway, Mark. Heavens on Earth: Utopian Communities in America, 1660-1880.
    2nd ed. New York: Dover, 1966.

16. Republished book

When a book is republished (e.g., by a different publisher or in a different binding), give the year of original publication immediately after the title, followed by a period. Then give the publication information for the book.

Austen, Jane. Emma. 1816. New York: Penguin, 1986.

17. Printed conference proceedings

Cite printed proceedings as a book.

Jackson, Janice, ed. Proceedings of the Dyson College Society of Fellows. New York: Pace UP, 1994.

18. Book published before 1900

Omit the publisher from the citation. The city and the year of publication are separated by a comma.

Kennedy, J. P. Horse-Shoe Robinson: A Tale of the Tory Ascendancy. Rev. ed. Philadelphia, 1865.

19. Preface, foreword, introduction, or afterword

First identify the author and then identify the name of the item being cited (Preface, Foreword, Introduction, or Afterword). Follow with the title of the book and the book's author preceded by the word *By*. Inclusive page numbers are included at the end of the publication information.

Monette, Paul. Foreword. A Rock and a Hard Place: One Boy's Triumphant Story. By Anthony Godby Johnson. New York: Crown-Random, 1993. xiii-xvii.

20. Article in a reference book

Treat an encyclopedia article or a dictionary entry as an entry from an anthology. Do not, however, cite the editor of the reference work. Begin an entry for a signed article with the author; begin an entry for an unsigned article with its title. (If the article is initialed, consult the list of names that correspond to the initials, printed elsewhere in the work.)

"Cochise." Encyclopedia of Indians of the Americas. St. Clair Shores, MI: Scholarly, 1974.

For familiar reference books it is not necessary to cite full publication information. List instead the edition *(ed.)* and the year of publication.

Fosco, Mariani. "Marco Polo." Encyclopaedia Britannica: Micropaedia. 1993 ed.

21. Pamphlet

Cite a pamphlet as a book. Be aware, however, that some publication information may be missing, as in the following example in which *N.p.* means "no place of publication" and *n.p.* following the colon means "no publisher."

Hastings, Gerald. To Your Good Health. N.p.: n.p., 1987.

22. Government publication

Because government publications differ widely from one another, documenting them can be confusing. If no author is given, begin the entry with the government agency issuing the document. For a congressional publication, include the number, session, and house of Congress as well as the type of document. Use recognizable abbreviations such as *HR* for House of Representatives and *GPO* for Government Printing Office for the publisher information.

United States. Dept. of Commerce. U.S. Industrial Outlook '92: Business Forecasts for 350 Industries. Washington: GPO, 1992.

---. Cong. House. Committee on Ways and Means. Hearings on Comprehensive Tax Reform. 106th Cong., 1st sess. 9 vols. Washington: GPO, 1986.

2   Periodicals

Periodicals such as scholarly journals, magazines, and newspapers supply useful, up-to-date information for research essays. Like the listing for a book, a basic Works Cited entry for a periodical consists of three elements: author, title, and publication information. These three elements are separated from one another by a period. Subsequent lines should be indented one-half inch (or five typed spaces). The entry ends with a period.

```
      ┌───── author ─────┐   ┌─────────── title ───────────┐
      Panikkar, Raimundo. "There Is No Outer without Inner Space."

indent  ┌──── publication information ────┐
spaces
          Cross Currents 43 (1993): 60-81.
```

Keep the following guidelines in mind when preparing periodical entries for the Works Cited list.

1. **Author:** An author's name should appear last name first, followed by a comma, then by the first and middle names or initials. Put a period after the author's name.

2. **Title:** Enclose the article title (and subtitle, if any) within quotation marks, and capitalize all major words (see 34e on capitalizing titles). Put a period at the end of the title, inside the closing quotation mark, followed by the publication information.

3. **Publication information:** Include the periodical title (copied from its cover), underlined, with introductory articles deleted (*New York Times,* not *The New York Times*); follow with one space. If appropriate, give the volume and issue numbers, followed by one space. Give the year of publication, in parentheses, followed by a colon and one space. For magazines and newspapers, list the day and month (abbreviated except for May, June, and July) of publication, with the day before the month, the month before the year (19 Dec. 1999). End the entry with inclusive page numbers of the entire article; do not use the abbreviations *p.* or *pp.*

23. Article in a journal paginated by volume

If a journal's pages are numbered consecutively from issue to issue, do not specify an issue number. Follow the journal title with the volume number in arabic numerals, but do not use the abbreviation *vol.*

Williams, Adelia. "Jean Tardieu: The Painterly Poem." Foreign Language Studies 18 (1991): 114-25.

24. Article in a journal paginated by issue

If pagination begins with "1" in each issue of a journal, identify the number of the issue immediately after the volume number. Separate the two numbers with a period, but do not add any space. Look for the issue number on the spine, the front cover, or the contents page.

Bender, Daniel. "Diversity Revisited, or Composition's Alien History." Rhetoric Review 12.1 (1987): 108-24.

25. Article in a magazine

Give the date of the issue (day, month, and year) immediately after the name of the magazine. Do not include a volume or issue number. Follow the date with a colon and the inclusive page number(s).

Howard, Bill. "Portable Computing: Power without the Pounds." PC Magazine Aug. 1993: 125-269.

Use the symbol "+" to indicate discontinuous paging when an article is interrupted and continues later in the magazine.

Jennings, Andrew. "Old Money and Murder in Chechnia." Nation 20 Sept. 1993: 265+.

26. Article with multiple authors

Treat an article with multiple authors as a book with more than one author. The article cited in the following example has seven authors.

Passino, Anne Wurtz, et al. "Personal Adjustment during Pregnancy and Adolescent Parenting." Adolescence 28 (1993): 97-122.

27. Article with a title within the title

If an article title contains an underlined or italicized title, keep the underlining or italics for that title. If an article title contains a quotation or a title within quotation marks, use single quotation marks around the quotation or the shorter title.

Hicks, David. "'Seeker for He Knows Not What': Hawthorne's Criticism of Emerson in the Summer of 1842." Nathaniel Hawthorne Review 17.1 (1991): 1-4.

28. Article in a newspaper

Follow the author and title of the article with the name of the newspaper (without the articles *a, an,* or *the*). Provide the date of publication, the section letter, and page numbers. Use a plus sign to indicate discontinuous paging if necessary. Provide the city of publication only if the newspaper is a regional and only if the city of publication is not evident from the paper's title.

Claiborne, William. "Boxes Full of Conspiracy? Researchers Dig into JFK Assassination Papers." Washington Post 24 Aug. 1993: A1+.

29. Article with an anonymous author

An unsigned article is alphabetized by the first major word in the article title (not *a, an,* or *the*).

"Democracy and Mega-Scandal." New Yorker 27 Sept. 1993: 6-8.

"Nissan Motors May Sell Some Stockholdings." Wall Street Journal 10 Sept. 1993: B4.

30. Editorial

Follow the title with the word *Editorial,* but do not underline it or place it within quotation marks. Begin the citation with the author's name if it is known.

"Another Tug-of-War over a Child." Editorial. Chicago Tribune 7 Sept. 1993: 20.

31. Letter to the editor

Follow the title (or the author if no title is given) with the word *Letter,* but do not underline it or place it within quotation marks.

Weber, Carl. "In Health Care, U.S. Is Best." Letter. New York Times 30 May 1990: A25.

32. Review

Begin with the name of the reviewer and the title of the review, if provided. Follow with *Rev. of* (meaning "review of") and the title of the work reviewed. Include all relevant publication information. If neither the reviewer nor the title of the review is identified, begin the entry with the abbreviation *Rev. of* followed by the title of the work reviewed; alphabetize such an entry according to the reviewed work's title. For reviews of performances, provide any relevant information about the production.

Jefferson, Margo. "The Department Store and the Culture It Created." Rev. of Land
     of Desire: Merchants, Power and the Rise of a New American Culture, by
     William Leach. New York Times 1 Dec. 1993: C24.

Rothstein, Edward. "Blood and Thunder from the Young Verdi." Rev. of
     I Lombardi. Metropolitan Opera House, New York. New York Times
     4 Dec. 1993: C11.

3   Other sources

33. Interview

Begin by identifying the person interviewed. Follow with the title of the interview (if there is one) in quotation marks. If there is no title, include the word *Interview* without underlining or quotation marks. Follow with a period and then give the necessary publication information. If the interview has not been published, provide relevant information—such as whether it was a personal interview, a telephone interview, or a televised interview.

Salter, James. "James Salter: The Art of Fiction XCCCIII." Interview. Paris Review
    127 (1993): 54-100.

Selzer, Richard. Telephone interview. 7 Jan. 1992.

34. Letter

Cite a published letter as a selection from an anthology. Identify the date of the letter after the title. If the letter is numbered, provide that number.

Keats, John. "To Benjamin Bailey." 22 Nov. 1817. Letter 31 of The Letters of John
    Keats. Ed. Maurice Buxton Forman. 4th ed. London: Oxford UP, 1952. 66-69.

For personal letters, follow this form.

Dillard, Annie. Letter to the author. 10 Apr. 1988.

For unpublished letters in archives, identify the name of the collection and the city and institution that houses it.

Kurowsky, Agnes von. Letter to Ernest Hemingway. 15 Feb. 1919. Hemingway
    Collection. John F. Kennedy Lib., Boston.

35. Lecture or speech

Begin with the speaker's name and follow with the title of the lecture or speech (if there is one) in quotation marks. If there is no title, use a descriptive word such as *Lecture* or *Keynote speech* (without underlining or quotation marks). Identify the meeting and sponsoring organization, if relevant. End the entry with the location (city) and date of the lecture or speech.

Anstendig, Linda. "Curriculum Design for the '90s: Developing Personal Growth
    and Social Consciousness." Conference on College Composition and Commu-
    nication. Boston. 19 Mar. 1991.

36. Dissertation

Enclose the title of an unpublished dissertation in quotation marks.
After the title, add *Diss.* (meaning "Dissertation") without quotation marks
or underlining, the name of the university granting the degree in shortened
form, and the year of acceptance.

Martin, Rebecca E. "The Spectacle of Suffering: Repetition and Closure in the
    Eighteenth-Century Gothic Novel." Diss. CUNY, 1994.

Cite a published dissertation as a book, but add relevant dissertation information. If the dissertation was published by University Micro-
films International (UMI), include the UMI number after the publication
information.

Kauta, John B. Analysis and Assessment of the Concept of Revelation in Karl
    Rahner's Theology: Its Application and Relationship to African Traditional
    Religions. Diss. Fordham U, 1992. Ann Arbor: UMI, 1993. 9300240.

When citing an abstract from *Dissertation Abstracts International (DAI)*,
include the *DAI* volume number, publication year, and page number after
the abstract title. The name of the university granting the degree follows the
DAI information.

Jenkins, Douglas Joseph. "Soldier Theatricals: 1940-1945." Diss. Bowling Green
    State U. DAI 53 (1993): 4133A.

37. Performance

List the title (if any) underlined, followed by the names of the key people involved in the performance. Also include the theater or concert hall, the
city, and the date of the performance. If the performance does not have a
title, use a word such as *Concert* or *Recital*. The organization of that information within the citation will depend on the aspect of the performance the
paper refers to. For example, when the work of an individual is the focus of
the text discussion, begin the entry with that person's name.

In the Summer House. By Jane Bowles. Dir. JoAnne Akalaitis. Perf. Dianne Wiest, Alina
    Arenal, and Jaime Tirelli. Vivian Beaumont Theatre, New York. 1 Aug. 1993.

Slatkin, Leonard, cond. St. Louis Symphony Orchestra. Concert. Carnegie Hall, New
    York. 23 Oct. 1994.

38. Musical composition

Begin the citation with the composer's name. The title of a musical composition, ballet, or opera is underlined, but a composition identified only by form,
number, and key is neither underlined nor placed in quotation marks. Cite a
published musical score as a book, including relevant publication information.

Beethoven, Ludwig van. Symphony no. 5 in C minor, op. 67.

Mozart, Wolfgang Amadeus. Don Giovanni.

39. Work of art

Include the artist's name, the title, and the museum or other repository
and its city. To cite a reproduction of the work in a book, include the book's
publication information at the end of the entry.

Bernini, Gianlorenzo. Apollo and Daphne. Galleria Borghese, Rome.

Moses, Grandma. The Barn Dance. Hammer Galleries, New York. Grandma Moses.
    By Otto Kallir. New York: Abrams, 1973. Illustration 940.

40. Film

Begin with the film's title followed by the director, producer, major performers, distributor, and year. But if citing an individual's work within that
film, begin your entry with that person's name and title.

The Age of Innocence. Dir. Martin Scorsese. Prod. Barbara DeFina. Perf. Daniel Day-
    Lewis, Michelle Pfeiffer, and Winona Ryder. Columbia, 1993.

Scorsese, Martin, dir. The Age of Innocence. Prod. Barbara DeFina. Perf. Daniel
    Day-Lewis, Michelle Pfeiffer, and Winona Ryder. Columbia, 1993.

41. Television or radio program

Begin with the program's title, underlined. Follow with the network, the
local station that broadcast the program, that station's location, and the date

of broadcast. Add information such as director, producer, and performers as appropriate. If citing an individual's work, begin the entry with that person's name.

Chantilly Lace. Dir. Linda Yellen. Prod. Steven Hewitt. Perf. Lindsay Crouse, Jill Eikenberry, and Martha Plimpton. Showtime. New York. 18 July 1993.

Friedson, Michael, and Felice Friedson. Jewish Horizons. WWNN-AM, Fort Lauderdale. 19 Sept. 1993.

48 Hours: State of Fear. Narr. Dan Rather. CBS. WHDH, Boston. 8 Dec. 1993.

42. Recording

An entry for a recording can begin with the name of the composer, the conductor, or the performer, depending on the emphasis of the research. Follow the name with the title of the recording, underlined unless the recording is a composition identified by form, number, and key (see sample entry 38). If relevant, identify the recording medium after the title. Conclude the entry with the manufacturer, any catalog number, and the year of issue, all separated by commas.

Bartoli, Cecilia. The Impatient Lover: Italian Songs by Beethoven, Schubert, Haydn, and Mozart. Compact disc. London, 440 297-2, 1993.

Gaines, Ernest. A Gathering of Old Men. American Audio Prose Library, 6051, 1986.

43. Videotape or videocassette

Identify the medium after the title. The rest of the citation resembles the form for a film (see sample entry 40).

The Dakota Conflict. Narr. Garrison Keillor. Videocassette. Filmic Archives, 1992.

44. Map or chart

Cite a map or chart as a book with an anonymous author. Add the word *Map* or *Chart* (without underlining or quotation marks) after identifying what the map or chart describes. Conclude with the publication information.

France. Map. Chicago: Rand, 1988.

45. Cartoon or comic strip

Begin the entry with the artist's name, followed with the title (if any) in quotation marks, and the label *Cartoon* or *Comic strip* (without underlining or quotation marks). Conclude with the appropriate publication information for a periodical.

Trudeau, Garry. "Doonesbury." Comic strip. Boston Globe 19 Sept. 1994: 23.

4   Electronic sources

The basic requirements for documenting electronic sources have remained consistent even as MLA guidelines have evolved to accommodate changes in electronic media. All citations must accurately identify the electronic source and provide clear and consistent directions for locating it. Whether accessed online or by CD-ROM, diskette, or magnetic tape, electronic sources are generally not as stable or closely regulated as print sources; as a result, their citation often demands more information than those for print. Judging the reliability of electronic sources also poses its own set of challenges. See 42c for guidance on evaluating electronic sources.

46. Online sources

The sixth edition of the *MLA Handbook for Writers of Research Papers* identifies fifteen possible components for documenting online sources. As with print sources, the precise number of elements you must cite for any one online source will vary depending on what the source is and how and in what forms it was published.

Online document

Basic citation for an online document includes five possible elements: author, title, print publication information, electronic publication information, and access information.

┌─ author ─┐ ┌──────── title ────────┐ ┌──────── print publication information ────────┐
Gore, Rick. "The Rise of Mammals." National Geographic Magazine Apr. 2003.

┌──────────── electronic publication information ────────────┐ ┌─
NationalGeographic.com. 2003. National Geographic Society. 21 Mar. 2003

┌──────────────── access information ────────────────┐
<http://magma.nationalgeographic.com/ngm/0304/feature1/index.html>.

The guidelines for citing the author and title conform to those for print publication. If no author is indicated, begin with the title. Enclose titles for articles, essays, stories, poems, and other short works in quotation marks and underline the titles for online books and Internet sites (with the exception of home pages).

Print publication information is required for online sources that indicate previous or simultaneous publication in print form. Cite the print information just as you would with a print publication. Remember to include the date of print publication and, if indicated, the name of the editor, compiler, and/or translator. Electronic publication information includes the title of the site (underlined), the version number (if given), the date of electronic publication or most recent update, and the name of the sponsoring organization (if any).

Access information consists of the access date and the source's Internet address, or uniform resource locator (URL). When citing a URL, be sure to include the access-mode identifier (such as *http, ftp, gopher, telnet, news*) and enclose the whole address in angle brackets < >. If the URL runs more than one line, make sure that each line break follows immediately after a slash within the URL.

The length or complexity of some URLs can make their complete and accurate citation difficult. In these instances, you may substitute the source's URL with the URL for the site's search page.

"Haile Selassie I." Encyclopaedia Britannica Online. 2002. Encyclopaedia Britannica.
    13 Jan. 2003 <http://search.eb.com/>.

List a site's home page when a source does not have a usable URL and when citing the search page is not feasible. If it is possible to navigate a short series of links from the home page to the source, follow the home page's URL with the word *Path* and a colon and then name the links, using semicolons to separate each link.

"Today's Featured Woman: Valentina Tereshkova." HistoryChannel.com. 2003. History Channel. 25 Mar. 2003. < http://historychannel.com/>. Path: Women's History; Women's History Month.

Remember, too, that URLs often change or only exist on the Internet for a short time. As a back up to your documentation, consider downloading or printing the material you use (see Tips about Downloading and Printing, p. 655).

Entire site

For reference databases, scholarly projects, journals, and professional sites, indicate the title (underlined), the editor or compiler (if given), the electronic publication information, and the access information.

Internet Classics Archive. Ed. Daniel C. Stevenson. 3 July 1998. MIT Program in
    Writing and Humanistic Studies, Massachusetts Institute of Technology. 13
    May 2002 <http://classics.mit.edu/index.html>.

A Guide to Contemporary Art in New England. 19 July 2003 <http://nearts.com>.

NYU Web. New York University. 4 Aug. 2003 <http://www.nyu.edu/>.

COURSE HOME PAGE

For course home pages, include the name of the instructor, the title of the course (neither underlined nor in quotation marks), the description *Course home page*, the course dates, department name, institution, and access information.

Dockray, Dawson. The Romantic Literature of the Highlands. Course home page.
    Sept. 2002-May 2003. School of English, University of St. Andrews. 7 Mar.
    2003 <http://www.st-andrews.ac.uk/~www_se/ug/en4075.html>.

PERSONAL HOME PAGE

For personal home pages, begin with the name of the person who created the site. Follow with the title or, if there is no title, the description *Home page*. Conclude with the date the site was last updated (if given) and the access information.

Chang, Kyle A. Home page. 20 Nov. 2001. 4 June 2001 <http://www.stern.nyu.edu/
    ~kac227/>.

Online book

For an entire online book, begin with the author's name (if given); follow with the title of the work (underlined); the name of the editor, compiler, or translator (if relevant); print publication information; and electronic publication information. Conclude with access information.

Sophocles. Antigone. Trans. E. H. Plumptre. Vol. VIII, Part 6. The Harvard Classics.
    New York: Collier, 1909-14. Bartleby.com: Great Books Online. 2001. 15 Apr.
    2003 < http://www.bartleby.com/8/6/>.

Wharton, Edith. The Age of Innocence. New York: D. Appleton and Company, 1920.
Electronic Text Center. Comp. Judy Boss. 1996. University of Virginia Library.
3 Apr. 2003 < http://etext.lib.virginia.edu/toc/modeng/public/WhaAgeo.html>.

When citing a part of an online book, insert the name of the part
between the author and the title. Place the name in quotation marks if the
part is a poem or essay.

Frost, Robert. "Meeting and Passing." Mountain Interval. New York: Holt, 1920.
Bartleby.com: Great Books Online. 1999. 1 June 2003 <http://www.bartleby.
com/ 119/>.

For online government publications, follow the guidelines for printed
government publications then add electronic access information.

United States. Dept. of Justice. Bureau of Justice Statistics. Compendium of
Federal Justice Statistics, 2000. Aug. 2002. 4 May 2003 < http://www.ojp.
usdoj.gov/ bjs/abstract/cfjs00.htm>.

Online periodical

In general, follow the procedure for citing print periodicals (see 43c-2),
and modify them by adding access information.

SCHOLARLY JOURNAL

Barnard, Rita. "Another Country: Amnesia and Memory in Contemporary South
Africa." Postmodern Culture 9.1 (1998). 29 Oct. 1999 <http://etexta.
ohiolink.edu:6873/ journals/postmodern_culture/v009/9.1r_barnard.html>.

NEWSPAPER OR NEWSWIRE

Maugh, Thomas H., II. "World of Physics Jolted by Finding on Neutrinos." Los
Angeles Times 5 June 1998. 5 June 1998 <http://latimes.com/HOME/
SCIENCE/ SCIENCETopstory.html>.

MAGAZINE

Landsberg, Steven E. "Who Shall Inherit the Earth?" Slate 1 May 1997. 3 June 1998
<http://slate.com/Economics/97-05-01/Economics.asp>.

REVIEW

Pinsker, Atanford. "The Stuff That Good Writing is Made Of." Rev. of Writing Was
Everything, by Alfred Kazin and How to Write: Advice and Reflections,

by Richard Rhodes. <u>Sewanee Review</u> 103.4 (1995): 14 pars. 7 June 1998
<http://sewanee.edu/Sreview/Pinsker 103.4.661.html>.

EDITORIAL

"Remembering Robert Kennedy." Editorial. <u>New York Times on the Web</u>. 7 June
1998. 7 June 1998 <http://www.nytimes.com/yr/mo/day/editorial/
07sun1.html>.

Other online sources

E-MAIL

Hoy, Pat. "Re: Mentoring." E-mail to Marion Bishop. 31 May 2001.

ONLINE POSTING

Bloom, Eric. "Unreal Computer Game." Online posting. 30 May 1998. 7 June 1998
<news:comp.edu.languages.natural>.

McCarty, Willard. "One More Than Ten." Online posting. 7 May 1998. Humanist
Discussion Group. 7 June 1998 <http://lists.village.virginia.edu/
lists_archive/Humanist/v12/2000.html>.

SYNCHRONOUS COMMUNICATION (MOOS, MUDS, IRC)

Haynes-Burton, Cynthia (Cyn). Online Conference on text-based reality "Writing
and Community: The Use of MOOs in the Teaching of Writing." 30 Apr. 1995.
LinguaMoo. 8 June 1998 <http://wwwpub.utdallas.edu/~cynthiah/
lingua_archive/Meridian-moo-seminar.txt>.

47. Source on CD-ROM, diskette, or magnetic tape

Citations for sources—including software programs—on electronic storage devices are distinguished according to whether the material is published
once, like a book; whether it is published in periodical or regularly updated
form, like a magazine; or whether it has a print equivalent or not.

Nonperiodical publication

Cite the publications as you would a book, but add the publication
medium. Begin with the author's name, followed by the title underlined;
editor, compiler, or translator (if relevant). Include the publication medium
(CD-ROM, Diskette, or Magnetic tape); edition, release, or version (if

relevant); place of publication; name of publisher/vendor; and date of publication. Cite as much of this information as is available.

Mann, Ron. <u>Poetry in Motion II</u>. CD-ROM. New York: Voyager. 1995.

To cite parts of a work, enclose the title of the part in quotation marks, and underline the title of the work as a whole.

"Modernism." <u>The Oxford English Dictionary</u>. 2nd ed. CD-ROM. New York: Oxford
    UP, 1992.

Periodical publication

When citing sources with print equivalents, begin with the author's name, followed by complete information for the print equivalent (see 43c-1-2). Follow this with the database name (if any), underlined; then identify the source as CD-ROM, diskette, or magnetic tape. Finally, give the database provider or vendor, if available, and the date of publication.

Lacayo, Richard. "This Land Is Whose Land?" <u>Time</u> 23 Oct. 1995: 68-71. <u>Academic
    ASAP</u>. CD-ROM. Infotrac. Dec. 1995.

For resources without print equivalents, list the author or the institution's name followed by a period. Then give the article's title and original date or inclusive dates, enclosed in quotation marks. Follow this with the database name (underlined) and identify the source as CD-ROM, diskette, or tape. Finally, give the location, provider or the vendor of the database (if available), and the date of the publication.

Levi Strauss. "The Levi Strauss Co.: Balance Sheet, 1/1/95-12/31/95." <u>Compact Dis-
    closure</u>. CD-ROM. New York: Digital Library Systems. Jan. 1996.

Multidisk publication

When citing a source that spans two or more disks, indicate either the total number of disks (if you are citing the entire publication) or a specific disk number (if you are citing material from only one disk). Enter this information after the publication medium.

<u>1898 Bartholomew's Atlas</u>. CD-ROM. 2 disks. London: S&N Genealogy Supplies,
    2001.

APA Documentation Style

The documentation style described in this section is that recommended in the *Publication Manual of the American Psychological Association* (5th ed. Washington: APA, 2001). This system, usually referred to as APA style, is used in psychology and in other social science

http://www.apastyle.org/elecref.html
Offers guidance for documenting Web sources in APA style.

disciplines, such as anthropology and sociology. But because variations exist among the documentation styles in the social sciences, you should check with your instructor about his or her preferred documentation style before beginning your paper.

Like the MLA style, the APA style includes brief in-text, parenthetical citations of borrowed material and lists at the end of the paper the sources cited. APA style, however, uses fewer abbreviations than does the MLA style. In addition, some publication data are included in APA parenthetical citations. Dates are important for readers and researchers in the social sciences since so much of the research in psychology and related disciplines updates, builds on, and corrects previous research.

The end-of-paper citations in APA style follow a pattern that, once learned, can be adapted easily to fit just about any desired work. Consult the accompanying chart of APA forms for an overview of the types of citations described in this section.

Directory of APA Sample Entries

In-Text, Parenthetical Citations (see 43d)

1. Author not named in text, 696
2. Author named in text, 696
3. Work with two authors, 696
4. Work with three to five authors, 697
5. Work with six or more authors, 697
6. Anonymous work, 697

43d   APA style for in-text, parenthetical citations

APA style uses two methods for citing borrowed material within the text: (1) Author and date are identified immediately following the borrowed material. (2) Author is identified in the text of the paper; the date is given immediately following the borrowed material. In-text, parenthetical citations provide readers with information needed to locate the source of borrowed information in the list of references at the end of the paper. In APA style, parenthetical citations identify what was borrowed from a source and when that source was published. Use the following guidelines when preparing parenthetical citations.

- Keep the citations concise, but provide all necessary information.

- Use an author's last name either in the text of the paper or in parentheses immediately after the borrowed material. Use an author's first initial and last name if two authors in the References share the same last name.

- Punctuate and format the parenthetical citations in the following manner.

   1. Place the parenthetical citation either at the end of the sentence or at a natural pause within the sentence. In either case, the citation should follow, as closely as possible, the material it refers to.

   2. If the citation is placed immediately following a quotation, place the citation after the closing quotation marks.

3. Place any punctuation marks in the text immediately following the closing parenthesis of the citation.
4. In block quotations, place the parenthetical citation following the final punctuation mark of the quotation.

- Include a page reference for the borrowed material.

1. Author not named in text

When an author is not identified in the text, place the author's last name and the year of publication in parentheses at a point where the citation does not interrupt the flow of your writing. Separate the author and date with a comma. Be sure that there is no confusion between what you are documenting and your own text.

During the Civil War, Thomas Carlyle supported the South, but after the war he admitted that he might have been wrong (Kaplan, 1983).

2. Author named in text

When an author is identified in the text, cite only the date within parentheses. If the same source is cited more than once in the same paragraph, you need not repeat the year in that and subsequent citations.

Kaplan (1983) analyzes Thomas Carlyle's admiration for strong leaders like Cromwell and Frederick the Great.

In citing a direct quotation, include a parenthetical reference to the page number(s). The abbreviation *p.* or *pp.* is included.

"We are never innocent travelers; we arrive with ideas about the place in our minds. These ideas may be more vivid than the place can sustain when we see it; they may be more resistant to change than the place itself" (Howe, 1993, p. 62).

Howe (1993) has observed that "we are never innocent travelers; we arrive with ideas about the place in our minds" (p. 62).

3. Work with two authors

Always cite the surnames of both authors in all text citations. Use an ampersand (&) to separate the authors' names in a parenthetical citation, but use the word *and* to separate their names in the text of the paper.

The New Orleans Center for the Creative Arts has produced successful performers such as Wynton Marsalis and Harry Connick, Jr. (Lichtenstein & Danker, 1993).

Lichtenstein and Danker (1993) demonstrate how the New Orleans Center for the Creative Arts has produced successful performers such as Wynton Marsalis and Harry Connick, Jr.

4. Work with three to five authors

If a work has more than two but fewer than six authors, cite them all in the first reference.

The Tivoli in Copenhagen, one of the world's best-known amusement parks, offers rides, games, fireworks, and other attractions (Bendure, Friary, Noble, Swaney, & Videon, 1993).

In subsequent references, however, cite only the first author followed by *et al.* (meaning "and others") neither italicized nor underlined.

According to Bendure et al. (1993), the Tivoli has no peers.

5. Work with six or more authors

When a work has six or more authors, cite the surname of the first author followed by *et al.* in all in-text citations. Include the names of all the authors in the end-of-paper list of references. The following example shows a sample citation for a work by Rorschbach, Aker, Zorn, Flugel, Erskine, and Zieffer.

As Rorschbach et al. (1993) have suggested, the consequences of radical demographic and cultural change on midsize cities of the American heartland have yet to be fully felt.

6. Anonymous work

Cite an anonymous work by using the first two or three words of the title in the in-text citation or parenthetically in place of the author's name. (See 40a on italicizing some titles.)

While many questions about the Iran-Contra affair persist, it seems unlikely any answers will be found ("Democracy," 1993).

7. Corporate author

Usually cite the full name of the corporate author in each in-text reference. If, however, the corporation's name is long or if an abbreviation for the company is easily recognized, abbreviate the corporate name in second and subsequent entries.

Recently published statistics show a decline in the incidence of cerebral palsy (United Cerebral Palsy Association [UCPA], 1994).

Governmental support for those with the disease cannot be curtailed (UCPA, 1994).

8. Author of two or more cited works

In referring to two or more of the same author's works published in the same year, distinguish between them in the parenthetical citations by alphabetizing the works in the reference list and providing each work with a lowercase letter. Thus, Annette Kolodny's "Dancing through the Minefield" would be labeled *Kolodny, 1981a,* while her "A Map for Rereading" would be designated *Kolodny, 1981b.*

9. Authors with the same last name

To distinguish works by authors with the same last name, use each author's first initial(s) in each citation.

E. Jones (1930) wrote a pioneering study of psychology and literature.

10. Two or more sources in a single citation

Cite two or more different authors in a single citation in alphabetical order and separated by a semicolon (Fetterley, 1978; Kolodny, 1975). Cite two or more works by the same author in a single citation in chronological order, separated by a comma (Flynn 1980, 1983).

11. Portions of a source

If you refer to a large portion of a source, identify it in the parenthetical citation by an abbreviation: *chap.* (chapter), *Vol.* (Volume), *Pt.* (Part).

A recent writer argues that religions are politically intermediate institutions, which should influence government and affect the political process but which should be little influenced by government (Carter, 1993, chap. 2).

12. Personal communication

Material such as letters, telephone conversations, messages from electronic bulletin boards, and personal interviews should be acknowledged in the text with the person's name, the identification *personal communication*, and the date. These sources are not included in the list of references because readers cannot retrieve them.

J. Holmes, president of Mayfair Fashions, predicts that formal evening gowns will become more popular next year (personal communication, December 29, 1993).

13. Web citations in-text

When you cite material obtained from the Internet, use the same author/date format as you would for a print document. If you are citing a specific part of a Web document, provide the chapter, figure, or table. If you quote a Web document, give page or paragraph numbers if you have them.

43e   APA style for content notes

Content notes (or footnotes) expand on or supplement information in a paper. Use APA-style content notes to clarify, illustrate, or explain an idea or to provide definitions and identify individuals and events. Make these notes as brief as possible so that they do not distract the reader from the text.

Use a superscript arabic number in the text immediately after the term or passage to be footnoted. Number any content note superscripts consecutively throughout the paper so they correspond to the notes themselves, which are typed on a separate page and placed at the end of the paper immediately before the list of references. Head this page "Footnotes."

To format content notes, indent five spaces and place the superscript number followed by the note. Double-space within and between the notes and place them in numerical order.

TEXT WITH SUPERSCRIPT

The age of the women involved, their marital status, and their economic well-being were important elements considered in designing the follow-up questionnaire.[1]

CONTENT NOTE

[1]Susan Crawford and Priscilla Denby, both of whom have extensive involvement with women's issues and social programs, provided helpful input and feedback throughout the study.

43f   APA style for the References list

APA style requires that all the sources of borrowed material in a paper be listed on a separate page at the end of the paper. This separate listing is called the "References." The References list should include only material that was used in the research and preparation of the paper.

Following the last page of the paper (but before any concluding notes or appendices) begin the list with the title "References" without quotation marks or underlining, centered, and an inch from the top of the page. The References list is paginated as the rest of the paper. Double-space between the title and the first entry on the list.

Arrange the citation entries in alphabetical order by authors' last names. If a source is anonymous, alphabetize it by using the first major word in its title (not *a, an,* or *the*). Begin each entry flush with the left margin, but indent all subsequent lines three spaces. Double-space within and between entries.

1   Books

A standard APA entry for a book consists of four elements: author, date of publication, title, and publication information. These four elements are separated from one another by a period. The entry concludes with a period. (Note that these formatting instructions are for preparing student papers. If you are submitting a paper to a journal for publication, refer to the *APA Publication Manual* for formatting guidelines.)

Keep the following guidelines in mind when preparing book entries for the References list.

1. **Author:** An author's name should appear last name first, followed by a comma and first and middle initials. Put a period after the author's name.

2. **Year of publication:** Enclose the year of publication in parentheses and follow with a period.

3. **Title:** Use italics. Capitalize the first word of the title, the first word of the subtitle, and any proper nouns. Separate the main title from the subtitle with a colon. Put a period after the complete title.

4. **Publication information:** Include the city of publication and the publisher, separated from one another with a colon. If two or more locations are given for the publisher, either give the location that is listed first on the title page or give the site of the publisher's home office. If the name of the city is not well known or if it is confusing, include a state or country abbreviation following a comma. Omit the word *Publisher* and abbreviations such as *Inc.* and *Co.* from the publisher's name. However, include the complete names of university presses and associations. Put a period after the publication information.

1. Book with one author

Emerson, G. (1976). *Winners and losers: Battles, retreats, gains, losses, and ruins from the Vietnam War.* New York: Norton.

2. Book with two or more authors

List all of the book's authors last name first followed by initials. Commas separate authors' names. An ampersand connects the final two names.

Bellah, R. N., Madsen, R., Sullivan, W., Swidler, A., & Tipton, S. M. (1985). *Habits of the heart: Individualism and commitment in American life.* Berkeley: University of California Press.

Lichtenstein, G., & Danker, L. (1993). *Musical gumbo: The music of New Orleans.* New York: Norton.

3. Book with an anonymous author

Begin the entry with the title. Alphabetize the entry using the first main word in the title (not *a, an,* or *the*). If "Anonymous" appears on the title page, then begin the entry with the word *Anonymous* and alphabetize the entry as if "Anonymous" were the author's name.

The world almanac and book of facts. (1983). New York: Newspaper Enterprise
   Association.

4. Book with an editor

Place the editor's name where an author's name would be placed. Note that the number of the cited volume is placed in parentheses after the title.

Syrett, H. C. (Ed.). (1986). *The papers of Alexander Hamilton* (Vol. 26). New York:
   Columbia University Press.

5. Selection from an anthology

Begin with the name of the author(s), the year of publication, and the title of the article or chapter neither underlined nor in quotation marks. Follow with the editor(s) listed in normal order with the abbreviation *Ed.* or *Eds.* in parentheses. Conclude the entry with the title of the book, the page numbers for the article or chapter, and the publication information.

Chrisman, N. J. (1985). Alcoholism: Illness or disease? In L. A. Bennett & G. M.
   Ames (Eds.), *The American experience with alcohol: Contrasting cultural
   perspectives* (pp. 7–21). New York: Plenum.

6. Book with a corporate author

Begin the entry with the corporate or group name and alphabetize the entry by the first major word in the name. When the same group is listed as both author and publisher, use the word *Author* at the end of the entry in place of the publisher's name.

National Geographic Society. (1988). *Discovering Britain and Ireland.* Washington,
   DC: Author.

7. Multivolume book

Include the abbreviation *Vol.* or *Vols.* and the number of volumes used in the paper. Place this information after the title, enclosed within parentheses, and place a period after the closing parenthesis. The following example indicates that both volumes were used in the paper.

Cohen, J., & Chiu, H. (1974). *People's China and international law: A documentary study* (Vols. 1–2). Princeton: Princeton University Press.

8. Translation

Include the names of the translator(s) in parentheses immediately following the title.

Le Goff, J. (1980). *Time, work, and culture in the Middle Ages* (A. Goldhammer, Trans.). Chicago: University of Chicago Press.

9. Revised edition

Indicate the appropriate edition in parentheses immediately after the title. Use the abbreviation *Rev. ed.* if the title page lists the book as a "Revised edition."

Pauk, W. (1993). *How to study in college* (5th ed.). Boston: Houghton Mifflin.

10. Republished book

Cite the date of original publication in parentheses at the close of the entry. The in-text citation should include both publication dates (*Veblen, 1899/1953*).

Veblen, T. (1953). *The theory of the leisure class: An economic study of institutions.* New York: New American Library. (Original work published 1899)

11. Two or more books by the same author

Begin each entry with the author's name followed by the year of publication. Arrange the entries chronologically, the earliest first.

Takaki, R. (1989). *Strangers from a different shore: A history of Asian Americans.* Boston: Little, Brown.

Takaki, R. (1993). *A different mirror: A history of multicultural America.* Boston: Little, Brown.

For two or more works by the same author published in the same year, arrange the entries alphabetically by the first main word in the title. Add lowercase letters (starting with *a*) to the entries (after the dates) to distinguish them from one another.

Gardner, H. (1982a). *Art, mind, and brain: A cognitive approach to creativity.* New
    York: Basic Books.

Gardner, H. (1982b). *Developmental psychology* (2nd ed.). Boston: Little, Brown.

12. Government publication

Begin the entry with the name of the government agency issuing the
publication (unless an author's name is provided). If the publication appears
in multiple volumes, indicate that, as in the second entry that follows.

U.S. Department of Commerce. (1992). *U.S. industrial outlook '92: Business fore-
    casts for 350 industries.* Washington, DC: U.S. Government Printing Office.

U.S. House of Representatives. Committee on Ways and Means. (1986). *Hearings on
    comprehensive tax reform* (Vols. 1–9). Washington, DC: U.S. Government
    Printing Office.

2   Periodicals

A standard periodical entry in APA style includes the same information
as an APA standard book entry: author, date of publication, title, and publication information. These elements are separated from one another by a period.
The entry ends with a period. (Note that these formatting instructions are for
preparing student papers. If you are submitting a paper to a journal for publication, refer to the *APA Publication Manual* for formatting guidelines.)

```
                    year of
                    publication
  ┌ author ┐    ┌    ┐ ┌─────── title ───────┐  ┌──────── subtitle ────────┐
Geertz, C. (1968). Thinking as a moral act: Dimensions of anthropological field-

  ┌─────────────────────┐
  work in the new states. Antioch Review, 28, 139–158.

indent three spaces           └── publication information ──┘
```

Keep the following guidelines in mind when preparing periodical entries for
the References list.

1. **Author:** An author's name should appear last name first, followed by a
    comma, then by the first and middle initials.

2. **Year of publication:** Give the year of publication. For magazines and newspapers, include the month and date of publication. Enclose the year of publication information in parentheses and follow with a period.

3. **Title:** The article title and subtitle are neither italicized nor set in quotation marks. Capitalize the first word of the title, the first word of the subtitle, and any proper nouns. Separate the main title from the subtitle with a colon. Put a period after the title.

4. **Publication information:** Begin with the complete title of the publication, with all the major words capitalized. Italicize the title. Provide the volume number (underlined and not preceded by the abbreviation *vol.*). End with the inclusive page numbers for the article. (APA includes the full sequence of page numbers.) Use the abbreviation *p.* or *pp.* for articles in newspapers but not journals or magazines. Put a period at the end of the publication information.

13. Article in a journal paginated by volume

Herzog, H. (1993). Human morality and animal research. *American Scholar, 62,* 337–349.

14. Article in a journal paginated by issue

If each issue in a volume begins with page 1, enclose the number of the issue in parentheses immediately after the volume number. Underline the volume number but not the issue number.

Livingston, H. (1980). Hamlet, Ernest Jones, and the critics. *Hamlet Studies, 2*(1), 25–33.

15. Article in a magazine

In citing the date, give the year first, followed by the month and day of publication, separated by a comma. For an article with discontinuous pages, use a comma to separate page numbers.

Klaeger, R. (1986, November). Hiring the recent college grad. *Video Manager,* 14, 20.

16. Article with an anonymous author

When no author is identified, begin with the title of the article. Alphabetize the entry by the first significant word in the title (in this example, by the word *talk*).

The talk of the town: Fanciers. (1990, December 31). *The New Yorker,* 28–29.

17. Article in a newspaper

Include the complete name of the publication after the article title. List all discontinuous page numbers.

Claiborne, W. (1993, August 24). Boxes full of conspiracy? Researchers dig into JFK
    assassination papers. *The Washington Post,* pp. 1A, 7A.

18. Editorial

Place the identifying label *Editorial* in brackets after the title of the piece. Note that no period follows the last word of the article title.

Another tug-of-war over a child [Editorial]. (1993, September 7). *The Chicago
    Tribune,* p. 20.

19. Letter to the editor

Place the words *Letter to the Editor* in brackets after the title of the piece. Note that no period follows the last word of the article title.

Deonarine, B. (1993, August). Basketball as a way out [Letter to the editor].
    Harper's, 77–78.

20. Review

Begin the entry with the reviewer and/or the title of the review, if provided. Follow with the date of publication. In brackets, include the identifying label *Review of* and the title of the piece that was reviewed. If neither the reviewer nor the title of the review is identified, begin the entry with the bracketed information; alphabetize such an entry according to the reviewed work's title.

Daynard, R. A. (1979). [Review of the book *Watergate and the Constitution*].
    American Journal of Legal History, 23, 368–370.

3   Other sources

21. Abstract

If only the abstract of a work is used, identify the author, year of publication, title, and full, original publication information for that work. Include the citation for the collection of abstracts parenthetically at the end of the entry.

Parked, K. R. (1992). Mental health in the oil industry: A comparative study of onshore and offshore employees. *Psychological Medicine, 22,* 997–1009. (From *Psychological Abstracts,* 1993, *80,* Abstract No. 27688)

22. Published interview

Begin with the interviewer's name followed by the date. Place the identifying label *Interview with* in brackets, then name the person interviewed.

Zunes, S. (1993, October). [Interview with George McGovern]. *The Progressive,* 34–37.

23. Dissertation

Italicize the title of an unpublished dissertation, and follow with the words *Unpublished doctoral dissertation* and the university granting the degree.

Etiegni, L. W. (1990). *Wood ash recycling and land disposal.* Unpublished doctoral dissertation, University of Idaho, Moscow.

When citing an abstract from *Dissertation Abstracts International (DAI),* do not italicize the dissertation title. The words *Doctoral dissertation* and the name of the university granting the degree parenthetically follow the abstract title. Include the *DAI* volume number, publication year, and page number.

Jenkins, D. J. (1993). Soldier theatricals. 1940–1945 (Doctoral dissertation, Bowling Green State University, 1992). *Dissertation Abstracts International, 53,* 4133A.

24. Report

Cite a report as you would a book, but include after the title any identifying number the report may have.

Jones, S. (1991). *Traffic flow and safety in mid-size urban communities* (Report No. TR-11). Albany: New York State Transportation Authority.

25. Film

Begin the citation with the name or names of those responsible for the production, followed by their titles in parentheses. Identify the medium in brackets after the title. Provide the city and name of the distributor.

Scorsese, M. (Director), & DeFina, B. (Producer). (1993). *The age of innocence* [Film]. Hollywood: Columbia Pictures.

26. Videotape or videocassette

Begin the citation with the name of the major contributor and that individual's title. State the medium after the title of the work enclosed in brackets, but use parentheses if an identifying number is given. End with publication information.

Keillor, G. (Narrator). (1992). *The Dakota conflict* (Videocassette No. 5790A). Botsford, CT: Filmic Archives.

27. Television or radio program

Begin the citation by identifying those responsible for creating the program and their titles.

Shapiro, E. (Director), Clifford, T. (Producer), & Rather, D. (Anchor and Reporter). (1993, December 8). *48 hours: State of fear.* Boston: WHDH, CBS.

28. Map or chart

Cite maps and charts as anonymous works. Use the words *Map* or *Chart* (without underlining or quotation marks) after the title, enclosed in brackets.

Hearing, language, social skills, motor skills [Chart]. (1981). Duluth: University of Minnesota, Department of Communicative Disorders.

4   Electronic sources

The Publication Manual of the APA, fifth ed. (2001), contains references to citing electronic sources, but the APA has posted additional guidelines for the Internet and other electronic sources on its Web page <http://www.apa.org/elecref.html>. The formats are similar to those used for print sources.

Email

Email is cited like other personal communications, such as letters. Because it cannot be retrieved by the reader, email is not included in the list of references at the end of the paper. However, it is identified within the paper itself, as in this illustration:

According to I. M. Scofield (personal communication, October 27, 1999), the project
has been a success.

An entire Web site

To refer to an entire site (not a specific document on the site), a parenthetical citation in the text is sufficient, as in the following example. No reference entry is needed.

PsycPORT provides access to a wide variety of news stories about psychology
(http://www.psycport.com/).

A specific document on a Web site

Documents on a Web site are treated in much the same way as print
documents. To cite Internet sources in APA format, (a) list complete information on author, date, title of article and/or larger work title, and pagination in the same format as for print sources. Then (b) provide the date you
retrieved the document, followed by the complete URL. Preserve slashes,
mechanics, and spaces within the address, without adding any final
period. The first example is an article from an online version of a journal
that contains all the information provided in its print equivalent. The second example comes from an online newspaper that does not have page
numbers.

Article in an online journal

Parrott, A. C. (1999). Does cigarette smoking cause stress? *American Psychologist,*
54, 817–820. Retrieved October 29, 1999 from the http://www.apa.org/journals/
amp/amp5410817.html

Article in an online newspaper

Azar, B., & Martin, S. (1999, October). APA's Council of Representatives endorses
new standards for testing, high school psychology. *APA Monitor Online.*
Retrieved October 29, 1999 from the http://www.apa.org/monitor/
oct99/in1.html

CMS Documentation Style

43g CMS style for footnotes (or endnotes)
and bibliography

Many disciplines, including history, philosophy, political science, economics, and business, use the citation system established by *The Chicago Manual of Style,* 14th edition (Chicago: University of Chicago Press, 1993), which features in-text numbered note references linked to endnotes describing the works cited, plus a bibliography for full reference details. Some instructors in other disciplines may prefer this system as well. You will likely encounter note and bibliography style in your research.

1 Bibliography entries

Format the bibliography as you would an MLA-style Works Cited list (see 43c). If you use footnotes, place your bibliography in the same place as you would a Works Cited list—after the last page of your paper. If you use endnotes rather than footnotes, place the bibliography after the page(s) of notes.

2 Notes—endnotes or footnotes

Endnotes, which are placed together at the end of a paper, or **footnotes** at the bottom (or foot) of a page, provide publication information about sources you quote, paraphrase, summarize, or otherwise refer to in the text of a paper. When using the note system of documentation, place superscript numbers (raised slightly above the line—[1]) in the text of the paper. Place the number at the end of the sentence, clause, or phrase containing the material that you are documenting. Superscript numbers should be typed with no space between the letter or punctuation mark that precedes it. Number the citations sequentially throughout the paper. Each number will correspond to an entry in your footnotes or list of endnotes.

TEXT

As Janetta Benton has noted, gargoyles are usually located in "visually inaccessible locations,"[1] peripheral to the medieval cathedral. She also speculates that gargoyle sculptors can be compared with medieval manuscript illuminators in their artistic freedom and imaginativeness.[2]

NOTES

1. Janetta Rebold Benton, *The Medieval Menagerie: Animals in the Art of the Middle Ages* (New York: Abbeville, 1992), 57.

2. Benton, 58-59.

Use the following guidelines when writing with endnotes or footnotes.

- Place all endnotes at the end of the paper. Start a new page with the heading "Notes" (without underlining or quotation marks), centered and one inch from the top margin of the page. Double-space to the first note entry and between entries. This system is recommended by CMS and is widely preferred to footnotes.

- Place footnotes at the base of the page where the superscript number appears. The first line of the footnote begins four line spaces from the last line of text on the page. Single-space within a footnote, but double-space between footnotes.

- Indent each note five spaces from the left margin to the number. Follow the number with a period and one space. (Subsequent lines in an entry do not indent.)

- For the first occurrence of the standard note, begin the entry with the author's name in normal word order followed by a comma, the title of the source, the publication information in parentheses, followed by a comma and the page number(s).

- For the second and subsequent references to a source, use a shortened form of the entry consisting of the author's last name followed by a comma and the page number(s). When you use the shortened form of the entry for multiple citations to more than one work by the same author, include an abbreviated title in the entry.

BOOKS

Book with one author

1. Janetta Rebold Benton, *The Medieval Menagerie: Animals in the Art of the Middle Ages* (New York: Abbeville, 1992), 57.

Book with two or three authors

2. Grace Lichtenstein and Laura Danker, *Musical Gumbo: The Music of New Orleans* (New York: W. W. Norton, 1993), 124.

Book with more than three authors

3. Glenda Bendure et al., *Scandinavian and Baltic Europe on a Shoestring* (Berkeley: Lonely Planet, 1993), 26.

Book with an anonymous author

4. *The World Almanac and Book of Facts* (New York: NEA, 1983), 264–68.

Book with an author and an editor

5. George Orwell, *Orwell: The War Commentaries*, ed. W. J. West (New York: Pantheon, 1985), 210.

Book with an editor

6. Linda A. Bennett and Genevieve M. Ames, eds., *The American Experience with Alcohol: Contrasting Cultural Perspectives* (New York: Plenum, 1985), 15.

Selection from an anthology

7. Noel J. Chrisman, "Alcoholism: Illness or Disease?" in *The American Experience with Alcohol: Contrasting Cultural Perspectives*, ed. Linda A. Bennett and Genevieve M. Ames (New York: Plenum, 1985), 7–21.

Multivolume work

8. Joseph Blotner, *Faulkner: A Biography* (New York: Random House, 1974), 1:257.

PERIODICALS

Article in a journal paginated by volume

9. Adelia Williams, "Jean Tardieu: The Painterly Poem," *Foreign Language Studies* 18 (1991): 119.

Article in a journal paginated by issue

10. Daniel Bender, "Diversity Revisited, or Composition's Alien History," *Rhetoric Review* 12, no. 1 (1987): 115.

Article in a magazine

11. Bill Howard, "Portable Computing: Power without the Pounds," *PC Magazine*, August 1993, 254.

Article in a newspaper

12. William Claiborne, "Boxes Full of Conspiracy? Researchers Dig into JFK Assassination Papers," *Washington Post*, 24 August 1993, sec. A, pp. 1, 4.

SHORTENED FORMS

Second and subsequent notes to the same source appear in a shortened form that lists the author's last name and page number only. Note that entries 14 and 15 show two works by the same author.

13. Howard, 254.
14. Benton, *Menagerie*, 145.
15. Benton, "Perspective," 34.

CSE Documentation Style

The CSE (formerly CBE, for Council of Biology Editors) styles of writing and documentation are described in *Scientific Style and Format: The CBE Manual for Authors, Editors, and Publishers*, 6th ed. (New York: Cambridge UP, 1994). Just as with MLA and APA styles of documentation, the CSE system includes both in-text, parenthetical citations and a list of end-of-paper references that contains more detailed bibliographic information about the sources cited. The CSE styles of in-text citation include the name-year system, which closely resembles APA style, and the citation-sequence system. This section explains and illustrates CSE in-text forms for both the name-year system and the citation-sequence system. The section also includes guidelines for preparing the CSE end-of-paper reference list.

43h   CSE style for in-text, parenthetical citations

1   The name-year system

To use the name-year system for in-text, parenthetical citations, provide the author's name and the publication year in parentheses. Do not separate author and date with a comma.

Edwin Hubble confirmed Heber Curtis's hypothesis that spiral nebulae are galaxies of stars (Ferris 1988).

If the author's name is mentioned in the text, use only the date in parentheses.

Ferris explains that Edwin Hubble confirmed Heber Curtis's hypothesis that spiral nebulae are galaxies of stars (1988).

To cite a work by an organization or agency when no author is listed, use the corporate or group name as the author.

The Child Health Encyclopedia notes that one infant in a hundred is born with some type of heart defect (Boston Children's Medical Center 1975).

To distinguish between one of two or more works published by the same author in a single year, assign letters to the books according to the alphabetical order of the titles' first major word (excluding *a, an,* or *the*). For example, to differentiate between I. Bernard Cohen's *The Birth of the New Physics* and his *Revolution in Science,* both published in 1985, cite the first book as *Cohen 1985a* and the second as *Cohen 1985b.*

2   The citation-sequence system

The citation-sequence system for in-text, parenthetical citations involves using parenthetical arabic numerals to identify the sources. This system has two variations. The *order-of-first-mention* variation provides reference numbers for each work in the order in which they appear in the paper and lists the full citations in that order in the reference list. Alternatively, the *alphabetized* variation allocates in-text reference numbers for works as they appear in the alphabetized list of references at the end of the paper.

ORDER OF FIRST MENTION

According to Gregory, Einstein drew on Planck's formula as it was then used to describe oscillations of matter (1). Once Einstein applied Planck's work to light, the age of relativity, as Ferris (2) suggests, was born.

ALPHABETICAL ORDER

According to Gregory, Einstein drew on Planck's formula as it was then used to describe oscillations in matter (2). Once Einstein applied Planck's work to light, the age of relativity, as Ferris (1) suggests, was born.

Whichever method you use, use it consistently and make sure the in-text citations correspond in number to the references listed at the end of the paper.

43i CSE style for the References list

The separate list of references that appears at the end of the paper is the reference list. This list can be titled *References* or *Cited References* and should be formatted much the same way as the reference list described in the APA documentation style (see 43f).

The arrangement of the entries in the reference list depends upon the system of in-text citation used in the paper. If the name-year system is used in the paper, arrange the entries in the reference list alphabetically. Take care to double-space within and between items in the reference list and begin each entry at the left margin (any subsequent lines should indent three spaces). If either of the citation-sequence systems is used in the paper, each citation in the reference list will begin with the number used in the text. Follow the number with a period and two spaces to the entry (any subsequent lines should align on the first letter of the entry). (See 43f for how to organize the reference lists.)

http://www.wisc.edu/
writing/Handbook/
DocCBE6.html
Offers the latest edition of the
complete CSE (CBE) manual.

Keep the following guidelines in mind when preparing book entries for the reference list.

1. **Number:** Assign a number to each entry only if a numbered in-text citation system is used.

2. **Author:** An author's name should appear last name first, followed by a comma and middle initials. Do not insert periods or spaces between initials.

Put a period after the author's name. (Alphabetize the reference list by the author's last name if you are using the name-year system of in-text citation.)

3. **Title:** Capitalize the first word of the title and any proper nouns. Do not underline or italicize. Separate the main title from the subtitle with a colon. Put a period after the title.

4. **Publication information:** For a book, include the city of publication and the full name of the publisher, separated from one another with a colon. Put a semicolon after the publisher's name and provide the year of publication. Put a period after the publication year, followed by total number of pages for all book entries.

1 Books

The following citations are done in the citation-sequence format.

Book with one author

1. Ferris, T. Coming of age in the Milky Way. New York: Doubleday; 1988. 495 p.
2. Gregory, B. Inventing reality: physics as language. New York: Wiley; 1990. 230 p.

Book with two authors

3. Hazen, RM, Trefil, J. Science matters: achieving scientific literacy. New York: Doubleday; 1991. 294 p.

Book with a corporate author

4. Boston Children's Medical Center. Child health encyclopedia: the complete guide for parents. New York: Dell; 1975. 576 p.

Book with an editor

5. Held, A., editor. General relativity and gravitation. Volume 2, One hundred years after the birth of Albert Einstein. New York: Perseus Books; 1980. 558 p.

2 Periodicals

When citing periodical articles, keep the following in mind.

1. **Journal titles:** Abbreviate the title of the journal unless it is one word. Do not underline it. For example, the *Journal of Molecular Biology* would be abbreviated *J. Mol. Biol.*

2. **Publication information:** Provide the volume number (in arabic numerals) followed by a colon and the inclusive page numbers (without the abbreviations *p.* or *pp.*). For journal articles, conclude with a semicolon followed by the year of publication and a final period.

Article in journal paginated by volume

6. Rickey, VF. Isaac Newton: man, myth, and mathematics. Coll Math J 1987; 18:362-89.

Article in journal paginated by issue

7. Eisenkraft, A, Kirkpatrick, L. Atwood's marvelous machines. Quantum 1993; 3(1):42-5.

Article in a newspaper

8. Stevens, WM. In now data on climate changes, decades, not centuries, count. New York Times 1993 Dec 7; Sect C4 (col. 1).

3   Other sources

Media sources

9. Kroopnick S. Treasures of the Titanic [Videocassette]. New York: Cabin Fever; 1988. VHS.

Computer disk

10. The New Grolier multimedia encyclopedia [CD-ROM program]. Danbury, CT: Electronic Publishing; 1993. 2 MB RAM, 1 MB hard drive space, Microsoft Windows 3.1 with Multimedia Extensions 2.21.

Chart

11. Department of Communicative Disorders. Duluth: University of Minnesota. Hearing, language, social skills, motor skills [chart]; 1981.

For information about variations of these formats, consult the *CBE Manual*. Also, see the accompanying chart that lists style manuals you can refer to for additional information on documenting sources in various disciplines.

RESEARCH HINT   Whenever you are assigned a research paper, make certain you know the documentation style your instructor expects you to use. If you have questions, ask.

If a style manual is unavailable and you are uncertain about documentation practices, ask a faculty member or a librarian for the name of a reputable journal in the field in which you are working. Follow the citation style used in the articles in that journal as a model, but do not hesitate to ask your instructor for assistance.

Style Manuals in the Disciplines

Biology	*Scientific Style and Format: The CBE Manual for Authors, Editors, and Publishers.* 6th ed. New York: Cambridge UP, 1994.
Chemistry	Dodd, Janet S., ed. *The American Chemical Society Style Guide: A Manual for Authors and Editors.* 2nd ed. Washington: ACS, 1997.
Education	National Education Association. *NEA Style Manual for Writers and Editors.* Rev. ed. Washington, DC: NEA, 1974.
General	Turabian, Kate L. *A Manual for Writers of Term Papers, Theses, and Dissertations.* 6th ed. Chicago: U of Chicago P, 1996.
	University of Chicago Press Editorial Staff. *The Chicago Manual of Style.* 14th ed. Chicago: U of Chicago P, 1993.
Law	Garner, Diane L., and Diane H. Smith. *The Complete Guide to Citing Government Information Resources: A Manual for Writers and Librarians.* Bethesda, MD: Cong. Info. Serv., 1993.

(continued)

Languages and Literature	Gibaldi, Joseph. *MLA Handbook for Writers of Research Papers*. 6th ed. New York: MLA, 2003.
Mathematics	American Mathematical Society. *A Manual for Authors of Mathematical Papers*. Rev. 8th ed. Providence: AMS, 1990.
Physics	American Institute of Physics. *AIP Style Manual*. 4th ed. New York: AIP, 1990.
Psychology	*Publication Manual of the American Psychological Association*. 5th ed. Washington: APA, 2001.
Political Science	Kelley, Jean P., et al., eds. *Style Manual for Political Science*. Rev. ed. Washington: American Political Science Association, 2001.

44 *Reading Two Research Essays*

This chapter presents two student research essays. One is an argumentative essay by Ericka Kostka using the documentation style recommended in the *MLA Handbook for Writers of Research Papers* (MLA style). The other is an excerpt from a literature review and analytical essay by Rosette Schleifer using the documentation style recommended in the *Publication Manual of the American Psychological Association* (APA style).

Reading and analyzing these essays will help you see how writers move from their research, notes, and drafts to a properly formatted final version of the essay that is ready for an audience. Annotations accompanying the sample essays point out important features and offer advice that you can use in your essays. See Chapter 43 for more information on MLA and APA documentation styles.

44a   Sample research essay in MLA style

You saw in Chapters 39 and 40 how Ericka Kostka researched and started writing an essay on the gray wolf. Her complete essay follows, accompanied by detailed explanatory annotations on facing pages. Within the annotations are "WRITING NOTES" and "WRITING HINTS." The NOTES have been included to help you understand how Kostka made key decisions about organization, revision, and other matters as she composed her essay and incorporated evidence. The HINTS offer practical advice that you can apply when writing your own essays.

1. Cover page format. Provide a separate cover sheet if your instructor requests it and if you are including an outline of the paper (as Kostka does). About one-third of the way down on her cover page, Kostka gives the title of her essay, her own name (preceded by "by"), and information about the course (course number, section, instructor's name, and the date)—all centered and double-spaced.

If your instructor does not require a cover sheet, place your name, course information, and date on the first page of your essay, double-spaced as shown here. If you do use a cover page, you do not need to repeat all of this information on the first essay page. Instead, use the first-page format of page 1 of Kostka's essay.

1

Preserving the Wild:

The Gray Wolf in Yellowstone

by

Ericka Kostka

Expos 16, Section 10

Professor Ed Miller

December 20, 1997

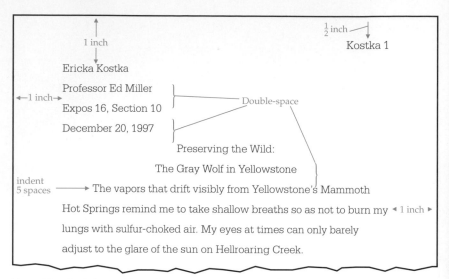

Format for First Page without Cover Page

2. Outline format. If your instructor asks for a final, formal outline, place it after the cover page but before the first page of your essay. Number the outline pages with lowercase roman numerals in the upper right-hand corner, placing your last name just before each page number. Center the heading "Outline" 1 inch from the top of the page.

> WRITING NOTE   Kostka wrote an informal topic outline when she began organizing and drafting her essay (see 40g-2); that outline guided her as she wrote to clarify her ideas and eventually evolved into the formal sentence outline required as part of the assignment.

3. Outline content. Kostka includes her thesis statement in her outline so that readers can recognize the logical relationships among the parts of her essay. Each main division of her outline (identified by roman numerals) relates to the thesis statement; subdivisions (identified by capital letters and arabic numerals) relate to the main divisions. The thesis also appears in the second paragraph of Kostka's essay (see p. 1 of her essay). (For more on constructing outlines, see 1f-1.)

$\frac{1}{2}$ inch
1 inch   Kostka i

Outline

Thesis Statement: Given that the evidence strongly indicates that wolf populations are important to the predator-prey balance of nature and that repopulation can be viable for both the gray wolf and its opponents, we should reverse the one-sided concessions that were forced upon a now-endangered population by supporting the program to restore wolves in the park and by keeping their endangered classification until the population is restored.

    I. Wolves wandered freely throughout the Yellowstone area for two million years until the government launched an intense extermination effort.

        A. Because of the wolves' predatory nature, the park considered wolves a danger to animal herds within the park.

        B. Folklore about bad wolves being a threat to humans intensified opposition to the wolf.

        C. Considerable opposition came from stockgrowers who blamed the wolf for all of their losses.

   II. As a result of the assault on the gray wolf over the last eighty years, the species is now classified as endangered.

  III. Yellowstone is considered to be the prime location for the repopulation effort.

        A. Environmentalists estimate that the park's wildlife population can support several packs totaling a population of about one hundred wolves.

        B. The wolf's presence in the park would restore the predator-prey balance that was destroyed with the elimination of the wolf.

Kostka ii

IV. Concerned that the return of the predator will bring economic disaster
    upon them, sheep and cattle ranchers have lobbied to gain political
    support from officials in the states surrounding the park.

    A. Opponents to repopulation fear having no recourse against
    wolves that might stray from the park and threaten their
    livestock.

    B. Opponents seek to remove the wolf from the endangered species
    list.

        1. Wolves that wander out of the park could be shot if no longer
       classified as endangered.

        2. Some biologists regard declassification as an acceptable
       compromise to get past a political stalemate on the issue of
       wolf repopulation.

V. Removing the gray wolf from federal protection could only be a hindrance to recovery.

    A. It could grease the political gears, but at the expense of an open
    season on still-endangered animals.

    B. Only under federal protection will wolves have a chance of sur-
    viving in the inevitable event that their pioneering instincts lead
    them into the outer zone of recovery.

VI. Reintroducing wolves as an experimental population, as permitted
    under a 1986 amendment to the Endangered Species Act and launched
    in 1995, is more acceptable than taking wolves off the endangered
    species list.

    A. Wolves should remain under federal protection from the public, while federal agents are allowed by the reintroduction program to remove or destroy wolves that become a problem for ranchers.

    B. Collaring wolves with radio transmitters can allow federal control over animals that wander outside the park's boundaries.

    C. Stockgrowers are being reimbursed for livestock damage.

        1. Compensation is being paid from a fund established by the Defenders of Wildlife.

        2. Based on losses in Minnesota under a similar wolf-recovery program, losses and costs are estimated to be minimal.

VII. Political opposition runs counter to popular support for wolf repopulation.

    A. The effectiveness of the park's educational program has been undercut by uninformed political opponents.

    B. The public strongly favored wolf repopulation even before the reintroduction program was launched.

$\frac{1}{2}$ inch

1 inch

Kostka 1

Double-space ⎰

Preserving the Wild: 4

The Gray Wolf in Yellowstone   5

1   The vapors that drift visibly from Yellowstone's Mammoth Hot

1 inch   Springs remind me to take shallow breaths so as not to burn my lungs with

sulfur-choked air. My eyes at times can only barely adjust to the glare of the

sun on Hellroaring Creek. A single stroke of blue crayon on paper was my

childhood representation of the flat plane above what was to me Massachu-

setts sky. I never was able to make accommodations in my sketchbook for

the western sky arching overhead, encasing its land in a dome more bril-

liant than crystal.   6

indent **2**   Adjustments are invariably in order when people and nature come
5 letter
spaces   into contact. My purpose for venturing to Yellowstone was to experience

its wild beauty, so I adapted myself to it. But when we hold our own inten-   7

tions primary, the concessions can tilt harshly the other way. The elimina-

tion of the gray wolf from Yellowstone National Park during the early part

of this century marked a major ecological concession to the interests of

stockgrowers. Over the past decade, an experimental program to repopu-

late Yellowstone with wolves in accordance with the Endangered Species

Act has met with objections similar to the justifications originally given

for eradicating wolves from the Rocky Mountains. These objections range

from lingering unsupported superstitions about the wolf to economic con-

cerns that an effective recovery plan should address. Given that the evi-   8

dence strongly indicates that wolf populations are important to nature's

4. Title. Select a title that gives readers a clear sense of your topic and that sparks their curiosity. Kostka combines a general sense of her topic ("Preserving the Wild") with a more specific reference to the problem she explores in her essay in a subtitle ("The Gray Wolf in Yellowstone"). Readers can infer from her title that preserving the wolf is important to Kostka and to her argument.

5. Paper format. The margins of the paper are 1 inch all around. Because Kostka includes a title page, she begins the first page of her paper with the title typed 1 inch from the top of the page (always double-space a title of more than one line) and double-spaced to the first line of text. The title is not enclosed in quotation marks or underlined. The entire essay is double-spaced. All paragraphs indent five letter spaces. Pages are numbered consecutively beginning with the first page of the essay; place page numbers in the upper right corner, following your last name, one-half inch from the top of the page.

6. Beginning the essay. A good beginning or introduction for an essay entices readers to keep reading, foreshadows the development of the rest of the essay, and states the thesis (see 5a on beginning paragraphs).

> WRITING NOTE   Kostka's beginning consists of two paragraphs. She starts on a personal note in the first paragraph, but in the third sentence of the second paragraph, she shifts to a more objective presentation of the topic she will address in her essay: reintroducing wolves into Yellowstone.

> WRITING HINT   Research essays need not include personal experience as evidence, but they can when such experience establishes the writer's commitment to the subject. However, all research essays need to be grounded in evidence derived from other, more objective sources (books, articles, and so forth). Kostka's shift to a more objective stance suggests the thoroughness of her research and gives readers a preview of what follows in the middle of her essay. (To see how Kostka selected a topic of interest to her, see 39b.)

7. Audience considerations. When Kostka started writing, she thought about what her audience needed to know in order to understand her essay. Because she was writing for an audience of generalists who may have only passing knowledge of the debate over wolves in Yellowstone, she knew she needed to provide some explanation. Had she been writing for an audience of specialists, she might have omitted this brief overview. Kostka also considered how to persuade her audience of the reasonableness of her thesis. She shows an awareness of the various interest groups involved in the debate over reintroducing wolves. (See 1d and 40f for more on considering audience.)

8. Thesis placement. Kostka strategically places her thesis at the end of her introduction for two reasons: her thesis has the most impact in that position,

Kostka 2

predator-prey balance and that repopulation can be viable for both the gray
wolf and its opponents, we should reverse the one-sided concessions that
were forced upon a now-endangered population and support the program
to restore wolves in the park, while keeping them classified as endangered
until their recovery is complete.

3   Wolves wandered freely throughout Yellowstone for two million years   9
until the government launched an intensive extermination effort. Because of
their predatory nature, wolves were regarded as "a decided menace to the   10
herds of elk, deer, mountain sheep, and antelope" (McNamee 12). Government hunters used guns, traps, and poisons during their war on Yellowstone   11
wolves between 1915 and 1926. The campaign ended in 1926 when the
National Park Service, established in 1916, succeeded in eliminating the
gray wolf from Yellowstone. The charter called for the Park Service "to con-
serve the scenery and the natural historic objects and wildlife . . . and to provide the enjoyment of the same in such manner and by such means as will   12
leave them unimpaired for the enjoyment of future generations" (qtd. in
Williams 32). Although there had been a few sightings of a lone wolf over the
previous sixty years in the area, it has been widely held by park officials and
biologists that a viable population of wolves no longer existed in the park
prior to their reintroduction in January of 1995. Candace Savage, who has for
years been studying the demise of the wolf in North America, points out the   13
irony inherent in the loss of the original population: "Although the wolf has

and it helps prepare her readers for the argument that immediately follows. (To see how Kostka arrived at her thesis, see 40e.)

> WRITING HINT   The thesis need not always fall at the end of the introduction, but that terminal position is the place of greatest emphasis.

9. From outline to essay. Paragraphs 3–5 constitute the first section of the middle of Kostka's essay and correspond to part I of her outline (see p. i).

> WRITING NOTE   In paragraphs 3–5, Kostka provides important background information about how the wolf became an endangered species, but she also renders judgments and prepares readers for the argument that she will offer in support of her thesis.

10. Quoting sources. In paragraph 3, Kostka uses three quotations from sources to provide historical background and lend authority to her argument.

> WRITING NOTE   Kostka uses the first two quotations because they highlight an interesting contradiction between the park's presumed mission of preserving wildlife and its official stance regarding the wolf as a "menace." Notice how smoothly Kostka blends the quoted words into her own sentences.

11. Parenthetical citation, author not named in text. Because Kostka does not introduce the quotation by naming the author, she places the author's name and the page number in parentheses immediately after the quotation.

12. Altered quotations. The ellipses used in the quotation indicate that Williams omitted words from the park's mission statement when he quoted it. (See 40d-3 on quoting with ellipses.)

13. Use of authority. Kostka establishes Candace Savage's authority as a wolf expert of long standing as a way of strengthening her argument.

the greatest natural range of any mammal except ourselves, it is now extinct

over much of its former range" (29).   14

4   Centuries of folklore made a powerful case against the wolf and fed a

lack of sympathy for its plight. Wolves have been depicted as vicious from

Brothers Grimm tales to old-timers' yarns. These accounts wrongly paint

the wolf as a danger to humans. Ted Williams argues that organizations

such as the Common Man Institute provide inflammatory information to

hunters and ranchers "which they, their elected officials, and their lobby   15

groups trustingly quote in public" (41). Dick Mader, founder of the institute,

has compared the wolf to mass murderer Ted Bundy. "As a kid," Mader

recalls, "I had heard them old-timers tell about these wolf kills. . . . When I

was a kid, the older people were absolutely one thousand percent agin' the

wolf" (qtd. in Williams 41). In spite of this image that the wolf is a threat to

humans, experts agree that there has never been an attack by a nonrabid

wolf on a human in North America (Gallagher 38). The same cannot be said   16

of many popular dog breeds or Feral domestic dogs, according to Jack

Rosenberger (qtd. in McNamee 340).

5   More divisive than the imagined threats to humans are the threats   17

that predatory wolves pose to cattle and sheep that ranchers rely on for

their livelihood. It was for this reason that wolves were systematically

hunted down and eliminated from many western regions. Though some of

the perceived threat has been exaggerated, wolves proved an easy target

14. Parenthetical citation, author named in text. Because Kostka introduces the quotation by naming the author, she gives only the page number in the parenthetical citation.

15. Quoting effectively and for impact. Kostka effectively uses Ted Williams's assessment of those who oppose wolves. She also makes good use of Dick Mader's words to expose his bias and undercut his claims. Kostka had to work through a few drafts to integrate the source material and eliminate the awkward blending of the words of her two sources. Compare this early draft with the final version in paragraph 4 of her essay.

Early draft

These accounts wrongly paint the wolf as a danger to humans. Dick Mader, founder of the Common Man Institute "think tank that funnels information to western hunters and ranchers and which they, their elected officials, and their lobby groups trustingly quote in public," has compared the wolf to mass murderer Ted Bundy (Williams 41). Tales Dick Mader heard as a child helped to form his fearful perceptions of wolves. "As a kid," Mader recalls, "I had heard them old-timers tell about these wolf kills. . . . When I was a kid, the older people were absolutely one thousand percent agin' the wolf" (qtd. in Williams 41).

Kostka's revised paragraph clarifies Williams's argument and makes it easier to see how she uses both Williams and Mader to support her claims.

> WRITING HINT Introducing quotations properly not only helps clarify the meaning of borrowed material but also makes your paragraphs easier to read and understand. (See Guidelines for Quoting in 40d-3 and 40i for more on integrating source material.)

16. Engaging readers by using understatement. In the last sentence in paragraph 4, Kostka implies (but also documents) that some dogs are more vicious than wolves. She seems to be asking, "Why all the fuss about the threat of wolves?" The sentence undercuts the reliability of the folklore about wolves.

> WRITING HINT Sometimes it is more effective to imply something than to say it straight out, thereby inviting readers to infer and become involved in figuring out the writer's judgment.

17. The topic sentence. Each of Kostka's paragraphs is tight and well constructed. She includes a topic sentence that states the paragraph's main idea so her readers know where the paragraph is going and how it relates to her thesis. The paragraph develops this main idea.

Kostka 4

18

for human frustration. Journalist John Skow relates that ranchers who lost

their entire herds to harsh winters irrationally spent large amounts of

money and energy to take vengeance on wolves. Skow reminds us that

"Barry Lopez, in his haunting book <u>Of Wolves and Men</u>, tells of wolves

drenched with gasoline and set afire, wolves pulled apart by horses." Notes

Skow, "You can't dismember an April blizzard" (13).

6   As a result of the assault on the gray wolf over the last eighty years,   19

the species is now classified as endangered. Given that there were but

1,200 wolves in Minnesota and 50 in Wisconsin and Michigan by the mid-

1980s, "if a new disease hit these populations, it could spell the end of the

species in the continental United States" (Begley 74). The Endangered

Species Act of 1973 mandates that federal agencies, such as the Park Ser-

vice, take "all methods and procedures necessary" to restore species that

have been driven to virtual extinction (qtd. in Williams 32). In accordance

with this act, an experimental program for wolf repopulation has been

launched successfully by the Northern Rocky Mountain Recovery Team

established by the U.S. Fish and Wildlife Service. While some wolf pups

have been lost, the program in its second year reported the arrival of new

pups, giving promise for the future (U.S. Fish and Wildlife Service).

7   Yellowstone is considered to be the prime location for the   20

repopulation effort. America's leading wolf expert, L. David Mech, explains

that Yellowstone "is a place that literally begs to have wolves. It's teeming   21

with prey" (qtd. in Williams 32). Mech believes that wolves can   22

WRITING NOTE   Kostka often places her topic sentences at or near the beginning of paragraphs, as she does in paragraph 5.

18. Summarizing and quoting. Citing authorities can strengthen your case and convince readers of your point. Here Kostka makes good use of two authorities on wolves in order to undercut the claims of the stockgrowers.

WRITING NOTE   Kostka first summarizes John Skow to capture the essence of his remarks. She then follows with Skow's exact words (on a second wolf authority, Barry Lopez) because these ironic and compelling quotations reinforce her idea about wolves being used as scapegoats.

19. From outline to essay. Paragraph 6 constitutes part II of Kostka's outline. It is also a **transitional paragraph** that points back to previous paragraphs and prepares readers for the argument that follows.

WRITING NOTE   Kostka wants to alert readers to a shift from earlier paragraphs on history and background to the upcoming paragraphs about the Park Service's mandate and the experimental program.

20. From outline to essay. Paragraphs 7 and 8 constitute part III of Kostka's outline. In them, she presents the environmentalists' point of view.

21. Use of authority. In paragraph 5 Kostka used authority to undercut her opposition (see annotation 18). In paragraph 6, she used an authority from an environmentalist organization she had located on the Internet. In paragraph 7, she also uses authority to strengthen her position favoring the reintroduction of wolves.

WRITING HINT   Strengthen your case by citing authorities, but be sure to include their credentials as Kostka does for L. David Mech, "America's leading wolf expert" (see 40l on incorporating evidence).

22. Parenthetical citation for an indirect source. Kostka found this quotation of Mech's in an article by Williams. To acknowledge that she is citing one writer's report of someone else's words, she uses the abbreviation *qtd. in* (meaning "quoted in"). In Kostka's Works Cited entry for this quotation, Mech is not cited.

Kostka 5

help re-balance the park's ecosystem. With its vast terrain and abundant populations of elk, deer, bighorn sheep, and bison, Yellowstone is definitely ideal wolf country. Environmentalists estimate that the park's wildlife population can support several packs totaling a population of about one hundred wolves (Satchell 29). That goal seems within reach soon; there were "forty, free wild wolves in the Greater Yellowstone Ecosystem" by the summer of 1996 (McNamee 321).

8   More appropriate than focusing on the park's ability to support the wolves is considering the critical role that the reintroduced wolf can play for   23
the area's ecosystem. The wolf's presence can restore the predator-prey balance that was destroyed with its elimination. Yellowstone's few grizzlies and coyotes cannot contain the exploding populations of their hoofed prey. Some observers noted that without evolutionary pressure, "the inflated ungulate [hoofed] herds are overgrazing and destroying the range" (Gal-   24
lagher 37). Rodger Schlickeisen, President of Defenders of Wildlife, reports that the wolf's return "has begun changing a huge ecosystem from one largely dominated by the comparatively passive activity of browsing and grazing animals to one greatly influenced by the more dynamic dining habits of our top predator." According to Schlickeisen, "The wolf is once again exerting its powerful evolutionary influence" (1-2). Christine Hager, in an independent assessment, argues persuasively that "we must preserve wolves in order to maintain the rich biodiversity that this planet needs to exist and continue its cyclic processes" (5). Far from posing an unfair threat   25

WRITING HINT   When citing indirectly always name the author of the original source either in your paragraph, as Kostka does, or in a parenthetical citation. Placing the authority's name and credentials in the text of the essay is often more effective than placing the authority's name within parentheses.

23. Evaluating evidence. Kostka relies on articles from print sources and from the Internet for her evidence. In paragraphs 7 and 8 she uses six sources (Williams, Satchell, McNamee, and Gallagher from print sources; Schlickeisen and Hager from the Internet) to present the environmentalists' case.

WRITING NOTE   Kostka realizes that three of her sources are environmental publications that may appear biased. To strengthen her claim in her paragraphs about the need for predators, she provides factual information; to keep the presentation balanced, she uses a summary from an environmental publication and a quotation from a more neutral publication. This fair and reasonable presentation makes Kostka's point clear: reintroducing the wolf makes ecological sense.

WRITING HINT   You will need to decide what sources to consider (see 40b), what sources to read critically (see 40c), and then what evidence to incorporate into your essay (see 40i). As a general rule, use evidence that will support your thesis and help your readers understand it. But do not ignore contradictory evidence.

24. Altering quotations. Using brackets, Kostka provides a definition of the unusual word *ungulate.*

25. Reflecting. Your research essay should not be a compilation of the ideas of other writers and researchers. It should contain what you think about your sources. After you have cited evidence, be sure to reflect on how that evidence supports your idea. Your reflections make the essay your own (see 40d-4 and 40i-2 on reflecting).

WRITING NOTE   Notice how effectively Kostka ends paragraph 8; she restates and reflects on her idea about the need for wolves in the park.

to the hoofed herds of Yellowstone, wolves are now restoring a natural cycle
of population control.

9   Wildlife biologist John Weaver's optimism about the suitability of Yellowstone for wolf recovery is far more reasonable than placing confidence in
the political process associated with this program. Concerned that the
return of the predator is in danger of bringing disaster upon them, sheep
and cattle ranchers have lobbied for political support from officials in the
states surrounding the park. They have emphasized their fear of having no   26
recourse against wolves that might stray from the park and threaten livestock. Bob Budd, director of the Wyoming Stockgrowers' Association in
Cheyenne, explained the concern:

> We're not antiwildlife, we're the people who've preserved the   27
> open spaces that provide their food and habitat, but we don't
> want wolves at Yellowstone for the simple reason that there's
> no way to control them when they inevitably move outside
> the park. There are no legal mechanisms in place that specify
> what will happen when we have some stock killed by wolves.
> (qtd. in Gallagher 41)

One legal mechanism that ranchers and their lobbyists sought was removal   28
of the wolf from the endangered species list. If the wolf were declassified to
"threatened" or removed from the list entirely, wolves that kill livestock
could be killed.

10   Joe Helle, the influential spokesman for the National Wool Growers
Association, had indicated that wolf recovery would be acceptable only if

26. From outline to essay. Paragraphs 9 and 10 constitute part IV of Kostka's outline. In these paragraphs she presents the concerns of the stockgrowers. As Kostka presents their argument, she also notes the conditions they sought.

WRITING NOTE   In paragraphs 9 and 10, Kostka offers a clear and logical presentation of the stockgrowers' concerns, showing that she understands both sides in this complicated debate. She also begins to intensify her argument and to use information about the Endangered Species Act. By stating the stockgrowers' conditions for accepting wolf repopulation, she effectively limits their objections and lays the groundwork for the solution she offers later in the essay.

27. Incorporating a long quotation. Quotations longer than four typed lines must be indented ten spaces or one inch from the left margin and set off from the rest of the essay. Do not enclose these block quotations in quotation marks. Double-space, and place the parenthetical citation at the end of the block quotation after the closing punctuation. (Place parenthetical citations for shorter quotations within the sentence, before the closing punctuation.)

    Introducing long quotations. To introduce the block quotation within paragraph 9, Kostka states the name of her source and his credentials, followed by a colon. She makes it clear that her source is an authority; it is also clear where the source material begins (after the colon) and where it ends (just before the parenthetical citation).

WRITING HINT   Use long quotations sparingly because too many of them interrupt the flow of your essay and give the impression that you are relying more on your sources than on your own thinking and reflection.

28. Reflecting. Kostka's ending for paragraph 9 is effective. Instead of concluding with Budd's long quotation, she reflects on it, putting his concerns in perspective and highlighting the consequences of declassification. She ends the paragraph with her own concerns rather than with Budd's.

unrestricted killing of wolves were permitted in the outer zone of the proposed management areas. Under the recovery guidelines, wolves have complete protection in Zone One, Yellowstone Park and four adjacent wilderness areas, and equal protection with other interests so that management decisions could go either way in Zone Two, the national forest lands surrounding Yellowstone. Beyond these areas, in Zone Three, ranching and other interests take priority over wolves. As endangered animals, wolves can be captured and relocated from Zone Two or Three by wildlife management officials should they come into conflict with other interests. They cannot, however, be killed either by officials or by the public under their present classification (USFWS Impact Statement). Should wolves become declassified, they could expect no federal protection in Zone Three. Such action would allow private citizens to shoot, trap, or poison wolves that stray into this outer zone (Cauble 26-27).

11   I believe that any move toward declassification would set a danger-   29
ous precedent. The species is endangered, and the Endangered Species Act mandates that recovery plans be in place to restore the wolf population. Removing the gray wolf from federal protection could only be a hindrance to recovery. Declassification might grease some political gears, but at the expense of an open season on still-endangered animals.

12   Bill Schneider claims there is little doubt that most wolves, given
their nomadic nature and their propensity to travel hundreds of miles, will   30
eventually reach the grazing lands of the outer zone. "As surely as the wolf howls at night, this will happen," Schneider believes (9). But it is self-

29. From outline to essay. Paragraphs 11 and 12 constitute part V of Kostka's outline. In them, she argues against declassification and asserts that the wolf will need federal protection to survive.

Using personal pronouns. In paragraphs 11 and 12, Kostka begins to present her own solution to the wolf problem using the personal pronoun "I" for the first time since her introduction to the essay.

WRITING HINT   Using "I" in a formal, objective research essay must always be weighed carefully. Does it show acceptance of responsibility for one's own ideas or does it seem too personal and inappropriate? Kostka's use of "I" is effective. Her readers know just where she stands and why, and her objective tone is not undermined. Consult your instructor about using "I" in formal research writing.

30. Being reasonable. In earlier paragraphs, Kostka acknowledges the legitimacy of the stockgrowers' claims. Careful and reasonable consideration of opposing points of view can only strengthen her argument. In paragraph 12, Kostka reiterates the reasonableness of the stockgrowers' concern but objects to their solution, pointing to the contradiction of "killing" wolves as part of a "recovery" plan.

defeating to kill wolves who stray into Zone Three when they do so as a
condition of a recovery act. Only under federal protection will wolves have a
chance of surviving in the inevitable event that their pioneering instincts   31
lead them into the outer zone of recovery.

13   The alternative compromise was reintroducing wolves as an experi-   32
mental population in December of 1995, as allowed for under a 1986 amendment to the Endangered Species Act (Parnall 83). This leaves wolves under
federal protection from the public, while allowing agents to remove or
destroy wolves that become an excessive problem for ranchers. Collaring
wolves permits effective control over nuisance animals. As biologist John   33
Weaver explains, radio tracking collars can be equipped with "remote-controlled tranquilizing darts . . . that could greatly facilitate the capture of
problem animals" (qtd. in Cauble 29). Under the reintroduction program,
wolves can be subject to reasonable federal control, rather than to the
vengeance of those ranchers whose hatred for them has been deeply
rooted. The process of reintroduction has not been easy, but it appears to be
working (McNamee 321).

14   Because wolves will probably kill livestock in their ventures onto   34
grazing lands, economic damage suffered by ranchers is an important concern. I believe it is unreasonable to allow a rancher to kill an endangered
animal, since ranchers can now be compensated for losses as part of the
program. Reimbursement for livestock damage is an economically sound
provision of recovery. The cost of such compensation is quite low, consider-

31. Kostka's solution. The final sentence of paragraph 12 stirs readers' interest as it provides a transition to Kostka's solution to the wolf repopulation problem; everything in the essay has been leading to this solution, and everything that follows will justify and explain it.

32. From outline to essay. Paragraphs 13–15 constitute part VI of Kostka's outline. In these paragraphs, she argues for federal protection of the wolf—her solution.

33. Combining summary and quotation to eliminate a block quotation. In paragraph 13 Kostka combines summary and quotation. She quotes only the part of Weaver's explanation that she cannot summarize effectively. In an excerpt from an earlier draft, Kostka originally quoted more of Weaver, but she decided to revise this draft to eliminate the block quotation. The language was not cogent or memorable, and she was using too many long quotations. Compare this draft with the final version.

Early draft

Wildlife biologist John Weaver made this observation:

> Each wolf released in Yellowstone would be wearing a radio collar, enabling researchers to keep tabs on its wanderings. The collars may be equipped with remote-controlled tranquilizing darts, a new device that could greatly facilitate the capture of problem animals. (Cauble 29)

Under this proposal, wolves would be subject to reasonable federal control, rather than to the vengeance of ranchers whose hatred tends to be deeply rooted.

(See also annotation 27 on incorporating long quotations.)

34. Evaluating evidence. As Kostka explains her solution to the wolf repopulation problem in paragraphs 14 and 15, she cites five sources, more than she has used in any other section of her essay. She clearly has her opponents, the stockgrowers, in mind as she brings together information from these sources. Notice how her use of evidence is sensitive and fair even as she rebuts the stockgrowers' argument.

> **WRITING HINT** Kostka evaluated her evidence to determine how best to make her point. You will also need to assess your evidence and decide about how much of it to use and where to place it.

Kostka 9

ing how few stock animals are being lost to wolves. Ranchers' predictions
and accounts of extensive losses tend to be greatly exaggerated. In Minnesota, which boasts a successful recovery program and an established wolf
population, only one-fifth of 1 percent of the 12,000 farms lost even one ani-   35
mal to wolves in any year by the mid-1980s (Begley 74). Ordinarily, only
about ten animals were killed each year by wolves (Edwards 378).[1]   36

15   The Yellowstone area has less livestock than Minnesota, and has far
fewer wolves. Stock losses are therefore estimated to be even smaller than
those affecting Minnesota farmers (Gallagher 41). In the rare instances that
stock damage occurs, ranchers are being compensated from a fund established by the Defenders of Wildlife (Skow 13). I believe that the current compensation program, which is similar to that used in Minnesota, is a more
direct and consistent way to deal with any economic loss that may affect
western sheep and cattle growers as a result of wolf recovery than allowing
ranchers to kill an endangered species. Diane Edwards, writing in Science   37
News, explains that biologists "have set a goal of 10 breeding pairs" producing offspring for three consecutive years (379). Declassification must only
be allowed after the recovery goal has been reached and the gray wolf is no
longer considered to be on the verge of extinction. Until then, stock loss can
continue to be matched with cash.

16   Volatile western politics has provided an enduring obstacle to a real-   38
istic public image of the wolf. Political pressure prior to the reintroduction

35. Incorporating numerical data. Kostka's discussion of the Minnesota program, which begins here in paragraph 14 and continues in paragraph 15, involves the introduction of numerical data or statistics that serve her argument in two ways: (1) the data suggest that her proposal is reasonable because it has worked successfully elsewhere; and (2) the data allow her to further undercut the stockgrowers' exaggerated predictions about losses. Such statistical data can be persuasive because the numbers are verifiable and carry scientific weight.

> WRITING HINT   Numerical data can be integrated into the text, or they can be presented in table, chart, or graph form when their complexity or importance warrants an illustration within the text. Whatever you decide, introduce data as you would other material from sources; document them properly.

36. Using an explanatory note. The superscript arabic number 1 in paragraph 14 refers readers to an explanatory note that provides additional information about the Minnesota experiment; the note appears at the end of Kostka's essay on a page titled *Notes*.

> WRITING HINT   Use explanatory notes when you want to provide incidental information, whether definitions or explanations, that would be disruptive if placed in the body of your essay. (See 43b for guidelines on preparing explanatory notes in MLA style.)

37. Revising. Always think about the best way to present evidence to your audience; revise to clarify or improve your presentation.

Early draft

Biologists "have set a goal of 10 breeding pairs": producing offspring for three consecutive years (Edwards 379). Declassification must only be . . . .

> WRITING HINT   Compare the way Kostka incorporated Edwards's quotation in an earlier draft with her revised use of it in paragraph 15 of the final draft.

Kostka decided to revise the introduction to the Edwards quotation. She named Edwards and the source (*Science News*) in the text rather than parenthetically, sensing that such a revision would make the quotation more persuasive.

38. From outline to essay. Paragraphs 16–18 constitute part VII of Kostka's outline. In these paragraphs she argues against the political opposition and points to the public's approval of wolves in the park.

Kostka 10

program hindered the park's educational programs on the issue of wolf recovery. Influential members of Congress from surrounding states criticized the park's efforts as being biased in favor of repopulation. Montana Representative Pat Williams further questioned "the appropriateness of providing the public with <u>information</u> . . . about wolf reintroduction" (qtd. in Williams 38). Our national parks are supposed to provide information to visitors about aspects of the ecosystem. I would certainly expect the park to have had a bias in favor of reintroduction, given that its function is to preserve wildlife for future generations. Yellowstone should uphold the interests of the wild, not those of the prevailing political view. But the park buckled under the political pressure. According to Ted Williams, the park not only stopped mailing educational material, it also canceled its slide show on the wolf, stopped writing about restoring the wolf population, and prohibited selling wolf posters at the park (38).

39

17   Political figures opposing park education programs, with an eye to special interest groups, would prefer the public to be exposed to the unsupported rhetoric that they offer as testimony on the wolf. Ted Williams reports that despite lack of evidence to support his claim, Wyoming Senator Alan Simpson "has asserted that wolves eat people" (Williams 36). Misinformation about the wolf, even among elected officials, makes it more critical than ever that the National Park Service should adhere to its educational efforts so the public can make informed judgments.

39. Incorporating a paraphrase and avoiding plagiarism. Use a paraphrase when you want to convey in your own words the essence of a source and a sense of its structure or order (see 40d-2).

> WRITING HINT   Kostka makes effective use of Williams's emphatic order in this paraphrase that concludes paragraph 16. Realizing that she needed evidence to support her contention about the park caving in to political pressure, she took her paraphrase from the following note card:
>
> ---
>
> Williams, "Waiting for Wolves," p. 38   Effects of
>   Politics
>
> P / As a result of political opposition, the Park Service stopped mailing educational material about wolves, canceled its slide show on the wolf, stopped writing about restoring the wolf population, and prohibited selling wolf posters in the park. / P
>
> // This is the essence of Williams's case about the effects of politics on the educational program. He makes this case convincingly, citing considerable details. No hesitation on my part to accept these conclusions. //

Notice how Kostka wove the material into her paragraph. The text flows smoothly, and you can distinguish her ideas from those of her source. However, it took Kostka a few drafts to get it right. When working on an earlier version of the paragraph, she double-checked the paraphrase against her note card and discovered that she had not properly acknowledged Williams and that she was combining her reflections with his ideas. She was running the risk of unintentionally plagiarizing from her source. Here is the first draft of the paragraph:

The park, however, buckled under the pressure and stopped mailing educational packets. It also canceled its slide show on the wolf, stopped writing about restoring the wolf population, and prohibited the selling of pro-wolf-restoration posters at the park (Williams 38).

To address these problems, Kostka introduced the paraphrase with the words *According to Ted Williams* and she replaced Williams's words with her own.

Kostka 11

18   Despite political pressure that curbed the National Park Service's educational programs, public support for wolf recovery was high on the eve of reintroduction. A poll of the park's visitors showed that 74 percent agreed "having wolves in the park would improve the Yellowstone experience," and 60 percent agreed "if wolves can't return to Yellowstone on their own, then we should put them back ourselves" (McNamee).[2] The public had the right   40 idea and provided a good foundation for the reintroduction program.

19   Returning wolves to Yellowstone can return natural balance to its ecosystem and spare the gray wolf from endangerment. In the words of wildlife ecologist Renee Askins, "If we can't preserve wildness in Yellowstone, where can we preserve it?" (qtd. in Skow 13). Even Joe Helle, a vocal critic of the repopulation program, indicated that he did not object to the concept of recovery. "If wolves were declassified in Zone Three and if the [zone boundaries] were acceptable," he said, "we probably wouldn't oppose reintroduction of wolves in Yellowstone" (qtd. in Cauble 27). Helle's words   41 give continued hope that the standoff between restorationists and their opponents might gradually ease off through the ongoing efforts of the recovery program to offer stockgrowers economic compensation for losses, while not allowing wholesale killing of wolves that wander out of the park's boundaries. If ranchers and restorationists can continue to show willingness to make compromises, we can hope that the wolf will again be part of our world under the embracing western sky.

40. Using reference notes. The superscript arabic number 2 refers to a reference note that appears on a page titled Notes at the end of Kostka's essay. Reference notes refer to supplementary sources that can provide additional information for interested readers. (See 43b on preparing notes in MLA style.)

41. Ending the essay. An essay's ending should provide a fresh, closing perspective rather than merely restate the thesis and supporting points (see 9b on ending paragraphs).

WRITING NOTE Kostka's ending is especially effective because she brings in an ecologist and a stockgrower from sources she has already cited to provide a final perspective on her thesis—proposing the retention of wolves in Yellowstone and the retention, as well, of the endangered classification until the population is restored. She also reminds readers that she seeks consensus between the "restorationists and their opponents." Hers is a plea for reasonable compromise under that "embracing western sky" that she introduces in paragraph 1 of her essay and that she returns to so skillfully here in her ending.

Kostka 12

Notes

[1] L. David Mech believes that public attitudes about the wolf have 42
"changed dramatically" over the last decade or so. Mech managed the
recovery program in Minnesota, and he makes this strong claim: "Even
Minnesota farmers, some of whom actually sustain livestock losses to
wolves, showed surprising tolerance of the animal." Mech's survey showed
that "only 24 percent" thought wolves should be forced to live elsewhere
than Northern Minnesota.

[2] In the Harvard Environmental Law Review, Harry R. Bader (517-33) 43
argues convincingly that public support is crucial to effective implementa- 44
tion of recovery plans; he is especially thorough in his analysis of the legal
obligations associated with the recovery plan for reintroducing wolves into
Yellowstone.

Kostka 13

Works Cited 45

Bader, Harry R. "Wolf Conservation: The Importance of Following Endan- 46
gered Species Recovery Plans." Harvard Environmental Law Review
13 (1989): 517-33.

42. Explanatory notes. Use explanatory notes for incidental comments or for information that does not relate directly to your thesis or idea and that would be disruptive if placed in the body of your essay. You can use these notes to clarify, illustrate, or further explain your idea; to provide definitions; and to identify individuals and events.

WRITING NOTE   Kostka chose to include this additional information in an explanatory note because it is related to the topic of her paragraph (see paragraph 14 of the essay), but it does not address directly the paragraph's main idea. Including the information in the paragraph would have been disruptive.

WRITING HINT   Always add a Works Cited entry for sources discussed in explanatory notes. The source for the note (the foreword to *Wolves*) appears in the Works Cited list under Mech's name (see annotation 47 for more on formatting notes).

43. Reference notes. Use reference notes to direct readers to additional supplementary sources.

WRITING NOTE   Kostka included these sources because they confirmed her research. She wanted her readers to be aware of the sources.

WRITING HINT   Be aware that you need to provide a Works Cited entry for each source that appears in the reference notes (as Kostka does on p. 11 of her essay).

44. Formatting explanatory and reference notes. To identify these notes in the body of your essay, insert a superscript arabic number immediately after the term or passage you wish to comment about, as Kostka does on pages 7 and 9 of her essay. That number corresponds to this listing of notes placed on a separate page at the end of the essay. I head this page *Notes* (centered, 1 inch below the top of the page) and place the page or pages immediately before your Works Cited list. The first line of each note should be indented five spaces, and a superscript number followed by a space should mark the beginning of the note. Double-space within and between the notes and place them in numerical order. (See 43b for more details on using and formatting explanatory and reference notes.)

45. Formatting the Works Cited list. A list of the sources cited in your essay—commonly called a bibliography—appears at the end of all research papers. In the MLA style, this list of sources is titled *Works Cited*. Entries appear in alphabetical order by the author's last name (if no author's name is provided, alphabetize by the first letter of the title). Entries are double-spaced. The first line of the entry should be typed flush with the left margin; subsequent lines should be indented five spaces. (See 43c for detailed formatting guidelines and examples.)

46. Entry for an article in a journal paged consecutively throughout an annual volume. Invert the author's name (last name, first name). Include the title of the article in quotation marks, followed by the name of the journal, underlined. Give the volume number followed by the year of publication (in parentheses), a colon, and the inclusive page numbers for the article.

Kostka 14

Begley, Sharon. "Crying Wolf in Yellowstone." Newsweek 16 Dec. 1985: 74.   47

Cauble, Christopher. "Return of the Native." National Parks July-Aug.   48
     1986: 24-29.

Edwards, Diane. "Recall of the Wild Wolf." Science News 13 June 1987:
     378-79.

Gallagher, Winifred. "Return of the Wild." Mother Earth Sept.-Oct. 1990:
34+.

Lopez, Barry. Of Wolves and Men. New York: Scribner's, 1978.   49

McIntyre, Rick. A Society of Wolves: National Parks and the Battle over the
     Wolf. Stillwater, Oklahoma: Voyageur, 1993.

McNamee, Tom. "Yellowstone's Missing Element." Audubon Jan. 1986:
     12+.

Mech, L. David. Foreword. Wolves. By Candace Savage. San Francisco: 50
     Sierra Club, 1988.

Parnall, Peter. "A Wolf in the Eye." Audubon Jan. 1988: 78+.

Satchell, Michael. "The New Call of the Wild." U.S. News & World Report
     29 Oct. 1990: 29.

Savage, Candace. Wolves. San Francisco: Sierra Club, 1988.

Schlickeisen, Rodger. "Wolf Recovery's Significance." Defenders   51
     Magazine Summer 1997. Defenders of Wildlife. 1997. 9 Oct. 1997
     <http://www.defenders.org/defenders/issu97.html>.

Schneider, Bill. "The Return of the Wolf." National Parks July-Aug. 1981:
     7+.

47. Entry for an article in a weekly magazine. Invert the author's name. Include the name of the article in quotation marks followed by the name of the periodical, underlined. Give the date of publication and then page number(s) for the entry. If the pages of the article are discontinuous (interrupted by other articles), use a plus sign after the page number—75+.

48. Entry for an article in a monthly magazine. Use the same format as for a weekly magazine (see annotation 48).

49. Entry for a book with one author. Invert the author's name. Underline the title. Include the city of publication, publisher, and year of publication.

50. Foreword. Invert the name of the foreword's author, followed by the word *Foreword* (without underlining or quotation marks, but followed by a period). Include the title of the book, underlined, the book's author preceded by the word *By*, and publication information. At the end of the entry, identify inclusive page numbers in lowercase roman numerals if such numerals are used in the source. No page numbers are given in this entry because the foreword has no page numbers.

51. Entry for publication from a Web site—source with print equivalent. Use the same format as citations for print periodicals (see 43c). After the print information, add the name of the site, the date the site was published or last updated, and the sponsors' name, as available. Always include the date you accessed the site and the electronic address (URL), placed inside angle brackets.

Kostka 14

Skow, John. "The Brawl of the Wild." Time 6 Nov. 1989: 13-14.

U.S. Fish and Wildlife Service. "Gray Wolf Recovery: Weekly   52

　　　Progress Report. Week October 28-November 3, 1997." IWC

　　　Yellowstone Updates 17 Nov. 1997. 18 Nov.

　　　1997<http://www.wolf.org/wolfnews/ystone/ylwoct28.html>.

Williams, Ted. "Waiting for Wolves to Howl in Yellowstone."

　　　Audubon Nov. 1990: 32+.

52. Entry for publication from a Web site—source with no print equivalent. Begin with the name of the creator of the site. Then give the title of the site, underlined. If there is no title, give a brief description of the site. Follow this with the editor or compiler of the site or project, the date of electronic publication or latest electronic update, and the name of the institution sponsoring the site. Always include the date you accessed the site and the electronic address (URL), placed inside angle brackets.

44b Sample research essay in APA style

In an independent research class, Rosette Schleifer was asked to write a research paper related to social or organizational psychology; she decided to focus on the development of intimate relations. Schleifer's instructor asked her to consider early and more recent studies in the field as a way of learning how experiments in psychology are conducted and how theories evolve as a result of criticism, questioning, and new experiments. Schleifer's audience would be the instructor and the members of her class, and her purpose would be to inform her audience about the adequacy of theories that attempt to account for intimate relations and to demonstrate an awareness of the specialized vocabulary associated with these theories.

Excerpts from Schleifer's essay follow. It is documented in APA style and is accompanied by annotations that highlight the organization and format of her paper and her findings. (See 43d–f for more on APA style.)

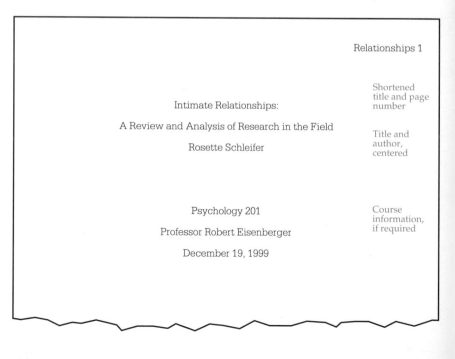

Relationships 1

Shortened title and page number

Intimate Relationships:

A Review and Analysis of Research in the Field

Rosette Schleifer

Title and author, centered

Psychology 201

Professor Robert Eisenberger

December 19, 1999

Course information, if required

Place abstract
on a separate
page; center
heading

Abstract

Researchers over the last two decades have attempted to construct frameworks to account for the development of intimate relationships between humans. A review and analysis of this research suggest that no single framework or theoretical perspective adequately accounts for the complexity of intimate relationships; researchers interested in understanding the phenomenon must depend on a number of these frameworks rather than any single one.

Conclusion

Abstract sum-
marizes sub-
ject, methods,
findings, and
conclusion

Introduction
presents an
overview of
the paper

Intimate Relationships:

A Review and Analysis of Research in the Field

People tend to take the development of intimate personal relationships for

granted. Trying to understand these relationships based exclusively on the

nature of their intimacy (whatever that intimacy may indicate) can cause

investigators to ignore the evolutionary process that leads to the formation

of intimacy and to the many factors that contribute to its development.

Focusing on development rather than on the fact of intimacy reveals how

the level and depth of relationships change over time and how those

changes are related to the way in which the relationships developed in the

first place. "Relationships develop in steps, not in slopes" (Duck, 1988,

p. 48).

Description
of how the
research was
conducted

Method

Over the last two decades, researchers have formulated a number of

theoretical frameworks to account for intimacy in personal relationships.

This review of the work of eleven researchers focuses on whether any single

framework provides a comprehensive explanation of the nature of intimacy

in personal relationships and a sense of just how intimacy develops.

Summary of data col-
lected and how they
were analyzed

Results

Several psychological processes underlie the development of intimate

relationships. As these close relationships develop over time, several

changes take place as interaction between people increases and as

partners increase their investment in the relationship. In time, a sense of

"WE-NESS" develops (Pearlman & Duck, 1987, p. 31). Investigators trying to

understand this complex development try to determine just how people

exchange information when they first meet and how these exchanges alter

relationships over time. While several different frameworks may partially

explain how these intimate relationships develop, a multiplicity of existing

theories is needed to understand the process. Therefore, researchers cannot

rely exclusively on one framework; instead, they need to study several.

Presentation of con-
clusions based on an
interpretation of the
surveyed literature

Discussion

Theory
of social
pene-
tration
intro-
duced

Both early and recent studies regard the theory of *social penetration* as a

basis for understanding the formation of relationships. According to Taylor

(1968), social penetration "provides a framework for describing the

development of interpersonal relationships" (p. 79). The theory suggests

that "reciprocal behaviors transpire between individuals during the

development of an intimate relationship" (p. 79). These behaviors include

the exchange of information and the exchange of expressions of both

positive and negative affects and mutual activities (p. 79). Furthermore,

two dimensions affect our understanding of penetration and interpersonal

development. The breadth of penetration describes the amount of interaction

Relationships 5

per unit of time. The depth of penetration refers to the degree of interaction

in an allotted exchange.

Concept
of self-dis-
closure
intro-
duced
and ex-
plained

Jourard and Lasakow (1958) conducted considerable research related

to the social penetration theory, focusing on *self-disclosure*, which involves

how much people are willing to make themselves known to others. Jourard

and Lasakow developed a self-disclosure rating scale that has been used in

studies other than their own. They found that in terms of self-disclosure,

whites disclosed more information than blacks, and females disclosed more

than males. Their results did not indicate a difference in self-disclosure

between married and unmarried subjects. But married subjects did tend to

disclose more to their spouses than to others with whom they had intimate

relationships. Jourard and Lasakow concluded that married subjects

"redistributed self-disclosure to their respective spouses" (p. 96). Their

studies helped indicate that self-disclosure is, in fact, measurable. Other

studies stemmed from their work, and the results of these subsequent

studies turned out to be both critical and supportive. . . .

APA-style reference
list appears on a sepa-
rate page; heading is
centered

Relationships 6

References

Entries in alphabetical
order, by authors'
names

Aron, A., Aron, E., Tudor, M., & Nelson, G. (1991). Close relationships as

including other in the self. *Journal of Personality and Social Psychology,*

60(2), 241–253.

Last names
first; initials
only for first
names

Certner, B. (1973). Exchange of self-disclosure in same sexed groups of

strangers. *Journal of Counseling and Clinical Psychology, 40*(2), 292–297.

Cozby, P. (1973). Self-disclosure: A literature review. *Psychology Bulletin,*

79, 73–91.

First line of
each entry is
flush with left
margin

Duck, S. (1988). *Handbook of personal relationships: Theory, research and*

inventions. New York: Wiley.

Jourard, S. M., & Lasakow, P. (1958). Some factors in self-disclosure. *Journal*

of Abnormal and Social Psychology, 56, 91–98.

Subsequent
lines of each
entry are
indented
three spaces

Pearlman, D., & Duck, S. W. (Eds.). (1987). *Intimate relationships:*

Development, dynamics, and deterioration. Newbury Park, CA: Sage.

Stephen, T. (1984). A symbolic exchange framework for the development of

intimate relationships. *Human Relations, 37*(5), 393–408.

Taylor, D. (1968). The development of interpersonal relationships: Social

penetration processes. *Journal of Social Psychology, 75,* 79–90.

Tierny, M. M. (1999). An intimate look at Internet relationships. Retrieved

October 29, 1999 from http://www.hightensionwires.com

VanLear, C., Jr. (1987). The formation of social relationships: A longitudinal

study of social penetration. *Human Communication Research, 13*(3),

299–322.

PART 9   WRITING FOR SPECIAL PURPOSES

45   *The Visual Design of Documents*

In this chapter we discuss how to design documents that enable you to communicate more effectively. We consider format, typeface, and the use of space, along with the use of graphics to add visual interest and to enhance, clarify, and emphasize key information and ideas.

45a   Designing documents

In writing for academic and professional purposes, your primary concern is to communicate information and convey ideas. You accomplish these goals through carefully selected language and tightly organized structures. In ordering your words, however, you should also consider how they appear on the page. The visual appearance of your writing affects your audience just as your words do. Your manner of presentation is part of your message, just as the matter you present is.

1   General design considerations

Titles

Titles should be centered on the page. They may be printed in the same size and font of type as the essay or paper, or in a larger or bolder typeface. Positioning the title and emphasizing it draws readers' attention to your paper's central concern.

Headings

Headings within a paper or report break the text into chunks, which are more easily digested by your readers. Page after page of print is less inviting than pages that include the visual "breaks" of headings and subheadings. Strategically placed headings focus your readers on specific aspects of your general topic. By glancing at your headings, readers can gain a quick overview of the specific content elements you have included.

Block quotations

Quotations of more than four lines of prose and three lines of poetry are set off visually as a *block* rather than being run into the text of your writing. This visual separation indicates that you are quoting more than a few words or sentences. The block of quotation enables the reader to shift gears and prepare to hear the voice of another writer.

Graphs and charts

Graphs and charts add to the communicative possibilities of your papers and reports. Such visual aids display information efficiently in far less space than it would take to explain their information content in words. In addition, graphs and charts provide an alternative way of presenting data. They allow you to introduce variety into your papers and reports. They can provide visual relief for readers, and they can make a strong impression as well.

2   Designing documents

Pagination

Number the pages of your document, omitting a page number from the title page. Begin numbering the first page of text consecutively with arabic numerals, usually in the upper right corner. Do not put parentheses around your numbers or periods after them. Many word processing programs can paginate your document for you.

Margins and spacing

Most often, your academic papers should be typed and double-spaced. You should indent your paragraphs one-half inch, or five spaces. In some circumstances, such as preparing science lab reports or reports for business courses, you may use single-spacing.

Computer Tip

Numbering Your Pages

You should always number the pages of an essay, paper, or report. Most word processors can do this for you automatically, if you instruct them to do so. Find, on the HELP menu, the words for "pages," "page numbering," "headers," and "footers." Select the appropriate commands to get the results you want. Look too for commands to control the position of the numbers on the page—and for the command that allows you to suppress or eliminate the numbering from particular pages, such as the first page, which should not be numbered.

You should always *justify,* or align, the lines of print to the left margin of your writing. You can indent for new paragraphs and for lists and block quotations. Check with your instructor about aligning, or justifying, the right margin. In printed books such as this one, both right and left margins are justified. In academic papers, however, it is common to leave the right margin *unjustified,* or ragged, to avoid overlarge spaces between words to create a right-column alignment, and also to avoid hyphenation for line breaks. (Many word-processing programs can be formatted to run with or without hyphenation.)

Type size and style

Almost all word processing programs provide options for selecting various type sizes and typefaces, or *fonts.* When you write papers and reports for your courses, it is generally best to select a standard size and font. A common easy-to-read 10- or 11-point size in a simple font keeps the emphasis on your writing. Using script fonts or italics may seem appealing, but these are difficult to read for more than a few lines at a time. In addition, stick with a single font and type size for your academic papers and reports—except for headings and titles, as explained earlier. The most commonly used font is Times Roman.

Highlighting

You may occasionally highlight words with italics, boldface, or capital letters. Using these techniques of emphasis too often, however, can be distracting. Most often, it is best to use these features only for headings and titles. In this book **boldface** is used to introduce key terms and *italics* to highlight words and phrases in textual illustration and exercise examples.

Headings

Use headings to announce the focus of sections within your writing. Most of your academic papers will probably not require headings. For longer reports and research papers, however, headings can help focus readers' attention on particular aspects of your topic. Some disciplines, moreover, have established conventions for report headings. See Chapter 44 on the parts of a report in the sciences and in the social sciences.

Lists

You may wish to use a list in a paper or report. Bulleted lists allow you to isolate and emphasize key points. They can also enhance the visual appeal of a document.

In using bulleted lists, however, be careful not to make them too long. Lists of more than ten items should be grouped into two categories. Also, try to keep the items in the list to a single line each. And be sure that the items are grammatically parallel.

You may use a bullet (•), a dash (–), or an asterisk (*) for each item in your list. In some instances, you may wish to number the items rather than use bullets.

White space

The space around the print on a page acts like a frame for a picture. It focuses the reader's attention on the printed text; it also creates a contrast between the dark print and the complementary white background against which that print stands out. For most academic writing, frame your pages with margins of 1 to 1½ inches all around, depending on the audience, purpose, and content of your document. Avoid creating lines of type that run nearly across the entire page or from top to bottom. Long lines of print and tiny margins give the page a crowded, unappealing look.

Use white space generally to create a clean, neat, balanced appearance for your documents. Breaking your print text with space makes it both more attractive to readers and easier for them to comprehend. Besides using white space around your words, consider its use around any visuals you may include.

45b Creating and using visuals

Visuals can help you present your ideas with clarity and emphasis. You can use them as support for a mostly written document, or you can make them the centerpiece of a document that is supported by a brief written text.

The kinds of visuals most frequently used in academic writing include tables, charts, and graphs. Tables present information in columns and rows, usually in numerical form. Charts and graphs present information so that relationships among different elements are apparent. Drawings, diagrams, and other more common images can be used to illustrate a process or describe the parts of something.

Tables and charts are familiar visual elements in business and scientific writing. When you include tables and charts in your academic papers and reports, it is standard procedure to number your tables and to provide titles for charts and graphs. The specific elements described in the tables and graphs should be made clear for your readers. In addition, you should provide a link between your visuals and your written text, either in the text itself or in a caption or subtitle to accompany the visuals you include.

At their best, the graphics you use will complement the information you convey through writing. Try to avoid overloading your document with graphics—they will overwhelm the content of your writing. On the other hand, avoid saving your graphics until the end of the document. Strive, instead, for a balance between text and graphics, always considering how graphics can enhance, clarify, and accentuate what you communicate through words.

Guidelines for Combining Graphics with Writing

- Use a flowchart, table, or outline to preview or review.
- Use a chart, diagram, or map to orient readers.
- Use a flowchart or diagram to illustrate sequential or hierarchical relationships.
- Use a bar graph, pie chart, or simple table to emphasize key relationships.
- Use a complex graph, table, or diagram to analyze or summarize data.
- Use a facsimile of a source to illustrate originals.
- Use a photo, cartoon, or other image to arouse interest.

In preparing your visuals, strive for a neat, clean appearance, with plenty of white space around them to increase their attractiveness and ability to communicate. Your visuals should complement your written text, add to it, or summarize information more efficiently than words can express rather than repeating in visual form what you say in writing.

Consider the following examples of visuals—a pie chart, a line graph, and a bar graph. Notice how the information presented is clearly labeled.

Pie chart

This *pie chart* illustrates how state lottery proceeds for a thirty-year period 1964–1995 were allocated. Although the information could be presented in alternative formats such as a list, table, or bar graph, the pie chart lets readers see the relative weight in percentages for each area of allocation. In general, use pie charts to portray relationships among parts and a whole.

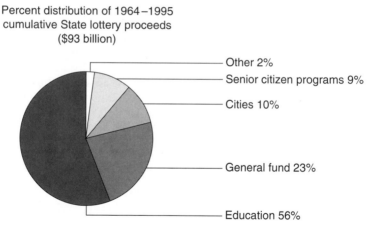

Percent distribution of 1964–1995
cumulative State lottery proceeds
($93 billion)

Other 2%
Senior citizen programs 9%
Cities 10%
General fund 23%
Education 56%

Sample Pie Chart

Line graph

The sample *line graph* represents media usage by consumers for a ten-year period. Each line represents a different type of media. The direction of each line indicates an increase or decrease in the use of particular media. Use line graphs to display trends and multiple line graphs to compare trends over time.

Media Usage by Consumers: 1989 to 1999

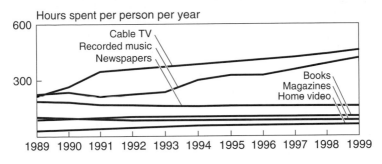

Sample Line Graph

Bar graph

The sample *bar graph* describes software sales for 1994 and 1995 in millions of dollars. Different types of software programs are included with the most used on top and the least used on the bottom. Use bar graphs to display comparative information visually.

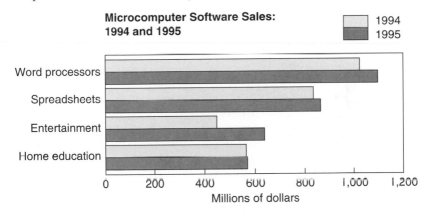

Sample Bar Graph

All charts adapted from the U.S. Bureau of the Census. From *The American Almanac 1996–1997 Statistical Abstract of the United States,* Hoover's, Inc., Austin, Texas, 1997, 296, 558.

Guidelines for Using Visuals

- Provide a caption or legend for each visual.
- Make sure the details of your visuals are clear and readable.
- Number your visuals.
- Provide a lead-in comment in your written text to introduce each visual.
- For complex visuals that contain multiple kinds of information, explain what the visual illustrates.
- Credit the source for visuals you do not create yourself.

Writing and Designing for the World Wide Web

46a Composing Web pages

The creation of Web pages has become a popular assignment in writing classes. You may be asked to (or you may want to) create a Web page on a particular topic of interest. As with all writing, composing a Web page requires you to plan, draft, and revise; understand your audience; and carefully select and arrange your material.

In general, Web pages contain three basic elements: **text** written by you, **links** to other appropriate Web pages on the Internet, and interesting and appropriate **graphics**. In more advanced Web pages—and this is recommended only for those with either some Web experience or sufficient time and motivation to learn—animations, sounds, movies, tables, and frames are included.

Web pages are written in a special computer code or language called "HTML" (for **H**yper**T**ext **M**arkup Language). While HTML is not particularly difficult to learn and may be done by hand, it is much simpler and quicker to produce your work in a Web page layout program. These programs make creating Web pages as simple as using a word processor. They allow you to make the page look almost the way you want it to, and then the software actually writes the necessary HTML code for you. In fact, many versions of word processing programs such as AppleWorks, WordPerfect, and Microsoft Word have the capability of converting a word-processed document into HTML, though by necessity they are less powerful and less accurate.

Characteristics of good Web pages

In general, your pages should meet the following criteria:

- **Content.** Be sure you have a reason to create the page. Composing a Web page is *real writing*: millions of people may see your page. Don't waste their time. The rule is "value-added"—if you are not adding anything of value to the Web, do not add anything at all. A page of nothing but links to other Web pages or pictures of your cat is best left off the Web. Add original content, something that may be useful and interesting for other Web users.

- **Graphics.** On the Web, the visual often rivals the textual in importance, and the two working together create effects that could not be achieved by either alone. Use graphics sparingly but effectively. In most cases, images that move, flash, beep, or buzz simply annoy your viewers, even if they seem clever at the time you create the page.

- **Ease of Navigation**. Moving around your Web site must be easy and intuitive. Make sure your viewers know how to find something on your site and how to get back to where they started. Avoid dead-end pages, which have no links on them for your viewer to move to. Use a table of contents and make it easy for your viewers to get to it from anywhere in your site.

- **Scannability**. Make your pages easy to scan. A viewer should be able to judge the content and value of your page almost instantly, simply by scanning it. Make sure your major points are visually highlighted.

- **Personality.** Give your viewers a sense of who you are. Your page should reflect your tastes, values, and viewpoints. It should also establish you as a credible source of information and interpretation. Viewers of your page are likely to want to know what gives you the authority to compose and publish this particular Web page.

46b　The World Wide Web: Rules and conventions

Web pages written in HTML are basically simple text files; they are made up of nothing but numbers, letters, and basic punctuation marks. That is what makes them usable on nearly every computer in the world. As such, you could write all your Web pages by hand in an elementary text editor such as SimpleText on the Macintosh or NotePad on Windows, but it would be tedious.

While it is possible to compose this code by hand from scratch, if your pages are complex, the task of doing so is overwhelming for beginning Web page designers. It is simpler to use a Web page editor, which works basically like a word processor. You type in your text, format it the way you want it to appear, add your graphical material, and when you save the file, it is saved as correct HTML, just as if you had added every tag by hand. Even word processors can save (or "export") their normal word processing files as HTML text files, with all the necessary HTML tags inserted. For even slightly more complex pages, however, you should consider using a Web page editor such as Adobe GoLive, Microsoft Front Page, or Claris Home Page.

One warning is in order: if you are accustomed to desktop publishing programs such as QuarkXPress or Adobe PageMaker, even with top-of-the-line Web page editors, you will need to give up the notion that you have complete control of how a page appears. HTML is a "page formatting" language, not a precise page layout language. The page you create will look slightly different on different computers. There's nothing you can do about that.

The Web uses certain conventions to name the files. File names must have the extension ".htm" or ".html" appended to them. This signifies to a computer's Web browser program (such as Netscape Navigator or Microsoft Internet Explorer) that the file is a real Web page and it should display the page according to the embedded tags it comes across in the text. The home page, the first page a user normally comes to when accessing a site, must be named "index.html" or "index.htm." Web browsers expect to find a page named "index.html" in every Web site, and they display that page first when a viewer accesses a Web site.

In most instances, case doesn't matter, so in theory a file may be named either "MyFile.html" or "myfile.html," and the file names will be interchangeable. Unfortunately, this is not always true. It is best to use all lowercase for all file names, even names that would ordinarily be capitalized, such as "english.html."

Graphics files must be in one of two formats: GIF (Graphics Interchange Format) or JPEG (Joint Photographic Experts Group), and the file extensions must be, respectively, ".gif" or ".jpg." Browsers cannot display other kinds of graphics files.

46c Planning and organizing

The first important point to keep in mind as you are planning your site is to learn to think hypertextually. Hypertext, the underlying concept of the World Wide Web, is the linking together of different pages in a hierarchical organization. The normal reading process of an essay or book is linear: you start at the beginning and read through to the end. In a hypertext document such as a Web site, the viewer has multiple options of where to start and what to read next. The viewer decides what to read in what order. Thus you cannot count on a viewer starting at the beginning of your Web site and reading through to the end. In fact, with the exception of the home page index.html, there is no beginning or end.

Visualize your site as a number of short pages that may be read in any order, the most important of which may be accessed from your site's home page. In this sense, the home page functions as a table of contents, providing an easily scanned overview of the topics of your site.

1   Finding a subject, purpose, and audience

Since composing a Web page and a Web site is just another form of writing, all the techniques you have learned from earlier chapters apply here. If you are assigned a subject for a Web page, you can skip the first step of finding a subject.

http://www.wwwscribe.com
Provides extensive advice about Web authoring and Web searching.

If not, search your journals, do some brainstorming on paper or in groups, question what you see and hear, or pick a controversy that you have some feelings about. Remember, Web pages grow and evolve just as written compositions do, so you will modify and revise whatever subject you choose anyway.

Your sense of purpose and your sense of audience work closely together. Not only do you have to arrive at a clear purpose for your Web page, but also you should achieve that purpose with a specific audience in mind. Are you trying to convince or persuade *someone*, or to inform *someone*? Who are they? How much do they know? What do they need to know?

2   Finding external Web pages to link to

You almost certainly will want to provide links to other relevant Web sites on your page. As part of your research for your Web page, you should make a running list of Web sites you visit as you research.

3   Finding graphical material to use

There is a huge store of graphical material available on the Web for your use. Usually any search engine or directory can locate an overwhelming amount of graphics in short order. There are two issues to be aware of, however.

First, it is often difficult to find what you want. If you want simple decorative or thematic clip-art, that is easy to find. If you want a *particular* image—say a picture of Albert Einstein or of the Space Shuttle—that will require a concentrated search. By using the search engines judiciously and refining your queries, you often will be able to find what you want.

The second perhaps more troublesome issue is copyright violations. Just as with text, every image you find on the Web is automatically copyrighted by its owner. You need to find images that the owner has allowed free use of (there are thousands of free clip-art sites that give blanket permission, although often this permission is restricted to nonprofit sites—read the fine print on the Web site where you get the image) or contact the owner of the image.

4   Creating a storyboard

For Web sites of more than a few connected pages, it is best to start with a storyboard, a visual outline of your project that shows each page and the hypertext links to and from it. It is very similar to the concept of "mapping" introduced in Chapter 1. If the design of the site is simple, you can sketch it out on a large sheet of paper; if it is more complex, you may want to use multiple sheets of paper, one Web page per sheet, and indicate how and where the pages are linked by pieces of string or some other device.

To make your storyboard, take a large sheet of paper, turn it sideways, and at the top draw a small box, labeled "Home Page." Insert a row of small boxes underneath your home page box, and draw a line from each one to the home page box. Draw one box for each topic you intend to link to the home page.

For a site on Robert B. Parker, linked to your home page, as a start, you expect that you will have pages on the author's life, his works, reviews and critical analyses of his works, the television show *Spenser: For Hire,* and links to other useful sites. You will discover more as you develop your site, but these are enough to begin. The first level of links from your home page, as represented in your storyboard, will look like Figure 1.

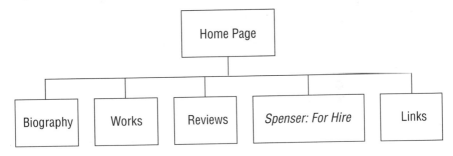

Figure 1

Figure 2 shows a sample of a storyboard and the first few levels of a Web site on the works of Robert B. Parker.

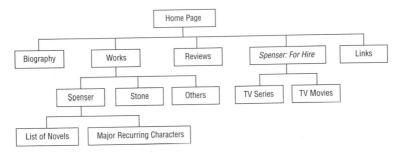

Figure 2

46d Using Netscape Composer

While not as powerful as top Web site creators such as Adobe GoLive or Microsoft FrontPage, the "Composer" module of Netscape Communicator (Netscape 4.0 and greater) rivals the middle-of-the-road programs in power and ease of use, and it has the added benefit of being free, so that it is readily available on most campuses. In addition, the Macintosh and Windows versions are nearly identical in all respects, and the Web page files you create on a Mac may be viewed and edited on a Windows PC, and vice versa. Following is an overview of Web page features.

1 Text

Basic text options are headings, centering, and lists. Long pages (not recommended anyway) may be visually divided by "Horizontal Rules" such as this:

In general, the text you compose should appear in regular size and typeface. As in any document, boldface and italics should be used sparingly. Use Headings (a specific HTML term) to indicate titles and subsections. HTML allows for 6 sizes of headings; normally, page titles should be in Heading 1 or 2.

Any list-like items may be placed into a "bulleted list" (again, a specific HTML term):

- This is list item 1
- This is list item 2
- This is list item 3

2 Links

A link is the "hot" text (usually shown in blue and underlined) that transports the reader to another Web page somewhere else on the Internet. Netscape Composer allows you to select text by dragging your mouse over text, and then entering into a box the URL (i.e., the Web address, which begins with "http://") of the page where the reader should go next. One variation on the URL is the "mailto" tag: instead of providing the user with an "http://"-type Web address, you provide an e-mail address, usually your own. When the user clicks on the link, the mail module on the user's computer is called forth, an e-mail message is preaddressed to the e-mail address specified, and the user only needs to compose the message and send it to you.

A link to another Web page looks like this: **http://members.xoom.com/ parkersbooks/index.html**

A mailto link looks like this: **mailto:chev39@flashmail.com**

3   Graphics

HTML was designed to be a text markup language, a way of providing users with standardized features for displaying text on one another's computers. Early on it included basic provisions for slipping graphics into the stream of text. Although this provision for graphics was neither elegant nor flexible, it helped give the World Wide Web true multimedia capabilities. Unlike its clumsy predecessors, ftp and gopher, the HTML-based Web included pictures and colors, and eventually sound and moving pictures. The Web has become a much more integrated medium with the combination of graphics and text creating a powerful rhetorical and emotional effect.

46e   Testing and revising your Web pages

Before you go public with your Web pages, revision is in order. Your pages will need to be re-thought out, reconsidered, and re-examined for subject, purpose, audience, and content. But at heart, all revision—whether it is of text or Web pages—begins with an awareness of audience. Review your pages slowly and carefully. Try to give your Web pages some cooling off time; get away from them for a while and try to come back to them with fresh eyes, as if you were a stranger to the Web site. That is how they will strike your viewer. Moreover, it helps to have some trusted peers review your work and provide you with some audience feedback.

1   Test for broken links

The most obvious problem, and the simplest one to check out, is links on your page that do not work. These are known as broken links, and they may have a number of causes. To test your links, you must load your page into a Web browser such as Netscape Navigator. To view your page in Navigator while you are composing it in Composer, click on the steering wheel View in Navigator icon on the toolbar.

Click on each link on each page, making sure that it displays the correct page. If you find any broken links, correct them. For internal links—links to other pages within your Web site—the most common cause of broken links is that you have saved the file to which the link refers in the wrong place on your hard drive. Move the file into your Web site's directory and redo the link. (This particular problem may not show up until you have uploaded your site to your Web server—see below. If a broken link appears then, the solution is the same.)

For broken external links (links to other sites out on the Web), the most common culprit is simple misspelling or mistyping of the page's address. Web addresses can be very complex, and one wrong character will make the address unusable. Find the page again, if you can, and double-check the address you typed into the link. The next most common culprit is the actual disappearance of the page you are linking to. Either it no longer exists at all, or it has been moved to another address by its owner. This is a common occurrence. There usually is nothing you can do except remove the link. On rare occasions, you may be able to track down the page's new location and re-establish the link.

2 Test for cross-platform compatibility

One of the challenges facing the composer of Web pages is making a page look acceptable on a variety of browsers and computer systems. Even if you get your page to look exactly the way you want it to when you create it, you cannot count on everyone having the same computer, browser, and version number that you do. For this reason, it is essential that you test your page, both before and after uploading it, on as many different browsers and systems as possible. At the very least you should keep a copy of the most recent versions of Internet Explorer and Netscape on your computer (they are both free), and test your pages in both. When you discover incompatibilities, you should find a middle ground, a version of your Web page that looks acceptably well on most browsers and systems. When you revise your pages, you will have to make some compromises.

3   Revise for style and overall appeal

If you have browsed the Web much at all, you know that there are many pages that are simply ugly—they lack style, they use colors that clash and irritate, they are confusing to view, and they simply create a bad impression on the viewer. While a complete discussion of the aesthetics of Web page design is beyond the scope of this chapter, here are a few guidelines to help you avoid the most common stylistic mistakes.

1. Limit your graphics both in size (physical size and file size) and number.
2. Make sure they are necessary and appropriate. Be sure that they really add something essential to your page.
3. Avoid frivolous and overly cute images that have no relationship to the content of the page.

4   Revise for content

This is probably your most familiar task as a writer. As with essays or other papers you may write, your Web pages must have a focus, purpose, and clear conception of the intended audience. The advice on revision given in Chapter 1 applies to Web pages also.

Consider all levels of your content: start with the major issues of purpose and focus. Does this page really have a purpose for existing? If so, do you (and your potential viewers) have a clear understanding of what it is, based on the content of the site? Revise your pages until there is nothing extra that will distract and nothing missing that will confuse the viewer.

Is the writing on the pages clear and concise? Web viewers tend to be impatient with extra text; cut your writing to its most concise form. Delete extra words; make list-like prose (a long series of items in sentences) into bulleted lists.

5   Revise to improve navigability

A good Web site needs to have absolutely clear, logical, and predictable navigation (the system of links within your Web site from page to page). If there is any possibility that your viewers may have a difficult time finding information or moving around your site, or if there is any possibility a viewer could get lost in your site and not be able to find a way back, you should revise the navigation system. There should be no "dead-end" pages—pages with no links at all, causing your viewer to feel trapped. Every page in your Web site must have at least a link back to your home page. Ideally, there will be links to other appropriate pages in your site and external links as well. Try to make each page present a consistent look and feel: always put the link to your home page at the bottom or in a column down the left side of the page.

46f   Uploading your Web site

The final step in the creation of your Web site is to publish (or copy) it to a Web server where it can be viewed by the rest of the world. This process involves using a special technique known as FTP (for "File Transfer Protocol") to transfer your file from your folder to your Web server. You will need some information before you can FTP your files to your Web server. Ask the Webmaster of your chosen host or find the information online. Usually the the information on uploading is clear and easy to follow.

Often, sending files via FTP from your computer can be a complicated process, requiring the use of special FTP software, but fortunately Netscape Composer can handle this for you. Before you actually begin the upload, however, you need to set up Composer. To do this, first you need to know your host's "server name." This is simply the name of the computer where you will be transferring your files. It will usually be "something dot something dot com." Second, you need to know the name of your specific account (usually your username or user ID) and your password—those were selected (or they were assigned to you) when you established your Internet account.

Click on the Publish icon in the toolbar (or select Publish from the File menu).

The first time you do this, you will need to give Composer your ftp information. We will assume you have set up a Web site with the free hosting service "xoom.com." According to their documentation, the name of their server is "ftp.xoom.com"; the account name you have set up is "parkersbooks." Enter that information, along with your account's password.

Enter your server name in the "Publish files to this location" box, followed by the "index.html" file name. Check the "All files in the page's folder" button and click "Select All," so that all the other files in your site will be uploaded automatically at the same time.

Now, when you click the Publish button, your Web site will be uploaded. Its address (its "URL") in this case will be http://members. xoom.com/parkersbooks/index.html. You should immediately access your Web site after it has been uploaded and double-check to make sure all the graphics display and all the links work. If everything looks good, then you are done, for a while.

47 *Business Writing*

The business world requires a great deal of writing. This writing is typically task oriented and time constrained. Reports, letters, and responses to memos, job postings, and email require quick and efficient response. Deadlines are critical. Equally important, business writing needs to be concise, direct, and purposeful.

This chapter explains the conventions of business writing and shows how to write memos, letters, reports, and proposals. It also explains how to write a résumé.

47a Writing business memos and letters

Business letters and *memorandums* (or *memos*) are the most frequently used types of writing in business. Memos are used to communicate within a company. When writing to a company or organization and for communication between them, business letters are the appropriate form of correspondence.

http://www.colostate.edu/ Depts/WritingCenter/ references/documents/ bletter/page1.htm
Provides a guide to writing business correspondence.

Business letters are more formal than memos, whose informality typically reflects the closer relationship between writers and readers. In selecting the tone for both memos and letters, use common sense. Let your relationship with your reader determine how formal you need to be. In cases where you are unsure, use a more formal rather than a less formal tone. In all your letters and memos, however, be courteous.

As with most business writing, you need to follow certain conventions of formatting. The following sections will help you determine the appropriate tone and format for your business memos and letters.

1 Memos and Email

Memos and email serve a number of purposes. Primarily, they maintain open channels of communication within a company—colleagues keep one another apprised of events with informal memos and email. Emails and memos also serve as a permanent record of decisions made and actions undertaken. They may contain information regarding approaches to problems, or they may express attitudes toward or changes in company policies.

Memos and email contain evidence that can be used to enhance or diminish your job performance. Thus, it is a good idea to avoid writing anything ungracious or unkind in your memos or emails. In particular, be careful to avoid biased language (see Chapter 26). In writing memos and email, keep the accompanying conventions in mind.

Conventions of Business Memos

- Follow the proper format, identifying the date of the memo, its audience, sender, and subject at the top of the page.
- Single-space long memos; double-space short ones.
- Initial the memo next to your name.
- Keep the memo brief and to the point.
- Engage your readers by focusing on essential matters, one idea per paragraph. Begin with the most important idea.
- Conclude with a gesture of goodwill.

---

2 Business letters

Unlike memos, which are the preferred form of written correspondence within a company, business letters serve as a company's primary means of external communication. A business letter is also the appropriate form of communication for an individual writing to a company. Whether you are writing to seek information, place an order, request an adjustment, lodge a complaint, or attend to some other business matter, you should follow the principles of business communication listed in the chart at the bottom of this page.

Computer Tip

Creating an Itemized List

Business correspondence relies heavily on itemized lists, which are often bulleted. Set off each item with a bullet, asterisk, or other marker that visually highlights your list. Be sure to introduce your list with a sentence explaining the topic or purpose of the list. Be sure also to keep your listed items in parallel grammatical form.

Guidelines for Writing Business Letters

- Direct your letter to an individual.
- Use a courteous opening and maintain a polite tone.
- State your reason for writing at the outset.
- Be clear about what you want.
- State your appreciation of the reader's concern and interest.
- Conclude with a polite gesture of thanks.
- Indicate an enclosure with the abbreviation *enc.* (plural *encs.*).
- Identify anyone else receiving a copy of the letter. Use *c.* for one copy to a single individual and *cc.* for copies to two or more people.
- Be consistent in using the block or modified block format.
- Single-space within paragraphs and double-space between paragraphs.
- Proofread your letter carefully.
- Always remember to sign your letter.

You should also use one of the standard formats for business letters: block or modified block. *Block format* aligns everything at the left margin. *Modified block* format indents as illustrated here and in 47b. Whichever format you use, be sure to observe the conventions of spacing as illustrated in the sample letters.

SAMPLE ENVELOPE

Boris Rodzinski
1234 Gray Street
Glen Ellyn, IL 54321

Ms. Angela Hernandez
Publicity Department
Cannon Electric Company
35 Harvest Drive
Chicago, IL 35791

Sample Business Letter in Block Format

return address	1234 Gray Street Glen Ellyn, IL 54321
date	April 25, 1999
line space	
inside address	Ms. Angela Hernandez Publicity Department Cannon Electric Company 35 Harvest Drive Chicago, IL 35791
line space	
salutation	Dear Ms. Hernandez:
line space	I am writing to request information about your company's products and services for a research paper I am preparing for my marketing course at Northwestern University. The instructor suggested that in addition to the usual library research, we could gain a different perspective by reading publications produced by various companies. Hence my request.
line space	I am a senior marketing major with a special interest in electrical products and services. I am particularly interested in research and development your company may be engaged in as well as in your company's relationship with suppliers and clients.
line space	I appreciate your taking the time to send me any company publications you think suitable. And if there were the slightest chance you would have time to speak with me in person, I would be happy to come to Cannon Electric at a time convenient for you.
line space	Sincerely yours,
closing	
4 line spaces	*Boris Rodzinski*
signature	Boris Rodzinski
name, typed	c. Professor K. Evancie

47b   Writing job application letters

Like business letters and memos, **job application letters** require a clear sense of purpose, a courteous tone, and care in observing conventions of formatting. An application letter should be more than a mere cover letter announcing that you are sending a résumé and applying for a job. Instead, let your application letter indicate who you are, what you have accomplished, and how you can contribute to a company or organization.

Tailor your letter to each job you apply for. Be sure to indicate where you heard about the job opening, why you are applying, and how your education and experience qualify you for it. Also include a request for an interview.

Guidelines for Writing a Job Application Letter

- Indicate how you learned of the job opening.
- Identify the job or position you are applying for.
- Provide evidence of your qualifications for the job.
- Provide specific information about your background and accomplishments.
- Ask for an interview.
- Note that a copy of your résumé is enclosed.
- Be courteous and confident.
- Pay attention to appearances. Use high-quality $8\frac{1}{2} \times 11$-inch bond paper (for both your letter and résumé). Be sure your letter is neat and error free.
- Type your name below your signature, and do not forget to sign your letter.

Sample Job Application Letter in Modified Block Format

April 21, 2000
North Hall
Pace University
Pleasantville, NY 10530

Dr. Adrienne Cherloux
Assistant Superintendent for Personnel
Dover High School
300 West McFarland Street
Dover, NJ 07801

Dear Dr. Cherloux:

Professor Samantha Darby, an instructor at Pace, recently conducted research in your school. She suggested I write you about the teaching position in psychology opening up in the fall. I will graduate next month with Honors, with a B.A. in psychology supplemented by a teaching certificate. Bilingual in Spanish and English, I am eager to teach in a public school. My résumé is enclosed.

During my four years at Pace, I focused on educational and social psychology, with a special interest in adolescent development. Having grown up in Puerto Rico, I wish to work in a high school with a large number of Spanish-speaking students. I understand their needs and would like to help them develop.

While pursuing my formal education, I coordinated a student network of volunteers to support the annual blood drive, provided child care for one of the local churches, and staffed a teen shelter one night a week. My volunteer work has given me insight into children's needs as well as a clear sense of how to organize groups of community helpers.

I would like to discuss my qualifications at an interview. I am especially interested in hearing more about your special programs for minorities. Please let me know where and when we can meet to discuss this exciting prospect. I look forward to hearing from you.

Sincerely,

Martha Kilmer

Martha Kilmer

enc. résumé

47c   Writing and formatting résumés

Your job application letter should be accompanied by a *résumé*, a succinct outline of your educational background and work experience, coupled with information about your related extracurricular activities and special skills or interests. Résumés may be arranged according to your specific job skills (a functional résumé) or according to the jobs you have held, beginning with the most recent (a chronological résumé). The accompanying sample résumé is arranged chronologically. Notice that the educational background and work experience begin with the most recent items and work backward. Employers will be more interested in your most recent work experience.

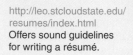
http://leo.stcloudstate.edu/
resumes/index.html
Offers sound guidelines
for writing a résumé.

Also be sure to include reference to the specific job for which you are applying or a general career objective. This will indicate precisely what you are interested in and will increase the likelihood that your letter and résumé will get into the hands of the right person.

And finally, if you include references, provide the names, addresses, and full titles of three professors, supervisors, or employers who have agreed to speak or write on your behalf. You have the option, however, of simply indicating that references can be furnished upon request. Use the guidelines on p. 788 in preparing your résumé.

Computer Tip

Using a Document Template

You can take advantage of document templates, which allow you to simply pour your information into a prearranged structure and let it fall into place. After you write (and save) the text for your document, select the desired template—a memo, résumé, or newsletter template, for example. Follow the instructions that accompany the template, including inserting your document into it.

Sample Résumé

Martha T. Kilmer
North Hall
Pace University
Pleasantville, NY 10570
914-555-3286

CAREER OBJECTIVE
To obtain a teaching position requiring Spanish/English language skills.

EDUCATION
Pace University, Pleasantville, New York
B.A. in Psychology with Honors; anticipated graduation 5/03
New York State Teaching Certificate, Grades 7-12
Flores High School, Hato Bay, Puerto Rico, diploma 1999
Salutatorian; Recipient of Principal's Award for Leadership

EXPERIENCE
Pace University, Psychology Department, Pleasantville, NY
Research Assistant, Professor Samantha Darby. Recruited and processed subjects in a cross-sectional computerized study of mental imagery in adults, children, and teenagers. June 2002 to March 2003.

Rindge Teen Shelter, Department of Human Services, Mt. Kisco, NY
Youth Coordinator. Staffed the shelter one night a week. Served as friend and counselor to drop-in teenagers. Prepared weekly workshops on issues of adolescence. September 2001 to May 2002.

SKILLS
Fully bilingual in Spanish and English.

ACTIVITIES
Coordinator for Neighborhood Development Program, a public service and community action program.

REFERENCES
Available upon request from the Pace University Career Service Office, Pleasantville, NY 10570.

Guidelines for Writing a Résumé

- Place your name, address, and phone number at the top of the page.
- Include clearly labeled categories for career objective, education, work experience, special skills, activities, and references.
- Include dates for graduation and for time at each job.
- If you are preparing a chronological résumé, place educational and work experience in reverse chronological order, beginning with the most recent job.
- Provide a brief description of your responsibilities at each job.
- Include a title for each job or position held.
- Try to keep the résumé to a single page so it can be scanned quickly.
- Use a uniform type size for headings, a different type size for information beneath the headings. If you are working with a word processing program, take advantage of the available lettering and formatting options.
- Space your categories evenly and make your résumé as pleasing to the eye as you can. Leave ample space between entries, avoid crowding, and be sure the résumé is perfect in appearance.

47d Writing business correspondence as email

Follow the same guidelines for business letters you send by email as for those you send via conventional mail. Express your purpose clearly, write succinctly and grammatically, and maintain a courteous and professional tone. Since email letters tend to be less formal than traditionally printed

Guidelines for Email Business Letters

- Identify your main topic in the subject line.
- Provide necessary context and background in your opening sentence.
- Clarify your purpose quickly.
- Zero in on the main point early.
- Try to keep your message to a single screen.

ones, you may adopt a slightly less formal style, but be careful to avoid collo-quialisms and an overly breezy casual style.

Keep in mind the guidelines shown in the chart on p. 788 when you use email for business correspondence.

47e Preparing a scannable résumé

An increasing number of corporations and institutions have begun scan-ning hard-copy résumés to establish a database of potential new employees. Thus, you may want to prepare both a traditional and a scannable résumé, particularly if you are applying to high-tech organizations.

There are some important differences between traditional and scannable résumés. Because computer scanning of résumés capitalizes on key word searches, and since key words tend to be nouns rather than verbs or adjectives, a scannable résumé needs to be noun-heavy rather than verb-heavy. In a tradi-tional résumé you would emphasize what you accomplished with verbs such as "produced," "maintained," "developed." In a scannable résumé you should shift to nouns and noun phrases such as "product manager," "maintenance control," "software developer." In addition, you should create a category for your key word descriptors and place it early to allow for quick identification of your key abilities.

Another linguistic difference between traditional and scannable résumés involves using technical language, or jargon. While maintaining clarity in your writing, you can introduce the jargon of the trade into your résumé to demonstrate your familiarity with its language and culture.

Because computer scanners vary in their ability to distinguish letters and other kinds of symbols on paper, you should make your paper résumé as easy to read and scan as possible. The following guidelines can help you prepare a scannable résumé.

Guidelines for a Scannable Résumé

- Use standard size white paper.
- Prepare an original, not a photocopy.

(continued)

- Print in black on a laser or ink-jet machine.
- Use a standard typeface and a 10- to 14-point font size.
- Avoid italics and underlining.
- Avoid lines, boxes, and graphics.
- Space letters normally, without kerning.
- Begin each line at the left margin—no columns.

On the opposite page is a scannable version of Martha Kilmer's résumé.

Martha T. Kilmer
North Hall
Pace University
Pleasantville, NY 10570
914-555-3286

KEY WORDS: Bilingual teacher, Spanish/English teacher, research experience, youth coordinator, counselor, public service, community action, psychology major.

OBJECTIVE: Teaching position with Spanish/English language skills.

EDUCATION: Bachelor of Arts, Pace University, May 2003
Major: Psychology (Honors Program)
New York State Teaching Certificate, Grades 7-12.

EXPERIENCE: Research Assistant, Psychology Department, Pace University, June 2002-March 2003. Recruiter for a computerized study of mental imagery in adults, children, and teenagers. Processor of data and statistical information for the study.

Youth Coordinator, Rindge Teen Shelter, Department of Human Services, Mt. Kisco, NY, September 2001-May 2002. Counselor and mentor to drop-in teenagers at the youth shelter. Workshop leader on adolescent concerns and issues.

SKILLS: Bilingual in Spanish and English.

ACTIVITIES: Coordinator for Neighborhood Development Program, a public service and community action program.

REFERENCES: Available from the Pace University Career Service Office, Pleasantville, NY 10570.

47f   Preparing an Internet résumé

You may also wish to post a résumé on the Web, where your résumé is a hyperlink on your home page. Like scannable résumés, Web-based résumés differ from traditional ones. Try to take advantage of the way the Web works by keeping your résumé brief and viewable without scrolling and by including more detail through links.

Guidelines for a Web-based Résumé

- Follow the guidelines for designing a Web site (see Chapter 46).

- Provide links to enhance your résumé with examples of your work, or with more detailed explanations of your accomplishments.

- Put essential information on one easily viewable page.

- Place the most important information—contact data, education, and work experience—in the topmost 300 pixels.

- Include relevant graphics—your photograph—and relevant artwork and images via links to scanned photos or images.

- Provide a practical title for users to easily identify the pages as your résumé.

- Keep your résumé current, and include the most recent date you revise your résumé.

48 *Writing and Making Oral Presentations*

In many business situations and in many college courses, you will be required to make oral presentations. Everything you have learned about business writing and about writing generally can be applied to preparing your oral presentations. For example, be sure to consider your audience and the purpose and occasion of your presentation. (See Chapter 1 for advice on considering audience, purpose, and occasion.)

Attend as well to the organization of your presentation as you would to written work, using your beginning to grab the attention of your audience and ending it with something you want them to remember. Use the middle of your presentation to explain, illustrate, support, and otherwise develop your ideas.

When you speak before a group, however, other considerations obtain. The following are among the most important:

- Reducing nervousness
- Speaking from notes or a prepared text
- Maintaining posture and using gestures
- Using a rostrum, lectern, or desk
- Using visuals and props
- Making team presentations

48a Reducing nervousness during oral presentations

To some degree, most people become nervous when they are required to speak in public, even when the audience is small and known to the speaker. This is partly the result of the greater formality of the "oral presentation" as compared with group conversation.

One thing you can do to reduce nervousness is to think of your audience as interested listeners in an extended conversation. You talk first; their turn comes later. To increase a conversational feeling in public speaking, you might inject a few questions into your text, even if you do not actually expect your audience to answer them. Also, leave time at the end of your presentation for a few questions in turn from your listeners.

Other strategies for staying calm include taking a few deep breaths before you begin, speaking a bit more slowly than usual, and finding a few friendly faces in the audience to focus on.

Perhaps the best way to reduce nervousness, however, is to be completely prepared. Know your presentation inside out. Practice it both silently and aloud. This is important not only for helping you remember your material, but also for timing and for identifying potential difficulties. A well-written text that uses short sentences, vivid language, and relevant examples will make the job of learning your presentation easier.

48b Using notes or a prepared text

You may be required to speak with or without notes, with or without a fully prepared text. Or you may be given a choice. When you use notes, it is easiest to read them from index cards arranged in the sequence you will use them. Write outlines or very brief key phrases and transitions on the cards, and write larger than usual. Doing this will make your note cards easier to read while you are speaking.

If you work from a script or a written text, make a relatively narrow column with wide margins, and mark the text for emphasis. Use plenty of paper, typing with triple or quadruple spacing for greater ease in reading. **Boldface** key words. USE CAPS for emphasis. Underline words you want to stress. You may also wish to add brief reminders to yourself to *slow down* or *pause* at strategic points.

In addition, end each page with a sentence. Doing this will give you time to pause as you turn the page. Finally, in using note cards, keep them in your hands, placing used cards on the bottom of the stack. In using a prepared text, do the same if you are holding your speech text without a stand for support. If you speak from a rostrum or lectern, simply turn each finished page over and set it aside.

48c Body language: posture and gestures

When you stand (or sit) before your audience, do so with your head up and shoulders back. Stand tall and erect. Don't be afraid to smile, and be sure to look at your audience. Many speakers have a tendency to look only at one member of the audience or to only one side of a room when speaking. Shift your gaze to different members of the audience, looking to both sides as well as to front and back.

To what extent you use hand gestures will depend in part on the kind of speech you are giving. A persuasive speech, for example, may benefit from more emphatic gestures than you would use in an informative speech. Your use of gesture will also depend on your general tendency to use your hands when you talk. People who gesture a lot in normal conversation may wish to temper this tendency in oral presentations. Conversely, people who gesture little in everyday speaking situations may wish to increase their use of gesture when they speak in public.

One way to decide how to modify your use of gesture is to practice before a mirror so you can see your gestures. Another is to get a friend or family member to listen to your presentation. Ask your listener to pay particular attention to your use of gestures.

48d   Using a rostrum or lectern

Some oral presentations are given from behind a lectern or rostrum. In others the presenter must stand with no place to lean against, hide behind, or place notes or a prepared text. Be sure you know whether you will have a lectern or other support for your notes or speech text. Perhaps you will be seated behind a desk or at a table.

Knowing the physical circumstances of your presentations can help in your decisions about how to prepare your notes or text. They might also affect decisions about how you dress for the occasion. Will your feet or legs be showing? Will any parts of your body receive emphasis—your head and shoulders if you are standing behind a rostrum, for example? If so, how will that information affect decisions about your dress and your posture?

In using a lectern or a rostrum for your presentation, you may wish to step out from behind it during the course of your presentation. You might do this to emphasize a point, to establish a closer intimacy with your audience, or to use a visual display.

Some speakers like to lean on the lectern, putting their hands on its sides or its platform to steady themselves. Others are more comfortable sitting on or behind a desk with their notes or text to their side or in front of them. Let the tone of the occasion, the nature of the audience, and your purpose and inclination help you decide, when that decision isn't made for you.

48e Using visuals

You may be required to use visuals in an oral presentation, or you may opt to do so. Visuals can enhance a presentation. They can also separate a speaker from his or her audience.

In creating visuals for a presentation, make sure they are large enough for your audience to see easily. What is easily viewable by you at close range will often not be seen at all by a person ten or twenty feet away. Also, be sure your visuals are clearly written, legible, and not overly cluttered. As with notes you make for yourself, keep the information on your visuals to the key points. You can elaborate on them either from your notes or from memory.

In using an overhead projector, be careful that you are not in the line of vision of any members of your audience. In using a chart, diagram, or blackboard with images behind you, be careful not to turn your back repeatedly to your audience. Stand, instead, to the side of your visual display so your audience can see you and it at the same time. use a pointer or your finger to highlight key words or visual details.

Keep in mind as well that any visuals should help clarify your presentation. They should neither confuse listeners nor distract them. Nor should they simply replicate your text.

Everything said here about the use of slides projected via an overhead projector applies as well to PowerPoint slides.

48f Making team presentations

More and more in business and in classes where oral presentations are required, team presentations are common. If you are part of a team making an oral presentation, be sure you meet with the other team members to discuss your individual responsibilities. Make sure you understand your precise role, especially what aspect of the group's work you will present. Be sure as well that you know what the others are doing in their presentations, including the sources, types of materials, visuals, and handouts they may include. Devise your presentation so that it complements those of your teammates.

49 *Writing Essay Examinations*

Writing strong essay exams is essential for success in many college courses. Time constraints make answering essay examination questions a challenge. To write essay exam answers that demonstrate your grasp of a subject, you will have to write efficiently and effectively. This chapter provides advice to help you do just that. It begins with some advice about pre-exam preparation, continues with tips about key words found in typical exam questions, and concludes with guidelines for writing and reviewing your exam response.

49a Preparing for the essay exam

Effective preparation for an exam includes careful note taking during class and completing reading assignments. In reviewing your notes for an essay exam, look for patterns and connections among facts, examples, theories, and other forms of information. Essay exams typically require students to synthesize information gleaned from lectures and readings, to explain relationships among important events and ideas, and to evaluate information.

Before the test, study the course material carefully. Form a study group with a few other students, and compare both your notes and your understanding of the important concepts and skills taught in the course. Try to rehearse for the test by anticipating and composing possible essay exam questions. Creating and answering test questions gives you an opportunity to prepare yourself for the types of questions you will be asked. It may also help you feel less nervous when faced with the actual test.

Throughout your preparation—note taking, independent study, group work—try to collect evidence to support your ideas. Identify key concepts you are likely to be asked about, and develop your own thesis or idea to explain and elaborate on each of them. Remember that good essays involve both a clear thesis or a strong idea and ample evidence to support it.

49b Considering the exam question and planning your answer

Read each question on the exam carefully, at least twice. Avoid jumping to a hasty conclusion about its intent. Look carefully at the directions—at the specific words of each question. Does the question ask you to "identify"? To "explain"? To "compare"? To "evaluate"? To do more than one of these or other things? The chart on page 800 outlines the common terms to look for as you read the exam question.

Once you have read the question and understood what you are being asked to do, allow yourself a few minutes to think before you begin writing your answer. Spend some time considering what you want to say and how you might go about using what you know to support your idea. You will find that you can remember quite a bit in even a few minutes of thinking—if you are well prepared. Collect your thoughts and begin to sort them. Also consider how much time you have to answer the question, and then allot your time sensibly. For example, if your exam includes two essay questions in a 50-minute period, and if the questions are equally weighted, plan to devote 25 minutes to answering each question.

Begin with some preliminary writing—jotting a few rough notes in no special order. You can arrange your notes later by numbering them as you prepare to write your response. The very act of putting pen on paper should stimulate further thought and help you make connections among all the material that you have studied and learned. You can also order your notes in a rough outline, noting how you can begin and end your essay and identifying some points to cover in between. By making a rough sketch of where you are heading and how you plan to get there, you will decrease the chances of forgetting an important point. You will also enhance the organization and readability of your answer. Even in your rough preliminary notes, try to include a thesis statement that responds concretely and specifically to the question.

49c Writing and reviewing your answer

As you write, be sure to respond directly to the question. Avoid vagueness and bland generalizations. Also avoid trying to throw everything you can think of into your answer; instead, tackle the question head on. Avoiding a direct response to the question will deprive your answer of clarity and focus and will diminish the point you wish to make.

Key Terms to Look for in Essay Exam Questions

Identify means to name, indicate, or specify. Some essay exams include *identify* as part of a question that asks you to do more to answer the question: "identify and explain" or "identify and discuss."

> Identify three prominent African American scientists and explain their contributions to their respective fields.

Explain means to provide reasons for, to lay out causes, effects, implications, ramifications. Explanations can be simple or complex, general or specific; they can include sparse or full detail. The time limit for an essay response will determine how much or how little explanation you should provide. If you are unsure about how much information to include in an explanation, ask your instructor for clarification.

> Explain how a legislative proposal becomes a law.

Discuss means to talk or write about. The instruction is not specific, and as a result, it is important to know how much flexibility you have with your answer. *Discuss* is often used to mean *explain*.

> Discuss Thoreau's reasons for leaving Walden Pond.

Define means to provide a definition, to point out characteristic features, to identify limits, or to put something into a category. Definitions can be brief or extended. An essay question that asks you to define a term or concept may also require that you examine, explain, elucidate, exemplify, list, characterize, or discuss the various aspects or elements of your definition.

> Define the concept of multiculturalism. Discuss the social and political issues the debate about multiculturalism has raised.

Compare and contrast means to consider the similarities and differences between two items or ideas.

> Compare and contrast Woody Allen's movie comedies with those of Mel Brooks. Consider Allen and Brooks as both actors and directors.

(continued)

Analyze means to break into parts in order to yield insight. To do an analysis of something involves examining it closely and carefully, looking at its details and at its component parts.

Analyze the structure and function of a red blood cell.

Evaluate means to assess or make a judgment about. You may be asked to evaluate the claims made by competing theories or to evaluate the performance of a nonprofit organization. Evaluation often involves comparison and explanation.

Evaluate Mel Gibson's performance in the 1991 film of Shakespeare's *Hamlet*.

For example, consider the following question: Discuss the economic factors that led up to the Civil War. This very specific question requires an answer that addresses economic factors only—not political, military, or religious ones (unless, of course, you can show how those other kinds of factors directly relate to the economic issues the question calls for). You also do not want to answer a broad question too narrowly. Respond to a question that asks how divorce affects children in the United States by providing information, statistics, evidence, and arguments specifically about all kinds of effects of divorce on children (social and psychological effects as well as financial and other effects). You should not stray from the question, however, by discussing the causes of divorce or its effects on divorcing couples. The most important thing you can do in writing an essay exam is to attend carefully to what the question asks for and then to be specific and thorough in providing an answer that demonstrates what you know.

WRITING HINT   When you find yourself running short of time in an essay exam, map out the direction your essay would take if you had time to complete it. Provide an outline for the instructor, showing him or her what you intended to discuss. Depending on how specific you can make the outline and on how accurate and thorough you have been up to that point, you should receive a better grade than if you simply stop midstream.

Essay Exam Checklist

- Prepare for the exam in advance.
- Consider the question, pace yourself, and plan your answer.
- Think before you write.
- Jot some rough notes and perhaps sketch an outline.
- Devise a thesis for your response.
- Write quickly, and be sure you respond to the question.
- Leave time to review your answer.

Glossary of Usage

This glossary provides guidance for using commonly confused words and phrases. The advice offered reflects standard usage for academic and professional writing. It also reflects current opinion among practicing writers on what is considered appropriate for publication. For additional guidance on matters of usage, consult a current dictionary.

a, an Use *a* before words that begin with consonant sounds: *a* book, *a* historical argument. Use *an* before words beginning with a vowel sound: *an* argument, *an* honest mistake.

accept, except *Accept* is a verb that means "to receive." She *accepted* his apology. As a preposition, *except* means "to leave out." *Except* for anchovies, he enjoyed all kinds of pizza toppings.

advice, advise *Advice*, a noun, means a "suggestion": Their *advice* was to take a double major. The verb *advise* means "to give advice": I *advise* you to write a letter expressing your appreciation for the special scholarship.

affect, effect The verb *affect* means "to influence" or "move emotionally": Excessive drinking *affected* their judgment. As a verb, *effect* means "to bring about": She wished to *effect* radical change. As a noun, *effect* signifies a result: The *effects* of the war were staggering.

aggravate, irritate *Aggravate* is sometimes used colloquially to mean *irritate*. Restrict this sense of aggravate to informal situations; in other writing situations observe the following distinction: To *aggravate* means "to make worse." He *aggravated* his back injury when he moved the refrigerator. To *irritate* means "to annoy." His behavior *irritated* her.

agree to, agree with *Agree to* indicates approval; *agree with* suggests shared views. They did not *agree with* every detail in the contract, but they *agreed to* its provisions and decided to sign it.

all ready, already *All ready* means "fully prepared"; *already* means "previously" or "before now." We were *all ready* to leave for our trip, having *already* made plane and hotel reservations.

all right, alright Spell *all right* as two words rather than as *alright*.

all together, altogether *All together* means that all are gathered in a group in one place: The committee had never been *all together*. *Altogether* means "entirely": They were *altogether* opposed to the idea.

allude, elude *Allude* means "to refer to": During her lecture the professor *alluded* to numerous historical events. *Elude* means "to evade or avoid": The runner *eluded* tacklers as he ran down the field.

allusion, illusion An *allusion* is an indirect reference to a person, event, or thing: The *allusion* was to Elvis Presley's habit of gyrating his pelvis in performance. An *illusion* is a deceptive appearance: *Illusions* about the glamor of movie acting draw many to Hollywood.

a lot, alot Spell *a lot* as two words rather than as *alot*. Avoid using the colloquial *a lot* in formal writing to mean "a large amount" or "many."

a.m., p.m. Use these abbreviations only with numbers to indicate time (*2 a.m., 4 p.m.*), not to replace the words *morning* and *afternoon*.

among, between *Among* indicates relationships among three or more people or things; *between* indicates relationships between two people or things. The proposals were considered *among* the club's four officers; they had to decide *between* retaining their present mission or going in an entirely new direction. You may, however, use *between* for three or more people or things to emphasize relationships of each to another. The chess tournament progressed with exciting games *between* the club's ten best players.

amount, number *Amount* indicates a quantity of something noncountable; *number* refers to things that can be counted. A large *number* of people expended a significant *amount* of effort.

and/or This construction is sometimes used in business or legal writing to indicate that either or both of two things apply: We wanted to buy a new car *and/or* truck. Avoid using *and/or* in formal writing. Instead, write out the options: We wanted to buy a new car, a new truck, or both.

anxious, eager *Anxious* means "uneasy or worried": He was *anxious* about his upcoming interview. *Eager* lacks the apprehension of *anxious*, indicating instead "being desirous of something": They were *eager* to begin eating.

anybody, any body; anyone, any one *Anybody* and *anyone* are indefinite pronouns that refer to people but not to particular individuals. Can't *anybody* here play this game? Isn't there *anyone* who can tell me how to get to the Brooklyn Bridge? *Any body* and *any one* both refer to specific though unidentified things or individuals: *Any body* of information can be used as a starting point for research. *Any one* of you may begin. Follow the same guidelines for *nobody, no body,* and *no one*. Note: *no one* is always two words (not *noone*).

as Avoid using *as* to mean *because, since,* or *while;* using *as* to substitute for these more precise words can result in vagueness or ambiguity. *As* they were preparing for the long journey, they decided to have a hearty breakfast. (It is not clear here whether *as* means *because* or *while*.)

as, like Use *as* to indicate equivalence; use *like* to indicate resemblance. *As* a lecturer, Dr. Benton is outstanding. (Dr. Benton = a lecturer.) *Like* other art historians who offer seasonal lecture series, she has an avid following. (*Like* = similar to.) Use *as* (not *like*) in clauses: You should do *as* I say, not *as* I do.

assure, ensure, insure These related words have particular areas of reference. *Insure*, for example, means "to protect against financial loss": They were *insured* against damages from earthquakes and hurricanes. *Ensure* does not carry this specialized meaning but signifies more generally "to make certain": To *ensure* your place in the class, you must pay your tuition on time. *Assure* generally means "to promise": They were *assured* that there would be no additional charges.

awful, awfully Avoid *awful* to mean "bad" and *awfully* to mean "very"—at least in formal and academic writing, even though you may use these words this way in casual conversation. Literally, if something is *awful* it suggests that it inspires awe or wonder.

awhile, a while *Awhile* means "for a short time"; *a while* means "a time." *Awhile* is an adverb and *while* is a noun: We relaxed *awhile* before studying for *a while* longer. The article and noun (*a while*) can be an object of a preposition (*for*).

bad, badly *Bad* is an adjective and *badly* an adverb: They had not been treated *badly*, but they nonetheless felt *bad* about what had happened.

being as, being that Avoid using these expressions in place of *since* or *because*: Because [not *being that*] she completed her work early, she was able to go home.

beside, besides *Beside* is a preposition meaning "next to": Place the chair in the corner *beside* the small table. *Besides*, as an adverb, means "moreover": *Besides*, there is always tomorrow. As a preposition, *besides* means "in addition to": *Besides* an excellent emergency room, the hospital boasts a state-of-the-art neonatal unit.

burst, bust *Burst* is a verb whose principal parts are *burst, burst, burst*. It means "to explode or break apart." *Bust* is a slang word meaning "to be locked up." It is also a nonstandard form for the verb *break*. The bubble *burst* (not *busted* or *bursted*).

but, however, yet Any of these words can be used to express contrast. They should never be combined.

can, may *Can* indicates an ability to do something; *may* suggests possibility. We *can* learn how to play chess. We *may* even become grand masters. Use *may* rather than *can* to request permission: *May* I go now?

can't, couldn't Reserve these contractions for informal writing. In formal writing, use *cannot* and *could not*.

center around Avoid this expression in formal writing; instead use *center on*. The proposal *centers on* increased spending for public works.

cite, sight, site *Cite* means "to mention" or "to identify a source": In her speech she *cited* a recent article published in the *New England Journal of Medicine*. *Sight* means "to view" (verb) or "a view" (noun): Astronomers recently *sighted* what they believe is a previously undiscovered planet. A *site* is a place or location: This is a perfect *site* to pitch a tent.

compare to, compare with Use *compare to* when stressing similarities only: Robert Burns *compares* his love *to* a red, red rose. Use *compare with* for noting similarities and differences: The class was asked to *compare* Vincent van Gogh's self-portraits *with* the self-portraits of Frida Kahlo.

complement, compliment *Complement* means "to add to" or "to go well with": Their trip north *complemented* their southern journey of the summer before. *Compliment* means "to praise": He *complimented* her on the outstanding speech she gave as valedictorian.

comprise, compose *Comprise* is sometimes mistakenly used to mean *consist*. *Comprise* means "to embrace or include"; *compose* means "to make up or consist." The main proposal *comprises* numerous subproposals; the whole plan is *composed* of four parts.

continual, continuous *Continual* means "repeated at frequent or regular intervals": The *continual* attempts to persuade me to buy were unsuccessful. *Continuous* means "ongoing": The music was *continuous,* never stopping for more than the normal break between songs.

credible, credulous *Credible* means "believable"; *credulous* means "believing too easily." His story was hardly *credible*. Some who heard it, however, were *credulous* and wanted to hear more.

criteria, criterion The words refer to standards of evaluation. *Criterion* is singular; *criteria* is plural. The *criteria* used to evaluate candidates were numerous and diverse.

data It has become acceptable to use *data* with a singular verb as well as in the plural: The *data was* gathered under the auspices of the American Council of Churches. The *data were* not clearly supportive of either position.

device, devise *Device,* a noun, refers to an instrument; *devise,* a verb, means "to fashion." Together, they invented a *device* to extract paper entangled in computer printers. They worked a long time before they were able to *devise* a solution to the problem.

different from, different than Though the preferred form, *different from* is being joined more and more by *different than* in print as well as in conversation. Their statistics were not very *different from* ours. His statistics were not very *different than* what we had expected.

disinterested, uninterested To be *disinterested* is to be "impartial"; to be *uninterested* means "to be not interested." The judge in the case was *disinterested*. He remained *uninterested* in politics all his life.

due to Use as an adjective following a form of the verb *to be:* The victory *was due to* a persistent and unyielding defense. Avoid using this phrase as a preposition: The committee chair canceled the meeting *because of* (not *due to*) the hurricane.

eager See *anxious, eager.*

effect See *affect, effect.*

elicit, illicit *Elicit* means "to evoke" or "to draw out": The advertisement for subsidized housing *elicited* many applications. *Illicit* means "illegal": The gang had been involved in *illicit* activities for years.

elude See *allude, elude.*

eminent, imminent *Eminent* means "distinguished or prominent": They sought to hire one of the most *eminent* scholars in the field. *Imminent* means "about to happen": The arrival of the performer was *imminent.*

ensure See *assure, ensure.*

especially, specially *Especially* means "particularly"; *specially* means "for a particular reason." She *especially* wanted to visit the Louvre, where she expected to buy a *specially* chosen gift for her grandfather.

every day, everyday Use *every day* to mean "each day"—an adjective with a noun. Use *everyday* as an adjective that modifies another noun. It was an *everyday* outfit, comfortable and simple—one that could be worn *every day.*

every one, everyone *Everyone* is an indefinite pronoun referring to a group as a whole: *Everyone* participated. *Every one,* an adjective followed by a noun, refers to each member of a group individually: *Every one* of the committee members favored the new plan.

except See *accept, except.*

explicit, implicit *Explicit* means "expressed directly or outright": Her *explicit* instructions were to deposit the money by noon in the savings account. *Implicit* means "implied or suggested": They had an *implicit* understanding between them.

farther, further *Farther* indicates distance only: The museum was *farther* away than I thought. *Further* indicates either distance or degree: When he took office in January 1992, President Clinton attempted to stimulate the economy *further.*

fewer, less Use *fewer* for countable items and *less* for noncountable ones: *Fewer* television programs today portray people smoking than those of a decade ago. There is *less* attention paid to survival skills than there used to be. See also *amount, number.*

flaunt, flout To *flaunt* means "to display" or "to show off": If you've got it, *flaunt* it. To *flout* means "to defy": Georgia O'Keeffe *flouted* many conventions of the art world.

former, latter These words work together to refer to the first and second of two things respectively: Louis Armstrong and Duke Ellington were both important American jazz musicians. The *former* was a trumpet player, the *latter* a pianist.

further See *farther, further.*

good, well *Good* is an adjective: He continued in *good* health *well* into his nineties. *Well* is often an adverb (though it can function as an adjective with verbs denoting a state of being or feeling): She performed *well* during the gymnastics competition. He did not feel *well* after eating a *good* two pounds of cole slaw.

hanged, hung The past participle of *hang* is both *hanged* and *hung.* Use *hanged* when referring to executions; use *hung* to mean "suspended." People are *hanged*; pictures are *hung.*

herself, himself, myself, yourself These *-self* pronouns are both reflexive (they refer to an antecedent) and intensive (they intensify an antecedent): I, *myself,* could not go. Do not use these pronouns in place of subjective or objective pronouns: The award went to Barbara and her (not *herself*). No one but you (not *yourself*) can make that decision.

hopefully *Hopefully* means "with hope": The quarterback watched his last pass *hopefully*. Avoid using *hopefully* to mean "it is hoped": We *hoped* the pass would not be intercepted. *Not: Hopefully* the pass would not be intercepted.

however, but, yet See *but, however, yet*.

hung See *hanged, hung*.

if, whether To express doubt, use *whether:* They were uncertain *whether* the game would be telecast in their region. To express an alternative, use *whether or not: Whether or not* you can come, please call next week. Use *if* in an adverbial clause expressing a condition: *If* you can make it, we'd very much like to have you join us.

illicit See *elicit, illicit*.

illusion See *allusion, illusion*.

imminent See *eminent, imminent*.

implicit See *explicit, implicit*.

imply, infer *Imply* means "to suggest"; *infer* means "to interpret or make a guess based on evidence." Readers *infer* what writers *imply*.

in, into, in to *In* suggests a stationary place or position; *into* indicates movement toward a place or position. While she was *in* the pool, the phone rang. When he dived *into* the pool, he made a terrific splash. Use *in to* when *to* is part of an infinitive: She went *in to* answer the phone.

infer See *imply, infer*.

insure See *assure, insure*.

irregardless, regardless *Irregardless* is nonstandard for *regardless. Regardless* (not *irregardless*) of their political connections, they still had to obey the traffic laws.

irritate See *aggravate, irritate*.

its, it's Use *its* only as a possessive adjective: The cat licked *its* fur. Use *it's* to mean "it is" or "it has": *It's* only a ten-minute walk. *It's* been raining steadily.

kind of, sort of Both expressions are informal for "rather." You may use them in formal writing, if *kind* and *sort* function as nouns: The panda is related to the raccoon; it is not a *kind of* bear. Avoid informal usages like the following in college writing: It was *kind of* an intriguing explanation. Instead write: It was an intriguing explanation.

later, latter *Later* means "after some time," or "more late": It was *later* than we thought. *Latter* refers to the second of two things mentioned: It is the *latter* date that I prefer. Do not use *latter* when referring to the last of three or more items. See also *former, latter*.

latter See *former, latter* and *later, latter*.

lay, lie *Lie* means "to recline"; *lay* means "to put or place." I wanted to *lie* down and take a nap. Please *lay* the eyeglass case on the bookcase.

leave, let *Leave* means "to depart from" or "to let remain": She had to *leave* early. *Let* means "to allow to" or "to permit": The instructor *let* the class go early.

less, fewer See *fewer, less.*

lie, lay See *lay, lie.*

like See *as, like.*

lose, loose *Lose* is a verb with many meanings, including "to suffer defeat": I hope our team doesn't *lose* the game. *Loose* is usually an adjective, meaning "not firmly attached": This knot is too *loose.* As a verb *loose* means "to set free": They *loosed* the hounds for the foxhunt.

may, can See *can, may.*

maybe, may be *Maybe* is an adverb meaning "perhaps"; *may be* is a verb. *Maybe* I'll travel this summer. It *may be* more difficult than you think.

might of Use *might have.* They *might have* come early. (*Of* is never used as a verb, only a preposition.)

Ms. This abbreviation was invented during the 1960s to provide women with a title parallel to Mr. for men. Midway between *Mrs.* and *Miss, Ms.* is deliberately ambiguous about a woman's marital status. When using *Ms.* with a full name, use the woman's first name and not her husband's name: *Ms.* Emily Beauford (*not* Ms. John Beauford).

nor Use with *neither* within a sentence: *Neither* Joanne *nor* her sister had ever gone abroad. When *nor* begins a sentence, place the verb before the subject: *Nor* had their parents been informed. Do not use *nor* when the verb is already in the negative: I am *not* offended *or* angry. You may also write: I am *neither* offended *nor* angry (since the verb *am* is positive).

number See *amount, number.*

OK, O.K., okay All of these are informal expressions suitable for conversation, but not for formal writing.

percent, percentage *Percent* suggests a specific figure; *percentage* is a more general term. The retention rate at Notre Dame is nearly 99 *percent.* A high *percentage* of college students are not graduated from the schools they attended as freshmen.

phenomena Plural of *phenomenon:* Certain ocean *phenomena* baffle biologists.

principal, principle *Principal* refers either to a sum of money or to the leader or head of an entity such as a school: They collected their interest each month but they left the *principal* untouched. The *principal* decided to hold an assembly to address disciplinary problems in the school. *Principle* means "a fundamental belief": They refused to comply as a matter of *principle.*

quotation, quote *Quotation* is a noun and *quote* is a verb. Former President Bush was *quoted* as saying, "Read my lips; no new taxes." It was a *quotation* that would haunt him during his unsuccessful campaign for reelection.

raise, rise *Raise* means "to lift": Please *raise* the shade. *Rise* means "to get up": I will *rise* tomorrow before 6 a.m.

real, really *Real* is an adjective; *really* is an adverb. Avoid using *real* to mean "very." The purchase they made was a *real* value. The dinner was *very* good. It was a *really* exciting game.

reason is because This is a redundant construction to be avoided. Use either *because* or the *reason...that* instead. The *reason* they couldn't come was *that* they had a prior commitment. They couldn't come *because* they had a prior commitment. *Not:* The reason they couldn't come was because they had a prior commitment.

respectively, respectfully *Respectively* means "in the order given." *Respectfully* means "with respect." Alpha and omega are, *respectively,* the first and last letters of the Greek alphabet. The children behaved *respectfully* in the presence of their family's guests.

rise See *raise, rise.*

set, sit *Set* means "to put or place": Would you *set* this cup on the counter? *Sit* means to "seat oneself": May I *sit* on this antique chair?

shall, will Use *shall* for polite questions in the first person: *Shall* we go? *Shall* I begin? Use *will* for other instances involving future tense: We *will* not be able to meet you tomorrow. We *will* be leaving for vacation.

should of Use *should have.* We *should have* avoided the freeway at rush hour.

sight, site See *cite, sight, site.*

somebody, some body; someone, some one *Somebody* and *someone* refer to people but not to particular individuals: *Somebody* ought to fix that wheel. Would *someone* please close the door? *Some body* is a noun modified by an adjective; *some one* is a pronoun modified by an adjective: *Some* governing *body* will decide the issue. *Some one* of you will be the new club president.

sometime, some time, sometimes *Sometime* means "at an indefinite future time": We will get around to seeing them *sometime.* *Some time* means "a period of time": We would like to spend *some time* with them on our next vacation. *Sometimes* means "occasionally": *Sometimes* I lose my concentration.

specially See *especially, specially.*

sure, surely *Sure* is an adjective; *surely* is an adverb. She was *sure* of one thing at least. *Surely,* you have made a mistake. Avoid using *sure* as an intensifier or as an adverb in formal writing. Not: She was *sure* clever. Or: *Sure,* I agree. (Though such usage is fine in conversation.)

than, then The conjunction *than* is used in comparisons; the adverb *then* indicates time. Throughout the 1980s, the Mets had a better baseball team *than* the Yankees. *Then* in the next decade, things changed.

that, which, who *That, which,* and *who* are all relative pronouns. Use *that* to refer to things or people, *which* to refer only to things, and *who* to refer only to people. For his thirtieth birthday, she bought him the gift *that* he had not wanted to buy for himself.

The opportunity, *which* will not readily come again, must not be passed by. Among the many attendees were some *who* couldn't wait to leave.

their, there, they're *Their* is a possessive pronoun; *there* is an adverb indicating place and is used in the common expressions "there is" and "there are"; *they're* is a contraction meaning "they are." When George Eliot and Jane Austen wrote *their* great novels, *there* were few creative opportunities for women, besides writing. Please put the books over *there*. *They're* unable to come until after the game begins.

then See *than, then.*

'til, till, until The contraction *'til* should be avoided in formal writing. *Till* and *until* are both acceptable, though many writers prefer to use *until* in academic writing.

to, too, two *To* is a preposition; *too* means "also" or "excessively"; *two* is a number. The quarterback faked a handoff *to* the fullback and threw over the middle *to* the tight end. You *too* may one day enjoy a chance to travel. You ate *too* much and you ate *too* fast. You'd better take *two* antacids.

toward, towards Both are acceptable.

uninterested See *disinterested, uninterested.*

unique *Unique* means "the only one of its kind." Avoid using modifiers or intensifiers with *unique*. "Very unique" or "the most unique" are meaningless expressions.

use, utilize *Utilize* means "to put to use." Avoid the term *utilize* when *use* will convey your meaning equally well. The mayor urged city residents and commuters to *use* (not *utilize*) public transportation during the week of the festival.

well See *good, well.*

whether, if See *if, whether.*

which, that Although *which* may be used before both restrictive and nonrestrictive clauses, many writers prefer to use it only with nonrestrictive clauses containing nonessential information: The car, *which* was parked behind the house, had been badly damaged. (The essential point here is that the car had been badly damaged. Where it was parked is not as important.) *That* is used only with restrictive clauses: The car *that* was parked behind the house had been badly damaged. (In this case where the car was parked is essential information identifying which car had been badly damaged: that is, the car parked behind the house.)

who, whom Use *who* when a sentence requires a subject pronoun: *Who* will be able to come? Use *whom* when a sentence requires an object pronoun: *Whom* did you tell? In most instances, for relative clauses, use *who* before a verb. Mariela, *who* is Danish, speaks four languages. Before a noun or pronoun, use *whom*: Mariela, *whom* I have just met, speaks four languages.

whose, who's *Whose* is a possessive adjective; *who's* is a contraction meaning "who is." *Whose* umbrella is this? *Who's* responsible for this wonderful dessert?

your, you're *Your* is a possessive adjective; *you're* is a contraction for "you are." *Your* idea was well received by the committee. *You're* one of the most courageous people I've ever met.

Glossary of Terms

This glossary lists and defines selected grammatical and rhetorical terms used throughout the *Handbook*. For fuller explanations of terms and additional examples, see the relevant sections cited within most definitions.

absolute phrase A group of words often consisting of a participle and its subject. An absolute phrase modifies an independent clause as a whole. *The game over,* the team left the field. See 29g.

abstract noun A noun that names concepts, ideas, or qualities: *justice, democracy, generosity.* See 26b.

acronym A word formed from the initial letters of a group of words: *NAFTA* (or *Nafta*) for North American Free Trade Agreement. See 26e and 36b.

active voice The verb form in which the grammatical subject is the agent and the direct object is the receiver of the verb's action. See 10j. See also *passive voice.*

adjective A word that modifies a noun or pronoun: a *bright* light. See 12a.

adjective clause A clause modifying a noun or pronoun in another clause. See 9d.

adjective phrase A prepositional phrase that functions as an adjective. See 9c-1. See also *prepositional phrase.*

adverb A word that modifies a verb, an adjective, or another adverb: *quickly, now.* See 12a.

adverb clause A clause that modifies a verb, adjective, another adverb, or an entire sentence. See 9d.

adverb phrase A prepositional phrase that functions as an adverb. See 9c-1. See also *prepositional phrase.*

agreement Correspondence of a verb with its subject in person and number, and of a pronoun with its antecedent in number and gender. See *subject–verb agreement,* 14a–j; and *pronoun–antecedent agreement,* 14k–n.

analogy A comparison of similar features of two different things in order to clarify, illustrate, or explain an idea. See 5e-9.

antecedent The noun that a pronoun refers to: Bill and *his* friends. See 11b and 14k–n.

appositive A noun, noun phrase, or pronoun that renames the noun or pronoun it immediately follows: my favorite day, *Saturday.* See 11f.

archaism An obsolete word: *gadzooks.* See 26e.

article A type of determiner that precedes a noun: *a, an,* or *the.* See 11a and 15c.

ASCII Acronym meaning American Standard Code for Information Interchange. This basic format permits transfer of text files between and among different computers and programs.

auxiliary verb Also called a *helping verb,* an auxiliary verb combines with a main verb to form a complete verb or verb phrase: We *will* attend. See 10b, 15i, and 15j.

balanced sentence A sentence that includes two clauses in grammatically parallel structure: *We retreated* while *they advanced.* See 23b.

base form The main form of the verb that indicates an action or state of being in the present: (I) *do,* (you) *hear,* (they) *go.* See 10a.

biased language Prejudiced language that stereotypes or unfairly denigrates members of a group. See Chapter 26.

bibliography A list of primary and secondary sources used in writing an essay, paper, or report. In MLA documentation style, this list is called *Works Cited;* in APA documentation style it is called *References.* See 43c and 43f.

Boolean term A word such as *and* or *or* that helps Internet and other database searchers restrict their searches with multiple words. *Example:* Graywolf and New England.

browser A World Wide Web program for accessing and getting around on the Internet. Netscape Navigator and Microsoft Internet Explorer are two of the more popular ones.

case The changes in form a noun or pronoun undergoes to indicate whether it functions as subject, object, or possessor: *they, them, their; Tom, Tom's.* See 11c–d and 31a.

clause A group of words that contains a subject and a predicate. See 9d. See also *dependent clause; independent clause.*

cliché A trite expression: *last but not least.* See 26h.

collective noun A noun that names a group of people or things: *team, family, committee.* See 11a and 14e.

colloquialism A word or expression appropriate to ordinary conversation, especially in informal situations, but not to academic writing. See 26c-1.

comma splice Two independent clauses incorrectly separated by a comma instead of a period. See Chapter 17.

common noun A noun that refers to classes—to any person, place, thing, concept, or general quality: *student, city, cloud, idea, wisdom.* See 11a.

comparative The form of an adjective (*more eager*) or adverb (*less quickly*) involving a comparison of more or less, greater or lesser. See 12e.

complement A word or group of words that completes the meaning of a subject or a direct object by renaming or describing it. See 9b-3.

complete predicate The verb in a sentence plus its modifiers, complements, and objects. See 10a.

complete subject The simple subject plus any additional modifying words or phrases. See 9a-1.

complex sentence A single independent clause with one or more dependent clauses. See 9f-2.

compound-complex sentence Two or more independent clauses and at least one dependent clause. See 9f-2.

compound noun Two nouns combined to form a single word: *moonstone*. See 11a and 27d-3.

compound predicate Two or more verbs that have the same subject. See 9a-2.

compound sentence Two or more independent clauses joined by a coordinating conjunction, without any dependent clauses. See 9f-2.

compound subject Two or more simple subjects joined by a coordinating or correlative conjunction. See 9a-1 and 14c.

concrete noun A noun that names things recognizable through the sense of sight, hearing, touch, taste, or smell: *salt, pumpkin*. See 26b.

conjunction A word that links words, phrases, and clauses to one another: *bread* and *butter*. See 13c.

conjunctive adverb An adverb that emphasizes the relationship in meaning between two independent clauses: *therefore, however*. See 13c-4.

connotation Secondary associations of a word beyond its primary dictionary meaning. See 26a. See also *denotation*.

contraction A shortened form of a word or group of words: *can't* for *cannot* and *wouldn't* for *would not*. See 31c.

coordinating conjunction A conjunction that joins words and phrases as well as independent clauses: *and, but, or, nor, for, so,* and *yet*. See 13c-1.

coordination The arrangement of two or more words, phrases, or clauses to indicate equal importance. See 22a.

correlative conjunction A paired conjunction that links words, phrases, and clauses: *bothand*. See 13c-2.

count noun A noun that can be counted and can take both a plural and singular form: *acorns, oaks, pens*. See 15a–d.

cumulative sentence A sentence that begins with the independent clause and adds modifying phrases as the sentence goes along. See 24c-1. See also *periodic sentence*.

cyber- A prefix indicating something created or existing electronically or online. *Example:* cybergame, cybernovel.

dangling modifier Words, phrases, or clauses that do not modify anything in a sentence while seeming to do so: *Concerned about hurricane-force winds,* the dinner was postponed. See 18i–j.

declarative sentence A sentence that makes a statement. See 9f-1.

deductive reasoning Also called *deduction*. The process of reasoning from a general principle to a particular instance. See 7b-1.

definite article The definite article *the* refers to particular nouns. See 15c. See also *indefinite article*.

demonstrative adjective An adjective that points to the nouns they replace: *this* poster; *these* flyers.

demonstrative pronoun A pronoun that points to a particular thing: *This* is an ugly poster; *those* are useless flyers. See 11b.

denotation The dictionary meaning of a word. See 26a. See also *connotation*.

dependent clause A group of words that begins with a relative pronoun or a subordinating conjunction: *before the game begins*. A dependent clause has both a subject and a verb but cannot stand alone as a sentence. See 9d and 16d.

determiner A word or group of words that introduces a noun. Some determiners signal that a noun is to follow: *a, an, the*. Other determiners indicate quantity by indicating how much or how many: *three, few, some*. See 11a and 15b.

dialect Language that uses expressions distinctive to a particular group or region. See 26f-2.

diction A writer's selection of words. See Chapter 26.

direct address Speech or writing directed at some individual or group: *I'll speak to you later, Sean*. See 15p, 19e, and 32a.

direct discourse Also called *direct quotation*. Reproducing the exact words of a real or imagined speaker in writing, requiring the use of quotation marks: W. T. Sherman once said, *"War is hell."* See 15p, 19e, and 32a. See also *indirect discourse*.

direct object A noun or pronoun that receives the action of a transitive verb in a sentence. See 9b-1. See also *indirect object*.

directory A list or group of related computer files, also known as a folder.

direct question A sentence that asks a question and ends with a question mark. See 28b and 32i-3. See also *indirect question*.

domain name A two-part name that uses symbols and letters to identify a computer server on the Internet. The first part of the name (before the dot [.]) designates the organization or server; the second part (after the dot [.]) indicates the kind of organization identified, as for example .gov for government or .edu for education organizations.

double comparison A nonstandard form using two comparative adjectives where only one is necessary: *more better*, for example. See 12e-2.

double negative A nonstandard form using two negatives where only one is necessary: *wouldn't never*, for example. See 12f.

double superlative A nonstandard form using two superlatives where only one is needed: *most best*, for example. See 12e-2.

download To move data electronically, usually from a server to a PC and often for printing.

ellipses Three equally spaced dots signifying that words have been omitted from a quotation: *And I have miles . . . before I sleep.* See 33d.

elliptical construction A grammatical construction that deliberately omits words for the sake of economy and emphasis. See 11g and 20c.

e-mail (electronic mail) Electronic messages sent or received through programs that allow for asynchronous communication. An e-mail address is a string of characters that identify a location for sending and receiving e-mail.

emoticons ASCII characters used to indicate moods or facial expressions in online writing. A smile, for example is indicated by :-) while ;-/ indicates a frown.

enthymeme An argument with an unstated premise. See 7b-1.

etymology The origin or historical derivation of words.

euphemism An evasive, inoffensive term used as a substitute for a more direct and possibly offensive one. See 26g.

exclamatory sentence A sentence that expresses strong feeling by making an exclamation: *Oh what a moment that was!* See 9f-1.

expletive A construction that begins with the word *here, there,* or *it* and is followed by a form of the verb *to be: There is* an expletive in this sentence. See 25b-5.

faulty predication A sentence error in which subject and predicate do not make sense together, resulting in an illogical construction and a mixed sentence. See 21b.

figurative language Language that is not meant literally. See 26i. See also *irony; metaphor; simile.*

finite verb A verb that combines with a subject to make an independent clause that expresses action, occurrence, or a state of being. Finite verbs indicate tense, person, number, voice, and mood. See Chapters 10 and 16. See also *verbal.*

flaming Personal attacks in e-mail or other forms of electronic communication.

formal language Represents the standard level of discourse suitable for academic writing. See 26c. See also *informal language.*

FTP (file transfer protocol) Electronic commands for transferring files between computers on the Internet.

fused sentence Also known as a *run-on sentence.* A sentence error in which two sentences are run together without a punctuation mark between them. See Chapter 17. See also *comma splice.*

future perfect progressive tense A verb tense that indicates a continuing action that will end at a future time: *We will have been playing.* See 10h-6.

future perfect tense A verb tense that indicates that an action will be completed at some future time: *We will have played.* See 10g-3.

future progressive tense A verb tense that suggests continuing action in the future: *We will be playing.* See 10h-3.

future tense A verb tense indicating action that has not yet begun: *We will play.* See 10f-3.

gerund A verbal ending in *-ing* that functions as a noun in a sentence: *Smoking* is prohibited. See 9c-2.

gerund phrase A group of words consisting of a gerund with related modifiers, objects, or complements. See 9c-2.

gopher Programs that access information on the Internet through hierarchically arranged menus.

grammar Principles or conventions that govern the way a language works by describing the system of relationships among words and conveying acceptable language patterns. See Chapters 9–15.

helping verb An auxiliary verb that accompanies the main verb in a sentence: *We were* driving. See 10b.

hit An electronic connection on the World Wide Web.

homonyms Words that sound alike but are spelled differently: *one* and *won*. See 27b.

HTML (Hypertext Markup Language) An electronic coding system for creating Web pages, which indicates how browsers should display images of text and graphics on screen.

hyperbole A type of figurative language involving excessive exaggeration. See 26i. See also *figurative language.*

hyperlink (hotlink) Connections between points on the Web.

hypertext Any document coded in HTML that includes hyperlinks.

hypothesis A generalization that a researcher or writer tests by observation or experiment.

idiomatic expression (or idiom) An expression whose meaning differs from the meaning of its individual words: *get into the swing.*

imperative mood A form of a verb that gives directions or expresses a request or command: *Come at noon.* See Chapter 10 and 19c.

imperative sentence A sentence that gives directions or expresses a request or a command. See 9f-1.

incomplete sentence A sentence missing essential words, phrases, or clauses. See 21c–e.

indefinite article The indefinite articles *a* and *an* refer to generalized nouns. See 15c. See also *definite article.*

indefinite pronoun A pronoun that refers to an unspecified person (*somebody*) or thing (*anything*). See 11b, 14d, and 14k.

independent clause A group of words consisting of a subject and a predicate. An independent clause can stand alone as a sentence. See 9d.

indicative mood The mood of verbs in which they state a fact, declare an opinion, or ask a question: *The bird has flown* from the nest. See Chapter 10 and 19c.

indirect discourse Also called *indirect quotation.* A paraphrased comment that does not repeat exactly what someone has said or written and that does not take quotation marks: Francis Macomber said that *he was no longer afraid.* (See 15p, 19e, and 32a.) See also *paraphrase; direct discourse.*

indirect object A noun or pronoun that indicates *to whom* or *for whom* the action of a verb in a sentence is performed. See 9b-1. See also *direct object.*

indirect question A sentence that reports a question and ends with a period rather than a question mark: *We asked if they could come.* See 15p, 28b, and 32h. See also *direct question.*

inductive reasoning Also called *induction.* The process of reasoning from the specific instance to the general case. See 7b.

inference A tentative conclusion based on observation of facts and details. See 2d-1 and 4a.

infinitive In the present, a verbal consisting of the base form of the verb and *to* (*to win*); in the past, a verbal that includes *to,* the past participle of *have,* and the past participle of the verb (*to have won*). Infinitives can function as nouns, adjectives, or adverbs. See 9c-2.

infinitive phrase A group of words consisting of an infinitive with its related modifiers, objects, or complements. Infinitive phrases can function as nouns, adjectives, or adverbs. See 9c-2.

informal language Casual and conversational language, typically used in everyday situations. See 26c. See also *formal language.*

intensifier A word that emphasizes another word or phrase, sometimes unnecessarily: *very* nice. See 25b-1.

intensive pronoun A *-self* form of a pronoun that emphasizes its antecedent: *yourself.* See 11b.

interjection An emphatic word or phrase that expresses surprise or emotion: *Wow!* or *Hey!* See 13d.

Internet A worldwide network that links computers and provides access to the World Wide Web.

Internet service provider (ISP) An individual or group that provides access to the Internet, such as America Online.

interrogative pronoun A pronoun that introduces a question (*who, which, what*). See 11b.

interrogative sentence A sentence that asks a question. See 9f-1.

interrupting modifier A misplaced modifier that disrupts the continuity of thought in a sentence. See 18e–h.

intransitive verb A verb that does not take a direct object: The whistle *blew.* See 10d-2. See also *transitive verb.*

invention techniques The ways that writers generate ideas. See also *mapping.*

inverted word order Reversing the order of subject and verb (so that the subject follows rather than precedes the verb) for variety and emphasis. *From our combined efforts came a new idea.* See 14h and 25a-3. See also *standard word order.*

irony A type of figurative language in which the intended meaning is the opposite of the words used: *War is kind.* See 26i. See also *figurative language.*

irregular verb A verb that forms the past tense and past participle in ways other than adding *-d, -ed,* or *-t: begin, began, begun.* See 10c.

jargon Specialized or technical language that a general audience might not understand. See 26d.

keyword A word or phrase used for searching computer databases.

linking verb A verb that joins the subject of a sentence to a subject complement. Linking verbs indicate conditions, states of being, or sense experience: *It will rain; He was tired; They are cold.* See 10d-1.

listserv The central server that controls ongoing e-mail discussion group activity.

main clause See *independent clause.*

mapping Also called *mind map.* An invention technique used to generate ideas and to organize them. See 1f-2.

mass noun Also called a *noncount noun.* Names things that cannot be counted: *sugar, dust, music.* Mass or noncount nouns are used only in the singular. See 15a–d. See also *count noun.*

mechanics Conventions governing the use of abbreviations, capital letters, hyphens, italics, and numbers. See Chapters 34–38.

metaphor A type of figurative language involving a direct comparison of dissimilar things: *He is a dynamo.* See 26i-1. See also *figurative language.*

misplaced modifier A modifier that is positioned in a sentence so that it is unclear which word, phrase, or clause is modified: Writers who read *often* will make use of that reading. See 18a–d.

mixed metaphor A type of figurative language involving an inconsistent or a ludicrous comparison. See 26i-1. See also *figurative language.*

mixed sentence A sentence that combines incompatible grammatical structures or includes an illogical relationship between subject and predicate, resulting in a confusion of meaning. See 21a–b.

modal auxiliary verbs Also called *modals.* Combine with main verbs to indicate necessity (*must*), obligation (*should, ought*), permission (*may*), or possibility (*might*). See 10b.

modifier A word or phrase that functions as an adjective or adverb to limit or qualify the meaning of a word, phrase, or clause. See Chapter 12 and Chapter 18.

mood A writer's or speaker's attitude indicated by a verb's action, whether imperative, indicative, or subjunctive. See Chapter 10 and 19c.

morpheme The smallest meaningful unit into which a word can be divided. In the word *prehistoric*, the prefix *pre-* (meaning "before") is a morpheme.

neologism A newly coined word that is not yet widely used. See 26e.

nominalization Using nouns rather than verbs to carry the meaning of a sentence. See 25b-6.

noncount noun See *mass noun*.

nonfinite verb See *verbal*.

nonrestrictive element A word, phrase, or clause that does not limit the element it modifies while providing information not essential to understanding the main clause of the sentence. A nonrestrictive element is set off with commas. See 29c. See also *restrictive element*.

nonstandard Words, expressions, or constructions that do not conform to the conventions of spoken and written English.

noun Names a person, place, thing, concept, or quality. Nouns can be common (*disk*), proper (*Sharon*), abstract (*innocence*), concrete (*ketchup*), collective (*class*), or mass (*weather*). See 11a and 26b.

noun clause A clause that typically begins with a relative pronoun and functions as a subject, an object, or a complement in a sentence. See 9d.

noun phrase A group of words consisting of a noun and its modifiers that functions as a subject, an object, or a complement in a sentence. See 9c-1.

number The quantity indicated by a verb, whether singular or plural. See 14a–j.

object A word or group of words, functioning as a noun or pronoun, that is influenced by a verb (direct object), a verbal (indirect object), or a preposition (object of a preposition). See 9b.

object complement A noun or adjective that follows a direct object and describes or renames it. See 9b-3.

objective case The case or function of a pronoun when it is the direct or indirect object of a verb or verbal, the object of a preposition, the subject of an infinitive, or an appositive to an object. See 15c.

object of a preposition A noun or pronoun that follows a preposition and completes its meaning. See 9b-2.

parallelism The use of a similar grammatical form for two or more coordinate words, phrases, or clauses to achieve clarity, elegance, or equivalence. See 5c-5, Chapter 23, and 25a-1.

paraphrase A restatement of another person's ideas or evidence in different words. See 40d-2. See also *indirect discourse*.

parenthetical citation A form of citing sources in parentheses directly after the source has been quoted, summarized, or paraphrased. See 43a, 43d, and 43h.

participial adjective A participle that functions as an adjective: the *growing* child, for example. See 10c-2.

participial phrase A group of words consisting of a present or past participle and accompanying modifiers, objects, or complements that functions as an adjective. See 10c.

participle A verbal that functions as an adjective. Present participles end in *-ing* (*burning*); past participles of regular verbs end in *-d* or *-ed* (*burned*). See 9c-2 and 10a.

parts of speech The categories into which words are grouped according to their grammatical function in sentences: verbs, nouns, pronouns, adjectives, adverbs, prepositions, conjunctions, and interjections. See Chapters 10–13.

passive construction A construction in which the subject of a sentence receives the action of a verb: *The ball was thrown.* See 10k.

passive voice The verb form in which the grammatical subject receives the verb's action, rather than directing that action as in the *active voice*. See 10k. See also *active voice.*

past participle The third principal part of the verb that includes qualities of both an adjective and a verb. The past participle usually ends in *-d* or *-ed*. See 10a, 10i-2, and 15h.

past perfect progressive tense A verb tense that suggests a continuing action that ended before another action: *They had been skiing.* See 10h-5.

past perfect tense A verb tense that designates an action that has been completed prior to another past action: *They had hiked.* See 10g-2.

past progressive tense A verb tense that conveys a continuing past action: *They were walking.* See 10h-2.

past tense A verb tense indicating action that occurred in the past, and which does not extend into the present: *They watched; They ate.* Regular past tense verbs take the ending *-d, -t,* or *-ed;* irregular verbs do not. See 10a, 10c, and 10f-2.

perfect tenses Verb tenses that indicate an action that has been completed before another action begins or an action finished by a specific time. See 10g and 15j.

periodic sentence A sentence that begins with modifiers and ends with an independent clause that is emphasized at the end of the sentence. See 24c-2. See also *cumulative sentence.*

person The form of a verb or pronoun that shows whether the subject is speaking (first person—*I, we*), being spoken to (second person—*you*), or being spoken about (third person—*he, she, it, they*). See 10a, 11b, and Chapter 14.

personal pronoun A pronoun that refers to a person or a thing. *we, you, they, him, her, it.* See 11b.

phrasal verb A verb that combines with prepositions to form a multi-word verb: *give up,* for example. See 15m.

phrase A group of related words that does not form a complete sentence and that functions as a noun, verb, or modifier. See 9c.

plagiarism The act of misrepresenting another person's words or ideas as your own by using those words or ideas without giving credit to the source. To avoid plagiarism, sources must be acknowledged with accurate documentation. See Chapter 41.

positive The simple form of an adjective that does not suggest comparison. See 12e. See also *comparative; superlative.*

possessive adjective A personal pronoun that functions as an adjective by modifying nouns and indicating ownership: *their* house; *her* car. See 12h and 15f.

possessive case Indicates when a pronoun shows ownership: *your, yours.* See 11c-3.

predicate The part of a sentence containing the finite verb. The predicate describes what the subject is doing or experiencing or what is being done to the subject: The car *rolled;* We *were asleep.* See 9a. See also *simple predicate; complete predicate; compound predicate.*

predicate adjective An adjective used as a subject complement: Hillary was *elated.* See 9b-3.

predicate nominative Also called *predicate noun.* A noun or pronoun complement: Bill is a nonstop *talker.* See 9b-3.

prefix A letter or group of letters attached to the beginning of a word that partly indicates its meaning: *pre*bake, meaning bake in advance.

premise An assumption basic to an argument. A syllogism consists of a major premise, a minor premise, and a conclusion. See Chapter 7.

preposition A word that indicates the relationship between a noun or pronoun and other words in a sentence. See 9c-1 and 13a–b.

prepositional phrase A group of words consisting of a preposition, its object, and any of the object's modifiers. Prepositional phrases function as adjectives or adverbs. See 9c-1.

present participle The *-ing* form of the verb, which functions as an adjective: *sewing, speaking.* See 10a.

present perfect progressive tense A verb tense that indicates action that began in the past and continues into the present: *I have been reading.* See 10h-4.

present perfect tense A verb tense that indicates that an action or its effects, begun in the past, either ended at some time in the past or continues into the present: *He had listened.* See 10g-1.

present progressive tense A verb tense that conveys a sense of ongoing action: *We are eating.* See 10h-1.

present tense The verb tense that designates action occurring at the time of speaking or writing; also used to indicate habitual actions and to express general truths: When you *speak,* they *listen.* See 10f-1.

primary source An original work of art or literature, a diary, speech, film, interview, correspondence, or other firsthand account. See 39c. See also *secondary source.*

principal parts Three forms of a verb: base form, past tense form, and past participle. See 10a and 10c.

progressive tenses Verb tenses indicating action that is continuing in the present, past, or future. See 10h.

pronoun A word that takes the place of a noun. See 11b.

proper noun Names specific persons, places, things, concepts, or qualities. See 11a.

purpose A writer's reason for writing, such as to inform, explain, or persuade. See 1d-3.

quotation An exact repetition or report of the words another has spoken or written. See 40d-3. See also *direct discourse; indirect discourse.*

reciprocal pronoun A pronoun that indicates each of two things has the same relationship toward the other: *each other.* See 11b.

reflexive pronoun A *-self* form of the pronoun that refers to the subject of the clause in which it appears. See 11b.

regionalism A word or expression commonly used in a particular geographic region. See 26f-1.

regular verb A verb that forms its past tense and past participle by adding *-d* or *-ed* (or in some cases *-t*) to the base form. See 10c.

relative clause A clause introduced by a relative pronoun. See 9d.

relative pronoun A pronoun that introduces a clause that modifies a noun or pronoun: *who, which, that.* See 11b and 14g.

restrictive clause A clause serving as an adjective or adverb that limits or restricts the meaning of the word(s) modified. See 29c.

restrictive element A word, phrase, or clause that limits or restricts the meaning of the element it modifies while providing information essential to understanding the main clause of a sentence. It is never set off with commas. See 29c. See also *nonrestrictive element.*

root The unchanging part of a word that takes a prefix or a suffix: inter*vene*; bi*lingual.*

run-on sentence See *fused sentence.*

schwa An unstressed vowel sound in a word: comp*e*tent. See 27e.

search engine A type of program, such as Excite or Yahoo! on the Web that permits users to search for information using key words.

secondary source A source or reference that explains or describes an original work or other type of primary source. See 39c. See also *primary source.*

sentence A group of words that includes a subject and a predicate. A sentence begins with a capital letter and ends with a mark of end punctuation. See 9a, Chapters 16–25, and Chapter 28.

sentence fragment A group of words that begins with a capital letter and ends with end punctuation but is grammatically incomplete. See Chapter 16.

sexist language A type of biased or prejudiced language that discriminates against females or males on the basis of gender. See 26k.

shift An abrupt change from one verb tense, mood, or voice to another, or from one pronoun person or number to another, which results in confusing writing. See Chapter 19.

simile A type of figurative language involving a comparison using *like, as,* or *as though: They sing like angels.* See 26i-2. See also *figurative language.*

simple predicate The verb of a sentence. See 9a-2.

simple sentence A single independent clause. See 9f-2.

simple subject A subject consisting of a single noun or pronoun. See 9a-1.

simple tenses Verbs in the past, present, and future tenses. See 10f.

slang Informal usage in vocabulary and idiom, often playful, and quickly outdated. See 26c-2.

split infinitive Separating an infinitive by putting one or more words between *to* and the verb: *to boldly go.* Avoid split infinitives in writing. See 18g.

squinting modifier An ambiguous modifier that appears to modify both the words before and after it: The decision we made *ultimately* concerns me. See 18d.

standard English English as used by educated speakers and writers in the business and academic worlds. See also *nonstandard.*

standard word order The usual word order of the English sentence: subject, predicate, object: *We saw the movie.* See also *inverted word order.*

stereotypes Unfair assumptions made about members of a group based on insufficient evidence. See 7b and Chapter 26.

subject The grammatical part of a sentence indicating what it is about. See 9a. See also *complete subject; compound subject; simple subject.*

subject complement A noun or adjective that follows a linking verb and identifies or describes the subject of the sentence. See 9b-3.

subjective case The case of a pronoun when it is the subject of a clause, a subject complement, or an appositive to a subject or a subject complement. See 11c–d.

subject–verb agreement See *agreement.*

subjunctive mood The mood of a verb expressing wishes, stipulating demands or requirements, or making statements contrary to fact: I wish I *were* rich. See Chapter 10.

subordinate clause See *dependent clause.*

subordinating conjunction A conjunction that introduces a dependent (or subordinate) clause indicating the relationship of the dependent clause to the main or independent clause of a sentence. See 9d and 13c-3.

subordination The arrangement of two or more words, phrases, or clauses to distinguish a main term, action, or idea from less important ones. See 22b.

suffix A letter or group of letters attached to the end of a word that partly indicates its meaning: regard*less*, meaning without regard.

summary A compressed version of a text in which writers explain the text's meaning in their own words. See 2b-4 and 40d-1.

superlative The form of an adjective that suggests the most or least of something: *highest; least.* See 12e. See also *comparative.*

syllogism An argument arranged in three parts: a major premise, a minor premise, and a conclusion. See Chapter 7.

synonym Words with the same or similar meaning: *joy* and *happiness.*

syntax The sequence of words in a sentence. See also *inverted word order; standard word order.*

tag question A question added on to the end of a sentence: It was a good film, *wasn't it?* See 29h.

tense The time of a verb's action or state of being, such as past, present, and future. See 10f–i.

thesis The main idea of an essay or report written as a single declarative sentence. See 7b and 40e.

tone A writer's attitude toward the subject conveyed to readers through diction, syntax, and other stylistic elements. See 1d-3 and 4b-2.

topic The broad subject of a piece of writing. See 6b and 39b.

topic sentence The sentence that expresses the main idea of a paragraph. See Chapter 5.

transitional expression A word or phrase that signals connections among ideas and creates coherence in a piece of writing: *for instance; on the other hand.* See 5c-3, 24b-1, and 29f.

transitive verb A verb that takes a direct object: He *washed* the car. See 10d-2. See also *intransitive verb.*

URL (uniform resource locator) A series of characters that identify the address of a home page or a Web site. The URL for the *Scribner Handbook for Writers* is http://www.abacon.com/DiYanni

usage The conventional ways of using words, phrases, and expressions.

verb A part of the predicate of a sentence that describes an action or occurrence or indicates a state of being. Verbs change form to indicate tense, voice, mood, person, or number. See Chapter 10.

verbal A verb form that functions as a noun or a modifier rather than as a verb in a sentence. Verbals may be infinitives, present or past participles, and gerunds. See 9c-2 and 10d-3.

verbal phrase A group of words consisting of a verbal and related modifiers, objects, or complements. Verbal phrases function as nouns or modifiers. See 9c-2.

verb phrase A group of words consisting of a main verb and its auxiliary verbs. A verb phrase functions as the predicate in a sentence or clause. See 9c-1.

voice The attribute of a verb that indicates whether its subject acts (*active voice*) or is acted upon (*passive voice*). See 10j–k. See also *active voice; passive voice.*

World Wide Web (WWW) An international service linking hypertext data on the Internet. It includes Web sites, or locations.

Credits

Index

REVISION SYMBOLS

Boldface numbers and letters refer to Handbook chapters and sections.

b	abbreviation **36**	¶ dev	paragraph development needed **5**
d	form of adjective/adverb **12**	prep	inappropriate preposition **13, 15n**
gr	agreement **14**		
wk	awkward diction or construction **19, 21, 26**	pron	incorrect pronoun form **11**
ias	biased language **26**	ref	unclear pronoun reference **20**
a	case **11**	rep	unnecessary repetition **25b**
ap	capitalization **34**	sp	spelling error **27**
oh	coherence **5**	shift	inconsistent, shifted construction **19**
ord	coordination **22**		
s	comma splice **17**	sub	sentence subordination **22**
	diction, word choice **26**	t	verb tense error **10f–i, 19b**
m	dangling modifier **18i j**	trans	transition needed **22 24**
ev	development needed **1–3, 5–8, 39–40**	var	sentence variety needed **24**
		vb	verb form error **10a–e**
oc	check documentation **40–41, 43**	w	wordy **25b, 26b–d**
nph	emphasis needed **25**	ww/wc	wrong word; word choice **26–27**
ag	sentence fragment **16**	//	faulty parallelism **23**
	fused sentence **17**	.?!	end punctuation **28**
ph	hyphen **38**	:	colon **30f–k**
ea dev	develop ideas, thinking, or reading **1–3, 5–8**	'	apostrophe **31**
m	interrupting modifier **18e–h**	—	dash **33a**
c	incomplete construction **16, 21**	( )	parentheses **33b**
l	italics **35**	[ ]	brackets **33c**
	awkward diction or construction **19, 21, 26**	. . .	ellipses **33d**
	lower-case letter **34**	/	slash **33e**
	logic **7b–c**	;	semicolon **30a–e**
n	misplaced modifier **18a–d**	" "	quotation marks **32**
x	mixed construction **21**	,	comma **29**
¶	no paragraph needed **5**	⌒	close up
m	number **37**	∧	insert a missing element
	paragraph **5**	ℐ	delete
		∿	transpose order

USEFUL CHECKLISTS

THINKING AND DEVELOPING IDEAS

READING AND RESEARCH

WRITING PROCESSES